HANDBOOK OF SOCIAL CAPITAL

Handbook of Social Capital
The Troika of Sociology, Political Science and Economics

Edited by

Gert Tinggaard Svendsen

Professor of Public Policy, Aarhus University, Denmark

Gunnar Lind Haase Svendsen

Professor (w.s.r.) of Rural Sociology, University of Southern Denmark, Denmark

Edward Elgar
Cheltenham, UK • Northampton, MA, USA

Published by
Edward Elgar Publishing Limited
The Lypiatts
15 Lansdown Road
Cheltenham
Glos GL50 2JA
UK

Edward Elgar Publishing, Inc.
William Pratt House
9 Dewey Court
Northampton
Massachusetts 01060
USA

Paperback edition 2010

A catalogue record for this book
is available from the British Library

Library of Congress Control Number: 2008943823

Mixed Sources
Product group from well-managed
forests and other controlled sources
www.fsc.org Cert no. SA-COC-1565
© 1996 Forest Stewardship Council

ISBN 978 1 84542 323 0 (cased)
ISBN 978 1 84980 433 2 (paperback)

Printed and bound by MPG Books Group, UK

Contents

Contributors

T.K. Ahn is Associate Professor of Public Administration at Korea University. His recent research focuses on experiments on endogenous group and network formation for collective action and political communication. Recent publications include an edited volume, *Foundations of Social Capital* (with Elinor Ostrom 2003), *A Dynamic Model of Generalized Social Trust* (with J. Esarey, 2008), and *Endogenous Group Formation* (with R.M. Isaac and T. Salmon, 2008).

Thora Margareta Bertilsson, Professor in Sociology at the University of Copenhagen, Denmark. Her research interests are: social theory, methods of inquiry, sociology of professions, science/technology. Latest publication: 'Pragmatism rediscovered: the relevance of Peirce for social science' in Patrick Baert and Bryan Turner (eds) *Pragmatism and European Social Theory* (Oxford: Bardwell Press, 2007).

Christian Bjørnskov is an Associate Professor of Economics at Aarhus School of Business, Aarhus University. His research interests include the study of informal institutions and the political and economic effects of political ideology. He has published papers in international journals within economics, political science and sociology.

D. Douglas Caulkins, B.A. Carleton College, PhD in Anthropology from Cornell University, has published on social capital in Norway, entrepreneurship in the UK, and identity in Celtic populations. He is the Donald L. Wilson Professor of Enterprise and Leadership at Grinnell College, Grinnell, Iowa 50112, USA. Email: caulkins@grinnell.edu.

Robert Chase is Senior Social Development Economist in the World Bank's Social Development Department. He coordinates the Department's work on social capital, focusing particularly on how to translate the extensive research findings on social capital into operational guidance for World Bank operations that follow a community driven development (CDD) approach. In addition, he manages production of the East Asia Regions Community Driven Development Flagship Study. This work brings together evidence from the World Bank's CDD work, summarizing what seems to work best and what works least well as a guide to new CDD operations. Prior to joining the World Bank in 2002, he was a member of the faculty of

Johns Hopkins School for Advanced International Studies, coordinating the development economics programme. His academic research considers impact evaluation of community initiatives, the social effects of policy change, and strategies for improved development assistance.

Rikke Nørding Christensen is a PhD student at the Department of Economics, Aarhus School of Business, Aarhus University, Denmark. Previously, she worked for the World Bank from 1999 to 2007, mainly focusing on social capital issues and impact evaluation in World Bank projects in Asia and Africa. Email: rinc@asb.dk.

Gil S. Epstein is Professor of Economics at Bar-Ilan University, Israel. He is an Associate Editor of the *Journal of Population Economics* and a Research Fellow at IZA. He has published papers on migration and public policy, public choice, political economy and labour economics in leading economics journals and co-authored the book *Endogenous Public Policy and Contests* (Springer).

Lars P. Feld, Full Professor of Economics, particularly Public Economics at the University of Heidelberg; Member of the Scientific Advisory Board to the German Federal Finance Ministry; Research Professor at the Centre for European Economic Research (ZEW) Mannheim; Managing Editor of the *Perspektiven der Wirtschaftspolitik* of the Verein für Socialpolitik; Research Fellow of the SIAW-HSG at the University of St Gallen, of CESifo Munich and of CREMA Basel; President of the European Public Choice Society. Born 1966; 1993 Master in Economics (Dipl.-Volksw.), University of Saarland, Saarbrücken; 1999 Dr Oec and 2002 Habilitation, University of St Gallen; 1998 Visiting Fellow at the University of Southern California and at the Université de Rennes 1 (France); 2002–06 Professor of Economics at the University of Marburg. Research Interests: Public Economics, Public Choice, Fiscal Psychology. Numerous articles in, among others, the *Journal of Public Economics, European Economic Review, Scandinavian Journal of Economics, Public Choice, Economic Policy, Kyklos, Economic Inquiry, Regional Science and Urban Economics, European Journal of Political Economy* and *German Economic Review*. Postal address: University of Heidelberg, Alfred-Weber-Institute of Economics, Grabengasse 14, D-69117 Heidelberg, Germany. Email: lars.feld@awi.uni-heidelberg.de.

Peter Graeff is a senior researcher at the faculty of Sociology, University of Bielefeld. His main areas of interest are positive and negative social capital, deviance and social networks as they are expressed in, for instance, corruption, trust and volunteering. He has also contributed in the fields of statistics and methodology, social inequality and conflict, and military sociology.

Peter Gundelach is Professor at the Department of Sociology, University of Copenhagen. He is the Danish national coordinator of the European Values Survey and has published several books and articles on national identity and values in a Danish and comparative perspective. Email: pg@soc.ku.dk.

Francisco Herreros is a research fellow at the Spanish National Research Council (CSIC). His most recent book is *The Problem of Forming Social Capital. Why Trust?* (New York: Palgrave, 2004). He has published articles on social capital, trust, democratic theory and political violence in *Rationality and Society, Comparative Political Studies, International Political Science Review, Journal of Peace Research, Political Studies, European Journal of Political Theory, Canadian Journal of Political Science* and *European Political Science*. Contact: herreros@ceacs.march.es.

Christian Hjorth-Andersen, Professor of Economics at the University of Copenhagen and editor of *The Danish Journal of Economics*. His principal interest is cultural economics. He has published a number of books and papers in journals of economics covering subjects in environmental economics, industrial economics and cultural economics.

Veronica Nyhan Jones is a Social Development Specialist at the World Bank. She has worked for over a decade as a social capital practitioner, applying this lens to capacity building for community development in Africa, Roma empowerment in the Balkans, and corporate social responsibility related to extractive industries. She has a Master's degree in Public Policy from Harvard University's Kennedy School of Government. Email: vnyhan@worldbank.org.

Henrik Jordahl, Associate Professor of Economics, is directing a research programme on the service sector at the Research Institute of Industrial Economics (IFN) in Stockholm. Contact information: Research Institute of Industrial Economics (IFN), Box 55665, SE 102 15, Stockholm, Sweden. Email: henrik.jordahl@ifn.se; www.ifn.se/hj.

Natalia Letki is an Assistant Professor at the Political Science Department of Collegium Civitas, Warsaw, Poland. Her research interests focus on the relation of social capital, social trust, civic morality and political participation to the institutional (political and economic) context in the new and established democracies. In 2005 she received a Western Political Science Association award for the best article published in the Political Research Quarterly in 2004. She is currently a recipient of the POWROTY/ HOMING grant from the Polish Science Foundation. Her most recent publications include 'Does diversity erode social cohesion? Social capital and race in British neighbourhoods', *Political Studies*, 2008, **56** (1), 99–126; 'Investigating the roots of civic morality: trust, social capital, and institutional performance', *Political Behavior*, 2006, **28** (4), 305–25.

Peter Nannestad, dr.scient.pol., is Professor of Public Policy at the Department of Political Science, Aarhus University. His research interests include immigration, integration, and social capital. He has published on these topics in i.a. *International Migration Review*, *European Journal of Political Economy* and *Journal of Ethnic and Migration Studies*.

Elinor Ostrom is Arthur F. Bentley Professor of Political Science; Co-Director of the Workshop in Political Theory and Policy Analysis, Indiana University, Bloomington; and Founding Director, Center for the Study of Institutional Diversity, Arizona State University. Her books include *Governing the Commons*; *Rules, Games, and Common-Pool Resources* (with Roy Gardner and James Walker); *Local Commons and Global Interdependence* (with Robert Keohane); *The Commons in the New Millennium* (with Nives Dolšak); *The Samaritan's Dilemma: The Political Economy of Development Aid* (with Clark Gibson, Krister Andersson and Sujai Shivakumar) and *Understanding Institutional Diversity*.

Martin Paldam, Professor, dr.oecon, School of Economics and Management (since 1975), Aarhus University. Also Honorary Professor of Economics at Deakin University, Melbourne, Australia Has written about 230 publications of which half are published in international journals and edited books. The rest is mostly in Danish. Contact: mpaldam@econ.au.dk; and URL: www.martin.paldam.dk.

Roger Patulny is a Research Fellow at the Social Policy Research Centre at the University of New South Wales, Australia, where he is engaged in evaluations of national community strengthening and mental health strategies. He was previously Research Fellow at the University of Surrey, UK, where he was engaged in quantitative analysis of social and political trust using European Social Survey and British Household Panel Survey. His research interests include social capital, welfare, trust, mental health, and the sociology of emotions.

Michael Bang Petersen is an Assistant Professor at the Department of Political Science, Aarhus University, Denmark (email: michael@ps.au. dk). His research is on the context-sensitivity of opinion formation processes, neuroscience of politics and the evolutionary psychology of party identification, social welfare and criminal justice. He has been a visiting scholar at the Center for Evolutionary Psychology, University of California, Santa Barbara.

Anders Poulsen is a lecturer at the School of Economics at University of East Anglia, Norwich, UK. His research areas are experimental economics, behavioural economics, and game theory.

Andreas Roepstorff is an Associate Professor at the Department of Social Anthropology, and at the Center for Functionally Integrative Neuroscience, University of Aarhus. He has published on anthropology of knowledge, cognitive science, brain imaging, and basic neuroscience. Currently, his research focuses on understanding the brain in context and communication. Contact address: CFIN, Aarhus University Hospital Building 14A, Nørrebrogade 44, DK-8000 Aarhus C, Denmark.

Bo Rothstein has held the August Röhss Chair in Political Science at Göteborg University in Sweden since 1994. He works within comparative institutional theory and his main research interests are social and welfare policy, trust, social capital and, most recently, corruption. He received his PhD from the University of Lund in 1986 and was assistant/associate professor at the Department of Government at Uppsala University 1986–94. He has been a visiting scholar at the Russell Sage Foundation, Cornell University, Harvard University, Collegium Budapest Center for Advanced Study, Australian National University, University of Edinburgh and at the University of Washington in Seattle. He has been Visiting Professor at Harvard University and Adjunct Professor at University of Bergen and University of Southern Denmark. He has been invited to give lectures at many leading universities including Princeton, Yale, Brown, Humboldt University Berlin, London School of Economics and Political Science and Ritsumekian University in Kyoto. Among his publications in English are *The Social Democratic State: The Swedish Model and the Bureaucratic Problems of Social Reforms* (University of Pittsburgh Press, 1996); *Just Institutions Matter: The Moral and Political Logic of the Universal Welfare State* (Cambridge University Press, 1998), *Restructuring the Welfare State* (edited volume with Sven Steinmo, Palgrave Macmillan, 2003); *Creating Social Trust in Post-Socialist Societies* (edited volume with Janos Kornai and Susan Rose-Ackerman, Palgrave Macmillan, 2004) and *Social Traps* *and the Problem of Trust* (Cambridge University Press, 2005). His scholarly articles have appeared in journals such as *Comparative Politics*, *The Journal of Theoretical Politics*, *Politics & Society*, *Rationality and Society*, *World Politics and Comparative Political Studies*. He is a regular contributor in the Swedish public debate about politics and social policy.

Fabio Sabatini received his PhD in Economics from the University of Rome, La Sapienza, and is currently a Research Fellow at the University of Siena. He has written numerous articles on social capital and he is the author and editor of *Social Capital Gateway*, a website providing resources for the social sciences.

Søren Serritzlew is an Associate Professor at the Department of Political Science, Aarhus University, Denmark. His research interests include decision making in public organizations, coalition formation and the impact of economic incentives. He can be reached at soren@ps.au.dk.

Kim Mannemar Sønderskov is a PhD student at the Department of Political Science, Aarhus University, Denmark. His research is on the role of generalized trust in collective action with special focus on citizens' behaviour in relation to environmental issues. He is about to embark on a larger project on the effects of immigration on generalized trust. Email: ks@ps.au.dk.

Gert Tinggaard Svendsen is Professor of Public Policy, Department of Political Science, Aarhus University, Denmark. He earned his PhD (Econ.) in 1996 and a MSc (Pol.Sci.) in 1991. Director of the Danish Social Capital Project (SoCap) since 2002. Visiting scholar at the University of Maryland, Department of Economics (1994–95), and member of a steering committee on Social Capital in the World Bank (1997–99). Author of seven books and about 50 scientific articles in international journals (cf. homepage of the author, http: www.ps.au.dk/gts). In addition, Svendsen is a member of the 'Editorial Board of Public Choice' and former Chair of the 'Danish Public Choice Association' (2004–06).

Gunnar Lind Haase Svendsen is an Associate Professor of Social Relations at the Danish Institute of Rural Research, University of Southern Denmark. His research interests include social capital theory, discourse theory, historical institutionalism, anthropological fieldwork and civic movements. He has published papers in international journals within sociology, history and economics. He is author of *The Creation and Destruction of Social Capital: Entrepreneurship, Co-operative Movements and Institutions* (together with Gert T. Svendsen, London: Edward Elgar, 2004).

Eric M. Uslaner is Professor of Government and Politics at the University of Maryland–College Park, USA (euslaner@gvpt.umd.edu). He is the author of 120 articles and the author/editor of 12 books, including *The Moral Foundations of Trust* (Cambridge University Press, 2002) and *Corruption, Inequality, and the Rule of Law: The Bulging Pocket Makes the Easy Life* (Cambridge University Press, 2008).

Ralph Weber is Lecturer in Political Science at the University of St Gallen, teaching the history of political ideas and political theory. He holds a doctoral degree from the same university. His research interests include Confucianism, hermeneutical and methodological aspects of comparative philosophy, and Chinese political theory.

Michael Woolcock is currently on external service leave from the Development Research Group at the World Bank as Professor of Social Science and Development Policy at the University of Manchester, where he is also Research Director of the Brooks World Poverty Institute. His research focuses on the role of social institutions in the survival and mobility strategies of the poor, and the mechanisms by which they negotiate solutions to local conflict. He has an MA and PhD in sociology from Brown University. Email: michael.woolcock@manchester.ac.uk.

Preface

In his utopian book *The Glass Bead Game* from 1946, Herman Hesse gives a detailed account of a truly interdisciplinary research community living in the remote mountain area of Castalia around the year 2400. Castalia is a contemplative and peace-loving community. Its members are truth-seekers unconstrained by narrow disciplinary boundaries. Rather, they enjoy an 'almost paradisal freedom' and are able to 'inform themselves in all sciences, mix the most diverging areas of study [and] fall in love with six or eight sciences at the same time'. In our view, this is exactly what social capital research is about: seeking the truth and becoming enamoured of many disciplines simultaneously, supported by complete mastery of one's own field of endeavour. Excellent though it may be, no discipline should isolate itself from the rest of academia. Hence, the subtitle of the book, *The Troika of Social Capital*, suggests that more disciplines should play an active part in this interdisciplinary research agenda – and not just three, but six or eight sciences, or even more. This will allow even more sophisticated truth-seeking: something every scientist should aspire to achieve.

We are most grateful to Edward Elgar Publishing for asking us to edit this handbook of interdisciplinary research on social capital. We hope the book will contribute to the academic and popular discussions of social capital and improve the quality of policy making across the world. Warmest thanks to our dynamic colleagues, who contributed to this volume. Without their help, it surely would not have been written at all.

Special thanks for skilful editorial and language assistance and a wonderful sense of humour to Else Løvdal Nielsen, and to Anne-Grethe Gammelgaard for bailing us out at the very last minute. We also want to thank Susanne Strandbjerg Nielsen, who has been a brilliant student help to us all. We deeply appreciate all those not mentioned here who also helped us in various aspects of the work presented here. Needless to say, any remaining errors or shortcomings are our own. Last, but not least, grateful love songs to our wives and children.

We dedicate this book to one of the most courageous truth-seekers of our time, Aleksandr Solzhenitsyn (1918–2008). He dared to speak the truth in a society ruled by distrust.

1 The troika of sociology, political science and economics

Gert Tinggaard Svendsen and
Gunnar Lind Haase Svendsen

Many common efforts succeeded in accomplishing that task which many more isolated efforts were not able to accomplish. (Carl von Linné, translated from the Swedish in Ulrik, 1867)

1.1 The troika of social capital

The Russian word *troika* ('threesome') denotes a sleigh or wagon pulled by three horses abreast. A simultaneous, harmonious and steady pull by all three horses sends the sleigh flying without exhausting the horses. In contrast, if one horse pulls too hard, or if one pulls less than the others, the sleigh will lose momentum and, at worst, overturn. The difficult act of driving a troika implies exact coordination, discipline and understanding to ensure smooth and skilful handling.

We find that 'troika' is an appropriate metaphor for the three disciplines that have mostly 'pulled' social capital research, namely sociology, political science and economics. The main idea in this book is that the most important synergy effect of a balanced team of horses hitched in troika is to account for tangible as well as intangible assets or 'forms of capital' at the same level of analysis (cf. Bourdieu, 1986), thus overcoming the artificial demarcation between economic and non-economic areas of research. This means that intangible forms of capital, for example, cultural and social capital, should be accounted for alongside the more traditional, visible capitals such as physical and economic capital. In such an approach, culture is seen as no less economic than economics, and vice versa, and various forms of intangible, normative resources such as trust, cooperative skills, tolerance, optimism and happiness are included in the equation so as to avoid what economist John F. Tomer (2002: 421) has termed 'mainstream theory's most notable failure'.

The notion of social capital implies that all three disciplines recognize the power inherent in network cooperation – invisible, but arguably with highly visible effects. However, not all disciplines are comfortable with numerous network types. A main theme in this book is therefore to further develop what we see as a useful main distinction between *bridging* and *bonding* types of social capital – something that poses serious academic challenges if we aim for a well-balanced troika.

Disciplinary privilege is a persistent problem in academia (Baron and Hannan, 1994) and must, in our view, be strenuously avoided in social capital research. Social capital certainly holds multidisciplinary promise. However, the difficulties associated with crossing disciplinary boundaries should not be underestimated. This is evident in the diversity of conceptions of social capital's most important proxy, namely trust. Recent works (among them Sobel, 2002; Herreros, 2004) suggest that multidisciplinary approaches to social capital should be carried out by operationalizing social capital as trust, that is, trust in, and therefore willingness to cooperate with, other people.

There is much debate within social capital analysis over whether trust is a strict historical norm (Fukuyama, 1995; Putnam, 2000) or a rational choice based on information (Dasgupta, 1988; Gambetta, 1988; Good, 1988). The rational choice perspective of economics is that lack of information concerning other people undermines trust. This is the subject of the famous Prisoner's Dilemma game (see, for example, Herreros, 2004: 44ff.). However, sociologists such as Luhmann oppose the rational choice perspective, arguing that we trust when we lack information. For Luhmann (2000), the primary function of trust is to help individuals cope with the increasing social complexity and uncertainty that characterizes post-industrial/modern society. If we lack information – as we most certainly do in complex society – we have to trust or action of any kind would be impossible. We would, for example, be paralysed each morning before even reaching the front door if we were to gather all the information necessary to calculate the risk of being hit by a car when we step outside.

Trust is thus manifested in two distinct entities with different dynamics, measurements and policy implications (Patulny, 2004). This is especially so when viewed through the lenses of different disciplines working out of concert. These disciplines need to work together – and a good, simple metaphor is needed to bring this point across. We have therefore chosen the metaphor of the troika to visualize cooperation between the disciplines.

We have identified key disciplines within the humanities, which we believe would help the troika run: economy primarily focusing on *transaction costs*, political science focusing on *institutions* and social studies focusing on the *norms* that regulate the behaviour of social groups (see Figure 1.1). Again, we stress that this does not imply a segregation of economic and non-economic studies. On the contrary, economic, social and cultural issues should be incorporated within all three approaches.

How do we in this setting address the important issues of cultural norms, political institutions and transaction costs within a unified theoretical

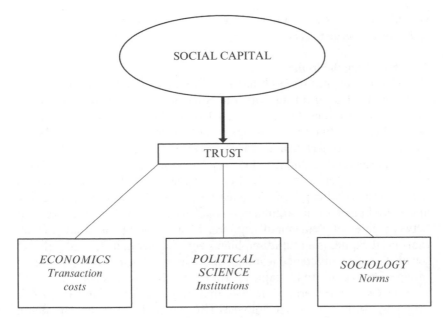

*Figure 1.1   The 'troika' of human sciences: social capital operationalized
as trust and combining three foci from three disciplines*

framework without over-privileging one discipline? The overall purpose
of this book is to achieve this aim by balancing the troika of sociology,
political science and economics.

This model echoes the ideas of Anheier and Kendall (2000: 14), who
identify three approaches to the study of trust: market transactions within
economics, social order within sociology and networks of social ties within
political science. We venture to suggest three directions that advance
Anheier and Kendall's work.

First, in our view, social capital studies should not be confined to the
view of networks of political science; they should be properly integrated
with economics and sociology. Second, the disciplines should be understood in terms of their focus on the aspects versus the outcomes of social
capital. Economics and political science largely concentrate on the *outcomes* of social capital – reduced transaction costs and improved functioning of political institutions – while sociology focuses on *aspects* of social
capital, that is, norms such as norms of trust. These foci could be expanded
to provide each discipline with a view of both outcomes and aspects (a
point we shall return to). And third, that a neo-capital theory focusing on
social capital in the context of *all* forms of capital and explaining how they
convert into each other (Bourdieu, 1986; Svendsen and Svendsen, 2003)

should constitute the overall framework for the three disciplines if we are to harvest synergy effects.

1.2   Balancing the troika

Recent social capital research has been productive and promising, albeit problematic. The problems with the concept have been discussed thoroughly (for example, Portes, 1998, 2000; Kadushin, 2004), and largely reflect those identified by sociologists such as Portes and Landolt (1996). These can be summarized as a lack of conceptual clarity, issues with causality and measurement, and the 'downside' of social capital is ignored. These problems have yet to be resolved despite the rise and fall of theoretical debate over social capital in the past ten years. The lack of resolution – and indeed much of the argument – is due to lingering territorial disputes between different academic disciplines. Despite the much-vaunted claim that social capital is a multidisciplinary concept, economists and political scientists assign different meanings and foci in debate, and sociologists rarely seem to come to the table except to criticize the concept.

A review of the literature reveals that even though social capital was originally formulated by sociologists (Bourdieu, 1986; Coleman, 1990), it has been adopted mostly within economic (for example, Sobel, 2002; Dasgupta and Serageldin, 2000) and political science (for example, Putnam, 2000) theory and research. This is unfortunate as sociology has important positive contributions to make – contributions that might constructively address some of the main criticisms that have been raised. In particular, we believe that sociological contributions are indispensable if we are to further develop and apply the important distinction between *bonding* and *bridging* types of networks.

In *Bowling Alone*, Putnam (2000) uses the bridging/bonding typology, but not in a strictly systematic way. He defines bridging social capital as open networks that are 'outward looking and encompass people across diverse social cleavages' (ibid.: 22), while bonding social capital consists of 'inward looking [networks that] tend to reinforce exclusive identities and homogeneous groups' (ibid.).

The dynamics of bonding and bridging networks are, however, more sophisticated than suggested by Putnam. From a sociological point of view bridging networks that transcend group cleavages such as Putnam's civic groups can be seen as guided by norms and morals of generalized trust (Uslaner, 2002; Mansbridge, 1999) that compensate for lack of information concerning strangers (Luhmann, 2000). In contrast, closed and exclusive bonding networks can be described as operating on the basis of members learning and making use of scarce information concerning appropriate forms of behaviour and etiquette. This precious information

– what Bourdieu (1986) in a power reproduction perspective calls cultural capital – is more than mere education or Becker's human capital. Rather, the fact that cultural capital encompasses 'etiquette' means that it serves as a way to distinguish insiders from outsiders as it comprises a set of cues and signals that facilitate the process of trusting people within the group ahead of people outside the group. Such ideas suggest that different mechanisms are at work in bonding and bridging and that they have different positive and negative implications (Patulny and Svendsen, 2007).

Portes and Landolt (1996) were the first to distinguish between positive and negative social capital. Positive social capital derived from social control is typically found in the forms that Portes (1998: 10) terms rule enforcement, bounded solidarity and enforceable trust, all of which generate fairly equal positive outcomes for all members of a group. Negative social capital also involves enforceable rules, but generates negative outcomes for the group (for instance downward-levelling norms), or positive outcomes for some members at the expense of others (organized crime). Given the more tightly structured and exclusive nature of bonding social capital, more negative aspects will typically be associated with such capital.

1.3 Cross-disciplinary thinking

Numerous works – in literature and philosophy as well as in economics and social science – suggest that network cooperation is profitable. Economists have long assumed that such profit occurs when single actors provide each other with valuable information and services (Herreros, 2004). However, networking also contains a social value that quite often remains unrecognized by economists. This is fundamental to sociology and philosophy, and has led to severe criticism of the doctrine of Economic Man formulated by Adam Smith. Philosophical critics suggest that economics either under-socializes man or reduces him to a metaphysical 'free will'. For example, German philosopher Arthur Schopenhauer (1977: 48) says that explaining human acts as products of purely free will is to accept effects without causes: 'Unter Voraussetzung der Willensfreiheit wäre jede menschliche Handlung ein unerklärliches Wunder, - eine Wirkung ohne Ursache'. This criticism is important, not as an attack on the economic depiction of exchange in networks driven by self-interest and free will, but rather to understand 'interest' in the broad sense of the word associated with culture.

Many economists acknowledge that the social and economic dimensions of networking can only be separated in an artificial way. Thus, even a hard-core economist such as Paul Krugman (1998) rejects one-sided economic formalism and emphasizes the importance of cultural factors alongside the single human scientist's rational intuitions. However, despite works dedicated to bridging the gap between economics and other disciplines – for example, economic sociology, new institutional economics and the social capital agenda – serious gaps remain between the disciplines (Baron and Hannan, 1994; Lebaron, 2000; Bourdieu, 2003). The real problem is how we go about entrenching cross-disciplinary thinking. It might not be difficult for us to link other disciplines to our work, but it is very hard to to start *thinking* cross-disciplinarily and integrate ideas and premises into our various core ideas.

The origins of cross-disciplinary thinking can be traced through critiques of orthodox, economic thinking, for instance the German *Methodenstreit* in the last decades of the nineteenth century; Durkheim's (1908: 5) rejection of the theory of economic materialism, which posits that economic life is the 'underlying structure' (*substructure*) of social life; Veblen's (1908) rejection of 'hedonistic (classical-Austrian) economics' that ignores 'intangible assets'; Polanyi's (1957: 3) aversion against the 'stark utopia' of 'a self-adjusting market'; Bourdieu's (2000) more recent advocacy of an anthropological economy aimed at replacing the empirically uncontested idea of homo economicus; or a similar critique of economic belief (*la croyance économique*) raised by Fréderic Lebaron (2000). The most recent occurrence is Woolcock's (2000) depiction of social capital as closing the artificial gap between economics and sociology.

These scholars do *not* reject that social relationships can be utilized as an economic resource in the here and now. But they *do* reject the idea that people only plan and carry out strategies in a strictly (economic) rational manner. Strategies are embedded in complex cultural 'games' and their outcomes are therefore unpredictable to a greater or lesser extent.[1] Agency and motivation are lost in an over-rational world, a point formulated so eloquently by Fyodor Dostoyevsky in his *Notes from the Underground* (1997: 11), when the I person reflects:

> [S]cience itself will teach man . . . that he never has really had any caprice or will of his own, and that he himself is something of the nature of a piano-key or the stop of an organ, and that there are, besides, things called the laws of nature; so that everything he does is not done by his willing it, but is done of itself, by the laws of nature . . . Of course, there is no guaranteeing . . . that it will not be, for instance, frightfully dull then (for what will one have to do when everything will be calculated and tabulated?)

This point needs repeating as many economists have yet to grasp it. Rational action is not the only motivating force in complex social systems. At the same time, we do not reject economic concepts as witness the usefulness of the term 'capital'. Despite evident problems, the concept of social capital contains a healthy dose of scepticism towards parsimonious economic laws of nature or metaphysical free wills while not over-socializing human beings. Working within the social capital framework might therefore teach us to think in a truly cross-disciplinary way without losing footholds in our individual sub-disciplines.

Overall, cross-disciplinary thinking is important. It helps researchers to think about observable phenomena in a multitude of ways and paves the way for new scopes, strengthening otherwise narrow analyses. This is stressed in a publication on qualitative assessment of social capital from the World Bank (Dudwick et al., 2006), which advocates simultaneous use of quantitative and qualitative methodologies.

1.4   Bridging and bonding

More than ten years have passed since Baron and Hannan (1994: 1122) somewhat derisively dismissed an expanding number of capitals within sociology as a 'plethora'. Since then, however, the new forms of capital appear to have gained increasing acceptance as they have been 'disciplined', not least social capital.

At the beginning of the new millennium it seems increasingly likely that such forms of capital will form the foundation of a new socio-economics. That is the logical outcome of social capital research. We suggest it be termed *Bourdieuconomics*, in honour of the French sociologist, who has played such an important role in establishing the legitimacy and structural interaction between the different forms of capital (Svendsen and Svendsen, 2003). Bourdieu envisioned such a neo-capital framework in his outline of *a general science of the economy of practices*, which aims to place visible and invisible forms of capital at the same level of analysis by reintroducing capital 'in all its forms and not only in the one form which is recognized by economic theory' (Bourdieu, 1986: 242; see also Bourdieu, 1979: 261ff.).

To create an environment conducive to a neo-capital theory we find it essential to consider the positive as well as the negative externalities associated with any particular form of capital, and social capital is no exception. The new bridging/bonding distinction within the social capital agenda offers much promise. Despite various weaknesses, we believe it can help make the troika of economics, political science and sociology run more smoothly by including qualitative work as well. This would ensure a more exact measurement of social capital not only as a non-excludable but also an excludable good at all levels, thus serving to hitch sociology to the troika again.

Most social capital research has hitherto measured social capital as generalized trust (Sobel, 2002; Uslaner, 2006). This thin trust has been associated with inclusive networks and provision of collective goods, that is, *bridging* social capital. Generalized trust of this nature is normative and related to morals and faith in strangers rather than to information, because people trust above and beyond what their rational calculations tell them is appropriate (Mansbridge, 1999).

In contrast, thick trust within families, kinship groups and networks of close friends, or *bonding* social capital, has been associated only with the provision of private goods, where *excessive* bonding leads to negative societal outcomes (Putnam, 2000). Such particularized trust is linked to information and experience with specific other people (Uslaner 2002), and ties in with economic concepts of rational trust (Patulny, 2004).

We emphasize this distinction here to clarify the contributions of different disciplines. Generalized trust is normative and can therefore most appropriately be studied within politics and sociology, while particularized trust is rational and better suited to economics. These two kinds of trust respectively promote non-excludable public goods by generalized trust and excludable private goods by particularized trust.

Different forms of trust require different networks to take effect. This brings us to the distinction between bonding and bridging social capital in relation to the three disciplines. We suggest – with respect to policy recommendations – that a *harmonious mix* of bridging/bonding social capital seems to be the solution (Svendsen and Svendsen, 2004: 3). Figure 1.2 suggests how this optimal mix between bonding and bridging might be accomplished in relation to balancing the troika of social capital, ensuring that proper attention is paid to both bridging (+) and bonding (+ –).

When conceived of in terms of a collection of outcomes with a variety of these combinations – and the varied and multiple causes of such a collection – a harmonious blend of bonding and bridging becomes a question of human happiness. Therefore the question of just what *actually* constitutes a harmonious mix in any given situation is essential and should be investigated empirically. This may require the qualitative and inductively oriented methods from sociology, anthropology and history (Svendsen, 2006) in certain circumstances. These include investigations into bonding capital at the local level, where positive and negative effects are most ambiguous. Such investigations should, however, also link to quantitative examinations of the extent and linkages of social capital at the aggregate national and international levels, focusing primarily upon bridging and the appropriate outcomes to which it can be linked.

Ultimately all studies will likely take place within the framework we have termed Bourdieuconomics – a general science of the economy of practices – or in a similar theoretical framework. Bourdieuconomics seeks to analyse material and non-material forms of capital at the same level by using a neo-capital framework, and it accounts for structural causes as well as material and non-material outcomes (Svendsen and Svendsen, 2003).

Social capital

+ Bridging

Open networks across social cleavages
Inclusion
Generalized trust

+/− Bonding

Closed, inward-looking networks
Exclusion
Particularized trust

+ Primary networks
Family, close friends

Voluntary associations with open membership (sports clubs, cooperative associations)

− Excessive bonding social capital
Hell's Angels, the Mafia, al-Qaeda, KKK

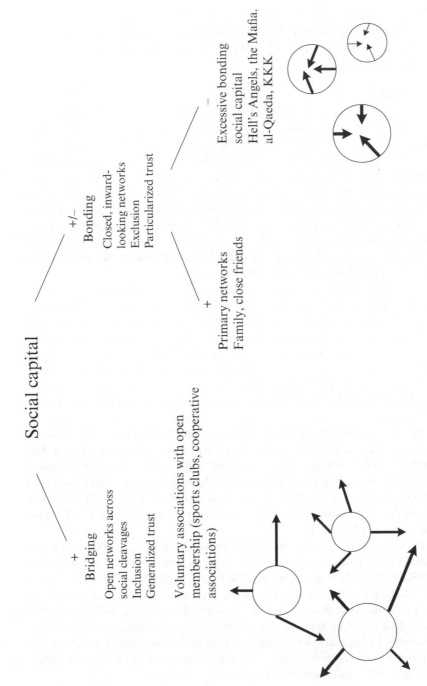

Figure 1.2 Bridging and bonding social capital

9

The approach has yet to be fully developed, but will continue the process of improving the dialogue between disciplines, encouraging the development of interdisciplinary work and perspectives, serving to help the troika of social capital run smoothly.

1.5   Outline

Social capital research claims to be interdisciplinary, but in practice it has been divided into three seminal research strings: sociology, political science and economics. Our main objective here is to balance the troika of sociology, political science and economics by offering important contributions to the study of *bonding* and *bridging* social capital networks. We repeat that bridging networks can be seen as guided by norms of generalized trust that produce positive externalities, while bonding networks are guided by information and particularized trust, thereby giving rise to exclusion. Social research links bonding to qualitative examinations of non-excludable and excludable goods and bridging to quantitative analysis of the externalities of social capital (Patulny and Svendsen, 2007).

Thus, more bridging social capital is required if international research is to embrace both the bright and the more shadowy aspects of social capital, that is, the bridging and excessively bonding social capital of economics, political science and sociology. The approaches used by economists, political scientists and sociologists are all necessary. The way to accomplish this feat is to get *all* three horses to pull the sleigh with similar force in order to keep it from overturning. We have therefore arranged the following 23 chapters into eight thematic parts and *not* according to academic discipline.

Part I deals with classical group theory and cooperation. Elinor Ostrom and T.K. Ahn summarize the seminal contributions of the social capital literature and link the meaning of social capital to collective action (Chapter 2). Anders Poulsen goes on to review evidence from experiments on group behaviour and the incentive to free ride (Chapter 3). Douglas Caulkins closes Part I by developing a grid-group analysis related to social capital and culture (Chapter 4).

Part II turns to more recent explanations why cooperation in fact occurs. Based on evidence from the growing discipline of cognitive neuroscience, Michael Bang Petersen, Andreas Roepstorff and Søren Serritzlew review recent studies on activities within the brain when cooperation or non-cooperation takes place (Chapter 5). Next, Peter Gundelach argues that humour and jokes may be yet another way to facilitate positive social effects and cooperation (Chapter 6). Ralph Weber closes Part II with an exploration of the religio-philosophical roots of cooperation with special emphasis on Confucianism (Chapter 7).

Part III looks into the importance to social capital of corruption and the quality of institutions. Eric M. Uslaner presents the concept of an inequality trap and the relationship between corruption, inequality and trust (Chapter 8). Peter Graeff takes up the problem of corruption and analyses micro-sociological preconditions for the presence of corruption norms and their influence on social capital (Chapter 9). Writing about East-Central Europe, Natalia Letki highlights the impact on social capital of moving from one set of institutions to a new on (Chapter 10).

Part IV uses the modern welfare state as an example of high-quality institutions. Francisco Herreros treats the state as a third-party enforcer that can create a general environment that creates fertile ground for trust to grow (Chapter 11). Bo Rothstein discusses what a universal welfare state is and whether it produces social capital or not (Chapter 12). Thora Margareta Bertilsson and Christian Hjorth-Andersen describe how trust operates in mediating equity and efficiency and examine whether the Scandinavian welfare model can be exported (Chapter 13). Part V illustrates the role of the state as public good provider. Lars P. Feld demonstrates that tax compliance – a necessary precondition for financing public goods – is shaped by the social capital present in society (Chapter 14). Kim Mannemar Sønderskov investigates the environmental effects on social capital and reviews the rapidly expanding literature within this field (Chapter 15). Fabio Sabatini addresses the relationship between social capital and the labour market (Chapter 16).

Part VI calls attention to migration and integration. Gil S. Epstein considers how migrants make their locational choices and how their social capital formation is affected (Chapter 17). Peter Nannestad asks whether social capital can help solve integration problems in Western European welfare states (Chapter 18).

Part VII focuses on the economic aspects of social capital. Henrik Jordahl finds that economic inequality reduces trust (Chapter 19). Christian Bjørnskov surveys the association between social capital and economic growth (Chapter 20), and Martin Paldam relates macroeconomic factors to generalized trust and income (Chapter 21).

Part VII closes by rethinking how social capital is measured in practice. Veronica Nyhan Jones and Michael Woolcock describe the qualitative and quantitative toolkits that have been field-tested by various groups of researchers inside and outside the World Bank (Chapter 22). In line with these methodological considerations, Roger Patulny emphasizes quantitative measures across countries (Chapter 23), while Robert Chase and Rikke Nørding Christensen combine qualitative and quantitative measures in the case of Thai rural villages (Chapter 24).

Overall, the main result of the book is that the bridging and bonding distinction in social capital is a viable conceptual tool, clearing the road for an elegant and powerful troika in future research.

Note

1. As an aside, Bourdieu realized this quite early on, and it seems to be the main reason why he did not continue his close cooperation with French econometricians during the 1950s (Lebaron, 2003)

References

Anheier, H.K. and J. Kendall (2000), 'Trust and voluntary organisations: three theoretical approaches', Civil Society working paper 5, Centre for Civil Society (LSE), London.
Baron, J.N. and M.T. Hannan (1994), 'The impact of economics on contemporary sociology', *Journal of Economic Issues*, **32**, 1111–46.
Bourdieu, P. (1979), 'Le capital social', *Actes de la recherche en sciences sociales*, **31**, 2–3.
Bourdieu, P. (1986), 'The forms of capital' in J. Richardson (ed.), *Handbook of Theory and Research in the Sociology of Education*, New York: Greenwood Press, pp. 241–58.
Bourdieu, P. (2000), *Les Structures Sociales de L'économie* (The Social Structures of the Economy), Paris: Seuil.
Bourdieu, P. (2003), *Firing Back: Against the Tyranny of the Market*, New York: New Press.
Coleman, J.S. (1990), *Foundations of Social Theory*, Cambridge, MA: Harvard University Press.
Dasgupta, P. (1988), 'Trust as a commodity', in D. Gambetta (ed.), *Trust: Making and Breaking Cooperative Relations*, Oxford: Basil Blackwell, pp. 49–72.
Dasgupta, P. and I. Serageldin (eds) (2000), *Social Capital: A Multi-faceted Perspective*, Washington, DC: World Bank.
Dostoyevsky, F.M. (1997), *Notes From the Underground*, Internet resource, Project Gutenberg, www.gutenberg.org (accessed 4 May 2005). (First published in 1864.)
Dudwick, N., K. Kuehnast, V.N. Jones and M. Woolcock, (2006), *Analyzing Social Capital in Context: A Guide to Using Qualitative Methods and Data*, Washington, DC: World Bank.
Durkheim, E. (1908) *Débat sur l'économie politique et les sciences socials*, Édition électronique par Jean-Marie Tremblay, http://pages.infinit.nct/sociojmt (accessed 20 September 2004).
Fukuyama, F. (1995), *Trust. The Social Virtues and the Creation of Prosperity*, London: Hamish Hamilton.
Gambetta, D.E. (ed.) (1988), *Trust: Making and Breaking Cooperative* Relations, Oxford and New York: Blackwell.
Good, D. (1988), 'Individuals, interpersonal relations, and trust', in D. E. Gambetta (ed.), *Trust: Making and Breaking Cooperative Relations*, Oxford and New York: Blackwell, pp. 131–85.
Herreros, F. (2004), *The Problem of Forming Social Capital: Why Trust?*, New York and Houndmills: Palgrave Macmillan.
Kadushin, C. (2004), 'Too much investment in social capital?', *Social Networks*, **26**, 75–90.
Krugman, P. (1998), 'Two cheers for formalism', *The Economic Journal*, **108**, 1829–36.
Lebaron, F. (2000), *La Croyance Économique*, Paris: Seuil.
Luhmann, N. (2000), *Vertrauen. Ein Mechanismus der Reduktion sozialer Komplexität*, Stuttgart: Lucius & Lucius. (First published in 1968.)
Mansbridge, J. (1999), 'Altruistic trust', in Marc E. Warren (ed.), *Democracy and Trust*, Cambridge: Cambridge University Press, pp. 290–309.
Patulny, R. (2004), 'Social capital norms, networks and practices – a critical evaluation', SPRC discussion paper, no 134, University of NSW, Sydney, June.
Patulny, R. and G.L.H. Svendsen (2007), 'Exploring the social capital grid: bonding, bridging, qualitative, quantitative', *International Journal of Sociology and Social Policy*, **27** (1/2), 32–51.

Polanyi, K. (1957), *The Great Transformation: The Political and Economic Origins of Our Time*, Boston, MA: Beacon Hill. (First published in 1944.)

Portes, A. (1998), 'Social capital: its origins and applications in modern sociology', *Annual Review of Sociology*, **24**, 1–24.

Portes, A. (2000), 'The two meanings of social capital', *Sociological Forum*, **15**, 1–12.

Portes, A. and P. Landolt (1996), 'Unsolved mysteries: the Tocqueville files II – the downside of social capital', *The American Prospect*, **26**, 18–21.

Putnam, R.D. (2000), *Bowling Alone. The Collapse and Revival of American Community*, New York: Simon & Schuster.

Schopenhauer, A. (1977), *Preisschrift über die Freiheit des Willens*, in *Arthur Schopenhauer Werke in zehn Bänden*, band VI Zürich: Diogenes Verlag. (First published in 1839.)

Sobel, J. (2002), 'Can we trust social capital?', *Journal of Economic Literature*, **40**, 139–54.

Svendsen, G.L.H. (2006), 'Studying social capital *in situ*. An anthropological approach', *Theory and Society*, **1**, 39–70.

Svendsen, G.L.H. and G.T. Svendsen (2003), 'On the wealth of nations: Bourdieuconomics and social capital', *Theory and Society*, **32**, 607–31.

Svendsen, G.L.H. and G.T. Svendsen (2004), *The Creation and Destruction of Social Capital: Entrepreneurship, Co-operative Movements and Institutions*, Cheltenham, UK and Northampton, MA: Edward Elgar.

Tomer, J.F. (2002), 'Intangible factors in the Eastern European transition: a socio-economic analysis', *Post-Communist Economies*, **4**, 421–44.

Ulrik, F.F. (ed.) (1867), *Arbejderforeninger til gjensidig Hjælp*, Copenhagen: Gyldendalske Boghandel.

Uslaner, E. (2002), *The Moral Foundations of Trust*, Cambridge: Cambridge University Press.

Uslaner, E.M. (2006), 'Does diversity drive down trust?', FEEM working paper, no. 69.2006, University of Maryland, Department of Government and Politics, http://ssrn.com/abstract=903051 (accessed on 16 February 2007).

Veblen, T.B. (1908), *Political Science Quarterly*, **23** (1), 112–28.

Woolcock, M. (2000), 'Social capital and its meanings', *National Institute for Governance Seminar*, Canberra Bulletin of Public Administration, Canberra, pp. 17–19.

PART I

WHY COOPERATION?
CLASSICAL
EXPLANATIONS

2 The meaning of social capital and its link to collective action*
Elinor Ostrom and T.K. Ahn

The rapid growth of social capital literature

Few social scientific concepts have gathered so much attention and so many followers in such a short period of time than the concept of social capital. The fundamental idea can be traced back at least to Tocqueville (1945), Hanifan (1920), Jacobs (1961) and Loury (1977). Bourdieu (1986) used the term 'social capital' to express ideas that foretold the current meaning of the term. Schultz (1961) and Becker (1962, 1964), among other economists, articulated theories of 'human' capital in the 1960s, paving the way to a broader understanding of 'capital'.

It was only toward the end of the last century, however, that James Coleman (1988) carried out the first systematic conceptualization of the concept of social capital. Social capital has slowly gained recognition, and important theoretical developments have been made (for example, see Burt, 1992). The publication of Robert Putnam and colleagues' celebrated book, *Making Democracy Work*, in 1993 unleashed social capital research into its current widespread and lively phase of development. The growth of interest in this subject is reflected in Table 2.1. The number of citations to articles and books overtly using the concept of social capital has escalated from two citations in 1991 to 443 citations in 2006.

Now, we encounter 'social capital' in every corner of the social sciences, and researchers are tackling a wide variety of questions including: the relationship between personal networks and political participation (Lake and Huckfeldt, 1998), the challenge of building effective developmental policies (Gibson et al., 2005), the difference in the industrial structures of the capitalist economies (Fukuyama, 1995), the poor performance of the African economies (Collier and Gunning, 1999), the health and satisfaction of citizens (Kawachi et al., 1997) and the impact of active team-sport programs to offset the higher potential for student disturbances in large urban schools (Langbein and Bess, 2002).

The reason for this rapid growth of the social capital literature lies in part in the limits of the 'standard' approaches to the problems of economic development and political order. Abundant anomalies have accumulated that call for careful examination of the factors that were left out of earlier

Table 2.1   Citations in Web of Science *on social capital**

Year	Number of citations
1991	2
1992	3
1993	15
1994	12
1995	27
1996	37
1997	61
1998	102
1999	127
2000	150
2001	220
2002	251
2003	291
2004	300
2005	403
2006	443

Note: *Includes Science Citation, Social Science Citation, and Humanities Indexes.
Thanks to Charlotte Hess for doing this search.

theories. The differential political and economic performance across
nations and communities, for example, could not be answered satisfactorily without seriously studying the omitted factors: trust and norms of
reciprocity, networks and forms of civic engagement, and both formal and
informal institutions.

The social capital approach takes these factors seriously as *causes* of
behavior and collective social outcomes. The social capital approach does
this in ways that are consistent with continued and lively development of
neoclassical economics and rational choice approaches. In sum, the social
capital approach improves the knowledge of macro political and economic
phenomena by expanding the factors to be incorporated in such knowledge
and by constructing richer causality among those factors, and by achieving these without dismissing the insights from neoclassical economics and
rational choice theories.

Abundant, and often valid, criticisms of the concept have also levied
against it (Arrow, 1999; Solow, 1999; Fine, 2001; Durlauf, 2002 – to name
a few). Solow notes that much of the social capital research is plagued by
'vague ideas' and 'casual empiricism'. Academic research can be afflicted
by fads and fashions just as much as any other field. We believe, however,
that the concept of social capital can be defined carefully. It is a useful

concept that should take its place alongside physical and human capital as core concepts of great usefulness to the social sciences.

Social capital and the second-generation theories of collective action

Collective-action theories – especially with their lively development into behavioral, evolutionary and indirect evolutionary versions – will, and should, provide further analytical foundations for future social capital research. The economic and political performances of societies, from villages to international communities, depend critically on how the members of a community solve the problem of collective action. Contemporary theorists of social capital, almost without exception, open their discourse by placing the problem of collective action at the center of economic and political problems. The linkage of collective-action theories and the social capital approach is, however, at best, incomplete up to now. Social capital researchers use the collective-action paradigm primarily to *frame* their research problems. Incorporating forms of social capital, such as trustworthiness, networks and institutions, into a collective-action framework is a frequent approach in narratives, but is less frequent in analytically rigorous formal models.[1]

A fundamental limitation exists for the first-generation collective-action models, however, because many assume homogeneous, selfish individuals. The meanings of trust and norms either cannot be properly understood, or may only be captured to a limited extent, from the perspective of the first-generation collective-action models. Second-generation theories of collective action are informed by decades of experimental studies influenced by behavioral and evolutionary game-theoretic models. This section discusses how the forms of social capital, their particular configurations, and their interaction with other factors facilitate collective action from the perspective of a fledgling second-generation collective-action theory (see Ostrom, 1998, 2005).[2]

What is social capital?

Let us clarify our own definition of social capital. All forms of capital involve the creation of assets by allocating resources that could be used up in immediate consumption to create assets that generate a potential flow of benefits over a future time horizon. Capital in its most basic sense is a set of assets capable of generating future benefits for at least some individuals (Lachmann, 1978). The set of individuals involved may be relatively small, such as a family or a work team, or quite large, such as the participants in an economy or a political system. The flow of benefits generated by capital may all be positive or a smaller group may be benefited while a larger group is harmed. The latter can occur when social capital is used to facilitate collusion among a smaller group leading to high benefits for those involved and generating negative externalities for others. This *dark side* of social capital can involve police gaining trust in each other to collude so as not to report excessive force used by another police officer (Langbein and Jorstad, 2002), corporations or nations colluding with one another to create cartels (Hoffman and Libecap, 1995) or members of the Mafia colluding to undertake illegal, economic activities (Gambetta, 1988).

Capital always involves *multiple* forms. Examples of physical capital include roads, irrigation systems, schools, factories and the machinery inside factories. Human capital includes many kinds of different forms of knowledge and personal skills (Schultz, 1961). For some purposes, scholars can reasonably attach a value to a particular form of physical or human capital – a factory or a college degree. To do so requires substantial knowledge about the date of acquisition, the specific sector, the amount of maintenance invested over time and the future demands for this particular type of capital. With even more assumptions, one can measure aggregations – the industrial capital of a nation or its educational achievement. Whether the assigned aggregate value of a particular form of capital is meaningful depends on the question being asked, the detailed type of information contained in the estimate and the accounting formulas being used.

Given the diversity of forms of physical and human capital, it is not surprising that multiple forms of social capital exist. We have selected three types of social capital that are particularly important in the study of collective action: (1) trustworthiness, (2) networks and (3) formal and informal rules or institutions. We view social capital as an attribute of individuals and of their relationships that enhance their ability to solve collective-action problems. The relevant forms of social capital and their specific roles need to be provided by the theoretical framework in which the concept is located. We regard second-generation collective-action theories as the organizing tool for social capital discourse. Therefore, this section provides a brief discussion of second-generation theories of collective action.

Second-generation collective-action theories
Theories of collective action concern settings in which there is a group of individuals, a common interest among them, and potential conflict between the common interest and each individual's interest. Collective-action problems arise whenever individuals face alternative courses of actions between short-term self-regarding choices and one that, if followed by a large enough number of individuals in a group, benefits all. The problem is one of overcoming selfish incentives and achieving mutually beneficial cooperative ways of getting things done. Solving the dilemma

of collective action is not easy; whatever others do, an individual is always better off in the short run by choosing not to cooperate with others. The Prisoner's Dilemma game characterizes the situation succinctly. It has been considered the central problem of political science (Ostrom, 1998).

The first generation of collective-action theories (Olson, 1965; Hardin, 1968) concluded that individuals could not achieve joint benefits when left by themselves. The ways of overcoming the supposed inability of individuals to solve these problems included regulation by an external authority, provision of selective incentives or privatization. The first-generation collective-action theories were a valid criticism of the naive belief that individuals with common interests would voluntarily act to achieve those common interests, expressed by earlier group theorists such as Bentley (1949) and Truman (1958). Research on collective action has shown that the first-generation theories, while not entirely wrong, represent only the limiting case of the ways that collective-action situations are structured and how individuals cope with them (Blomquist, 1992; Bolton and Ockenfels, 2000; NRC, 2002 – to name just a few relevant studies).

At the core of the first-generation theories of collective action is an image of atomized, selfish and fully rational individuals. In the field, individuals do not live in an atomized world. Many collective-action problems are embedded in pre-existing networks, organizations or other ongoing relationships among individuals. Second, the universal selfishness assumption has been repeatedly rejected by empirical research conducted in the field and the experimental laboratory (see Camerer, 2003). Individuals do exist, who are concerned only with their own immediate material gains, but a significant proportion of individuals do have non-selfish utility functions (Frey, 1994, 1997). Further, non-selfish individuals also differ among themselves in terms of the extent to which they presuppose universal selfishness. Second-generation collective-action theories acknowledge the existence of multiple types of individuals as a core principle of modeling (Ostrom, 2005). In addition to the standard non-cooperative game theory that has been the key modeling tool of the first-generation collective-action theories, second-generation theories also use behavioral and evolutionary game theories (Gintis, 2000; Henrich, 2004). Many models of collective action based on behavioral or evolutionary game theories still use the solution concepts of the standard noncooperative game theory to address new kinds of questions that are particularly relevant to social capital research. For example, one of the main concerns of behavioral game theory is the problem of social motivations (Rabin, 1993; Fehr and Schmidt, 1999; Bolton and Ockenfels, 2000; Charness and Rabin, 2002), which has a direct implication to the discussion of trust and trustworthiness in social capital research. Another example is the problem of endogenous preferences, a key issue in the evolutionary game-theoretic approach to collective action (Bowles, 1998, 2000; Güth and Yaari, 1992; Güth and Kliemt, 1998; Güth et al., 2000), that provides a way to model the historical interaction between the institutional structures and the quality of citizenship described by Putnam et al. (1993).

Forms of social capital, trust, and collective action
In this section, we present our views on the forms of social capital, how they enhance trust among people and, thus, breed cooperation in a collective-action situation. We emphasize two points. First, social capital is a rubric. What is fundamental is how collective action is achieved. Various aspects of collective action can be studied without resorting to the concept of social capital, but in some contexts, the concept of social capital helps to unravel puzzles. Social capital provides a synthesizing approach to how cultural, social and institutional aspects of communities of various sizes jointly affect their capacity of dealing with collective-action problems.

Second, the ideas fundamental to a social capital approach cannot be entirely captured by the first-generation collective-action theories that tend to reduce trust, trustworthiness and norms to incentives embedded in social structures of interaction. It is essential to couple social capital to the second-generation theories of collective action that regard heterogeneous preferences seriously. What is important is to recognize genuine trustworthiness, defined in terms of preferences that are consistent with conditional cooperation, as independent and non-reducible reasons why some communities achieve collective action while others fail. Many social capital researchers are not conscious, let alone explicit, about the underlying version of collective-action theories on which their discussions of social capital and trust are built.

Trust as linkage between the forms of social capital and collective action
The various forms of social capital contribute to successful collective action, almost always, by enhancing trust among the actors. In other words, trust is the core link between social capital and collective action. Trust is enhanced when individuals are trustworthy, are networked with one another and are within institutions that reward honest behavior. These relationships are shown in Figure 2.1.

We agree with Torsvik (2000) that trust itself is not a form of social capital but an outcome of the forms of social capital linking them to successful collective action. The existence of trust among a group of individuals can often be explained as a result of the other forms of social capital such as trustworthiness of people, networks, and institutions.

Drawing on Gambetta (2000), we define trust as 'a particular level of

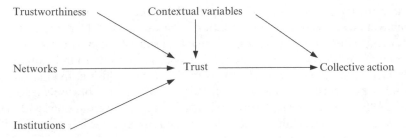

Figure 2.1   *Trust, forms of social capital and their linkage to achieving collective action*

the subjective probability with which an agent assesses that another agent or group of agents will perform a particular action'. Thus, trust allows the trustor to take an action involving risk of loss if the trustee does not perform the reciprocating action (Ostrom, and Walker, 2003). Another crucial aspect of trust is that it involves an opportunity for both the trustor and the trustee to enhance their welfare.

Let us think of a business transaction in which agent A has to pay before agent B delivers the desired good. If A pays the price and B delivers the good, both are better off than in the absence of the transaction. Agent B might be tempted not to deliver the good even after A has paid the price. This lack of trustworthiness would leave agent A with a net loss. If A does not trust B in the first place and refuses to complete the transaction, B will have lost an opportunity to sell their product and thus increase their wealth. Thus, trust and trustworthiness are essential for the completion of many complex transactions in modern life. As Kenneth Arrow (1972: 357), pointed out: 'Virtually every commercial transaction has within itself an element of trust, certainly any transaction conducted over a period of time. It can be plausibly argued that much of economic backwardness in the world can be explained by a lack of mutual confidence.'

Theoretically, the subjective belief of a trustor can be independent of objective conditions. One can falsely trust someone who is not trustworthy and experience losses. It is quite reasonable, however, to assume that trust as a subjective belief cannot be sustained in the long run unless it is verified frequently enough by the behavior of the trusted (Yamagishi, 2001; Yamagishi et al., 1999). When trust is defined as a subjective *belief* about a trustee's unobservable or not-yet-observed *behavior*, it is possible that an untrustworthy individual trusts another agent. Saying that A, who would not repay what he borrowed from B, however, trusts B to repay what B might borrow from A, is highly unlikely.[3]

The variants of the Prisoner's Dilemma game in standard non-cooperative game theory provide ample examples where the expectations of others' behavior in collective-action situations can be reduced to other factors. Repetitive interaction among individuals – a sign of a robust network and an important form of social capital – provides incentives to individuals to build a reputation of being trustworthy. Even very selfish individuals may not betray the trustor under those circumstances. In fact, precisely because he is selfish and he wishes to obtain gains from future transactions with the trustor, a selfish individual embedded in assured repetitive interactions will be more likely to reciprocate trust.

Dense horizontal networks – referred to as bonding social capital – with the capability of efficiently transmitting information across the network members also create incentives to behave in a trustworthy manner even for those who have only selfish motivations (see discussion in Svendsen and Svendsen, 2004, and this volume). Suppose that, though the transaction between A and B is not of a repetitive nature, there are other agents, C and D, who obtain information about the transaction and condition their future transactions with A on whether A behaves trustworthily in their transaction with B. Then again, A has an incentive not to betray B, not because of the prospects for future gain from transactions with B, but in expectation of those from C and D. Anirudh Krishna (2002) and Mark Baker (2005) provide carefully researched studies of local communities in India and how bonding social capital enables local residents to engage in challenging forms of collective action – establishing new investments in development activities and coping effectively with landslides and other environmental threats.

The possibility of sustaining cooperation via reputation in widespread networks connecting individuals who do not live in the same community and cannot establish close face-to-face networks – bridging social capital – has sparked interest in medieval guilds (Greif et al., 1994), law merchants (Milgrom et al., 1990), international trade associations (Maggi, 1999) and eBay's feedback system (Malaga, 2001; Standifird, 2001; Janssen, 2006; Resnick et al., 2006). Krishna (2002) and Baker (2005) also document that many successful local communities in India rely on both close bonding forms of social capital as well as bridging forms. By linking the close relationships within a local community to external actors who have new knowledge, larger stores of financial capital, and political connections, communities characterized by both bonding and bridging capital are more effective in solving big problems than those who have only close networks or loose connections to the outside world. Granovetter (1973) illustrated the power of weak ties long before the term 'bridging' social capital was coined.

Institutional rules also create incentives for the parties of transactions to behave trustworthily. They can influence behavior directly by establishing mechanisms of rewards and punishment or indirectly to help individuals govern themselves by providing information, technical advice, alternative conflict-resolution mechanisms and so forth. When effective formal or informal rules-in-use exist that specify punishments to be imposed on those who do not keep contracts, they affect a trustor's assessment of the trustee's future behavior. Intentionally not delivering the goods after receiving the payment for them constitutes a crime. The quality of a rule-in-use, or a statute as a form of social capital, depends not only on content but more critically on how they are actually implemented (Freitag, 2006).

We have so far examined how networks and institutions enhance trust among individuals in a collective-action situation. In sum, they change the incentive structure of the trustee. As a result, the trustor knows the incentive structure the trustee faces given the repetitive nature of the interaction, the existence of other network members who observe the trustee's behavior, and the rules and laws that punish or reward the trustee. Common understanding between the trustor and trustee regarding the existence and functioning of those factors encourages them both to engage in productive transactions.

Trustworthiness as a form of social capital
Trust cannot always be explained entirely by the incentives embedded in the structure of social interactions. The trustworthiness of trustees often results from the characteristics of the trustees themselves. Imagine a transaction that occurs in absolute absence of other forms of social capital: no repetition, no networks and no possibility of external sanctions. An example is a local villager being asked for help by a lost traveler who promises some reward in the future. Another example is a first mover in a single-play sequential Prisoner's Dilemma experiment conducted in a double-blind procedure. Both face a decision whether or not to trust the other's pure motivation. In those cases, the probability assessments by the trustors depend only on their belief regarding the trustees' motivation. Having neither any specific information about the trustee's trustworthiness nor the structural incentives the trustee faces, a trustor regards the trustee as representing a population of heterogeneous individuals. The individual who wants to be trusted in these cases is represented as coming from a population in the trustor's mind. The distribution of trustworthy individuals in this hypothetical population is based on the trustee's observable characteristics (if these can, indeed, be observed), such as appearance, dress, gender, age, language and so forth (see Frey and Bohnet, 1996).

The above examples are presented to abstract a trustor's belief about a trustee's motivation as an independent source of the trustor's expectation of the trustee's behavior. We emphasize that individuals' intrinsic values are an independent reason for behaving cooperatively and reserve the term trustworthiness primarily to refer to such non-selfish motives. In the language of game theory, trustworthiness refers to the characteristics of the trustee's preference. As numerous one-shot experiments using prisoner's dilemma type monetary payoff structures have shown (see, for example, Ahn et al., 2003), a significant number of individuals in the trustee's position do choose to reciprocate. At the same time, not all do. The fact that the magnitude of the gains from exploitation matters (Ahn et al., 2001; Clark and Sefton, 2001) indicates that individuals are distributed on a continuous scale of trustworthiness. In other words, the size of the internal parameter that the individual assigns to behaving in a trustworthy manner varies across individuals (Crawford and Ostrom, 2005). Behavioral game theorists (Fehr and Schmidt, 1999; Bolton and Ockenfels, 2000) have developed formal models to reflect such motivational heterogeneity.

Unless trustworthiness as preference is recognized as an independent reason for behaving cooperatively, the concept of generalized trust loses meaning. Generalized trust, borrowing Yamagishi's (2001: 143) definition, is a baseline expectation of others' trustworthiness.[4] We add, not necessarily reflecting Yamagishi's view, that the generalized trust reflects the average level of trustworthiness in a society. If trustworthiness is primarily an effect of networks and ongoing relationships, as Russell Hardin (2002) argues, it truly is difficult to conceive of 'general' trust or 'average' level of trustworthiness. Then again, social capital itself is more or less irrelevant beyond the confines of a network. But if one acknowledges that among multiple communities of a comparable size, from villages to nations, the average trustworthiness of people may differ and it affects the way collective-action problems are solved across communities, the concept of general trust and the underlying general trustworthiness become quite meaningful. Social capital can then become a useful rubric to refer to them along with other cooperation-enhancing factors for a society.

The potential of modern market economies and democratic political orders makes it imperative for individuals to deal with others beyond the confines of intimate relations and close networks. The very condition for a successful market economy and democracy is that a vast number of people relate in a trustworthy manner when dealing with others – many of whom do not know one another and cannot incorporate repeated interaction or a network – to achieve collective actions of various scales. Many of these relationships can properly be characterized as a single-shot situation, or one that is repeated a very small number of times. The establishment and maintenance of such social relationships depend on the trustworthiness of people that cannot be explained away by the incentives provided by the structure.

The trustworthiness of a population can be formalized in game theory by introducing a generic utility function that contains a 'type' parameter (Crawford and Ostrom, 2005). Suppose the parameter takes a value of 0 for purely selfish individuals, whose cooperative behavior can only be induced by other forms of social capital, and a value of 1 for those who are entirely trustworthy, who would behave cooperatively in the absolute absence of other cooperation-enhancing social capital. Then, the statistics of the parameter, its mean value and variance and so forth, is an independent input to the trustor's probability assessment when faced with an anonymous individual or individuals in a collective-action situation. The evidence suggests that few individuals are truly unconditional altruists who cooperate or trust others no matter what! Rather, in addition to networks and institutions, considerations of equity and fairness also affect the likelihood of individuals adopting conditional cooperation in collective-action situations (Fehr and Schmidt, 1999; Bolton and Ockenfels, 2000; Ahn et al., 2003).

Reciprocity is an internalized personal moral norm as well as a pattern of social exchange. Ostrom (1998: 10) defines reciprocity as involving a family of strategies in collective-action situations including:

> (1) an effort to identify who else is involved, (2) an assessment of the likelihood that others are conditional cooperators, (3) a decision to cooperate initially with others if others are trusted to be conditional cooperators, (4) a refusal to cooperate with those who do not reciprocate, and (5) punishment of those who betray trust.

As the above definition indicates, trust and trustworthiness are integral elements of reciprocity. An individual who abides by the norm of reciprocity is trustworthy. The information about others' trustworthiness is an essential input to a reciprocal individual's decision whether or not to cooperate. That the norm of reciprocity prevails in a society implies that a significant proportion of individuals in the society are trustworthy.

Reciprocity as a prevailing pattern of interaction among individuals is, in game-theoretic terms, an efficient equilibrium of repeated social dilemma games with multiple types of individuals and incomplete information. For reciprocity to prevail as patterns of social interaction, trustworthy individuals need not only to overcome the temptation to free-ride but they also need to coordinate their actions successfully.

Networks
As Putnam and colleagues (1993) point out, dense networks of social exchange are a crucial condition for the rise of the norm of generalized reciprocity. When trustworthy individuals who are willing to cooperate with

others constitute only a small minority of a society's whole population, one condition for them to survive, prosper and spread is to establish a network among them. Evolutionary theorists (Axelrod, 1981, 1984; Heiner, 2002; Richerson and Boyd, 2005; Trivers, 1971) have shown that when reciprocal agents using conditionally cooperative strategies have a higher chance to interact with one another than with the surrounding population in general, they can invade a population composed of agents who always defect. Information regarding a potential transaction partner's trustworthiness is crucial when trustworthy individuals try to initiate cooperation (Ahn et al., 2007). Dense social networks also encourage the development of reciprocity norms through the transmission of information across individuals about who is trustworthy and who is not.

Institutions – formal and informal rules as a form of social capital
We define institutions in broad terms as prescriptions that specify what actions (or outcomes) are required, prohibited or permitted, and the sanctions authorized if the rules are not followed (Ostrom et al., 1994: 38; Crawford and Ostrom, 2005). Institutions are thus the rules of a game that people devise (North, 1990). Rules are the results of human beings' efforts to establish order and increase predictability of social outcomes. Rules can be used to increase the welfare of many individuals or, if collective-choice processes are controlled by a well-organized subgroup, to benefit that group more than others.[5]

Written laws, administrative regulations, court decisions and so forth are formal rules written on paper and enforced by public authority. Grootaert (1998) considers the view of social capital that encompasses formalized institutional structures (including governments, political regimes, court systems, as well as civil and political liberties). Many scholars (for example, Fuller, 1981; Taylor, 1982) have argued that legal rules and formal institutions are an ineffective means to solve collective-action problems, and sometimes might even undermine the very basis of social cooperation. This view is a valid criticism to Hobbesian tradition in which the state is regarded as the inevitable and omnipotent solution to the collective-action problem (see Ostrom, 1991, 1997). We think that this criticism, however, should not be stretched so far as to deny the significant role of formal laws at national, regional, and local levels in sustaining and facilitating social cooperation. First formal laws, or the characteristics of a political system broadly understood, can encourage or discourage individuals' efforts to voluntarily solve their collective-action problems. Though no authoritarian regime can completely demolish peoples' will and ability to self-organize to deal with the problems they face on a daily basis, whether or not a regime explicitly allows and even encourages those activities makes a big difference for the fate of self-governance. Therefore, a rule of law, a democratic atmosphere and a well-structured government (if these exist) are valuable social capital for any society.

Formal laws themselves are often major sources of working rules especially when backed with close monitoring and sanctioning by public authorities. The difference between working rules and formal laws depends on the contexts in which the working rules operate and the extent that formal laws apply to those contexts. No formal law can completely cover the exigencies arising in daily life, thus working rules may basically involve filling in the lacunae left in general systems of law. However, when the mandates from relevant laws and official regulations are deemed impractical or improper, individuals may devise their own working rules that 'assign *de facto* rights and duties that are contrary to the *de jure* rights and duties' (Ostrom, 1992: 20).

To provide themselves with working rules to deal with their collective-action problems, individuals need to invest time and resources to devise, revise, monitor and sanction. Common understanding among the involved individuals regarding what actions and outcomes are expected of themselves and of others is essential for a sustainable set of working rules (Aoki, 2007). While the difficulties of sustaining long-term collective action are substantial, the benefits of creating local organizations and selecting locals as leaders who are rewarded for their performance can offset these high costs. Instead of presuming that individuals face an impossible task, we are better advised to assume that it is *possible*, even though difficult, for those facing severe collective-action problems to overcome them. To do so, they need sufficient local autonomy to invest in the social and physical capital involved in building systems and monitoring performance.

No general set of formal rules exist that guarantee successful development of working rules in all contexts. The rules used by individuals to structure their patterns of relationships may enhance or retard the creation of other forms of social capital and affect the level and impact of human and physical capital. Rules relate to patterns of activities at several levels including day-to-day operational activities all the way to constitutional activities that create and re-create the general patterns of authority in a society. The type of rules that individuals will find productive depends upon the kinds of norms and patterns of reciprocity that already exist. Similarly, patterns of trust and reciprocity will depend to a large extent upon the types of rules that are crafted in any polity.

Self-governing systems in any arena of social interaction tend to be more efficient and stable not because of any magical effects of grassroots participation itself but because of the social capital in the form of effective working rules those systems are more likely to develop and preserve, the networks that the participants have created and the norms they have adopted. For example, many scholars have found it hard to understand why the 'primitive' irrigation systems built by the farmers themselves significantly outperform those that have been improved by the construction of modern, permanent, concrete and steel headworks, often funded by donors and constructed by professional engineering firms (Ostrom, 1999).

Many factors contribute to these results, most of them related to the incentives of key participants in the finance, design, construction, operation and maintenance of differently organized irrigation systems. On farmer-governed irrigation systems, farmers craft their own rules to counteract the perverse incentives that they face given the physical and cultural setting in which they are enmeshed (Joshi et al., 2000). These rules are frequently invisible to project planners when they design new physical systems. In project planning, most effort focuses on how to improve physical capital, such as creating permanent headworks, that affects various aspects of the *technical* operation of a system. How these variables affect the incentives of participants is rarely explored. Unless the changes in physical infrastructure are undertaken with a consciousness that they will affect the incentives of participants – sometimes in perverse manners – projects intended to do good may generate harm instead. In other words, investment in physical capital that does not also include efforts to improve social capital and the fit between social and physical capital hardly guarantees desired consequences (Gibson et al., 2005).

Simply agreeing on an initial set of rules, on the other hand, is rarely enough. Working out exactly what these rules mean in practice takes time. If those learning how to use a set of rules do not trust one another, further investments are needed in extensive monitoring activities (Ostrom and Nagendra, 2006). Appropriate sanctions for non-conformance must be developed. Conditions under which exceptions to rules can be made without endangering the basic ordering principles must also be discovered and discussed. Conflict over rule interpretation and adjustment will occur, which if no facilities for conflict resolution are available, may destroy the process of building capital before it gets very far. The time it takes to develop a workable set of rules, known to all relevant parties, is always substantial (Dietz et al., 2003).

Part of learning through experience is what happens when things go wrong. In all practical affairs, many things can go wrong. Everyone may not have received the same information about joint objectives, processes to be followed and how one process feeds into another. Some may do their part while others fail to perform. Some may want to interpret a rule in a way that is harmful to the interests of others. There may not be fair and objective conflict-resolution processes available. Conflict may destroy prior lessons about how to work together and may reinforce prior doubts about the reliability and trustworthiness of some participants.

Thus, social capital is not only created, it can be weakened, destroyed, strengthened or transformed. Social capital can be characterized as outdated, up to date or ahead of its time. It may enhance the outcomes of a few without any impact on others. Or, advantages to the few may come at the expense of others. Alternatively, the advantages to a few may also generate positive benefits for others. A system of government based upon military command and use of instruments of force can also destroy other forms of social capital while building its own.

Notes

* We are deeply appreciative of support that we have received from the National Science Foundation, the Ford Foundation and the MacArthur Foundation, and the fabulous editing by Patty Lezotte.
1. For several ambitious attempts to formalize the concept of social capital and its effects, see Annen (2002a, 2002b) and Henning (2002).
2. The following section draws on Ostrom and Ahn (2001), but is substantially revised.
3. Using one's own view of what one would do in a situation has repeatedly been found to be a good predictor of one's expectations about what someone else would do in that situation. In social dilemma situations, those that choose the more cooperative strategies usually have a higher expectation that others will also cooperate than those who do not cooperate (see Orbell et al., 1984; Orbell and Dawes, 1991).
4. Yamagishi's discussion of trust focuses on its relationship with social intelligence; a higher level of social intelligence allows a person to entertain a correspondingly higher level of trust. This appears to consider trust as an individual's disposition. What is not clear in his discussion is whether a person's default expectation of others' trustworthiness also reflects the objective level of trustworthiness of others.
5. Berman (1983: 557) noted in his discussion of the importance of legal systems that the 'legal ordering is itself a form of capital'.

References

Ahn, T.K., Justin Esarey and John Scholz (2007), 'Reputation and cooperation in voluntary exchange: comparing local and central institutions', paper presented at the American Political Science Association meeting, Chicago, 29 August–3 September.

Ahn, T.K., Elinor Ostrom and James Walker (2003), 'Heterogeneous preferences and collective action', *Public Choice*, **117** (3–4), 295–314.

Ahn, T.K., Elinor Ostrom, David Schmidt, Robert Shupp and James Walker (2001), 'Cooperation in PD games: fear, greed, and history of play', *Public Choice*, **106** (1/2), 137–55.

Annen, Kurt (2002a), 'Social capital, inclusive networks, and economic performance', paper presented at the Public Choice Society meeting, San Diego, 22–24 March.

Annen, Kurt (2002b), 'Social norms, communication, and community enforcement', working paper, Washington University, Department of Economics, St Louis, MO.

Aoki, Masahiko (2007), 'Endogenizing institutions and institutional change', *Journal of Institutional Economics*, **3** (1), 1–31.

Arrow, Kenneth (1972), 'Gifts and exchanges', *Philosophy and Public Affairs*, **1**, 343–62.

Arrow, Kenneth (1999), 'Observations on social capital', in Partha Dasgupta and Ismail Serageldin (eds), *Social Capital: A Multifaceted Perspective*, Washington, DC: World Bank, pp. 3–5.

Axelrod, Robert (1981), 'The emergence of cooperation among egoists', *American Political Science Review*, **75** (2), 306–18.

Axelrod, Robert (1984), *The Evolution of Cooperation*, New York: Basic Books.

Baker, Mark (2005), *The Kuhls of Kangra: Community-Managed Irrigation in the Western Himalaya*, Seattle, WA: University of Washington Press.

Becker, Gary S. (1962), 'Investment in human capital: a theoretical analysis', *Journal of Political Economy*, **70** (5), 9–49.

Becker, Gary S. (1964), *Human Capital*, New York: Columbia University Press.

Bentley, A. (1949), *The Process of Government*, Evanston, IL: Principia Press.

Berman, Harold J. (1983), *Law and Revolution: The Formation of the Western Legal Tradition*, Cambridge, MA: Harvard University Press.

Blomquist, William (1992), *Dividing the Waters: Governing Groundwater in Southern California*, San Francisco, CA: ICS Press.

Bolton, Gary and Axel Ockenfels (2000), 'ERC: a theory of equity, reciprocity, and competition', *American Economic Review*, **90**, 166–93.

Bourdieu, Pierre (1986), 'Forms of capital', in John G. Richardson (ed.), *Handbook of Theory and Research for the Sociology of Education*, New York: Greenwood Press, pp. 241–58.

Bowles, Samuel (1998), 'Endogenous preferences: the cultural consequences of markets and other economic institutions', *Journal of Economic Literature*, **36**, 75–111.

Bowles, Samuel (2000), 'Individual interactions, group conflicts, and the evolution of preferences', in Steve Durlauf and Peyton Young (eds), *Social Dynamics*, Washington, DC: Brookings Institution.

Burt, Ronald S. (1992), *Structural Holes: The Social Structure of Competition,* Cambridge, MA: Harvard University Press.

Camerer, Colin F. (2003), *Behavioral Game Theory: Experiments in Strategic Interaction*, Princeton, NJ: Princeton University Press.

Charness, Gary and Matthew Rabin (2002), 'Understanding social preferences with simple tests', *Quarterly Journal of Economics*, **117** (3), 817–69.

Clark, Kenneth and Martin Sefton (2001), 'The sequential prisoner's dilemma: evidence on reciprocation', *Economic Journal*, **111**, 51–68.

Coleman, James S. (1988), 'Social capital in the creation of human capital', *American Journal of Sociology*, **94** (supplement), S95–S120.

Collier, Paul and Jan Willem Gunning (1999), 'Explaining African economic performance', *Journal of Economic Literature*, **37**, 64–111.

Crawford, Sue E.S. and Elinor Ostrom (2005), 'A grammar of institutions', in Elinor Ostrom (ed.), *Understanding Institutional Diversity*, Princeton, NJ: Princeton University Press, pp. 137–74. Originally published in *American Political Science Review*, **89** (3) (1995), 582–600.

Dietz, Thomas, Elinor Ostrom and Paul Stern (2003), 'The struggle to govern the commons', *Science*, **302** (5652), 1907–12.

Durlauf, Steven N. (2002), 'Bowling alone: a review essay', *Journal of Economic Behavior and Organization*, **47** (3), 259–74.

Fehr, Ernst and Klaus Schmidt (1999), 'A theory of fairness, competition, and cooperation', *Quarterly Journal of Economics*, **114**, 817–68.

Fine, Ben (2001), *Social Capital versus Social Theory: Political Economy and Social Science at the Turn of the Millennium*, London: Routledge.

Freitag, M. (2006), 'Bowling the state back in: political institutions and the creation of social capital', *European Journal of Political Research*, **45**, 123–52.

Frey, Bruno S. (1994), 'How intrinsic motivation is crowded out and in', *Rationality and Society*, **6**, 334–52.

Frey, Bruno S. (1997), *Not Just for the Money: An Economic Theory of Personal Motivation*, Cheltenham, UK and Northampton, MA, USA: Edward Elgar.

Frey, Bruno S. and Iris Bohnet (1996), 'Cooperation, communication, and communitarianism: an experimental approach', *Journal of Political Philosophy*, **4** (4), 322–36.

Fukuyama, Francis (1995), *Trust: The Social Virtues and the Creation of Prosperity*, New York: Free Press.

Fuller, Lon (1981), *The Problem of Social Order*, Durham, NC: Duke University Press.

Gambetta, Diego (1988), 'Mafia: the price of distrust', in Diego Gambetta (ed.), *Trust: Making and Breaking Cooperative Relations*, London: Basil Blackwell, pp. 158–75.

Gambetta, Diego (2000), 'Can we trust trust?', in Diego Gambetta (ed.), *Trust: Making and Breaking Cooperative Relations*, Oxford: University of Oxford, Department of Sociology, electronic edition, pp. 213–37.

Gibson, Clark, Krister Andersson, Elinor Ostrom and Sujai Shivakumar (2005), *The Samaritan's Dilemma: The Political Economy of Development Aid*, New York: Oxford University Press.

Gintis, Herbert (2000), *Game Theory Evolving*, Princeton, NJ: Princeton University Press.

Granovetter, Mark (1973), 'The strength of weak ties', *American Journal of Sociology*, **78**, 1360–80.

Greif, Avner, Paul Milgrom and Barry R. Weingast (1994), 'Coordination, commitment, and enforcement: the case of the merchant guild', *Journal of Political Economy*, **102** (4), 745–76.

Grootaert, Christiaan (1998), 'Social capital, household welfare and poverty in Indonesia', Social Capital Initiative working paper, no. 2148, World Bank, Washington, DC.

Güth, Werner and Menahem Yaari (1992), 'An evolutionary approach to explaining reciprocal behavior in a simple strategic game', in Ulrich Witt (ed.), *Explaining Process and Change: Approaches to Evolutionary Economics*, Ann Arbor, MI: University of Michigan Press, pp. 23–34.

Güth, Werner and Hartmut Kliemt (1998), 'The indirect evolutionary approach: bridging the gap between rationality and adaptation', *Rationality and Society*, **10** (3), 377–99.

Güth, Werner, Hartmut Kliemt and Bezalel Peleg (2000), 'Co-evolution of preferences and information in simple games of trust', *German Economic Review*, **1** (1), 83–110.

Hanifan, L.J. (1920), *The Community Center*, Boston, MA: Silver, Burdett & Co.

Hardin, Garrett (1968), 'The tragedy of the commons', *Science*, **162**, 1243–8.

Hardin, Russell (2002), *Trust and Trustworthiness*, New York: Russell Sage Foundation.

Heiner, Ron (2002), 'Robust evolution of contingent-cooperation in pure one-shot prisoners' dilemmas', working paper, James Buchanan Center for Political Economy, Fairfax, VA.

Henning, Christian H.C.A. (2002), 'On the conception of social capital in the framework of a generalized version of Coleman's linear system of action', paper presented at the Public Choice Society meeting, San Diego, 22–24 March.

Henrich, Joe (2004), 'Cultural group selection, co-evolutionary processes and larger-scale cooperation', *Journal of Economic Behavior and Organization*, **53** (1), 85–8.

Hoffman, Elizabeth and Gary Libecap (1995), 'The failure of government-sponsored cartels and development of federal farm policy', *Economic Inquiry*, **33**, 365–82.

Jacobs, Jane (1961), *The Death and Life of Great American Cities*, New York: Random House.

Janssen, Marco (2006), 'Evolution of cooperation when feedback to reputation scores is voluntary', *Journal of Artificial Societies and Social Simulation*, **9** (1), http://jasss.soc.surrey. ac.uk/9/1/17.html (accessed 12 September 2007).

Joshi, Neeraj, Elinor Ostrom, Ganesh Shivakoti and Wai Fung Lam (2000), 'Institutional opportunities and constraints in the performance of farmer-managed irrigation systems in Nepal', *Asia-Pacific Journal of Rural Development*, **10** (2), 67–92.

Kawachi, Ichiro, Bruce P. Kennedy and Kimberly Lochner (1997), 'Long live community: social capital as public health', *The American Prospect*, (November/December), 56–9.

Krishna, Anirudh (2002), *Active Social Capital: Tracing the Roots of Development and Democracy*, New York: Columbia University Press.

Lachmann, Ludwig M. (1978), *Capital and Its Structure*, Kansas City, MO: Sheed Andrews and McMeel.

Lake, Ronald La Due and Robert Huckfeldt (1998), 'Social capital, social networks, and political participation', *Political Psychology*, **19** (3), 567–84.

Langbein, Laura and Roseana Bess (2002), 'Sports in school: source of amity or antipathy', *Social Science Quarterly*, **83**, 2, 436–54.
Langbein, Laura and Connie M. Jorstad (2002), 'Productivity in the workplace: cops, culture, communication, cooperation, and collusion', working paper, Washington, DC: School of Public Affairs, American University.
Loury, Glenn (1977), 'A dynamic theory of racial income differences', in P.A. Wallace and A. LeMund (eds), *Women, Minorities, and Employment Discrimination*, Lexington, MA: Lexington Books, pp. 153–88.
Maggi, Giovanni (1999), 'The role of multilateral institutions in international trade cooperation', *American Economic Review*, **89** (1), 190–214.
Malaga, Ross A. (2001), 'Web-based reputation management system: problems and suggested solutions', *Electronic Commerce Research*, **1**, 403–17.
Milgrom, Paul R., Douglass C. North and Barry R. Weingast (1990), 'The role of institutions in the revival of trade: the law merchant, private judges, and the champagne fairs', *Economics & Politics*, **2** (1), 1–23.
National Research Council (NRC) (2002), *The Drama of the Commons*, Committee on the Human Dimensions of Global Change, Elinor Ostrom, Thomas Dietz, Nives Dolšak, Paul Stern, Susan Stonich and Elke Weber (eds), Washington, DC: National Academy Press.
North, Douglass C. (1990), *Institutions, Institutional Change, and Economic Performance*, New York: Cambridge University Press.
Olson, Mancur (1965), *The Logic of Collective Action: Public Goods and the Theory of Groups*, Cambridge, MA: Harvard University Press.
Orbell, John M. and Robyn M. Dawes (1991), 'A "cognitive miser" theory of cooperators' advantage', *American Political Science Review*, **85**, 515–28.
Orbell, John M., Peregrine Schwartz-Shea and Randy Simmons (1984), 'Do cooperators exit more readily than defectors?', *American Political Science Review*, **78**, 147–62.
Ostrom, Elinor (1992), *Crafting Institutions for Self-Governing Irrigation Systems*, San Francisco, CA: ICS Press.
Ostrom, Elinor (1998), 'A behavioral approach to the rational choice theory of collective action', *American Political Science Review*, **92** (1), 1–22.
Ostrom, Elinor (1999), 'Social capital: a fad or a fundamental concept', in Partha Dasgupta and Ismail Serageldin (eds), *Social Capital: A Multifaceted Perspective*, Washington, DC: World Bank, pp. 172–214.
Ostrom, Elinor (2005), *Understanding Institutional Diversity*, Princeton, NJ: Princeton University Press.
Ostrom, Elinor and T.K. Ahn (2001), 'A social science perspective on social capital', report commissioned by the Enquete Commission of the German Federal Government.
Ostrom, Elinor and Harini Nagendra (2006), 'Insights on linking forests, trees, and people from the air, on the ground, and in the laboratory', *Proceedings of the National Academy of Sciences (PNAS)*, **103** (51), 19224–31.
Ostrom, Elinor and James Walker (eds) (2003), *Trust and Reciprocity: Interdisciplinary Lessons from Experimental Research*, New York: Russell Sage Foundation.
Ostrom, Elinor, Roy Gardner and James Walker (1994), *Rules, Games, and Common-Pool Resources*, Ann Arbor, MI: University of Michigan Press.
Ostrom, Vincent (1991), *The Meaning of American Federalism: Constituting a Self-Governing Society*, San Francisco, CA: ICS Press.
Ostrom, Vincent (1997), *The Meaning of Democracy and the Vulnerability of Democracies: A Response to Tocqueville's Challenge*, Ann Arbor, MI: University of Michigan Press.
Putnam, Robert, with Robert Leonardi and Raffaella Nanetti (1993), *Making Democracy Work*, Princeton, NJ: Princeton University Press.
Rabin, Matthew (1993), 'Incorporating fairness into game theory and economics', *American Economic Review*, **83** (5), 1281–302.
Resnick, Paul, Richard Zeckhauser, John Swanson and Kate Lockwood (2006), 'The value of reputation on eBay: a controlled experiment', *Experimental Economics*, **9** (2), 79–101.

Richerson, Peter J. and Robert Boyd (2005), *Not by Genes Alone: How Culture Transformed Human Evolution*, Chicago, IL: University of Chicago Press.

Schultz, Theodore (1961), 'Investment in human capital', *American Economic Review*, **51**, 1-17.

Solow, Robert M. (1999), 'Notes on social capital and economic performance', in Partha Dasgupta and Ismail Serageldin (eds), *Social Capital: A Multifaceted Perspective*, Washington, DC: World Bank, pp. 6–9.

Standifird, Stephen S. (2001), 'Reputation and e-commerce: eBay auctions and the asymmetrical impact of positive and negative ratings', *Journal of Management*, **27**, 279–95.

Svendsen, Gert Tinggaard and Gunnar Lind Haase Svendsen (2004), *The Creation and Destruction of Social Capital: Entrepreneurship, Co-operative Movements and Institutions*, Cheltenham, UK and Northampton, MA, USA: Edward Elgar.

Taylor, Michael (1982), *Community, Anarchy, and Liberty*, Cambridge: Cambridge University Press.

Tocqueville, Alexis de (1945), *Democracy in America*, New York: Alfred A. Knopf. (First published in two volumes in 1835 and 1840.)

Torsvik, Gaute (2000), 'Social capital and economic development', *Rationality and Society*, **12** (4), 451–76.

Trivers, R.L. (1971), 'The evolution of reciprocal altruism', *Quarterly Review of Biology*, **46**, 35–57.

Truman, D.B. (1958), *The Governmental Process*, New York: Knopf.

Yamagishi, Toshio (2001), 'Trust as a form of social intelligence', in Karen Cook (ed.), *Trust in Society*, New York: Russell Sage Foundation, pp. 121–47.

Yamagishi, Toshio, Masako Kikushi and Motoko Kosugi (1999), 'Trust, gullibility, and social intelligence', *Asian Journal of Social Psychology*, **2** (1), 145–61.

3 Cooperation: evidence from experiments[1]
Anders Poulsen

3.1 Introduction

Most social capital researchers consider the ability of groups, regions and entire societies to cooperate as a crucial, if not defining, aspect of social capital; see, for example, Putnam (1993) and Coleman (1988). Among well-known examples of cooperation are a group of neighbours who look after each others' houses, thereby reducing break-ins and theft; reprimanding the local youth for transgressing, thus keeping crime low; residents removing snow from a public driveway; not littering in the local park; joining a local volunteer association that fights crime, vandalism and graffiti; a buyer and seller who each does his or her part of the deal without cheating the other side; taking part in a consumer boycott; keeping the thermostat low during a winter fuel shortage; not shirking in teams; restraining one's resource use in common pool resource situations, such as fishing in international waters; paying taxes; not collecting illegitimate social welfare payments; voting; avoiding proliferation of nuclear weapons, and reducing greenhouse gasses.[2]

In all these situations, there is no central coercive authority (state, 'police officer', or world government) that, through the use of fines, prison sentences, taxes or subsidies, get people to cooperate. Even if one exists, it may be weak or corrupt, and so unable to effectively sanction opportunistic behaviour. Cooperation must instead be based on incentives that are locally provided, by the group members themselves. The fundamental problem is that in these situations each individual group member has an incentive to not cooperate (for example, litter, over-fish or let other team members do most of the work on the joint project), regardless of what the other group members do. When all group members behave in this free-riding manner, the overall result for the group is worse than if all had cooperated. Individual rationality leads to collective irrationality.

In this chapter we think of social capital as a group's ability to generate high and stable levels of cooperation in difficult situations such as those described above. In this survey we describe the literature using economic experiments.[3] This literature is novel and rapidly expanding, and it has produced several interesting and important insights. Our survey will also show that many economists recently have become interested in concepts and questions that were previously thought to lie outside the domain of economic analysis.[4]

What is the experimental evidence on cooperation? We first consider the experimental evidence on how much groups cooperate. We then survey the findings on why group members cooperate. We then. describe the features of an economic or social situation that promote, or hinder, to cooperation.

What is the value of an experimental approach to measuring and understanding cooperation? Experiments allow us to control the context in which people make decisions and hence provide us with clean data on the extent and determinants of cooperation. By comparing the degree of cooperation in two experiments that differ only in the presence of some variable, it becomes possible to evaluate the significance of this, and only this, variable. Second, in the economic experiments we shall review subjects earn money and how much depends on the outcomes. The subjects' cooperation decisions thus have real implications, as is clearly the case in real situations. A weakness of the experimental approach is the artificiality of the laboratory environment. As we shall see below, however, economists have recently turned to field experiments; see the survey in Harrison and List (2004). As with any other empirical research method, the experimental approach has advantages and disadvantages, and it should be seen as complementary to other research methods. For introductions to and surveys on experimental economics, the reader is referred to Camerer (2003), Davis and Holt (1993), Kagel and Roth (1995), and Roth (1987).

Owing to space constraints, this chapter is selective and not intended to be an exhaustive survey of the experimental findings on cooperation.[5] We have instead assigned priority to some of the recent findings.

The rest of the chapter is organized as follows. In Section 3.2 we describe a simple and frequently used model of cooperation. Section 3.3 describes a representative cooperation experiment. Section 3.4 describes the role of reciprocity and trust for cooperation. In Section 3.5 we describe the features that have been shown to be important determinants of cooperation. We sum up and conclude in Section 3.6. Section 3.7 outlines some future research.

3.2 Cooperation

Most experimental studies of cooperation are based on a model known as the Prisoner's Dilemma.[6] In this model, each group member has two choices, 'Cooperate' (C) and 'Defect' (D). The meaning of these choices depends on the context. The C choice could mean 'Help to fight crime in the neighbourhood', and D could mean 'Stay home and watch television'. Each group member is assumed to choose between C and D without knowing the other members' choices.[7] The Prisoner's Dilemma game is used to model 'collective action problems' (Olson, 1971), the 'tragedy

	C	D
C	6.6	3.7
D	7.3	4.4

Figure 3.1   A two-person Prisoner's Dilemma

of the commons' (Hardin, 1968) and 'social dilemmas' (Dawes, 1980). It also models voluntary contributions to the production of a public good (Ledyard, 1995).[8] Most of the experiments we consider in this survey belong to the latter category.

The Prisoner's Dilemma for a group with just two members, say Smith and Jones, is shown in Figure 3.1. Smith chooses between the rows, and Jones chooses between the columns. The numbers in the figure indicate the material reward that each person obtains, depending on his own and the other group member's choice.[9] We assume, in line with most traditional economic theory, that each group member seeks to achieve an outcome that gives him or her the highest material reward; the plausibility of this assumption is discussed in Section 3.4. We see from the figure that the best outcome for the group is when the entire group cooperates (there is then no time to watch television, but also no crime – and the latter outcome is plausibly the more valuable to each group member). The worst outcome for the group is when no one cooperates (there will be plenty of crime and people will watch television at home not daring to walk outside in the evenings). But we also see that each individual group member prefers the outcome where he or she defects (watches television) and the *other* group member cooperates (that is, the other group member does all the hard work fighting crime, which benefits *all* neighbours, including the neighbour watching television at home).

What will Smith and Jones choose? Regardless of what Jones is thought to do, Smith prefers to defect (D) rather than to cooperate (C). Similarly, no matter what Jones believes Smith will do, Jones is better off defecting. According to economic theory, Smith and Jones will therefore each decide to defect, so the outcome is (D,D). But both group members would be better off if they had both chosen to cooperate. In the language of economics, both choosing D is the only Nash equilibrium of the situation. A Nash equilibrium is a situation where each group member chooses his or her most preferred action, given the choices made by the other group members. See Binmore (1992) for a detailed argument.[10]

3.3 How much do people cooperate?

The prediction of universal defection developed in the previous section was based on economic theory. How much do people cooperate in practice? Let us consider a recent experiment, by Fehr and Gächter (2000a). In each session of their experiment, there were 24 subjects. The subjects interacted for ten periods. In each of those periods, the subjects were randomly divided into six four-person groups. Subjects knew that there were a finite number of periods.[11] Group members did not know the identity of other group members and could not communicate in any way. Only neutral wordings were used in the instructions and on the computer screens.

In each period, a four-person group faced the following version of the Prisoner's Dilemma. Each person was given 20 tokens that had a monetary value. A subject could either keep these tokens for himself or could contribute all or some of them to a joint project. Keeping tokens is the same as defecting (consume a private good, such as watch television); contributing tokens to the joint project corresponds to contributing to a public good (fight crime in the neighbourhood). The total number of tokens that the group members decided to contribute to the joint project was multiplied by a number (0.4) and the resulting number gave the total amount of the public good. *Each* group member then received this amount. The number 0.4 represents how productive the contributions were in producing the joint project (public good).[12] A subject's total earnings was given by the sum of the tokens he kept for himself (watching television) and the quantity of the public good that was produced (low crime levels).[13] At the end of each period, each group member learned the other group members' contributions, and this was repeated for ten rounds. A subject's total earnings equalled the sum of the ten individual period earnings. Once the experiment was over, the earnings were converted into real money.

In this experiment, as in the Prisoner's Dilemma, the group's total earnings is maximized when all group members contribute everything to the joint project. However, no matter how much the other group members contribute, each individual is best off when he or she contributes zero tokens to the public good.[14] It follows that the economic prediction is that there will be no contributions to joint project (the public good) – universal defection occurs in every period.[15]

The main findings of the experiment were the following. In the initial periods, contribution rates were high (exceeding 30 per cent), but they decreased over time. Towards the end, most subjects did not contribute anything to the joint project. The average number of tokens contributed to the joint project was 3.7 (a contribution rate of 18.5 per cent). In the final period, the average contribution rate was only 9.5 per cent (see Fehr and Gächter, 2000a: table 3).

This finding, that initial cooperation is significant but deteriorates over time, is typical in the literature. See for example Keser and van Winden (2000), Ledyard (1995), and Fehr and Schmidt (1999). A recent survey is Gächter (2006). Typically, subjects start out contributing between 40 per cent and 60 per cent of their endowment to the joint project; see Sally (1995). These contribution rates tend to fall over time, however, and towards the end most subjects consistently keep all their endowment. The initial high cooperation cannot be sustained by the group. Similar results have been found for the Prisoner's Dilemma (Figure 3.1); see Dawes (1980) and Sally (1995).

3.4   Why do some people cooperate? The role of reciprocity and trust
How can we explain that there is a significant degree of cooperation in the group, but that it tends to fall over time?

3.4.1   Reciprocity
One plausible explanation is that there are different 'types' of subjects in the population from which groups are formed. A subject's type refers to his value system and desires, or, as economists call it, his preferences. Some people prefer to always defect; this is the self-interested Homo Economicus type of person that populates traditional economic models. But other subjects prefer to contribute to the public good *if* they expect the other group members will do the same; otherwise they prefer not to contribute. This type of behaviour is called *conditional cooperation* or *reciprocity*; see Fehr and Gächter (2000a, 2000b) and Sugden (1984).[16]

In the Prisoner's Dilemma, a reciprocal group member *prefers* to cooperate if he or she expects the other group members to cooperate; and he prefers to defect if he believes the other group members will defect. In other words, a reciprocally motivated person is not guided solely by a desire to maximize his or her material returns, as is Homo Economicus.[17] Reciprocity, together with inequity aversion (Fehr and Schmidt, 1999; see also Bolton and Ockenfels, 2000) are important manifestations of the more general finding that people preferences are concerned with more than just their own money earnings; this is referred to as *social preferences*; see Camerer and Fehr (2005, 2006), Sobel (2005) and Schram (2000). For a theoretical analysis of social capital and social preferences, see Poulsen and Svendsen (2005).

There is now considerable experimental evidence that a substantial proportion of subjects are motivated by reciprocity in cooperation, and other situations.

In the experiment by Fischbacher et al. (2001), it was found that 50 per cent of subjects could be classified as reciprocal (conditional cooperators), 30 per cent could be classified as self-interested (free-riders), and the remaining 20 per cent of subjects displayed other kinds of behaviour. See also Bardsley and Moffatt (2007), Croson (2007) and Fischbacher and Gächter (2006).

In the field experiment by Frey and Meier (2004), students enrolling at the University of Zurich made higher (lower) donations to a charitable university fund when they were informed that a high (low) proportion of other students had made similar donations.

Gächter (2006) described other public goods experiments.[18]

The insight that there is a substantial proportion of reciprocally motivated people in the population allows us to understand the experimentally observed decline in cooperation over time, described in Section 3.3. It is due to the interaction between reciprocal and self-interested people in the group. What happens is that the reciprocally minded subjects 'give up' contributing, since they dislike being the only ones who contribute, and since they cannot directly discipline or punish the defecting subjects. Resigning, the reciprocally oriented subjects decide that the best they can do is to not contribute anything. Cooperation thus falls over time. See also Fischbacher et al. (2001).

3.4.2 Trust

A reciprocally minded person is willing to cooperate if he or she believes that the other group members are going to cooperate, too. Otherwise, he or she prefers to defect. It follows that a reciprocal person's *beliefs* about what other people in the group will do is crucial. To get cooperation, it is not enough to have reciprocity; the reciprocal people must believe other people will cooperate.[19] Anything that affects the reciprocal group members' beliefs affect how willing they are to cooperate. See Gächter (2006) for a detailed discussion.

We can thus say that a reciprocal person cooperates if he or she *trusts* that other people will cooperate. To trust in our context is thus to be sufficiently convinced that other people in the group will also cooperate. See Hardin (2003) for a discussion. The concept of trust is, of course, crucial to social capital research. The relationship between trust and cooperation that we postulate here is oversimplified. See the other chapters in this handbook and Cook and Cooper (2003) for a discussion. There is also an experimental literature specifically investigating the formation of trust in certain situations. See for example Ostrom and Walker (2003) and Camerer (2003: ch. 2).

What determines the extent to which a reciprocal person will trust that other group members will cooperate, and hence will cooperate him or herself? In the next section we describe some experimental findings.

3.5   What promotes cooperation?

The findings described in the previous section led experimental economists to investigate which factors could increase and stabilize cooperation.

3.5.1   Punishing free-riders

The important experiment by Fehr and Gächter (2000a), described in Section 3.3, also considered the situation where group members could punish other group members.[20] This was done in the following way. After group members had made their contribution decisions (how many tokens to keep for themselves and how many to contribute to the joint project), each group member learned how much each of the other group members had contributed. A group member could then punish other group members by assigning a number of 'punishment points' to the latter, and these reduced the latter's money earnings. Punishment was costly in that it also reduced the punisher's own money earnings.

Theoretically, since punishment is costly for the punisher, no rational and self-interested person should punish. Knowing that, no one will contribute. The prediction is therefore that costly punishment should not make a difference – contributions will remain at zero and no one will punish.[21] However, Fehr and Gächter find that the opportunity to punish low contributors had a dramatically positive impact on contribution rates. With punishment, people start out contributing more than without punishment, and on average the contribution rate with punishment is 58 per cent, much higher than the 18.5 per cent observed under no punishment. Importantly, the contribution rates no longer fall over time. Indeed, there are situations where they increase over time. In the last period, the average contribution rate with punishment is more than 61 per cent, a dramatic increase relative to the no-punishment setting.

The experimental data show that punishment raises contribution. This increases the group's total earnings. But recall that punishment is costly, both for the punished and the one meting out the punishments. What is the net effect on overall welfare? The data reveal that in the early periods, the net effect on welfare is negative, while it tends to be positive in later periods. See also the discussion in Page et al. (2005: fn. 15).

Why does the opportunity to punish increase cooperation? The reciprocators punish the free-riders, even though doing so reduces the reciprocators' own earnings. In particular, the less a subject contributes relative to the average contribution in the group, the more he or she tends to be punished (see table 5 in Fehr and Gächter, 2000a). Realizing this, the selfish types increase their contribution in order to avoid punishment. All this acts to increase the reciprocators' trust that the other groups members will indeed cooperate, hence inducing them to cooperate. This observation, that reciprocity can 'discipline' self-interested people's behaviour in groups, is discussed further in Fehr and Schmidt (1999). Following Fehr and Gächter's seminal experiment, other experiments have reached much the same conclusions and have explored other issues concerning punishment. See Carpenter (2007), Fehr and Gächter (2002), Falk et al. (2005), Masclet and Villeval (2006) and Nikiforakis (2008).

Punishment is very effective in generating high and stable cooperation. Note, however, a key requirement for punishment to work: The reciprocal group members must have information about individual group members' contributions. Without such detailed information, punishments cannot be targeted towards free-riders, and in this case the deterrent effects of punishment is likely to be much smaller.

3.5.2   Counter-punishment – can we really govern ourselves?

The previous section seems to convey a positive message: when there are opportunities for reciprocally minded people to mete out informal and decentralized punishments, we can generate high and stable cooperation in groups. We do not need a central coercive authority, a Hobbesian Leviathan, to rule us. We can, apparently, govern ourselves.

Recent research has, however, shown that this may be a too simplistic and optimistic conclusion. Note that in the experiment described in Section 3.5.1, a person who is punished cannot punish back. That is, he or she cannot take revenge. But if punishment is an option, then counter-punishment seems equally plausible.[22] What happens when counter-punishment is possible? Does the fear of reprisal deter reciprocally minded people from punishing, and does this increase free-riding? Does it lead to bloody vendettas destroying most of the social surplus? Nikiforakis (2008) conducts an experiment with counter-punishment. As in Fehr and Gächter (2000a), subjects first decide on how much to contribute to the joint project, and they can then punish other group members at a second stage. But Nikiforakis adds a third stage where subjects are informed of who (if any) punished them and where a punished subject can punish back, by assigning 'counter-punishment' points to those who punished him or her. Counter-punishment is costly, as is punishment.[23]

The experimental data show that counter-punishment reduces overall cooperation. Contributions with counter-punishment are below those where only punishment is possible. Cooperation is lowest when no form of punishment is possible (the standard set-up), investigated in Section 3.3. In the final period, cooperation under counter-punishment is almost as low as when no punishment is possible. Counter-punishment thus neutralizes the beneficial effects of punishment, observed in Section 3.5.1. When the punished can punish the punishers, it seems that we end up not being able to govern ourselves.

Denant-Boemont et al. (2005) extends Nikiforakis' design in several ways. They allow for several rounds of punishment (punishment followed by counter-punishment followed by counter-counter-punishment). In this case, there are costly vendettas, and overall group welfare can even be lower than when punishments are allowed and individual contributions to the joint project would be zero (the basic situation studied in Section 3.3).

These experimental findings on the effects of counter-punishment are important and sobering. Once we realize that punishment can, and is likely to be accompanied by counter-punishment, informal decentralized punishment does not seem to be the panacea we may initially have thought. It seems that for punishment to be socially desirable, either counter-punishment must somehow be prevented or, at a minimum, it must not be possible for free-riders to identify *who* punished them.

3.5.3   Non-monetary punishment

Masclet et al. (2003) observe that the efficacy of (one-sided) punishments (see Section 3.5.1) to increase cooperation could be due either to the fact that punishment lowers the free-riders' money earnings from making low contributions, or due to the fact that punishments express *disapproval*. If even free-riders experience a psychic welfare loss from disapproval (shame or guilt), this can induce them to increase contributions, even though the disapproval has no monetary implications.

Masclet et al. accordingly run an experiment where punishment is non-monetary and only expresses disapproval.[24] They run the same no-punishment and monetary punishment treatment as in Fehr and Gächter (2000a), and a new treatment, where instead of assigning monetary punishments, subjects could assign 'disapproval points' to other specific group members. It was free to assign this kind of punishment and it did not reduce the recipient's earnings.

Expressing disapproval was in the early periods of the experiment as efficient as monetary punishment in raising cooperation.

In subsequent periods, however, monetary punishment is more effective. Nevertheless, since non-monetary punishment is 'cheaper' than monetary punishment, the group's overall earnings are as high as in the case of one-sided monetary punishment. Allowing subjects to express disapproval that has no monetary consequences per se thus raises cooperation and earnings.[25]

3.5.4 Isolating free-riders

An alternative to punishment is to expel defectors from the group.[26] Expulsion only works when people can be prevented from consuming the benefit that the group produces. Clearly, one cannot prevent defectors from benefiting from a clean atmosphere. Expulsion thus works with smaller groups producing benefits that are more or less specific to the group. In economic terminology, the benefit produced by the group can be non-rival but must be excludable. A professional society, say of doctors or builders, can decide to take away the certificate of a member who is thought to have behaved antisocially. Or, the management may decide to remove a free-riding employee from the team.

Expulsion is likely to be costly for the group, both because it may be difficult and time-consuming to expel other people from the group, and it is likely to be psychologically unpleasant. Indeed, since expulsion is costly, Homo Economicus will never want to pay to expel other group members. Knowing this, no one will fear being expelled; contributions will be as low (namely zero) as without the possibility of group expulsion.

Cinyabuguma et al. (2005) run an experiment with group expulsion.[27] Subjects received 10 experimental dollars that could be put either on a 'private account' (kept by the subject) or on a 'joint account' (the public good). A group had 16 members and the group interacted for 15 periods. This fixed number of periods was known by the subjects. At the first stage, group members decided on contributions to the public good. At a second stage, each subject saw other group members' contributions and could then secretly vote to expel other group members. The votes were then added up and shown to all subjects on their computer screens. If half or more of all group members had voted to expel any given group member, that group member was expelled for the remainder of the 15 periods. Expulsion meant being moved to a second group. This group, which consisted of all the expelled individuals, faced a similar public goods situation, but each expelled individual was given fewer experimental dollars. If a group member was expelled, all the remaining group members paid a cost, equal to 25 experimental cents. Expulsion was thus costly. But note that attempts to expel (vote) was not costly per se.

What happened in the experiment? The economic prediction fared badly. There was frequent voting to expel other group members and typically between one and four subjects were driven out of the group. Compared to when no expulsion is available, expulsion results in very high cooperation rates. On average, more than 90 per cent of the experimental money was contributed to the group account.

It is the low-contributing group members who were driven out. The data analysis shows that it is the anticipation of this that increases cooperation.

Also, the possibility of expulsion led to higher overall earnings (even when including the earnings of the expelled group members), relative to when expulsion was not an option.

3.5.5   Avoiding free-riders

Rather than expelling free-riders, it may be possible to avoid meeting them in the first place, or to distance oneself from them. This requires that one can get information about other people's past cooperation/defection record. If so, endogenous formation of groups can allow cooperators to cluster and prevent exploitation by free riders.

This may have the same positive impact on cooperation as group expulsion and punishment, but it avoids the costs associated with these methods.

Page et al. (2005) experimentally studied a situation where subjects could seek out new group members.[28] In each session, there were 16 subjects participated. Groups consisted of four members and there were 20 periods. As usual, this was commonly known. At the end of periods 3, 6, 9, 12, 15 and 18, each subject was shown a list of all the other 15 subjects' contributions in all previous periods on his computer screen. Each subject then indicated a preference for which three of the other 15 subjects he would like to form a new group with. It was costly to indicate a preference for new group members. A subject could decide not to rank other group members. If this was chosen, the computer assigned the number 8 to every other subject. Once all subjects had completed such a ranking, the computer formed four new groups by first identifying those four subjects for whom the sum of each other's rankings were the highest. These four subjects were put in the same group. A similar matching algorithm was used to form the second, third and fourth group. Once the new groups were formed, group members resumed their contribution decisions.[29]

The data show that the endogenous formation of new groups improves cooperation. On average the rate of cooperation with endogenous groups was 70 per cent, while it was only 28 per cent without regrouping. Page et al. also compare endogenous groups with costly punishment, studied in Section 3.5.1. In terms of subjects' overall earnings, regrouping is preferable. The reason is that whereas punishment is costly both for the punisher and the one he or she punishes, the only cost of regrouping is the cost of ranking other group members (this can be interpreted as a 'transportation cost', incurred when finding new group members).

What kind of group members were endogenously grouped together? Not surprisingly, subjects in general expressed a preference to be matched with those who had contributed a lot in the past. As a result, there was a clear separation: the four people who had previously been making the highest contributions were able to get together in the same group; of the remaining subjects, the four highest got together to form the second group, and so on. Finally, the four least contributing individuals ended up in the last group.

The experiment by Page et al. shows that when individuals have sufficient information about other individuals' past behaviour and when they can influence with whom they interact, there can arise a socially beneficial segregation of people into different cooperativeness.[30]

3.5.6 Communication

Why not just let people talk about the situation before they decide on how much to cooperate? According to orthodox economic theory, such communication should not matter, for talk does not change the material incentives of the situation. Homo Economicus does therefore not assign any credibility to other peoples' free messages.[31]

The claim that free and non-binding communication is worthless in stimulating cooperation has, however, been proven squarely wrong. Numerous experiments (mostly by social psychologists, see Sally, 1995, for a survey), indicate that allowing people to communicate before deciding how much to contribute significantly raises contribution rates, relative to when communication is ruled out. In a meta-study, Sally (1995), it was found that communication raises cooperation by 40 per cent.

Communication can improve cooperation for many reasons. It can help group members to better understand the situation, in particular that the group is best off when all people cooperate; it allows for exchanges of promises and threats; it can activate social norms, minimize 'social distance' between group members and create a group identity (we return to this in Section 3.5.7); see Brosig et al. (2003) for a discussion. Just being able to *see* other subjects' faces can have a positive effect on cooperation; see Sally (1995) and Eckel and Wilson (2002).

What kind of communication is best for cooperation? Communication can be face to face, taking place around a table or via a video conference; it can be message based, such as communicating with others in a chat room, or by exchanging emails; it can be purely auditory (telephone). As already described, economic theory has traditionally been of little help in shedding light on this question, because it has treated any communication as 'cheap'. This is, however, changing. Some recent economic experiments investigating the relative efficacy of the various communication methods on the ability of groups to cooperate are Bochet et al. (2006) and Brosig et al. (2003). These studies find that face-to-face communication is the most efficient communication method.[32] One possible explanation is that face-to-face communication is most effective at revealing other peoples' intentions and trustworthiness; this in turn indicates that the primary reason why communication generates additional cooperation is that it somehow fosters solidarity and group identity.

3.5.7   Group identity

According to the traditional economic approach, people's main motivation is to maximize their material returns. Being a member of a group can affect behaviour only in so far as it affects an individual's material benefits and costs; but it cannot affect the individual's motivation itself. Social psychologists have, however, long emphasized that group membership can exert a separate influence on motivation. See, for example, Tajfel (1982). If a group member identifies with the group, the resulting group identity can affect the individual's motivation. The individual can assign larger weight to the group's overall interests, and this can lead to more cooperation. There is, however, a side-effect: outgroup members may receive a worse treatment. This is known as ingroup–outgroup bias or ingroup favouritism (see Dawes et al., 1988; Bicchieri, 2002; Hewstone et al., 2002).

Chen and Li (2006) experimentally test social identification theory (Tajfel, 1982) according to which belonging to even completely arbitrarily created groups can affect behaviour.[33] The experiment consisted of three stages. At the first stage, two groups were formed on the basis of subjects' preferences between paintings by Klee or Kandinsky. Each subject knew his or her group assignment (Klee or Kandinsky) and how many subjects were in the group. This first stage corresponds to what social psychologists call the formation of 'minimal groups' (Tajfel, 1982). At the second stage of the experiment, each subject allocated money between pairs of other subjects. The allocating subject knew the two other members' group affiliation (Kandisky or Klee). At the third stage, each subject allocated money between him/herself and another subject, and once more the other person's group affiliation was known.

According to economic theory, a subject will not condition his behaviour on either his own or on other subjects' group affiliation. Nevertheless, Chen and Li find that group affiliation does matter. At the second stage, subjects are significantly more generous towards people from the same group than people from the other group. When allocating money between members from the same group (in or outgroup), no group affiliation effect is observed. Similarly, at the third stage, when interacting with an ingroup member, subjects are considerably more cooperative, generous, and forgiving than when interacting with outgroup subjects. They are also more willing to take actions that maximize total surplus. All this can be seen as the effects of group identity. Although the groups were created artificially and membership had no effect on earnings per se, group affiliation matters for the subsequent observed behaviour.

An important question, then, is how are the overall earnings affected by the created group identities? Chen and Li used a control treatment with subjects who had not been exposed to the first and second stages, described above. These subjects made stage three choices without any notions of group affiliation. The data from the main treatment show that ingroup earnings increase, but earnings fall when people from different groups interact. Moreover, the net effect on overall earnings is negative. Thus overall, compared with the control, the engineering of group identity led to an overall *decrease* in earnings.[34]

Charness et al. (2006) and Eckel and Grossman (2005) also experimentally explore the role of group identity for cooperation (both are laboratory experiments).[35] They find weaker results than Chen and Li (2006). Charness et al. find that a minimal group condition is not enough to generate more cooperation in a Prisoner's Dilemma game. But if the group has a stake in each member's earnings and if other group members observe a group member's choice, there is less cooperation when members of different groups meet. In this sense, the group as a whole becomes more aggressive. The overall effect can be to lower the overall social earnings. Eckel and Grossman (2005), in a public good experiment framed as team production, also find that weak manipulation of team identity (such as assigning different colours to different groups) does not suffice to generate more cooperation. Only a stronger manipulation, such as inter-group competition where the group that produces most gets a prize, has a significant positive effect on cooperation. For some interesting field experiments documenting various degrees of ingroup-favouritism, see Ferhstman and Gneezy (2001), Goette et al. (2006), and Ruffle and Sosis (2006).

Overall, the evidence thus shows that group identity can be fostered, but the evidence is mixed regarding how easy it is to generate it. In some experiments, it was enough to divide people into groups based on their preference between different artists. In other experiments, a stronger manipulation was required. Second, it remains unclear what the overall effect on social welfare is from creating group identity. This depends on whether or not the positive effect from increased ingroup cooperation outweighs the detrimental effects from increased hostility when dealing with outgroup members.

3.6 Engineering cooperation: a summary

What have experiments taught us about cooperation? In the basic cooperation situation, studied in Section 3.3, we saw that people tend to start out with a high cooperation rate. This is due to the presence of reciprocal subjects. But over time cooperation deteriorates, since the presence of free riding subjects discourages reciprocators, who as a consequence 'give up' and start to defect, too.

What can ensure high and enduring cooperation? There are several methods. Punishments that reduce the earnings of the free-riders, but also of the punishers, work very well. The problem is that punishments can trigger counter-punishments (and counter-counter-punishments), and the associated costs may outweigh the gains from higher cooperation. Another mechanism is non-monetary punishment, such as expressing disapproval. This is a cheaper method, since it does not reduce the material earnings of the group. But is it less effective in raising cooperation and an open issue is what happens if the sanctioned can express counter-disapproval. A more radical but effective approach is to expel free-riders. This may, of course, be physically impossible or for other reasons morally problematic. If, over time, reciprocally motivated people can seek out each other and avoid free-riders, the resulting segregation can generate more co-operation.

Communication, especially face-to-face, is very effective in increasing cooperation, and it is cheap. If the group is large, such a communication method may however be impossible. Creating a group identity can give more cooperation within the group, but there may be less cooperation when individuals interact with outgroup members. The overall effect on society's welfare can thus be negative.

3.7 Some unresolved issues

Let us very briefly mention two areas that seem interesting to investigate further. The first area concerns reciprocity. As is clear from this survey, it is the presence of reciprocally motivated people who, although materially costly, are willing to punish free-riders that is the raw resource that cooperation thrives on. If there is no reciprocity, there will be no or very little cooperation. One crucial question is, why are these people willing to punish – is it due to social norms or may there even be a biological basis for punishment? The reader is referred to Knoch et al. (2006) and De Quervain et al. (2004), and the references therein. The potential role played by biological and neurological factors is explored by the emerging field of neuroeconomics. See Camerer et al. (2005).

Another important issue facing many modern societies is: How can we raise the proportion of reciprocally oriented people in society? We know very little about this. Education by parents and teachers, the presence of role models, but also society's institutional make-up seem to matter for which 'types' (reciprocity, self-interest) will flourish.[36]

The second promising area is experimental analysis of centralized sanctioning institutions (the state). How do they arise and, compared to the decentralized institutions we have described in this chapter, how effective are they? There are relative few such experiments (see, for example, Kosfeld et al., 2006) and scope for much more experimental work.

Notes

1. I thank Daniel Zizzo and the editors for helpful comments. All errors are mine.
2. Many of these examples are from Dawes (1980).
3. The main difference between 'economic' experiments and other social science experiments is that economists pay their subjects for the choices they make and that they do not use deception.
4. The growing research field known as 'behavioural economics' (see, for example, Mullainathan and Thaler, 2000; Camerer, 2003; Camerer et al., 2004) is a testimony of this.
5. See Dawes (1980), Ledyard (1995) and Kollock (1998).
6. See, for example, Kollock (1998) for the history of this extremely important and influential model of cooperation.
7. Or, more generally, group members are unable to make binding agreements about what each group member should do.
8. Public goods are goods and activities that no group member can be excluded from enjoying and where consumption of the public good by one group member does not reduce other group members' consumption possibilities. Classic examples of public goods are national defence, clean environment and a crime-free neighbourhood.
9. To make sense of the numbers, assume Smith and Jones must each decide either to spend 4 hours watching television or 4 hours fighting crime. The total reward to each person is the sum of his reward from watching television (the private good) and his reward from enjoying low crime (the public good). Assume that each hour spent in front of the television gives reward 1, while each hour spent out fighting crime gives a reward of $3/4$ to *both* neighbours (low crime is a public good). If both neighbours watch television, each gets reward $1 \times 4 + (3/4)(0 + 0) = 4$. If, however, both neighbours spend their time fighting crime, each gets reward $1 \times 0 + (3/4)(4 + 4) = 6$. But if Jones fights crime and Smith watches television, Smith gets reward $1 \times 4 + (3/4)(0 + 4) = 7$, and Jones gets $1 \times 0 + (3/4)(0 + 4) = 3$. Similarly the other way around.
10. In this analysis, we implicitly assumed Smith and Jones only faced the decision situation once. More generally, however, the conclusion that universal defection occurs holds whenever the situation is encountered a fixed and known number of periods. It is also possible that the group perceives that a given situation will be repeated indefinitely. In this situation, cooperation can occur if group members are sufficiently forward-looking. See Binmore (1992). In this survey, we consider the first class of situations, since these are regarded as the most problematic.
11. The random re-shuffling of groups after each period ensures that it is very unlikely that two subjects interact repeatedly. This is a 'Stranger' matching protocol; see Andreoni (1988). This minimizes the extent of other factors influencing cooperation, such as repeated game effects. Fehr and Gächter also consider a 'Partner'-treatment where the same group members repeat for ten periods. The results for this treatment are similar to Stranger treatment, and here we only consider the Stranger treatment.
12. In symbols, let g_i denote group member i's contribution to the joint project, where i = 1, 2, 3, 4. When all four members have made their contribution decisions, member i's earnings are: $20 - g_i + 0.4 \times (g_1 + g_2 + g_3 + g_4)$. In the previous section, we used the number 0.75 instead of 0.4; see fn. 9.
13. This situation is known as the 'voluntary contribution mechanism' (see, for example, Dawes and Thaler, 1988). It can be thought of as a continuous version of the Prisoner's Dilemma, since subjects can choose intermediate levels of cooperation (contributing to the joint project) or defecting (keeping money). The outcome where a group member keeps (contributes) all tokens, is like playing 'C' ('D') in the Prisoner's Dilemma.
14. If in any period each group member contributes all the 20 tokens to the joint project,

each member gets a reward equal to $1 \times 0 + 0.4 \times (20 + 20 + 20 + 20) = 32$. This is higher than the 20 tokens each member gets if they all keep their tokens (only watch television). However, the additional (or marginal) return to any individual member from keeping a token is 1, while the additional return from contributing to the joint project is only 0.4. This implies that any *individual* group member's earnings is highest when he/ she keeps all 20 tokens, regardless of what the other group members decide to do. All group members are therefore predicted to defect.

15. This theoretical prediction follows from the fact that there is a finite number of periods and from the fact that groups were randomly re-shuffled each period. See Fehr and Gächter (2000a) for details.

16. It is important to distinguish reciprocity from altruism. An altruist can prefer to cooperate in the Prisoner's Dilemma even if he or she expects the other group members to defect. Altruism is unconditional cooperation and hence conceptually very different from reciprocity. Altruism also seems to be be empirically less relevant than reciprocity in explaining cooperation. See Fehr and Schmidt (1999) and Gächter (2006); but see also Andreoni et al. (2007).

17. Reciprocity-based cooperation is different from the self-interested cooperation typically emphasized by game theorists and economists. The latter sort of cooperation requres a very long time horizon and sufficiently forward-looking and patient individuals (see, for example, Binmore, 1992). Reciprocity, on the other hand, can generate cooperation even if the situation is only encountered once. This also makes reciprocity different from evolutionary models of cooperation, based on Tit-for-Tat and other strategies (Axelrod, 1984); see Sethi and Somanathan (2003).

18. Reciprocity is also experimentally documented in many other decision situations, such as bargaining and distributional situations. See Fehr and Schmidt (1999) and Camerer (2003). Sethi and Somanathan (2003) surveys the literature on reciprocity. Reciprocity has also been found to influence the behaviour of third parties; this is called *indirect* reciprocity. See Seinen and Schram (2006).

19. Suppose two reciprocal persons face the Prisoner's Dilemma game, and suppose each knows the other is reciprocal. If each person is pessimistic and believes the other person will defect, it is best to defect. If each person is optimistic and believes it is sufficiently likely that the other person will cooperate, then each will cooperate. In the language of game theory, both mutual cooperation and mutual defection are Nash equilibria.

20. Another experiment investigating punishment is Ostrom et al. (1992).

21. For a theoretical analysis of a related situation, see Sethi (1996).

22. One can imagine a conversation of the form: 'You are not going to invite me to dinner because I did not help with the voluntary work last week? Well, in that case I'm not going to drive your kids to the next football match!'

23. One restriction of Nikiforakis' design is that punished subjects can only punish those who punished them at the second stage. See Deanant-Boemont et al. (2005).

24. An experiment combining monetary and non-monetary punishment is Noussair and Tucker (2005). See also Rege and Telle (2004) and Gächter and Fehr (1999).

25. In Masclet et al.'s experiment, subjects expressed disapproval by sending messages via a computer. Presumably, if subjects interacted face to face, the dispproval effect would be even stronger; see Section 3.5.6. But note also that Masclet et al. did not allow a subject who received disapproval to return the disapproval ('counter-disapprove'), cf. Section 3.5.2.

26. See Hirshleifer and Ramusen (1989) for a theoretical model of ostracism.

27. A related experiment is Maier-Rigaud et al. (2005).

28. A closely related experiment is Gächter and Thöni (2005).

29. Note an important feature of the group formation process: two individuals are likely to be assigned to the same group only if *both* would like to be together. In other words, a defector, who is likely to rank cooperators highly, cannot unilaterally decide to be with cooperators (since the latter are likely to give the defectors a very low rank). This can be contrasted with the experiment in Ehrhardt and Keser (1999), where a defector can join any group. Coricelli et al. (2003) study some related matching protocols.

30. Other experiments investigating the impact of the group formation process on overall cooperation is Bohnet and Kübler (2005), and Gunnthorsdottir et al. (2007). For experiments investigating the role of information about past behaviour, see Seinen and Schram (2006) and the references therein.
31. Economists typically consider verbal statements that are not backed up by credible threats or promises as having no credibility and being merely 'cheap talk'. See Farrell and Rabin (1996) for a review of the literature.
32. Face-to-face communication also improves peoples' ability to reach agreement in negotiation situations. See Roth (1995).
33. Their experiment does not use the Prisoner's Dilemma situation, but considers related situations, and the experiment is interesting enough to be reported here in some detail.
34. For a similar finding in a somewhat different context, see Hargreaves Heap and Zizzo (2006).
35. Zizzo (2005) explores the strength of group identity ('common fate') in bargaining and coordination games. See also Cookson (2000) for how cooperation is sensitive to the experimental framing of the situation.
36. See Bisin and Verdier (2001) for a formal model of the intergenerational transmission of preferences. See also Poulsen and Poulsen (2006) for a model that endogenizes the proportion of reciprocity and other preference types.

References

Andreoni, A. (1988), 'Why free ride? Strategies and learning in public goods experiments', *Journal of Public Economics*, **37**, 291–304.
Andreoni, A., W. Harbaugh and L. Vesterlund (2007), 'Altruism in experiments', *The New Palgrave Dictionary of Economics*, 2nd edn, Basingstoke, Hampshire; New York: Palgrave Macmillan.
Axelrod, R. (1984), *The Evolution of Co-operation*, New York, NY: Basic Books.
Bardsley, N. and P. Moffatt (2007), 'The experimetrics of public goods: inferring motivations from contributions', *Theory and Decision*, **62**, 161–93.
Bicchieri, C. (2002), 'Group identity, norms, and communication in social dilemmas', *Rationality and Society*, **14** (2), 192–228.
Binmore, K. (1992), *Fun and Games: A Text in Game Theory*, Lexington, MA: D.C. Heath.
Bisin, A. and T. Verdier (2001), 'The economics of cultural transmission and the dynamics of preferences', *Journal of Economic Theory*, **97** (2), 298–319.
Bochet, O., T. Page, and L. Putterman (2006), 'Communication and punishment in voluntary contribution games', *Journal of Economic Behavior and Organization*, **60**, 11–26.
Bohnet, I. and D. Kübler (2005), 'Compensating the cooperators: is sorting in the prisoner's dilemma possible?', *Journal of Economic Behavior and Organization*, **56** (1), 61–76.
Bolton, G. and A. Ockenfels (2000), 'ERC: a theory of equity, reciprocity, and competition', *American Economic Review*, **90** (1), 166–93.
Brosig, J., A. Ockenfels and J. Weimann (2003), 'The effect of communication media on cooperation', *German Economic Review*, **4** (2), 217–41.
Camerer, C. (2003), *Behavioral Game Theory*, Princeton, NJ: Princeton University Press.
Camerer, C. and E. Fehr (2005), 'Measuring social norms and preferences using experimental games: a guide for social scientists', in J. Henrich, R. Boyd, S. Bowles, C. Camerer, E. Fehr and H. Gintis (eds), *Foundations of Human Sociality: Economic Experiments and Ethnographic Evidence from Fifteen Small-Scale Societies*, Oxford: Oxford University Press, pp. 55–96.
Camerer, C. and E. Fehr (2006), 'When does "economic man" dominate social behavior?', *Science*, **311**, 47–52.
Camerer, C., G. Loewenstein and D. Prelec (2005), 'Neuroeconomics: how neuroscience can inform economics', *Journal of Economic Literature*, **43**, 9–64.
Camerer, C., G. Loewenstein and M. Rabin (eds) (2004), *Advances in Behavioral Economics*, Princeton, NJ: Princeton University Press.

Carpenter, J. (2007), 'The demand for punishment', *Journal of Economic Behavior and Organization*, **62** (4), 522–42.

Charness, G., L. Rigotti and A. Rustichini (2006), 'Individual behavior and group membership', working paper, available online at the Social Science Research Network, http://ssrn.com/abstract=894685.

Chen, Y. and S. Li (2006), 'Group identity and social preferences', working paper, available at http://www.si.umich.edu/~yanchen/papers/Chen_Li_identity_20080711.pdf and forthcoming in the *American Economic Review* 2008.

Cinyabuguma, M., T. Page and L. Putterman (2005), 'Cooperation under the threat of expulsion in a public goods experiment', *Journal of Public Economics*, **89**, 1421–35.

Coleman, J. (1988), 'Social capital in the creation of human capital', *American Journal of Sociology*, **94** (S1), 95–120.

Cook, K. and R. Cooper (2003), 'Experimental studies of cooperation, trust, and social exchange', in E. Ostrom and J. Walker (eds), *Trust and Reciprocity: Interdisciplinary Lessons from Experimental Research*, New York: Russell Sage Foundation, pp. 209–44.

Cookson, R. (2000), 'Framing effects in public goods experiments', *Experimental Economics*, **3**, 55–79.

Coricelli, G., D. Fehr and G. Fellner (2003), 'Partner selection in public goods experiments', Max Planck Institute of Economics, Strategic Interaction Group, discussion paper 2003-13.

Croson, R. (2007), 'Theories of commitment, altruism and reciprocity: evidence from linear public goods games', *Economic Inquiry*, **45** (2), 199–216.

Davis, D. and C. Holt (1993), *Experimental Economics*, Princeton, NJ: Princeton University Press.

Dawes, R. (1980), 'Social dilemmas', *Annual Review of Psychology*, **31**, 169–93.

Dawes, R. and R. Thaler (1988), 'Anomalies: cooperation', *Journal of Economic Perspectives*, **2** (3), 187–97.

Dawes, R., A. van de Kragt and J. Orbell (1988), 'Not me or thee but we: the importance of group identity in eliciting cooperation in dilemma situations: experimental manipulations', *Acta Psychologica*, **68**, 83–97.

De Quervain, D., U. Fischbacher, V. Treyer, M. Schellhammer, U. Schnyder, A. Buck and E. Fehr (2004), 'The neural basis of altruistic punishment', *Science*, **305**, 1254–58.

Denant-Boemont, L., D. Masclet and C. Noussair (2005), 'Punishment, counter-punishment, and sanction enforcement in a social dilemma', unpublished working paper.

Eckel, C. and P. Grossman (2005), 'Managing diversity by creating team identity', *Journal of Economic Behavior and Organization*, **58**, 371–92.

Eckel, C. and R. Wilson (2002), 'The human face of game theory: trust and reciprocity in sequential games', in E. Ostrom and J. Walker (eds), *Trust and Reciprocity: Interdisciplinary Lessons from Experimental Research*, New York: Russell Sage Foundation, pp. 245–75.

Ehrhardt, K. and K. Keser (1999), 'Mobility and cooperation: on the run', CIRANO working paper no. 99s-24.

Falk, A., E. Fehr and U. Fischbacher (2005), 'Driving forces behind informal sanctions', *Econometrica*, **73** (6), 2017–30.

Farrell, J. and M. Rabin (1996), 'Cheap talk', *Journal of Economic Perspectives*, **10** (3), 103–18.

Fehr, E. and S. Gächter (2000a), 'Cooperation and punishment in public goods experiments', *American Economic Review*, **90** (4), 980–94.

Fehr, E. and S. Gächter (2000b), 'Fairness and retaliation: the economics of reciprocity', *Journal of Economic Perspectives*, **14** (3), 159–81.

Fehr, E. and S. Gächter (2002), 'Altruistic punishment in humans', *Nature*, **415**, 137–40.

Fehr, E. and K. Schmidt (1999), 'A theory of fairness, competition, and cooperation', *Quarterly Journal of Economics*, **114** (3), 816–68.

Fershtman, C. and U. Gneezy (2001), 'Discrimination in a segmented society: an experimental approach', *Quarterly Journal of Economics*, **116**, 351–78.

Fischbacher, U. and S. Gächter (2006), 'Heterogeneous social preferences and the dynamics of free riding in public goods experiments', working paper no. 261, Institute for Empirical Research in Economics, University of Zurich.

Fischbacher, U., S. Gächter and E. Fehr (2001), 'Are people conditionally cooperative? Evidence from a public goods experiment', *Economics Letters*, **71**, 397–404.

Frey, B. and S. Meier (2004), 'Social comparisons and pro-social behavior: testing "conditional cooperation" in a field experiment', *American Economic Review*, **94** (5), 1717–22.

Gächter, S. (2006), 'Conditional cooperation: behavioral regularities from the lab and the field and their policy implications', CeDEx discussion paper no. 2006–03, University of Nottingham.

Gächter, S. and E. Fehr (1999), 'Collective action as a social exchange', *Journal of Economic Behavior and Organization*, **39** (4), 341–69.

Gächter, S. and C. Thöni (2005), 'Social learning and voluntary cooperation among like-minded people', *Journal of the European Economic Association*, **3**, 303–14.

Goette, L., D. Huffman and S. Meier (2006), 'The impact of group membership on cooperation and norm enforcement: evidence using random assignment to real social groups', IZA discussion paper no. 2020, Institute for the Study of Labor (IZA).

Gunnthorsdottir, A., D. Houser and K. McCabe (2007), 'Disposition, history and contributions in public goods experiments', *Journal of Economic Behavior and Organization*, **62**, 304–15.

Hardin, G. (1968), 'The tragedy of the commons', *Science*, **162**, 1243–8.

Hardin, R. (2003), 'Gaming trust', in E. Ostrom and J. Walker (eds), *Trust and Reciprocity: Interdisciplinary Lessons from Experimental Research*, New York: Russell Sage Foundation, pp. 80–101.

Hargreaves Heap, S. and D. Zizzo (2006), 'The value of groups', available at: http://ssrn.com/abstract=951619.

Harrison, G. and J. List (2004), 'Field experiments', *Journal of Economic Literature*, **42** (4), 1009–55.

Hewstone, M., M. Rubin and H. Willis (2002), 'Intergroup bias', *Annual Review of Psychology*, **53**, 575–604.

Hirshleifer, D. and E. Rasmusen (1989), 'Cooperation in a repeated prisoner's dilemma with ostracism', *Journal of Economic Behavior and Organization*, **12**, 87–106.

Kagel, J. and A. Roth (eds) (1995), *The Handbook of Experimental Economics*, Princeton, NJ: Princeton University Press.

Keser, K. and F. van Winden (2000), 'Conditional cooperation and voluntary contributions to public goods', *Scandinavian Journal of Economics*, **102** (1), 23–39.

Knoch, D., A. Pascual-Leone, K. Meyer, V. Treyer and E. Fehr (2006), 'Diminishing reciprocal fairness by disrupting the right prefrontal vertex', *Science*, **314**, 829–32.

Kollock, P. (1998), 'Social dilemma: the anatomy of cooperation', *Annual Review of Sociology*, **24**, 183–214.

Kosfeld, M., A. Okada and A. Riedl (2006), 'Institution formation in public goods games', IZA discussion paper, no. 2288.

Ledyard, J. (1995), 'Public goods: a survey of experimental research', in J. Kagel and A. Roth (eds), *The Handbook of Experimental Economics*, Princeton, NJ: Princeton University Press, pp. 111–94.

Maier-Rigaud, F., P. Martinsson and G. Staffiero (2005), 'Ostracism and the provision of a public good – experimental evidence', preprints of the Max Planck Institute for Research on Collective Goods, Bonn, no. 24.

Masclet, D. and M.-C. Villeval (2006), 'Punishment, inequality and emotions', GATE-CNRS working paper 06-04.

Masclet, D., C. Noussair, S. Tucker and M.-C. Villeval (2003), 'Monetary and nonmonetary punishment in the voluntary contributions mechanism', *American Economic Review*, **93** (1), 366–80.

Mullainathan, S. and R. Thaler (2000), 'Behavioral economics', NBER working paper no. 7948.

Nikiforakis, N. (2008), 'Punishment and counter-Punishment in public good games: can we really govern ourselves?', *Journal of Public Economics*, **92** (1–2), 91–112.

Noussair, C. and S. Tucker (2005), 'Combining monetary and social sanctions to promote cooperation', *Economic Inquiry*, **43** (3), 649–60.

Olson, M. (1971), *The Logic of Collective Action: Public Goods and the Theory of Groups*, Cambridge, MA: Harvard University Press.

Ostrom, E. and J. Walker (2003), *Trust and Reciprocity: Interdisciplinary Lessons from Experimental Research*, New York: Russell Sage Foundation.

Ostrom, E., J. Walker and R. Gardner (1992), 'Covenants with and without a sword: self-governance is possible', *American Political Science Review*, **86** (2), 404–17.

Page, T., L. Putterman and B. Unel (2005), 'Voluntary association in public goods experiments: reciprocity, mimicry and efficiency', *Economic Journal*, **115**, 1032–53.

Poulsen, A. and O. Poulsen (2006), 'Endogenous preferences and social dilemma institutions', *Journal of Institutional and Theoretical Economics*, **162** (4), 627–60.

Poulsen, A. and G. Svendsen (2005), 'Social capital and endogenous preferences', *Public Choice*, **123** (1–2), 171–96.

Putnam, R. (1993), *Making Democracy Work. Civic Traditions in Modern Italy*, Princeton, NJ: Princeton University Press.

Rege, M. and K. Telle (2004), 'The impact of social approval and framing on cooperation in public good situations', *Journal of Public Economics*, **88**, 1625–44.

Roth, A. (ed.) (1987), *Laboratory Experimentation in Economics: Six Points of View*, Cambridge: Cambridge University Press.

Roth, A. (1995), 'Bargaining experiments', in J. Kagel and A. Roth (eds), *The Handbook of Experimental Economics*, Princeton, NJ: Princeton University Press, pp. 253–92.

Ruffle, B. and R. Sosis (2006), 'Cooperation and the in-group-outgroup-bias: a field test on Israeli kibbutz members and city residents', *Journal of Economic Behavior and Organization*, **60**, 147–63.

Sally, D. (1995), 'Conversation and cooperation in social dilemmas – a meta-analysis of experiments from 1958 to 1982', *Rationality and Society*, **7** (1), 58–92.

Schram, A. (2000), 'Sorting out the seeking: the economics of individual motivations', *Public Choice*, **103**, 231–58.

Seinen, I. and A. Schram (2006), 'Social status and group norms: indirect reciprocity in a repeated helping experiment', *European Economic Review*, **50**, 581–602.

Sethi, R. (1996), 'Evolutionary stability and social norms', *Journal of Economic Behavior and Organization*, **29** (1), 113–40.

Sethi, R. and E. Somanathan (2003), 'Understanding reciprocity', *Journal of Economic Behavior and Organization*, **50**, 1–27.

Sobel, J. (2005), 'Interdependent preferences and reciprocity', *Journal of Economic Literature*, **43** (2), 392–436.

Sugden, R. (1984), 'Reciprocity: the supply of public goods through voluntary contributions', *Economic Journal*, **94**, 772–87.

Tajfel, H. (1982), 'Social psychology of intergroup relations', *Annual Review of Psychology*, **33**, 1–39.

Zizzo, D. (2005), 'You are not in my boat: common fate and discrimination against outgroup members', available at: http://ssrn.com/abstract=675223.

4 Grid-group analysis*
D. Douglas Caulkins

4.1 Introduction: the development of a framework

British anthropologist Mary Douglas (1921–2007) insisted that anthropological theory should be useful in the study of complex industrial societies. 'If she had to be recalled for a single achievement', contends her biographer, Richard Fardon (2007), 'it would be as the anthropologist who took the techniques of a particularly vibrant period of research into non-western societies and applied them to her own, western milieu.' Douglas used insights from small-scale societies to develop a two-dimensional theoretical framework, grid-group analysis, that reveals four different but relatively stable forms of social organization that incorporate different types and degrees of social capital. In keeping with the 'troika' theme of this volume, Douglas's work had an impact on other social sciences, including economics (Douglas and Isherwood, 1979), political science (Douglas and Wildavsky, 1983; Thompson et al., 1990) and sociology and anthropology (Mars, 1982; Gross and Rayner, 1985; Caulkins and Peters, 2002). Until shortly before her death, Mary Douglas pursued the implications of her theoretical perspective for some of our most challenging social problems, such as the confrontation between mainstream societies and paramilitary enclave organizations, such as Al Qaeda.

A theoretical framework of wide utility, Grid/group analysis underwent a long process of elaboration by Mary Douglas and others (Douglas, 1978, 1989, 1992; Douglas and Wildavsky, 1982; Mars, 1982; Mars and Nicod, 1984; Gross and Rayner, 1985; Schwarz and Thompson, 1990; Thompson et al., 1990, 1999; Douglas and Ney, 1998), following the first publication of the basic ideas of grid-group in natural symbols (Douglas, 1970). She noted that all social organizations have at least two types of control, 'grid' (external controls) and 'group' (controls internal to a group). The group dimension is 'exerted for and by the group, a personal control exercised by members over each other' (Douglas, 2005: 4). Grid, in contrast, encompasses 'a rich variety of anonymous controls that do not directly stem from or support the group' including 'collective responses to climate, technology, work' and other aspects of the web of institutions (Douglas, 2005: 4–5). The 'group' or 'incorporation' dimension ranges from low to high, indicating the degree to which individuals are embedded within bounded social groups. As Douglas observes,

> Rules of admission to a group can be strong or weak, making it more or less
> exclusive; the life-support a group gives to its members can be complete, or
> partial. For any social context we can recognize appropriate measures of group
> commitment, whether to ancient lineage, to a learned profession or to a regi-
> ment or a church. (Douglas, 1982: 3)

As noted elsewhere (Caulkins and Peters, 2002), the group dimension is
theoretically similar if not identical to 'bonding' social capital as defined by
a variety of social capital theorists (Coleman, 1990; Putnam, 1995, 2000),
including Portes and associates (Portes and Sensenbrenner, 1993; Portes
and Landolt, 1996; Portes, 1998) who also identify 'positive' social capital.
The idea of positive bonding social capital was anticipated in Naroll's
concept of 'moralnets', or networks of associates sharing a set of values
(Naroll, 1983; Caulkins, 1995a).

   In this chapter I explore, first, the parallels between the grid and group
dimension and bonding and bridging social capital in order to delineate
an integrated framework. Second, I describe the four resulting culture
types and show how they can stimulate fruitful theorizing about large- and
small-scale social changes. Finally, I conclude with a consideration of the
Mary Douglas's advice on dealing with our most pressing problems of
international conflict.

4.2   Group and bonding social capital

Measures of the group dimension include frequency of interaction and the
mutuality and scope of the relationship (Mars, 1982: 27). Are the individuals in frequent face-to-face contact, do they have associates or colleagues
in common, and do they interact in a variety of contexts? In addition,
is there a strong boundary that demarcates the group? Positive answers
indicate high group measurement or high bonding social capital. Bonding
social capital is described in virtually identical terms: 'closed systems of
social networks inherent in the structure of relations between persons and
among persons within a collectivity' (Zhou and Bankston, 1994: 824; see
also Coleman, 1990; Portes and Sensenbrenner, 1993; Sanders and Nee,
1996; McLean et al., 2002).

   Low group measurement signifies a loosely connected, ramifying network
in which the individuals in different sectors of the network may not know
each other, lacking the 'bounded solidarity' (Portes, 1998) and 'closure'
(Coleman, 1990) of bonding social capital.

   Gross and Rayner (1985), who have devoted attention to measurement
issues, suggest the five measures of the group dimension listed in Table 4.1.

Table 4.1   Gross and Rayner's group measures

Group measure	Definition
1. Proximity	Measure of closeness of group members, frequency of interactions
2. Transitivity	Likelihood that if member 1 interacts with member 2 and 2 interacts with 3, then 1 will interact with 3
3. Frequency	Proportion of time a group member spends in some activity with other members
4. Scope	Diversity of a member's interactive involvement in group activities
5. Impermeability	Likelihood that a non-member who satisfies membership requirements will actually gain membership

Source: Gross and Rayner (1985: 70–73).

4.3   Grid and bridging social capital

'Grid', the second dimension of the framework, indicates the degree to which an individual is constrained by external rules. Douglas (1982: 3) suggests, 'the possibilities should run from maximum regulation to maximum freedom, the military regiment with its prescribed behavior and rigid timetabling, contrasted at the other end with the free life, uncommitted, unregulated'.

Grid can be measured by at least four variables (Mars, 1982: 25). First, autonomy varies inversely with grid. The greater the choice or control over one's actions, the lower the grid. Second, the more insulated the individual (or other unit) from others, the higher the grid. The insulation can be physical, as is the case with an executive office remote from the rest of a business operation, or structural, as occurs when an executive secretary filters all business contacts between the outside world and his boss. Insulation can also be filtered normatively, in which certain kinds of information are routinely kept from someone in order to preserve his innocence. A political operative's illegal or immoral activities in service of party interests, for example, may not be shared with the politicians that he serves. Finally, individuals may be insulated symbolically, for example, by wearing special clothing, such as a prison uniform.

The third and fourth indicators of grid are reciprocity and competition. The environment is high grid if the range of possible reciprocities – ways of exchanging resources – is constrained. A firm in which it is proper only for the managing director to distribute Christmas gifts is higher grid than a firm in which all staff members, regardless of position, are free to exchange gifts. Finally, a highly competitive environment, a marketplace, is low

Table 4.2   Gross and Rayner's grid measures

Grid measure	Definition
1. Specialization	Number of possible roles a group member assumes in a given time span
2. Asymmetry	Measure of lack of symmetry in role exchanges among group members
3. Entitlement	Proportion of ascribed v. achieved roles in the group
4. Accountability	Amount of member interactions in which one is dominant and the other subordinate

Source: Gross and Rayner (1985: 80–81).

grid. The more constrained the possibilities for competition, the higher the grid.

Low grid environments foster innovation
The more the individual is expected to create his own role, and the more his transacting with others is entirely up to himself, the better advised he is to corner a little resource, to specialize, or at least to offer an improved version of what everyone else can do. Hence we recognize in low-grid conditions the tendency to cultivate idiosyncrasy – and this fits well with the general tolerance of deviance (Douglas, 1982: 240).

As Douglas (1982: 240) notes, low grid is favorable to the development and expansion of science and the arts. In their methodological statement, Gross and Rayner suggest the measures of grid listed in Table 4.2.

In one recent statement of grid/group theory, Douglas and Ney (1998: 100–102) describe these two dimensions as 'structure' (grid) and 'incorporation' (group). This terminology helps to illuminate another important insight: grid is also a measure of 'bridging' social capital (Putnam, 2000). Bridging social capital provides a linkage of trust among individuals and groups that may not have face-to-face relations. In this sense bridging social capital resembles the idea of 'imagined community' (Anderson, 1983) of persons who share some collective identity but are not necessarily known to each other. In high group (bonding social capital)/high grid (bridging social capital) contexts, persons have the advantage of a close-knit support group and linkage to other groups.

In the study of local voluntary organizations in Norway, for example, I found that dozens of organizations might be linked to each other by slightly overlapping membership. No one person belonged to all of the organizations in a cluster of overlapping groups, but there was still a sense of connection among the organizations that formed an ideological cluster or imagined community (Caulkins, 2004a). Some organizations were highly sectarian, pledged to a particular ideology that linked them to some other organizations but separated them from others that were ideological opponents. Not all of the 160 organizations were connected together by bonding social capital, contrary to the assumptions of some theorists of democratic structures (Eckstein, 1966; Putnam, 1996). Instead, local government agencies that connected with all the organizations, regardless of their ideological content, provided the bridging social capital and reinforced trust in the local 'imagined community'.

Low group, high grid structures, however, form a kind of clientelism, in which an individual, lacking a support group and bonding social capital, is linked to a single patron who controls the options available to the individual. Battered women, controlled by their dominating partner, as we shall see, constitute one example of such a structural relation.

The two dimensions each form a continuum between strong (or high) or weak (or low) values, producing a fourfold typology that describes the major stable forms of social organization and associated social values, according to Douglas. In most diagrammatic representations, Grid is considered the vertical axis of increasing strength, from low to high, and Group is the horizontal axis of increasing strength. Figure 4.1 shows the relationship between grid-group and bonding and bridging social capital in each of the quadrants. Within each quadrant I have included the terms often used to describe the character of the social organization found there.

Two of these types, individualism (Quadrant A) and hierarchy (Quadrant C), are very familiar in social science, but social science is enriched by the addition of the other stable forms as well (Wildavsky, 1989: 59). The grid-group framework has proved useful for the study of modern nations as well as for smaller social organizations, such as firms and even families. Political scientist Aaron Wildavsky (1989: 59), one of Mary Douglas's frequent collaborators, contends that countries, as well as other social units, are conglomerations of the four forms of social organization, although 'at any one time a single culture may be more powerful than others in certain spheres of life'. While social organizations ranging in scale from small firms to large nations may contain all four quadrants simultaneously, they are not necessarily in equal balance. Over time, the relative dominance can shift from one sector to another. England, for example, was more hierarchical than the United States, at least, before Prime Minister Margaret Thatcher's campaign to push Great Britain down grid and down group, toward what she termed the individualistic 'Enterprise Culture' (Hargreaves Heap and Ross, 1992). Thus, every group has a cultural bias, a tendency toward a particular configuration of grid and group (or structure and incorporation) that may change rapidly or very slowly, depending on the nature of the external and internal forces for

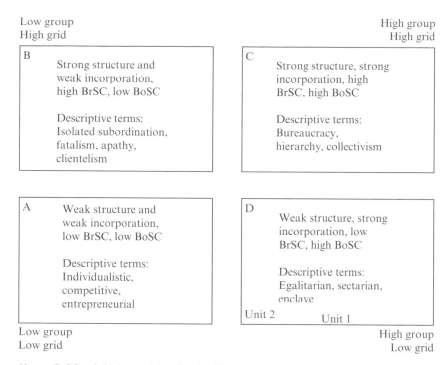

Low group
High grid

High group
High grid

B   Strong structure and
weak incorporation,
high BrSC, low BoSC

Descriptive terms:
Isolated subordination,
fatalism, apathy,
clientelism

C   Strong structure, strong
incorporation, high
BrSC, high BoSC

Descriptive terms:
Bureaucracy,
hierarchy, collectivism

A   Weak structure and
weak incorporation,
low BrSC, low BoSC

Descriptive terms:
Individualistic,
competitive,
entrepreneurial

D   Weak structure, strong
incorporation, low
BrSC, high BoSC

Descriptive terms:
Egalitarian, sectarian,
enclave

Unit 2   Unit 1

Low group
Low grid

High group
Low grid

Note: BrSC = bridging social capital; BoSC = bonding social capital.

Figure 4.1   Grid-group and bonding/bridging social capital

change. National elections are often fought to persuade the electorate to shift the cultural balance more toward one quadrant or another.

Both grid (structure) and group (incorporation) are continuous dimensions, so that concrete social units could be located at different coordinates within a quadrant. For example, Units 1 and 2 (Figure 4.1) are both in the D quadrant, but Unit 1 has a higher group score and lower grid score than Unit 2. Unit 1, therefore, is a more extreme example of the egalitarian or enclave quadrant. A nearly infinite variety of concrete social units can be accommodated in this framework, each differing in grid/group coordinates. For example, some of the sectarian Norwegian voluntary organizations mentioned earlier have moved up-grid in the century since their founding and, like Unit 2 in Figure 4.1, have become much more similar to hierarchical organizations in the C quadrant.

Significantly, grid-group theorists contend that 'none of the modes of organizing social life is viable on its own' (Wildavsky, 1989: 65).

Hierarchies need something – anarchic individualists, authority-less egalitarians, apathetic fatalists – to sit on top of. Egalitarians need something – unfair competition, inequitable hierarchy, non-participant fatalists – to criticize. Fatalists require an external source of control to tell them what to do. 'What a wonderful place the world would be', say the adherents of each culture, 'if only everyone were like us', conveniently ignoring that it is only the presence in the world of people who are not like them that enables them to be the way they are (Wildavsky, 1989: 65).

The four structures need each other to define their identity, since each embodies different conceptions of the world. 'It is the differences and distances from others that defines one's own cultural identity', Wildavsky (1989: 65) argues.

The contention that all four quadrants are found in any empirical situation is both theoretically and methodologically important and encourages any researcher to look carefully for all the contending structures. For example, in a study of regional economic development in the UK, I found that many engineers who previously worked in the research and development divisions of large, hierarchical multinational corporations had been terminated when the corporation 'downsized' their operations. In some cases the research and development (R&D) engineers were then hired to continue work on their projects, not as regular employees, but as independent consultants on short contracts. This moved them up grid and down group, toward the isolated quadrant, where they remained unless they found other employment or more clients as independent consultants. Otherwise they were totally dependent on the multinational corporation but without the benefit of continuous employment once the current project was completed. For employees who had envisioned serving their entire careers with the multinational corporation, this required a major life adjustment (Caulkins, 1992).

Other former R&D staff members became 'accidental' entrepreneurs and, rather than work on contract with their previous employer, started up new firms. 'This is the best thing that could have happened to me', said one engineer recently terminated from a hierarchical corporation, 'since I never would have decided to launch my own business otherwise.' Several newly unemployed engineers founded new firms that evolved rapidly from a classic individualistic start-up firm into an egalitarian organization staffed by like-minded individuals (Caulkins, 1995b; Caulkins and Weiner, 1998, 1999). The new firms typically had very flat organizational structures and a sectarian belief in the high quality of the product and the inspired mission of the firm. The biography of Intel Corporation co-founder Robert Noyce (Berlin, 2005) describes not only the egalitarian structure of the early Intel Corporation, but also the transition up-grid to a more hierarchical organization as the increased size and complexity of the organization required the increasing imposition of systems and procedures. Noyce's own view (Noyce, 1983) as well as that of other entrepreneurs whose firms were moving up-grid (Caulkins, 2004b), represents a kind of nostalgia for the earlier, egalitarian stage of the organization.

4.4   Four types of cultures

The general characteristics of social organization and culture in each quadrant are as follows.

Quadrant A

Entrepreneurial individualism describes the environment of the classical entrepreneur that 'allows options for negotiating contracts or choosing allies and in consequence it also allows for individual mobility up and down whatever the current scale of prestige and influence' (Douglas, 1982: 4). Individuals are responsible only for themselves and not for the weak or the needy, unless they willingly accept that responsibility (Gross and Rayner, 1985: 7). When things go wrong, individualists blame bad luck or personal incompetence (Wildavsky, 1989: 67): 'People may be dumb, as economic individualists say, but markets are always smart.' In this quadrant, both bonding and bridging social capital are poorly developed. The individualist's social networks are not the kind of closed, dense networks that typify bonding social capital. Instead, the individualist thrives on widely ramifying connections with others who can be tapped to gain access to a variety of resources.

On the level of the nation state, all four cultures are present to some degree. The political culture of the United States, according to Thompson et al. (1990: 255) is an alliance of individualism and hierarchy, with an essential element of egalitarian critique of the extremes of both individualism and hierarchy.

Quadrant B

Isolated subordination is an environment in which the behavior of individuals is strongly regulated according to their socially assigned classifications (Gross and Rayner, 1985: 8). It can be a hierarchical environment in which many individuals are segregated from the decision-making process. Often these are stigmatized individuals who 'do as they are told, without the protection and privileges of group membership' (Douglas, 1982: 4). When things go wrong, fatalists blame fate. At the level of the nation state, Italy is characterized by 'a fatalistic way of life, in which group involvement is low and social prescriptions are high', according to Thompson et al. (1990: 248), who reanalyse the studies of political culture by Almond and Verba (1963). While fatalism might be a dominant culture in Italy, the other types are also present.

Quadrant C
Most recently Douglas (2005) has suggested that this quadrant should be called 'positional' rather than hierarchical, since the latter term is often construed as a pejorative term. This quadrant is structured by positional rules of heredity, gender, age or other criteria that control expected behavior. Seniority rather than merit is the criterion for promotion. 'Loyalty is rewarded and hierarchy respected: an individual knows his place in a world that is securely bounded and stratified', according to Douglas (1982: 4). This is a collective environment in which everyone suffers together in bad times. Blame is often attributed to deviants who do not value the system (Wildavsky, 1989: 67) since to blame the system would be self-destructive. Again on the level of the nation state, Thompson et al. (1990: 251) note that German political culture 'is readily recognizable as a hierarchical culture in which individuals identify with the system but believe that their participation should be limited to its proper sphere'.

Quadrant D
In an environment of sectarianism or egalitarian enclavism, the external group boundary is a constant preoccupation. For this reason, organizations in this quadrant regard themselves as unique, as mavericks that are categorically different from other organizations with which they might be compared. 'Egalitarians try to manipulate the other cultures by incessant criticism', according to Wildavsky (1989: 65) and 'coerce one another by attributing inequalities to corruption and duplicity'. For egalitarians, the majority system, whether dominated by individualists or hierarchies, is corrupting and a constant threat to their way of life. On the level of the nation, the strongly hierarchical political culture of Germany incorporates the Green Party, a critical egalitarian or enclavist culture (Thompson, et al., 1990: 252). The distinction between 'them and us' is critically important because the world outside can infect or pollute the group, destroying the quality and purity of its actions, thoughts, and products.

In a study of social capital and voluntary organizations in a community in Norway during the late twentieth century, I found that many of the contemporary voluntary groups were products of nineteenth-century sectarian political and religious movements, such as Haugianism (Caulkins, 2004a, 2001). These D quadrant organizations were highly critical of A and C quadrant organizations in the same commune. When I explained my project of studying all of the organizations in the commune, the leader of one sectarian organization asked me skeptically, 'How can you talk with those other people?' Sectarian enclaves look inward, rather than outward.

The success of enclave organizations can be measured by the quality of their product rather than profit, turnover, or other measures (see for example, Hamilton, 1987: 75). This preoccupation with quality for its own sake makes the sectarians more like artisans than classical entrepreneurs (Stanworth and Curran, 1976). In addition to the threat of pollution from outside, organizations in this quadrant perceive a constant danger of treachery from inside, so that scapegoating and the expulsion of unworthy members of the group occurs from time to time. Other aspects of interpersonal relations are ambiguous and negotiable. The concept of leadership implies inequality for enclavists and therefore is not appealing, except when the organization is under threat. Then charismatic leadership may be accepted (Wildavsky, 1989: 69). As Gross and Rayner suggest, 'Leadership tends to be charismatic and lacking in clear rules for succession. Extreme cases are represented by certain religious and political cults whose members interact with each other on an egalitarian basis' (1985: 10).

Outsiders may perceive the sectarian organization or network as deviant, while for insiders the egalitarian structure and deeply felt concern for an alternative morality is at the same time a matter of pride and an indictment of the dominant organizations in the environment.

The grid-group framework allows systematic comparison between different levels and types of social units: intersocietal comparisons (for example, the US and Italy), intrasocietal comparisons (different corporations in the US), or comparisons of the same unit at different points in time (for example, British Rail before and after privatization). Grid-group analysis is a dynamic, rather than static, framework (Thompson et al., 1990). The present location of an individual or organization is not necessarily its ultimate destiny, as persons can migrate between quadrants and organizations as their situations change. The framework can illuminate these changes on a micro-structural level as well as macro-structural level.

In an ethnographic field study of former battered or abused women and their partners, for example, Stiles and Caulkins (1989) found that most of the women, regardless of their quadrant before they became involved in an abusive relationship, were driven down-group and up-grid by a process of 'abusive isolation' in which the male forced the woman to break off or restrict her relationships with friends, family or coworkers, and imposed an increasing number of restrictions on her behavior. For example, some men disabled their partner's car so that they could not leave home for any reason during the absence of the man and without his permission. In short, the women were driven into the 'isolated' quadrant where they often stayed for extended periods, fatalistically concluding that they were to blame for their situation. 'He wanted total control over everything I did', said one woman of her husband, 'and I was intimidated enough to think that I deserved that treatment.' Some of these women were finally recruited into an egalitarian organization of women with experience of abuse in which they were taught that they were not to blame personally for their situation and were helped to develop positive self-images. As a result of joining the support organization, many were able to leave the abusive relationship and to start over, with the help and solidarity of the other members of the organization. These women went from the isolation quadrant to the egalitarian/sectarian quadrant, clearly benefiting from positive bonding social capital. Many women started in the hierarchical quadrant with an authoritarian father as head of the family and then developed a relationship with a partner, moving progressively into the isolation quadrant, and subsequently escaping into the egalitarian quadrant, recruited by a group of women who had similar experiences of abuse.

As asserted earlier, every large-scale social unit potentially contains all four types (Thompson et al., 1990: 87–99; Douglas and Ney, 1998: 104). 'A well-run community' Douglas (2005: 13) contends, 'needs some hierarchy in the sphere of government, some enterprise on the part of Individualists, some criticism from Enclaves, and it cannot avoid having some passive members in the sector of Isolates.' Over the long term social organization is dependent on having an entrepreneurial, innovative, shifting sector (Quadrant A), a hierarchical structural repository of tradition, well-defined roles and certain loyalties (Quadrant C), a self-confident, solidary group of activist-critics who disparage both the hierarchists and the individualists (Quadrant D), and a group of fatalists who are manipulated by whoever is in power (Quadrant B).

As Douglas and Ney suggest, each culture type is useful for different organizational purposes:

> When a complex coordination has advantages, it makes sense to develop the top right pattern and to cultivate the values and attitudes that justify it. When individual initiative is needed, it makes sense to develop the bottom left pattern and the values that go with it. When concerted protest is needed, it makes sense to sink individual differences and go for the egalitarian group. And so on. (1998: 103)

According to grid/group theory, everyone has a cultural bias, including, of course, the social scientist. Mary Douglas (2003: 15), a devout member of the Catholic Church all her life, recommended that everyone discover his or her preferred cultural bias and affirmed that 'at heart I like hierarchy best'. She claims that the forms of social organization have great power in shaping personhood and identity (Douglas and Ney, 1998).

The two-dimensional diagram presents a set of limits within which the individual can move around. Personally, I believe the limits are real, that it is not possible to stay in two parts of the diagram at once, and that the moral justifications which people give for what they want to do are the hard edge of social change. If they wish for change, they will adopt different justifications; if they want continuity, they will call upon those principles which uphold the present order (Douglas, 1982: 4).

4.5   High grid and high group: bridging social capital
The criticisms of Putnam's early conception of social capital (for example, McLean et al., 2002) are to some degree answered by focusing on the difference between bonding and bridging social capital. Bonding social capital unites members of the same group or category and strengthens group boundaries, while bridging social capital links different social networks or groups and mitigates the focus on group boundaries (Caulkins, 2004a).

The grid group framework helps us to interpret and reinterpret the social organization of contending social groups. Svendsen (2006), for example, describes the dilemma of a small rural community in which the elderly villagers find themselves often opposed to the newcomers, most of whom are from the Copenhagen region, living on social transfer payments. The two populations were often distrustful of each other. The 'Copenhageners' had few contacts with the locals. We can interpret the locals as connected in a hierarchical structure, connected to local government and a wealth of local voluntary organizations that provide bridging social capital. The 'Copenhageners', a category rather than an interacting group, are either isolated (quadrant B) or linked in small groups with bonding social capital (quadrant D) in small enclaves.

Similarly, a historical analysis of Irish ethnic identity in a small Nebraska (US) town shows how a small enclave came to move up grid when the state government invited towns to create ethnic festivals as a part of the centennial celebration of Nebraska statehood. The ethnic identity of a minority of the population of the town – only 20 per cent claimed Irish heritage – became the identity of the whole town when the state government declared it the 'Irish Capital of Nebraska'. The city government and a series of civic organizations became the managers of the collective identity, linking all sectors of the town and sponsoring a commercially important Saint Patrick's Day celebration that drew hundreds of outsiders into the town's restaurants, pubs and motels (Caulkins, 2006; French, 2007).

The problem of conflicting expectations by ethnic/national groups with differential grid-group placement is illustrated in a study of industries in which the management is predominantly English and the workers predominantly Welsh (Caulkins and Weiner, 1999). Welsh concepts of personhood emphasize egalitarianism, emotionalism, martyrdom (or sacrifice for the good of the group) (Caulkins et al., 2000; Trosset and Caulkins, 2001), all of which fit well in the sectarian/egalitarian quadrant. The Welsh workers attributed opposite characteristics to their English managers: hierarchy, lack of emotion and rationality, all fitting neatly within the hierarchy quadrant. Thus, the Welsh workers saw their managers as having a different culture, quite out of sympathy with their own.

This situation, in which an ethno-national divide separates two cultures, calls for bridging social capital in order to avoid 'social traps' (Rothstein, 2005) in which populations become locked into their own groups through bonding social capital in the absence of appropriate bridges. Ironically, part of the solution has been provided by a Welsh Nationalist politician whose heroic hunger strike helped secure the funds for the Welsh language television channel, S4C. Gwynfor Evans, a former Member of Parliament from Wales, was active in promoting a voluntary organization, aptly named *Pont* (bridge), for uniting the interests of the English and Welsh populations in Wales.

4.6   Conclusion: problems of extreme bureaucracies and enclaves
Two organizational types toward the high end of the group or incorporation continuum are especially problematic. These are the highest extreme of quadrant C and the lowest extremes of quadrant D.

The highest level of quadrant C, marked by hyper-developed rules, represents the territory of bureaucracy. Here the constraints limit the possibilities of productive bridging between divisions of an organization or a nation state. The bridges between different units become, in effect, toll bridges, in which the transaction costs are very high because actions are constrained by extensive rules.

The lowest levels of grid in quadrant D produce extreme enclavist organizations that may be extremely hostile to other sectors of society, so hostile that they may deny the essential humanity of other parts of society. Some rebel and terrorist groups have evolved into enclavist organizations. In the last few years Mary Douglas was especially interested in the problem of extreme enclaves. She notes that they have been particularly important in recent history as a frequent and effective organizational form for terrorists.

The objective of Al-Qaeda, more global and transnational, is to overturn the Arab chiefs who fail to adhere to the Islamic Sharia rules, to destabilize the Western world, especially America, Russia and Israel, so as to liberate the Islamic world from domination (we observe that the enclave formation is uniquely well adapted to destabilizing and liberating) (Douglas, 2005: 14).

If the positional, individual and enclave quadrants are always in tension, as Douglas and her associates contend, then it might be possible in extreme circumstances for the individual and the positional organizations to join forces against an apparently more dangerous organization.

If the others combine to suppress the enclave, violence will erupt as the enclavists will not be silenced. Here lies the first of the normative lessons for our times, war on terrorism will not be won unless the enclave's consciousness of injustice be calmed: 'Do not attend solely to the policing without attending to the injustices that fuel subversive movements' (Douglas, 2005: 13).

One could hardly formulate a more elegant plea for the importance of extending bridging social capital into the enclaves that feel aggrieved in the national and international arenas of public life.

Note

*   For Mary Douglas (1921–2007): inspiring public intellectual, adventurous interdisciplinary thinker, demanding teacher and loyal mentor to several generations of scholars.

References

Almond, Gabriel and Sidney Verba (1963), *The Civic Culture: Political Attitudes and Democracy in Five Nations*, Princeton, NJ: Princeton University Press.

Anderson, Benedict (1983), *Imagined Communities: Reflections on the Origin and Spread of Nationalism*, London: Verso.

Berlin, Leslie (2005), *The Man Behind the Microchip: Robert Noyce and the Invention of Silicon Valley*, New York: Oxford University Press.

Caulkins, Douglas (1992), 'The unexpected entrepreneurs: small high technology firms and regional development in Wales and Northeast England', in Frances Abrahamer Rothstein and Michael Blim (eds), *Anthropology and the Global Factory: Studies in the New Industrialization of the Late Twentieth Century*, New York: Bergin & Garvey, pp. 119–35.

Caulkins, Douglas (1995a), 'Are Norwegian voluntary associations homogeneous moralnets? Reflections on Naroll's selection of Norway as a model society', *Cross-Cultural Research*, **29** (1), 43–57.

Caulkins, Douglas (1995b), 'High technology entrepreneurs in the peripheral regions of the United Kingdom', in Reginald Byron (ed.), *Economic Futures on the North Atlantic Margin: Selected Contributions to the Twelfth International Seminar on Marginal Regions*, Aldershot: Avebury Press, pp. 287–99.

Caulkins, D. Douglas (2001), 'Norway', in Melvin Ember and Carol R. Ember (eds), *Countries and Their Cultures*, New York: Macmillan Reference USA, pp. 1667–79.

Caulkins, Douglas (2004a), 'Organizational memberships and cross-cutting ties: a cluster analytic approach to the study of social capital', in Sanjeev Prakash and Per Selle (eds), *Investigating Social Capital: Comparative Perspectives on Civil Society, Participation and Governance*, New Delhi: Sage, pp. 162–83.

Caulkins, Douglas (2004b), 'Identifying culture as a threshold of shared knowledge: a consensus analysis method', *International Journal of Cross-Cultural Management*, **4** (3), 317–33.

Caulkins, D. (2006), 'From ethnic celebration to community festival: phases of formalization of social capital', conference on Reassessing Civil Society, the State, and Social Capital: Theory, Evidence, Policy, Hardanger, Norway, 11–13 May.

Caulkins, Douglas and Christina Peters (2002), 'Grid-group analysis, social capital, and entrepreneurship in North American immigrant groups', *Cross-Cultural Research*, **36** (1), 48–72.

Caulkins, Douglas and Elaine S. Weiner (1998), 'Finding a work culture that fits: egalitarian manufacturing firms in MidWales', *Anthropology of Work Review*, **19** (1), 27–31.
Caulkins, Douglas and Elaine S. Weiner (1999), 'Enterprise and resistance in the Celtic fringe: high growth, low growth and no growth firms', in Reginald Byron and John Hutson (eds), *Local Enterprise on the North Atlantic Margin: Selected Contributions to the Fourteenth International Seminar on Marginal Regions*, Aldershot: Ashgate Press, pp. 73–86.
Caulkins, Douglas, Carol Trosset, Anna Painter and Meredith Good (2000), 'Using scenarios to construct models of identity in multiethnic settings', *Field Methods*, **12** (4), 267–81.
Coleman, J.S. (1990), *Foundations of Social Theory*, Cambridge, MA: Harvard University Press.
Douglas, Mary (1970), *Natural Symbols*, London: Barrie & Rockcliff.
Douglas, Mary (1978), 'Cultural bias', Royal Anthropological Institute occasional paper, 35.
Douglas, Mary (1982), *Essays in the Sociology of Perception*, London: Routledge & Kegan Paul.
Douglas, Mary (1989), 'Culture and collective action', in Morris Freilich (ed.), *The Relevance of Culture*, New York: Bergin & Garvey, pp. 39–57.
Douglas, Mary (1992), *Risk and Blame: Essays in Cultural Theory*, London: Routledge & Kegan Paul.
Douglas, Mary (2003) *ILF Digest*, interview, pp. 1–23, www.wbsi.org/ilfdigest/interviews_apr.htm (accessed 6 November 2007).
Douglas, Mary (2005), 'Grid and group, new developments', prepared for Workshop on *Complexity and Cultural Theory in Honour of Michael Thompson*, London School of Economics, 27 June.
Douglas, Mary and Baron Isherwood (1979), *The World of Goods*, New York: Basic Books.
Douglas, Mary and Steven Ney (1998), *Missing Persons: A Critique of Personhood in the Social Sciences*, Berkeley, CA: University of California Press.
Douglas, Mary and Aron Wildavsky (1983), *Risk and Culture: An Essay on the Selection of Technological and Environmental Dangers*, Berkeley, CA: University of California Press.
Eckstein, Harry (1966), *Division and Cohesion in Democracy*, Princeton, NJ: Princeton University Press.
Fardon, Richard (2007), 'Dame Mary Douglas', *Guardian*, 18 May, available at http:www.guardian.co.uk/news/2007/may/18/guardianobituaries.obituaries.
French, Brigittine (2007), '"We're all Irish": transforming Irish identity in a Midwestern community', *New Hibernia Review*, **23** (1), 9–24.
Gross, Jonathan L. and Steve Rayner (1985), *Measuring Culture: A Paradigm for the Analysis of Social Organization*, New York: Columbia University Press.
Hamilton, R.T. (1987), 'Motivations and aspirations of business founders', *International Small Business Journal*, **6** (1), 70–78.
Hargreaves Heap, S. and A. Ross (1992), *Understanding the Enterprise Culture: Themes in the Work of Mary Douglas*, Edinburgh: Edinburgh University Press.
Mars, Gerald (1982), *Cheats at Work: An Anthropology of Workplace Crime*, London: Allen & Unwin.
Mars, Gerald and M. Nicod (1984), *The World of Waiters*, London: George Allen & Unwin.
McLean, Scott L., David Schultz and Manfred Steger (2002), *Social Capital: Critical Perspectives on Community and 'Bowling Alone'*, New York: New York University Press.
Naroll, Raoul (1983), *The Moral Order: An Introduction to the Human Situation*, Beverly Hills, CA: Sage Publications.
Noyce, Robert (1983), Personal communication, 5 May.
Portes, Alejandro (1998), 'Social capital: its origins and applications in modern sociology', *Annual Review of Sociology*, **24**, 1–24.
Portes, Alejandro and P. Landolt (1996), 'The downside of social capital', *The American Prospect*, **26**, 18–21.

Portes, Alejandro and J. Sensenbrenner (1993), 'Embeddedness and immigration: notes on the social determinants of economic action', *American Journal of Sociology*, **98**, 1320–50.

Putnam, Robert (1995), 'Bowling alone: Americans' declining social capital', *Journal of Democracy*, **6** (1), 65–78.

Putnam, Robert (1996), 'The strange disappearance of civic America', *The American Prospect*, **24**, 34–48.

Putnam, Robert (2000), *Bowling Alone: The Collapse and Revival of American Community*, New York: Simon & Schuster.

Rothstein, Bo (2005), *Social Traps and the Problem of Trust*, Cambridge: Cambridge University Press.

Sanders, Jimy M. and Victor Nee (1996), 'Immigrant self-employment: the family as social capital and the value of human capital', *American Sociological Review*, **61**, 231–49.

Schwarz, Michiel and Michael Thompson (1990), *Divided We Stand: Redefining Politics, Technology and Social Choice*, Philadelphia, PA: University of Pennsylvania Press.

Stanworth, John and James Curran (1976), 'Growth and the small firm – an alternative view', *Journal of Management Studies*, **13**, 95–110.

Stiles, Julie L. and Douglas Caulkins (1989), 'Prisoners in their own homes: a structural and cognitive interpretation of the problems of battered women', presentation at Iowa Academy of Science meetings, Storm Lake, Iowa, 22 April.

Svendsen, Gunnar L.H. (2006), 'Studying social capital *in situ*: a qualitative approach', *Theory and Society*, **3**, 39–70.

Thompson, Michael, Richard Ellis and Aaron Wildavsky (1990), *Cultural Theory*, Boulder, CO: Westview Press.

Thompson, Michael, Per Selle and Gunnar Grendstad (1999), *Culture Theory as Political Science*, London: Routledge.

Trosset, Carol and Douglas Caulkins (2001), 'Triangulation and confirmation in the study of Welsh concepts of personhood', *Journal of Anthropological Research*, **57** (1), 61–81.

Wildavsky, Aaron (1989), 'Frames of reference come from cultures: a predictive theory', in Morris Freilich (ed.), *The Relevance of Culture*, New York: Bergin & Garvey.

Zhou, Min and Carl L. Bankston (1994), 'Social capital and the adaptation of the second generation: the case of Vietnamese youth in New Orleans', *International Migration Review*, **28**, 821–45.

PART II

WHY COOPERATION?
RECENT EXPLANATIONS

5 Social capital in the brain?
Michael Bang Petersen, Andreas Roepstorff and Søren Serritzlew

Introduction

The social capital concept has demonstrated its relevance. To name a few examples, it is crucial for understanding determinants of economic growth (Knack and Keefer, 1997), how democracy works (Putnam, 1993a), and more fundamentally, cooperation in collective action problems. But social capital is also a contested concept. There is no clear consensus on how to define it, some say that it is ambiguous, and some even that it should be abandoned (Arrow, 2000: 4). One of the hotly debated topics relates to the psychological basis of cooperation. Is cooperation grounded in rational calculations, directed by strong social norms or soaked in affective and emotional motivations? Such core questions directly pertain to how social capital is translated into cooperative behavior by individual minds. The alternatives presented in the debate draw on significantly different models of the human actor, and as long as answers to these questions remain unclear, so will other core concepts such as cooperation and social capital.

This chapter reviews recent studies from the growing discipline of cognitive neuroscience. By offering the social sciences radically new kinds of data on psychological processes, these studies have the potential to shed new light on the psychological basis of cooperation and related questions. The message of this chapter is that the neuroscientific evidence strongly suggests that cooperative behavior is a real phenomenon motivated by the elicitation of context-sensitive emotional systems that primarily operate in situations of a moral character. However, it is also necessary to approach the new field of cognitive neuroscience with caution. We will return to this aspect in the conclusion.

The next section describes the contested nature of the social capital concept in more detail. We then move on to a description of the potential of cognitive neuroscience to shed light on some of the contested issues. This paves the way for a review of a series of studies where neuroscientific methods were used to investigate when and how cooperation emerges in experimental economic games. Based on this review, the idea of context-sensitive moral emotions is advanced. The chapter concludes with a discussion of, first, how the findings from neuroscience relate to the social capital literature; second, some limitations of the neuroscience perspective, and third, how to proceed further.

Social capital: potentials and pitfalls

Why do people cooperate? That is one of the big puzzles in experimental economics and public choice. It is easy to predict how people should behave in, for example, the classic ultimatum game. In this game two players are to divide a dollar – or often more – between them. The first player proposes how to divide the amount. The second player either accepts the deal and receives his part or rejects it. In this case neither player receives anything. A rational and selfish actor should accept any positive amount, so the first player should propose a division that favors him and leave only a very small amount for the second player. It turns out that in reality this rarely happens. Starting with Güth et al. (1982) many experiments have shown that subjects usually offer more balanced splits, and meager offers are routinely rejected even when stakes are very high. In Indonesia unbalanced proposals were turned down even in situations with stakes as high as three months' expenditure of the average participant (Cameron, 1999). Hence, though it should be a trivial task for a rational and selfish actor to maximize his payoffs in the ultimatum game, it turns out that actual behavior is different, and that the seemingly rational strategy of splits favoring oneself turns out in practice to be inferior to more equal splits. Similar differences between theory and reality are evident in other types of games. In the one-shot Prisoner's Dilemma game it is never individually rational to cooperate (although mutual cooperation maximizes joint payoffs). In experiments, however, subjects cooperate much more than would be expected theoretically (Ahn et al., 2001). This is also true when, from a theoretical point of view, cooperation is especially unlikely, for instance when the temptation to defect and the penalty for being a sucker (that is, to cooperate while the other subject defects) are high. In other bargaining games subjects tend to contribute to a public good, also when it is apparently not individually rational to do so, and even in the absence of sanctions (Yamagishi, 1988). Another interesting fact, which the social capital approach may help explain, is that the over-tendency to cooperate varies slightly in different cultures. In the ultimatum game, Japanese and Israeli subjects on average offer more uneven splits than American and Yugoslavian subjects (Roth et al., 1991). In the public good game experiments, American subjects contributed more to the public good than their Japanese counterparts (Yamagishi, 1988).

In other words, people tend to cooperate more than they should according to theories based on the assumption that people are selfish and rational, and they do so to different degrees. This kind of behavior is not puzzling in the social capital perspective; it is exactly what one would expect. Coleman (1988: S98) defines social capital by what it does: it is

> a variety of different entities, with two elements in common: they all consist of some aspect of social structures, and they facilitate certain actions of actors – whether persons or corporate actors – within the structure . . . Unlike other forms of capital, social capital inheres in the structure of relations between actors and among actors.

Social capital can facilitate cooperation or in other ways explain deviations from rational behavior. As Putnam (1993b: 35–6) puts it, social capital refers to 'features of social organization, such as networks, norms, and trust, that facilitate coordination and cooperation for mutual benefit'. In groups with high levels of social capital cooperative behavior can be facilitated by high levels of trust, strong norms of reciprocity or behavior based on motives other than selfish ones (although certain fractions within the social capital approach tend to favor one of these explanations over the others, for example, reciprocity over trust or vice versa). Since the amount of social capital varies – and it does, there are dramatic country differences in levels of trust (Inglehart et al., 2004: A165; Paldam and Svendsen, forthcoming) – the different levels of excess cooperation are also understandable. Owing to social capital, cooperation is easier in some groups or areas than in others.

The social capital approach has shown its relevance by providing the concepts necessary for understanding and solving several old puzzles. But it is also fair to say that the approach is fuzzy. First, there is no consensus on how to define it (Sobel, 2002: 146ff.). According to Coleman's functionalist definition (and Putnam's, see 1993a: 167), social capital is a property of the social structure; something that characterizes the settings or atmosphere in which individuals interact, and which affects how they interact. Portes (1998: 5) argues that this definition is vague. In order to avoid tautological statements, he holds that it would be helpful to exclude from the definition the sources and effects of social capital. Other researchers understand social capital as something possessed by individuals (see Portes, 1998: 6), or as a preference to cooperate (Poulsen and Svendsen, 2005: 172). Social capital is higher in societies of people who are more likely to choose cooperative strategies. Second, central concepts in the social capital approach are elusive. Concepts such as trust and reciprocity are integral to many social capital arguments, but they are considerably more 'elastic' than the rigid concepts of rationality and selfishness in the public choice approach. Although the social capital literature has been very successful in its empirical investigations of cooperation, these considerations leave one wondering whether the social capital literature has been equally successful in explaining cooperation.

Consensus on how to understand trust and reciprocity, and ultimately social capital, is not likely to arise from elaborate discussions of the strengths and weaknesses of various definitions. One probable but not very satisfying source of consolidation is the empirical market place. In Friedman's 'as if' logic (1953: 18), the critical test of a theory is whether it works, not whether assumptions and definitions are correct. His famous leaf example is illustrative:

> Consider the density of leaves around a tree. I suggest the hypothesis that the leaves are positioned as if each leaf deliberately sought to maximize the amount of sunlight it receives, given the position of its neighbors, as if it knew the physical laws determining the amount of sunlight that would be received in various positions . . . Despite the apparent falsity of the 'assumptions' of the hypothesis, it has great plausibility because of the conformity of its implications with observation. (Friedman, 1953: 19-20)

Empirical studies show which concepts are more fruitful, and the quotations on the empirical stock exchange of the most useful understandings of the concepts will increase.

The pitfall here is that definitions and assumptions selected in that way risk being tautological. Many actions can be explained as results of rational and selfish behavior as long as convenient – and fruitful – assumptions on preferences can be made. As Wildavsky (1993: 155) phrases it:

> Explanations based on self-interest give the appearance of mattering more than they actually do, as well, because they are often interpreted retrospectively to cover whatever happens. Why did a person sacrifice life or limb in a particular instance? Because that act was in the person's self-interest or the person wouldn't have done it.

Various combinations and understandings of trust and reciprocity, and hence social capital, will in just the same way be able to explain just about any level of cooperation in a particular setting.

Another potential way to sharpen and define the central concepts is to look to other disciplines. In the following sections we follow this strategy. We do not claim that the concepts of trust and reciprocity – independently or together – define social capital, only that they are essential in most practical applications of the social capital approach. However, it is still contested whether trust and reciprocity are just the artificial expression of what is essentially strategic behavior of rational agents. By shedding some light on these concepts from the perspective of cognitive neuroscience, we hope to bring more nuances to the understanding of them. Particularly, we will argue that both appear to tap into processes and brain regions typically associated with emotions.

The potential of cognitive neuroscience
The empirical basis of social science theories is most often behavioral data. One problem with such data is that they only indirectly shed light on what most theories really are concerned with: the reasons for behaving in a certain way. The social capital literature is an example in point, as cooperative behavior is a well-established empirical fact. The real controversy regards why cooperative behavior happens: Is it self-interest, trust, social capital, and so on? Traditionally, we infer these whys by analysing the contingencies of behavior, that is, the conditions under which it is present or not.

Cognitive neuroscience offers a qualitatively distinct kind of data. Breakthroughs in technologies such as the development of functional PET (Positron Emission Tomography) and fMRI (Functional Magnetic Resonance Imaging) allow the study of physiological correlates of brain activity when individuals act, solve problems, make decisions, form expectations and so forth. Briefly, these methods give a physiological measure of the activity in particular brain regions as a function of some task a person is performing while being scanned. Both techniques are based on the finding that the brain directs blood flow to active regions, probably to ensure sufficient oxygen and glucose for the task at hand. Most PET experiments use a tiny amount of radioactive water to track local changes in blood saturation, while fMRI measures the magnetic properties of the blood, which is a function of the availability of oxygenated hemoglobin, and therefore affected by the relation between changes in activity and blood flow. It should be noted that both techniques provide indirect measures of brain activity with a relatively coarse (a matter of seconds, at best) time resolution, and that the precise relation between the measures and the underlying brain activity is (still) a matter of debate (Frackowiak et al., 2004).

As the knowledge about the functions of different brain regions expand, we may be able to get an idea about what processes underlie diverse cognitive tasks. In the end, this means that through the neuroscientific approach we get a more direct glimpse of the whys of behavior. Not surprisingly, the use of neuroscience in the social sciences is growing rapidly. Religious cognition (Saver and Rabin, 1997; Persinger and Healey, 2002), group relations (Harris and Fiske, 2006), the formation of political attitudes (Lieberman et al., 2003; Morris et al., 2003) and many other social science topics have been subject to neuroscientific inquiry. In this chapter, however, we focus solely on one of the intersections between neuroscience and the social sciences, neuroeconomics (Glimcher, 2003; Camerer et al., 2005). The social capital literature has for a long time recognized the importance of studies in experimental economics focusing on cooperation in the Prisoner's Dilemma game, the ultimatum game, and so on.

Table 5.1   *Overview of central studies in neuroeconomics relevant to social capital*

Study	Central results
McCabe et al. (2001)	Increased activation in brain regions involved in reading intentions during cooperation with human partners
Rilling et al. (2002)	Increased activation in brain's reward centers under mutual cooperation
Sanfey et al. (2003)	Increased activation in brain regions linked to anger and disgust when turning down unfair offers
Zak et al. (2004)	Oxytocin is released as a response to intentional signals of trust
De Quervain et al. (2004)	Increased activation in brain's reward centers when engaging in altruistic punishment
Kosfeld et al. (2005)	Oxytocin increases trustworthy behavior
Singer et al. (2006)	Less activation in brain regions involved in empathy and increased activation in brain's reward centers when unfair opponents are punished

As neuroeconomics is largely preoccupied with applying neuroscientific techniques to such experiments, this field holds an immediate promise of delivering important insights about social capital.

The social capital approach to understanding cooperation and interaction is flexible and it is not simplistic, but neither is it simple. Despite differences in methodology, objects of study and scientific tradition, the social capital approach could perhaps become more simple – but not simplistic – by learning from neuroeconomics. Below we discuss a number of recent studies. They are briefly summarized in Table 5.1.

Neuroscience of trust and reciprocity
One of the first neuroeconomic studies to investigate the neural correlates of trust and reciprocity was conducted by McCabe and colleagues (2001). Although the reporting of the data and the level of statistical significance obtained do not quite meet contemporary standards, the issues touched upon are instructive for the approach as such. While being fMRI scanned, the subjects were exposed to a simple two-player reciprocal trust game in which they either played against a human or a computer for cash rewards. Based on behavioral analysis, the subjects were pooled into two groups, one where subjects showed cooperative behavior against the human opponent, but not against the computer, and one where they showed no significant cooperative behavior, regardless of opponent. An analysis of the brain

scans revealed a pattern of (weak) activations mainly in the prefrontal cortex in the first group when the subjects cooperated with persons, while subjects in the second group showed no significant differences in brain scans between the two conditions. Notably, one of the strongest activations while cooperating appeared in the medial prefrontal cortex near an area also implicated in 'theory-of-mind' like tasks, that is, tasks where an individual takes into account the other person's knowledge or perspective (Gallagher et al., 2002; Gallagher and Frith, 2003). For the current discussion, we can draw three relevant aspects from the McCabe study:

1. The degree to which subjects engage in cooperative relations in reciprocal exchanges is not evenly distributed within a randomly selected population (only about 50 per cent sought to collaborate with the human opponent).
2. The choice of a cooperative strategy seems to be contingent upon a contextual analysis of the exchange situation and of the nature of the opponent (no subjects attempted a systematic collaboration with the computer).
3. Opting for a collaborative strategy makes for particular neuronal signatures (in this particular case a pattern of mainly prefrontal activity including putative 'intentional stance' regions).

Since then, a broad range of studies have examined in more detail various phases in cooperative and non-cooperative exchanges. In a paradigmatic study Sanfey and colleagues (2003) examined interactions in a variation of the ultimatum game. Briefly, subjects received offers from humans and computer opponents presenting them with a share of a known sum varying from 50/50 (fair) split to a 10/90 split (unfair). If the offer was accepted both parties would get their share; if the offer was rejected, however, everything would be lost. All fair offers were accepted, but contrary to rational choice theory, a significant proportion of unfair offers were rejected with a large intersubject variability (from 0 to 100 per cent rejection rate). An analysis of the brain scans revealed a significant difference in the BOLD (blood oxygen level-dependent) signal in the right dorsolateral prefrontal cortex (a typical 'cognitive' area) and anterior insula (a typical 'emotional' area associated with feelings of anger and disgust) when subjects were presented with an unfair offer from a human opponent. Regression analysis revealed a between-subject linear correlation between acceptance rate and activity in right anterior insula, and also a highly significant difference between right anterior insula activity in unfair situations where offers were rejected, compared to unfair situations where they were accepted. This suggests, the authors conclude, that the areas of the anterior insula and dorsolateral prefrontal cortex represent the twin demands of the ultimatum game task, the emotional goal of resisting unfairness and the cognitive goal of accumulating money. Further, as activity in the 'emotional' region was a strong predictor of rejection, 'models of decision-making cannot afford to ignore emotion as a vital and dynamic component of our decisions and choices in the real world'. (Sanfey et al., 2003: 1758).

Although the interpretation may be somewhat heavy-handed, Sanfey's study was paradigmatic because it demonstrated that a balance between 'emotional' and 'cognitive' constraints on decision-making in an interactive game was translated into brain activities. Economic interactions have therefore become research tools, also for studying other aspects of cognition and emotion. In one study, Tanya Singer and colleagues (2006) first exposed subjects to variations of Prisoner's Dilemma interactions with opponents who were either instructed to be fair or blatantly unfair. Interview ratings classified unfair opponents as significantly more unattractive and unpleasant and significantly less likeable. Subsequently, the subjects were scanned while they and their fair and unfair opponents were subjected to painful electrical stimulations. Analysis revealed that, particularly in men, there was significantly less activity in 'empathy' regions of the brain (in this study anterior insula and anterior cingulate cortex), when unfair subjects received electric shocks compared to when fair subjects got shocks. Further, again in men only, there was significant activity in a so-called 'reward' area of the brain (nucleus accumbens) when unfair opponents received electric shocks, and it was correlated with the desire for revenge. In other words, an unfair offer is not only often rejected on what appears to be emotional grounds (the Sanfey et al. story). Acting unfairly seems to make individuals less attractive and likeable, and if pain is inflicted on such individuals their opponents are less likely to react with empathy: in fact, these individuals may trigger the sweet pleasure of revenge in those they treated so badly.

One of the key figures in the neuroeconomic investigations of human interactions is the Swiss economist Ernst Fehr. From a background in labor market economics (Fehr 2004), he moved to an investigation of 'fairness', first in behavioral experimental economics. Through a number of high-profile pharmacological, fMRI and TMS experiments (for example, de Quervain et al., 2004; Knoch et al., 2006; Kosfeld et al., 2005), his research group has now taken these questions to the brain. Their study of 'altruistic punishment' (de Quervain et al., 2004) is exemplary in this regard. They used a simple economic trusting game where subjects were given the option to punish – at a cost – defectors who failed to reciprocate donations. Contextual modifications allowed for different scenarios where the opponents were constructed as responsible for the defection or as bound entirely by the rules of the game. Only in conditions where opponents were perceived as having a choice did defection give rise to a desire for punishment. The crucial examination was a PET scanning of the decision to punish and the results were quite stunning. When subjects meted out a costly punishment, there was activity in the caudate nucleus, a typical reward area. Furthermore, the activity in this region was correlated with the desire for revenge and the costs of getting it. In line with the study by Singer et al. (2006), the material costs of punishment seem to be outweighed by the pleasure of seeing justice served.

This is a highly interesting expansion on the neuroeconomic literature because the focus is shifted from the decision making process to the evaluation of the opponent. It is when the opponent is perceived as having some element of choice that the interaction acquires moral potential. The decision to punish seems to involve and be correlated with activity in deep-brain structures, in this case reward regions. There are also significant correlations with activity in cortical regions, but interestingly and potentially of ideological stripe, this aspect is hardly discussed. In any case, the paper is *gefundenes Fressen* for a social capital approach because it indicates that even in an interaction with a stranger one may never meet again, most subjects will incur significant costs to punish violations of a norm to reciprocate and that there seems to be neuronal correlates of this desire.

In a later high-profile paper, the group shifted focus to examine whether neuronal manipulation affected how trusting people would be with strangers in a simple economic game (Kosfeld et al., 2005). Briefly, subjects were exposed to oxytocin, a neuropeptide known to play a role in social attachment and affiliation in non-human mammals. They then subjected them to a 'trust game' where they could give money to an opponent in the hope that he would return their investment. The neuropharmocological intervention significantly increased the invested sum, suggesting that 'trust' and cooperative behavior may be affected by neuronal mechanisms beyond conscious rational decisions. As picked up by Damasio in a commentary (2005), one should in the future perhaps beware of political operators who generously spray the crowd with oxytocin at rallies for their candidates. While Kosfeld et al. (2005) deal with the behavioral consequences of exogenously induced oxytocin, a study by Zak et al. (2004) investigates when oxytocin is released by the brain endogenously. In this study, the researchers also examined behavior using a trust game. More precisely, they compared two versions of the game. In the first version participants had to choose whether to trust another participant with an investment. In the second version, this choice was determined randomly by drawing a numbered ball from an urn. The results revealed that the oxytocin levels of the participants were nearly twice as high if they were entrusted with an investment, but only if it was done intentionally (as in the first version). Importantly, the average monetary transfers in the two versions was identical, indicating that it is not benefits per se that release oxytocin, but only signals of pro-social intentions. These two oxytocin studies suggest a neurochemical mechanism linked to the emergence of reciprocity. Oxytocin appears to be released by intentional pro-social acts, which in turn motivate pro-social behavior. Reciprocal social interaction may therefore arise due to emotional reactions to (perceived) mutual good intentions. In real life interactions this simple mechanism is obviously also useful in various forms of deceptions and manipulation, for example, in the science fiction-like concept of spraying oxytocin in a board room (Damasio, 2005), and, in more realistic situations, intentional manipulations of the perceptions of the interaction.

The idea that reciprocity may be grounded in emotions is also supported by an earlier fMRI-study conducted by Rilling et al. (2002). Players engaged in mutual cooperation showed significantly increased activation in neural circuits that have been linked to reward processing (for example, nucleus accumbens and the caudate nucleus). Furthermore, the activation in the reward centers increased with consecutive outcomes of mutual cooperation. This might seem surprising given that mutual cooperation is less profitable than cheating (defection-cooperation), but the authors interpret the effect as the neural foundation of a subjective emotional reinforcement of reciprocal interactions, which motivates us to resist the temptation to cheat. Thus, participants also considered mutual cooperation the most personally satisfying outcome.

Emotions and the importance of context

The studies cited above appear to lend empirical support to an important claim made by at least some social capital-theorists, namely, that humans are not only directed by narrow self-interest. They are also at times motivated by notions of cooperation and of fairness. Importantly, both at the behavioral and the neuronal levels, there seem to be particular markers of these traits. The links between experiencing unfairness and subsequent action appears to be 'emotional' in the sense that typical emotional regions in the brain become activated, and that particular interactive valence is attached to opponents who behave either unfairly or pro-socially. It is these observations about the importance of emotions that form the core message from neuroscience to the social capital literature. Furthermore, situations of cooperation entail, apparently, an interpretation of the opponent as intentional and human. We elaborate on these observations below.

It is a current trend in neuroscience to study emotions as fundamental motivating forces in human decision-making (Damasio, 1994, 2004;

LeDoux, 1996). We can conceptualize the emotions evoked in the studies described above (such as sympathy, anger and disgust) as belonging to a category of *moral emotions* owing to their ability to promote unselfish behavior (Haidt, 2003). Important brain regions activated when such emotions are evoked are the amygdala, various subcortical nuclei and the insula (Moll et al., 2002). Interestingly, people are seemingly often unaware of the processes leading to the execution of these emotions (LeDoux, 1996). This might relate to the fact that the regions vital to emotional processing are buried deep beneath the brain centers involved in controlled, conscious processing such as the prefrontal cortex (Lieberman, 2003). This lends support to the claim that behavior in dilemmas of cooperation is not always motivated by conscious assessments of self-interest.

When emotions are introduced into the equation, it not only becomes necessary to acknowledge the existence of moral motives; one must also acknowledge the endogenous nature of these motivations. In the words of Damasio (2004: 58), one may conceive of the brain regions for the elicitation of such specific emotions as 'locks that open only if the appropriate keys fit', the keys being the stimuli present in a situation (see also Damasio, 1994; Gazzaniga et al., 2002; LeDoux, 1996; Tooby et al., 2005). This means that the emotions of interest here are motivational *states* rather than *traits*, that is, they emerge at a given moment in a particular situation. In this way, the emotions, which neuroscience documents as an important ingredient in decision-making, are something very different from the preferences in rational choice theory. Where preferences generally are conceived to be both exogenous to the decision-making context and stable across situations (see, for example, Shepsle, 1989), emotionally grounded motivations are triggered by the very context in which a decision is made.

As the emotional system is highly context-sensitive, we should expect moral emotions to be operative only under particular circumstances. As described above, a basic method in neuroeconomical studies is to compare brain activity when subjects play against a human partner with the activity elicited when they play against a computer. Apart from the experimental heuristics of this approach, it also provides substantial information about the context specificity of the experience of interactive exchanges. In the experiments discussed above, human–computer interactions elicit moral response to a lesser extent than do human–human interactions. In the McCabe et al. (2001) study of the Prisoner's Dilemma, the activity of cooperators in the prefrontal cortex, a region involved in inhibiting impulses (see also Knoch et al., 2006), is only higher in human-human interactions compared to human–computer interactions. Highly uneven offers made by computers in the ultimatum game appear not to activate anger and disgust patterns (Sanfey et al., 2003), nor do subjects feel pleasure when they reject such offers (de Quervain et al., 2004; see discussion of this experiment below). Interestingly, this contextual understanding of an interaction is not necessarily the result of a 'correct' reading of the situation. This is exemplified in Gallagher et al.'s study of intentional stance by way of a rock-paper-scissors game (2002). Subjects were here led to believe that they either played against a rule-bound computer program or a human opponent, when during scanning they actually played a random sequence. Both the experience of the game as validated by interviews and the brain activity recorded by PET scanning pointed to a marked difference between these two conditions. As expressed by one subject: 'I could clearly feel the other person there, whereas I felt nothing from the computer.'

The crucial question is how these human-computer interactions should be interpreted. Blount (1995) was among the first to investigate such interactions through behavioral observations. She claims that people reason about computer behavior in the same way they reason about environmental events, that is, as produced by chance rather than by the good or bad intentions of humans (although, along the lines of the Gallagher et al. finding, this difference may be a result of the contextual framing rather than the 'real' nature of the interaction (see also Jack and Roepstorff, 2002)). This interpretation is reinforced by a recent brain-imaging study investigating human-computer interactions in more detail. In this study, Rilling et al. (2004) shows that areas involved in figuring out the intentions of others (anterior paracingulate cortex and superior temporal sulcus) can also – under the right circumstances – be activated when playing what is perceived to be a computer opponent. Thus, a Prisoner's Dilemma game where the response of the computer was contingent upon the response of the subject showed much more 'human interaction like' patterns (Rilling et al., 2004). In tandem, these observations imply that the putative ascription of morality to an interaction depends on a (not necessarily consciously made) contextual analysis of an interaction as 'human' (and that it may be a matter of degree rather than kind). Further, behavioral data suggest that this contextual analysis also involves asking questions about matters of obligation. Thus, in the ultimatum game participants share the understanding that endowments won in a quiz should not be split as evenly as endowments provisionally distributed by the experimenter (Hoffman McCabe et al., 1994). When endowments are earned rather than assigned, people seem to feel less obligated to consider the interests of others.

In sum, the elicitation of moral emotions appears related to contexts where the opponent is perceived, first, as capable of understanding the situation from more than one perspective; second, as capable of acting with a certain level of freedom, and third, as obligated to take into account the act's welfare consequences for other people. Morality is thus a matter of framing, and as institutions and political developments foster relevant frames on certain issues or domains, they effectively become part of a moral economy. The market is a classic example of a context in which one is largely allowed to act without considering the general welfare consequences of one's acts. In line with this, a large literature shows how moral motivations are 'crowded out' when social exchanges are moved from a non-market context and into a market context (Frey, 1997; Le Grand, 2003). For example, people may be more willing to donate blood if they are *not* paid to do so, that is, when it is a gift rather than an exchange on the market (Titmuss, 1970). Similarly, interactions can be moved into a moral domain by fostering the expectation that people are obligated to consider these interactions from the perspective of others and revise their acts if there is a potential for negative impacts on the welfare of others. Smoking is a clear example (see Rozin and Singh, 1999). Over a decade political campaigns have transformed smoking from a non-issue into a moral one, in which the smoker is obligated to consider how his vice impacts bystanders. If he fails to do so, reactions of anger and disgust are quickly elicited. Another example of direct relevance to social capital literature is environmental behavior which the advent of post-materialistic values has moved into a trust-regulated moral domain (see Sønderskov, 2008). In this way, the neuroeconomic experiments described here underscore the claim of some social capital theorists regarding the importance of the institutional context for human motivations (for example, Ostrom, 1998). An implication of this perspective is that a certain reservoir of social capital is probably not sufficient to guarantee collective action. A likely necessary condition is that the problem is perceived as a moral matter, in which the intertwinement of people's interests and their capability and obligation to act accordingly is clear.

Conclusion

In this chapter, we have reviewed a series of studies in neuroeconomics. These studies demonstrate that reciprocal social interactions are, psychologically speaking, motivated by emotional dynamics that emerge outside conscious awareness in situations where the participants are mutually perceived as capable of and obligated to consider each other's interests. Neuroeconomics thus sheds light on the psychological basis of cooperation and, furthermore, points to important conditions that must be fulfilled for cooperation to emerge.

This conclusion can be taken as support for the relevance of the social capital tradition. Although operating at very different levels, both the social capital and the neuroeconomic approach reject, partly on experimental grounds, partly on theoretical ones, a simple 'rational man' approach, in which decisions are based solely on short-term selfish cal-culations. In addition, both approaches identify elements like trust and reciprocity as central explanatory variables in group behavior as well as in individual actions. The significance of trust, reciprocity and emotion in neuroeconomic studies indicates that these phenomena are more than just artificial consequences of selfish and rational motivations. When another human being trusts you, it is not necessarily because he is confident that you cannot afford to renege on your promise. And if you do so, he will probably feel angry, and perhaps even make a costly effort to get revenge. If you return a favor, reciprocate, your motivation is likely to be a feeling of obligation or desire to do so, and not just a calculation that it will pay off. The social capital approach operates with concepts that are more than rationality in disguise and they are essential to understanding human behavior. However, the social capital approach is also diverse. While the conclusion about the importance of context-sensitive emotions will be in line with some perspectives in the social capital tradition, it might be at odds with other more rationalistic approaches to social capital.

In one reading of these parallels between social capital and neuroeconom-ics, current neuroeconomics proves 'social capital theory' right in that the key concepts of the approach, trust, emotions, and reciprocity, are found in the brain. The problem with such an interpretation is that it uncritically links two very different levels of explanation where concepts take on very different meanings, while bracketing out the epistemological and ontologi-cal differences that separate these levels. For instance, the finding about the link between oxytocin and cooperation is intriguing, but like much current neuroeconomic research it cries out for proper contextualization. It can be taken along a path of radical reductionism, as illustrated by Zak and Fakhar (2006), who claim to identify cross-national correlations between the consumption of plant-based estrogens, a precursor of oxytocin, and levels of trust. In a mild reductionism, Damasio (2005) suggests that current marketing techniques may provide stimuli that naturally release oxytocin. It would also lend itself nicely to a social capital explanation; if trust is about social capital and social capital is about a particular social and interpersonal context, and oxytocin is released in particular contexts, for example in social bonding processes (Uvnäs-Moberg et al., 2005), then social capital may be all about creating an environment that triggers the release of oxytocin. However, a satisfying explanation must look into how decision-making emerges in a balance between these different factors and how it merges with contextual evaluations and the experience and exertion of agency. That level of neurobiological explanation has yet to be achieved and it may be a long way down the line.

Although the current state of cognitive neuroscience allows us to emphasize the importance of emotion, a basic problem is that the approach as such does not provide the tools required to develop more comprehensive understandings of these emotions. Our knowledge of neural processes is still (and may always be) too limited to help us infer the answers to questions such as 'How are specific emotional systems structured?', 'When are they elicited?' and 'What kind of motivations do they foster?' simply by examining patterns of brain activity. Thus, to be able to venture deeper into exactly how emotions form the backbone of social cooperation, we are in need of meta-theoretical guidance.

Different possibilities suggest themselves. One might look to the discipline of evolutionary psychology, where emotions are described as biological information processing systems that evolved to help our ancestors deal with recurrent reproductive problems (Tooby and Cosmides, 1990; Cosmides and Tooby, 2000). Through knowledge of ancestral environments, evolutionary processes and the structure of the recurrent problems, this approach may offer detailed hypotheses about the architecture of human emotions and the situations in which they are elicited (Barkow et al., 1992). Another possible way forward would involve a more sociological focus on actual persons, how they interact, and how configurations of the social interact with the biological (Latour, 2006; Rose, 2006). Our review of the literature suggests that trust and reciprocity are highly contextual elements that appear to be applied only in particular reflexive situations of interaction. They occur when person A interacts with another person B and A imagines that B is in a situation where she can take A's position into account and act with that in mind. While this acknowledges how particular biological configurations allow humans to construct others as persons equipped with perspective taking, intentionality, emotions, and so on (Frith and Frith, 1999, 2006), it stresses how the identification of key social capital effects like trust and reciprocity, both at the level of brains and interactions, are consequences of reflexive sociality in action.

References

Ahn, T.K., E. Ostrom, D. Schmidt, R. Shupp and J. Warker (2001), 'Co-operation in PD games, fear, greed and history of play', *Public Choice*, **106**: 137–55.

Arrow, Kenneth J. (2000), 'Observations on social capital', in Partha Dasgupta and Ismail Serageldin (eds), *Social Capital. A Multifaceted Perspective*, Washington, DC: World Bank.

Barkow, Jerome H., Leda Cosmides and John Tooby (eds) (1992), *The Adapted Mind*, Oxford: Oxford University Press.

Blount, Sally (1995), 'When social outcomes aren't fair: the effect of causal attributions on preferences', *Organizational Behavior and Human Decision Processes*, **63** (2), 131–44.

Camerer, Colin, George Loewenstein and Drazen Prelec (2005), 'Neuroeconomics: how neuroscience can inform economics', *Journal of Economic Literature*, **43** (1), 9–64.

Cameron, Lisa (1999), 'Raising the stakes in the ultimatum game: experimental evidence from Indonesia', *Economic Inquiry*, **37**, 47–59.

Coleman, J.S. (1988), 'Social capital in the creation of human-capital', *American Journal of Sociology*, **94**, S95–S120.

Cosmides, Leda and John Tooby (2000), 'Evolutionary psychology and the emotions', in Michael Lewis and Jeannette M. Haviland-Jones (eds), *Handbook of Emotions*, 2nd edn, New York and London: Guilford Press, pp. 91–115.

Damasio, Antonio (1994), *Descartes' Error*, New York: HarperCollins Books.

Damasio, Antonio (2004), *Looking for Spinoza*, New York: Vintage Books.

Damasio, Antonio (2005), 'Human behaviour: brain trust', *Nature*, **435**, 571–2.

De Quervain, Dominique J.F., Urs Fischbacher, Valerie Treyer, Melanie Schellhammer, Schnyder Ulrich, Alfred Buck and Ernst Fehr (2004), 'The neural basis of altruistic punishment', *Science*, **305**, 1254–8.

Fehr, Ernst (2004), 'The productivity of failures', *Nature*, **428**, 701.

Frackowiak, R.S.J., Karl J. Friston, Christopher D. Frith, Raymond J. Dolan, Cathy J. Price, Semir Zeki, John Ashburner and William D. Penny (eds) (2004), *Human Brain Function*, Boston, MA: Elsevier Academic Press.

Frey, Bruno S. (1997), *Not Just for the Money. An Economic Theory of Personal Motivation*, Cheltenham, UK and Lyme, USA: Edward Elgar.

Friedman, Milton (1953), *Essays in Positive Economics*, Chicago, IL: University of Chicago Press.

Frith, C.D. and U. Frith (1999), 'Interacting minds – a biological basis', *Science*, **286**, 1692–5.

Frith, C.D. and U. Frith (2006), 'How we predict what other people are going to do', *Brain Research*, **1079**, 36–46.

Gallagher, H.L. and C.D. Frith (2003), 'Functional imaging of "theory of mind"', *Trends in Cognitive Science*, **7**, 77–83.

Gallagher, H., A.I. Jack, A. Roepstorff and C.D. Frith (2002), 'Imagining the intentional stance in a competitive game', *NeuroImage*, **16**, 814–21.

Gazzaniga, M.S., R. Ivry and G.R. Mangun (2002), *Cognitive Neuroscience: The Biology of the Mind*, 2nd edn, London and New York: W.W. Norton.

Glimcher, Paul (2003), *Decisions, Uncertainty, and the Brain. The Science of Neuroeconomics*, Cambridge, MA: MIT Press.

Güth, Werner, Rolf Schmittberger and Bernd Schwarze (1982), 'An experimental analysis of ultimatum bargaining', *Journal of Economic Behavior and Organization*, **3**, 367–88.

Haidt, Jonathan (2003), 'The moral emotions', in Richard J. Davidson, Klaus R. Scherer and H. Hill Goldsmith (eds), *Handbook of Affective Sciences*, Oxford: Oxford University Press, pp. 852–70.

Harris, Lasana T. and Susan T. Fiske (2006), 'Dehumanizing the lowest of the low: neuroimaging responses to extreme out-groups', *Psychological Science*, **17** (10), 847–53.

Hoffman, Elizabeth, Kevin McCabe, Keith Shachat and Vernon Smith (1994), 'Preferences, property rights, and anonymity in bargaining games', *Games and Economic Behavior*, **7** (3), 346–80.

Inglehart, Ronald, Miguel Basáñez, Jaime Díez-Medrano, Loek Halmann and Ruud Luijkx (eds) (2004), *Human Beliefs and Values. A Cross-cultural Sourcebook Based on the 1999– 2002 Values Surveys*, Coyoacan: Siglo XXI Editores.

Jack, A.I. and A. Roepstorff (2002), 'Introspection and cognitive brain mapping: from stimulus-response to script-report', *Trends in Cognitive Sciences*, **6**, 333–9.

Knack, Stephen and Philip Keefer (1997), 'Does social capital have an economic payoff? A cross-country investigation', *Quarterly Journal of Economics*, **112** (4), 1251–88.

Knoch, Daria, Alvaro Pascual-Leone, Kaspar Meyer, Valerie Treyer and Ernst Fehr (2006), 'Diminishing reciprocal fairness by disrupting the right prefrontal cortex', *Science*, **314**, 829–32.

Kosfeld, M., M. Heinrichs, P.J. Zak, U. Fischbacher and E. Fehr (2005), 'Oxytocin increases trust in humans', *Nature*, **435**, 673–6.

Latour, B. (2006), *Reassembling the Social. An Introduction to Actor-Network Theory*, Oxford: Oxford University Press.

LeDoux, Joseph (1996), *The Emotional Brain*, New York: Touchstone.

Le Grand, Julian (2003), *Motivation, Agency, and Public Policy. Of Knights and Knaves, Pawns and Queens*, Oxford: Oxford University Press.

Lieberman, Matthew D. (2003), 'Reflective and reflexive judgment processes: a social cognitive neuroscience approach', in J.P. Forgas, K.R. Williams and W. von Hippel (eds), *Social Judgments: Implicit and Explicit Processes*, New York: Cambridge University Press, pp. 44–67.

Lieberman, M.D., D. Schreiber and K.N. Ochsner (2003), 'Is political thinking like riding a bicycle? How cognitive neuroscience can inform research on political thinking', *Political Psychology*, **24**, 681–704.

McCabe, Kevin, Daniel Houser, Lee Ryan, Vernon Smith and Theodore Trouard (2001), 'A functional imaging study of cooperation in two-person reciprocal exchange', *Proceedings of the National Academy of Science*, **98** (20), 11832–5.

Moll, Jorge, Ricardo de Oliveira-Souza, Paul J. Eslinger, Ivanei E. Bramati, Janaina Mourao-Miranda, Pedro Angelo Andreiuolo and Luiz Pessoa (2002), 'The neural correlates of moral sensitivity: a functional magnetic resonance imaging investigation of basic and moral emotions', *The Journal of Neuroscience*, **22** (7), 2730–36.

Morris, James P., Nancy K. Squires, Charles S. Taber and Milton Lodge (2003), 'Activation of political attitudes: a psychophysiological examination of the hot cognition hypothesis', *Political Psychology*, **24** (4), 727–45.

Ostrom, Elinor (1998), 'A behavioral approach to the rational choice theory of collective action: presidential address, American Political Science Association', *American Political Science Review*, **92**, 1–22.

Paldam, Martin and Gert T. Svendsen (forthcoming), *Trust, Social Capital and Economic Growth: An International Comparison*, Cheltenham, UK and Northampton, MA, USA: Edward Elgar.

Persinger, Michael A. and Faye Healey (2002), 'Experimental facilitation of the sensed presence: possible intercalation between hemispheres induced by complex magnetic fields', *The Journal of Nervous and Mental Diseases*, **190** (8), 533–41.

Portes, A. (1998), 'Social capital: its origins and applications in modern sociology', *Annual Review of Sociology*, **24**, 1–24.

Poulsen, A. and G.T. Svendsen (2005), 'Social capital and endogenous preferences', *Public Choice*, **123** (1–2), 171–96.

Putnam, Robert D. (1993a), *Making Democracy Work: Civic Traditions in Modern Italy*, Princeton, NJ: Princeton University Press.

Putnam, Robert D. (1993b), 'The prosperous community. Social capital and public life', *American Prospect*, **4** (13), 35–42.

Rilling, James K., Alan G. Sanfey, Jessica A. Aronson, Leigh E. Nystrom and Jonathan D. Cohen (2004), 'The neural correlates of theory of mind within interpersonal interactions', *NeuroImage*, **22**, 1694–703.

Rilling, James K., David A. Gutman, Thorsten R. Zeh, Giuseppe Pagnoni, Gregory S. Berns and Clinton D. Kilts (2002), 'A neural basis for social cooperation', *Neuron*, **35**, 395–405.

Rose, N. (2006), *The Politics of Life Itself. Biomedicine, Power and Subjectivity in the Twenty First Century*, Princeton, NJ: Princeton University Press.

Roth, Alvin E., Vesna Prasnikar, Masahiro Okuno-Fujiwara and Shmuel Zamir (1991), 'Bargaining and market behavior in Jerusalem, Ljubljana, Pittsburgh, and Tokyo: an experimental study', *American Economic Review*, **81**, 1068–95.

Rozin, Paul and Leher Singh (1999), 'The moralization of cigarette smoking in the United States', *Journal of Consumer Psychology*, **8** (3), 321–37.

Sanfey, Alan G., James K. Rilling, Jessica A. Aronson, Leigh E. Nystrom and Jonathan D. Cohen (2003), 'The neural basis of economic decision-making in the ultimatum game', *Science*, **300**, 1755–8.

Saver, Jeffrey L. and John Rabin (1997), 'The neural substrates of religious experience', *Journal of Neuropsychiatry*, **9** (3), 498–510.

Shepsle, Kenneth A. (1989), 'Studying institutions. Some lessons from the rational choice approach', *Journal of Theoretical Politics*, **1** (2), 131–47.

Singer, T., B. Seymour, J.P. O'Doherty, K.E. Stephan, R.J. Dolan and C.D. Frith (2006), 'Empathic neural responses are modulated by the perceived fairness of others', *Nature*, **439**, 466–9.

Sobel, J. (2002), 'Can we trust social capital?', *Journal of Economic Literature*, **40** (1), 139–54.

Sønderskov, Kim M. (2008), 'Environmental group membership, collective action and generalised trust', *Environmental Politics*, **17** (1), 78–94.

Titmuss, Richard M. (1970), *The Gift Relationship: From Human Blood to Social Policy*, London: Allen & Unwin.

Tooby, John and Leda Cosmides (1990), 'The past explains the present: emotional adaptations and the structure of ancestral environments', *Ethology and Sociobiology*, **11**, 375–424.

Tooby, John, Leda Cosmides and H. Clark Barrett (2005), 'Resolving the debate on innate ideas', in Peter Carruthers, S. Laurence and Steve Stich (eds), *The Innate Mind: Structure and Content*, New York: Oxford University Press, pp. 305–37.

Uvnäs-Moberg, Kerstin, Ingemar Arn and David Magnusson (2005), 'The psychobiology of emotion: the role of the oxytocinergic system', *International Journal of Behavioral Medicine*, **12** (2), 59–65.

Wildavsky, Aaron (1993), 'Why self-interest means less outside of a social context: cultural contributions to a theory of rational choices', *Journal of Theoretical Politics*, **6** (2), 131–59.

Yamagishi, Toshio (1988), 'The provision of a sanctioning system in the United States and Japan', *Social Psychology Quarterly*, **51** (3), 265–71.

Zak, P.J. and A. Fakhar (2006), 'Neuroactive hormones and interpersonal trust: international evidence', *Economics & Human Biology*, **4**, 412–29.

Zak, Paul J., Robert Kurzban and William T. Matzner (2004), 'The neurobiology of trust', *Annals of the New York Academy of Sciences*, **1032**, 224–7.

6 Humour
Peter Gundelach

Introduction

Humour is social. 'We rarely laugh alone and never tell ourselves jokes out loud or play jokes on ourselves' (Fine, 1983: 176). Everybody enjoys a good laugh and in a book like this it lays near at hand to compare the pleasant effects of humour with the positive effects of social capital. Intuitively humour and social capital seem to be interrelated and have positive social effects. In this sense humour may be seen as an element in creating social capital and thus an asset for instance in relation to the performance of groups.

Such positive functions of humour will be considered in detail below but initially it should be noted that both in studies of humour and social capital there is a 'nice guy tendency'. Researchers tend to overlook the negative sides of jokes and other types of humour (Billig, 2001a). For instance, humour may create seemingly negative, stereotypical pictures of other groups and in other cases jokes may be used to marginalize group members. In totalitarian regimes people have been arrested for telling jokes that are critical towards the regime. Likewise, there may also be a tendency to overlook the downside of social capital (Portes and Landholt, 1996; Portes, 1998) for instance where groups or communities are closed, have a strong exclusion mechanism and may hinder economic and social development. It seems that humour and social capital are reminiscent of each other in the sense that their functions depend on the character of the phenomenon and the social context.

In *Bowling Alone* Putnam (2000: 22) made a distinction between bonding and bridging social capital. Bridging refers to social capital that encompasses people across diverse social cleavages and bonding refers to inward-looking networks that tend to strengthen exclusive identities. As mentioned, humour at first glance may be seen as a bonding mechanism in the sense that it creates group unity and group boundaries – but it is often a mechanism that represents a useful, surplus, playful element of social life. On the one hand, humour may unite a group and have a positive effect on the functions of a group. One the other hand, humour may be used to ridicule other people (and create closure) but it also has an anarchistic play-fulness that challenges the negative sides of social capital. For instance, a group may use jokes to create a negative image of another group. However, this does not mean that the other group in fact is considered inferior or even that the joke-teller perceives that there is an element of truth in the joke (Davies, 2002). In many cases a joke is simply a way to play. Thus telling a joke may be a bonding mechanism but it does not follow that such bonding prevents bridging.

The jokes which are studied below are primarily connected to work groups and ethnic groups because it may be expected that the relationship between humour and social capital is different in the two contexts. The chapter begins by looking at work groups in a Putnam perspective. Here we should expect that humour may strengthen the bonds of the group and improve its performance – a relationship that is in line with Putnam's general argument about the positive function of social capital. However, a closer analysis shows that humour may have many different consequences depending on the situation as well of the participants. Next ethnic humour is discussed because it may be hypothesized such humour creates an us–them cleavage and that, consequently, ethnic jokes prevent bridging. There are examples of such a mechanism and that ethnic jokes create bonding, but as it will be shown humour is also a bridging mechanism because the joke-teller and the target of the joke often feel related and joke-telling is a form of ritual that creates a feeling of affiliation between the two groups. Finally, the chapter studies humour at the personal level, using Pierre Bourdieu's theory of capital. It will be shown that at the individual level jokes are just as multifaceted as at the group level. Humour plays a role in many different types of situations. Humour may bond or bridge depending on the situation, the type of humour and on the relationship between the participants.

Humour as a micro-mechanism in creating group identity in work groups

Humour serves a wide range of functions at work, one of which is to foster collegiality. For instance, an analysis of interactions in workplaces showed that one of the most important functions of humour was the construction and maintenance of good relations with fellow workers (Holmes, 2006). Humour may strengthen social capital by creating network and trust among members and humour may have positive economic effects because humour seems to facilitate a well-functioning group and increase the performance of the group. The feeling of belonging and cohesion and the creation of mutual trust increase the group's performance, that is, have economic effects.

Humour is a part of the life of all social groups but it may have different kinds of consequences, depending on the group and the participants. An example of the positive sides of humour may be found in Terrion and Ashforth's (2002) study of how a group of Canadian police officers who participated in a six-week Executive Development Course changed from 'I' to 'we'. During the six weeks a strong group identity was created. Jokes, teasing and conversational joking were important mechanisms to create group identity.

Terrion and Ashforth report that when the participants introduced themselves on the first day of the course, many of them did this with gentle putdowns as for instance when a French speaker said 'I'm trying to learn English, so if you'll help me out'. Jokes and teasing became important parts of the interaction of the group. Such putdown humour is very common. It may be classified as a 'superiority' type of humour where we laugh at the perceived weakness of the target. During the course the use of putdown humour went through different phases, from putdowns of oneself, to putdowns of shared identities, to putdowns of external groups and finally to putdowns of each other.

Putdown jokes of external groups create an us–them distinction. The group is convinced it is better or superior to other groups. In this way the joke is an element in social bonding that tends to create a closure in relation to other groups. In some ways this is instrumental. Jokes become a way of knitting the group together and creating a common culture of belonging to a group – in this case of executive personnel. Joke-telling created a small group culture, 'it creates comfort in group life and serves to maintain group relationship by building communalities' (Fine and De Sourcey, 2005: 2). Humour also provides the members with a network and possibly opportunities for interactions that are instrumental for the carrying out of the duties of the participants when they finish the course.

During the course a member of the group suggested to begin each day by telling a joke and eventually joking became a ritual. Telling jokes about outsiders strengthened the cohesion in the group but not everybody approved of the jokes that were told. For instance, one member told a sexist joke. On several later occasions this joke was retold and recognized as a very popular joke. The joke had what Goffman has called a 'referential afterlife' (cf. Fine and De Sourcey, 2005: 2). Several of the participants considered the joke equivocal – although they did not voice a criticism in the group, only to the researchers. In spite of the criticism they laughed and it appears that it was not the content of the joke, but rather the laughing that was important. Even though there often was variability in how members interpreted the joke, Terrion and Ashforth (2002) argue that the potential multiplicity of meanings that may have facilitated group development by enabling members to interact as if they shared perceptions. Laughing became a ritual that would knit the group together but at the same time several members of the group felt that the sexist joke was inappropriate, not funny. They laughed but at the same time they probably distanced themselves a little from the joke-teller. Thus joke-telling and laughing may create distance, tension and possibly hostility even among those who laugh at a joke because it is a social convention to participate in laughing, but it may also indicate that all group members like each other and share the pleasure of laughing together and to contribute to the feeling of group cohesion.

Joking may also strengthen the group norms. For instance Baarts (2006) has shown how teasing is a strong element in conversations among a Danish crew of construction workers. Even though Denmark is a so-called wet alcohol culture, where beer plays an important role, drinking beer was neither formally nor informally accepted at this particular workplace – or for that matter at Danish workplaces in general. Among the workers drinking beer was seen as dangerous because it threatened safety at work. Baarts tells an example of how members of the work crew tease each other with stories of their alleged drinking. The target may hit back and tease other members and in this way the positions of the members are negotiated while at the same time the jokes indirectly refer to a strong norm about trust and safety at work.

In such ways humour may be a powerful tool in building more cohesive groups (McGhee and Goldstein, 1983) and this is important, because often cohesive groups work together better in pursuing common goals especially in situations where there are high performance expectations. Such insights have (of course) created opportunities for management consultants who help managers to use humour functionally at the workplace. One example of the perceived benefits of humour comes from a company called Humour Incorporated. At the website of this company you can read the following: 'When humour is incorporated into your outlook it won't cure all your problems instantly, but it will change your life for the better. When you're laughing, it's impossible to be angry. Instead of battling with negative emotions, your frame of mind will allow you to rationally deal with the situation.'[1] The website continues by promising that in a 'happy workplace' there is less absenteeism, illness and turnover, and the customers are more satisfied.

No doubt such a piece of advertising from a company that sells humour promises more than it can keep. It is interesting, however, to see the use of humour as a kind of social engineering and what in a critical – dark side – analysis may be understood as a kind of manipulation where management by using humour induce employees to work harder.

In general, humour creates social capital in a work group. However, depending on the situation and the character of the jokes, the humour may have bonding or bridging effects or perhaps both effects at the same times. Joking at the expense of a group member may create group cohesion but it may also result in negative feelings in a group (even though this does not need to be the case, cf. below) and as with the example of sexist jokes the climate of a group may prevent members of the group voicing critical remarks about, for instance, discriminating jokes. This means that even though humour in general helps to create social bonds in a group it may also have negative consequences for individual members. In work groups jokes about outsiders may create or reproduce stereotypical perceptions. In this way the jokes are similar to ethnic jokes.

Ethnic jokes
Ethnic jokes are often regarded as congruent with the weak form of the superiority theory of humour (Davies, 2002: 12). 'In laughing at ethnic jokes we are laughing at comically defective attributes ascribed to others. The jokes play with superiority and disparagement' (Davies, 2002: 13).

The ethnic jokes create an us–them division. When we tell jokes about other ethnic groups the idea of the joke is to ridicule the group by using a negative stereotypical image. But this does not necessarily mean that the joke-teller actually feels superior or hostile to the ethnic group that is the butt of the joke. Whether or not this is the case is an empirical question (Davies, 2002: 13). When someone tells an ethnic joke the listeners already know that it will play with the fact that some ethnic groups are 'inferior' in one way or the other, but at the same time there is a feeling of affiliation with the group that is the butt of the joke.

This paradox can be explained with the character of ethnic jokes. In general, people only tell ethnic jokes about groups that they have a relationship with. Radcliffe-Brown defines a joking relationship as 'a relation between two persons in which one is by custom permitted, and in some cases required, to tease or make fun of the other, who in turn is required to make no offence' (1940: 195). Radcliffe-Brown interprets the functions of joking relationships in a structural-functional theoretical framework. However, as argued by Apte (1985), jokes and joking relationships can be studied as social phenomena without reference to structural-functional theory. They can simply be studied as peculiar types of social relations.

Joking ethnic relationships are social relations where citizens from one nation tease people from another nation. The jokes are usually based on national stereotypes. It can only occur between nations that are somehow related to each other, for instance between North America and Britain or among the Nordic countries. In some cases the teasing is reciprocal as is the case with Norway and Sweden, and in other cases it is unidirectional: Danes tease Norwegians and Swedes but there are very few jokes about the Danes in Norway and Sweden (Gundelach, 2000).

Such joking relationships are to some extent institutionalized because they reflect the nation state as a social unit. In that sense ethnic jokes may be seen as an element of what Billig (1995) has termed banal nationalism because they confirm a picture of the world as one comprising nations that are experienced as real or objective entities. National identity is strengthened by joking relationships because the joking relationship can be used to illustrate the national stereotypes that different nations have towards each other. For instance, in many cases when a Scot meets a Brit it is socially expected that jokes are exchanged. This at the same time creates a bond (an us–them description) and a bridging (telling the joke across national boundaries) Davies (1996) has classified the jokes into two types: jokes that consider the butt of the joke as canny (for instance, jokes about the Scots) or jokes that consider the butt of the joke as stupid (for instance, jokes about the Poles). However, even though the jokes apparently assign certain characteristics to other people there is no reason to believe that the jokes represent some kind of perceived reality. For instance, even though Americans like to tell jokes about the dirty Poles there is no empirical evidence that Americans tend to dislike Poles or to consider them as dirty (Davies, 2002). Similarly, when Danes tell jokes about the rigid and formal Swedes and the naive Norwegians, this does not mean that they distance themselves from these nations. In fact, a survey showed just the contrary, that is, that when the Danes were asked what nation they would like to belong to other than their own a large majority chose the other Scandinavian countries (Gundelach, 2000).

Ethnic jokes usually create an unsympathetic picture of the other ethnic group but the butt of the jokes is participating in a imagined joking relationship. The ethnic joke indicates the joke-teller's superiority but the butt of the joke is placed in a favourable position because it is, so to speak, selected as a butt among many other possible ethnic groups. A person from an ethnic group that is exposed to the joke and ridiculed may feel embarrassed but also have a feeling of bonding. In this sense ethnic jokes are a mixture of bonding and bridging.

Ethnic jokes occur primarily between ethnic groups that already have some kind of relationship. However, it is not enough for joking to occur that there is a relationship between two ethnic groups, not even a hostile relationship. For instance Davies reports that during the Second World War very few Americans or Britons told jokes about the Japanese in spite of the fact that Japanese generally were seen as 'treacherous, fiendish, fanatical, and cruel' (Davies, 2002: 211) and Davies concludes that theories of humour that explain playful aggression in terms of real aggression have very little predictive power. This does not mean that there are no jokes between hostile groups but it is important to note that probably there are many more jokes among groups that have a positive relationship or some kind of feeling of affinity towards each other, such as the Americans and English, the English and the Irish, the French and the Belgians and the Norwegians and the Swedes.

Another side of creating group identity is to develop concepts or expressions that are specific to the group. Word plays may be used jokingly to create a special in-group terminology that bonds the participants. For instance in a small expatriate Uruguayan community in Gainesville, Florida, some residents refer to themselves as *Galiesbiano* (gay/lesbian) instead of using the more appropriate translation *Gainesvileano* (Moyna, 1994). As argued by Boxer and Cortés-Conde (1997: 281) other Spanish-speaking people in the larger community would have an understanding of the terminology, but the special meaning could only be appreciated by those who created it. Such use of the language is also common in ethnic jokes. The storyteller may use an adaptation of an expression from the language of the target's mother tongue to make the joke sound even more funny (for instance, talk with a French accent, talk slowly as the Finns are supposed to do, and so on).

Finally, it should be noted that ethnic jokes have some similarity to jokes that are told about sexual minorities, in the sense that in both cases the jokes are ways of creating boundaries between groups and ways of stigmatizing specific groups. There are many jokes where gay men and lesbians are the butts of jokes but the humour is also turned the other way around as a counter-hegemonic version of humour that is related to jokes about sexual minorities, in ways of dressing, movies and so on that challenges 'heteronormativity' (Sands, 1996). In this sense 'in addition to affirming the lives and communities of sexual minorities, many instances of gay and lesbian humour cheerfully undermine the notion of fixed sexual identities per se' (Sands, 1996: 508). This example shows how groups can use what, in the eyes of the majority, may seem to be self-mocking but in fact has a liberating and bridging consequence.

Self-mocking jokes
Self-mocking jokes are jokes people tell about their own group, in the case of ethnic groups jokes that are told about one's own people. Jewish jokes are famous but such jokes are also told among the Scots (Davies, 2002). Jokes about the Scots paint a picture of the calculating canny Scotsmen and Jewish jokes show the Jews as outsiders, enemies or deserters. A typical joke about the thrifty Scots goes like this: 'Angus called in to see his friend Donald to find he was stripping the wallpaper from the walls. Rather obviously, he remarked "You're decorating, I see", to which Donald replied "Nae. I'm moving house".'[2]

In self-mocking jokes humour plays a double role: strengthening in-groups feelings and at the same time playing with the stigmatization that is part of the joke. In fact in some cases jokes are ways of promoting a certain ethnic group even if the joke presents the ethnic group less favourably. A Scot may, for instance, tell a joke about the canny Scots, and there are many examples of joke collections of Scottish jokes that have been produced by Scots. The intention is to playfully advance the Scottish. Of course, this does not mean that the listeners will perceive the joke in the same way. Once a joke is told the joke-teller has no control of its reception. In some cases the joke may even have the opposite effect of what was intended – in the above example that the audience see it as confirming their belief in Scottish canniness (Davies, 2002: 221).

In his book, *Community*, Joseph Gusfield's (1975) tells the joke told about a dying Jew who in his last hour asks to be converted to Christianity. His sons plead against it but the old man wins out, is converted and given the last rites of the church. The children cannot understand why their father, always a devout and orthodox Jew, should renounce his lifelong faith and they prevail on him to explain. With his dying breath the old man rises up in bed and shouts: 'Better one of *them* should die than one of *us*.'

Gusfield reads two lessons out of this history. That the old Jew clearly defines the us–them cleavage, and that the joke shows that even if the father apparently is irrational he is in fact rational because he dies within the communal fold (Gusfield, 1975: 24). The joke is funny because it shows how people identify themselves and others as belonging to a certain community or association and how the character of people is created.

In general, telling jokes about oneself may be analysed as a bonding activity that brings a message of unity of the group and exclusion of other groups. However, the Jewish joke is not just a way of creating an us–them contradiction. It is also a way of telling that this particular Jew wishes to create an us–them contradiction and from the joke-teller's point of view to argue that such a construction is debatable.

Thus the apparent bonding jokes may have potential for bridging. Again we find a complicated relationship between social capital and joking. This is also seen when we move from the group level to the individual level.

Biting and bonding

As argued by Portes (2000) and other scholars social capital has an individualistic as well as a collective aspect. While the collective aspect – in a Putnam perspective as indicated above – often relates to social capital as an asset, individual social capital – as theorized by Bourdieu – is related to the social positions and struggles for power and recognition in groups. To Bourdieu, capital is linked to a field. Bourdieu distinguishes between economic, cultural and social capital, and is also interested in the social composition and the totality of an individual's forms of capital (Bourdieu, 1986; 1989).

Bourdieu also argues that in principle researchers may identify many different fields, that is, areas of struggle and positioning in, for instance, groups. It would possibly be to exaggerate if we identified humour as a field but it is evident that humour may be used for exclusion and social positioning. Telling jokes, conversational joking or other types of humour are strong ways of using the language. The skills to tell a good joke may be admired – or feared – by members of a group. In this sense the skills of telling jokes may be part of a person's social capital. Furthermore, since joking is closely related to an intimate and playful use of language it will of course tend to exclude persons who have less skills in eloquence.

In other cases the exclusion is related to the person's social characteristics. For instance there may be created a distinction between men's and women's use of humour, and labels such as 'feminist joking' (Kotthof, 2006) illustrate how humour creates boundaries and social categories. Also telling explicit sexist jokes may function as a closure mechanism. Men and women tend to tell sexist jokes about the other sex only when the other sex is not present. However, as mentioned by Terrion and Ashforth (2002), people may laugh at jokes that they consider improper for a normative point of view simply because laughing together is a way of showing group affiliation.

The role of humour in social positioning may at first glance seem relatively uncomplicated: humour reproduces social positions and hierarchy. In a classical study of faculty meetings at a psychiatric clinic, Coser (1960) showed that humour tended to reproduce the power structure and the cultural capital (using Bourdieu's terminology) of the individuals (for instance, senior staff members' jokes about junior staff members but never vice versa) and there are many examples of situations where people use putdown humour to elevate themselves at the target's expense and indeed the more disliked the target, the funnier the putdown is perceived.

However, teasing and joke-telling may also be seen as part of a joking relationship as described above only in this case at the individual level. People often tease people they know well and whom they like (Kotthoff, 2006: 16), and in some cases the direction of joking and teasing and authority is reversed. In the previously mentioned study of police officers in a newly established group, Terrion and Ashforth (2002), the most popular putdown jokes were those that targeted popular group members; indeed Terrion and Ashforth argue that it was precisely because the members enjoyed a high status that they were safe to laugh at. Some of Terrion and Ashforth's respondents claimed that they would never tell a joke about someone that they did not like.

This example shows that the bridging and bonding mechanisms are not only important at an aggregate level but also at the individual level. In some groups teasing may be seen as bonding in the negative sense, that is, it excludes or marginalizes persons who have low status or are marginal to the group. But in other cases the jokes have positive functions. They signal that the group has reached a level of 'maturity' where joking and teasing is a sign of unity and homogeneity. Thus in a new group different kinds of humour are also indicative of the development of the group. In the beginning the members of the group tend to tell jokes (that is, stories that target other groups) but gradually – and if it is felt to be safe – the humour will be directed at other members, that is, teasing.

Teasing – joking about someone present – is the most dangerous and most threatening kind of humour. The butt of the teasing becomes the focus of the group's attention. Teasing runs along a continuum from bonding to nipping and biting (Boxer and Cortés-Conde, 1997: 279) and it may be strongly situation specific and depending on non-verbal features of the conversation whether the tease is one that bonds, nips or bites – and sometimes teasing may have all of these consequences.

Nipping or biting are part of many everyday conversations especially among persons who are related in some way: among colleagues, husband and wife, parents and children. In such cases teasing, joking conversation or other types of humour are used to correct others, to ridicule or embarrass them.

Teasing may create positive and negative reactions in a group and create specific roles and social positions among the members. Self-teasing (mocking oneself) is another way of showing humour. Self-teasing will often be a (at least temporary) way of bridging because one of the functions of self-teasing is to make the speaker self-effacing allowing the addressee to perceive them as approachable. Boxer and Córtes-Conde (1997: 281) refer to the following conversation between two female strangers in a swimming pool:

Ann: What is this (i.e. swimming) supposed to do for you?
Barb: Your legs mostly. I don't think it does much for your stomach.
Ann: Oh, I am not interested in the thighs. They're beyond hope.

In this case Ann's joking may be seen as a way of opening possibilities for conversation, that is, for bridging at a personal level. Bridging in this sense is very common in everyday conversation among strangers. For instance, the use of irony is a culturally acceptable way of telling an audience 'that the speaker has a sense of wit and thus has the potential of functioning to create a momentary bond' (Boxer and Córtes-Conde, 1997: 288). Joking with strangers is a way of showing that you are a kind or approachable person. It is a way of breaking the ice and to smooth what may be interpreted potentially as a shaky situation.

The use of irony or putdown jokes about oneself is behaviour that is strongly situation dependent. Among strangers it may break the ice but among close relatives or friends irony may sometimes tend to bite or nip. If such types of conversational joking are used among intimates, they may be interpreted as biting. The same remark or joke may have an opposite effect in different social settings.

Conclusion

It has correctly been stated that words are never innocent or neutral (Baarts, 2006) and jokes may have positive or negative effects on social capital both bridging or bonding. However, in many cases jokes do not have fixed tendencies. The same joke may be seen as funny by some listeners, an insult to others and simply incomprehensible to another. Jokes may have positive consequences and create a pleasant atmosphere. People who tell jokes are strongly appreciated in a group and joke-telling and laughter produce a stronger group feeling and a sense of continuity in a group. By contrast, jokes may have negative consequences for the individual or the group. In extreme cases people have been arrested by an authoritarian regime for telling jokes and, more generally, there are examples of strong negative attitudes towards people who tell a bad or 'improper' joke. And jokes may be an expression of extreme racist humour where violence is a matter of humour (Billig, 2001b).

The situation-specific element in humour and the differences in interpretations in jokes and teasing do not mean that humour cannot be studied by the social sciences, but one should not make too fixed conclusions. In relation to social capital this chapter has shown that humour may be bonding as well as bridging, and have positive as well as negative effects. The problem is that it is difficult to make generalizations about the functions of humour. The same joke may in some cases be interpreted as funny and help to make stronger bonds among group members, and in other cases it may create hostility. In some cases the joke even plays with the negative sides of bonding, as in the Jewish joke about the dying father mentioned above.

Joking like this is part of innumerable everyday situations. One type of joke is a storytelling that is directed towards people outside the group. When told, the joke may create a boundary for the groups and a bond between the joker and the listeners. Another bonding situation may be seen with jokes that are plays on words. This in itself makes the conversation easier and more pleasant. Joking creates a feeling of affiliation and sympathy among group members.

The bonding is on a continuum from weak to strong. At one extreme, bonding is, temporarily, just a play with words – a way to ease the climate of a group. At another extreme, joking is a way of creating negative stereotypes that may have impact on the behaviour of group members. An example of the first case is a couple of close female friends who joke about men. It is fun to tell a joke and laughing creates bonding, but the joke is not a reflection of the women's' perception of men and it has no attitudinal or behavioural consequences (Boxer and Córtes-Conde, 1997). The joke is simply told because it is fun to tell a joke and to feel the bonding it creates. At the other extreme are jokes among conflicting nations or denominations where the jokes create hostility against the butt of the joke, as, for instance, jokes in war propaganda.

Jokes may also create hostility from the addressee of the jokes without having consequences for the groups where jokes are told. For a Dane, a telling example is the so-called Mohammed cartoon crisis where a Danish newspaper, *Jyllands-Posten*, in 2005 published a number of cartoons that were a satire of Mohammed and thus could be perceived as an insult by Muslims. As a reaction to publishing there were demonstrations in several Arab countries, burnings of the Danish flag and a consumer boycott of Danish products. The reactions in Denmark were mixed but it would be fair to say that the negative reactions from Arab countries did not create stronger bonds among the Danes and in general it did not create hostility against the Arab countries. There were some strong reactions against the flag-burning but, according to a number of qualitative interviews, many Danes considered the burning of the flag an unimportant incident (Gundelach et al., 2008).

The relationship between social capital and humour is intriguing. Humour creates in-group feelings: This may result in a well-functioning group, but some kinds of humour also has the form of teasing or mocking group members. Even in such situations joke-telling creates an us-them relationship and confirm some kind of affiliation between the joke-teller and the target of the group.

Even though humour often results in bonding types of social capital, it also has a potential for bridging. Irony and self-mocking may be a way whereby a person can show that he/she is approachable and nice. However, in other cases irony is a verbal bite, for instance among siblings or spouses.

The study of humour is interesting precisely because humour is so anarchistic and does not lend itself to simple interpretations. For instance, attempts to show the negative consequences of ethnic jokes or to confuse jokes with reality have proven to be wrong. There is no reason to believe that jokes have political impact or that groups that are chosen for ridicule are looked upon as particularly negative (Davies, 2002). And even though joking may create stronger bonds in a group, it may also crease tension and hostility.

An unsubstantiated anecdote about Sigmund Freud tells that after a lecture on sexual symbols somebody ask Freud to comment on the fact that he smoked a lot of cigars. Freud answered that 'sometimes a cigar is just a cigar'. In the same way, humour can be classified into various types, attributed with a lot of positive and negative functions, and scrutinized under the social science microscope, but humour is also an anarchistic play with words and a way of making people laugh. After all, sometimes a joke is just a joke.

Notes

1. http://www.humourincorporated.com/ (accessed April 2007).
2. http://scotlandvacations.com/JokesPage1.htm (accessed 28 March 2007).

References

Apte, Mahadev L. (1985), *Humor and Laughter. An Anthropological Approach*, Ithaca, NY: Cornell University Press.
Baarts, Charlotte (2006), 'Druk, bajere og løgnehistorier – om humor og fællesskab på en byggeplads', *Dansk Sociologi*, **17** (1), 67–83.
Billig, Michael (1995), *Banal Nationalism*, London: Sage Publications.
Billig, Michael (2001a), 'Humour and embarrassment: limits of the "Nice-Guy" theories of social life', *Theory, Culture and Society*, **18** (5), 23–43.
Billig, Michael (2001b), 'Humour and hatred: the racist jokes of the Ku Klux Klan', *Discourse & Society*, **12** (3), 267–89.
Bourdieu, Pierre (1986), *Distinction. A Social Critique of the Judgement of Taste*, London: Routledge & Kegan Paul.
Bourdieu, Pierre (1989), 'Social space and symbolic power', *Sociological Theory*, **7** (1), 14–25.
Boxer, Diana and Florencia Cortés-Conde (1997), 'From bonding to biting: conversational joking and identity display', *Journal of Pragmatics*, **27**, 275–94.
Coser, Rose L. (1960), 'Laughter among colleagues', *Psychiatry*, **23** (81), 95.
Davies, Christie (1996), *Ethnic Humor Around the World*, Bloomington, IN: Indiana University Press.
Davies, Christie (1998), 'Ethnic jokes, moral values and social boundaries', *British Journal of Sociology*, **33** (3), 383–403.
Davies, Christie (2002), *The Mirth of Nations*, New Brunswick, NJ: Transaction.
Fine, Gary Alan (1983), 'Handbook of humor research, vol. 1', in P.E. McGhee and J.H. Goldstein (eds), *Sociological Approaches to the Study of Humor*, New York: Springer, pp. 159–82.
Fine, Gary Alan and Michaela De Sourcey (2005), 'Joking cultures: humor themes as social regulation in group life', *Humor*, **18** (1), 1–22.
Gundelach, Peter (2000), 'Joking relationships and national identity in Scandinavia', *Acta Sociologica*, **43** (1), 113–22.
Gundelach, Peter, Hans Raun Iversen and Margit Warburg (2008), *I hjertet af Danmark*, København: Hans Reitzels Forlag.
Gusfield, Joseph R. (1975), *Community. A Critical Response*, New York: Harper & Row.
Holmes, Janet (2006), 'Sharing a laugh: pragmatic aspects of humor and gender in the workplace', *Journal of Pragmatics*, **38** (1), 25–50.

Kotthoff, Helga (2006), 'Gender and humor: the state of the art', *Journal of Pragmatics*, **38** (1), 4–25.

McGhee, Paul E. and Jeffrey H. Goldstein (1983), *Handbook of Humor Research*, vols 1–2, New York: Springer Verlag.

Moyna, Irene, (1994), 'Nosotros los americanos: humorous code-switching and borrowing as a means to defuse culture shock', unpublished paper, University of Florida.

Portes, Alejandro (1998), 'Social capital: its origins and applications in modern sociology', *Annual Review of Sociology*, **24**, 1–24.

Portes, Alejandro (2000), 'The two meanings of social capital', *Sociological Forum*, **15** (1), 1–12.

Portes, Alejandro and Patricia Landholt (1996), 'The downside of social capital', *The American Prospect*, **26**, 18–21.

Putnam, Robert D. (2000), *Bowling Alone. The Collapse and Revival of American Community*, New York: Simon & Schuster.

Radcliffe-Brown, A.R. (1940), 'On joking relationships', *Africa*, **12** (3), 195–210.

Sands, Kathleen M. (1996), 'Ifs, ands, and butts: theological reflection on humor', *Journal of the American Academy of Religion*, **64** (3), 499–523.

Terrion, Jenepher Lennox and Blake E. Ashforth (2002), 'From "I" to "we". The role of putdown humor and identity in the development of a temporary group', *Human Relations*, **55** (1), 56–88.

7   Religio-philosophical roots
Ralph Weber

Introduction

Throughout the ever-growing corpus of literature on social capital, two very different ways of thinking and writing stand out in the social sciences. One makes use of the concept of social capital heuristically, that is, as analytical tool, to investigate an actor's resources that originate from that actor's relation to a specific social structure; the other conceives of social capital as a measurable entity present in different social groups in varying quantities – often, but not always, the higher the quantity the better for the group. To divide the wide-ranging debates over social capital into these two camps is simplifying, but demarcates a major dividing line, on the one side or the other of which every social scientist concerned with social capital chiefly falls. This division is also useful for structuring the present religio-philosophical reflection on social capital. Such reflection is indeed apposite. For reasons of expediency or, worse, ignorance, social scientists of both camps more often than not disregard religious and philosophical thought and relegate their own research's contingency to the background. This chapter seeks to illustrate – by adopting a Confucian viewpoint – how religio-philosophical reflection may contribute to making social enquiry more effective.

Little if any of the existing literature on social capital that deals with religion or philosophy targets the concept itself. Yet, regardless whether social capital is used as tool applied to some social structure or whether it is taken as entity to be measured across different groups, the social scientist in question engages in or relies on a conceptualization of this tool or that entity. Every conceptualization, in turn, is contingent on specific cultural factors, some of which – to be the focus of this chapter – can be traced to constitutive texts of religious and philosophical traditions. Reflection of the religio-philosophical background against which a given conceptualization of social capital is formulated assures that social scientists neither read too much nor too little into the results of their research. Moreover, the concept's contingency becomes an issue if social capital is researched cross-culturally and across spheres of influence of different religio-philosophical traditions. The ethnocentrism in such research is obvious and perhaps unavoidable, but important to note. Even more congenial to the concerns of social scientists: wholesale disregard of the religio-philosophical traditions that form part of, and inform, the social context under scrutiny may simply block the view toward alternative conceptualizations or result in rather poor and misguided operationalization. Finally, a social scientist's conceptualization is necessarily in one way or other tied to language and – in a multilingual context – dependent on far-reaching choices of translation. The choice of terminology, in turn, is never made in a political vacuum, and the term 'social capital' has met criticism for '"enshrining" a certain definition of social reality' (Smith and Kulynych, 2002: 152). From this perspective, every practice of merely adopting or positing a definition of social capital before engaging in analysis or before presenting empirical findings eventually falls short. To be clear, the concern here addressed is not about curtailing empirical research, but about drawing attention to some of its limits. Responsible empirical researchers of course will, when faced with completely unexpected results, review and possibly revise their conceptual and operational assumptions. Still, the need for conceptual work per se is evident, for instance in the case when results meet expectations squarely despite ill-informed conceptualization or operationalization.

Religio-philosophical reflection of social capital precisely means to engage in conceptual work from one specific perspective among many. It is understood that a full account of how such reflection may contribute to the manifold debates over social capital is beyond scope and possibility of the present chapter. Only some elements of prominent conceptions of social capital will be attended and some problems of contingency and vocabulary be expounded, so as to lay out several points of departure for further thorough religio-philosophical reflection. Furthermore, though the concept of social capital may be reflected upon from a variety of religious and philosophical traditions, only one tradition will be engaged: the reflections presented in this chapter draw from texts (and interpretations thereof) considered constitutive of the Confucian tradition, named after the historical figure of Confucius (Kongzi, 551–479 BC).

This chapter is divided in three parts. First, I state reasons for the adopted viewpoint and make transparent my understanding of Confucianism as a religio-philosophical tradition. Second, I discuss social capital as analytical tool based on selected writings by James Coleman. I contrast his 'rational actor' with the Confucian 'actor' and inquire into some Confucian forms of social capital. Third, I turn to social capital conceptualized as measurable entity. Particularly, I engage writings by Robert Putnam, who is a major voice in the debates over social capital, and Francis Fukuyama, who relates trust and social capital directly to Confucianism. In the conclusions, I roughly adumbrate what a Confucian conceptualization of social capital could look like before underlining the need to broaden the debate on social capital even beyond the social sciences.

Confucianism as religio-philosophical tradition

Choosing Confucianism over other, equally legitimate, viewpoints has the advantage that a seemingly maximal hermeneutical distance to those religious and philosophical traditions in which the concept of social capital has its origins is established.[1] Issues of contingency might thus be detected more easily. Moreover, Confucianism is commonly said to inform the social context of China proper, as well as that of adjacent countries such as Japan and South Korea. An analysis using the concept of social capital or an assessment of the amount of social capital with regard, say, to a specific Chinese social context thus requires consideration of Confucianism.

A few remarks qualifying the here-adopted understanding of Confucianism are in order. First, the status of Confucianism as religion or philosophy has been the subject of many debates. Given the Latin and Greek roots and subsequent prominent histories of the terms 'religion' and 'philosophy', it is not astonishing that those adhering strictly to these roots and histories conclude that Confucianism is neither religion nor philosophy. Others who employ a more inclusive understanding of the terms reach precisely the contrary conclusion. Perhaps, the question is misguided. Wilfred Cantwell Smith suggestively observed that 'the question "Is Confucianism a religion?" is one that the West has never been able to answer, and China never able to ask' (Smith, 1991: 69). A similar point could be made as to the question of philosophy. For the purposes of this chapter, I – rather than be bogged down in metaphysical argument – pursue a pragmatic approach. As Confucianism continues to be in some way meaningful (regardless of whether religiously or philosophically) to millions of people, and as the scholarly community treats it as either religion or philosophy, I here refer to it as a religio-philosophical tradition, the term reflecting the stated ambiguity.

Secondly, the Confucian tradition is not monolithic. Different strands of religio-philosophical Confucianism are easily identified and commentators usually align with one of these – some stressing Mencius (Mengzi, *c.* 372–289 BC) more than Xunzi (*c.* 310–238 BC), some considering Zhu Xi (AD 1130–1200) as paramount, and so on. Moreover, there are other forms of Confucianism, markedly not of religio-philosophical character. For instance, religio-philosophical Confucianism is complexly related to and burdened by those forms of politicized Confucianism that have repeatedly served to provide legitimacy for imperial politics. Religio-philosophical Confucianism cannot and should not be confused with these. To do so would be tantamount to mistaking Stalinism for the writings of Marx or the Crusades for the teachings of the Bible. Though certainly related, there is good reason for a differentiated treatment.

Thirdly, to claim influence of Confucianism on Chinese social contexts is not to say that the influence is exclusive or fully determinant. Obviously, other religious and philosophical traditions such as Daoism, Buddhism, Chinese Marxism-Leninism, and even Liberalism have informed and continue to inform these contexts. To what extent traditions in general exert influence on social contexts is itself a disputed matter, yet it would be a rather bold argument to deny any such influence. It is an understanding of Confucianism along these lines that guides the following religio-philosophical reflection on the concept of social capital.

Social capital as analytical tool
Social scientists who employ social capital as analytical tool often rely or build on the influential definitions by Pierre Bourdieu or James Coleman. Lacking space for discussing both, I only focus on Coleman. He defines social capital by its function as a 'particular kind of resource available to an actor', and highlights two elements common to all variations of social capital: 'they all consist of some aspect of social structures, and they facilitate certain actions of actors – whether persons or corporate actors – within the structure' (Coleman, 1988: 98). Social capital, in this view, is not an attribute plainly of either actor or structure, but 'inheres in the structure of relations between actors' (Coleman, 1988: 98).

That Coleman applies social capital heuristically is most conspicuous when he refers to 'using the concept of social capital' (Coleman, 1990: 304). He admits that the concept may not lead to the discovery of new social processes, but rather obliterates otherwise important differences 'between types of social relations' (Coleman, 1990: 305). Its main value, however, is that 'it identifies certain aspects of social structure by their function', that is, their value to actors as resources helpful for achieving pursued interests. Although Coleman takes considerable interest in the 'mathematics of social action', he is not concerned about calculating or measuring social capital as an entity and is unsure whether it will be of future use as a quantitative concept in the way financial, physical or human capital are. The value of the concept of social capital 'lies primarily in its usefulness for qualitative analyses of social systems and for those quantitative analyses that employ qualitative indicators' (Coleman, 1990: 305–6).

Coleman's interest in social capital as 'a conceptual tool' is motivated by an attempt to steer between two extreme conceptualizations of the actor, respectively exemplified by the tendency of sociologists toward an 'oversocialized' (Wrong, 1961) and of economists toward an 'undersocialized' concept of man (Granovetter, 1985). The concept of social capital is a tool through which Coleman seeks to combine work of new institutional economists and agency-oriented sociologists, though he is clear that his point of departure is 'a theory of rational action, in which each actor has control over certain resources and interests in certain resources and events' (Coleman, 1988: 98). It is, however, a 'simple structural fact' that actors are not fully in control of their actions; other actors also exert partial or complete control over them (Coleman, 1990: 29). Hence, Coleman's conceptualization is that of a rational actor who is not acting wholly independently, not arriving at goals wholly alone and not pursuing exclusively selfish interests (Coleman, 1990: 301). For Coleman, '"empirical reality" is such that "persons" actions are shaped, redirected [and] constrained by the social context' (Coleman, 1988: 96).

Coleman's rational actor versus the Confucian image of the co-creator
Coleman's concept of social capital relies on a specific conceptualization of what is an 'actor'. His actor is explicitly rational – though not in the straightforward sense of consistently acting in accordance with self-interest. Rationality, for Coleman, consists in the actor's construction of an internal constitution in which the rights, resources and interests of various actors are reflected and through which actions come about. Rationality thus understood promises 'maximum viability' for the actor. Coleman even sees in this conceptualization of the actor 'the starting point for a theory of the self' (Coleman,1990: 949).

As far as a social scientific analyst who employs social capital as a tool may attend to only one specific form of social capital and to only one specific social structure at a time, Coleman emphasizes context greatly. If Coleman's concept is used to analyse a specific Chinese social context, his conceptualization of the rational actor must measure up to those conceptualizations relevant to the context, lest the situation under scrutiny be misconstrued. What, then, is the Confucian view of 'actor' and 'rationality'? Given the conceptual resources of Confucianism, analogues to these concepts are utterly difficult to construct.

The 'actor' in Confucianism is best understood as a co-creative centre of relationships. The expression 'centre of relationships' indicates that a person is constantly immersed in a complex web of social contexts. These social contexts constitute the moral playground on and through which a Confucian seeks to engage in self-cultivation (*xiuyang* or *xiushen*), the single most important religious task in the radically this-worldly oriented Confucianism. The contemporary Confucian Tu Wei-ming, drawing on the Confucian classic *Daxue* (The Great Learning), has visualized these different social contexts as a series of concentric circles (Tu, 1985: 175).[2] First and foremost, the family constitutes one's primary social context. Self-cultivation here implies to relate meaningfully to one's parents, one's siblings, or one's children. Confucian family virtues such as filial piety

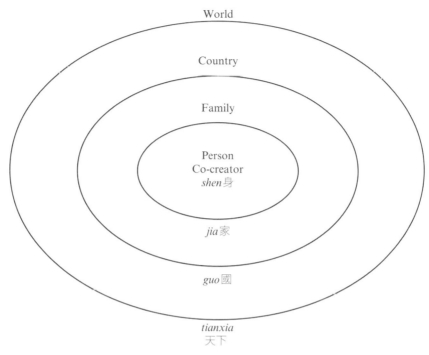

World

Country

Family

Person
Co-creator
shen 身

jia 家

guo 國

tianxia
天下

Figure 7.1   The Confucian co-creator amid the circles suggested in the
Daxue *(The Great Learning)*

(*xiao*) and parental love (*ci*) or ancestor worship are ritually defined and communally acknowledged (though not written in stone), and spell out how to relate to one's family, to those living and those dead.

Self-cultivation, however, also means to expand one's sensitivity beyond the family. Expansion in this context does not mean emulation, for the difference between family members and non-family members changes the virtues and sensitivities in question. For instance, the virtue of respect (*jing*), cultivated within the family domain, is to be expanded to further circles – from fellow villagers, fellow countrymen and countrywomen, to strangers – yet the respect offered to these people is unlike the one felt for one's parents, simply because they are one's parents. This is not to deny that a friend may be as highly respected as one's parents are; what is denied is that it is the same kind of respect. Although the *Daxue* merely mentions three circles (see Figure 7.1), namely the family (*jia*), the country (*guo*), and the world (*tianxia*), more circles may easily be suggested. Tu Wei-ming, for example, lists: self, family, neighbourhood, kinship (or clan), community, country (or state, nation), world, cosmos and beyond (Tu, 1985: 175–81).

Obviously, these circles may be drawn up differently depending on time and context.

The movement of expanding one's sensitivity is captured in religious terms by the notion 'self-transcendence' or, in Tu's other expression, by 'ultimate self-transformation as a communal act' (Tu, 1985: 64). Self-transcendence, to be sure, does not mean self-denial. One's body (*shen*) as well as one's heart-and-mind (*xin*) is to be cultivated, that is, affirmed and not denied. What is to be transcended are one's 'selfish desires' (*si yu*), which, according to the Ming-dynasty Confucian Wang Yangming (Wang Shouren, AD 1472–1529), arise *inter alia* from drawing excessive distinctions between oneself and others (Wang [~1527] 2000: 509). Indeed, the other plays an important role as to the cultivating of oneself. There is no 'self' without the other. For the self-cultivating Confucian, self and other are mutually implicated. Toward the other, one should expand one's sensitivity, and the other it is who should be gradually included. In Confucianism, an 'actor' is unthinkable as an 'individual' separate from 'society'. Rather, a person is thought of as a co-creator, that is, as 'actor' amid innumerable other 'actors' – the actions of whom are co-determined by those of others. Under such a view, each and every action, that is to be religio-philosophically meaningful, is a communal action, that is, a co-creative action drawing on and likely creating, so to say, 'social capital'.

The sensibility expressed by the Confucian image of the co-creator is similar to that of Coleman's 'simple structural fact', which holds that actors are not fully in control of their actions. This similarity is, however, not to belie fundamental differences. Coleman's methodological individualism as well as his version of an individual's rationality are both alien to Confucianism. Rationality, in whatever version, builds on its contrast to sensibilities, sentiments or habits; inasmuch as the emphasis is on thinking, rationality is often based on a concomitant mind–body distinction. These distinctions are exceedingly difficult to accommodate with regard to Confucianism, given the latter's markedly non-dichotomous conceptual resources. Notwithstanding, the similarities between Coleman's actor and the Confucian co-creator do suggest that further religio-philosophical reflection may open up new perspectives as to the concept of social capital in order to construct a workable tool for identifying relevant 'actors' and relevant 'social structures' in a Chinese social context.

Coleman's versus Confucian forms of social capital
Coleman further intimates the concept of social capital by distinguishing several 'forms of social capital', such as those found in the reciprocity of obligations/expectations, norms coupled with effective sanctions, 'information potential' and 'authority relations' (Coleman, 1988: 102–5, 1990:

310–11). These forms, however, do not exhaust the multifaceted concept of social capital, and neither does Coleman claim that they do. Coleman states that 'all social relations and social structures facilitate some forms of social capital' (Coleman, 1988: 105). It is hence far from inconceivable that research into Chinese social contexts and religio-philosophical reflection of Confucianism would bring to light specific (Confucian) forms of social capital – at least in so far as these Chinese social contexts have been or are indeed informed by Confucianism.

For instance, there is the case of community granaries (*shecang*) and academies (*shuyuan*) founded by 'voluntary association[s] of Confucian intellectuals and officials' during the Song-dynasty (AD 960–1279), as the historian Hoyt Cleveland Tillman explains. He uses the term 'fellowship' to capture the social, political and philosophical interaction and networking that occurred at the time to an unprecedented degree comprising activities such as: 'personal visits, exchanged letters, group discussions and debates, funeral eulogies, marriage alliances, shrine building and rituals, special terminology, training in academies, passing members' examination essays, recommending and promoting members in the bureaucracy, etc.' (Tillman, 2004: 124). With a view to the present day, Tillman seems to argue that a better understanding of 'Confucian ideals and networks' will affect 'our conception of a possible role for Confucianism within social networks and in the modern quest for civil society' (Tillman, 2004: 142). Drawing on such historical research may help to construct Confucian forms of social capital and, in return, to make for a better fit between the concept and a given Chinese social context.

Furthermore, there may be Chinese forms of social capital that are not, or not as clearly, related to Confucianism. A prime candidate is the Chinese notion of *guanxi*, roughly translatable as 'connections', 'relation', 'relationships' or in its verbal form as 'to relate to'. *Guanxi* is not a classical Confucian notion. Yet, many scholars who understand it as authentic expression of what is Chinese link *guanxi* to the paramount emphasis of Confucianism on human-relatedness (Gold et al., 2002: 10). At a conceptual level, it is strongly interlaced with other Chinese notions such as *ganqing* (sentiment), *renqing* (human feeling), *mianzi* (face) as well as *bao* (reciprocity), and in current usage is invested with positive and, more frequently, negative meanings (Gold et al., 2002: 6). The relevance of *guanxi* for understanding virtually any Chinese social context is largely agreed upon. Some particular social ties, which *guanxi* build and build on, are listed in Table 7.1.

The distinction between ascribed and achieved characteristics is telling inasmuch as research on social capital predominantly leans towards examining the latter (apart from a frequent emphasis on family relations). Still,

Table 7.1   Characteristics of social ties related to guanxi

Ascribed/primordial	Achieved
Kinship Native place Ethnicity	Attending the same school (even if not at the same time) Serving in the same military unit Shared experiences (e.g. the Long March) Doing business

Source: See Gold et al. (2002: 6).

guanxi and social capital are easily enough brought into association. Gold et al. acknowledge a general resemblance between the Chinese notion of *guanxi* and Bourdieu's concept of social capital. Yet upon closer examination, they argue, *guanxi* discloses itself as 'imparting a special significance to interpersonal relations' that makes it a genuinely Chinese concept and sets it apart from the concept of social capital. Two idiosyncrasies of *guanxi* prompt them to claim dissemblance between the two concepts. Firstly, *guanxi* forms the ground on which a heavily ritualized and distinct 'gift economy' flourishes in China. Secondly, *guanxi* is never devoid of sentiment and therefore not purely instrumentalist (Gold et al., 2002: 7–8). Smart, who discusses *guanxi* in the context of the exchange of gifts and in contrast to bribery, agrees that these 'social connections' may openly be pursued for 'instrumentalist aims'; yet, on a more fundamental level, they are inextricably tied to 'the continued existence of personal relationships' (Smart, 1993: 398–9). It is a matter of perspective whether these idiosyncrasies recommend treating *guanxi* as a concept wholly different from that of social capital or as an additional, a Chinese, form of social capital. Smart, at least, readily speaks of 'the social capital achieved through *guanxi*' (Smart, 1993: 399).

Another way of thinking about Confucian forms of social capital is to reflect on Coleman's forms of social capital from a Confucian perspective. Coleman points out that performing a good deed often entails a complicated pattern of reciprocity, that is, an expectation, on the one, and an obligation, on the other side. The resulting social capital is analytically separable into two dimensions, which Coleman lists: 'trustworthiness of the social environment, which means that obligations will be repaid, and the actual extent of obligations held' (Coleman, 1988: 102). Any social structure differs with regard to these dimensions and so does any actor with regard to the latter. These differences arise for many reasons, one of which Coleman suggests is cultural diversity in such patterns of reciprocity (Coleman, 1988: 103). I need not elaborate on the point that 'trustworthiness', 'obligation' or 'reciprocity' are problematic terms when applied to a Chinese social context, given the prominent role that similar – but not completely commensurable – notions such as *xin* (trust, trustworthy), *yi* (appropriateness, right, duty) or *shu* (reciprocity, deference) play in Confucianism.

As to Coleman's second form of social capital, which addresses the role of norms in the creation of social capital, a final caveat is to be issued. Coleman, for instance, deems the prescriptive norm 'that one should forego self-interest and act in the interests of the collectivity' a particularly important form of social capital (Coleman, 1988: 104). Obviously, there is a set of similar, but different norms informing the actions of 'actors' in a Chinese social context. Some noted passages in the *Lunyu* (the famous *Analects*, a collection of short conversations between Confucius and his disciples) come to mind. Consider, for instance, what is often called the Confucian Golden Rule and variously, but predominantly negatively, stated in the *Analects* (5:12, 12:2, 15:24). In one of these, Zigong, a disciple of Confucius, asks whether there is 'one expression that can be acted upon until the end of one's days', whereupon Confucius claims this expression to be *shu* (reciprocity, deference): 'do not impose on others what you yourself do not want' (Ames and Rosemont, 1998: 189). Mencius has later formulated the sentence decidedly in the positive, which makes it sound to the Christian ear all the more like Matthew 7.12. The point is that even norms as temptingly alike as these are still norms formulated against and within a specific religio-philosophical background, which will inform not only the practical relevance and bindingness of norms but also, more fundamentally, the very concept of 'norm' (as well as the concept of 'concept'). What is and what ought to be are questions that have received countless answers in the course of history, and whether or not one draws a distinction between the two arguably is itself a highly contingent matter.

Social capital as measurable entity

Social capital is also conceptualized as an entity that is measurable with regard to different communities, countries or even cultural regions. Social capital is then understood as something 'out there' and a high level of which is said to induce economic prosperity and, by some accounts, to further the cause of the common good, so to speak, political prosperity. In analogy with physical and human capital, there may be more or less of it and its stock can be augmented or depleted. Social capital, however, is less tangible and less fungible than these other forms of capital. More broadly conceived, social capital is sometimes linked to norms of civility and is said to be – along a neo-Tocquevillean line of thought – essential for the flourishing of civil society and, in turn, of democracy. Although the reference to Tocqueville does not stand close examination (cf. Lichterman, 2006), it does indicate a shared orientation toward value-statements about social groups. This second way of conceptualizing social capital is widely used by economists and political scientists for explaining and even forecasting developments around the world.

Putnam's conceptual shift
Social capital, when understood as an entity inherent in a social group, is most often associated with the work of Robert Putnam, who defines social capital as 'features of social life – networks, norms, and trust – that enable participants to act together more effectively to pursue shared objectives' (Putnam, 1995b: 664–5). Notoriously, Putnam's thesis of a decline of such social capital in the United States has incited a great deal of research litera-ture as well as outspoken criticism as regards, for instance, the data backing his thesis (Ladd, 1996) or the conceptual shift toward a de-contextualized and moralized usage of social capital (Edwards and Foley, 1998). With a view to the concept of social capital, Putnam's conceptualization is poign-antly depicted in the following statement:

> The central idea of social capital, in my view, is that networks and the associated norms of reciprocity have value. They have value for the people who are in them, and they have, at least in some instances, demonstrable externalities, so that there are both public and private faces of social capital. I focus largely on the external, or public, returns to social capital, but I think that is not at all incon-sistent with the idea that there are also private returns. (Putnam, 2001: 41)

The differences compared with Coleman's conceptualization are striking. Whereas Coleman is interested in social capital as a tool to analyse an actor's 'private returns' in a specific social context, Putnam is in its 'exter-nal' or 'public' manifestation. Social capital is no longer assessed qualita-tively as an attribute of the relation between an actor and a specific social structure, but is conceptualized as quantitatively measurable in individuals or in social groups. This change of focus comes along with a weighty con-ceptual shift – from a specific actor and a specific social structure to some 'public', that is, from an emphasis on context to a generalized good of a social group.

Putnam measures social capital according to data generated by several surveys. In each of these, individuals are asked a set of questions. The results of all surveys are combined into a single measure and a social capital index is thus established. Measuring social capital in this manner is haunted by the charge of 'logical circularity', that is, of simultaneously considering social capital both 'a cause and an effect' (Portes, 1998: 19). Putnam is clear that what he intends to measure are consequences of social capital, but that he cannot rule out the possibility that the 'arrow of effects' might really run 'to social capital instead of from social capital' (Putnam, 2001: 51). For instance, does trust lead to the formation of social capital or vice versa? The issue of directionality is far from being settled. Still, in Putnam's conceptualization, social capital is treated as a property that is measurable at the individual level. By means of aggregation, the individual property is then turned into a property of a social group.[3] Eventually, the level of social capital, say, in Madison, in Dane County, in Wisconsin or in the United States can be positively determined.

From the outset, Putnam has acknowledged that social capital is 'not a unidimensional concept' (Putnam, 1995a: 76). For instance, he distinguishes formal and informal kinds and he has popularized the distinction between 'bonding' and 'bridging' kinds of social capital (Putnam, 2000: 22). Furthermore, Putnam urges that 'we need to think about its multiple dimensions' (Putnam, 2001: 41). The acknowledged multiplicity is, however, in no way conceived as an insurmountable barrier to measuring social capital. Putnam is confident that 'the development of theoretically coherent and empirically valid typologies or dimensions' of social capital is feasible – though he admits that this is not to be expected in the near future (Putnam, 2001: 42). The scope of these typologies or dimensions is not restricted to assessing social capital with regard to one social group, but, eventually, is to make possible a 'cross-national, reliable measurement of social capital' (Putnam, 2001: 51). Concerning China, this implies not only that there will be a measure to assess the amount of social capital there (which, for that purpose, could be China specific), but also that the measure will allow for meaningful comparisons across the globe (which, then, would need to be unspecific).

Fukuyama, low-trust China and Confucian familism
The work of Francis Fukuyama on social capital (Fukuyama, 1995; 2001; 2002) takes up the concept of social capital as measurable entity and presents broad cross-national and cross-cultural comparisons. Fukuyama identifies one of the 'world's major cultural groups' as the 'Confucian'. Each of these groups – which he seems to denominate at will either ethnically or religiously ('Western, Islamic, Confucian, Japanese, Hindu, and so on') – boasts a level of trust as a 'single, pervasive cultural characteristic' (Fukuyama, 1995: 5–7). Fukuyama's interest lies in the relationship between cultural and economic life, and his thesis is that the level of trust in a society decides on a 'nation's well-being' and 'its ability to compete' (Fukuyama, 1995: 7). In his view, trust is 'the expectation that arises within a community of regular, honest, and cooperative behaviour, based on commonly shared norms, on the part of other members of that community' and social capital is 'a capability that arises from the prevalence of trust in

a society or in certain parts of it' (Fukuyama, 1995: 26). The problem of directionality shows up again. Whereas Putnam considers 'social trust' as a 'consequence' (and therefore a suitable 'proxy') of social capital (Putnam, 2001: 45), Fukuyama appears to conceive of social capital as a function of trust. Inasmuch as social capital is, in Fukuyama's account, distinctly 'created and transmitted through cultural mechanisms like religion, tradition, or historical habit' (Fukuyama, 1995: 26), his prominent comments on 'Chinese Confucianism' in relation to trust and social capital might lend themselves to a religio-philosophical reflection on the concept of social capital.

Fukuyama draws up 'Confucianism' in very broad strokes. For instance, he repeatedly speaks of 'orthodox Confucianism' (Fukuyama, 1995: 86), which is a misnomer par excellence in religio-philosophical Confucianism, where there is no overseeing body that lays down the right faith and where 'orthodoxy' (the correct teaching) is indistinguishable from 'orthopraxy' (the correct practice). More seriously, Fukuyama blurs notions such as 'culture', 'nation', 'society' and 'community', which results in a somewhat confused argument on the influence of 'Confucianism' on the level of trust and social capital in China and in Japan. On the one hand, his main argument runs as follows: the Japanese is different from the Confucian cultural group. Because of cultural characteristics, Japan has quickly developed 'large, modern corporations' and, judged by the prevalence of '*keiretsu* networks' and '*iemoto*-type organizations', exhibits a high level of trust (Fukuyama, 1995: 53, 57). Chinese societies (Taiwan, Hong Kong, Singapore and the People's Republic of China) are burdened by the pervasive cultural influence of 'Confucianism', particularly 'Confucian' familism, and are therefore low-trust societies. On the other hand, Fukuyama admits that 'Japan and China are both Confucian societies and share many cultural traits', though he is quick to assert that there are striking differences 'that become evident in all aspects of social life' (Fukuyama, 1995: 57).

Fukuyama seems to notice the apparent inconsistency and tries to solve it by claiming that 'orthodox Chinese Confucianism' is 'very different from its Japanese offshoot, with important consequences for business organization' (Fukuyama, 1995: 86). Unfortunately, he thereby rather accentuates the inconsistency. Is he saying there is a kind of Confucianism in Japan (different from those in Confucian societies) that makes for different possibilities of business organizations? Or is he saying the negative influence of Confucianism on trust and social capital is, in the Japanese case, rendered ineffective by non-Confucian, Japanese cultural or other traits? What is evident is that Fukuyama is taken in by a specific understanding of Confucianism, one that tends to treat Confucianism as a proxy for Chinese society and to make it the scapegoat for all social ills.

Although Fukuyama underlines that 'the true essence of Chinese Confucianism was never political Confucianism at all but rather what Tu Wei-ming calls the "Confucian personal ethic"' (Fukuyama, 1995: 85), his reading of the latter is rather reminiscent of politicised Confucianism and his comments on Confucianism as 'ethical teaching' are quickly, and tellingly, intermingled with comments on 'Chinese society'. Statements, such as that on the duty to the family trumping all other duties or that 'there is no concept of individual conscience that can lead an individual to contradict [paternal authority]' (Fukuyama, 1995: 85–6), are imprecise and misrepresent religio-philosophical Confucianism grossly. The Chinese scholar Hsieh Yu-wei (Xie Youwei, 1901–76), employing a similar terminology, has affirmed that in Confucianism an 'individual', for instance, must 'decide by his own conscience' on the course of action when in conflict with 'community' (Hsieh, 1968: 320).

Chinese familism, the cornerstone of Fukuyama's argument that 'Chinese Confucianism' leads to low levels of trust and social capital, goes directly against contemporary interpretations of religio-philosophical Confucianism. For Fukuyama, the Confucian family is a paradigm of bonding social capital and its putatively negative externalities, and there is nothing in Confucianism to act as a counterbalance. However, self-transcendence in religio-philosophical Confucianism precisely means not to further nepotism or familism, but to show concern and feel duty beyond the family, that is, to generate bridging social capital. Tu Wei-ming writes:

> But if we extend sympathy only to our parents, we take no more than the initial step toward self-realization. By embodying our closest kin in our sensitivity, we may have gone beyond egoism, but without the learned ability to enter into fruitful communication outside the immediate family, we are still confined to nepotism. Like egoism, nepotism fails to extend our sensitivity to embody a larger network of human relationships and thus limits our capacity for self-realization. Similarly, parochialism, ethnocentrism, and chauvinistic nationalism are all varying degrees of human insensitivity. (Tu, 1985: 176)

A similar argument is advanced by political philosopher Joseph Chan, who takes issue with the mistaken view that, 'in classical Confucianism, the basic principles and virtues of the family and clan are extended without much revision to the social and political spheres' and explores specific Confucian non-familial principles and virtues (Chan, 2004: 61). Furthermore, as regards the purportedly absolute authority of the father in the Confucian family, Chan cites the Confucian texts *Xunzi* and *The Classic of Filial Piety* to illustrate that a son may be required to remonstrate with his father, for how could, as the latter text pointedly asks, 'blind obedience of a son to every command of his father be regarded as filial piety?' (Chan, 2004: 69).

These glimpses into contemporary interpretations of religio-philosophical Confucianism serve to suggest that it would be rather precipitate to close the case for Confucianism with regard to social capital because of some ostensibly inherent familism or some awkward denial of 'individual conscience'. Rather, and in contrast to Fukuyama's call to redirect research on social capital away from conceptual matters to a more 'pragmatic agenda' (Fukuyama, 2002: 23), more conceptual work and more religio-philosophical reflection are necessary.

Conclusions
The reflections in this chapter have mainly engaged the concept of social capital through some selected writings of James Coleman, Robert Putnam and Francis Fukuyama. Adopting the perspective of religio-philosophical Confucianism has served to highlight some contingencies of their conceptualizations of social capital. I have suggested several points of departure for further religio-philosophical reflection of social capital, understood as an important complement to the efforts undertaken in the social sciences. Most points raised, however, require further elaboration. For instance, it would be a worthwhile effort to spell out in more detail a conceptualization of Confucian social capital based on self-cultivation and concentric circles: engaging in 'bridging' forms of social capital could turn out to be a prerequisite for the flourishing of meaningful 'bonding' forms and vice versa, while the line dividing 'positive' and 'negative' forms of social capital would be destabilised. Very clearly, Confucianism understood as a religio-philosophical tradition offers rich resources from which to construct a Confucian variant of what the editors of this handbook in their introduction call 'a *harmonious mix* of bridging/bonding social capital'. For the moment, it is to be hoped for that the present reflections from a Confucian viewpoint will be further pursued and also be supplemented by reflections from perspectives of other traditions.

To end with, the question of generalized trust may serve to illustrate the use of religio-philosophical reflection and conceptual work to social scientists. The question, to be clear, is a proxy often used in combination with other questions to measure social capital around the globe and reads: 'Generally speaking, do you believe that most people can be trusted or can't you be too careful in dealing with people?' Even if the problem of translation can be overcome, how could one ever be confident – in the absence of thorough local knowledge – that the question is a meaningful question for the concrete person who is filling out the questionnaire? Do we all share an understanding of when we speak 'concretely' and when we do so 'generally'? What might 'to trust', 'to be careful' and 'to deal with people' mean in a specific social and religio-philosophical context? Who is included in the idea of 'people'? A neighbour? An acquaintance? A compatriot? What about someone of similar ethnic appearance? Or someone who speaks the same dialect? Or the same language? Finally, how would we interpret an interviewee who in all earnestness ticks off both options? These are some of the many issues 'someone' might raise with regard to a survey that employs the generalized trust question. Yet, still, that 'someone' is well advised to show interest for and to take seriously the very findings of that survey. Religio-philosophical reflection, conceptual work and empirical research should not go entirely separate ways.

Notes

1. For a conceptual history of the concept of social capital, see with regard to economic sociology the article by Michael Woolcock (1998) and with regard to methodological considerations and an emphasis on the work of John Dewey the article by James Farr (2004).
2. In his seminal work of 1947, the Chinese sociologist Fei Xiaotong (1910–2005) brought up – drawing on the ancient dictionary *Shiming* (The Explanation of Names) – the metaphor of 'concentric circles' to convey the meaning of the Confucian term renlun (human relationships), which, he writes, 'signifies the ripplelike effect created from circles of relationships that spread out from the self, an effect that produces a pattern of discrete circles' (Fei, 1992: 65).
3. A similar approach of micro-to-macro transition by aggregation is visible in the work of those researchers who psychologize social capital. For them, social capital 'is an aggregate concept that has its basis in individual behavior, attitudes, and predispositions' (Brehm and Rahn, 1997: 1000).

References

Ames, Roger T. and Henry Rosemont, Jr (1998), *The Analects of Confucius: A Philosophical Translation*, New York: Ballantine Books.
Brehm, J. and W. Rahn (1997), 'Individual-level evidence for the causes and consequences of social capital', *American Journal of Political Science*, **41** (3), 999–1023.
Chan, Joseph (2004), 'Exploring the non-familial in Confucian political philosophy', in Hahm Chaihark and Daniel A. Bell (eds), *The Politics of Affective Relations: East Asia and Beyond*, Lanham, MD: Lexington Books, pp. 61–72.
Coleman, J.S. (1988), 'Social capital in the creation of human capital', *The American Journal of Sociology*, **94**, Supplement: Organizations and Institutions: Sociological and Economic Approaches to the Analysis of Social Structure, 95–120.
Coleman, J.S. (1990), *Foundations of Social Theory*, Cambridge, MA and London: The Belknap Press of Harvard University Press.
Edwards, B. and M.W. Foley (1998), 'Civil society and social capital beyond putnam', *The American Behavioral Scientist*, **42** (1), 124–39.
Farr, J. (2004), 'Social capital: a conceptual history', *Political Theory*, **32** (1), 6–33.
Fei, Xiaotong (1992), *From the Soil: The Foundation of Chinese Society*, trans. Gary G. Hamilton and Wang Zheng, Berkeley, CA: University of California Press.
Fukuyama, Francis (1995), *Trust: The Social Virtues and the Creation of Prosperity*, New York: Free Press.
Fukuyama, Francis (2001), 'Social capital, civil society and development', *Third World Quarterly*, **22** (1), 7–20.

Fukuyama, Francis (2002), 'Social capital and development: the coming agenda', *SAIS Review*, **22** (1), 23–37.

Gold, Thomas, Doug Guthrie and David Wank (2002), 'An introduction to the study of *guanxi*', in Thomas Gold, Doug Guthrie and David Wank (eds), *Social Connections in China: Institutions, Culture, and the Changing Nature of Guanxi*, Cambridge: Cambridge University Press, pp. 3–20.

Granovetter, M. (1985), 'Economic action and social structure: the problem of embeddedness', *The American Journal of Sociology*, **91** (3), 481–510.

Hsieh, Yu-wei (1968), 'The status of the individual in Chinese ethics', in Charles Moore (ed.), *The Chinese Mind*, Honolulu: East-West Center, pp. 307–22.

Ladd, E.C. (1996), 'The data just don't show erosion of America's "social capital"', *The Public Perspective*, **7** (4), 1, 5–6.

Lichterman, P. (2006), 'Social capital or group style? Rescuing Tocqueville's insights on civic engagement', *Theory and Society*, **35** (5/6), 529–63.

Portes, A. (1998), 'Social capital: its origins and applications in modern sociology', *Annual Review of Sociology*, **24**, 1–24.

Putnam, Robert D. (1995a), 'Bowling alone: America's declining social capital', *Journal of Democracy*, **6** (1), 65–78.

Putnam, Robert D. (1995b), 'Tuning in, tuning out: the strange disappearance of social capital in America', *PS: Political Science and Politics*, **28** (4), 664–83.

Putnam, Robert D. (2000), *Bowling Alone. The Collapse and Revival of American Community*, New York: Simon & Schuster.

Putnam, Robert D. (2001), 'Social capital: measurement and consequences', *ISUMA: Canadian Journal of Policy Research*, **2** (1), 41–51.

Smart, A. (1993), 'Gifts, bribes, and guanxi: a reconsideration of Bourdieu's social capital', *Cultural Anthropology*, **8** (3), 388–408.

Smith, S.S. and J. Kulynych (2002), 'It may be social, but why is it capital? The social construction of social capital and the politics of language', *Politics & Society*, **30** (1), 149–86.

Smith, Wilfred C. (1991), *The Meaning and End of Religion*, Minneapolis, MN: Fortress Press.

Tillman, Hoyt C. (2004), 'Selected Confucian networks and values in society and the economy', in Hahm Chaihark and Daniel A. Bell (eds), *The Politics of Affective Relations: East Asia and Beyond*, Lanham, MD: Lexington Books, pp. 121–47.

Tu, Wei-ming (1985), *Confucian Thought: Selfhood as Creative Transformation*, Albany, NY: State University of New York Press.

Wang Yangming (~1527), *Daxuewen* [Inquiry on the Great Learning], reprinted in Zhong Zhian and Zhang Zhonggang (eds) (2000), *Wang Shouren: Chuanxilu* [Wang Shouren: Instructions for Practical Living], Jinan: Shandong Friendship Press, pp. 509–14.

Woolcock, M. (1998), 'Social capital and economic development: toward a theoretical synthesis and policy framework', *Theory and Society*, **27** (2), 151–208.

Wrong, D.H. (1961), 'The oversocialized conception of man in modern sociology', *American Sociological Review*, **26** (2), 183–93.

PART III

CORRUPTION AND THE QUALITY OF INSTITUTIONS

8 Corruption[1]
Eric M. Uslaner

Corruption flouts rules of fairness and gives some people advantages that others don't have. Corruption transfers resources from the mass public to the elites – and generally from the poor to the rich (Tanzi, 1998). It acts as an extra tax on citizens, leaving less money for public expenditures (Mauro, 1998: 7). Corrupt governments have less money to spend on their own projects, pushing down the salaries of public employees. In turn, these lower-level staffers will be more likely to extort funds from the public purse. Government employees in corrupt societies will thus spend more time lining their own pockets than serving the public. Corruption thus leads to lower levels of economic growth and to ineffective government (Mauro, 1998: 5).

The roots of corruption lie in the unequal distribution of resources in a society. Economic inequality provides a fertile breeding ground for corruption – and, in turn, it leads to further inequalities. The connection between inequality and the quality of government is not necessarily so simple: as the former Communist nations of Central and Eastern Europe show, you can have plenty of corruption without economic inequality. The path from inequality to corruption may be indirect – through generalized trust – but the connection is key to understanding why some societies are more corrupt than others. When we trust people who may be different from ourselves, we will be more predisposed to treat them honestly – and profiting from corruption will seem unseemly. When we distrust strangers, especially if we believe that they are trying to cheat us, our moral compunctions against corrupt behavior become less compelling. Corruption and inequality wreak havoc with our moral sense. Della Porta and Vannucci (1999: 146) argue that pervasive corruption makes people less willing to condemn it as immoral. As corruption becomes widespread, it becomes deeply entrenched in a society (Mauro, 2004: 16). People begin to believe that dishonesty is the only way to get things done (Gambetta, 2002: 55).

The argument from inequality to low trust to corruption – and back again both to low trust and greater inequality (what I call the 'inequality trap') – stands in contrast to the more common approach to explaining corruption as stemming from deficient institutions. The roots of corruption are largely *not* institutional, but rather stem from economic inequality and a mistrusting culture, which itself stems from an unequal distribution of wealth. There is one institution that does shape corruption: the *fairness of the legal system*.

The inequality trap is hard to break. I posit a model where inequality, mistrust, and corruption are mutually reinforcing:

$$\text{inequality} \rightarrow \text{low trust} \rightarrow \text{corruption} \rightarrow \text{more inequality}$$

The most compelling argument for the notion of an inequality trap is that corruption is *sticky*. There is little evidence that countries can escape the curse of corruption easily – or at all. The r^2 between the 2004 Transparency International (TI) estimates of corruption – I use TI measures in the aggregate analyses to follow – and the historical estimates for 1980–85 across 52 countries is .742. Any theoretical perspective on corruption must take into account its persistence over time.

My argument stands in contrast to more traditional institutional accounts of corruption, which often suggest that the cure for malfeasance is to put the corrupt politicians in jail. If we do so (and we ought to do so), they will be replaced by other corrupt leaders. Nor do we need a reformed system of government that either centralizes power to herd in independent 'entrepreneurs' who extort businesses or average citizens (Treisman, 1999) or decentralizes power to prevent an all-powerful 'grabbing hand' (DiFrancesco and Gitelman, 1984: 618; Fisman and Gatti, 2000). In contrast to corruption, political institutions are not so sticky. The r^2 for political rights from 1973 to 2003 is .165 and for civil liberties it is .263 (both N = 77). Even excluding countries that were Communist in 1973, the respective r^2 values increase only to .264 and .375 (N = 67). More critically, changes in political rights and civil liberties from 1973 to 2003 are unrelated to changes in corruption from 1980–85 to 2004 (r^2 = .007 and .038 respectively, N = 38). Moving the democratization measures forward to 1988 does not improve the fit with changes in corruption (r^2 = .004 and .0005 for political rights and civil liberties, N = 39).

My argument on the sources of corruption is largely pessimistic: corruption is not easy to eradicate if it is largely based upon the distribution of resources (economic inequality) and a society's culture (trust in people who may be different from yourself). Changing institutions may not be easy, but its difficulty pales by comparison with reshaping a society's culture or its distribution of wealth (and power). Corruption, inequality, and trust are all 'sticky': they don't change much over time. Yet, all is not lost: policy choices that countries make also shape corruption. Countries that have very high levels of regulation of business have more corruption. In turn, the level of regulation is shaped by the fairness of the legal system, the openness of the economy, and whether the government is military or civilian.

Inequality and corruption

The link between inequality and corruption seems compelling. Corruption is exploitive. Not all corruption is linked to inequality. 'Grand' corruption refers to malfeasance of considerable magnitude by people who exploit their positions to get rich (or become richer) – political or business leaders. So grand corruption is all about extending the advantages of those already well endowed. 'Petty corruption', small-scale payoffs to doctors, police officers and even university professors, very common in the formerly Communist nations of Central and Eastern Europe (and many poor countries) is different in kind, if not in spirit. Petty corruption, or 'honest graft' as New York City political boss George Washington Plunkitt called it (Riordan, 1948), does not enrich those who practice it. It may depend upon an inequitable distribution of wealth – there should be no need to make 'gift' payments in a properly functioning market economy.

It does not exacerbate the gap between the rich and the poor – and may actually narrow it by providing some small benefits to the middle-class bureaucrats, teachers and doctors who benefit from it. With the sort of aggregate data we have on corruption indicators, there is no clear way to separate either the causes or effects of inequality on big and little corruption. Survey data can help us do so (see Kornai, 2000; Miller et al., 2001). But the distinction is not so critical to an examination of the factors underlying corruption at the aggregate level for two reasons.

Inequality promotes corruption in many ways. Glaeser et al. (2003: 2–3) argue:

> inequality is detrimental to the security of property rights, and therefore to growth, because it enables the rich to subvert the political, regulatory, and legal institutions of society for their own benefit. If one person is sufficiently richer than another, and courts are corruptible, then the legal system will favor the rich, not the just. Likewise, if political and regulatory institutions can be moved by wealth or influence, they will favor the established, not the efficient. This in turn leads the initially well situated to pursue socially harmful acts, recognizing that the legal, political, and regulatory systems will not hold them accountable. Inequality can encourage institutional subversion in two distinct ways. First, the havenots can redistribute from the haves through violence, the political process, or other means. Such Robin Hood redistribution jeopardizes property rights, and deters investment by the rich.

Similarly, You and Kaghram (2005, italics in original) argue: 'The rich, as interest groups, firms, or individuals may use bribery or connections to influence law-implementing processes (*bureaucratic corruption*) and to buy favorable interpretations of the law (*judicial corruption*).'

Inequality breeds corruption by: (1) leading ordinary citizens to see the system as stacked against them (Uslaner, 2002: 181–3); (2) creating a sense of dependency of ordinary citizens and a sense of pessimism for the future, which in turn undermines the moral dictates of treating your neighbors honestly, and (3) distorting the key institutions of fairness in society, the courts, which ordinary citizens see as their protectors against evil-doers, especially those with more influence than they have (see also Glaeser et al., 2003; and You and Khagram, 2005).

Economic inequality creates political leaders who make patronage a virtue rather than a vice, since it provided jobs for ordinary citizens. These leaders *help* their constituents, but more critically *they help themselves*. Inequality breeds corruption – and to a dependency of the poor on the political leaders. Inequality leads to *clientelism* – leaders establish themselves as monopoly providers of benefits for average citizens. These leaders are not accountable to their constituents as democratic theory would have us believe. When some groups are richer than others, inequality breeds resentment of one group against another – as we see in several transition countries where ethnic conflict has reemerged after transition. The conflicts in the former Yugoslavia, reflected in ethnic cleansing by Serbia in Bosnia, and the reemergence of long-standing group tensions and nationalist politics in Romania and Hungary – are compounded by perceptions of economic inequality (Verdery, 1993). These strong in-group preferences tend to be reproduced over time as trust is largely learned early in life from one's parents (Uslaner, 2002: ch. 6).

There may well be the trappings of democracy, with regularly scheduled elections, so that the link between democratic and honest government may not be as strong as we might initially expect.[2] The political boss is well entrenched in his position. His party reigns supreme in the area. Potential opponents don't have the resources to mount a real challenge – and, even if they tried, the boss can count on the support of the legions whose jobs he controls through his patronage machine.

Unequal wealth leads people to feel less constrained about cheating others (Mauro, 1998: 12) and about evading taxes (Owsiak, 2003: 73; Uslaner, 2003). Where corruption is widespread, people realize that they are not the masters of their own fate – and they lose faith that their future will be bright. People become resigned to their fate. In the World Values Survey waves 1–3 (1981, 1990, 1995–97), respondents who believed that corruption was widespread in their country were significantly *less likely to believe that they could get ahead by hard work rather than by luck or having connections*. The zero-order correlation is modest (as we might expect with a sample of almost 60,000, tau-b = .061) – but 34 percent of people in societies where corruption was seen as widespread thought the only way you could get ahead was by luck, compared to 29 percent in honest societies.

If people feel that they have been treated unfairly by the police or in the courts, they are less likely to have faith in the legal system. The justice system is especially important for two reasons. First, a corrupt court system can shield dishonest elites from retribution. Second, the courts, more than any other branch of the polity, are *presumed to be neutral and fair*. We appeal 'unjust' decisions to the judiciary – and our vernacular includes the phrase 'court of last resort', suggesting that *somewhere there must be justice*. Rothstein and Stolle (2002) argue that there are two dimensions to the legal system: fairness and efficiency. Fairness, I argue, is the key to the connection between law and corruption *because it reflects the advantages that some people have over others*. The efficiency of the courts should not matter so much for corruption – since rounding up the corrupt leaders and putting them in jail only makes room for a new group of miscreants, doing little to address the underlying causes of corruption.

When people have little faith in the fairness of the legal system, there are few incentives to obey the law. When Russian oil entrepreneur Mikhail Khodorkovsky confessed his sins of relying on 'beeznissmeny' (stealing, lying and sometimes killing) and promised to become scrupulously honest in early 2003, Russians regarded this pledge as 'startling'. When he was arrested and charged with tax evasion and extortion under orders from President Vladimir Putin ten months later, the average Russian was unphased: about the same share of people approved of his arrest as disapproved of it (Tavernise, 2003). The arrest of Khodorkovsky stands out as exceptional: corrupt officials and business people are rarely held to account. While crime spiraled in Russia after the fall of Communism, *conviction rates plummeted* (Varese, 1997). Russians (and many others) are deluged with fake goods on sale everywhere – from vacations complete with photos (so that errant husbands might convince their wives that they are on 'fishing trips') to bogus caviar, phony diplomas and term papers (including portions of President Vladimir Putin's doctoral dissertation), and fake VIP stickers and flashing blue lights for your car so that other cars will let you avoid Moscow's traffic. About half of all consumer goods are bogus in Russia (Murphy, 2006).

Russians are hardly exceptional. Nigerian con artists engage in a wide range of scams (including many of those email messages we get promising us riches if we send back our bank account details) under the rubric of '419' (four-one-nine), from the Nigerian criminal code on financial fraud. The poor may find their humble houses sold from under them by '419' scammers and they paint 'This House Not for Sale: Beware of "419"' on their outside walls (Packer, 2006: 72). As in Russia, there is little recourse. The police are not the purveyors of justice, but rather are complicit in illicit deals (Mbaku, 1998: 258).

The story of the inequality trap is that corruption persists over long periods of time. Corruption has a legacy in Romania at least as far back as the Ottoman empire (Sampson, 2005: 18). In Ottoman times, Romania was run by Greek princes (the Phanariotes) who bought their positions from the sultans, which they financed through extortion from ordinary citizens. Each local ruler could be challenged by other princes and bidding wars for power were common (Mungiu-Pippidi, 1997). The decline of the Ottoman empire and the independence of Romania did not lead to more honest government: 'From the first king of Romania (and the concession of the first railroad) to the last king and government before WWII, state property and the role of the state in developing Romania were accompanied by widespread influence-peddling and corruption' (Mungiu-Pippidi, 1997). Indeed, Romanians ruefully boast of their exceptional levels of corruption: They say, 'La no cal la nimeni', or 'No one has it the way we do' (Sampson, 2005: 20).

Since trust rests upon a foundation of fairness and especially equality, the link from inequality to low trust to high corruption is straightforward.

Some preliminary evidence

Fairness of the legal system is not equivalent to economic inequality – and the connection between the two is not as strong as we might suppose. I use a measure of legal fairness developed by the Economist Intelligence Unit; it only covers 60 countries, so I derived estimated values for other countries by imputation.[3] Economic inequality is measured by the Gini index from Deininger and Squire (1996). Overall, the fit between these two indicators of equality (equal treatment before the law and equal distribution of wealth) is not strong. For 88 nations, $r^2 = .131$. The correlation is depressed by the former and present Communist nations that largely have unfair legal systems but more equitable distributions of income.[4] For many years, this equality was imposed from above by a command economy – but even as inequality has grown sharply, it has not approached the level of capitalist economies. Overall, we see relatively high economic equality matched with both low and high levels of judicial fairness. When I remove the Eastern bloc countries, the r^2 rises to .279 – still rather modest. Fairness of the legal system is *not* the same as economic inequality.

The plot of inequality and corruption is striking: Across 85 countries, there is a weak (at best) relationship. The r^2 is a paltry .082, suggesting no relationship at all between inequality and corruption. When I remove the former and present Communist regimes, there is a moderate fit between the two indicators ($r^2 = .246$, N = 62) when the former and present Communist countries are excluded. With a bivariate r^2 of this magnitude, it should not take much effort to see it vanish in a multivariate analysis.

The connection with fairness of the legal system is far stronger – and this is hardly surprising. While I took care to find an indicator of the fairness of the legal system that is *not* based upon an underlying measure, it is hardly surprising that corruption flourishes where the courts give special treatment to some over others – and where court procedures are not transparent. The least fair legal systems have a mean corruption score of 2.82, while the most fair systems have a mean of 8.78 (high scores indicate greater transparency, less corruption). The fit between legal fairness and corruption is very strong: $r^2 = .722$ for the 55 cases of the original EIU data and .733 for the 86 cases including the imputed scores.[5]

There are good theoretical reasons to believe that corruption stems from economic inequality as well as the fairness of the legal system. But the evidence does not seem compelling. Have we reached a dead end?

Trust, inequality and corruption
Not at all. There *is* a link between inequality and corruption, but it is not direct, at least not in aggregate analyses. Inequality leads to corruption because it leads to resentment of out-groups and enhanced in-group identity. Generalized trust, the value that is predicated upon the belief that many others are part of your moral community, is the foundation of the 'well-ordered society'. When we believe that 'most people can be trusted', we are more likely to give of ourselves and to look out for the welfare of others. When we believe that 'you can't be too careful in dealing with people', we are likely to be on our guard and to feel little compunction in taking advantage of others who may not have our best interests in mind.

Generalized trust is predicated on the notion of a common bond between classes and races and on egalitarian values (Seligman, 1997: 36–37, 41).[6] Faith in others leads to empathy for those who do not fare well, and ultimately to a redistribution of resources from the well-off to the poor. If we believe that we have a shared fate with others, and especially people who are different from ourselves, then gross inequalities in wealth and status will seem to violate norms of fairness. Generalized trust rests upon the psychological foundations of optimism and control and the economic foundation of an equitable distribution of resources. Optimism and control lead people to believe that the world is a good place, it is going to get better and that you can make it better. Economic equality promotes both optimism and the belief that we all have a shared fate, across races, ethnic groups and *classes*.

Corruption, of course, depends upon trust – or honor among thieves. As it takes two to tango, it takes *at least two to bribe*. Corrupt officials need to be sure that their 'partners' *will deliver* on their promises (Lambsdorff, 2002). Corruption thrives upon trust, but it cannot be based upon the notion of widespread goodwill and common interests in a society underlying generalized trust. Entrance into a corruption network is not easy. Members of a conspiracy of graft cannot simply assume that others are trustworthy (as generalized trusters do). Treating strangers *as if* they were trustworthy (also as trusters do) can be hazardous at best.

Instead, corruption thrives on *particularized trust*, where people only have faith in their own kind (or their own small circle of malefactors). Particularized trusters strongly distrust outsiders. They fear that people of different backgrounds will exploit them – and in a dog-eat-dog world, you have little choice to strike first before someone exploits you. Plunkitt saw his opportunities and took them – worrying that someone else might get there first and leave nothing for him. Gambetta (1993) argued that the Mafia took root in Southern Italy because there were strong in-group ties and weak generalized trust there.

Where is generalized trust high and where is it low? *Across a wide set of nations, across the American states, and over time in the United States – the only country with a long enough time series on the standard survey question on trust*[7] *– the strongest predictor of trust is the level of economic inequality.* As economic inequality increases, trust declines (Uslaner, 2002: chs 6, 8; Uslaner and Brown, 2005). Optimism for the future makes less sense when there is more economic inequality. People at the bottom of the income distribution will be less sanguine that they too share in society's bounty. The distribution of resources plays a key role in establishing the belief that people share a common destiny – and have similar fundamental values. When resources are distributed more equally, people are more likely to perceive a common stake with others. If there is a strong skew in wealth, people at each end may feel that they have little in common with others. In highly unequal societies, people will stick with their own kind. Perceptions of injustice will reinforce negative stereotypes of other groups, making trust and accommodation more difficult (Boix and Posner, 1998: 693).

Seligman (1997, 36–7, 41) argues that trust *cannot* take root in a hierarchical culture. Such societies have rigid social orders marked by strong class divisions that persist across generations. Feudal systems and societies based on castes dictate what people can and can not do based upon the circumstances of their birth. Social relations are based on expectations of what people must do, not on their talents or personalities. Trust is not the lubricant of cooperation in such traditional societies. The assumption that others share your beliefs is counterintuitive, since strict class divisions make it unlikely that others actually have the same values as people in other classes.

A history of poverty with little likelihood of any improvement led to social distrust in the Italian village of Montegrano that Edward Banfield (1958: 110) described in the 1950s: 'any advantage that may be given to another is necessarily at the expense of one's own family. Therefore, one cannot afford the luxury of charity, which is giving others more than their due, or even justice, which is giving them their due'. Montegrano is a mean world, where daily life is 'brutal and senseless' (Banfield, 1958: 109), much like Hobbes's 'nasty, brutish, and short' existence. All who stand outside the immediate family are 'potential enemies', battling for the meager bounty that nature has provided. People seek to protect themselves from the 'threat of calamity' (Banfield, 1958: 110).

Inequality leads to low levels of trust in strangers. What trust remains is entirely within your group, so there are few moral sanctions for cheating people of a different background. Inequality thus breeds corruption indirectly – by turning people inward and reducing the sanctions, both external and internal, of taking advantage of others. So I posit an indirect link from inequality to corruption:

inequality → low generalized trust and high in-group trust → corruption

Trust and corruption *are* linked. I show the connection in Figure 8.1 (see also Uslaner, 2004). The graph is a bit difficult to read because it is difficult to fit the country abbreviations into the graph since many countries have similar values on both variables. The trust question comes from the World Values Survey – and to increase the number of cases, I imputed values on this measure as well.[8] Here we see a more robust fit than in the connection between inequality and corruption: $r^2 = .420$ for 83 cases.[9]

Just as corruption is 'sticky', inequality and trust do not change much over time, either. The r^2 for the most commonly used measures of economic inequality (Deininger and Squire, 1996) between 1980 and 1990 is substantial at .676 for a sample of 42 countries. A new inequality data base developed by James Galbraith extends measures of inequality further back in time and across more countries. The r^2 between economic inequality in *1963* and economic inequality in *1996* is .706 (for 37 countries). The r^2 between generalized trust, as measured in the 1981, 1990–95 World Values Surveys across between 1980 and the 1990s is .81 for the 22 nations included in both waves – the r^2 between generalized trust in 1990 and 1995 is also robust (.851, N = 28). The persistence of corruption follows the stability of inequality and trust over time. Institutions seem far more malleable than inequality, trust or especially corruption. This is the foundation of the inequality trap.

A summary of the evidence
I can do little more here than to summarize the evidence I have marshalled for the inequality trap in Uslaner (2008). I present evidence from both

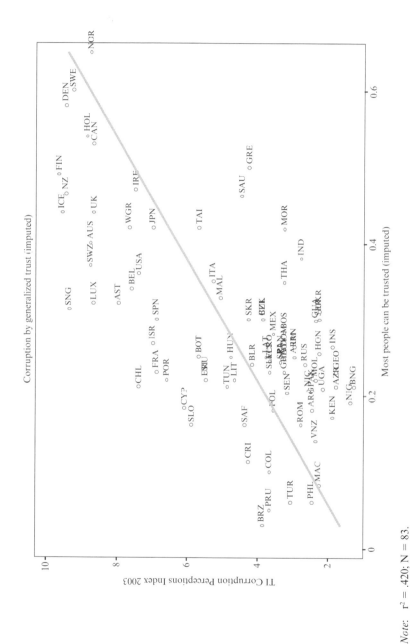

Corruption by generalized trust (imputed)

Most people can be trusted (imputed)

TI Corruption Perceptions Index 2003

Note: r² = .420; N = 83.

Figure 8.1   Corruption by generalized trust (imputed)

136

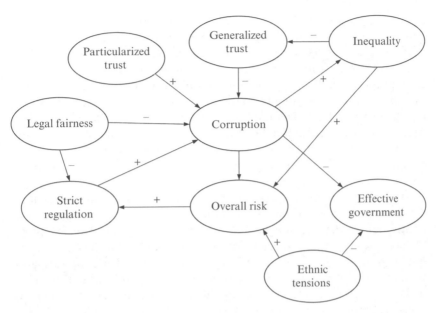

Figure 8.2   Model of inequality, trust, corruption and effective government

aggregate-level statistical models and from the analyses of surveys. Most critically, I present a simultaneous equation model of corruption, trust, inequality (as well as the level of strangling regulation of business, the overall risk level of an economy and a measure of government effectiveness). I find strong support for the inequality trap argument across 61 nations. See Figure 8.2 for a summary of the model, which is more complex than I can consider here (see Uslaner, 2008: ch. 3 for the full model). Economic inequality strongly lowers the level of generalized trust, and trust in turn is the most powerful determinant of corruption. Since particularized trust should lead to greater corruption, I sought a measure of faith only in one's own kind. There are no comparable data available cross-nationally. So I must rely upon a proxy for particularized trust: whether a state restricts members of minority religions from converting others to their faith. This measure comes from the State and Religion data set of Fox (2006). While at best an approximation – perhaps a crude one – it does tap the idea of only trusting one's own in-group. Religious fundamentalists tend to trust only people of their own faith – and when they do participate in civic life, they join exclusively religious organizations (Schoenfeld, 1978: 64; Uslaner, 2001; 2002, 87–8). Restrictions on conversion are the mark of fundamentalist domination of the state – and I use this measure as a proxy for particularized trust. Such restrictions are indicative of high in-group trust and low tolerance toward out-groups. This measure of particularized trust leads to higher levels of corruption, as does an unfair legal system.

Policy also matters, however: strangling regulations on business (requiring permissions from many officials) presents more opportunities for corruption. An unfair legal system not only leads directly to corruption, but also to more strangling regulations – so it has both direct and indirect effects on corruption. The level of democracy does *not* matter, nor do a number of other institutional factors such as the structure of the electoral system, whether a polity is centralized or decentralized, or the pay of the civil servants. A free (and widely read) media similarly does not lead to less corruption in this model.

In turn, corruption has a powerful effect in leading to more inequality. Across a wide range of policy outcomes – ranging from economic competitiveness to the ethical behavior of business firms to multiple measures of social expenditures (especially on education and public health) and the quality of life, an honest government matters more for better performance than an efficient state. For the American states, there is also a powerful relation between both levels of inequality and trust and reporters' perceptions of corruption (see also Uslaner, 2006).

Government effectivness, as measured by an index constructed from perceptions of businesspeople in the Executive Opinion Survey of the World Economic Forum in 2004 (see Uslaner, 2008: ch. 3), does not have an independent effect on corruption – but rather is shaped by corruption. The major factor shaping government effectiveness is the level of ethnic tensions in a country. More highly corrupt countries not only have greater inequality, but also more shaky economies (as measured by the International Country Risk Guide of Political Risk Services, see Uslaner, 2008: ch. 3). A risky economy also leads to a less fair legal system, so it indirectly shapes corruption (as well as being a consequence of malfeasance).

I also consider corruption perceptions across a range of countries and blocs, focusing especially on transition countries. While former Communist nations have traditionally lower levels of inequality, the disparity between the rich and the poor has been increasing sharply since transition. In transition countries, most people believe that the only way you can become rich is by being dishonest. So people link grand corruption, but not petty corruption, to inequality and here there is a more direct link between perceptions of corruption and beliefs about the inequitable distribution of resources. There is also a link from perceptions of inequality to lower trust – and people who are less trusting also perceive far more grand corruption. Perceptions of rising inequality and high levels of corruption also lead to demands of redistribution of income from the rich to the poor, as I show from a survey of Romanians. In Estonia, Slovakia and Romania, elites are far less likely to see high levels of corruption than are ordinary citizens – and in Estonia, trust and corruption perceptions are more strongly linked for ordinary citizens than for elites (especially entrepreneurs).

Similar results hold for Africa, especially Nigeria, when I analyse Afrobarometer surveys. Africa is a classic case of the inequality trap – with persistent high inequality, low trust and high corruption. Perceptions of grand corruption, but not petty malfeasance, lead people to perceive greater inequality – and where people see a less equitable distribution of wealth and an unfair legal system they are more likely to see high-level corruption. Corruption creates social divisions between the rich and the poor – and thus less trust across classes and groups – but in turn people who are disadvantaged are most likely to perceive corruption.

Where corruption is weaker, the link to trust and especially to inequality is far weaker, generally insignificant. The Nordic countries (Denmark, Finland, Norway and Sweden) have the most trusting populations in the world – and have very little corruption and a strongly egalitarian distribution of wealth. So it is not surprising to see little connection among trust, perceptions of inequality and views about corruption. There is also no link in Hong Kong (where trust is moderate, as is inequality) and Botswana (where trust and egalitarianism are both low) – both countries that have escaped the inequality trap and have honest governments. While both countries – as well as Singapore – have reduced (even eradicated) malfeasance by strong anti-corruption agencies, their success is not easily replicable. Each of these countries has worked hard to develop a sense of social solidarity by reducing high levels of inequality and promoting multicultural (or multitribal) cooperation in the face of external threats.

In contrast anti-corruption agencies in many other countries, especially in Africa, have not been successful in fighting corruption – sometimes they even cover it up – and Nigerians' faith in their commission reflected both their perceptions about high-level corruption and economic inequality – as well as low trust in people generally. When people have lost faith in each other and believe that their leaders are corrupt and inequality is rampant, they will have little faith that another bureaucracy could combat corruption.

Reprise

Corruption is 'bad social capital'. It is dishonesty, to be sure, but it is more than that. It exploits the poor and powerless to grant more riches and power to people who already have great wealth. There is no easy way out of this inequality trap. Few countries become markedly less corrupt over time – and inequality and trust are also remarkably sticky. Institutional change seems to have little effect on corruption: The two great 'success stories' in combating corruption, Hong Kong and Singapore, are not democracies. Combatting corruption means tackling inequality. And the policies that work best to reduce inequality and promote trust – universalistic social welfare policies – also depend upon honest governments to deliver the goods and upon a social compact to provide benefits such as universal education and health care to the rich and the poor alike. High levels of corruption mean that services may not be provided and the inequity underlying grand corruption will lead to more radical demands for redistribution – and policies that might alleviate, but not resolve, fundamental inequalities (Rothstein and Uslaner, 2005). 'Bad social capital' seems self-perpetuating.

Notes

1. This chapter summarizes Uslaner (2008). I am grateful to the Russell Sage Foundation and the Carnegie Corporation for a grant on a related project that is encompassed in my work on the United States and to the General Research Board of the University of Maryland–College Park, for a Faculty Research Award in the Spring 2006 semester; and to Bo Rothstein, Jong-sung You, Gabriel Badescu, Ronald King, Paul Sum, Kems Adu-Gyan, Michael Bratton, Nick Duncan, John Helliwell, Karen Kaufmann, Lawrence Khoo, Mark Lichbach, Anton Oleynik, Jon (Siew Tiem) Quah and Leonard Sebastian for helpful comments and discussions and to Mitchell Brown for research assistance.

2. The r^2 between the 2003 Transparency International Corruption Perceptions Index and the trichotomized 2003 Freedom House index (not free, partially free, and free) is just .216.

3. I am grateful to Elizabeth Anderson of the Economist Intelligence Unit for providing the data on legal fairness. The variables I used for the imputation are: gross national product per capita (from the State Failure Data Set), the tenure of the executive and a dummy variable for having a parliamentary system (from the Database of Political Institutions), the Freedom House composite indicator of democracy trichotomized for 2003, and the distance of a country from the equator (from Jong-sung You). All variables had positive coefficients. The R^2 is .769, the standard error of the estimate is .647 (N = 53)

4. Within the former and present Communist countries, there is also a negative relationship between economic inequality and legal fairness (r = −.357, N = 23, r = −.526, N = 17 for the original, non-imputed, data). The East bloc nations reduce the overall goodness of fit since they lie on a separate and less steep regression line.

5. I plot only the original scores, which are integer values. The imputed scores are not generally integer values and the plot was unreadable.

6. The following section is derived from Uslaner (2004), which in turn summarizes Uslaner (2002).

7. The question, 'Generally speaking, do you believe that most people can be trusted, or can't you be too careful in dealing with people?', was asked first in cross-national samples, in *The Civic Culture* in 1960 (Almond and Verba, 1963). It has been regularly asked in the General Social Survey in the United States and periodically in the American National Election Studies. Cross-nationally, it has been asked in each wave of the World Values Survey. The measure here comes from the 1990 and 1995 waves (most recent figure used). For an analysis of why the question refers to trust in strangers and a more general defense of the question, see Uslaner (2002: ch. 3). The cross-national analysis omits countries with a legacy of Communism. I do not do so here, but I do omit China, since it has an anomalously high trust value (see Uslaner, 2002: 226, n. 6).

8. The variables used to impute trust are: gross national product per capital; the value of imports of goods and services; legislative effectiveness; head of state type; tenure of

executive (all from the State Failure Data Set); distance from the equator (from Jong-sung You of Harvard University); and openness of the economy (from Sachs and Warner, 1997; data available at www.cid.harvard.edu/ciddata/ciddata.html).The $R^2 = .657$, standard error of the estimate $= .087$, $N = 63$.

9. Three outliers stand out – Saudi Arabia, Morocco and Greece, all of which likely have estimates of trust that seem unrealistically high. The Greek estimate of trust is from the World Values Survey, which places it between Canada and Finland and far ahead of more similar states such as Italy, Turkey and Spain. Greek scholars have told me that they question this score. The values for Saudi Arabia and Morocco are close to New Zealand and Finland, on the one hand, and West Germany and Great Britain on the other. These values are imputed and thus may not be as reliable. Without these countries, the R^2 rises to .478.

References

Almond, Gabriel and Sidney Verba (1963), *The Civic Culture*, Princeton, NJ: Princeton University Press.

Banfield, Edward (1958), *The Moral Basis of a Backward Society*, New York: Free Press.

Boix, Carles and Daniel N. Posner (1998), 'Social capital: explaining its origins and effects on government performance', *British Journal of Political Science*, **28**, 686–74.

Deininger, Klaus and Lyn Squire (1996), 'A new data set: measuring economic income inequality', *World Bank Economic Review*, **10**, 565–92.

Della Porta, Dontella and Alberto Vannucci (1999), *Corrupt Exchanges: Actors, Resources, and Mechanisms of Political Corruption*, New York: Aldine de Gruyter.

DiFrancesco, Wayne and Zvi Gitelman (1984), 'Soviet political culture and "covert participation" in policy implementation', *American Political Science Review*, **78**, 603–21.

Fisman, Raymond and Roberta Gatti (2000), *Decentralization and Corruption: Evidence Across Countries*, Washington, DC: World Bank.

Fox, Jonathan (2006), 'World separation of religion and state into the 21st century', *Comparative Political Studies*, **39**, 537–69.

Gambetta, Diego (1993), *The Sicilian Mafia: The Business of Private Protection*, Cambridge, MA: Harvard University Press.

Gambetta, Diego (2002), 'Corruption: An Analytical Map', in Stephen Kotkin and Andras Sajo (eds), *Political Corruption in Transition: A Skeptic's Handbook*, Budapest: CEU Press.

Glaeser, Edward L., Jose Scheinkman and A. Shleifer (2003), 'The injustice of inequality', *Journal of Monetary Economics*, **50**, 199–222.

Kornai, Janos (2000), 'Hidden in an envelope: gratitude payments to medical doctors in Hungary', www.colbud.hu/honesty-trust/kornai/pub01.PDF.

Lambsdorff, Johann Graf (2002), 'What nurtures corrupt deals? on the role of confidence and transaction costs', in Donna della Porta and Susan Rose-Ackerman (eds), *Corrupt Exchanges*, Baden Baden: Nomos Verlag, pp. 20–36.

Mauro, Paolo (1998), 'Corruption: causes, consequences, and agenda for further research', *Finance and Development* (International Monetary Fund), March, 11–14.

Mauro, Paolo (2004), 'The persistence of corruption and slow economic growth', IMF Staff Papers, 51, 1, Washington: International Monetary Fund.

Mbaku, John Mukum (1998), 'Corruption and the crisis of institutional reforms in Africa', in John Mukum Mbaku (eds), *Corruption and the Crisis of Institutional Reforms in Africa*, Lewiston, ME: Edward Mellen Press, pp. 237–62.

Miller, William L., Ase B. Grodeland and Tatyana Y. Koshechkina (2001), *A Culture of Corruption: Coping with Government in Post-Communist Europe*, Budapest: CEU Press.

Mungiu-Pippidi, Alina (1997), 'Crime and corruption after communism: breaking free at last: tales of corruption from the postcommunist Balkans', *East European Constitutional Review*, www.law.nyu.edu/eecr/vol6num4/feature/breakingfree.html (accessed 28 September 2006).

Murphy, Kim (2006), 'Forging ahead in Moscow', *Los Angeles Times*, 10 July, www.latimes. com/news/nationworld/la-fg-fakes19jul10,0,5893954.story?coll-la-home-headlines.

Owsiak, Stanislaw (2003), 'The ethics of tax collection', *Finance and Common Good*, **13/14**, 65–77.

Packer, George (2006), 'The megacity: decoding the chaos of Lagos', *The New Yorker*, 13 November, 63–75.

Riordan, William (1948), *Plunkitt of Tammany Hall*, New York: Alfred A. Knopf.

Rothstein, Bo and Dietlind Stolle (2002), 'How political institutions create and destroy social capital: an institutional theory of generalized trust', paper prepared for delivery at the Annual Meeting of the American Political Science Association, Boston, August–September. Galbraith data available at: http://utip.gov.utexas.edu/data.html.

Rothstein, Bo and Eric M. Uslaner (2005), 'All for all: equality and social trust', *World Politics*, **58** (October), 41–72.

Sachs, Jeffrey D. and Andrew M. Warner (1997), 'Natural resource abundance and economic growth', Harvard University Center for International Development, www2.cid.harvard. edu/Warner's%20Files/Natresf5.pdf (accessed 5 December 2005).

Sampson, Steven (2005), 'Integrity warriors: global morality and the anticorruption movement in the Balkans', in Chris Shore and Dieter Hall (eds), *Corruption: Anthropological Perspectives*, London: Routledge. Pages from manuscript.

Schoenfeld, Eugen (1978), 'Image of man: the effect of religion on trust', *Review of Religious Research*, **20**, 61–7.

Seligman, Adam B. (1997), *The Problem of Trust*, Princeton, NJ: Princeton University Press.

Tanzi, Vito (1998), 'Corruption around the world: causes, consequences, scope and cures', *IMF Staff Papers*, **45**, 559–94.

Tavernise, Sabrina (2003), 'Russia is mostly unmoved by the troubles of its tycoons', *New York Times*, Washington edition, 3 November, A3.

Treisman, Daniel (1999), 'Decentralization and corruption: why are federal states perceived to be more corrupt?', presented at the Annual Meeting of the American Political Science Association, September, Atlanta.

Uslaner, Eric M. (2001), 'Volunteering and social capital: how trust and religion shape civic participation in the United States', in Paul Dekker and Eric M. Uslaner (eds), *Social Capital and Participation in Everyday Life*, London: Routledge, pp. 104–17.

Uslaner, Eric M. (2002), *The Moral Foundations of Trust*, New York: Cambridge University Press.

Uslaner, Eric M. (2003), 'Trust and civic engagement in East and West', in Gabriel Badescu and Eric M. Uslaner (eds), *Social Capital and the Transition to Democracy*, London: Routledge, pp. 81–94.

Uslaner, Eric M. (2004), 'Trust and corruption', in Johann Graf Lambsdorff, Markus Taube and Matthias Schramm (eds), *Corruption and the New Institutional Economics*, London: Routledge, pp. 76–92.

Uslaner, Eric M. (2006), 'The civil state: trust, polarization, and the quality of state government', in Jeffrey Cohen (ed.), *Public Opinion in State Politics*, Stanford, CA: Stanford University Press, pp. 142–62.

Uslaner, Eric M. (2008), *Corruption, Inequality, and Trust*: The Bulging Pocket Makes the Easy Life, New York: Cambridge University Press.

Uslaner, Eric M. and Mitchell Brown (2005), 'Inequality, trust, and civic engagement', *American Politics Research*, **31**, 868–94.

Varese, Frederico (1997), *The Russian Mafia: Private Protection in a New Market Economy*, Oxford: Oxford University Press.

Verdery, Katherine (1993), 'Nationalism and national sentiment in post-socialist Romania', *Slavic Review*, **52**, 179–203.

World Values Survey (1981, 1990, 1995–97), N.d. Machine-readable database (Waves 1–3), www.worldvaluessurvey.org.

You, Jong-sung and Sanjeev Khagram (2005), 'A comparative study of inequality and corruption', *American Sociological Review*, **70** (February), 136–57.

9 Social capital: the dark side
Peter Graeff

Introduction

In the past decade, the concept of social capital gained tremendous popularity in social science literature. Beside the classical factors of production and human capital, it has now a proper place in the academic discussion. Social capital occurs when people use social relationships to accomplish personal goals. While this idea was picked up in various theoretical concepts, the positive consequences of social capital dominated the scientific debate. Especially if social capital is associated with people's participation in networks and with interpersonal trust, it was identified as an important resource to solve collective problems (Putnam, 1993). It does have an economic pay-off in the sense that economies with bigger stocks of social capital are more prosperous and grow faster (Knack and Keefer, 1997).

But in order to understand the forces driving social capital relationships and to get a more complete picture, negative implications of the social processes deserve attention as well. In literature, negative consequences are inherently part of special social bonds. They are, however, seldom considered as those.

Take as an example the distinction between bridging and bonding social capital (Putnam, 2000). These categories refer to the type of cohesion when people are brought together: bridging social capital emerges among heterogeneous group members and bonding social capital takes place among homogeneous members. Bonding ties are aiming at the social network itself and do leave little space for people with different characteristics than those the group members already possess. Typical examples are ethnic groups or institutions that compete with other social groups and gain privileges at their expense. In contrast, bridging social capital refers to those ties that are open for people not belonging to the network yet such as ecumenical movements that try to reduce existing conflicts between religious groups.

Even if Putnam (2000) states that this distinction is rather a matter of degree and not a categorization, so that no social group can be exactly labelled as bonding or bridging, the preponderance of examples with negative societal consequences of social capital belong to those groups with a stronger tendency for bonding ties. Therefore, it might be useful to assess the effect of different social capital types for society as a whole (Larsen et al., 2004) or other social groups in particular. In criminology, almost every offence that is committed with the help of others relies on bonding ties which become vital for the success and the survival of the group. Consequently, socially deviant actions that come at the expense of other members in society hardly reveal properties of bridging ties.

Although interest in the adverse effects of social capital seems to be increasing, only a few theoretical and empirical contributions exist so far (Portes, 1998; Putnam, 2000; Fisman and Miguel, 2006). The goal of this contribution is to examine a special form of bonding social capital, namely the negative consequences of corruption norms, and to investigate the conditions and forces of the actors at play. As a working definition, corruption norm can be understood as the expectation in a certain situation that an actor can usually offer or accept a corrupt deal.

The chapter is organized as follows. In the first section, I examine the link between norms and social capital. I explain why corruption norms must be regarded as social capital which, although it has the definition features of positive sociability, leads to negative consequences. In the second section, I examine the reasons for the special implications of corruption norms and refer to typical conditions of corrupt deals. Rational choice theory provides a fertile ground for analysing the actions and conditions of corrupt actors. In the third section, the preconditions, characteristics and implications of corruption norms are determined and some empirical results are reported. Finally, I embed the theoretical and empirical findings into the social capital debate.

Norms and social capital: definition and theoretical implications
In order to shed some light on the relationship between social capital, norms and corruption, using the Coleman approach as a starting point has the advantage of providing a theoretical basis of both social capital and norms. Almost all theorists agree that social capital is a feature of the relationship between persons. Referring to the insights of former researchers (such as Granovetter, 1985, or Lin, 1990), Coleman (1990: 302) provides this special notion of social capital: 'It is not a single entity, but a variety of different entities having two characteristics in common: They all consist of some aspects of a social structure and they facilitate certain actions of individuals who are within the structure.' Although the term 'social structure' needs clarification in actual social settings, referring to the criterion of action facilitation implies that the benefit of social capital lies in its function, namely the achievement of particular aims that would not be attainable otherwise. Different from other capital forms, social capital is not tradable and only restrictively fungible.[1] Therefore, it is not the 'private property' of the actors who are involved in the social capital relationship.

Norms can be considered as a special form of social capital. Norms adhere (like social capital) to the social structure; they are not a property or a feature of the actors themselves. Coleman (1990: 243) puts it this way: 'I will say that a norm concerning a specific action exists when the socially defined right to control the action is held by others. . . . this implies that there is a consensus in the social system or subsystem that the right to control the action is held by others.' With this definition, he aims at informally based agreements and refrains from laws and other legal measures which can be interpreted as norms, too. This definition implies that the maintenance of norms depends on their regular practice (Popitz, 1980: 10). On the individual level, actors 'feel' obliged to comply with social regularities. The actors' obligation is often supported by the threat of other people's sanctions (because other people hold the right to control the actions and to punish trespassing against the norms). In this sense, norms become behavioural rules and can be considered as driving actions 'if any departure of real behavior from the norm is followed by some punishment' (Homans, 1950: 123).

The social aim of norms lies in encouraging and restricting actions. Their emergence is tightly related to this aim. Norms provide (usually) positive consequences for people who obey these norms and this might be the major reason why groups or a society has an interest in establishing these norms. This reason is, however, 'functionalistic', and may not count as a real explanation for the emergence of norms because it is not clear what causes the actors to give up the right to control the action.

When explaining the emergence of norms, the (public) surmounting of externalities is a better approach. As a mechanism of social coordination, norms appear if actors are not able to eliminate externalities via market or negotiation activities. Consider administrative guidelines as an example. Those guidelines might cause externalities to public officials and citizens by making administrative processes more complicated than they should be. To overcome these externalities, public officials and citizens might find a way to reduce the administrative complexity. Usually, this is only possible by deviating from the official guidelines. If these deviations happen regularly (so that people can expect their occurrence) and if people will sanction others insistence on following the guidelines, a norm has emerged.[2]

The sanctioning of others is easier and more likely when social relationships are tighter. Small groups and close relationships have the best potential to maintain existing norms by punishing those who deviate. Friendships, for instance, sometimes develop their own set of norms. The friends' social closeness is tightly connected to upholding these norms. In families, special norms also emerge although it is more difficult to exclude someone from the family than from the friendship if he or she deviates.

Close socials nets (either based on family kinship or sympathy) establish and maintain group norms more efficiently than they maintain norms which are also valid outside the group. This is because the people who deviate and who sanction belong to the same group. Popitz (1980) perceives close social nets as a (small) 'society' on their own, differing from the public. Sanctions which are applied in groups due to norm trespassing differ from sanctions due to norm violations in general. The sanctioning of norm violations which could be prosecuted in the public could be done by everybody but the actual sanctioning is less likely. The prosecution of norm violations in close social nets could only be done by group members and is, therefore, more likely.

In a certain sense, norms can be treated as social capital. They make certain actions easier but they also prohibit some others. Coleman (1990: 311) provides some examples:

> A prescriptive norm that constitutes an especially important form of social capital within a collectivity is the norm that one should forgo self-interests to act in the interests of the collectivity. A norm of this sort, reinforced by social support, status, honor, and other rewards, is the social capital which builds young nations (and which dissipates as they grow older), strengthens families by leading members to act selflessly in the family's interest, facilitates the development of nascent social movements from a small group of dedicated, inward-looking, and mutually rewarding persons, and in general leads persons to work for the public good.

Such norms are mechanisms of social coordination and derive their social importance from their contribution to solve problems of procurement or public goods.

The positive character of this mechanism might entice one to consider its social consequences as unreservedly favourable although it is obvious that the facilitation of certain actions comes at the expense of restricting several others. Norms, for instance, that allow women to walk the streets at night also limit the actions of criminals (Coleman, 1990: 311).[3] Traditional rules that tie children to their family even as adults and aim at maintaining a strictly hierarchical family order may contribute to a family's stability and cohesion. But this happens at the expense of their family members' individuality and freedom.

As there is no norm (associated with social capital) that facilitates certain actions without restricting others, the social consequences of 'social capital norms' are not positive in any situation. Arguably, the assessment of actions as good or bad depends on the cultural settings, the political conditions and the social aims. But it seems worthwhile to note that the inherent ambiguity of norms due to the fact that they allow actions at the expense of constraining others suggests a 'dark' side of social capital as well.

Portes (1998) provides some negative examples of social capital when social control becomes too excessive. By these illustrations, the excessively bonding nature of social capital becomes clear. Referring to Waldinger (1995), he describes the strong social control processes that immigrants in their ethnic group are exposed to. The groups might create economic advantages for their members and generate a feeling of comradeship and solidarity. But this implicitly restricts relations with non-group members and limits exchanges with them. Communities or groups, in which social capital fosters the economic prosperity of their members by reducing transaction cost, realize their economic and social surplus most often by effectively enforcing certain group norms. A high degree of social control is a necessary prerequisite to solve the free-rider problem. The existence of social control also implies restrictions of individual freedom. For example, members of rural populations usually know each other personally and are, therefore, able to build up a strong social network and robust social ties. Under these conditions, it is easy to implement associations of neighbours that provide help, for instance, with homework, gardening or security. But these associations only work at the expense of restriction personal freedom and choices.[4]

Tight social networks can be excessively exacting to their members. They exchange individual freedoms for group care. Traditional families are a good example (Hofferth et al., 1999) because – according to Rumbaut (1977: 39) – 'family ties bind, but sometimes these bonds constrain rather than facilitate particular outcomes'. This aspect can be shown in countries where traditional family roles and systems still exist (as in China or in the south of Italy). Since tight social networks include demands on and duties of their members, family membership also implies responsibility for the wealth of other family members. In China, it is no exception that economically successful family members 'support' less successful ones. This has not only positive consequences as Portes (1998: 16) explains: 'Thus, cozy intergroup relations of the kind found in highly solidarity communities can give rise to a gigantic free-riding problem, as less diligent members enforce on the more successful all kinds of demands backed by shared normative structure.'

Another example of dark social capital appears when communities try to reduce the individuality of their members (which is more or less an attempt to bring more homogeneous people together). If, for instance, groups or solidarity communities compete with other groups, norms might be used as a tool to standardize and homogenize their members' behaviour and attitudes in order to align them with the group aims. A situation of competition forces a group to ensure that all members hold an attitude of solidarity. It is crucial that the group members believe that only a joint effort will prevail and that individual efforts are in vain. Portes (1998: 17) puts it this way: 'In these instances, individual success stories undermine group cohesion because the latter is precisely grounded on the alleged impossibility of such occurrences. The result is downward levelling norms that operate to keep members of a down-trodden group in place.'

Downward-levelling norms reduce the opportunity of single persons to reach the group aim and increase the members' dependence on the group. These norms apply often in gangs or military units in which the survival hinges on group solidarity. Even though the homogeneity of their members is the most crucial aspect, the supporting features of these relationships are bonding characteristics.

Another example of the harmful consequence of social capital (which is not explicitly related to norms) is associated with rent-seeking or lobbying that occurs if people or groups strive for artificial rents without investing into productive activities. The rent-seeking literature implies that well-established groups in a democratic system hamper economic and social prosperity by demanding excessively large shares of national resources for themselves (Olson, 1984) or by obstructing economic improvements. For society, the social capital of rent-seeking or lobbying groups leads – owing to the groups' goals particularistic character – to the negative social outcome which are imposed at the expense of the general public.

In all those cases, social capital can be also considered as a public 'evil' that does not lead to favourable social outcomes. The main idea inherent in all examples is the divergence of public norms and special group norms.

In order to analyse some dynamics underlying the processes of special group norms with negative externalities, corruption norms are further scrutinized since these provide good examples of 'dark' social capital.

Social capital and the social aspects of corruption

Corruption – in its broadest sense usually defined as the abuse of public positions for private gain (Nye, 1967) – involves several social aspects which are explained best by a three-actor model (Banfield, 1975). The 'principal' assigns (decision) power and resources to the agent. The 'agent' abuses his public position for private gain and grants the 'client' a benefit which was made possible by the corrupt deal. Only agent and client need to be real persons, the principal can also be a person (such as the leader of a department), but also an authority or department or the state itself. The agent breaks a rule (given by the principal or by formal law) in order to pass an illegal benefit to the client. This is how a corrupt deal or exchange takes place (see Figure 9.1).[5]

Corruption presupposes the breaking of a (formal or informal) contractual agreement between principal and agent. This contract concedes a sphere of responsibility and some decision latitude to the agent. The agent

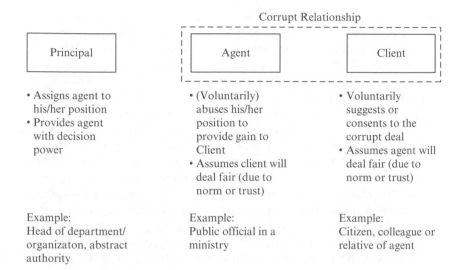

Figure 9.1   Three-actor model of corruption

takes advantage of this leeway on his and the client's behalf but without the principals' knowledge. Correspondingly, the client pays off the agent for the abuse of his position.

Within corrupt deals, all sorts of people and groups, such as families, friends, political parties or institutions, can be favoured. But the actual exchange always occurs between real people only – between legal people or organizations corruption is inconceivable. Corruptly behaving people are aware of the illegality of their exchange and try to be secretive about it. In most legal systems, corruption is treated as a voluntary act that involves deliberation. Since corrupt deals must be considered as organized and pre-meditated, the theoretical analysis of corrupt exchanges should analyse the decisions of the participants as well. One special characteristic of corrupt deals is the fact that actors voluntarily take part in the illegal exchange. In contrast, blackmail denotes a situation when an actor is forced to par-ticipate in an illegal exchange. The conditions and explanations of such criminal acts differ from those regarding corruption.

In literature, three characteristics of corruption can be found (which are used by most of the researchers – see Lambsdorff (2002) for an overview): a corrupt deal is illegal (and the perpetrators are liable to prosecution), the deals happen only in privacy[6] and the agreement cannot be imposed by bringing this case to court. The latter point suggests that the decision situ-ation must include certain conditions in order to let the actors consent to a corrupt offer (Graeff, 2005: 42): if the actors behave rationally (and this seems to be a reasonable assumption because corrupt deals occur deliberately *and* voluntarily), they will only accept or offer a corrupt exchange if every actor assumes that his partner will accomplish his part of the deal. This form of reciprocity is a necessary condition for making or accepting corrupt offers as long as the three mentioned situational circumstances are valid. The criminal act implies the risk of being sanctioned (Coleman, 1990: 147) and because every actor could expose the corrupt deal (at the expense of his own prosecution), the deliberate consent to corruption involves the belief that the corrupt exchange is beneficial to all participants. Evidently, the corrupt partners must also accept the negative externalities for non-participants as particularistic interests outweigh universalistic interests in every corrupt deal (what entails necessarily the emergence of negative external effects). Therefore, the corrupt deal should occur in private so that the negative externalities do not become public.

If we focus on the main part of the decision problem – namely, the 'reciprocity assumption' (that is, the question: 'when can I assume that my partner will accomplish his part of the deal') – two social mechanisms providing the subjective certainty about the success of an intended corrupt deal are conceivable: trust and norms.

Mechanisms of trust apply in situations in which the corrupt actors have specific knowledge about each other, most often because they have known each other for a long time or are, at least, acquaintances or even friends. The reciprocity originates from the same information background in the same way that the shared knowledge about each other simplifies the decision to make a corrupt offer. As it is likely that they will deal with each other again (because of their common 'history'), sanctions (outside the corrupt deal) for deviating from the corrupt agreement are possible. Corrupt exchanges relying on mutual trust can be arranged individually in accordance with the specific claims of the actors.[7]

While specific knowledge and trust, accordingly, provide subjective certainty about the the the mutual commitment to a prospective deal, another social mechanism applies if trust cannot be given owing to a lack of knowledge about the potential corruption partner. Norms are able to regulate corrupt deals in the absence of trust if those norms clearly define what a corruptly behaving actor should do. The general knowledge about how people should behave in certain corruption situations implies the reciprocity between actors if the situation actually happens. By this, a norm directs the illegal exchanges by suggesting what is 'normal' in such a situation.[8]

Preconditions, characteristics and implications of corruption norms
There are several examples of norms that foster corruption by implying the reciprocity between the agent and the client. They all accomplish

this by setting a behaviour frame in advance that involves social ties or obligations.

Among them, the Chinese *guanxi* networks have been broadly discussed in literature (Schweitzer, 2005). The term *guanxi* means certain forms of obligations between members of a network (Fan, 2002) which were important – in medieval China – to stabilize social and public relations and to secure economic exchanges (Schramm and Taube, 2005: 183). With the strengthening of the formal legal system in modern times, these very important and widespread networks get in the way of legal processing. This is because the network or group norms often clash with the laws. This leads to a competition between two norm systems or, as Schramm and Taube (2005: 192) put it: 'The same transaction that would be regarded as "corrupt" from the perspective of a universalistic system of order might constitute norm-conforming behaviour when seen from the perspective of a personalistic-bound ordering system like a *guanxi* network.'

In the modern understanding of the term, corruption always presupposes the distinction between the public and private role of the agent (Rose-Ackerman, 1999: 91). Depending on a society's level of functional differentiation, corruption becomes very likely if this distinction is blurred. This effect is aggravated by traditions which foster a personal mutual exchange. For example, in some African countries, gifts are an adequate feedback for services received, even if this service was provided by a public official in his line of duty. Formal agent–client relationships are perceived as queer and unnatural. In such a situation, bribes and gifts are hardly distinguishable. In general, it differs from country to country how public officials are perceived formally. The more the role might be interpreted as allowing informal exchanges (for example, the acceptance of gifts is probable), the more likely is the abuse of this public position.

Because corruption norms are closely tied to traditional attitudes and rules, they are the outcome of a learning process only. The traditional aspects ensure that they are frequently refreshed by regular repetition. They are not part of the biological endowment of a society, although they are deeply ingrained in the society's fabric.

Corruption norms do not emerge due to a lack of legal order. On the contrary, they arise because of existing legal norms or laws which – most probably – lead to a negative external effect.[9] Exact guidelines or laws can become grounds for planning agent–client matters beside the legal proceedings.

Corruption norms depend on cultural settings and differ among civilizations. This refers to the fact that what is perceived as an appropriate social private and public behaviour is the result of a social appraisal. In an extreme case, there is ambivalence about the assessment of corrupt deeds and deals due to insecurity about which norms are actually valid and legal (Blankenburg et al., 1999: 929). According to Schweitzer (2002), the assessment of actions as legal or illegal is only of secondary importance: whether a norm is valid or not depends on the political assessment, not on statutory law and is, therefore, a consequence of the distribution of power in a society.

The ambiguity of half-legal actions (subsuming herein also the blurred corruption deals) is only prevented by establishing *one* binding and reliable norm.

Usually, these processes in which contrasting norms are adjusted are triggered by public scandals (Tumber and Waisbord, 2004). Scandals rip the masks off the agents' faces that render them impersonal (Moodie, 1980) – scandals bring the accusation down to a personal level which is mostly feared by corrupt actors. The media play an important role in this norm adjustment process when they become an amplifier for different opinions. Because there are usually different views about what is right and wrong among the public, the mediating process of scandals by the media is not a very effective one.

As a social mechanism, corruption norms generate a social scope for actors who want to act in their own particular interest at the expense of universalistic interests. If these norms belong to traditional aspects of the society, the corrupt actions derived are mostly illegal but seldom illegitimate. Even in modern societies legal 'loopholes' exist which give actors an opportunity to harmonize particularistic and universalistic interests via corrupt exchanges (Smelser, 1971). In this situation, corruption norms serve as a social 'tool' to bring individual and public interests into accordance with each other. As part of the public system of norms, corruption norms allow actors to strive for their very own interest at the expense of the public. This begs the political question: to what degree is a society willing to accept this 'harmonization' given the evident disadvantages? If corruption norms are prevalent in a society a situation of 'systemic corruption' occurs in which politicians are among the beneficiaries and have very little interest to change the situation. 'Systemic corruption' occurs in those societies which are unable to solve conflicts in their normative systems (Schweitzer, 2002). If universalistic norms do not prevail over particularistic ones, people cannot be prevented from realizing their private gain at the expense of society as a whole. As mentioned before, solidarity groups (Popitz, 1980: 89) expand the opportunity to sanction behaviour deviating from inner group norms and make consequently the occurrence of corruption norms (contradicting existing norms) more likely.

The most crucial point about the characteristics of corruption norms is its necessary competition with existing legal norms. Corruption norms only exist in the shadow of public rules and regulations. They are dark social

Table 9.1   Preconditions, characteristics, and consequences of corruption
             norms

Preconditions for the emergence of corruption norms	Traditions implying a low degree of differentiation between the private and public roles Weakness of legal enforcement/strongly sanctioning group norm violations (Strong) existing legal guidelines or laws Norm ambiguity
Characteristics of corruption norms	Facilitating actions for group members in violation of universalistic rules Contradicting legal norms
Consequences of corruption norms	More corruption becomes more likely because the corrupt exchange no longer relies on a specific corruption partner Inefficient administration entailing a special relationship between politicians/public officials and citizens

capital in the way that they facilitate the actions of group members at the expense of universalistic statutes.

The existence of this dark social capital entails a special relationship between politics or the employees of the public administration and the citizens: namely, that formal aspects have become secondary and that administrative processing depends on the arbitrariness of people who use this social capital in their own interest.

The main issues about the features of corruption norms are summarized in Table 9.1.

Measuring corruption norms: an illustration
To measure corruption norms we can take advantage of the fact that they contradict existing norms. A strong attitude implying that particularistic interests are clearly favoured over universalistic ones might work as an indicator for the susceptibility of corrupt deals. Unfortunately, the empirical analysis is limited by a restriction: a direct measure for the divergence of legal and specific group norms is not available. One might manage this problem with the application of personal issues depicting 'strong' attitudes. In this sense, all types of issues with a clear particularistic character might apply as indicator for potential norm conflicts. The particularistic effect might be increased if the issue involves emotional content.

In every society, families are groups with the highest degree of intimacy and trust. The relationship between parents and children in modern society is (from the parents' point of view) less important owing to functionalistic reasons (such as a provision for old age) but valuable owing to emotional connections. It seems reasonable to suppose that norms referring to this private space might easily get in the way of universalistic rules.

In order to test this hypothesis, one could refer to the World Values Survey measures of 'family norms'. Among the variety of items which could be used, the item 'norm of respect for parents' seems to be a suitable one in order to depict a strong particularistic norm. This item reads: 'Regardless of what the qualities and faults of one's parents are, one must always love and respect them.'

The variable 'respect for parents' depicts the situation when family values do not depend on actual events or experiences, for example, the assessment of the parents is not oriented to universalistic values of the society.[10] The right to have their own assessments of their parents is not held by the children. This norm has a clear particularistic character. It does not have to jeopardize universalistic norms per se but it has the potential to do so.

In order to examine the impact of these variables in a multivariate model, two control variables were used. These turned out to be the strongest determinants of corruption (Treisman, 2000; Paldam, 2002; Uslaner, 2005; Paldam and Svendsen, 2006): the level of economic development and generalized trust. If this particularistic norm contributes to the explanation of corruption in a multivariate model, it should exert a significant effect on corruption even when the control variables are also considered in the model.

In order to test the proposed hypothesis, aggregated country for 61 nations are used, referring to the time period of the fourth wave of the World Value Survey (2001–03). The dependent variable is the Corruption Perception Index (CPI) published by Transparency International Berlin.

The CPI is the compilation of different survey data. It measures corruption from 0 (highest degree of corruption) to 10 (no corruption). To make results easier to interpret, for this analysis the scale is inverted so that high CPI scores indicate a high level of corruption. The measurement of perceived corruption includes assessments of the extent of illegal behaviour in a country in general.

The multivariate model yields this result:[11]

$$\text{Inverted CPI} = 6.62^{(*)} \text{ Intercept} + 0.04^{(**)} \text{ Norm of respect}$$
$$- 0.02^{(**)} \text{ Trust} - 1.53^{(**)} \text{ Ln GDP pc}$$

One asterisk in parentheses behind the regression coefficients denote the 10 per cent significance level (one tailed, estimated with White-corrected standard errors). Two asterisks indicate the 5 per cent significance level, accordingly. The model explains 75 per cent of the total variance.

Leaving the intercept out of interpretation, the other variables perform as theoretically expected. The stronger the norms of respect in a country, the higher the corruption level will be, which is indicated by the positive sign. This effect is significant on the 5 per cent level. Higher degrees of generalized trust and economic wealth curb corruption. These effects are also significant on the 5 per cent level.

These results can be cross-validated with smaller samples from earlier waves of the World Value Survey. The corruption increasing influence of the norm of respect always turns out to be significant, even controlled for the strongest determinants of corruption.

To test for potential influences of endogeneity, a two stages least squares (TSLS) regression was applied with the lagged variables of generalized trust (derived from earlier World Value Survey waves) and economic wealth as instruments. Since norms which are not directly associated with the moral assessment of non-family members are not affected by changes in the corruption level of a country, they can be treated as exogenous.

The TSLS estimation affirms the former results. The size of the *t*-values and the coefficients are more moderate but still significant with the sign in the expected direction.

These results show that particularistic norms add to the explanation of corruption, even when the strongest determinants are simultaneously considered. Corruption norms are antagonistic to the positive consequences of generalized trust and increases in wealth. This fits the theoretical expectations but also points to the fact that the negative consequences of social capital deserve a place in theory and empirics.

Conclusion

The danger of corruption norms lies in the fact that they provide the general knowledge about consenting to a corrupt offer regardless of the characteristics of the corruption partner. If norms drive the corrupt behaviour the partners are fungible. If trust is the source of the corrupt deal, the specific partner is not fungible. This difference points to theoretical expansion of social capital theory. Coleman (1990) suggests that social capital is not fungible, but this is not true if corruption norms are considered as mechanisms which facilitate achieving goals that are not attainable otherwise! There seems to be a difference between the implications of social capital which has, in sum, more positive social consequences (such as norms that prevent crimes) and social capital which must be considered as 'un-social' because of its inherent emphasis of particularistic elements. The latter property exists in conjunction with its bonding social capital features. Even when bonding social capital is defined by its social cohesion, this property can only exist if others are excluded. The exclusion is not a sufficient criterion for the occurrence of bonding social capital but it stands as a necessary one.

Established corruption norms suggest that corruption has become the normal state in a society. In return, the actual state of a society sets the frame of the people's expectation about how life will be. Here seems to be another difference to social capital theory which focuses on the positive consequences only: 'positive norms' are considered to be weak and fragile forms of social capital. But corruption norms which imply reciprocity between strangers can be stable forms of (negative) social capital when they (subjectively) affirm illegal events that tie their perpetrators together.

Corruption norms are the result of learning processes. This implies that already learned habits are generalized to similar situations. Fisman and Miguel (2006) demonstrate this effect in their study. Diplomats from high corruption countries who enjoy zero legal enforcement for parking violations (owing to their diplomatic immunity) commit significantly more parking violations than diplomats from countries with lower levels of corruption. Although this does not depict a corruption norm in terms of an agent–client relationship, it clearly shows that norms – as clues for actions in unknown settings or in dealing with strangers – are deeply internalized and will be transferred to other situations/countries as well. According to Durkheim (1925), the family is the first and most important institution leading a child's effort to become a member who fits in society. Families are the fundamental basis of society. But they are also the breeding ground for the particularistic tendencies which are responsible for the clash of norms that lead to corruption. The role of the family for the explanation of illegal transactions has been regarded often in literature. Ben-Porath (1980) emphasizes the importance of the identity of persons in order to establish exchange relationships with low transaction costs. The same happens in ongoing corrupt exchanges in which the actors decrease their transaction cost by generating mutual trust. On an aggregate level of society, these reductions of transaction cost can be achieved by norms, although certain transaction cost for the corrupt actors still remain.

If one wants to derive policy recommendations for tackling problems of corruption due to 'dark' social capital, at least two aspects can be focused on (see Table 9.2). As the exclusion of others is a distinctive feature of corrupt transaction, making administrative processes transparent seems to be more auspicious than simple monitoring measures. Because the problem lies in the social bonds not in the (incompleteness of) working contracts, the relevant aspects leading to corrupt transactions can only be monitored to a certain degree. Working in groups might also help to overcome

Table 9.2   Some features of 'dark' social capital and policy recommendations for combating corruption

Feature of 'dark' social capital	Policy recommendations
Exclusion of others	Transparent processing, not (only) monitoring
	Working in groups
Learning/generalization of norms	Development of non-corrupt codes of practice
	Providing incentives for obeying the rules
	(Providing information about the usefulness of these codes)

particularistic tendencies created to exclude other people. It is, however, not a magic bullet, as – even larger groups – tend to create their own rules and norms pretty fast.

People adapt to given situations, for example, working conditions. In other words, they learn how to manage difficulties or they pick up already established habits in organizations and firms. The fact that corruption norms are the product of a learning process is both a good and a bad message. On the one hand, it implies that people can get 'spoiled' by the organizations and firms they are working with. It also implies that they generalize their experiences to other institutions or companies if they change their place of employment. On the other hand, people might also pick up non-corrupt codes of practice if generally offered by the organization. For this, favourable ways of working and codes of conduct have to become explicit. If possible, these aspects should be part of the organizations overall concept. Because these 'good practices' should be clear for all, it might be advisable to offer incentives for meeting these commitments. Rewarding desired behaviour seems to be more useful than punishing deviations. As this 'positive' strategy to maintain certain practices should be deliberately reflected, it could also be of advantage to provide information about the overall usefulness of these practices.

It is contrary to every corrupt deal if information becomes known about it. Publicizing aspects of corruption norms is not only a good way for organizations to take action against it. The renewed interest in the consequences of corruption norms (at this point in time mostly documented by working papers, such as Lazzarini et al., 2005, Sandholtz and Gray, 2003, and Fisman and Miguel, 2006) should be considered in the framework of social capital theory. The reference to this framework ensures not only the existence of a common theoretical basis; it also adds to the theoretical development of this theory by enhancing the heuristic value of this concept.

Notes

1. If corrupt transactions are considered, social capital is fungible with respect to specific actions. This is true if actors work as mediators for initiating or facilitating corrupt deals (Graeff, 2005: 56).
2. If corruption is considered, it is often the case that public officials create opportunities to earn some extra money. If their behaviour has a norm status, red tape and administrative obstacles are used as reasons to offer corrupt or exploitative administrative short cuts. Thus, norms occur both by intention and by regular practice.
3. A normative argumentation would here deviate from a scientific one. Most people – even criminals themselves – would prefer living conditions in a society in which norms prohibit the occurrence of crimes. In most cases, it seems evident what should be forbidden by norms, rendering people that trespass these rules as bad persons. From this point of view, crimes are bad and offenders must be punished. Owing to the variety of possible perceptions of norms and rules and owing to the lack of objective criteria for favouring one norm or rule over all others, a scientific argumentation would refrain from treating norms as good or bad. Scientifically, it is, however, of interest to understand the mechanisms of how norms work regardless of their social appraisal. Then, one might make suggestions to restrain or promote the occurrence of norms in pursuit of certain political aims (that are no inherent part of the scientific perspective). These suggestions are the results of knowledge about norm mechanisms, not just the corollary of labelling a norm as good or bad.
4. The dilemma those communities face is one of the most fundamental problems that social sciences have ever tackled. Simmel (1995) discussed this problem already in 1903. He voiced his opinion for individual freedom and individual responsibility. Social capital approaches nowadays, however, tend to give priority to the benefits of solidarity groups.
5. Particularly when it comes to a journalistic understanding of corruption, the extent of meaning of this term also includes criminal behaviour of public officials which does not involve the participation of other people. In this sense, social aspects of corruption are rescinded. As a scientific term, this understanding bears the disadvantage that every crime by public officials must be labelled as corruption. Although the term 'corruption' is open to all sorts of interpretation, I use it – in line with the scientific literature – to denote an informal agreement between an actor in a public position and his client. The participants of this corrupt deal voluntarily consent to it and both benefit from it. Because the corrupt deal is advantageous for all participants, it is not to be confused with crimes like blackmailing or exploitation.
6. This point seems to be a bit troublesome when corruption norms are considered. Norms imply that other people have knowledge about the applicability of corrupt exchanges. The knowledge about the possibility of corruption seems not to be limited to the private sphere of the actors. To solve the problem, one has to distinguish between the knowledge about a corrupt deal and the deal itself. Because the corrupt actors can be prosecuted they have a vested interest that their exchange does not happen in public. From a sociological point of view, their interest for a private exchange results from the fact that their behaviour contradicts an existing norm.
7. In corrupt exchanges, knowledge is a major reason for the emergence of trust. It is, however, not the only one. For a more elaborate discussion about the conditions and the effects of trust in corrupt relationships, see Graeff (2005).
8. At first sight, both trust and norms seem to be able to contribute to the subjective certainty simultaneously. This idea only makes sense if one assumes that general knowledge about a transaction has equal value for the decision about a corrupt deal as does

specific knowledge. In practice, specific knowledge about a transaction partner usually crowds out general knowledge insofar as it allows for organizing the corrupt exchange in accordance with the needs and wishes of the transaction partner. Specific knowledge provides certainty about a deal with a specific person. General knowledge in the form of norms provides certainty regardless of a specific transaction partner.

On the one hand, a long-term corruption exchange might be initiated by norms. But if the reciprocity is not challenged during the exchange, specific knowledge about the trust-worthiness of the specific transaction partner becomes available. And a higher degree of trust is achieved the longer and the more beneficially the transaction lasts (Husted, 1994: 21). Then, general knowledge about how to behave in corruption situations is no longer necessary. Since specific knowledge is a positive function of the frequency of corrupt deals, general knowledge must be substituted by specific knowledge if a corrupt transaction (or legal transactions with the same partner as well) continue to happen.

On the other hand, a corrupt exchange with corruption partners who do not know each other cannot be explained by trust. As trust is a function of frequent transactions, it can not be taken as an initiating factor for corrupt deals between strangers.

9. Informal mechanisms which apply in case of a lack of public order are connected to the emergence of protection groups like neighbourhood watch or – in the case of a more general breakdown of public protection – Mafia systems (Gambetta, 1993).

10 There are other variables which measure family norms and which could be used to contrast to universalistic norms such as 'the importance of family' or 'the importance of friends'. In a bivariate correlation analysis, it turns out that the 'norm of respect for parents' is significantly negative associated with 'the importance of friends' and significantly positive correlated with 'the importance of family'. The negative correlation between the norm variable and the importance of friends suggests a trade-off between family and friends. The negative correlations with non family variables connote an inward orientation of the norm of respect variable. With reference to the other control variables, high respect for parents is connected with a low level of trust and wealth. The same inward orientation can be found in the correlations between the importance of families and the trust variable although they do not turn out to be significant. The 'importance of family' variable seems to be fairly unconnected to non-family variables in general. The opposite effect – a more outward-oriented attitude – can be found in the correlations between importance of friends and the trust variable.

11. Data for Generalized Trust and the Norm of Respect Variable are taken from the WVS 2001–2003. The GDP pc data (PPP) were taken from the World Indicator CD-Rom 2005. Data for CPI and GDP pc were averaged over 2001 to 2003.

References

Banfield, Edward C. (1975), 'Corruption as a feature of governmental organisation', *Journal of Law and Economics*, **18** (3), 587–605.

Ben-Porath, Yoram (1980), 'The f-connection: families, friends, and firms and the organization of exchange', *Population and Development Review*, **6** (1), 1–30.

Blankenburg, Erhard, Rainer Staudhammer and Heinz Steinert (1999), 'Political scandals and corruption issues in West Germany', in Arnold J. Heidenheimer, Michael Johnston and Victor T. LeVine (eds), *Political Corruption. A Handbook*, 5th edn, New Brunswick, NJ: Transaction, pp. 913–32.

Coleman, James S. (1990), *Foundations of Social Theory*, Cambridge, MA: The Belknap Press of Harvard University Press.

Durkheim, Emile (1925), *Moral Education. A Study in the Theory and Application of the Sociology of Education*, New York: Free Press.

Fan, Ying (2002), 'Questioning guanxi: definition, classification, and implications', *International Business Review*, **11** (5), 543–61.

Fisman, Ray and Edward Miguel (2006), 'Cultures of corruption: evidence from diplomatic parking tickets', paper presented on the USC FBE Applied Economics Workshop, April.

Gambetta, Diego (1993), *The Sicilian Mafia. The Business of Private Protection*, London: Harvard University Press.

Graeff, Peter (2005), 'Why should one trust in corruption? The linkage between corruption, norms and social capital', in Johann Graf Lambsdorff, Markus Taube and Matthias Schramm (eds), *The New Institutional Economics of Corruption*, New York: Routledge, pp. 40–58.

Granovetter, Marc (1985), 'Economic action, social structure, and embeddedness', *American Journal of Sociology*, **83**, 1420–43.

Hofferth, Sandra L., Johanne Boisjoly and Greg J. Duncan (1999), 'The development of social capital', *Rationality and Society*, **11** (1), 79–110.

Homans, George C. (1950), *The Human Group*, New York: Harcourt Brace.

Husted, Bryan W. (1994), 'Honor among thieves: a transaction-cost interpretation of corruption in third world countries', *Business Ethics Quarterly*, **4** (1), 17–27.

Knack, Stephen and Philip Keefer (1997), 'Does social capital have an economic payoff? A cross-country investigation', *Quarterly Journal of Economics*, **112**, 1251–88.

Lambsdorff, Johann Graf (2002), 'Making corrupt deals: contracting in the shadow of law', *Journal of Economic Behaviour and Organization*, **48**, 221–41.

Larsen, Larissa, Sharon L. Harlan, Bob Bolin, Edward J. Hackett, Diane Hope, Andrew Kirby, Amy Nelson, Tom R. Rex and Shaphard Wolf (2004), 'Bonding and bridging. Understanding the relationship between social capital and civic action', *Journal of Planning Education and Research*, **24**, 64–77.

Lazzarini, Sergio G., Gary J. Miller and Todd R. Zenger (2005), 'Order with some law: complementary vs. substitution of formal and informal arrangements', *Journal of Civil Society*, **1** (1), 75–95.

Lin, Nan (1990), 'Social resources and social mobility: a structural theory of status attainment', in Ronald L. Breiger (ed.), *Social Mobility and Social Structure*, Cambridge: Cambridge University Press, pp. 247–71.

Moodie, Graeme C. (1980), 'On political scandals and corruption', *Government and Opposition*, **15** (2), 202–22.

Nye, Joseph S. (1967), 'Corruption and political development: a cost-benefit analysis', *American Political Science Review*, **61** (2), 417–27.

Olson, Mancur (1984), *The Rise and Decline of Nations*, New Haven, CT: Yale University Press.

Paldam, Martin (2002), 'The cross-country pattern of corruption. Economics, culture and the seesaw dynamics', *European Journal of Political Economy*, **18**, 215–40.

Paldam, Martin and Gert Tinggaard Svendsen (eds) (2006), *Trust, Social Capital and Economic Growth: An International Comparison*, Cheltenham, UK and Northampton, MA, USA: Edward Elgar.

Popitz, Heinrich (1980), *Die normative Konstruktion von Gesellschaft*, Tübingen: Mohr.

Portes, Alejandro (1998), 'Social capital: its origins and applications in modern sociology', *Annual Review of Sociology*, **24**, 1–24.

Putnam, Robert D. (1993), *Making Democracy Work: Civic Traditions in Modern Italy*, Princeton, NJ: Princeton University Press.

Putnam, Robert D. (2000), *Bowling Alone. The Collapse and Revival of American Community*, New York: Simon & Schuster.

Rose-Ackerman, Susan (1999), *Corruption and Development. Causes, Consequences, and Reform*, Cambridge: Cambridge University Press.

Rumbaut, Ruben G. (1977), 'Ties that bind: immigration and immigrant families in the United States', in Alan Booth, Ann C. Crouter and Nancy S. Landale (eds), *Immigration and the Family: Research and Policy on US Immigrants*, Mahwah, NJ: Erlbaum, pp. 3–45.

Sandholtz, Wayne and Mark Gray (2003), 'International integration and national corruption', *International Organization*, **57**(4), 761–800.

Schramm, Matthias and Markus Taube (2005), 'Private ordering of corrupt transactions. The case of the Chinese guanxi networks and their challenge by a formal legal system', in Johann Graf Lambsdorff, Markus Taube and Matthias Schramm (eds), *The New Institutional Economics of Corruption*, New York: Routledge, pp. 181–97.

Schweitzer, Hartmut (2002), Ideas for developing a theory of corruption, unpublished manuscript.

Schweitzer, Hartmut (2005), 'Corruption – its spread and decline', in Johann Graf Lambsdorff, Markus Taube and Matthias Schramm (eds), *The New Institutional Economics of Corruption*, New York: Routledge, pp. 16–39.

Smelser, Neil J. (1971), 'Stability, instability and the analysis of political corruption', in Bernard Barber and Alex Inkeles (eds), *Stability and Social Change. In Honor of Talcott Parsons*, Boston, MA: Little, Brown & Co.

Simmel, Georg (1995), *Die Großstädte und das Geistesleben. Georg Simmel Gesamtausgabe 7*, Frankfurt am Main: Suhrkamp, pp. 116–31. (First published 1903.)

Treisman, Daniel (2000), 'The causes of corruption: a cross-national study', *Journal of Public Economics*, **76**, 399–457.

Tumber, Howard and Silvio R. Waisbord (2004), 'Introduction. Political scandals and media across democracies, Volume I', *American Behavioral Scientist*, **47** (8), 1031–9.

Waldinger, Roger (1995), 'The "other side" of embeddedness: a case study of the interplay between economy and ethnicity', *Ethnical Racial Studies*, **18**, 555–80.

Uslaner, Eric M. (2005), 'Trust and corruption', in Johann Graf Lambsdorff, Markus Taube and Matthias Schramm (eds), *The New Institutional Economics of Corruption*, New York: Routledge, pp. 76–91.

10 Social capital in East-Central Europe*
Natalia Letki

Introduction

Transformation in East-Central Europe (ECE) is now almost 18 years old. It has been an unprecedented event, due to its unexpectedness, but also its complexity. One of the key questions asked about the direction of changes in the post-communist states has been whether the transformation process was one of the ECE states simply 'catching up' with the mature Western democracies, or whether historical, cultural and political heritage created specific circumstances which would lead to different mechanisms than those observed in stable Western democracies. The former – 'modernization' – approach seemed to have prevailed, as almost all theories created on the basis of observation of mature democracies were being applied to ECE, with varying degrees of sensitivity. Social capital was among them.

When the concept of social capital swept the academic world in the early 1990s, it became popular in the new post-communist democracies of East-Central Europe as well. In many ways, it was a continuation of an already decade-long discussion of the importance of civil society for the quality of politics and economics. The concept of social capital, and social trust in particular, has been present in the research on post-communist transformation since. However, while the causes and consequences of trust and associational activism have been thoroughly examined in the stable context of Western democracies, the research on new democracies is rather more patchy. Research and recommendations from the leading social capital scholars point to the importance of building civic activism and interpersonal trust in transition, but at the same time there is a growing body of evidence pointing to the specificity of the post-communist context which needs to be taken into account when examining social capital.

This chapter attempts not only to review the existing literature on social capital in East-Central Europe, but also to ask some questions that have not been asked before. The key points discussed will refer to the following two issues: (1) the main dimensions of social capital in post-communist countries, and links between them, and (2) the relationship between social capital and the quality of democracy. The chapter also assesses levels of bridging social capital in the post-communist countries – the first analysis of this kind. Some of the questions asked in this chapter relate to the specificity of the post-communist context, but others refer to the issue of social capital more generally. In the latter case, the context of social, political and economic transformation that has been taking place in East-Central Europe since 1989 is a unique and useful background for attempts aimed at disentangling processes that are difficult to pin down in stable democracies.

The next section discusses the key dimensions of social capital: formal and informal networks and social trust, and their manifestations in the post-communist states of ECE. In particular, it tries to highlight that the balance and dependencies between these three dimensions is different in the post-communist countries than in established democracies. It later discusses bridging social capital on the example of ethnic relations. The section after that assesses the relevance of social capital for the development and quality of democracy in ECE, again stressing the specificity of the regimes in transition from communism to democracy. All these considerations are summarized in the 'Conclusions' section.

Dimensions of social capital in East-Central Europe
Theoretical definition of social capital refers to formal and informal networks and connections among people, that can be used for their individual and collective benefit (Putnam, 1996). It also encompasses norms of trust and reciprocity. The empirical definition is usually much more restricted, as it is constrained by the existing empirical indicators, falling into the above-mentioned attitudinal (trust and reciprocity) and behavioural (networks and participation) categories. Following Putnam's book on institutional performance of Italian regions (Putnam, 1993), it has become customary to use indicators referring to interpersonal trust/trust in other people and membership in voluntary associations as the key dimensions of social capital. Of course, informal networks and sociability have not been denied significance in fostering the creation of interpersonal trust, but they are more difficult to capture and analyse, especially in a cross-national context, therefore they are less frequently present in empirical research on social capital. So, since questions on 'trust in others' and membership in voluntary associations are readily available, they have become the most popular indicators of social capital, also in ECE.

Formal networks: civic associations
Civic engagement in East-Central Europe became the focus of scholarly interest long before the fall of the Berlin Wall. Dissident activities and independence movements formed in numerous European communist countries in the 1970s and 1980s stimulated emergence of interest in what was called 'the rebirth of civil society'. The events of the late 1980s and early 1990s confirmed the importance of voluntary civic activism for the existence and quality of democracy.

However, some scholars distinguish between civic activism constituting a leverage or counterbalance to the state ('civil society II'), as under communism in ECE, and civic activism being an ancillary to the democratic state, as in the democratic tradition of Alexis de Tocqueville, Adam Smith or Adam Ferguson ('civil society I') (Foley and Edwards, 1996). Foley and Edwards feared that the tradition of civic opposition to the state ('civil society II') may become a serious burden for the new democracies of East-Central Europe. However, once the democratic structures and provisions, such as freedom of speech, freedom of opinion or association, which are necessary for the existence of the 'civil society I', have been created, citizens started forming and joining groups and associations that are remarkably similar to those found in established Western democracies. Nevertheless, the sphere of civic activism in ECE remained in the focus of academic attention, and this interest can also be linked to the rise of the popularity of social capital concept, and its implications for democratizing countries.

It was soon noticed that after the initial wave of enthusiasm, citizens' interest in voluntary activism weakened: almost all ECE countries witnessed a significant decline in the association membership rates between the early and late 1990s (Barnes, 2006). Howard has conducted the most extensive and detailed analysis of formal civic activism in post-communist Europe, comparing it also with other post-authoritarian societies and 'older democracies' (Howard, 2002). His diagnosis points to the noticeable weakness of civic engagement, even in comparison with other new democracies: 'post-communist citizens have significantly and consistently lower levels of membership and participation than citizens of most other democratic countries, particularly when compared to citizens of post-authoritarian countries that have similar levels of economic development and political rights and civil liberties' (Howard, 2002: 147). Comparing levels of membership across three groups of countries, he found that the average number of memberships per person in 'older democracies' (for example, US, Australia, Sweden or Finland) is a 2.39, in post-authoritarian democracies (for example, South Africa, South Korea or Chile) this number is 1.82, while in the post-communist democracies of ECE it is a low 0.91 (Howard, 2002: 80). There are various possible reasons for such low levels of civic engagement: some authors mention general 'post-communist' distrust of formal organizations of any kind, others refer to the fact that 'organizations that evolve from the grassroots take time to grow' (Gibson, 2001: 66, see also Dowley and Silver, 2002; Howard, 2002; Barnes, 2006). However, Howard disagreed with the negative scenarios picturing a weak civil society as the key hindrance to the process of democratization. Instead, he perceives it as a 'distinctive element of post-communist democracy, a pattern that may well persist throughout the region for at least several decades'

(Howard, 2002: 150). His intuition is confirmed by research by Dowley and Silver, who have found no relationship between the level of associational membership and various dimensions of democracy across 20 post-communist states in the mid-1990s (2002; see also Evans and Letki, 2006).

Besides being not very strong in terms of number of members, at the individual level voluntary associations in ECE seem to be working in a similar way to that which has been found in established democracies. Similarly to what has been identified in the West, not all associations are alike (Stolle and Rochon, 2001). Letki has found that in post-communist Europe there exist three dimensions of associational membership: (1) community associations (for example, farmer associations, church groups, local groups and ethnic organizations), (2) professional/ lifestyle organizations (professional and business associations and sports clubs) and (3) labour organizations (trade unions and factory committees), where the labour organizations are by far the most popular type, owing to a legacy of high unionization under the communist regime (Letki, 2004, see also Evans and Letki, 2006). Their role as 'schools of democracy', that is, organizations socializing citizens into the habit of participation in politics, varies across the three types: the positive effect of membership in community associations on political participation is twice as strong as the effect of membership in any of the other two types. However, all three types are politically relevant. This finding shows that people 'specialize' in particular types of voluntary activism, with those holding multiple memberships choosing associations of a similar type. The 'socializing' effect of voluntary association membership has also been demonstrated by Bernhagen and Marsh in their analysis of unconventional (protest) political participation in post-communist Europe (Bernhagen and Marsh, 2007).

Norms: social trust
Expectations about the dramatically low levels of social capital in post-communist Europe extended beyond civic activism and civil society to what is considered their by-product, yet lies at the heart of the concept of social capital: norms of social trust and reciprocity. It was proclaimed that post-communist societies will suffer from a serious deficiency of interpersonal trust owing to low levels of citizens' interactions, but also as a result of the experience of totalitarianism and authoritarianism:

> only in democracies is trust a rational gamble. When the heavy hand of the state looms over society, it makes little sense to put too much faith in most other people . . . In totalitarian societies, it makes little sense to trust anyone but your family and your closest friends. In authoritarian societies, you might trust a somewhat larger circle. But only in democracies – and not even all of them – will you give trust to strangers (Uslaner, 1999: 141).[1]

Research comparing levels of interpersonal trust in ECE with established Western democracies suggests that, indeed, post-communist countries are, on average, 'trust poor'. At the same time, comparisons of proportions of respondents who believe that 'most people can be trusted' in various countries do not produce as clear-cut results as expected. Some post-communist states have similar or higher levels of social trust than established democracies, such as France, Belgium or Austria (Inglehart, 1997; Gibson, 2001). Contrary to the expectations of the social capital theory, not only did new ECE democracies emerge from the period of communism with some (rather than none) 'stocks of social trust', but also it appears that these stocks of social trust have been depleted as a result of the democratization process. Rose-Ackerman suggests that the inefficiency of the communist system generated strong and reliable networks of trust and reciprocity, which were the key resource used to cope with everyday life. 'This sense of community has been broken up by the move to the market and to democracy leading to a loss of trust and to an increase in opportunism' (Rose-Ackerman, 2001: 415, see also Letki and Evans, 2005). Such extensive networks of trust and reciprocity, reaching beyond the close circle of immediate family and friends, and their practical uses, have also been discussed by Åberg and Sandberg. They see such non-kin networks not only as a means of securing basic economic goods and social influence, but also as an important source of trust and norms of cooperation (Åberg and Sandberg, 2003). The importance of these networks for survival under conditions of economic scarcity, but also for creating horizontal links between people who would otherwise have little in common, has been empirically researched on the example of Russia by Rose and Ledeneva (Ledeneva, 1998; Rose, 2000, 2001).

Informal networks: friendship
Informal networks complement associational membership as a behavioural dimension of social capital that is responsible for creating norms of trust and reciprocity (Putnam, 2000). However, despite the expected weakness of civic associations in post-communist countries, research into social capital has not been extended to dimensions that would have been more relevant, due to the reasons described above, in the context of East-Central Europe. Therefore, there exists only very limited information about the extent and functions of informal sociability and links with friends, neighbours and colleagues in post-communist democracies. Below, I reconstruct existing research on this topic, and supplement it with the discussion of the bridging and bonding functions of friendship networks.

Conversation networks are often used as a measure of friendship networks. Asking individuals whether and how often they talk to each other and who their conversation partners are allows one not only to assess the extensiveness of a personal communication network, but also their type. For example, it is possible to detect whether individuals limit themselves to the company of their family, or whether they extend their contacts beyond family, to friends, neighbours and work colleagues. It is also possible to describe whether those non-family conversation partners are similar to or different from the respondent in terms of ethnicity, religion or social class. The former distinction refers directly to the notion of strong (family based) versus weak (beyond family) ties (Granovetter, 1973). The latter is tapping into the recently introduced distinction between bridging and bonding social capital, where bridging ties link individuals of different groups, while bonding social capital bonds individuals within their particular group. In short, 'bonding social capital brings together people who are like one another in important aspects (ethnicity, age, gender, social class, and so on), whereas bridging social capital refers to social networks that bring together people who are unlike one another' (Putnam, 2002: 11). While a certain degree of both types of social capital is necessary for social groups to form and interact with each other, bonding social capital emerges 'naturally' owing to people's preferences for socializing with those who are like them (McPherson et al., 2001), and it may result in reinforcing social divisions along racial, religious and class lines, thus undermining social cohesion. Bridging capital is more likely to have positive political and economic outcomes, but is more difficult to generate (Woolcock, 1998; Woolcock and Naryan, 2000).

There are several studies of informal networks in the post-communist states, and they all focus on the type, density and political relevance of conversation networks, stressing the distinction between 'strong' and 'weak' ties, defined as, respectively, contacts within and outside of family. Gibson's analysis of the extensiveness of conversation networks in post-communist Russia shows that in the beginning of the transition period over 75 per cent of Russians who reported being involved in conversation networks relied at least partly on weak ties, but that number decreased to around 60 per cent in 1995 (Gibson, 2001). At the same time, he discovered that conversation networks in Russia have high political capacity and are used to disseminate political ideas. Therefore, their weakening, in the context of underdeveloped associational activism, means a decline of the major channels of political communication available to the general public.

The political relevance of informal networks in ECE has also been observed by Igli , who compared the density and extensiveness of conversation networks in Serbia and Slovenia in the mid-1980s. Igli concluded that the type of personal networks that existed prior to the breakdown of communism was of a crucial importance for citizens' later patterns of political mobilization (Igli , 2003). Flap and Völker discussed informal friendship ties functioning as a leverage to the oppressive state in communist East Germany, and analysed their properties and social and political relevance in the post-communist period (Flap and Völker, 2003). Each of these studies points to the importance of friendship networks for social, political and economic life during the transition period. Also Pichler and Wallace (2007) concluded that citizens of East-Central Europe rely on weak ties much more often than people living in other European regions. Finally, using in-depth interviews conducted in several post-communist countries, Howard suggested that 'these active private networks are to some extent an alternative to, or a substitute for, the social ties that many people in non-post-communist societies typically acquire through voluntary organisations' (Howard, 2002: 153).

Bridging ties
While these studies distinguish between 'strong' and 'weak' types of networks, and discuss the functionality of 'weak' ties in the post-communist transition, they do not look at whether these ties are of a bridging or bonding type.[2] Ethnic divisions have been frequently discussed as an example of bridging vs. bonding social capital outside the ECE context, and although this distinction so far has not been applied to ethnic issues in post-communist countries, the salience of ethnic divisions in ECE has been noticed and widely discussed. For example, there exists literature on ethnic polarisation (for example, in respect to the experience of democracy or minorities' rights) or ethnic identity in post-communist societies (Brady and Kaplan, 2000; Evans and Lipsmeyer, 2001; Evans and Need, 2002), which provides indirect evidence for the scarcity of bridging social capital in some post-communist states. In particular, countries with one predominant minority group, such as Estonia, demonstrate a high degree of polarisation and very low levels of interactions across ethnic lines. The results of these studies also suggest that it is the majority/minority status that is the key social division, not ethnic group membership per se. This makes the ethnic majority/minority divide a suitable example of studying the presence of bridging social capital in East-Central Europe.

In the survey conducted in 1993[3] respondents ('egos') were asked to describe two people ('alters') who they talk to about politics most often, indicate ethnic and social background of these alters, as well as the relationship between the ego and the alters. Respondents could thus describe their kin and non-kin social ties.[4] While this question asked specifically about political conversation networks, recent research shows that such political networks and personal friendship networks largely overlap, which justifies using this survey item as a measure of the respondents' personal friendship networks (Klofstad et al., 2006). The proportions of respondents who, while discussing politics, rely at least partly on 'weak'/non-kin ties (that is, have at least one conversation partner from outside of the family circle) are similar across countries, as they vary only from around 87 per cent in Poland and the Czech and Slovak Republics to 91 per cent in Belarus.[5] Both representatives of the dominant and minority ethnic background were present in the sample.

Since our interest is in the presence of bridging ties, that is, those linking egos and alters from different ethnic backgrounds, we focus on egos from a majority ethnic background mentioning at least one alter of a minority ethnic status, and vice versa. However, countries vary significantly in terms of the size of their ethnic minorities (from just over 2 per cent in Poland to as much as 36 per cent in Estonia), making direct comparisons of frequency of such 'bridging' contacts impossible. Therefore, Figure 10.1 presents the difference between levels of bridging contacts among ethnic majorities and minorities in particular countries and the random probability of such contacts.[6] To control for the fact that ethnic background may influence the propensity of talking about politics in general, and determine likelihood of relying on weak versus strong ties, only respondents who talk about politics *and* have weak ties are taken into account in the analysis.

If people were choosing their conversation partners randomly, and not based on their ethnicity, the occurrence of 'bridging' contacts would equal their random probability. As Figure 10.1 shows, in all cases but one, the occurrence of bridging contacts is significantly lower than their random probability, that is, bonding contacts dominate in conversation networks. For example, in the Ukraine, the frequency of egos of a majority status having an alter of a minority status is 46.6 per cent lower than the random probability of such relationships, while in the case of Ukrainian minorities this divergence is even larger, at 62.2 per cent. Only in Poland do ethnic majority respondents report having at least one ethnic minority conversation partner at a level which is close to the level of random probability of such contacts, and there is no country where the frequency of such bridging contacts would be significantly higher than their random probability. Comparison across countries reveals, that with the exception of Estonia, the Czech Republic and Bulgaria, ethnic majorities form bridging ties slightly more often than ethnic minorities.

Although the discriminating effect is generally weaker among ethnic majority respondents, two countries stand out as particularly divided: Estonia and Bulgaria. In Bulgaria, ethnic majority egos list an ethnic minority alter 95.9 per cent less often than would result from random probability, while in Estonia both ethnic majority and minority egos name an alter from an opposite ethnic background between 88 and 90 per cent less often than if they were choosing their friends randomly, not discriminating

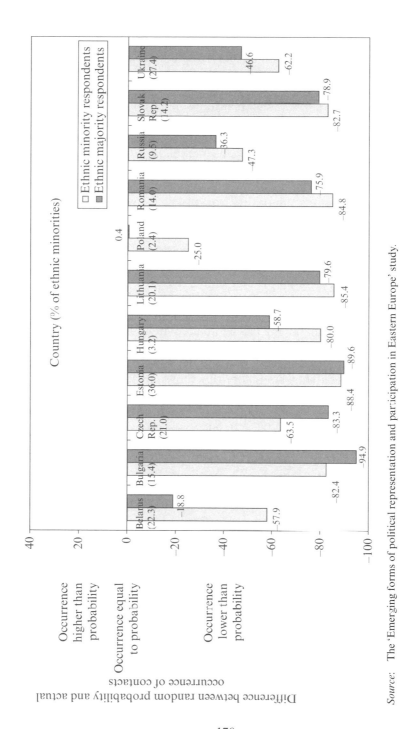

Source: The 'Emerging forms of political representation and participation in Eastern Europe' study.

Figure 10.1   Bridging non-kin contacts v. their random probability in East-Central Europe in 1993–94 (N = 11 312)

on the basis of ethnicity. These results suggest that in Bulgaria and Estonia ethnic groups lead largely separate, 'parallel', lives with extremely little contact across the ethnic divide. These observations correspond with research on ethnic conflict and ethnic discrimination in East-Central Europe, where both Bulgaria and Estonia appear particularly strongly antagonized (McIntosh et al., 1995; Evans, 1998; Evans and Need, 2002).

These results may seem extremely alarming. However, two caveats are in place: first, there is no research on established democracies that could serve as a baseline for comparisons, so we are able to interpret the above results only by comparing them across the countries within the area. Second, in most ECE countries ethnic minorities are strongly regionally segregated from the majority group, thus lowering their likelihood of encountering a majority alter.[7] However, using random probability of contacts across the ethnic divide as a baseline for comparisons, we are able to conclude that although ECE citizens form extensive 'weak' networks, their character is predominantly bonding.

Does social capital matter for post-communist democracy?
One of the main reasons for the popularity of social capital among academics and policy-makers is the utility ascribed to it. The consequences of social capital for institutional quality have been illustrated by Putnam's study on institutional reform in Italy, and have been further discussed by many other authors since (Putnam, 1993, see also Knack and Keefer, 1997; Boix and Posner, 1998; Woolcock, 1998). Civic activism encourages self-organization and generates norms of trust and reciprocity, thus lowering transaction costs, stimulating interactions among citizens, self-government and elite responsiveness. In short, social capital (activism and interpersonal trust) is seen as an important cultural factor stimulating both the economy and political institutions.

However, most of the studies investigating the benevolent effects of social capital on institutional functioning focus either on stable democratic contexts or on comparisons of states which vary in the degree of their democratic character. Causality of social phenomena is notoriously difficult to pin down, and the link between social capital and institutional quality is an example of such a difficult relationship. Putnam and his followers argue that social capital is an exogenous factor determining institutional performance, and as such is necessary for the consolidation of democracy and market economy in post-communist Europe (Putnam, 1993). Lack of social capital is dangerous for the newly emerging democracies: 'the rapid and successful transition to post-authoritarian modes of governance and the consolidation of liberal democratic regimes is seen to be greatly hindered by the absence of trust' (Offe, 1999: 43). This approach can be called *bottom up*, as here cultural factors, such as norms, attitudes and behaviour, determine institutional quality.

However, there is a growing body of literature and research suggesting that the mechanisms linking social capital with institutional performance in Western democracies are not readily applicable to other, less stable contexts. Observations of the relationship between dimensions of social capital and institutional performance in the context of post-communist transformation suggest a different, *top-down* approach. And so, Dowley and Silver (2002) have found that there is at best a very weak link between dimensions of social capital such as interpersonal trust and membership in voluntary associations, with quality of democracy across a number of post-communist states. Although Gibson (2001) identified strong interpersonal networks in Russia, he has found no link between trust in strangers and political culture. Moreover, Letki and Evans (2005) have discovered that countries more advanced along the democratization path in mid-1990s (for example, Hungary, Czech Republic) demonstrated lower levels of trust than those who were lagging behind (for example, Russia, Belarus or Ukraine). Marsh has discovered a negative relationship between civicness and support for democracy and reform in Russia (Marsh, 2000). Also using Russia as an illustration, Rose argued that formal and informal networks that constitute social capital are used to 'get things done' when government fails its citizens (1998, 2001). All these studies show that in the post-communist context the relationship between various components of social capital and institutional functioning is different to what has been identified in stable democracies.[8] It seems that the relationship between social capital and institutions needs to be reversed. For example, although civic activism contributed to the breakdown of communism and introduction of democracy, voluntary associational activism became possible only after democratic institutions had been introduced. Moreover, interpersonal trust and informal networks formed in response to the unstable and unpredictable institutional setting, such as the conditions of shortage under the communist rule, became weaker and less popular as political and economic transition progressed.

Figure 10.2 below illustrates the relationship between levels of interpersonal trust and development in democratization across 11 ECE states. The figure shows the effect of democracy on trust, and trust on subsequent levels of democracy, taking into account level of economic development. It demonstrates that the levels of social trust had no influence on the subsequent progress of democratization, while the development of democracy prior to 1993, when the survey was conducted, was a strong determinant of the levels of trust detected by the survey. Moreover, this effect is negative (a strong standardized coefficient of −0.693), which means that in the mid-1990s ECE countries with higher levels of democracy had lower stocks of

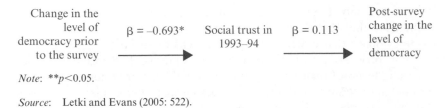

Note: **p<0.05.

Source: Letki and Evans (2005: 522).

Figure 10.2 *Democratization and social trust (controlling for the effect of economic development)*

social trust. This finding can only be understood and explained within the *top-down* framework described above.

Conclusions
Social capital has proven to be an attractive concept, and it has been applied to numerous contexts. Post-communist East-Central Europe has been no exception and, as discussed above, various dimensions of social capital and their consequences have been researched using survey, interview and institutional data from the 1990s. ECE has been treated predominantly as a background for confirming the analytical value of the social capital concept, but specific features of countries in transition from communism to market economy and democracy have proven, in some instances, its rather limited value.

Above, I described three main components of social capital: formal and informal networks and norms of trust and reciprocity. Research indicates that all three are present in the post-communist countries of East-Central Europe. However, following earlier findings from established democracies, as well as general principles of modern liberal democracy, researchers have focused predominantly on detecting and discussing formal involvement, at the expense of informal ties, although these informal ties were the key network resources available to ECE citizens under communism and in the early stages of transformation. As a result, attention has focused largely on the development of voluntary associations and civic activism, while informal networks have been researched much less often.

Despite very limited evidence that there exists any link at all between voluntary activism and trust in post-communist countries,[9] post-communist societies were predicted to suffer from low levels of trust and reciprocity owing to the weakness of formal associational structures. However, as research cited above shows, post-communist citizens continued relying on the networks of informal contacts created under communism, and thus cultivated their trust networks formed prior to 1989. The presence of social trust despite weakness of civil society suggests the importance of informal networks for generating trust and reciprocity.

Astonishingly, the very mechanisms of transition seemed to have contributed to the breakdown of these norms and networks. Moreover, there is no evidence that either low or high stocks of social capital interacted with the progress of transition: in the early and mid-1990s ECE countries varied in terms of their levels of interpersonal trust or voluntary activism (although their levels of informal networks were rather similar, see above), but by 2007 most of them have been classified as democracies and joined the European Union. It seems, therefore, that if the post-communist countries of East-Central Europe have been treated as an experiment field for testing the causality between culture (social capital) and institutions (democracy and free market), the evidence from this experiment points towards a limited, if at all present, effect of culture on institutions.[10] As some research quoted above shows, the type and quality of institutions, under communism and during the transition, are the major factors shaping attitudes and behaviour, such as formal and informal sociability and interpersonal trust and reciprocity.

However, the key conclusion of this chapter comes from its analysis of bridging ethnic contacts in post-communist Europe. Results presented above show that during the transition period bridging ethnic contacts have been at extremely low levels, and that in almost all ECE countries people tend to socialize with those of their own ethnicity. However, although the presence of bridging social capital is certainly important for social cohesion and the quality of social life, it does not seem to determine political or economic success. In fact, Estonia, who in the mid-1990s showed remarkably little bridging social capital, by 2000 has been one of the front-runners of the political and economic transition. Whereas, Belarus and Russia, with medium levels of bridging social capital in the mid-1990s, are at present the most undemocratic and economically inefficient states of the region. The above does not render the concept of social capital useless or redundant, but it does suggest that greater caution and sensitivity are needed when applying concepts created in the stable context of Western democracies to societies experiencing radically different social, political and economic circumstances.

Notes

*   I would like to thank Meredith Rolfe for useful comments on the earlier version of this paper.
1.   For a summary and criticism of this approach in reference to Russia, see Marsh (2000).
2.   Perhaps the one exception is work of Igli , who suggests that the different patterns of political mobilization in Serbia and Slovenia can be linked to the greater significance of ethnic and religious affiliation for friendship patterns in Serbia in comparison with Slovenia (Igli , 2003).
3.   1994 in Hungary and the Czech and Slovak Republics. The data used come from the study 'Emerging forms of political representation and participation in Eastern Europe',

directed by Geoffrey Evans, Stephen Whitefield, Anthony Heath and Clive Payne, part of stage II of the ESRC's East–West Programme.

4. The options were: 'Other family member in your household', 'Other family member not in your household', 'Co-worker', 'Neighbour' and 'Friend other than co-worker or neighbour'.

5. When the entire sample, including those who did not indicate any conversation networks, is taken into account, the proportion of those relying at least partly on weak ties varies from 42.7 per cent in the Slovak Republic to 58.5 per cent in Hungary.

6. Since respondents could name two alters, the probability of naming at least one alter from a given ethnic background B by an ego from an ethnic group A is $P = 1 - (1 - p_A)^2$, where P is the random probability, and p is the proportion of an ethnic group A.

7. I thank Hajdeja Igli for pointing this out.

8. Marsh finds a relationship between social capital and progress of democratization across Russian regions (Marsh, 2000). However, his index of social capital does not include trust or informal networks, instead focusing on formal involvement in the way analogous to the original index of civicness constructed by Putnam (1993).

9. Among the studies that attempted to find a relationship between these components and failed, are Dowley and Silver (2002), Evans and Letki (2006) and Howard (2002).

10. For an empirical investigation of the culture vs. institutions argument, see Muller and Seligson (1994).

References

Åberg, M. and M. Sandberg (2003), *Social Capital and Democratisation. Roots of Trust in Post-Communist Poland and Ukraine*, Aldershot: Ashgate.

Barnes, S.H. (2006), 'The changing political participation of postcommunist citizens', *International Journal of Sociology*, **36**, 76–98.

Bernhagen, P. and M. Marsh (2007), 'Voting and protesting: explaining citizen participation in old and new European democracies', *Democratization*, **14**, 44–72.

Boix, C. and D.N. Posner (1998), 'Social capital: explaining its origins and effects on governmental performance', *British Journal of Political Science*, **29**, 686–93.

Brady, H.E. and C.S. Kaplan (2000), 'Categorically wrong? Nominal versus graded measures of ethnic identity', *Studies in Comparative International Development*, **35**, 56–91.

Dowley, K.M. and B.D. Silver (2002), 'Social capital, ethnicity, and support for democracy in the post-communist states', *Europe-Asia Studies*, **54**, 505–27.

Evans, G. (1998), 'Ethnic schism and the consolidation of post-communist democracies: the case of Estonia', *Communist and Post-Communist Studies*, **30**, 57–74.

Evans, G. and N. Letki (2006), 'Understanding the relationship between social capital and political disaffection in the new post-communist democracies', in M. Torcal and J.R. Montero (eds), *Political Disaffection in Contemporary Democracies. Social Capital, Institutions, and Politics*, London and New York: Routledge, pp. 130–54.

Evans, G. and C. Lipsmeyer (2001), 'The democratic experience in divided societies: the Baltic States in comparative perspective', *Journal of Baltic Studies*, **32**, 379–400.

Evans, G. and A. Need (2002), 'Explaining ethnic polarization over attitudes towards minority rights in Eastern Europe: a multilevel analysis', *Social Science Research*, **31**, 653–80.

Flap, H. and B. Völker (2003), 'Communist societies, the velvet revolution, and weak ties: the case of East Germany', in G. Badescu and E.M. Uslaner (ed.), *Social Capital and the Transition to Democracy*, London and New York: Routledge, pp. 28–45.

Foley, M. and B. Edwards (1996), 'The paradox of civil society', *Journal of Democracy*, **7**, 38–52.

Gibson, J.L. (2001), 'Social networks, civil society, and the prospects for consolidating Russia's democratic transition', *American Journal of Political Science*, **45**, 51–69.

Granovetter, M.S. (1973), 'The strength of weak ties', *American Journal of Sociology*, **78**, 1360–80.

Howard, M.M. (2002), *The Weakness of Civil Society in Post-Communist Europe*, Cambridge: Cambridge University Press.

Igli , H. (2003), 'Trust networks and democratic transition: Yugoslavia in the mid-1980s', in G. Badescu and E.M. Uslaner (eds), *Social Capital and the Transition to Democracy*, London and New York: Routledge, pp. 10–27.

Inglehart, R. (1997), *Modernization and Postmodernization: Cultural, Economic, and Political Change in 43 Societies*, Princeton, NJ: Princeton University Press.

Klofstad, C., S.D. McClurg and M. Rolfe (2006), 'Family members, friends, and neighbors: differences in personal and political networks', paper presented at the Annual Meeting of the Midwest Political Science Association, Chicago, 20–23 April.

Knack, S. and P. Keefer (1997), 'Does social capital have an economic payoff? A cross-country investigation', *The Quarterly Journal of Economics*, **62**, 1251–88.

Ledeneva, A.V. (1998), *Russia's Economy of Favours: Blat, Networking and Informal Exchange*, Cambridge: Cambridge University Press.

Letki, N. (2004), 'Socialization for participation? Trust, membership and democratization in East-Central Europe', *Political Research Quarterly*, **57**, 665–79.

Letki, N. and G. Evans (2005), 'Endogenizing social trust: democratisation in East-Central Europe', *British Journal of Political Science*, **35**, 515–29.

Marsh, C. (2000), *Making Russian Democracy Work. Social Capital, Economic Development, and Democratization*, New York: Edwin Mellen Press.

McIntosh, M.E., M.A.M. Iver, D.G. Abele and D.B. Nolle (1995), 'Minority rights and majority rule: ethnic tolerance in Romania and Bulgaria', *Social Forces*, **73**, 939–67.

McPherson, M., L. Smith-Lovin and J.M. Cook (2001), 'Birds of a feather: homophily in social networks', *Annual Review of Sociology*, **27**, 415–44.

Muller, E.N. and M.A. Seligson (1994), 'Civic culture and democracy: the question of causal relationships', *American Political Science Review*, **88**, 635–52.

Offe, C. (1999), 'How can we trust our fellow citizens?', in M. Warren (ed.), *Democracy and Trust*, Cambridge: Cambridge University Press, pp. 42–87.

Pichler, F. and C. Wallace (2007), 'Patterns of formal and informal social capital in Europe', *European Sociological Review*, **23** (4), 423–45.

Putnam, R.D. (1993), *Making Democracy Work: Civic Traditions in Modern Italy*, Princeton, NJ: Princeton University Press.

Putnam, R.D. (1996), 'Who killed civic America?', *Prospect*, **7**, 66–72.

Putnam, R.D. (2000), *Bowling Alone. The Collapse and Revival of American Community*, New York: Simon & Schuster.

Putnam, R.D. (ed.) (2002), *Democracies in Flux. The Evolution of Social Capital in Contemporary Society*, Oxford: Oxford University Press.

Rose, R. (1998), 'Getting things done with social capital. New Russia barometer VII', Series: Studies in Public Policy, Centre for the Study of Public Policy, University of Strathclyde.

Rose, R. (2000), 'Uses of social capital in Russia: modern, pre-modern, and anti-modern', *Post-Soviet Affairs*, **16**, 33–57.

Rose, R. (2001), 'When government fails. Social capital in an antimodern Russia', in B. Edwards, M.W. Foley and M. Diani (eds), *Beyond Tocqueville. Civil Society and the Social Capital Debate in Comparative Perspective*, Hanover and London: Tufts University, pp. 56–69.

Rose-Ackerman, S. (2001), 'Trust and honesty in post-socialist societies', *KYKLOS*, **54**, 415–44.

Stolle, D. and T.R. Rochon (2001), 'Are all associations alike? Member diversity, associational type, and the creation of social capital', in B. Edwards, M. Foley and M. Diani (eds), *Beyond Tocqueville. Civil Society and the Social Capital Debate in Comparative Perspective*, Hanover: Tufts University, pp. 143–56.

Uslaner, E.M. (1999), 'Democracy and social capital', in M.E. Warren (ed.), *Democracy and Trust*, Cambridge: Cambridge University Press, pp. 213–39.

Woolcock, M. (1998), 'Social capital and economic development: toward a theoretical synthesis and policy framework', *Theory and Society*, **27**, 151–208.

Woolcock, M. and D. Naryan (2000), 'Social capital: implications for development theory, research, and policy', *The World Bank Research Observer*, **15**, 225–49.

PART IV

THE WELFARE STATE

11 The state
Francisco Herreros

Introduction

Does the state promote social trust? The literature on social capital does not always agree on this point. The now classical study about social capital, Putnam's *Making Democracy Work* (1993) totally disregarded a possible role of the state in the creation of interpersonal trust, focusing instead on a thesis of path dependence to explain the differences in the levels of social capital between the central and Northern Italian regions as compared with the South, arguing that those differences could be traced back to an initial gap in social capital between both territories in the period of the Italian city-republics of the eleventh to fifteenth centuries. In his posterior notorious work, *Bowling Alone* (Putnam, 2000), the state was hardly acquitted from the charge of destroying America's social capital. There are numerous examples in the literature on social capital of how social capital can be destroyed by conscious actions of the state, as the actions of the Spanish viceroys in the sixteenth and seventeenth centuries in Southern Italy (Padgen, 1988), the Italian state after the *Risorgimento* (Huysseune, 2003), or the communist regimes in Eastern Europe (Nichols, 1996: 634–8; Mondak and Gearing, 1998; Dowley and Silver, 2003; Flap and Völker, 2003; Iglic, 2003; Uslaner, 2003).

Not everything is bad news for the role of the state on social capital, though. A number of authors have claimed that the state can indeed be a positive factor in the development of social capital, at least measured as interpersonal trust. This line of research has presented two main arguments: according to some authors, the state can promote social trust acting as a third-party enforcer of private agreements (see, for example, Hardin, 1998; Huck, 1998; Levi, 1998; Offe, 1999; Guseva and Rona-Tas, 2001; Heimer, 2001; Rothstein, 2001; Darley, 2004). This means that in a trust relation the state acts as a guarantor of the fulfillment of trust by the trustee. The second argument considers that the state can promote trust by its role in the creation of more equal societies (Rothstein and Uslaner, 2005). Equality of opportunity and economic equality, the argument goes, promote the creation of social trust, and universal social policies contribute to the creation of both types of equality and thereby social trust.

In this chapter, I will offer various theoretical mechanisms and some empirical tests to prove that the state can indeed create interpersonal trust.

In my view, and contrary to most of the analysis mentioned above, the state as a third-party enforcer of contracts cannot create trust directly, but it can create an environment where trust has a possibility to grow. This is a mechanism for the creation of trust that is related, in a way, with a liberal conception of the state, to the effective enforcement of the rule of law. However, the welfare state can also promote the creation of trust, equalizing social relations and promoting advances in the levels of education and income, variables that are consistently related to trust in most empirical studies. In this chapter, I test whether the two modalities of the state, the liberal and the welfare state, can indeed create interpersonal trust, through a comparative analysis of 22 European countries from the 2002/03 wave of European Social Survey. The chapter is structured as follows. First, I offer a brief discussion of the literature about the role of the state in the creation of trust, and I present the two theoretical mechanisms that I defend in this chapter. Second, I present an empirical model to test these theoretical mechanisms.

The state and trust: theoretical mechanisms
As I have said before, one of the main arguments in favor of a positive role of the state in the creation of trust is that the state creates trust acting as a third-party enforcer of private agreements. The idea is that the truster can place his trust in the trustee because the state will sanction the trustee if he breaches the agreement. For example, if the truster and the trustee end a contract about, say, the selling of a house, and the contract is not finally enforced, the truster can count on the state institutions, in this case the judiciary, to put the contract into effect. It is a quite straightforward argument, but it is opened to an important criticism: acting as a third-party enforcer of private agreements the state does not promote trust, but cooperation. Indeed, it makes trust at a certain extent redundant. Uslaner (2002: 45, 47), for example, argues that trust is not encouraged by making people respect the law: courts may, at most, help to build some form of 'strategic trust'. According to Ullman-Margalit (2004: 65), in modern societies, the state acts as a substitute for trust: the state's enforcement of legally binding contracts does not generate trust, but in fact relieves society of the need for trust. Analysing issues of trust in the Internet, Helen Nissenbaum (2004) maintains that trust is incompatible with security and certainty. Therefore, the security provided by the existence of a third-party which enforces agreements will tend to replace rather than enhance trust. Similarly, Murnighan et al. (2004) have argued that the enforcement of a legal contract may in fact undermine internal understanding and mutual trust between the parties to an agreement. Finally, Torsvik (2000: 460) claims that the concept of trust is incompatible with the presence of a third party which enforces agreements.

These critiques are, in my view, well placed. One of the difficulties of the application of a rational choice framework to the analysis of trust is that, at least in definitions as that of Coleman (1990), as a decision to cooperate under uncertainty, trust is a redundant concept of cooperation. Other definitions of trust from a rational choice perspective, especially Hardin's (2002: 3) definition of trust as encapsulated interest, defined as 'I trust you because your interest encapsulates mine, which is to say that you have an interest in fulfilling my trust', allow us to disentangle the concept of trust from cooperation. But the idea that the state creates trust sanctioning the breaching of private agreements leads us again to a definition of trust virtually indistinguishable from cooperation. By sanctioning the breaching of private agreements, the state does foster cooperation, but does it foster trust? In principle, it does not. However, there is a possibility to rescue the role of the state on trust as a third-party enforcer of agreements.

My idea is that, by enforcing private agreements the state can at least create an environment within which trust can grow. This is a rather abstract idea, but let me clarify it a bit. We can distinguish two scenarios: a first one with an efficient state, and a second stateless scenario, or, alternatively, a situation where the state is highly inefficient. In each of the scenarios we have two players, A and B. The first is offering cooperation to the second, who has, in turn, to decide whether to honor this cooperative move or not. A has an initial expectation about B's trustworthiness, who, in turn, can be, to simplify things, one of two types: trustworthy or untrustworthy. Consider next how trust will evolve in each of the two scenarios.

First scenario: efficient state
In this scenario, as in the second one, the trustworthy B will always reciprocate A's cooperative move. The untrustworthy B, in turn, will reciprocate A's cooperation only if the probability of being sanctioned by the state if he betrays A is sufficiently high. In this scenario, we assume that this is the case: the state is efficient in the application of sanctions to opportunistic players. Therefore, both types of player B will behave exactly the same, although for different reasons: the trustworthy B will honor A's trust spontaneously, and the untrustworthy B will do it out of fear of being punished by the state. It is, to put it in terms of a signaling game, a pooling equilibrium. A characteristic of this type of equilibrium is that it does not offer player A new information about the type of player B. That is, player A remains with the same prior beliefs about B's trustworthiness that he had at the beginning of the game. From an evolutionary point of view (that is, thinking in long-term payoffs and what they mean for the survival or disappearance of types), given that the expected payoffs of both types of player B will be the same (as both reciprocate A's cooperation) there will

not be a crowding-out of types. That is, given that there is not one type of player that receives systematically lower payoffs than the other types, neither of them have reasons to change. Both the opportunistic type and the trustworthy type will survive. Equally, if we distinguish between different types of player A depending on how much they trust player B (that is, what is her expectation about player B's trustworthiness), differentiating for example between high trusters and low trusters, we see that all of them will receive the same expected payoffs, independently of how much they trust their fellow citizens. For example, imagine a situation where there are four people: a high truster, a low truster, a trustworthy person and an untrustworthy person. These people are newcomers to the neighborhood, so they do not know each other. Suppose that they live in the same building and they decide to install a parabolic antenna because they are all fans of the Champion's League and they want to see Real Madrid winning its tenth cup. They have to share the cost of the antenna. The trustworthy and untrustworthy persons ask their neighbors to pay in advance all the cost because they are at the moment facing unpredicted expenses. They promise to pay their share in a few days. Will they fulfill their promise? The trustworthy person will certainly do it for good motives. The first impulse of the untrustworthy would be not to pay his share. But in this case, the other neighbors can impel him to pay because (this is an assumption of the example) there is an extremely efficient judiciary procedure to assure compliance in these cases. So, the untrustworthy person will pay to avoid being fined by the judiciary. Notice that the high truster and the low truster person will achieve the same outcome here: their money will be returned. They have no reasons to change their beliefs about the other people's trustworthiness. The low truster has intact his reasons for not trusting other people. He is not made more trusting by this experience. The high truster has also not been made more trusting, but he at least can still be thinking that most people can be trusted.

This means that the intervention of an efficient state does not increase the probability of interpersonal trust but it does not destroy trust either. In other terms, high trusters are not crowded out by the intervention of the state, as it is claimed by some of the authors cited above that posit a trade-off relation between state and trust. With an efficient state, trust can grow, and it can be indeed a useful tool to achieve cooperation in examples of social exchange where the intervention of the state would be too costly to be efficient. This is most likely in coordination problems, where both parties are interested in a cooperative equilibrium but are not sure about the preferences of the other player. In coordination problems there are different possible equilibria and the picking of the efficient one can possibly depend on how much trust you have in the other player's intention of also picking that equilibrium. In these cases, therefore, mutual trust can be crucial to achieve a cooperative outcome (Herreros, 2003).

Second scenario: the state is relatively inefficient
As in the first scenario, a trustworthy player B will reciprocate a cooperative move by player A, because to always cooperate is her dominant strategy. However, the opportunistic player B will not reciprocate cooperation, because in this case the state will not punish him. The decision of A of whether to offer cooperation or not to B depends on how much trust she places on player's B good will. In the first scenario, as we have seen, A's expectations about player B's trustworthiness were irrelevant. In this second scenario, by contrast, trust is quite important. A high-truster player A will offer cooperation to player B, whereas a low truster player A will not offer cooperation. Moreover, in this case player A can update her expectations about player B's trustworthiness, given that each type of player B chooses opposite strategies. If player B reciprocates cooperation, player A will know for sure that she is dealing with a trustworthy player B, whereas if player B does not reciprocate cooperation, she can be sure that she is dealing with an opportunistic type. A cooperative outcome depends, therefore, both on dealing with a trustworthy type of player B and on being a high-truster player A. We can also consider the implications of this outcome from an evolutionary point of view. What will happen in successive encounters between the different types of players? We can assume that the expected payoffs of the opportunistic type of player B will be higher than the expected payoffs of the trustworthy player B. Therefore, we should expect that the 'nice type' of player B will progressively tend to disappear, as his payoffs are systematically lower than the payoffs of the opportunistic type. Regarding player A, we can distinguish, as we did in the first scenario, between high-truster and low-truster types of player A. The high-truster player A will have higher payoffs than the low-truster one depending on the percentage of 'nice types' of player B. As the probability of encountering trustworthy players B decreases, the expected payoffs of the low-truster type of player A will be higher than the expected payoffs of the high trusters. As the number of trustworthy players B diminishes, high trusters will systematically obtain lower payoffs than low trusters. In the long term, high trusters will tend to disappear.

Therefore, in this second scenario, where the state is ineffective, high trusters and trustworthy players will tend to disappear, to be crowded out, whereas low trusters and opportunistic types will survive. Without the state, trust disappears, and cooperation is very unlikely.

The two scenarios, the first with an effective state and the second with an ineffective one, show that the relation between state and trust is complex.

The presence of an effective state sanctioning non-cooperative behavior acts as a substitute of trust. It does not foster trust but it does not crowd it out either. It simply renders trust unnecessary for social cooperation in many instances, although trust can be useful in instances where the intervention of the state would be too costly or in coordination problems. However, the absence of the state, or the presence of an inefficient state, has the effect of crowding out high trusters. To sum up, more state does not foster trust but less state destroys trust. In a world with an efficient state there is, say, a friendly environment for the development of trust. In a stateless world, trust can not grow. We should expect, therefore, that a more efficient state would lead to more trust.[1]

This has been my first mechanism for the creation of trust through the action of the state: an efficient state creates an environment where trust can grow. Inefficient states do not allow for the growing of trust. This mechanism has to do with the liberal conception of the state: the presence of an effective rule of law. The rule of law implies that the law is applied impartially to everybody, and it is one of the cornerstones of the liberal conception of the state.

State strategies for forming social trust

However, it is not just the liberal version of the state that can promote trust. The welfare state can also foster social trust. First, the welfare state can promote the creation of trust through its impact on individual variables (that is, measurable attributes), as education and income. These variables are consistently associated to social trust in most empirical analyses. Second, Rothstein and Uslaner (2005) have pointed out the effects of equality of opportunity and material equality on trust. These forms of equality, especially material equality, are clearly promoted by the redistributive policies of the welfare state. According to Rothstein and Uslaner (2005: 47), both types of equality are essential for people to think that others 'share our fate', and this, in turn, is deemed essential to trust in other people. Another mechanism, in my view, through which equality can promote trust is through the equalizing of social relations that could be derived from certain actions of the state. This has to do with the idea that in unequal relations, trust is much more difficult to develop between the parties. I will develop next this mechanism.

Consider the basic model of a typical production contract between a principal (an employer) and an agent (an employee) as developed by Laffont and Martimort (2002: 32–5). In this model, the employer delegates to the agent the production of a quantity q of a given good. The value for the principal of the q units of the good is S(q). Its marginal value is positive and decreases in line with the quantity of goods produced. In the basic game, the worker can be either efficient or inefficient, which is expressed in two different levels of effort. Here we will just consider an observable level of effort, θ. In this model, the employer offers a contract to the worker, then the worker decides whether or not to accept the contract, and finally the contract is executed. The principal has to offer the agent a high enough salary for the agent to accept the contract. This is the agent's participation constraint: the principal must offer the agent a utility level that is at least as high as the utility level that the agent obtains outside the relationship. In this model there is no asymmetric information between the players. Therefore, the employer knows the level of effort θ made by the worker. If we define U_0 as the outside utility level of the worker and t as the transfer received by the agent, then he will accept the contract whenever $t - \theta q \geq U_0$. This can be expressed as $t \geq \theta q + U_0$. Therefore, the amount of the transfer necessary for the worker to accept the contract depends on the level of effort made by the worker and also on his outside utility level. The lower this outside utility level, the lower the salary offered by the employer.

We can understand this outside utility level as embodying the bargaining power of the worker with respect to the employer. It can be affected by the worker's resources. If he has recently inherited a large amount of money, the contract will probably not meet the participation constraint. We can also consider the outside utility level as dependent on the presence of other workers with different utility levels. That is, if there is a pool of workers with outside utility levels $U_1 < U_0$, the employer will offer the contract to one of them, and we can expect a convergence of outside utility to U_1 for all workers. Low outside utility levels means low bargaining power, and, therefore, an imbalance of resources between the parties to the agreement. What does this mean for the problem of trust? In a relation in which there is a clear imbalance of resources between the parties, there are no reasons to believe that the powerful will encapsulate the interest of the weak: it is difficult to attain trust between the parties. All agency relations are characterized by a conflict of interests between the principal and the agent; hence the certainty that the principal will not, at least in part, encapsulate the interest of the agent. However, we can consider respect for the other's interest as a continuum, from total encapsulation of the other person's interests to zero encapsulation, with medium levels in between. If the principal is powerful enough, he can completely disregard the agent's interest. In the case of this example of the basic model of a production contract, if there is this pool of workers with outside utility levels $U_1 < U_0$, the employer can completely disregard the worker's interest and hire another employee from that pool by paying him less. In this case, the worker is dependent on the employee. There is clearly an imbalance of power between them, and this is why it is highly improbable that the employer's interest will encapsulate the employee's.

Are there grounds for the stronger party – the employer – to trust the weaker one – the employee? In this case, the object of trust can be the level of effort θ displayed by the worker, assuming now that this level of effort can be high (θ_h) or low (θ_l) and it is the worker's private information. If this level of effort is worker's private information, then the employer has a problem of trust. How can the state contribute to the development of trust in these circumstances? The answer is by favoring one of the parties to the contract, namely the weaker one. Consider how public institutions can promote trust between the parties to the agreement outlined in the previous model of an agency relation. We can think of various ways, most of them relating to the legal treatment of labor unions. First, labor unions can provide their members with resources to increase their outside utility levels. If all the workers in an economic sector are members of a labor union, they can pool resources by forming a union in order to better resist pressure from the employer to accept lower wages. When labor unions are illegal, as in most European countries during the early phases of the Industrial Revolution and in many underdeveloped countries today, major obstacles (from repression to coordination problems) hinder the formation and consolidation of stable labor unions. Legal recognition of labor unions can eliminate some of these obstacles. A second, higher level of state involvement would involve creating incentives for workers to join unions; one example of these would be the tax breaks offered in some countries to people who join unions. This raises the outside utility level of the worker. The state could also recognize the unions as collective actors empowered to negotiate contracts with employers. The wage bargaining by collective social actors practiced in Northern European social democracies constitute one of the best-known examples of this type of arrangement. In all these cases, the state endows the weaker party to the agreement with additional resources in an attempt to level the playing field with the stronger party. However, the state may also establish external constraints to optimal contracts through legal guarantees. This is the theoretical rationale behind the recognition of labor rights by the state, beginning, notably, with Bismarck's regulations of primitive social security schemes in the 1860s. These regulations impose external constraints benefiting the weaker party to the contract. Whatever the extent of employers' power, they are obliged to provide better working conditions than they would do in the absence of such regulations.

Do these measures foster the development of interpersonal trust? They may foster relations of trust by giving the weaker party to the contract grounds to think that the stronger party has incentives to encapsulate the weaker party's interests. Whether by raising the outside utility level of the weaker party (the satisfaction with the amount of goods he can consume if he is not hired) or by imposing external constraints on the optimal contract, or both, public institutions force the stronger party to take the weaker party's interest into account, or at least to a greater extent it would do in the absence of state intervention. This should promote trust between the parties. As Miller (1992, 2001) has repeatedly argued, one of the obstacles to the development of relations of trust in interpersonal relations characterized by agency problems is the difficulties the principal has when it comes to making credible commitments. In this case, the credibility of the commitments is guaranteed by state regulation. If the principal has to fulfill given legal standards in the contract and if his relative power with respect to workers is reduced by the state reinforcing the latter's position, there are good grounds to think that the principal will be trustworthy.

Therefore, we have identified some mechanisms through which two versions of the state – the liberal state and the welfare state – can foster relations of trust. Some of them are related to the role of the state in the enforcing of private agreements, whereas others are related to the role of the state providing conditions of equality between the parties in those agreements, and conditions of social equality in general.

I test the hypotheses derived from the theoretical part in the next section. I will use data of 22 countries from the first wave (2002/03) of the European Social Survey. The countries are Austria, Belgium, the Czech Republic, Germany, Denmark, Spain, Finland, France, the United Kingdom, Greece, Hungary, Sweden, Switzerland, Ireland, Luxembourg, Italy, the Netherlands, Portugal, Poland and Norway.

The model
The empirical model combines two levels of data: contextual and individual levels. The most appropriate way of analysing both levels simultaneously is through a multilevel model (Jones and Bullen, 1994: 252–5; Goldstein, 1999: 5–36). Populations exhibit complex structures with many levels. This complexity in the data has usually been overlooked in traditional analyses. By using multilevel models we are able to model the different levels of the data simultaneously, gaining the potential for improving estimation, valid inference and a better substantive understanding of the social phenomenon. The multilevel model is able to measure how social trust is affected by the citizens' characteristics, as education or membership in associations, as well as by the efficacy of the institutional context. Moreover, the multilevel model allows analysing how these two levels interact (Jones and Bullen, 1994; Goldstein, 1999).

The dependent variable: social trust
The dependent variable is people's trust.[2] The indicator is the standard survey question: generally speaking, would you say that most people can be trusted, or that you cannot be too careful in dealing with people? The answer to this question in the European Social Survey is a scale from 0 to 10, 0 being no trust at all and 10 complete trust.

This variable as measured in surveys is problematic, especially from the point of view of a rationalistic definition of trust. To reconcile rationalistic definitions of trust with the idea of 'generalized trust', we can consider that the information requirement of a rational expectation implies that while certain forms of trust based on blind faith are excluded, it does not require full information about the other people's trustworthiness. In order to form that expectation, some pieces of information can be used but it does not assume full information about the other player's preferences to be considered rational. In most cases, the gathering of full information about other people's preferences will be very costly and inefficient (Popkin, 1991). Expectations of trust in strangers can be based on informational shortcuts, and one source for these expectations is the actions of the state.

The independent variables
The models include individual-level and country-level variables. The first independent variable at the country level is the efficacy of the state. I have claimed that an efficacious state creates an 'environment' where trust can grow, whereas the state's inefficacy destroys trust. The variable of the state's efficacy is the Public Institutions Index of the World Economic Forum's 2003–04 Global Competitiveness Report. It is the mean of two subindexes. The first is the 'Contracts and Law Subindex', that measures the independence of the judiciary, the protection of property rights, the neutrality of the government in the assigning of public contracts and the pervasiveness of organized crime. The second is the 'Corruption Subindex', which measures the pervasiveness of bribes in economic exchanges. Lowest values of the public institution index indicate low efficacy of public institutions and low corruption. The descriptives of the Public Institutions Index are shown in Table 11.1.

The second variable at the country level is public social expenditure. This variable has been included in the models to test whether the welfare state has an impact on social trust. The general mechanism for this relation was provided by Rothstein and Uslaner (2005): the equality of opportunities and material equality fostered by the welfare state promotes social trust. I have proposed a second mechanism, basically focused on how the equalization of social relations affects the incentives of both parties in an exchange.

Table 11.1   Public Institutions Index

Denmark	6.56
Finland	6.52
Sweden	6.28
Switzerland	6.20
Germany	6.10
Netherlands	6.02
United Kingdom	6.01
Luxembourg	5.92
Austria	5.83
Israel	5.82
Norway	5.73
Portugal	5.52
France	5.50
Ireland	5.46
Belgium	5.41
Spain	5.28
Hungary	5.18
Slovenia	5.11
Greece	4.71
Italy	4.56
Czech Republic	4.51
Poland	4.17

However, general levels of public social expenditures do not tell the whole story of the welfare state. For this reason, I have included a categorical variable to account for differences in the modalities of welfare states. I have considered Esping-Andersen's (1990) original typology of welfare states, as I did in a previous analysis of the influence of public expenditure on social capital (Herreros, 2004: 90–99). In the sample, liberal welfare states include Ireland and the United Kingdom, conservative welfare states include Belgium, Switzerland, Germany, Spain, France, Greece, Italy, Luxembourg, the Netherlands and Portugal, and social-democratic welfare states include Austria, Sweden, Norway, Denmark and Finland. I have added a fourth category of welfare states, the ex-communist ones. In a continuum from less to more de-commodification, communist states will be in the extreme of fully decommodification. Although the welfare states in those countries have been profoundly transformed since the demise of communism, most probably current welfare states in ex-communist countries still share certain characteristics that justify grouping them together in one apart category. In our sample, the ex-communist welfare states include the Czech Republic, Poland and Hungary.

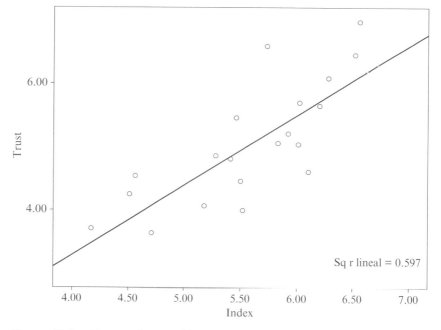

Figure 11.1   Trust and state efficacy

The independent variables at the individual level are education, income, participation in associations and gender. Education is a classical variable associated with trust. It is an ordinal variable that measures the years of education completed. Income is also a variable traditionally considered related to trust: higher income levels are usually regarded as predictors of high levels of trust. It ranges from 1 (lowest income level) to 12 (highest income level). Participation in associations has usually been considered a variable related to the development of social trust (Putnam, 1993, 2000; Stolle and Rochon, 1998; Wollebak and Selle, 2003). I have included this variable in the model as a classical 'social capital' variable in the explanation of social trust.

Results

Before presenting the results of the multilevel models, it could be useful to observe some relevant bivariate relations between social trust and our two main contextual variables: the state's efficacy and public social expenditure.

Figure 11.1 reflects the correlation between the average levels of social trust for each of the countries in the sample and the Public Institutions

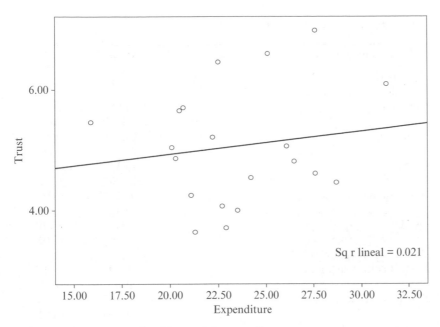

Figure 11.2   Trust and public social expenditure

Index. As we can see, there is a fairly strong correlation between both variables. Higher levels of state efficacy seem to be related to higher averages of social trust. This is coherent with the idea that in more efficient states there is a friendly environment for the growing of trust.

The correlation between public social expenditure and social trust is depicted in Figure 11.2. In this case, we can not observe a significant correlation between both variables. Part of the explanation for this low correlation lies in the presence of three ex-communist countries in the sample: the Czech Republic, Poland and Hungary. These are countries with relatively high levels of public social expenditure (above 20 per cent of GDP) and low levels of social trust. However, if we delete these cases from the dataset, the correlation between both variables actually falls, even if slightly. Therefore, it does not seem to be an appreciable correlation between levels of social expenditure and social trust, contrary to the predictions of the theoretical part.

To corroborate or to discard these simple correlations, I have estimated three multilevel lineal regression models. The results of the three models are shown in Table 11.2. The first model shows the variation across countries in terms of political trust. As we can see, there are significant differences across countries in the dependent variable.

Table 11.2   The state and social trust

Independent variables	Model 1	Model 2	Model 3
Fixed part			
Individual-level variables			
Constant	5.08***	4.09***	4.11***
	(0.22)	(1.47)	(1.47)
Education		0.07***	0.07***
		(0.003)	(0.006)
Income		0.03***	0.03***
		(0.007)	(0.007)
Associational membership		0.37***	0.37***
		(0.02)	(0.02)
Gender		−0.01	−0.01
		(0.02)	(0.02)
Country-level variables			
Public Institutions Index		0.35**	0.34**
		(0.16)	(0.16)
Public social expenditure		−0.05	−0.05
		(0.03)	(0.03)
Liberal welfare state		−1.08**	−0.99**
		(0.47)	(0.48)
Conservative welfare state		−1.19***	−1.20***
		(0.29)	(0.30)
Ex-communist welfare state		−1.58***	−1.75***
		(0.51)	(0.53)
Interaction education/liberal welfare state			−0.007
			(0.01)
Interaction education/conservative welfare state			0.001
			(0.008)
Interaction education/ex-communist welfare state			0.01
			(0.01)
Random part			
Between countries variation	0.92***	0.16***	0.16***
	(0.30)	(0.05)	(0.05)
Log likelihood	151113.70	150165.30	150162.80
N	33702	35221	35221

Note: ***Significant at 99 per cent; **significant at 95 per cent.

Model 2 includes the relevant variables of our analysis alongside other individual-level control variables. Among these individual-level variables, the results are in general terms the expected by the literature on social capital. Participation in associations, income and education are all related to the levels of social trust: more affluent and educated people tend to be more trusting, and members of associations tend to be more trusting than non-members. Gender, by contrast, is not significant.

As regards the relevant variables to test the arguments of the theoretical section, the model confirms the results of the correlations of Figures 11.1 and 11.2. The Public Institutions Index is significant and the sign of the coefficient is as expected: the more efficient the public institutions, the higher the levels of interpersonal trust. This result is coherent with the idea expressed in the theoretical section about the likely relationship between an efficient state and trust in others. By contrast, the variable of public social expenditure is not significant. There is not a relationship between the percentage of the state's social expenditure and trust.

Do these results mean that the welfare state does not have an effect on social trust? Not necessarily. Maybe the effect of the welfare state on trust does not depend on the level of expenditure, but on the type of welfare state. For this reason, I have differentiated between four types of welfare state, as I mentioned before: the social-democratic, the conservative, the liberal and the ex-communist. I have built four dummy variables (that is, a numerical variable with various categories that represent different subgroups in the sample) for each of the welfare state's types, and I have included in the model the dummy variables for the conservative, the liberal and the ex-communist type of welfare state. Therefore, the category of reference to interpret the coefficients of the three dummy variables is the social-democratic welfare state, corresponding in our sample, as we know, to Austria, Denmark, Sweden, Norway and Finland. As we can see, the type of welfare state does have an effect on social trust. People tend to be more trusting in social-democratic welfare states than in the other three types of welfare state. This has probably something to do with the universalistic social policies characteristic of this type of welfare state. According to Rothstein and Uslaner (2005), universal social policies are more effective than selective ones in creating material equality and equality of opportunities, and, thereby, more effective in creating trust.

We know, therefore, that the type of the welfare state does have an effect on the societal levels of social trust. Social-democratic welfare states foster the development of high trusting societies. However, is the effect of the welfare state on social trust evenly distributed among social groups? In general, social capital, both in terms of associational membership and social trust, tend to be unequally distributed among social classes (Wuthnow, 2002). Maybe universalistic welfare states do not only promote high levels of social trust, but also a more even distribution of this resource in society. In a previous work (Herreros, 2004), I found a positive relation between universalistic welfare states and equality in the distribution of social capital measured as participation in associations across social classes. Is this also the case for social trust? To test this idea, I have added three interaction terms between types of welfare state and education (as an indicator of social class) in the third model of Table 11.2. The results do not seem to confirm the hypothesis. The social-democratic welfare states do not redistribute the levels of social trust more evenly among social classes than the liberal, the conservative and the ex-communist models. That is, the interaction terms between the different types of welfare state and education are not significant. This clearly means that the type of welfare state does not have an effect on the levels of social trust of less educated people.

Conclusion

The state has indeed an effect on trust. In fact, two versions of the state seem to be related to the generation of social trust: the liberal model and the welfare state. The liberal model increases trust through the efficacy of public institutions. I have argued that this efficacy creates an 'environment' where trust can grow. This idea is slightly different to other theoretical developments about the role of the state as a third-party enforcer of private agreements on social trust. It predicts that trust will be destroyed in the absence of the state or where the state is highly inefficient, and that trust will most likely flourish in countries blessed with an efficient and impartial state. The results of the models seem to confirm this idea in general terms.

The welfare state has also a role to play. Although general levels of public social expenditure do not seem to affect the levels of trust in our sample of European countries, the type of welfare state is indeed relevant to create high-trusting societies. Trust is significantly higher in the social-democratic welfare state than in the other three types of welfare state included in the models. This can be related, as Rothstein and Uslaner (2005) claim, to the pre-eminence of universalistic policies in the social-democratic type of welfare state. However, it is also important to note that the unequal distribution of trust across social classes is virtually unaffected by the welfare state.

Notes

1. Does this mean that an efficient dictatorship will be more positive for the growing of trust than an inefficient democracy? The argument is, in principle, neutral to the type of regime. Empirically, however, one should expect, first, for the rule of law to be better grounded in a democracy than in a dictatorship, and, second, for the more efficient states to be over-whelmingly concentrated among democracies. Public institutions can be more effective in democracies perhaps because there is a relation between relatively high per capita GDP and democratic regimes, at least in the sense that per capita income has a strong impact on the survival of democracies (Przeworski et al., 2000), and more affluent countries tend to have more efficient bureaucracies. Rule of law and low levels of corruption can

also be related to democracy through mechanisms directly related to the type of regime: democracies are associated with electoral accountability and other institutional checks and balances as separation of powers, and these mechanisms should make corruption of public officials less likely, although there remain ample possibilities for corruption even in democracies (Rose-Ackerman, 1999).

2. In a regression model, the dependent variable is the explained variable, whereas the independent variables are the explanatory variables.

References

Coleman, James S. (1990), *Foundations of Social Theory*, Cambridge, MA, and London: Harvard University Press.

Darley, John M. (2004), 'Commitment, trust and worker effort expenditure in organization', in M. Kramer and K. S. Cook (eds), *Trust and Distrust in Organizations*, New York: Russell Sage, pp. 127–51.

Dowley, Kathleen M. and Brian D. Silver (2003), 'Social capital, ethnicity and support for democracy in the post-communist states', in G. Badescu and Uslaner (eds), *Social Capital and the Transition to Democracy*, London: Routledge, pp. 95–119.

Esping-Andersen, Gösta (1990), *The Three Worlds of Welfare Capitalism*, Princeton, NJ: Princeton University Press.

Flap, Henk and Beate Völker (2003), 'Communist societies, the velvet revolution, and weak ties', in G. Badescu and E. Uslaner (eds), *Social Capital and the Transition to Democracy*, London: Routledge, pp. 28–45.

Goldstein, K. (1999), *Watering the grassroots: Interest Groups, Lobbying and Participation*, Ann Arbor, MI: Michigan University Press.

Guseva, Alya and Akos Rona-Tas (2001), 'Uncertainty, risk and trust: Russian and American credit card markets compared', *American Sociological Review*, **66** (5), 623–46.

Hardin, Russell (1998), 'Trust in government', in V. Braithwaite and M. Levi (eds), *Trust and Governance*, New York: Russell Sage, pp. 9–27.

Hardin, Russell (2002), *Trust and Trustworthiness*, New York: Russell Sage.

Heimer, Carol A. (2001), 'Solving the problem of trust', in Karen S. Cook (ed.), *Trust in Society*, New York: Russell Sage, pp. 40–88.

Herreros, Francisco (2003), 'The dilemma of social democracy in 1914. Chauvinism or social dilemma?', *Rationality and Society*, **15** (3), 325–44.

Herreros, Francisco (2004), *The Problem of Forming Social Capital. Why Trust?*, New York and London: Palgrave.

Huck, Steffen (1998), 'Trust, treason and trials: an example of how the evolution of preferences can be driven by legal institutions', *The Journal of Law, Economics and Organization*, **14** (1), 44–60.

Huysseune, Michel (2003), 'Institutions and their impact on social capital and civic culture: the case of Italy', in M. Hooghe and D. Stolle (eds), *Generating Social Capital*, New York: Palgrave, pp. 211–30.

Iglic, Hajdeja (2003), 'Trust networks and democratic transition. Yugoslavia in the mid-1980s', in G. Badescu and E. Uslaner (eds), *Social Capital and the Transition to Democracy*, London: Routledge, pp. 10–27.

Jones, K. and N. Bullen, (1994), 'Contextual models of urban house prices: a comparison of fixed and random coefficients models developed by expansions', *Economic Geography*, **70**, 252–70.

Laffont, Jean-Jacques and David Martimort (2002), *The Theory of Incentives. The Principal–Agent Model*, Princeton, NJ: Princeton University Press.

Levi, Margaret (1998), 'A state of trust', in V. Braithwaite and M. Levi (eds), *Trust and Governance*, New York: Russell Sage, pp. 77–101.

Miller, Gary J. (1992), *Managerial Dilemmas. The Political Economy of Hierarchy*, Cambridge: Cambridge University Press.

Miller, Gary J. (2001), 'Why is trust necessary in organizations? The moral hazard of profit maximization', in Karen S. Cook (ed.), *Trust in Society*, New York: Russell Sage, pp. 307–31.

Mondak, Jeffrey and Adam F. Gearing (1998), 'Civic engagement in a post-communist state', *Political Psychology*, **19** (3), 615–37.

Murnighan, J. Keith, Deepak Malhotra and J. Mark Weber (2004), 'Paradoxes of trust: empirical and theoretical departures from a traditional model', in M. Kramer and K.S. Cook (eds), *Trust and Distrust in Organizations*, New York: Russell Sage, pp. 293–326.

Nichols, Thomas M. (1996), 'Russian democracy and social capital', *Social Science Information*, **35** (4), 649–52.

Nissenbaum, Helen (2004), 'Will security enhance trust online, or supplant it?', in M. Kramer and K.S. Cook (eds), *Trust and Distrust in Organizations*, New York: Russell Sage, pp. 155–88.

Offe, Claus (1999), 'How can we trust our fellow citizens', in Mark Warren (ed.), *Democracy and Trust*, Cambridge: Cambridge University Press, pp. 42–87.

Padgen, Anthony (1988), 'The destruction of trust and its economic consequences in the case of eighteenth-century Naples', in Diego Gambetta (ed.), *Trust*, London: Basil Blackwell, pp. 127–41.

Popkin, Samuel L. (1991), *The Rational Voter. Communication and Perception in Presidential Elections*, Chicago, IL: University of Chicago Press.

Przeworski, Adam, Michael E. Alvarez, José Antonio Cheibub and Fernando Limongi (2000), *Democracy and Development: Political Institutions and Well-Being in the World 1950–1990*, Cambridge: Cambridge University Press.

Putnam, Robert D. (1993), *Making Democracy Work. Civic Traditions in Modern Italy*, Princeton, NJ: Princeton University Press.

Putnam, Robert D. (2000), *Bowling Alone. The Collapse and Revival of American Community*, New York: Simon & Schuster.

Rose-Ackerman, Susan (1999), *Corruption and Government. Causes, Consequences and Reform*, New York: Cambridge University Press.

Rothstein, Bo (2001), 'Social capital in the social democratic welfare state', *Politics and Society*, **29** (2), 207–41.

Rothstein, Bo and Eric Uslaner (2005), 'All for all. Equality, corruption, and social trust', *World Politics*, **58**, 41–72.

Stolle, Dietlind and Thomas Rochon (1998), 'Are all associations alike? Member diversity, associational type and the creation of social capital', *American Behavioral Scientist*, **42** (1), 47–65.

Torsvik, Gaute (2000), 'Social capital and economic development. A plea for mechanisms', *Rationality and Society*, **12** (4), 451–76.

Ullman-Margalit, Edna (2004), 'Trust, distrust and in between', in R. Hardin (ed.), *Distrust*, New York: Russell Sage, pp. 60–82.

Uslaner, Eric (2002), *The Moral Foundations of Trust*, Cambridge: Cambridge University Press.

Uslaner, Eric (2003), 'Trust and civic engagement in East and West', in G. Badescu and E. Uslaner (eds), *Social Capital and the Transition to Democracy*, London: Routledge, pp. 81–94.

Wollebak, Dag and Per Selle (2003), 'The importance of passive membership for social capital formation', in M. Hooghe and D. Stolle (eds), *Generating Social Capital*, New York: Palgrave, pp. 67–88.

Wuthnow, R. (2002), 'The United States: bridging the privileged and the marginalized?', in Robert D. Putnam (ed.), *Democracies in Flux. The Evolution of Social Capital in Contemporary Society*, Oxford: Oxford University Press, pp. 59–102.

12 The universal welfare state
Bo Rothstein

What is a universal welfare state?

The large body of welfare state research that exists has to quite some extent been a taxonomic enterprise. Scholars in this field have put at lot of effort into constructing an adequate conceptual map that captures the extensive variation that exists in how different industrialized Western states are doing 'welfare' and what differentiates the one social program from the other (Flora, 1987; Goul Andersen and Hoff, 1996; Korpi and Palme, 1998; Rothstein, 1998; Swank, 1998; Kuhnle, 2000). Many scholars have come to single out the four Nordic countries as a special type of welfare state that has been labelled as 'the universal welfare state' (Esping-Andersen, 1990). By this is meant that there is a broad range of social services and benefits that are intended to cover the entire population throughout the different stages of life, and that the benefits are delivered on the basis of uniform rules for eligibility. A typical example would be universal childcare or universal child allowances that are distributed without any form of means-testing (that is, no individual screening is carried out). Universal health care or sickness insurances are other examples. This type of welfare policy may be distinguished from selective welfare programs that are intended to assist only those who cannot manage economically on their own hand. In a selective program, the specific needs and the economic situation of each person seeking assistance have to be scrutinized by some administrative process (Kumlin, 2004). A third type of welfare state is that in which benefits and services are distributed according to status group. In such systems, privileged groups of the population are singled out to receive more than the rest of society, a benefit originally intended as an award for loyalty to the state. The status-oriented compartmentalized social insurance schemes in Germany, which are tailored to its specific clientele, are a case in point (Rothstein and Stolle, 2003).

It should be noted that all modern welfare states are mixtures and that differences between various programs can be rather fine-grained. It is also the case that selectivity is carried out in a number of different ways. For example, there are programs that cater to almost the whole population except for the very wealthy and that are thus not singling out the poorest part of the population. Other welfare states have different programs for very broad categories of citizens based, for example, on occupational status

(Mau, 2003). Nevertheless, most welfare state and social policy researchers seem to have accepted the idea that it is reasonable to categorize different welfare states according to this universal-selectivity dimension based on what is their typical 'modus operandi' (Goodin et al., 1999; Scharpf and Schmidt, 2000; Huber and Stephens, 2001; Pontusson, 2005).

A number of important political and social consequences follow from how welfare states are organized. Firstly, since universal welfare states cater to a very large part of the population, the middle and professional classes are included in the programs. This has important electoral and political consequences because the welfare states in the Nordic countries are not primarily seen as only catering to the needs of 'the poor' (Rothstein and Uslaner, 2005). Secondly, a universal welfare system demands a high level of taxation for the simple reason that if (almost) everyone is included, the public coffers have to be big (Steinmo, 1993). Thirdly, a universal policy can be implemented without the large bureaucratic apparatus that is needed for carrying out the individualized means-testing that is needed in a selective welfare system (Rothstein, 1998). Fourthly, it is well known that means-testing often is perceived by clients as problematic from an integrity perspective and that social stigma often follows from being seen as a client in a selective program (Soss, 2000).

One way to illustrate the differences is to compare a person with low economic resources in these different systems, for example a single parent with low education (usually a woman). In a selective system, this is usually a person that does not work because she cannot afford daycare. It follows that she and her children have to exist on some form of selective benefits which, in addition to the integrity problems that follow from means-testing, usually also carries a social stigma. This is thus a person that can be seen as someone who does not contribute to society (not working and not paying taxes) but that survives on special benefits. In a universal system, this is usually a person that works because her children are in the public childcare or pre-school system as are (almost) everyone else's children. The implication is that this is a person that is usually able to get by without applying for social assistance by combining her (low) income with the universal benefits and services that goes to everyone. She is thus not seen as someone just benefiting from the welfare state and as being outside the social fabric (Sainsbury, 1999). Moreover, the services and benefits that she gets do not carry any special social stigma and her integrity is not violated by a bureaucratic process scrutinizing her economic and social situation.[1]

Admittedly, this is an ideal-type of reasoning and one should be wary of the great variation that exists between 'really existing' welfare states (Alber, 2006). Nevertheless, there is some empirical support for this argument about the social and political consequences of different welfare state models. This concerns not least the situation of children that grow up in low-resource single parent families (Rainwater and Smeeding, 2003). This chapter is organized as follows: the first section deals with the puzzle why the countries that have the most ambitious and encompassing social policies also seem to have the largest stock of social capital. The second section deals with the problem of causality – if the level of social capital can be seen as a causal factor behind variation in welfare state ambitions, or if the causality works the other way around. In this section is also a presentation of the relation between types of welfare state programs and economic redistribution. The last section presents a theory of how the causal mechanism(s) between social capital and welfare state policies can be understood.

Social capital and the Nordic puzzle
What has become particularly interesting from a social capital perspective is that the countries that most resemble the ideal-type universal welfare state model are also the countries that are richest in social capital. Although, as should be obvious from this volume, there are a great number of ways to conceptualize and measure social capital, there is by now overwhelming support for this claim. Both attitudinal measures about social trust and behavioral measures about social activities in formal organizations and informal networks support the fact that the Nordic countries are the richest in social capital (Uslaner, 2002; Delhey and Newton, 2005; Kääriäinen and Lehtonen, 2006; Bjørnskov, 2007; Job, 2007). For example, people in the Nordic countries are much more likely than people in other countries to believe that 'most other people can be trusted' (You, 2006). According to the 1995–97 World Value Study survey, the average stating that they believe that 'most people can be trusted' is 64 percent for the Nordic countries which is almost three times as high as the world average. People in the Nordic countries are also members and active in voluntary associations to a comparatively large extent (Vogel et al., 2003; van Oorschot et al., 2006). Moreover, for the Nordic countries there are no traces of the decline of social capital that has been reported for the United States (Larsen, 2007).

The high level of social capital in the Nordic countries can be seen as puzzling for several reasons. One is that not least in political and policy circles, social capital in the form of social networks and voluntary associations or, with another term, civil society organizations, has been seen as an alternative to the state (and the market and the family) for 'getting things done'. Voluntary organizations come in many forms, from sport clubs and cultural organizations to religious communities and mutual self-help organizations, to name a few. What they all have in common is that they represent an alternative form of organizational logic. It is not authority (or money or kinship) that is driving civil society but cooperation for mutual interests, and such organizations cannot thrive without trust between members and confidence between the rank and file and the leaders of these organizations. One could therefore expect that we should see a 'crowding out' effect such that the huge expansion of the responsibility of the government that the universal welfare state represents should be detrimental to the development of a vibrant civil society (Ostrom, 2000). Moreover, one could argue that in a society where the government takes on the responsibility for a large number of social needs, people do not have to develop and maintain trusting relations and invest in a social network (Wolfe, 1989; Scheepers et al., 2002). However, as stated above, the empirical reality contradicts these expectations. Studies show that social trust is highest in the Nordic countries and that citizens in these countries are among the most active in voluntary associations (van Oorschot and Arts, 2005). Thus, the relation between social capital and the Nordic type of universal welfare state presents us with a real puzzle.

Is social capital the cause or the effect of the universal welfare state?
There can be at least three general explanations for why high levels of social capital and 'big government' in the form of universal welfare systems go together. First, both the development and level of social capital in a country may be unrelated to its system of welfare and social policies. This argument would rest on an idea that the social, political and economic trajectories of social capital and the welfare state can live 'separate lives'. I consider this is a very unlikely scenario for a number of reasons. First, welfare states are about (different forms of) equality which has been shown to be important for the development of social trust (Uslaner, 2002; Dinesen, 2006; You, 2006). Secondly, the Nordic type of welfare states have historically been closely related to important nation-wide social movements such as the temperance movement, the labour movement, the farmers movement and the free churches to name a few. Historically, there is a direct link between civil society organizations and the welfare state in these countries going back to the late nineteenth century (Rothstein, 2002; Torpe, 2003; Wollebæck and Selle, 2003).

Thirdly, as will be shown below, citizens' perceptions of 'fairness' by government agencies have an impact on social trust and universal social policies contribute to this (Štulhofer, 2004; Kim, 2005; Uslaner, 2008). Finally, the three Scandinavian countries became internationally known for their consensual and collaborative forms of politics that were established during the economic crises of the 1930s, not least when it comes to arranging cooperative patterns of interaction between the major interest organizations and the state around the development of the welfare state.

The second general explanation for the puzzle is that a high level of social capital was necessary for the creation of the universal type of welfare state. In other words, the Nordic countries could build their encompassing system of social policies from the 1930s and onwards because they were already by then rich in social capital (Rothstein, 2005). In this scenario, the universal welfare state is to at least some extent caused by a high level of social capital. A country with a high level of social trust and an active voluntary sector is more likely to produce the kind of policies that are typical of the universal welfare states. This line of reasoning is of course difficult to evaluate since we lack most of the necessary type of data from this period. We have no surveys or systematic comparative studies of the voluntary sector from this period. However, there are patches of data and 'stories' that can be used to shed light on this theory and as I will show below, it can to some extent be substantiated (Trägårdh, 2007).

The third general explanation would be that the universal welfare state as such is a source of social capital (Kumlin, 2004). This would imply that either the outcome of what this type of welfare state produces enhances generalized trust and makes it more likely that people will be engaged in voluntary associations and/or develop rich informal social networks. Or it could be something in 'how it is done' that increases social capital. This latter argument implies that it is not the outcome of the various policies but the specific process of implementation in the universal welfare state that is important for creating social capital.

The universal welfare state as a redistributive machine

The universal welfare state is not only larger in terms of spending than other welfare states, but it is also more redistributive. This is somewhat counterintuitive since one would think that a selective welfare state that 'taxes the rich and gives to the poor' would accomplish more redistribution than a universal welfare program that in principle gives the same benefits and services to all groups regardless of their income. However, empirical research gives a clear answer that the Nordic welfare states accomplish more redistribution than other welfare states (Smeeding, 2005). The reason for this is that taxes are usually proportional on a percentage base (or progressive), while benefits and services are nominal. The net effect of this is a considerable redistribution from the rich to the poor, while on average the middle strata breaks even in this system. In fact, before taxes and transfers are taken into account, the Nordic type of economy produces as much economic inequality as the US economy. The 'pure (labour-) market logic' in the Nordic countries is thus not particularly prone to equality. The reason why a selective welfare state produces less redistribution seem to be that if the middle class perceives that benefits and services are only going to 'other people', they will not accept a high level of taxation (Rothstein,

2001). It also seem to be the case that services for the poor tend to become 'poor services', while if the middle and upper classes are included, they will demand high quality in, for example, health care, schools and care for the elderly.

The universal welfare state as an outcome of social capital
There are several reasons for why one could consider the universal welfare state as an effect of high levels of social capital. First, since the universal welfare state demands a high level of taxation, citizens must have a reasonable amount of trust that other citizens are willing to pay what they are supposed to. This can of course be accomplished by a draconian type of tax administration, but most research in this field show that brute force will not be enough. Some kind of quasi-voluntary compliance seems to be needed for securing that the state can collect enough taxes and one ingredient in this seems to be that the individual citizen comes to trust that most other citizens are taking on their share of the tax burden (Levi, 1998; Scholz, 1998). Without this initial trust in 'other people', one could argue that it would not have been possible to finance universal social policies.

A second argument is that at the time of the foundation of the universal welfare policies (mostly from the 1930s and onward), these were countries with hardly any ethnic or religious cleavages (although Finland still has a sizeable Swedish-speaking minority). Mistrust between different ethnic groups did not exist and it is reasonable to think that this would have been favorable for the existence of social trust.

Thirdly, although good comparative data is lacking, most historical research about the history of the Nordic countries underlines the importance of the so-called popular movements that arose during the latter part of the nineteenth century. An important historical research project about the Swedish nineteenth century labelled this period as the 'age of the associations' (Pettersson, 1995). Among these associations, the labour movement, the farmers' movement, the temperance movement and the free churches played a very special and important role. The popular mass movements saw themselves as protest movements against the bureaucratic, clerical, aristocratic and capitalist elite who dominated Scandinavia at the turn of the last century. The idea of a 'movement' implied that society should be changed and that the vehicle was mass organization from below. As organizations of both protest and self-help, the popular mass movements stood in sharp contrast to the charity organizations dominated by the middle and upper classes. In the official mythology, the popular mass movements were the major schools of democratic and organizational training, making the transition to democracy a relatively civilized affair in these countries (Lundström and Wijkström, 1997).

The major social conflict during this period in the Nordic countries was of course the tension between the labor movement and the capitalist class. However, what seems to be unique about the Nordic countries (with the notable exception of Finland) is the development of a very close collaboration between the state and the popular mass movements without destroying the autonomy of the latter (Klaussen and Selle, 1996). To illustrate the historical pattern, I focus on one aspect of the relationship between the state and the labor movement in Sweden. An especially interesting case was the establishment of the National Board for Social Affairs in 1912. According to the commission that prepared the bill, the task of this agency was not primarily poor-relief, a function handled by local authorities, but instead was nothing less than the so-called *labor question*. The commission argued that the problem was concentrated in the cities, where the rapid process of industrialization had led to a potentially dangerous situation with masses of workers who had become alienated from traditional local communities and other social bonds. In the words of the commission:

> The feeling of solidarity that has emerged among the working masses, in itself praiseworthy, is limited to themselves and they do not appear to wish to extend it to the whole society in which they share responsibility and play a part. This obviously poses a national danger, which must be removed in the common interest of everyone. Everywhere the government therefore faces the difficult task of mitigating conflicts of interest and repairing the cracks that are opening in the social structure. (Cited in Rothstein, 1992: 162)

The National Board for Social Affairs was established to handle this problem by implementing reforms in worker safety, labor exchanges and social housing and by overseeing the poor-relief system managed by the local authorities. Its mandate was to handle the labor question, and the preferred method was to *incorporate* representatives from this new and threatening social class into the state machinery. As a result of the commission's proposal, the chairmen of the national trade union conference (the LO) and of the employers' federation (the SAF) were given seats on the board of the agency and, following the corporatist principle, other representatives from the LO and the SAF were given seats on various subcommittees. The commission's argument supporting this arrangement was that the representatives from the organizations

> would behave as guardians not only of special interests but also of the interests of everyone, of society as a whole . . . It should certainly be expected that a representative body structured according to these principles, official and thus functioning with a sense of responsibility, should provide valuable support for the new social welfare administration. (Cited in Rothstein, 1992: 164)

Another illustration of this type of state-organized collaboration between the opposing interests can be found for the public employment exchanges. In many continental countries, this issue was hotly disputed because the party that controlled the employment exchanges had a very important influence in the many local industrial conflicts that were very common during this period. However, in Sweden, the local public employment exchanges were to be governed by a so-called parity principle, which meant that half the representatives on the board were taken from the local unions and the other half from the major employers (and the board was to be chaired by an impartial local civil servant). In a report from 1916 to the government regarding the operation of the local employment exchanges, the National Board for Social Affairs declared that 'no objection has appeared from any quarter against the organizational principles on which the publicly operated employment exchanges were based'. On the contrary, the board argued that it was these very principles that had made it possible for the system to grow and that had been pivotal for strengthening the confidence their operations enjoyed among both employer organizations and unions, 'which in our country have fortunately abstained from utilizing the employment service as a weapon in the social struggle, which in Germany has partially distorted the whole issue of labor exchanges'. The board also observed that

> Despite the sharp social and political conflicts that have emerged in other areas of public life between members of the employer and worker camps, on the boards of the labor exchanges the same persons have, in the experience of the National Board for Social Affairs, continued to cooperate faithfully in the interest of objectivity. (Cited in Rothstein, 1992: 165)

This type of corporatist relations spread quickly to other areas of the Swedish state and came to dominate the political culture of the Swedish model. It should also be noted that in Sweden, this pattern of interest accommodation was established before parliamentary democracy was enacted. Almost all areas of political intervention in the labour market (for example, workers pensions, accident compensation and the implementation of the eight-hour working day) were to be governed according to the collaborative principles. Moreover, in addition to how the labor movement was organized into the state, many other voluntary organizations were also incorporated into this pattern of governance. For example, the temperance movement was given the responsibility of handling the government's propaganda against widespread misuse of alcohol; the farmers' movement, the responsibility of handling subsidies to farming; small business organizations, the responsibility of implementing subsidies to support small business, and so on. A qualitative breakthrough came during the

Second World War, when nearly all parts of the wartime administrations incorporated the major interest organizations of each policy area. The argument that was put forward repeatedly was that this would create trust among the members and followers of the organizations for the process of implementing the policy in question (Rothstein, 1992).

This pattern of close collaboration between the state and the major organizations on the labor market can of course be seen as a contrast to other European countries where these relations ended in bloody conflicts, civil wars and ruthless dictatorships. However, it is noteworthy that in, for example, the Spanish case, recent historical analyses have argued that as late as 1931, the Spanish socialist party 'had collaborated with the government, taking a position that put them to the right even of the French Socialists at that time and brought them close to the . . .. Scandinavian Social Democrats'. It was a only few years later (in 1933–34) that the Spanish socialist party declared that it was going for 'a full-scale civil war' and put forward slogans such as 'Harmony? No! Class War! Hatred of the criminal bourgeoisie to the death!' (Payne, 2004: 31).

Why the class conflicts in the Scandinavian countries followed a collaborative and peaceful path is of course open to debate, but it is not unreasonable to point at the establishment of the neo-corporatist structures as described above (Rothstein, 2005). It should be noted that the Nordic countries were not always a peaceful part of the world characterized by collaboration and negotiations. Going back in history, Denmark and Sweden were arch-enemies and fought ten bloody wars between 1471 and 1814. Norway was under Danish rule until 1814 and then under Swedish rule until 1905. Finland had a terrible civil war in 1918 (including the use of concentration camps and organized killings of innocent civilians) and quite some social unrest in the 1930s. What was special with the Scandinavian countries is that the system of neo-corporatism that was established early in the twentieth century proved to be a successful way to build trustful relations between the opposing factions in society, which in its turn paved the way for the establishment of the universal welfare state.

The universal welfare state as a producer of social capital

The other possible explanation for the 'Nordic puzzle' may be that a universal welfare state creates social trust and social capital. One such reason may have to do with outcomes. Several studies show that economic inequality is detrimental to the development of social capital (Uslaner, 2002; Kääriäinen and Lehtonen, 2006; You, 2006). The logic for this would be that in societies with high levels of economic inequality and with few (or inefficient) policies in place for increasing equality of opportunity, there is less concern for people of different backgrounds. The rich and the poor in a country with a highly unequal distribution of wealth, such as Brazil, may live next to each other, but their lives do not intersect. Their children attend different schools, they use different health care services and, in many cases, the poor cannot afford either of these services. The rich are protected by both the police and private guards, while the poor see these as their natural enemies. In such societies, neither the rich nor the poor have a sense of shared fate with the other. Instead they are likely to fear and/or despise each other (Rothstein and Uslaner, 2005; Larsen, 2007).

One special feature of the universal welfare state is that the very universality of social services and benefits (including education) may increase not only economic equality but also the sense of equality of opportunity. Since optimism for the future is one key determinant of social trust, this makes less sense when there is more economic inequality. Moreover, the less fortunate have fewer reasons to be optimistic about their (or their children's) future if they sense that society is not giving them equality of opportunity. People at the bottom of the income distribution, or minorities that feel discriminated against, will be less sanguine that they too share in society's bounty (Uslaner, 2002).

Second, the distribution of resources and opportunities plays a key role in establishing the belief that people share a common destiny and have similar fundamental values. When resources and opportunities are distributed more equally, people are more likely to perceive a common stake with others and to see themselves as part of a larger social order. If there is a strong skew in wealth or in the possibilities to improve one's stake in life, people at each end may feel that they have little in common with others. In highly unequal societies, people are likely to stick with their own kind. Perceptions of injustice will reinforce negative stereotypes of other groups, making social trust and accommodation more difficult.

The importance of economic equality from the literature on social capital was until recently not on the agenda which, given what the data show, is something of a mystery. For example, while Robert Putnam points at the importance of economic inequality in his analysis of the decline of social capital in the US, it is not mentioned in his conclusion about 'what killed civic engagement?' Moreover, among the seven policy prescriptions for increasing social capital in the US that he presents, none touches upon increasing any form of equality (Putnam, 2000: 359ff., chs 15, 22). This is all the more surprising since the decline of social capital that Putnam finds in the US since the 1970s seems to be suspiciously related in time to a dramatic increase in economic inequality (Neckerman, 2004).

The same strange omission can be seen in the Russell Sage Foundation's large project on trust: among the 51 chapters in the four edited volumes, none is about economic inequality and none of the volumes has an index entry on equality or inequality (Hardin, 1998, 2004; Ostrom and Walker, 2003; Cook et al., 2005). The same goes for the three monographs that this project has produced (Hardin, 2002; Huo and Tyler, 2002; Cook et al., 2005). While political scientists and sociologists largely have neglected the importance of equality for creating social trust, economists have been more interested. Stephen Knack and Paul Zak at the World Bank have concluded that redistribution is one important policy option for governments to increase social trust. However, in a way that seems mandatory for economists, they add that they worry about the economic inefficiencies that they believe can be caused by such redistribution (Knack and Zak, 2002).

The second major reason for why a universal welfare state may generate social trust has to do with procedural fairness. The problem with means-testing from the perspective of procedural justice is that it places great demands both on public employees and on citizens seeking assistance. The public employee must actively interpret a general body of regulations and apply them to each individual seeking to qualify for a public service. The difficulty is that the regulations are seldom so exact that they provide completely unambiguous direction as to what is the right decision in an individual case. As Michael Lipsky shows in *Street-Level Bureaucracy* (1980), 'grassroots bureaucrats' must develop their own practice in interpreting the regulations in order to deal with this difficulty. This interpretive practice is frequently informal and less explicit in nature and, consequently, the bureaucracies applying the needs tests are easily suspected of using '*prejudice, stereotype, and ignorance as a basis for determination*' (emphases added) (Lipsky, 1980: 69). In other words, a program based on needs-testing implies a great scope for bureaucratic discretion. The citizen, for her part, has an incentive and opportunity in this situation to withhold relevant information from the bureaucrat and to try in various ways to convince the latter that she should qualify for the service in question. This easily escalates into a vicious spiral of distrust from the client, leading to increasing control from the bureaucrat (who, moreover, is equipped with a large amount of discretion) that in its turn results in still more distrust from the client, and so on.

Because of these complex and controversial decision-making processes, needs testing and bureaucratic discretionary power are often more difficult to reconcile with principles of procedural justice, compared with universal public services. Since selective welfare institutions must test each case individually, they are to a greater extent subject to the suspicion of cheating, arbitrariness and discrimination, compared with universal public agencies (Rothstein, 1998).

Another problem is that selective welfare programs often stigmatize recipients as 'welfare clients'. They demarcate the rich and the poor, and those at the bottom are made to feel that they are less worthy, not least because of the bureaucratic intrusion felt in the process of implementation. Universal programs are connected to citizens' rights, while selective welfare programs have trouble with legitimacy because they have to single out the 'deserving' from the 'non-deserving poor'. This will always imply discretionary decisions by street-level bureaucrats who may intrude on the personal integrity of clients (Soss, 2000). Denigrating recipients of means-tested government programs leads to social strains in two ways: The poor feel isolated and feel that others deem them unworthy. The denigration of welfare recipients feeds on public perceptions that the poor truly are responsible for their own poverty. Neither side sees a shared fate with the other. In contrast, universal programs do not cast aspersions on the responsibility of benefits and thus do not destroy trust. When they work well, they can even help to create trust by increasing feelings of equal treatment and equality of opportunity (Rothstein and Uslaner, 2005).

Conclusion

Historical macro-level explanations in the social sciences are difficult things. There are good arguments both for the idea that the Nordic-type welfare state is an effect of a initially high level of social capital or that it is cause for the high level of social capital. To solve this question is in all likelihood a 'hard case' (Stolle, 2003). However, one could think that it is a combination of both approaches that explains the high level of social capital in the Nordic welfare states. Following this line of reasoning, sequencing and so-called 'feedback' mechanism between the variables set societies on different (vicious or virtuous) circles that can be understood as paths from which it is difficult to deviate. One could think of this development in the following way: initially the Nordic societies had a stock of social capital that was not much higher than in other comparable countries, but it was high enough to create a small set of universal policies which in its turn increased the level of social capital so that in the next sequence it was possible to enact new or broaden the existing universal social policies, that served to further increase the level of social trust, and so on. However, it can also be the case that this path did not start out with an initially 'more than average' level of social capital but with a 'top-down' construction of some kind of universal social insurance policy that started this process. In any case, the explanation for why these societies are nowadays rich in social capital would be that at some 'formative moment' or 'critical juncture' they managed to set in motion a process in which universal social policy institutions and social capital became mutually reinforcing entities.

Note

1. It is interesting that the political metaphor 'welfare queen' does not exist in the Scandinavian languages.

References

Alber, J. (2006), 'Das "europäische Sozialmodell" und die USA', *Leviathan – Berliner Zeitschrift für Sozialwissenschaft*, **7** (2), 207–40.
Bjørnskov, C. (2007), 'Determinants of generalized trust: a cross-country comparison', *Public Choice*, **130** (1–2), 1–21.
Cook, K.S., R. Hardin and M. Levi (2005), *Cooperation without Trust?* New York: Russell Sage Foundation.
Delhey, J. and K. Newton, (2005), 'Predicting cross-national levels of social trust: global pattern or Nordic exceptionalism?', *European Sociological Review*, **21** (4), 311–27.
Dinesen, P.T. (2006), 'Social tillid, civilsamfund og institutioner – En empirisk analyse af årsager til social tillid i Europa', dissertation, Department of Political Science, Aarhus University.
Esping-Andersen, G. (1990), *The Three Worlds of Welfare Capitalism*, Cambridge: Polity Press.
Flora, P. (1987), *Growth to Limits: The Western European Welfare States since World War II*, Berlin and New York: de Gruyter.
Goodin, R.E., B. Headey, R. Muffles and H.-J. Dirven (1999), *The Real Worlds of Welfare Capitalism*, Cambridge: Cambridge University Press.
Goul Andersen, J. and J. Hoff (1996), *The Scandinavian Welfare States*, London: Macmillan.
Hardin, R. (1998), 'Trust in government', in V. Braithwaite and M. Levi (eds), *Trust & Governance*, New York: Russell Sage Foundation.
Hardin, R. (2002), *Trust and Trustworthiness*, New York: Russell Sage Foundation.
Hardin, R. (ed.) (2004), *Distrust*, New York: Russell Sage Foundation.
Huber, E. and J.D. Stephens (2001), *Development and Crisis of the Welfare State*, Chicago: The University of Chicago Press.
Huo, Y.J. and T.R. Tyler (2002), *Trust in the Law: Encouraging Public Cooperation with the Police and Courts*, New York: Russell Sage Foundation.
Job, J.A. (2007), 'Ripples of trust: reconciling rational and relational accounts of the source of trust', dissertation, Department of Sociology, Australian National University.
Kääriäinen, J. and H. Lehtonen (2006), 'The variety of social capital in welfare state regimes – a comparative study of 21 countries', *European Societies*, **8** (1), 27–57.
Kim, J.-Y. (2005), '"Bowling together" isn't a cure-all. The relationship between social capital and political trust in South Korea', *International Political Science Review*, **26** (2), 193–213.
Klaussen, K.K. and P. Selle (1996), 'The third sector in Sweden', *Voluntas*, **7**, 99–122.
Knack, S. and P. Zak (2002), 'Building trust: public policy, interpersonal trust and economic development', *Supreme Court Economic Review*, **10**, 91–107.
Korpi, W. and J. Palme (1998), 'The paradox of redistribution and strategies of equality: welfare state institutions, inequality, and poverty in the Western countries', *American Sociological Review*, **63** (5), 661–87.
Kuhnle, S. (ed.) (2000), *Survival of the European Welfare State*, London: Routledge.
Kumlin, S. (2004), *The Personal and the Political: How Personal Welfare State Experiences Affect Political Trust and Ideology*, New York: Palgrave/Macmillan.
Larsen, C.A. (2007), 'How welfare regimes generate and erode social capital – the impact of underclass phenomena', *Comparative Politics*, **40**, 83–102.
Levi, M. (1998), 'A state of trust', in V. Braithwaite and M. Levi (eds), *Trust & Governance*, New York: Russell Sage Foundation.
Lipsky, M. (1980), *Street-level Bureaucracy: Dilemmas of the Individual in Public Services*, New York: Russell Sage Foundation.

Lundström, T. and F. Wijkström (1997), *The Nonprofit Sector in Sweden*, Manchester: Manchester University Press.

Mau, S. (2003), *The Moral Economy of Welfare States: Britain and Germany Compared*, London: Routledge.

Neckerman, K. (ed.) (2004), *Social Inequality*, New York: Russell Sage Foundation.

Ostrom, E. (2000), 'Crowding out citizenship', *Scandinavian Political Studies*, **23** (1), 3–16.

Ostrom, E. and J. Walker (eds) (2003), *Trust & Reciprocity: Interdisciplinary Lessons from Experimental Research*, New York: Russell Sage Foundation.

Payne, S.G. (2004), *The Spanish Civil War, the Soviet Union and Communism*, New Haven, CT: Yale University Press.

Pettersson, L. (1995), 'In search of respectability', in L. Rudebeck and O. Törnqvist (eds), *Democratization and the Third World*, Uppsala: Institutionen för u-landskunskap, Uppsala universitet.

Pontusson, J. (2005), *Inequality and prosperity: Social Europe vs. Liberal America*, Ithaca, NY; London: Cornell University Press.

Putnam, R.D. (2000), *Bowling Alone: The Collapse and Revival of American Community*, New York: Simon & Schuster.

Rainwater, L. and T.M. Smeeding (2003), *Poor Kids in a Rich Country: America's Children in Comparative Perspective*, New York: Russell Sage Foundation.

Rothstein, B. (1992), *Den korporativa staten. Intresseorganisationer och statsförvaltning i svensk politik*, Stockholm: Norstedts.

Rothstein, B. (1998), *Just Institutions Matter: The Moral and Political Logic of the Universal Welfare State*, Cambridge: Cambridge University Press.

Rothstein, B. (2001), 'The universal welfare state as a social dilemma', *Rationality and Society*, **14** (2), 190–214.

Rothstein, B. (2002), 'Sweden: social capital in the social democratic state', in R.D. Putnam (ed.), *Democracies in Flux: The Evolution of Social Capital in Contemporary Society*, Oxford: Oxford University Press.

Rothstein, B. (2005), *Social Traps and the Problem of Trust*, Cambridge: Cambridge University Press.

Rothstein, B. and D. Stolle (2003), 'Social capital, impartiality, and the welfare state: an institutional approach', in M. Hooghe and D. Stolle (eds), *Generating Social Capital: The Role of Voluntary Associations, Institutions and Government Policy*, New York: Palgrave/Macmillan.

Rothstein, B. and E.M. Uslaner (2005), 'All for all. Equality, corruption and social trust', *World Politics*, **58** (3), 41–73.

Sainsbury, D. (1999), *Gender and Welfare State Regimes*, Oxford: Oxford University Press.

Scharpf, F.W. and V.A. Schmidt (2000), *Welfare and Work in the Open Economy: From Vulnerability to Competitiveness*, Oxford: Oxford University Press.

Scheepers, P., M. Te Grotenhuis and J. Gelissen (2002), 'Welfare states and dimensions of social capital: cross-national comparisons of social contacts in European countries', *European Societies*, **4** (2), 185–207.

Scholz, J.T. (1998), 'Trust, taxes and compliance', in V. Braithwaite and M. Levi (eds), *Trust & Governance*, New York: Russell Sage Foundation.

Smeeding, T.M. (2005), 'Public policy, economic inequality, and poverty: the United States in comparative perspective', *Social Science Quarterly*, **86** (5), 955–83.

Soss, J. (2000), *Unwanted Claims: The Politics of Participation in the U.S. Welfare System*, Ann Arbor, MI: University of Michigan Press.

Steinmo, S. (1993), *Taxation and Democracy. Swedish, British and American Approaches to Financing the Modern State*, New Haven, CT: Yale University Press.

Stolle, D. (2003), 'The sources of social capital', in M. Hooghe and D. Stolle (eds), *Generating Social Capital: Civil Society and Institutions in a Comparative Perspective*, New York: Palgrave/Macmillan.

Štulhofer, A. (2004), 'Perception of corruption and the erosion of social capital in Croatia 1995-2003', *Croatian Political Science Review*, **41**, 78–96.

Swank, D. (1998), 'Funding the welfare state: globalization and the taxation of business in advanced market economies', *Political Studies*, **46**, 671–92.
Torpe, L. (2003), 'Social capital in Denmark: a deviant case?', *Scandinavian Political Studies*, **26** (1), 27–48.
Trägårdh, L. (ed.) (2007), *State and Civil Society in Northern Europe*, New York: Berghahn Books.
Uslaner, E.M. (2002), *The Moral Foundation of Trust*, New York: Cambridge University Press.
Uslaner, E.M. (2008), *The Bulging Pocket and the Rule of Law. Corruption, Inequality and Trust*, New York: Cambridge University Press.
Van Oorschot, W. and W. Arts (2005), 'The social capital of European welfare states: the crowding out hypothesis revisited', *Journal of European Social Policy*, **15** (1), 5–26.
Van Oorschot, W., W. Arts and J. Gelissen (2006), 'Social capital in Europe – Measurement and social and regional distribution of a multifaceted phenomenon', *Acta Sociologica*, **49** (2), 149–167.
Vogel, J., E. Amna, I. Munck and L. Hall (2003), 'Membership and participation in associations in Sweden: welfare, social capital and schools for democracy', *Sociologisk Forskning* (2), 53–89.
Wolfe, A. (1989), *Whose Keeper? Social Science and Moral Obligation*, Berkeley, CA: University of California Press.
Wollebæck, D. and P. Selle (2003), 'Participation and social capital formation: Norway in a comparative perspective', *Scandinavian Political Studies*, **26** (1), 67–91.
You, J.-S. (2006), 'A comparative study of income inequality, corruption and social trust: how inequality and corruption reinforce each other and erode social trust', PhD dissertation, Harvard University, Kennedy School of Government.

13 The Nordic welfare state
Thora Margareta Bertilsson and Christian Hjorth-Andersen

13.1 Introduction

The Scandinavian countries stand out in the present world economy as both competitive and well-functioning societies.[1] This is an interesting observation in light of the fact that these societies, besides being wealthy also cultivate strong equity-values. This raises classic questions of compatibility between equity and efficiency: traditional views both in economics (Hayek, 1945) and in sociology (Schumpeter, 1976; Weber, 1978: 85–113; O'Connor, 1981) tend to propagate quite opposite views; too much focus on equity undermines efficiency, while efficiency in turn erodes equity. It may be unfair that one person is a professor and another person an asphalt worker but the gain in efficiency outweighs the costs of inequality.

On a more general level, we seek to address the old relationship of the state versus the market in a new light: what are the mechanisms by which equity under some conditions can translate into efficiency? Gösta Esping-Andersen has for decades been an ardent spokesman for the Nordic welfare mix, that heavily relying on tax-supported scheme of welfare subsidiaries for social and family care, in the long run, pools social resources better than any other model (Esping-Andersen, 1990, 1999, 2002, 2006). We are basically in agreement with Esping-Andersen here, but would like to stress the generic feature of the Nordic welfare states: the combined perspective of efficiency and equity was – and is – at the heart of its construction. From a social science point of view, such a combined perspective demands the cooperation between economists and sociologists in accounting for the success of such a state formation. Regrettably, such cooperation across the social sciences is often lacking, with the result that economists tend to look at efficiency measures, while sociologists (and political scientists) focus on problems of equity. In this text, we advance the thesis that a multitude of explanations is required in accounting for the apparent success of the Nordic welfare state. Economic and fiscal policies, the general character and the power of government and, not least, sociological explanations are needed for a fuller account of its success in a global perspective. Of particular interest, as we suggest in this chapter, is the intergenerational effect of what sociologists call 'social capital'. On the whole, and according

Table 13.1   GNI per capita, US$000s, 2004

Denmark	40 650
Finland	32 790
Norway	52 030
Sweden	35 770
European Monetary Union	27 630
United States	41 400
World	6 280

Source: World Bank database.

to opinion surveys, young people stubbornly support 'general welfare'. In this text we shall take a particular look at what economists call 'dynamic effects' of social capital; investments in public policies apparently 'pay off' on the level of individual and collective performance. The welfare mix in the case of the Nordic countries seemingly operates in a social environment of high 'institutional trust' between the populations and state systems (Rothstein and Stolle, 2003). Such institutional trust has considerable socio-economic payoffs.

In this chapter, we disregard differences between the Scandinavian countries and stress differences between these countries and the rest of the world. In Section 13.2, we briefly present some characteristics of these states. In Section 13.3, we offer some tentative explanations. We stress the overall consensual climate of these countries with regard to political goals to be pursued, and we explore in some detail how social trust operate in mediating equity and efficiency. Finally, we consider whether or not the welfare systems of these countries are easily exportable; in our view, these systems ('trust banks') are quite unique for the reason that they take generations to establish.

13.2   The Scandinavian welfare states at the turn of the millennium
In a global perspective, the Scandinavian countries are quite rich and at the same time they are characterized by a rather equal distribution of income.

In Table 13.1, we reproduce the average income in the four countries. The indicator used is the gross national income (GNI) per capita, a standard measure of the average income.

On average, the Scandinavian countries have an income per capita on a par with the United States. Norway is a little higher due to oil income, and Finland and Sweden a little lower, but as a rough measure it seems fair to

Table 13.2   The Gini index

Country	Gini index
Denmark	22.0
Finland	28.0
Norway	29.3
Sweden	25.7
Germany	28.0
United States	46.4

Note: The index refers to 2001–03.

Source: World Bank database.

say that the average income in the Scandinavian countries are comparable to the US, and they are certainly higher than the average of the European Union.[2]

At the same time, the Scandinavian countries rank high with respect to equality. The Gini index usually used to describe income equality is presented in Table 13.2. The Gini index may be computed in various ways, and the numbers presented here refer to households. Nevertheless, for our purposes, these distinctions are not crucial and it would seem that the Scandinavian countries are much more equitable than the United States but not markedly more equitable than, for example, Germany. The Scandinavian welfare states have a rather equal distribution of income in an international perspective but not necessarily in a European perspective. Moreover, the Scandinavian countries are not egalitarian countries. There are dollar billionaires in Scandinavia, too, and their numbers are presently increasing.

The traditional social democratic vision of the welfare society was not an egalitarian society but a society with equal opportunities. The son of the asphalt worker should have the same opportunities in life as the son of the professor. In that respect, these countries have enjoyed a moderate measure of success.[3]

These two tables essentially make our case: *there is no necessary trade-off between income and equality.* Apparently, high income can combine with a considerable equity. The Scandinavian countries provide evidence that there are alternatives to the American model; that wealth demands a considerable spread of income differences in the population to motivate individuals to climb the social ladder. On the other hand, we know for sure that equity under some conditions can lead to considerable reduction in collective wealth. The interesting question in this context is under what conditions and through which mechanisms equity can contribute to wealth?

The results concerning income equality in the Scandinavian countries are largely due to public redistribution, and these countries are notorious for their taxation. Indeed, taxation is higher in the Scandinavian countries than the Organisation for Economic Co-operation and Development (OECD) average or the US but not very much higher than some countries in continental Europe such as Germany or France. In light of the high tax pressures in the Scandinavian countries, especially in Sweden and Denmark, one would expect the population, especially the more wealthy segments, to partake actively in tax revolts: to express strong opinions in favour of tax reduction or to vote such political parties into power that offer to cut taxes. In fact, it seems that the opposite is true.

Typically, we expect the Nordic welfare countries to be run predomi-nantly by a social democratic government, alone or in a coalition. While clearly social democratic parties were the dominant actors in initiating and establishing general welfare, the picture today appears much more varied. Even when liberal-right parties are in power (as is currently the case in Scandinavia, with the exception of rich Norway!) these governments only seem to make minor changes in basic welfare institutions. Political parties even compete among themselves as to which represents the best and most sustainable welfare model.

Although measurements of the value-structures in the Nordic countries typically show equality to be a cherished value, it is also relevant to point out that the welfare theme stressing the value of equity in a population can serve instrumental means-ends value as well. For the middle classes, welfare services such as good childcare, free access to universities, good maternity and paternity conditions, and good hospitals are typically in their own best (economic) interests. Welfare services have both primary and secondary gains; primary gains are typically those that serve distribu-tive justice and target needy groups, but there are often considerable side effects now discovered by wide population groups.

From a sociological point of view, we feel ready to advance the thesis that the welfare state project in large measures in the Scandinavian coun-tries has become a successful middle-class project. Such a link can also help illuminate its great attraction among a wide spectrum of political parties. Such an outcome – that broad middle-class strata are the winners in the welfare game over time – may also shed light on numerous other indica-tors where people in the Nordic countries excel: they run high on indexes of happiness (Veenhoven, 2006); the fertility rate, also alarmingly low in Europe, is slightly better in these countries than in the rest of the continent. The suicide rate is not as high as once suggested by President Eisenhower in a famous speech in 1960 where he linked the suicide rate in Scandinavia to the welfare state's conception of security from cradle to grave, implying that people had nothing to live for. When it comes to such 'individualistic' contests as artistic expression, Danish film, for instance, occupies a top league position; sport activities of various kinds show continuous Nordic top achievements. Although the Nordic welfare states could be (and certainly have been) targeted by critics to induce the terror of normalcy and mediocrity, prevailing indicators report otherwise.

The prospects for the Scandinavian countries currently look good. They have a natural advantage in a future knowledge-based economy. There are dark clouds, of course. In an international world, it may be difficult to sustain the level of taxation necessary to support the welfare state. Furthermore, immigration from Third World countries poses serious problems for the welfare state. The welfare states have a highly qualified labour force as well as high minimum wages. Massive welfare clientism among immigrants can result in resentment, and even xenophobia, among the domestic population. Denmark is especially targeted, but similar concerns are found in the other Nordic countries as well. There are in fact signs that we may see the beginning of a new underclass: permanent unemployment, school leavers and a rising level of criminality. Such a prospect would certainly tarnish the picture of a general welfare state.

13.3   Explanations
So far, we have demonstrated that the Nordic welfare states do reasonably well from an economic point of view and reasonably well from a social point of view. The question is, why? It is beyond our knowledge, and indeed anybody's knowledge, to provide a definitive answer but we have some suggestions.

Family policy is of course central, as it enables women to enter the labour market, but we regard this observation as commonplace and already well documented. In a short chapter, it is not possible to give a thorough discussion, and we shall not enter into a discussion of purely economic aspects either, such as savings behaviour, capital accumulation, and so on, and though we will concentrate on 'social' explanations, it should not be forgotten that wealth creation is also a question of efficient production of mobile phones, trucks, oil and pigs.

We also skip a discussion of labour market and education policy. It would certainly be relevant to our topic but would require a rather extensive presentation.[4]

Table 13.3   Net total social expenditure, per cent of GNP

Country	Net total social expenditure
Denmark	26.4
Finland	22.6
Norway	23.6
Sweden	30.6
France	31.2
Germany	30.8
OECD-23	22.5
United States	24.5

Source: Adema and Ladaigue (2005).

13.4   The growth orientation of the welfare states

As an introduction, we think it is illuminating to think of welfare in the Nordic states in terms of the idea of surplus, once playing a prominent part in Marxist theory. The capitalist system produced a surplus, as the value of production was more than the amount necessary to sustain the labour class. This surplus was consumed (undeservedly) by the capitalists. In a sense, this idea may be transferred to the welfare states. The economic system produces a surplus in the sense that the value of production is larger than the amount necessary to satisfy the perceived consumption needs of the population. Thus, we get the simple equation: The larger the production, the larger the surplus and the higher the welfare. Hence, it is very much in the interest of the welfare state to promote an efficient economy as that means a larger surplus and higher welfare. This fact was clearly understood by the social democratic movement.

Furthermore, in a welfare state the choice is not just between consumption today and welfare today. It is very much the choice of welfare today or tomorrow. The welfare states are permanent. They expect to be in power for the foreseeable future. There are two important consequences of this fact.

One is that it is a mistake to think of the welfare states as spending exorbitantly on welfare! Adema and Ladaigue (2005) have produced figures for the OECD countries with respect to net total social expenditure. This concept quantifies the proportion of an economy's domestic production at the disposal of recipients of social benefits. Table 13.3 presents the available data.[5]

We see that the proportion to be used as social benefits is not markedly higher in Scandinavia than in the rest of the OECD. Sweden is a little higher than the OECD average but even Sweden does not have a higher proportion than, for example, Germany or France. Thus, the Nordic welfare states should be understood with an emphasis on 'state'. It is the institution of general taxation and general welfare schemes that characterizes these states rather than the amount disbursed as welfare. The Nordic welfare countries do not spend a disproportionate amount on welfare and thus do not drain the economic resources away from productive usages.

A second consequence is with respect to social policies. The fact that the welfare state may rightly assume that it will be in place not only today but also tomorrow will give an investment perspective on social expenditure that would otherwise be absent. Investment in prevention of personal malfunctioning – be it due to illness, unemployment or, for example, word blindness – becomes a sensible and, quite possibly, even profitable social policy. In Denmark, for example, all babies are regularly visited in their home by a nurse to check their health. This may well result in preventing health problems that could otherwise only have been treated later at a high cost in the public health system. Thus, such a policy measure may well be judged by a social cost–benefit analysis to be financially sound, but it would not be easy to implement unless the state paid the costs of the nurse as well as the later health costs.

13.5   Is government the problem?

Ronald Reagan and Margaret Thatcher introduced in the 1980s the slogan that government was not the solution to the problem – government was the problem. This way of thinking never took hold in the Nordic countries. In fact, the public sector is actually well regarded. Transparency International publishes an annual index of perceived corruption. Finland and Denmark top the list, with Sweden and Norway a few places behind.[6] Corruption is simply not perceived to be a major social problem. This may be due partly to tradition and partly to the fact that corruption does not thrive very well in small transparent societies.

Of course, the welfare state by its very nature involves substantial government regulation and administration. One danger to the public sector would be that it was considered by the citizens to be inefficient. This poses a specific problem for the welfare state. The basic economic fact is that it is very hard to measure efficiency in the public sector. While private firms may document improvements in efficiency as increasing profits or declining prices, this is not possible for the public sector. The public sector is thus very vulnerable to attacks that it is simply inefficient.

The supporters of the welfare state have long recognized this danger and have in fact introduced the slogan: '*We must reform the welfare state in order to conserve it!*' The consequence has been very marked efforts to modernize the substantial public sector, such as introducing new technology and new public management. The traditional concept of a public servant – a lifelong and virtually secure employment, pension rights and low pay – is rapidly disappearing. The public sector is increasingly using benchmarking and indicators to demonstrate their efficiency. Outsourcing to the private sector has become quite common even though it may seem contrary to the traditional ideas of the social democratic movement. However, the reform spirit of the welfare state has accepted the idea that outsourcing may be politically necessary and an acceptable compromise. For example, free dental care to schoolchildren may be a worthy objective of the welfare state. Nevertheless, if this principle is attacked as being inefficient, a compromise may be to insist that free care is still provided to all children but not necessarily at a public clinic.

Another aspect of the welfare state and the general trust in the welfare state is that it facilitates some solutions that are not (politically) possible elsewhere. To give a particular example of what we have in mind, we may mention the CPR system. The CPR stands for Central Personal Registry, and is a personal number issued to all persons in each of the Scandinavian countries. When a baby is born, it gets a CPR number which it will have for the remainder of its life. This CPR number is used in all connections between the person and the public sector thus saving a lot of administrative resources. In a welfare state, the range of applicability becomes very extensive: tax questions, social benefits of every kind, contacts with hospitals and the doctor, use of the library, payment of parking tickets, and so on. There can be no doubt that the introduction of the CPR system required substantial faith in the public sector as, obviously, the system could be used for a detailed monitoring of the citizens with consequent possibilities of abuse. Once in place, the system has proved to be remarkably successful and is widely used in the private sector as well.

13.6 The value of social capital, trust and legitimacy
The notion of social capital has gained increased attention, not only in sociology but also in the field of economics. In sociology, the writings of Pierre Bourdieu first made explicit use of the concept as 'the aggregate if the actual or potential resources which are linked to possession of a durable network of more or less institutionalized relationships of mutual acquaintance or recognition' (1985: 248). James Coleman (1988) reintroduced social capital to the Anglo-Saxon world in looking at such high-trust communities as global diamond trading. The concept was later widely popularized by Putnam's studies on the transformation of social life in modern USA (Putnam, 2000). More recently, economists have also taken

interest in 'social capital' (Paldam, 2004).[7] Economists have come to accept that not only labour and capital are important for sustained growth and prosperity but also a number of other factors traditionally studied within the discipline of sociology. The notion of social capital is easy to incorporate into a growth perspective as social capital will reduce transaction costs and facilitate trade and wealth creation.[8] So far, economists have learned that only a fraction (though a sizeable fraction) of the economic growth is attributable to growth in the labour force and in the capital stock. The part not explained by traditional economic factors is sometimes attributed to research and development (R&D), sometimes to 'culture' or 'social capital'.

While notoriously hard to define and measure exactly, the concept implies that there is a civic spirit in the population to cooperate, a substantial trust in other persons, and a substantial amount of agreement as to the pursuit of overriding social goals.

To these social values, sociologists and political scientists have also added more 'procedural' dimensions resting in the 'institutional trust' that people may have in government and the court system. Institutional trust can be translated into 'legitimacy', and serves as a belt of transmission between individuals and the wider social system (Parsons, 1964; Cohen and Arato, 1994). The Scandinavian countries would seem to qualify in all these respects (Rothstein and Stolle, 2003). In the continual measurements that Eurobarometer performs to survey the state of affairs on the European continent, the Scandinavian populations top the list on various indexes of both personal and impersonal trust (van Oorschot et al., 2006).

The amount of general trust is markedly higher in the Scandinavian countries than in the surrounding world. People tend to trust each other. Whether this is a consequence of the welfare state, or the welfare state is contingent upon this trust, is an open question. The sure thing is, however, that a high degree of trust, or generalized social capital, lowers the transaction costs and thus contributes to wealth creation – another aspect not incorporated into traditional economic models.

Seeking to specify in somewhat greater detail how the welfare state seems successful in producing (and profiting from) such institutional trust over time, we take notice of Coleman's seminal discussion in order to see how some of his remarks especially apply to intergenerational processes in the welfare state.

> Social capital is defined by its function. It is not a single entity but a variety of different entities, with two elements in common: they all consist of some aspects of social structures, and they facilitate certain actions of actors – whether persons or corporate actors – within the structure . . . A given form of social

capital that is valuable in facilitating certain actions may be useless or even harmful for others. (Coleman, 1988: 98)

In comparison with other more commonplace forms of capital such as physical (tools, cars) and human (number of PhD's and newborn babies), social capital, as Coleman notes, is somewhat less tangible 'for it exists in the *relations* among persons' (1988: 100–101). Clearly, in a society with a high degree of trustworthiness among its citizens, there are fewer transaction costs in terms of special control personnel and costly monitoring processes than in a society with little trust among its members.

Coleman mentions three sorts of mechanisms in operation to create social capital as a value in and for social action: (1) obligations, expectations, and trustworthiness of structures; (2) information channels, and (3) norms and effective sanctions. We next see how each of these mechanisms applies to the modern (Nordic) welfare state.

13.7 Obligations, expectations and trustworthiness

Since Marcel Mauss's *The Gift* (1990, first published in 1924) sociologists and anthropologists have been studying primitive gift economies, as the gift gives rise to expectations (on behalf of the gift-giver) as well as obligations on behalf of the gift-receiver to return the gift at a proper time. A non-returned gift can have serious repercussions, not only on the person inflicting the damage, but also on general group-life. Such breaches diminish general trust in the community, and can, if it is repeated, destroy community life.

As Mauss himself noted, the welfare state is in its construction a generalized and impersonalized 'gift economy' where the gift-giver and gift-receiver are no longer in personal contact with one another. The loss of 'thick community' can result in the loss of trust – unless some substitute in form of a general insurance system can restore the economy of trust. The transactions are now managed by the state as tax transference. Obligations and expectations are again maintained as institutional trust: via the tax slip, members give their allocations to the community in the expectation that their share will be returned, if and when these same members are in need. Such expectations in the case of the welfare state of the Nordic type is now carefully specified as a set of 'universal rights' with regard to parenthood, childcare, worker's rights, pension rights and so on (see Rothstein's contribution in this volume). In the language of Coleman, the citizens have great investments in such an economy of shared expectations/ obligations, but the wheel could not operate unless a sufficient number of such assets remain unobserved: 'The density of outstanding obligations means, in effect, that the overall usefulness of the tangible resources of that social structure is amplified by their availability to others when needed' (Coleman, 1988: 103).

Francis Fukuyama (1999) in his discussion of social capital makes a special point in noting that building up such capital of strongly shared expectations/obligations is more a task of 'second generation' economic reform. Such institutional trust cannot be modelled as social policy in the first place, but is rather to be seen as the by-products of first generation social policies. Also Coleman points out the 'intergenerational effects' of existing social capital; those givers who contribute in the first place are not necessarily among the receivers themselves, although their children and grandchildren can come to profit. Here, then, is an instance why the welfare state appears to be so robust among the younger generation: despite their many individual preferences at large, they appear as strong supporters of generalized welfare services.

Clearly, the institutional trust economy in the welfare state is heavily dependent upon not too many 'free-riders' taking benefits without paying their due. Not only will the actual economy sour, especially over time, but more serious is the breakdown of institutional trust: instead of shared cooperation among the citizens we will get a society of selfish individualists and/or communities.

13.8   Information channels

Coleman especially notes the importance of information in the creation and sustenance of social capital (1988: 104). 'Acquisition of information is costly' for the reason that it demands attention on behalf of social actors, and this, he says, is always in short supply. Hence, the acquisition of information is greatly facilitated if it can be 'down-loaded' free of charge from social relations already in operation for other purposes.

We have already noted the efficiency both for state and in the private sector of the central registration banks (CPR) in the Nordic welfare states. In many other countries, notably Great Britain, such CPR numbers are looked upon with great suspicion as it is seen as a threat to individual privacy and integrity. In all the Nordic states, CPR banks are heavily controlled by 'information laws' in order to preserve the integrity of the individuals. But certainly, the mere existence and further refinement of such central registration facilitates not only state and market operations but, increasingly, communication between citizens and authorities on all levels. Communication as to tax transference, pension accumulations, child maternity/paternity allotments and so on are now wholly computerized so that individuals can inform themselves as to their social rights and obligations without too much effort. Welfare institutions for more special services such as schools, hospitals and employment agencies also facilitate the general communication flow: students need only listen to their more well-informed colleagues to acquire vital information as to new and old policies. In this respect, it is worthwhile underscoring how cheap information has become in the welfare state – especially for the second- and third-generation members: while conversing on this and that, as a matter of course they are informed and assured of their 'rights'.

Surely, the reverse of the easy availability of such social information is the fact that people also have easy access to such information that can assist them as free-riders. Hence, the formal system of rights and obligations need to be sustained by an informal system of norms and sanctions.

13.9 Norms and effective sanctions

The third central factor in regenerating 'social capital' is, Coleman suggests, that norms and effective sanctions are in operation so that those who breach the contract of community are punished accordingly. Such norms have a moral character; they operate among individuals themselves on a face-to-face level to distribute honours and rewards and, if needed, sanctions.

As we have noticed earlier, the upholding of a shared norm and reward system in the Nordic countries were certainly much facilitated by the small and homogenous populations widely socialized into the Protestant ethic. We need to add yet another central dimension here, namely, the control of the class system. We are far from implying that 'social class' is not a factor in these countries, but the culturally mediated honour and reward systems appear to operate beyond class. A 'free-rider', whether in the working or the upper class, will experience difficulties to reach the top of the social hierarchy. Indeed, in the selection of elites in the public as well as in the private sectors, there are quite a few barriers an individual needs to overcome. This is due to the thorough organization of social life making purely individualized manoeuvres in pursuing careers – outside selection undertaken in existing associations – difficult to achieve. The 'cooperative spirit' needs to be deeply entrenched for these societies to functioning well. As suggested by Rothstein and Stolle (2003), the Nordic countries maintain a high level of social capital when measured as participation in community associations; the 'Bowling Alone' syndrome is seemingly not so widespread in these countries.

13.10 Closure of social networks

It is worth mentioning yet another dimension in Coleman's seminal text, namely, the character of social structure in a given society. All social relations and structures are generating some form of social capital either to support or to oppose formal system operations, but certain kinds of 'closures' are more effective in facilitating social capital than are others. Coleman mentions 'closures' as especially effective here. With closures, he refers to the circuit of information/relationships among the members of a group. In a group or network with no closures, much information is simply wasted as it is not fed back into the system of relationship: it is like opening up the windows with radiators controlled by thermostat; the heat is going out the window and it will quickly turn costly; the heating bills will be enormous.

The same system operates in social networks: if there are closures, that is, information circuit among its members, community feeling (or social capital) is greatly enhanced – it may operate to strengthen group life – or else, to oppose orders from above.

We have already pointed to efficient information channels in operation in the welfare states. In this regard, it can be suggested that such channels also operate as 'circuits' where people check up on one another. One could here point to the more flattened out social structures in the Nordic welfare states, especially in the workplace but certainly so also in government offices and in universities. Sociologists have suggested that an 'informalization ethos' has taken root in the Nordic welfare countries: in personal communications titles have largely disappeared. In comparison with continental Europe, the Nordic countries are characterized by much weaker social hierarchies. In the language of Granovetter (1973), one could suggest that the social structure in the Nordic countries be characterized by 'bridging' rather than 'bonding' ties: information flows quite easily up and down the social ladder. The flattening out of social structures can under certain conditions constitute a weakness, as for instance in military organizations preparing for war! But under more regular conditions, the flat structures allow for great inter-communication, and secure wide acceptance among those on the shop floor as their voice is being heard.[9]

The other side of the coin resulting from strong social capital accumulation is, however, that there is a systemically operating danger for dividing insiders and outsiders. Those who do not comply with the informal rule system are in danger of being excluded from the community. This may also explain why immigrants so far are having difficulties in gaining access to the labour market.

13.11   Concluding remarks
To some politicians and social scientists, the Scandinavian mix of equity and wealth may seem worthy of imitation. To others, there are less appealing aspects of the Nordic welfare states, for example the reduced role of the family and the problems that such reduction leads to (such as impersonal care, old people left alone).

However, *if* one would like to imitate this model of society the question arises as to whether or not it is at all possible. Of course, some elements may in principle rather easily be copied, for example the emphasis on education, labour market policy and research. Nevertheless, it would seem to us after considering the facts presented in this chapter that the answer in general would be negative. Other elements would seem to be dependent upon the nature of these countries. They are all small homogeneous countries.[10] The fact that they are small means that there can be no presumption that they can influence world affairs, and therefore they have a political climate that accepts adaptation to changing circumstances in the world. They are homogeneous with respect to language and culture, and that fact facilitated the introduction and consolidation of the welfare state. Early on, they inherited a favourable attitude towards the state that the welfare was able to profit from. The state has typically been seen as a solution rather than a problem. The welfare state today has evolved over more than a century, and owing to continual reform has been able to command general support. All these aspects make us believe that, in general, the Nordic welfare state is difficult to export. One may transfer physical capital to other countries but not social capital.

The evolution of a society is a complex process involving economic as well as sociological factors. Ignoring the sociological factors is as bad as ignoring the economic factors. In our view, social capital is a valuable concept as it helps in linking social and institutional behaviour. Furthermore, it helps in linking sociological and economic considerations. However, it can certainly not stand alone; its interaction and compounded effects with many other factors remain to be studied.

Notes

1. By Scandinavia, we understand in this chapter Denmark, Finland, Norway and Sweden. Iceland is a special case due to a small population and a very different geography but shares many aspects with the other Scandinavian countries. We use the terms Scandinavia and the Nordic countries interchangeably.
2. To some extent, it could be argued that this conclusion would seem to be dependent upon the inclusion of oil-rich Norway. However, a comparison with the US should take into account that the US is also a country with large natural resources.
3. For example, in a formal sense there is free education for all but the evidence suggests that admittance to higher education is nevertheless strongly biased towards the sons and daughters of the wealthy and the well-educated parents. Nevertheless, there has been some success. An American observer concludes (Solon, 2002: 64): 'At this stage, it seems reasonable to conclude that the United States and the United Kingdom appear to be less mobile societies than are Canada, Finland and Sweden.' Research available in the Danish language suggests that the same result would apply to Denmark.
4. The notion of corporate responsibility for employment is soundly rejected, and the state rather than the firm (or the family) provides the security net.
5. We are indebted to Esping-Andersen (2006) for this reference.
6. See http://www.transparency.org/.

7. As Alejandro Portes (1998) has noted, the economist Glen Loury already made use of the concept 'social capital' in 1977 in criticizing neo-classical explanations of racial income inequality as too 'individualistic' (Loury, 1977).
8. Lenin remarked that trust is fine but control is better. However, this was the point of view of a dictator. A modern economist would say that trust is cheap while control is costly!
9. These types of ties or closures are often referred to as 'consensus cultures': it is important to engage many people in decision-making. Such consensual processes also create obligations and expectations, and thus we are back into the basics of accumulating social capital over time: the 'rights' of people to be heard are now institutionalized in quite settled semi-legal procedures.
10. Economists have studied the relation between the income level and the size of the economy. From an economic point of view, see, for example, the summary by Alesina (2003) in his Joseph W. Schumpeter lecture, there are a number of advantages from being a large state. For example, the provision of public goods may be cheaper, and a larger market will foster economic growth. However, small states may join existing organizations such as defence organizations, and they may use the international market instead of the national market, and so there is no necessary or in fact empirical correlation between country size and income level.

References

Adema, W. and M. Ladaique (2005), 'Net social expenditure, 2005 edition: more comprehensive measures of social support', OECD social employment and migration working papers, no. 29.

Alesina, Alberto (2003), 'The size of countries: does it matter?', Joseph Schumpeter Lecture, *Journal of the European Economic Association*, **1** (2–3), 301–16.

Bourdieu, Pierre (1985), 'The forms of capital', in J.G. Richardson (ed.), *Handbook of Theory and Research for the Sociology of Education*, New York: Greenwood, pp. 241–58.

Cohen, Jean and Andrew Arato (1994), *Civil Society and Political Theory*, Cambridge, MA: MIT Press.

Coleman, James S. (1988), 'Social capital in the creation of human capital', *American Journal of Sociology*, **94**, 95–120.

Esping-Andersen, Gösta (1990), *The Three Worlds of Welfare Capitalism*, Oxford: Oxford University Press.

Esping-Andersen, Gösta (1999), *Social Foundations of Postindustrial Economies*, Oxford: Oxford University Press.

Esping-Andersen, Gösta (2002), *Why We Need a New Welfare State*, Oxford: Oxford University Press.

Esping-Andersen, Gösta (2006), 'An equitable social model', *Samfundsøkonomen*, **1**, 35–8.

Fukuyama, Francis (1999), 'Social capital and civil society', IMF Conference on Second Generation Reforms, 8–9 November, www.imf.org/external/pubs/ft/seminar/1999/reforms/fukuyama.htm, accessed 25 August 2008.

Hayek, Friedrich (1945), 'The use of knowledge in society', *The American Economic Review*, **4**, 519–30.

Granovetter, Mark (1973), 'The strength of weak ties', *American Journal of Sociology*, **78** (6), 1360–80.

Loury, Glen C. (1977), 'A dynamic theory of racial income differences', in P.A. Wallace and A.M. La Mond (eds), *Women, Minorities, and Employment Discrimination*, Lexington, MA: Heath, pp. 153–86.

Mauss, Marcel (1990), *The Gift: Forms and Functions of Exchange in Archaic Societies*, London: Routledge. Original in French 1924, Essay sur le Don.

O'Connor, James R. (1981), *The Fiscal Crises of the State*, London: Palgrave Macmillan.

Paldam, Martin (2004), 'The Nordic welfare state – success under stress', *European Journal of Political Economy*, **20**, 739–42.

Parsons, Talcott (1964), *The Social System*, New York: Free Press. (First published in 1951.)

Portes, Alejandro (1998), 'SOCIAL CAPITAL: its origins and applications in modern sociology', *Annual Review of Sociology*, **24**, 1–24.

Putnam, Robert (2000), *Bowling Alone: The Collapse and Revival of American Community*, New York: Simon & Schuster.

Rothstein, Bo and Dietlind Stolle (2003), 'Introduction: social capital in Scandinavia', Scandinavian Political Studies, **26** (1), 1–26.

Schumpeter, Joseph (1976), *Capitalism, Socialism, and Democracy*, London: George Allen & Unwin. First published in 1942.

Solon, Gary (2002), 'Cross-country differences in intergenerational earnings mobility', *Journal of Economic Perspectives*, **16** (3) 59–66.

van Oorschot, Wim, Wil Arts and John Gelissen (2006), 'Social capital in Europe: measurement and social and regional distribution of a multifaceted phenomenon', *Acta Sociologica, Journal of the Nordic Sociological Association*, **49** (2), 149–69.

Veenhoven, R. (2006), 'World database of happiness', www2.eur.nl/fsw/research/veenhoven/, accessed 27 April 2007.

Weber, Max (1978), *Economy and Society*, vol.1, Guenther Roth and Claus Wittich (eds), Berkeley, CA: University of California Press.

PART V

THE ROLE OF THE STATE

14 Tax compliance[1]
Lars P. Feld

14.1 Introduction

Tax compliance has gained considerable importance for tax policy during the last decade. The German case is particularly instructive in this respect as a policy of tax-cut-cum-base-broadening is accompanied by measures that supposedly reduce tax evasion and avoidance. The German government has hoped to increase tax compliance by fostering deterrence directly (for example, the Black Activities Act of 2004) or indirectly (through facilitated information exchange via the European Savings Directive in 2005), but also by a tax amnesty in 2003. The importance of compliance issues is, however, not only visible in Germany. In the USA discussion on fundamental tax reform, its potential to facilitate compliance is additionally debated (Gale and Holtzblatt, 2002; The President's Advisory Panel on Federal Tax Reform, 2005: ch. 6). In the UK, the Mirrlees Review, aiming at a fundamental reform of the UK tax system for the twenty-first century, includes a chapter on tax compliance as well (Slemrod et al., 2007). Such attention for tax compliance and administrative issues is a relatively new phenomenon as tax policy used to exclusively focus on efficiency and equity issues.

The main focus in the literature on tax compliance, and thus of policies to enhance tax honesty, is on deterrence. When we let this dominance of deterrence prevail in the beginning of our analysis, some interesting insights can be gained. Deterrence (and coercion) by the state in democratic societies governed by the rule of law usually implies the use of sanctions, if someone does not comply with the law, after such non-compliance behaviour is discovered in official investigations. With respect to tax compliance, deterrence is obtained by fines and, in severe cases, prison sentences as well as audits of taxpayers to increase the probability of detection. Allingham and Sandmo (1972) and Yitzhaki (1974) (henceforth ASY) provided the first analyses of tax compliance in which deterrence became the most important explanatory factor. They considered fines and audits as the (potential) costs of tax non-compliance, and tax rates and incomes of taxpayers on the benefits side of the evasion gamble. If a taxpayer has to pay a certain amount of money as punishment for not paying taxes honestly with a particular probability of being detected, she has an incentive to reduce tax non-compliance. However, she can gain a certain amount of money depending on the actual income she earns and on the marginal tax rate she faces.

For the assessment of costs and benefits, the expected amounts of fines and of tax advantages due to tax non-compliance play a role. Taxpayers make their calculations using subjective probabilities of being detected as a tax cheater as inferred from perceived auditing efforts of tax administrations. Moreover, the benefit–cost calculus depends on taxpayers' risk preferences, that is, whether they are risk-averse or risk-neutral. While the negative effect of expected punishment on non-compliance is robust to different risk preferences, the positive effects of the benefits – the additional income earned through tax cheating given a marginal income tax rate – depends on risk preference. With a decreasing absolute risk aversion, higher tax rates may induce less tax cheating (Andreoni et al., 1998).

Both, subjectively perceived probabilities of detection and risk preferences, provide challenges for the validity of the purely economic approach as they may be prone to misperceptions of individual taxpayers or tax authorities. Indeed, the ASY model of tax compliance does not perform particularly well, when it comes to explaining observed levels of tax compliance. The actual extent of deterrence in most industrialized countries is too low to explain the relatively high tax compliance: 'A purely economic analysis of the evasion gamble implies that most individuals would evade if they are "rational", because it is unlikely that cheaters will be caught and penalized' (Alm et al., 1992: 22). If this explanation gap were closed by relying on individual misperceptions of the probability of being caught or on particular risk preferences, the economic approach would be undermined however. On the one hand, risk aversion would need to be 10 to 15 times higher than actually observed in order to account for the present compliance rates in the US (Graetz and Wilde, 1985; Alm et al., 1992) or in Switzerland (Pommerehne and Frey, 1992; Frey and Feld, 2002). On the other hand, the economic approach relies on rational individuals, and saving an explanation of tax compliance which is based on this model by assuming irrationality questions the approach in general (Sandmo, 2006). Objective probabilities of detection and thus the ability of taxpayers to behave dishonestly might vary across different sub-groups of the population, but they are still far from complete even for those facing highest detection rates.[2]

Thus, additional factors which are not included in the pure economic approach of tax compliance must be considered to learn why people obey tax laws. Following simple intuition, an explanation of compliance by a reduction on deterrence appears to be insufficient. Each person could tell numerous anecdotes of individuals behaving honestly in very different contexts without any reliance on deterrence by the state. Moral behaviour often occurs and tax morale is a particular component of it. The ASY approach mentions tax morale as a determinant of tax compliance, but treats it as given and exogenous. Following the ASY reasoning, tax morale results from an individual's education and socialization and is therefore not affected by economic incentives. There is, however, mounting evidence that tax morale is systematically shaped by different factors which could be influenced, at least partly, by government policy (Torgler, 2007). Two promising influences rely on taxpayers' interactions with each other and with the government. When people perceive others to comply with tax laws, they also pay their taxes honestly (Feld and Tyran, 2002). Individuals conditionally cooperate. Similarly, taxpayers are willing to pay taxes honestly when they get public services in exchange which are worth paying for (Alm et al., 1993). Tax morale is endogenous and in turn affects tax compliance. Tax morale thus contributes to the social capital of a country such that this chapter's main question becomes: does social capital influence tax compliance?

If the pure deterrence approach is insufficient to explain actual levels of tax compliance satisfactorily, a policy that almost exclusively relies on deterrence is in danger of falling short of fighting tax non-compliance successfully. An understanding of what shapes tax morale is thus indispensable. In this chapter, I discuss to what extent social norms affect tax compliance, and whether and to what extent such norms can be influenced by government policy. This is done by drawing on empirical evidence for Germany and Switzerland. Following Feld and Frey (2007), tax compliance is considered as the result of an exchange relationship in which citizens/taxpayers pay their taxes in exchange for public goods and services. Before the elements of this exchange relationship are introduced, different manifestations of tax compliance and non-compliance as well as their measurement are briefly discussed (Section 14.2). In the case of black activities as an example of tax non-compliance, the role of social norms is empirically demonstrated in Section 14.3. In Section 14.4, the exchange relationship is characterized and the roles of deterrence and responsive regulation are determined. Section 14.5 offers conclusions.

14.2 Measuring tax (non-)compliance

Many people think of tax compliance as the opposite of tax evasion and may have in mind rich people not declaring the true capital income obtained from their assets. However, tax non-compliance is also involved when people are working in the shadow economy, or when the elderly donate capital to their heirs without thinking about inheritance and gift taxes. Equally important, large corporations pursue particular tax-saving strategies that might turn out to be illegal only after a court finally decides the case. It is thus useful to have a brief look at different forms of tax non-compliance and their measurement.

While the shadow economy includes economically legal but fiscally hidden activities in the sense of black work, it also comprises illegal activities like trade of illicit drugs, prostitution or other criminal activities (for broader discussions see Schneider and Enste, 2000; Feld and Larsen, 2005). Black, but otherwise legal activities in the shadow economy usually involve tax evasion, but taxes could also be evaded pursuing different activities than those in the shadow economy. This is, for example, the case when capital income earned in the official economy is not truthfully reported. Tax compliance can thus be understood opposite to the tax gap as the amount of the projected total tax base that tax authorities actually collect (Andreoni et al., 1998). Finally, tax morale usually refers to the residuum of tax compliance which cannot be explained by standard portfolio choice determinants and deterrence measures, but also captures the general attitude of respondents towards tax non-compliance. The different terms 'black activities', 'shadow economy', 'tax evasion', 'tax compliance' or 'tax morale' obviously are overlapping and not too clearly distinguished from each other, but are not identical and not synonymous as well.

When it comes to the measurement of different forms of tax non-compliance, these definitions appear to be less important because data on the extent of tax evasion or the size of the shadow economy are not easily available owing to their very clandestine nature anyway. In economics, several estimation methods have been developed to 'measure the unmeasurable' that are usually more or less closely linked to the one or the other aspect of tax evasion (Schneider and Enste, 2000; Feld and Larsen, 2005). Some of these methods rather capture the shadow economy or black activities by concentrating on the labour market, physical production or particular economic transactions. Others aim at a more comprehensive assessment of tax compliance.

There are indirect and direct methods of measurement. The first indirect method is called the income gap approach. It uses the basic definition in national accounts that the income measure should be the same as the expenditure measure of the domestic product. If there are statistical discrepancies, they might occur because the quality of the data is insufficient. However, it is highly implausible that these statistical discrepancies increase substantially over time. Thus, tax evasion explains why people in an economy buy more products and services than they officially have money for, given their earned income according to income tax declarations. In Europe, Larsen (2002) uses this method for Denmark and Gorodnichenko et al. (2007) for Russia. Pommerehne and Weck-Hannemann (1996) and Feld and Frey (2002b) apply it to measure Swiss tax evasion. In a similar fashion, the official participation rate in the labour market is compared with actual employment (Pedersen, 2003).

The second indirect measurement method is based on monetary approaches. On the one hand, the transactions approach, starting from the Fisher equation of the quantity theory of money, relates total nominal gross national product (GNP) to total transactions. The GNP of the shadow economy is obtained by subtracting official GNP from total nominal GNP, assuming a base year in which the ratio of total transactions to total nominal GNP was normal, that is, no shadow economy existed (Feige, 1989). On the other hand, the currency demand approach assumes that transactions in the shadow economy are more strongly done in cash than transactions in the official economy in order to leave no accounting traces (Kirchgässner, 1983; Schneider, 2004). The size of the shadow economy is then inferred by simulating currency demand with and without tax variables.

The third indirect method is the electricity consumption method (Schneider and Enste, 2000). It assumes that electricity serves as a good indicator of overall economic activity also assuming an electricity-to-gross domestic product (GDP) elasticity of close to one. Then, a calculation can be made of how large the actual total GDP of a country is. The difference from official GDP provides an estimate of the shadow economy.

The fourth indirect method is the hidden variable approach (Frey and Weck, 1984). Macroeconomic indicators, usually the labour participation rate, real GDP growth, currency demand and working hours, are used as indicator variables for the shadow economy and linked to explanatory variables such as tax rates or the regulatory burden using LISREL techniques (structural causal modelling techniques, or the DYMIMIC approach, see Schneider and Enste, 2000). With the hidden variable approach, only a relative assessment of the size of the shadow economy is possible such that analyses using this method often relate their estimates to the currency demand approach (Pickhardt and Sardà Pons, 2006). In contrast to the income gap method, the latter three approaches capture activities in the shadow economy, but not overall tax evasion as they are not able to account for undeclared income from capital.

There are three main direct methods. The first focuses on black activities, as a part of the shadow economy, by using surveys in which individuals are directly asked whether they have carried out black activities, either for cash payments or payments in kind (Feld and Larsen, 2005; Pedersen, 2003). The second direct method, applied by the US Internal Revenue Service (IRS), is based on actual tax auditing and other compliance methods (Engel and Hines, 1999). In 1963 the IRS started to conduct periodic tax audits (Taxpayer Compliance Measurement Program – TCMP) measuring understatement of income, overstatement of deductions and exemptions, and so on, for a random sample of individual income taxpayers. The data are used to calculate tax evasion for the whole population. The IRS also applies an income gap method for non-filers by calculating the discrepancy between the declared income and actual income of randomly audited individuals (Andreoni et al., 1998). The third direct method aims at measuring tax morale instead of tax evasion in surveys. For instance, the World Values Survey elicits tax morale for a representative sample of individuals by asking whether cheating on tax can be justified (Torgler, 2007).

Any of these indirect and direct methods has disadvantages. The income gap method has to cope with the unreliability of statistical errors. The monetary methods may overestimate the rationality of the money market. In addition, many transactions in the shadow economy take place without cash payments. As indirect methods minimize strategic problems that emerge if individuals are directly confronted with questions about tax honesty, it could be argued that the indirect methods provide for an upper boundary of tax evasion or the shadow economy. The survey approach is sensitive to the formulation of the questions, and participants in the survey may behave strategically and simply not tell the truth. Even in face-to-face interviews, which promote the greatest degree of participation in the survey, a respondent may simply lie. Moreover, household surveys include black activities by professional firms at most incompletely. The survey method may thus measure a lower limit of black activities in the economy. The tax auditing method is prone to sample selection bias, because the selection for audit is based on the properties of the tax returns submitted to the tax office and thus not independent of the probability of evading taxes. Those taxpayers identified as tax cheaters could be only the tip of the iceberg, because it is highly improbable that tax authorities would detect all tax cheaters even if they wanted to (Erard and Feinstein, 2007). The survey of individual tax morale only measures hypothetical tax morale and not real tax compliance. Nevertheless all methods taken together describe recent possibilities to measure the phenomenon.

14.3   The role of social norms for black activities

As noted in the introduction, Germany passed a Black Activities Act in 2004 which increased deterrence considerably. Before this change in law, in August 2004, the Rockwool Foundation carried out a representative survey among German households of which 2143 face-to-face interviews of persons aged between 18 and 74 years were available for a study conducted by Feld and Larsen (2005). Asking people whether they carry out black activities is a delicate task as respondents have incentives to reply dishonestly. It is possible to reduce such dishonesty by conducting a structured

Table 14.1   *Black activities in 2001 and 2004, respondents 18–74 years of age*

	Carried out black activities? (%)				No. of respondents
	Yes	No	Don't know	Total	
2001	10.4	86.7	2.8	100	5686
2004	8.8	89.9	1.3	100	2143

Source: Feld and Larsen (2005: table 6.1).

face-to-face interview with a questionnaire which is informed by the experiences from surveys on individual willingness to pay for public goods like environmental quality (see for the Contingent Valuation Method, Kopp et al., 1997). Still, it cannot be excluded that respondents did simply not tell the truth such that this survey method only provides for a lower bound of the shadow economy in Germany. The concrete question asked, after the questionnaire focused the attention of respondents only slowly on the black activities topic, reads (Feld and Larsen, 2005: 44):

> The next questions are about what are popularly called 'black activities' . . . In the case of black activities you work for someone else by mutually accepting that the remuneration is not taxed although it normally has to . . . Have you carried out activities of this kind during the past 12 months?

Similar formulations have been used in a number of surveys in Denmark since 1994. It is followed by questions about the kinds of black activity, the time spent on black activities, black hourly wages, and so on. The responses to the question are given in Table 14.1 and show that, in 2004, 8.8 per cent of the respondents carried out black activities. Compared with an earlier survey by the Rockwool Foundation (Pedersen, 2003), black activities thus declined from 10.4 per cent.

The extent of black activities as a percentage of the official GDP could be inferred on the basis of this question by additionally considering the number of working hours in black activities in relation to the working hours in the official economy, assuming that the productivity of workers in both sectors is the same. With this additional information, Feld and Larsen (2005: table 7.5) are able to report a decline of the size of the German shadow economy from 4.1 per cent of GDP in 2001 to 3.1 per cent in 2004.

These survey data from 2001 and 2004 could subsequently be used in multivariate econometric (statistical) analyses to explain the probability of conducting black activities. The dependent variable explained by the model is a binary variable which takes on the value of one if a person indicates she conducted black activities, and zero otherwise. The independent, explanatory variables comprise a set of socio-demographic characteristics like age, marital status, whether children live in the household, occupation, education, employment status (number of unemployed months), a regional dummy variable for West and East Germany, and home ownership. From the perspective of tax compliance theory, it is most interesting that the respondent's monthly net income, a variable measuring the individual's subjective probability of being caught and a measure of perceived punishment are elicited. Monthly net income is obtained for five different income classes. Individuals assessed their risk of being caught on a scale from very high to very low. The perceived punishment is calculated from a question in which respondents could choose between taxes due, fines or imprisonment, or combinations thereof. While income and probability of detection were thus proxied by continuous measures, punishment elicited by the survey is only a discrete measure with different punishment categories. A further shortcoming can be found in the insufficient responses to the questions about subjective tax burdens. Nevertheless, three of the four classic variables from the ASY model are included in the analysis.

Most importantly, the survey also contains questions about social norms. Respondents received eight alternative examples of cheating behaviour and had to assess on a scale from 1 to 10 whether they find this behaviour absolutely unacceptable or absolutely acceptable. Although respondents mostly evaluate the different activities as unacceptable, there are interesting differences between the different types. If someone receives welfare benefits and other transfers without entitlement, 73 per cent deem this behaviour as totally unacceptable. Taking a free ride on public transportation is absolutely unacceptable to 52 per cent of the respondents. Only 32.5 per cent think of carrying black activities as absolutely unacceptable. Differentiating the different kinds of black activities, there are additional interesting insights. If a private household hires a private person for black activities, 25.5 per cent assess this behaviour as absolutely unacceptable. If a private household hires a firm for black activities, 48.5 per cent of respondents find it absolutely unacceptable. If a firm has a private person carrying out black activities, 62.5 per cent evaluate this behaviour as totally unacceptable. If a firm hires another firm to carry out black activities, even 70.5 per cent assess it as absolutely unacceptable. Finally, tax evasion is less acceptable than carrying out black activities: 47.5 per cent deem tax evasion as absolutely unacceptable, which is about 15 percentage points more than in the case of carrying out black activities. The latter question about tax evasion corresponds to the measurement of tax morale in the World Value Survey.

Table 14.2 Summary of logistic regressions of the probability of
participating in black activities, 18–74-year-olds (inclusive),
Germany, 2004

	Men 2004		Women 2004	
	With full deterrence	With social norms	With full deterrence	With social norms
Income	*	*	ns	ns
Perceived risk of discovery	ns	ns	*	ns
Perceived penalty	ns	ns	ns	ns
Social norms	–	*	–	***
Age	***	***	***	***
Marital status	***	***	***	***
Children under 6	*	*	ns	ns
Education	***	***	ns	ns
Occupation	ns	ns	**	**
Length of unemployment (months)	ns	ns	***	***
Owner-occupier/ tenant	ns	ns	ns	ns
Region	*	*	ns	ns

Notes:
The dependent variable has the value 1 if the respondent has carried out black activities within the last 12 months, and the value 0 otherwise.
***: The variable is significant at the 1 per cent level.
 **: The variable is significant at the 5 per cent level.
  *: The variable is significant at the 10 per cent level.
 ns: The variable is not significant.
 Joint significance of several variables has been tested by Likelihood Ratio Tests.
 The sample has been drawn at the household level, and a weight has been applied to make the sample representative as to sex and age distribution and other characteristics of the total population.
 See Feld and Larsen (2005: 89) for the detailed set of results.

Source: Feld and Larsen (2005: table 10.2).

This model is estimated for men and women separately as the labour participation of both is different, and Logit-regressions are performed because the dependent variable is a binary variable, that is, with a value of one for those carrying out black activities and zero otherwise (for details, see Feld and Larsen, 2005: chs 6–10). The main results are summarized in Table 14.2. Starting with the socio-demographic factors across all regressions, age and marital status have significant influences on the probability of carrying out black activities. Black activities in Germany are more probably conducted by men under 50 years and by women younger than 40 years. Married men have a higher probability and married women a significantly lower probability of working in the shadow economy. With respect to the remaining variables, the regressions exhibit even more differentiated results for men and women. Children significantly raise black activities among men, but do not significantly influence black activities of women. Education has a highly significant influence for men, but not for women, with more highly educated men carrying out fewer black activities. Occupation is not significant for men, but for women, with retired women more probably working in the shadow economy. The length of unemployment has no significant effect on men's behaviour, but raises black activities among women. The differences between West and East Germany are not, or only marginally, significant and home ownership does not play any role.[3]

Turning to the traditional ASY variables (the pure economic approach), it is useful to distinguish the regression results with and without the inclusion of the social norms variables. In the full deterrence models without social norms, income has a marginally significant effect on men's black activities; the perceived risk of detection only has a marginally significant negative effect on the probability of black activities for women, and the perceived penalty has no effect at all. This is far from convincing evidence in favour of the ASY model. Including social norms, the most important results are, first, social norms have a highly significant impact on black activities in the case of women and of men, though only marginally in the latter case. Given that deterrence does not have any significant effect on male black activities, this is a remarkable result. Second, including the indicators of social norms, the perceived risk of being caught does not have any significant impact any more on women's probability of participating in black activities. For women and men, a higher acceptance of receiving welfare without entitlement results in a lower probability of carrying out black activities. For men, black activities become more probable for those who find carrying out black activities in general more acceptable. Women more strongly accepting black activities from private to private, firm to private and firm to firm have a higher probability of carrying out black activities. Black activities from private to firm lead to a lower probability of participating in black activities, although this does not reach any level of significance. These results indicate a positive relationship between social norms and black activities in particular for women: the less accepted different kinds of black activities are, the less probable are black activities. Only cheating on transfer payments leads to the opposite effects: The more accepted cheating is the less need exists to work in the shadow economy. It would then be easier to cheat on the transfer system. Feld and Larsen (2005) report further results according to which social norms are quantitatively more important than deterrence measures.

14.4 The psychological tax contract
The results for Germany indicate that the deterrence model of tax compliance is not sufficient to explain the individual probability of carrying out black activities. Social norms, in particular different expressions of tax morale, robustly and more strongly affect tax compliance. Similar results are reported by other authors.[4] If tax morale is thus important to understand tax compliance behaviour, the question becomes what affects individuals' tax morale. Feld and Frey (2007) refer to tax morale as an intrinsic motivation to pay taxes. The idea of intrinsic motivation stems from social psychology arguing that, under particular conditions, monetary (external) interventions undermine individuals' intrinsic motivation.[5] Rewarding people for activities has indirect negative consequences as they nurture the expectation of future rewards such that desired behaviour is undertaken only if rewards are provided. Frey (1997a) generalizes these results by extending it to control and punishment, which could crowd out intrinsic motivation if they are perceived as interferences into the privacy of individuals. Tax morale could thus be influenced by the behaviour of tax authorities.

Tax officials are aware of these effects of their actions on taxpayers' behaviour realizing that a disrespectful treatment of taxpayers undermines tax morale and thus increases the cost of raising taxes. Tax authorities will, however, only treat taxpayers respectfully when they can start from a non-negligible extent of tax morale. Tax officials at the same time perceive that tax payments do not solely depend on tax morale but that incentives play an important role. In particular, incentives are used to prevent taxpayers with low, or lacking, tax morale from exploiting the more honest taxpayers and to escape paying their due share. A combination of respectful treatment and incentives is necessary to shape successfully taxpayers' behaviour. The sole reliance on incentives, as suggested by a large part of the tax compliance literature, represents a special case which only applies under restrictive conditions. Such a special case occurs when the tax officials are convinced that individuals' tax morale is low or does not exist at all. In general, however, it is optimal to simultaneously use both respectful treatment as well as incentives. The higher the initial level of tax morale, and the stronger the crowding out effect, the less weight is put on incentives, and the more respectfully taxpayers are treated.

These considerations result in the perception of tax compliance as a psychological tax contract (Feld and Frey, 2007). It is an implicit or relational contract (Akerlof, 1982) between taxpayers and tax authorities which goes beyond material incentives and involves emotional ties and loyalties. It is called 'psychological' to clearly distinguish it from formal contracts, which are backed by the explicit and material sanctions they contain. In the psychological tax contract, punishment still plays a role in order to provide deterrence. But the satisfaction of taxpayers with what they get from the other contract party, that is, the government, influences their tax morale. Taxpayers' reward from that contract must be understood in a broad sense going beyond pure exchanges of goods and services for the payment of a tax price. In addition to such direct exchange components, the fairness of the procedures leading to particular political outcomes as well as the way the government and the taxpayers treat each other are part of the contractual relationship. A genuine reward is therefore obtained only if taxpayers as citizens have an inclusive, respectful relationship with the community. Both sides of the contract perceive each other as contract partners and treat each other with mutual respect. As deterrence and tax morale interact, it would be counterproductive to solely rely on punishment because tax morale can be undermined. A dynamic relationship results in which deterrence, fiscal exchange, but also decision-making procedures and the treatment of taxpayers play a role.

The social capital resulting when the psychological tax contract is upheld thus refers to the ability of taxpayers and tax authorities to cooperate, but also includes the ability of taxpayers to cooperate among themselves. The psychological tax contract subsequently shapes the social norms that affect tax compliance. The ability of cooperation between the parties involved in such a contract may vary across jurisdictions such that the social norm to pay taxes honestly, and thus tax compliance, also varies respectively. As is usually the case with implicit contracts, the psychological tax contract is vulnerable to external shocks. Wars, changes in the political system, escalating cheating behaviour or crime in general could erode the basic understanding and mutual trust among taxpayers and between taxpayers and the state.

The contractual metaphor has many advantages over traditional theoretical approaches. It first underlines that paying taxes is a quasi-voluntary act. Each party has to agree to the contents of the contract. In practice, it is seldom the case that each public good is individually contracted with each taxpayer for a certain tax price. However, a steady reduction in tax compliance need not only be interpreted as a violation of the law, but also as taxpayers' discontent with what they receive for their taxes. Second the contractual approach emphasizes the role of fair procedures decided upon at a constitutional stage. Tyler (1990) argues that people comply with the law in general if they perceive the process as fair that leads to this law. Most obviously, it will be difficult to think of a psychological tax contract in autocratic regimes. The inclusiveness of political decision-making could, however, also be very different in democratic regimes depending on the extent of citizens' involvement in political decision-making. Third, the way people are treated by the tax authorities affects cooperation levels. Again the analogy to private contracts is useful. If people can purchase a product from two different suppliers, they choose the one who is friendly and respectfully treating his customers and are even willing to pay a price for it. In a similar fashion, the way the tax office treats taxpayers plays a role.

At this procedural level, respectful treatment can be split into two different components. First, the procedures used by auditors in their contact with taxpayers are to be transparent and clear. In the case of unclear procedures and hidden actions, taxpayers feel helpless and get the impression that the state is doing what it wants to with its citizens. Such behaviour reduces their perception of being obliged to pay taxes. It creates a feeling of 'them or us'. Second, respectful treatment has a direct personal component in the sense of how the personality of taxpayers is respected by tax officials. If they treat taxpayers as partners in a psychological tax contract, instead of inferiors in a hierarchical relationship, taxpayers have incentives to pay taxes honestly. In addition, respectful treatment of taxpayers enforces the effects of emotions on compliance behaviour (see Grasmick and Bursik, 1990, for evidence).

Two opposite ways of treating taxpayers can be distinguished: (1) a respectful treatment supporting, and possibly raising, tax morale; (2) an authoritarian treatment undermining tax morale. The tax officials can choose between these extremes in many different ways. For instance, when they detect an error in the tax declaration, they can suspect the intent to cheat, and impose legal sanctions. Alternatively, the tax officials may give the taxpayer the benefit of the doubt and inquire about the reason for the error. If the taxpayer in question did not intend to cheat but simply made a mistake, he or she will most likely be offended by such disrespectful treatment by the tax authority. The feeling of being controlled in a negative way, and being suspected of tax cheating, tends to crowd out the intrinsic motivation to act as an honourable taxpayer and, as a consequence, tax morale will fall. In contrast, if the tax official makes an effort to locate the reason for the error by contacting the taxpayer in a friendly way, the taxpayer will appreciate this respectful treatment and tax morale will be upheld.

Given the requirements of a psychological tax contract, what role does deterrence play? Higher control intensities increase deterrence and thus tax compliance on the one hand, but may be perceived as intrusive by taxpayers and thus reduce tax compliance on the other hand (Scholz and Pinney, 1995; Kirchler, 1999). Feld and Frey (2002b) provide evidence that fines and penalties are part of a non-linear punishment schedule that allows for low levels of fines in the case of minor offences against the tax code in order to reduce taxpayers' perception of intrusiveness, but requires high penalties in cases of tax fraud or major convictions in order to make clear that the psychological tax contract is at stake. Minor and major offences could thereby be distinguished with respect to the amount evaded, but also to procedural categories, for example by differentiating between active tax fraud by manipulation of the balance sheet and passive tax evasion when taxpayers forget to report particular income components. Deterrence thus has two different aspects. On the one hand, in order to keep up a psychological tax contract between the tax office and the taxpayers, honest taxpayers must be confident that they are not exploited by dishonest tax cheaters. Thus, deterrence for major violations of the tax code reduces tax evasion. On the other hand, each taxpayer may make a mistake, so that minor offences can be penalized less without undermining the psychological tax contract. A non-linear punishment schedule with low fines for minor tax evasion and high penalties for tax fraud, will serve the purpose of shaping tax morale.

A particular mode of deterrence emerges when social control within a community is possible. Citizens may enforce the psychological tax contract with their fellow citizens in the community by ensuring that everybody is paying her fair share of the public good. Tax morale may be undermined if an honest taxpayer realizes that his neighbours get away with their tax dishonesty without sanction. Compared with deterrence by the government and the legal system, social control entails the additional risk for a potential tax cheater of losing reputation among her friends and relatives. Exerting social control is, however, not easy. In most countries, taxpayers are not informed about the extent of tax evasion of other taxpayers owing to tax secrecy laws. This may be different if a citizen can suspect that black activities are going on. Switzerland is different in that respect as it has a history of publishing tax registers from which taxpayers could get information on the tax payments of others and thus have the possibility to form expectations about the tax honesty of others. As the historic account by Schanz (1890) indicates, publication of tax registers frequently appeared in Switzerland in the nineteenth century. A mixture of moral suasion by and envy of their fellow citizens was supposed to increase the tax morale of tax cheaters. Schanz (1890, vol. I: 120) was, however, pessimistic about the success of published tax registers because he conjectured that honest taxpayers would reduce their tax compliance once they realized that their neighbours successfully evaded taxes. In recent times this practice has been abolished in some Swiss cantons and legally restricted in others which still allow publication of tax registers under particular conditions. Feld and Frey (2002a, 2002b) find no robust effect of publishing tax information on tax compliance.

From the perspective of standard economic theory, a direct incentive for tax compliance consists in the goods and services that the state provides to citizens for their tax payments (Mackscheidt, 1984; Smith and Stalans, 1991). If the analogy to private contracts is considered, the individual utility obtained from goods or services provides the foremost incentives to pay a price to get them. From the perspective of a psychological tax contract, respectful treatment occurs at two different levels of action, the traditional fiscal exchange and the procedural level. The fiscal exchange between the taxpayers and the state requires that citizens' tax payments are met by public services. According to the benefit principle of taxation, taxes are prices for certain public goods (Buchanan, 1976). However, the benefit principle does not necessarily imply that income redistribution becomes impossible and only infrastructural goods as well as public consumption goods are provided by the state. Citizens may perceive their tax payments as contributions to the 'bonum commune' such that they are willing to honestly declare their income even if they do not receive a full public good equivalent to their tax payments. Income redistribution is the more accepted by affluent citizens the more the political process is perceived to be fair and the more policy outcomes are legitimate.

Empirically, the more governments follow the benefit principle of taxation and provide public services according to the preferences of taxpayers in exchange for a reasonable tax price, the more taxpayers comply with the tax laws. Alm et al. (1992) and Alm et al. (1992a, 1992b, 1993) provide experimental evidence on the positive impact of fiscal exchange on tax compliance. Pommerehne, Hart and Frey (1994) use a simulation study design to analyse the impact of fiscal exchange on tax compliance. They show that tax compliance increases with reductions in government waste. Whenever redistribution of income is at stake, problems of tax evasion are pertinent. There are only few studies that consider the relationship between tax evasion and redistribution in a fiscal exchange setting. In their experiments, Güth and Mackscheidt (1985) chose a simple tax transfer scheme to come as close as possible to the principle of vertical equity, that is, take from the rich and give to the poor. They found that subjects had a compliance rate of 93 per cent. Becker et al. (1987) report, however, that evasion rises if taxpayers believe they will lose from redistribution. It appears that notions of fairness or justice shape the extent to which the fiscal exchange paradigm increases tax compliance. Kinsey and Grasmick (1993) report evidence that horizontal equity plays a role. If an individual's tax burden is of about the same magnitude as that of comparable others, tax compliance increases. They also report that vertical unfairness of the tax schedule increases tax evasion. Moreover, Scholz and Lubell (1998) emphasize the importance of trust in government for tax compliance.

The fiscal exchange relationship between taxpayers and the state therefore depends on the politico-economic framework within which the government acts. According to Alm et al. (1999), rational egoists should vote for the lowest control intensities and fines that are necessary to ensure compliance. However, the possibility for voters to vote directly on matters of content increases the legitimacy of policies and serves as an insurance against exaggerated government waste. Direct political participation particularly activates public spiritedness of taxpayers (Feld and Kirchgässner, 2000). In an experimental study, Feld and Tyran (2002) find that tax compliance is higher on average in an endogenous fine treatment in which subjects are allowed to approve or reject the proposal of a fine as compared to an exogenous fine treatment where the fine is imposed by the experimenter (see also Alm et al., 1999). The main explanation why people show higher tax morale if they are allowed to vote on a fine is legitimacy. Field studies by Pommerehne and Weck-Hannemann (1996), Pommerehne and Frey (1992) and Frey (1997b) provide support for the experimental findings focusing on tax evasion in the Swiss cantons between 1965 and 1978. Direct democratic political decision-making reduces tax evasion according to those studies. These results are replicated by Feld and Frey (2002b) and Frey and Feld (2002) by extending the sample to the period 1985 to 1995. Torgler (2005) provides evidence that direct democracy raises tax morale in the Swiss cantons. In addition, he reports findings that local autonomy as an indicator of fiscal federalism has a positive impact on tax morale. Güth et al. (2005) show experimental evidence for effects of fiscal decentralization on tax compliance. Subjects show higher tax morale if public goods are provided and financed regionally or locally because their taxes are spent on their own regional or local public goods.

The psychological tax contract is also supported by interactional justice, in particular a respectful treatment of taxpayers by tax authorities. In order to investigate the relationship between taxpayers and tax authorities, Feld and Frey (2002b) sent a survey to the tax authorities of the 26 Swiss cantons which asked detailed questions about the legal background of tax evasion, but also included questions on the treatment of taxpayers by tax authorities in day-to-day audits, in particular when a taxpayer is suspected of not declaring his or her true taxable income. According to this survey, the extent of respectful treatment of the taxpayers is captured by: (1) fully observing procedures based on formal and informal rules, that is, what happens typically if a taxpayer does not declare taxable income at all (procedures, fines), if a tax declaration is mistakenly filled out or, in a second stage, if taxpayers do not react? (2) Acknowledgment of individual citizens' rights and personality, that is, what does the tax administration do if taxpayers declared taxable income by mistake too high? Are there attempts to find out whether taxpayers intentionally or mistakenly declare too low a taxable income? Are mistakes in the tax declaration to the advantage or to the disadvantage of taxpayers?

With a sample of 26 Swiss cantons in the years 1970–95, the authors show that the tax authorities in Switzerland do indeed behave as if they were aware of the reaction of taxpayers to being treated with respect. According to the empirical findings, tax evasion is lower, the more fully the tax office observes formal and informal procedural rules. The observation of procedural rules is indicated by a distinction between friendly treatments, for example a respectful procedure, and unfriendly treatments, like an authoritarian procedure or the tax authorities' direct deterrence to fine. It can be shown that the friendly treatment has a stronger dampening effect on tax evasion particularly in cantons using referendums and initiatives in political decision-making, while the authoritarian procedure, the threat of deterrence, is particularly reducing tax evasion in representative democracies, but counter-productive in direct democracy. Moreover, Swiss citizens are the more respectfully treated by the tax authority the more strongly developed citizens' participation rights (Feld and Frey, 2002a).

14.5 Conclusions

In this chapter, it has been argued that tax compliance in its different manifestations cannot be the result of a pure deterrence by the state. The exemplary evidence on German black activities raises serious doubts that deterrence suffices and rather indicates that social norms like tax morale play an important role. Following Feld and Frey (2007) it is argued that citizens and the state develop their fiscal relationships according to a psychological tax contract. It establishes fiscal exchange between taxpayers and tax authorities which goes beyond pure exchanges and involves loyalties and ties between the contract partners. Tax morale is therefore a function of (1) the fiscal exchange where taxpayers get public services for the tax prices they pay, (2) the political procedures that lead to this exchange and (3) the personal relationship between the taxpayers and the tax administrators.

In particular the empirical evidence on Switzerland summarized in this chapter shows a family of tax jurisdictions where something like a psychological tax contract appears to be in place. There, the tax authorities take into account that the way they treat the taxpayers systematically affects the latter's tax morale, and therefore their willingness to pay taxes, which in turn affects the costs of raising taxes. In addition, tax compliance in Switzerland is shaped by direct democracy establishing a fiscal exchange relationship between taxpayers and the state. The arguments and the evidence in this chapter thus provide a perspective on tax compliance as shaped by the social capital present in a society.

Notes

1. I would like to thank Bruno Frey, Claus Larsen, Friedrich Schneider and Benno Torgler for our joint work on tax compliance that has fed into this chapter. The very stimulating discussions with them, in particular with Bruno Frey, have made me think about tax compliance in the way it is outlined in this chapter. I would also like to thank the editors for their encouraging comments.
2. In a recent paper on the effectiveness of the IRS, Erard and Feinstein (2007) report detection rates of 88 per cent for wage earners (excluding tip income), 47 per cent for recipients of rents and royalties and 32 per cent for self-employed individuals. The detection rate of capital income (including capital gains) is not reported. Even for wage earners these figures are not quite those close to 100 per cent claimed by Slemrod (2007).
3. The latter result should not be emphasized too much. In a recent paper, Feld and Torgler (2007) demonstrate that tax morale in East Germany, which was significantly higher than in West Germany when unification took place, subsequently converged to the lower West German levels. These differences between both parts of Germany are probably a mixture of differences in social norms and in institutions. But the convergence effect is certainly resulting from the East German disappointment as regards the process of unification and is thus in accordance with the arguments for a psychological tax contract as presented below.
4. See again Alm et al. (1992), Graetz and Wilde (1985), Skinner and Slemrod (1985) or Pommerehne and Frey (1992) who conclude that the risk aversion needed in order to raise compatibility with actual compliance rates is not supported by evidence. In a recent paper, Slemrod (2007) has questioned such an interpretation of the evidence by arguing that the way tax authorities collect information on taxpayer compliance matters such that the probability of detection increases considerably for large parts of the taxpaying population. His example draws on taxation of labour at source, but neglects that many workers do not need to underreport their true income earned in the official part of the economy, but could conduct black activities.
5. Headed by Deci (1971). Extensive surveys are given, for example, in Pittman and Heller (1987) and Lane (1991). For meta-analyses see Deci et al. (1999) and Cameron et al. (2001). That external interventions may crowd out intrinsic motivation is introduced into economics as 'Crowding Theory' (Frey, 1997a; Le Grand, 2003) and is supported by much empirical evidence (Frey and Jegen, 2001).

References

Akerlof, G.A. (1982), 'Labor contracts as partial gift exchange', *Quarterly Journal of Economics*, **84**, 488–500.

Allingham, M.G. and A. Sandmo (1972), 'Income tax evasion: a theoretical analysis', *Journal of Public Economics*, **1**, 323–38.

Alm, J., B.R. Jackson and M. McKee (1992a), 'Institutional uncertainty and taxpayer compliance', *American Economic Review*, **82**, 1018–26.

Alm, J., B.R. Jackson and M. McKee (1992b), 'Estimating the determinants of taxpayer compliance with experimental data', *National Tax Journal*, **45**, 107–14.

Alm, J., B.R. Jackson and M. McKee (1993), 'Fiscal exchange, collective decision institutions and tax compliance', *Journal of Economic Behavior and Organization*, **22**, 285–303.

Alm, J., G.H. McClelland and W.D. Schulze (1992), 'Why do people pay taxes?', *Journal of Public Economics*, **48**, 21–38.

Alm, J., G.H. McClelland and W.D. Schulze (1999), 'Changing the social norm of tax compliance by voting', *Kyklos*, **52**, 141–71.
Andreoni, J., B. Erard and J. Feinstein (1998), 'Tax compliance', *Journal of Economic Literature*, **36**, 818–60.
Becker, W., H.-J. Büchner and Simon Sleeking (1987), 'The impact of public transfer expenditures on tax evasion: an experimental approach', *Journal of Public Economics*, **34**, 243–52.
Buchanan, J.M. (1976), 'Taxation in fiscal exchange', *Journal of Public Economics*, **6**, 17–29.
Cameron, J.A., K.M. Banko and W.D. Pierce (2001), 'Pervasive negative effects of rewards on intrinsic motivation: the myth continues', *Behavioral Analyst*, **24**, 1–44.
Deci, E.L. (1971), 'Effects of externally mediated rewards on intrinsic motivation', *Journal of Personality and Social Psychology*, **18**, 105–15.
Deci, E.L., R. Koestner and R.M. Ryan (1999), 'A meta-analytic review of experiments examining the effects of extrinsic rewards on intrinsic motivation', *Psychological Bulletin*, **125**, 627–68.
Engel, E. and J.R. Hines (1999), 'Understanding tax evasion dynamics', NBER working paper, no. 6903, NBER, Cambridge, MA.
Erard, B. and J. Feinstein (2007), 'Econometric models for multi-stage audit process: an application to the IRS National Research Program', in J. Alm, J. Martinez-Vazquez and B. Torgler (eds), *Tax Compliance and Tax Evasion*, London: Routledge.
Feige, E.L. (1989), *The Underground Economies: Tax Evasion and Information Distortion*, Cambridge: Cambridge University Press.
Feld, L.P. and B.S. Frey (2002a), 'Trust breeds trust: how taxpayers are treated', *Economics of Governance*, **3**, 87–99.
Feld, L.P. and B.S. Frey (2002b), 'The tax authority and the taxpayer: an exploratory analysis', unpublished manuscript, University of Zurich.
Feld, L.P. and B.S. Frey (2007), 'Tax compliance as the result of a psychological tax contract: the role of incentives and responsive regulation', *Law and Policy*, **29**, 102–20.
Feld, L.P. and G. Kirchgässner (2000), 'Direct democracy, political culture and the outcome of economic policy: a report on the Swiss experience', *European Journal of Political Economy*, **16**, 287–306.
Feld, L.P. and C. Larsen (2005), *Black Activities in Germany in 2001 and in 2004. A Comparison Based on Survey Data*, Copenhagen: Rockwool Foundation.
Feld, L.P. and B. Torgler (2007), 'Tax morale after the re-unification of Germany: results from a quasi-natural experiment', CESifo working paper, no. 1921, February.
Feld, L.P. and J.-R. Tyran (2002), 'Tax evasion and voting: an experimental analysis', *Kyklos*, **55**, 197–22.
Frey, B.S. (1997a), *Not Just for The Money. An Economic Theory of Personal Motivation*, Cheltenham, UK and Lyme, USA: Edward Elgar.
Frey, B.S. (1997b), 'A constitution for knaves crowds out civic virtues', *Economic Journal*, **107**, 1043–53.
Frey, B.S. and L.P. Feld (2002), 'Deterrence and morale in taxation: an empirical analysis', CESifo working paper, no. 760, August.
Frey, B.S. and R. Jegen (2001), 'Motivation crowding theory: a survey of empirical evidence', *Journal of Economic Surveys*, **15**, 589–611.
Frey, B.S. and H. Weck (1984), 'The hidden economy as an "unobserved" variable', *European Economic Review*, **26**, 33–53.
Gale, W.G. and J. Holtzblatt (2002), 'The role of administrative issues in tax reform: simplicity, compliance, and administration', in G.R. Zodrow and P. Mieszkowski (eds), *United States Tax Reform in the 21st Century*, Cambridge: Cambridge University Press, pp. 179–214.
Gorodnichenko, Y., J. Martinez-Vazquez and K. Sabirianova Peter (2007), 'Myth and reality of flat tax reform: tax evasion and real side response of Russian households', in J. Alm, J. Martinez-Vazquez and B. Torgler (eds), *Tax Compliance and Tax Evasion*, London: Routledge.

Graetz, M.J. and L.L. Wilde (1985), 'The economics of tax compliance: facts and fantasy', *National Tax Journal*, **38**, 355–63.

Grasmick, H.G. and R.J. Bursik (1990), 'Conscience, significant others, and rational choice: extending the deterrence model', *Law and Society Review*, **24**, 837–61.

Güth, W. and K. Mackscheidt (1985), 'Die Erforschung der Steuermoral', working paper, University of Cologne.

Güth, W., V. Levati and R. Sausgruber (2005), 'Tax morale and (de-)centralization: an experimental study', *Public Choice*, **125**, 171–88.

Kinsey, K.A. and H.G. Grasmick (1993), 'Did the Tax Reform Act of 1986 improve compliance? Three studies of pre- and post-TRA compliance attitudes', *Law and Policy*, **15**, 239–325.

Kirchgässner, G. (1983), 'Size and development of the West German shadow economy, 1955–1980', *Journal of Institutional and Theoretical Economics*, **139**, 197–214.

Kirchler, E. (1999), 'Reactance to taxation: employers' attitudes towards taxes', *Journal of Socio-Economics*, **28**, 131–38.

Kopp, R.J., W.W. Pommerehne and N. Schwarz (1997), *Determining the Value of Non-Marketed Goods: Economic, Psychological, and Policy Relevant Aspects of Contingent Valuation Methods*, Boston, MA: Kluwer.

Lane, R.E. (1991), *The Market Experience*, Cambridge: Cambridge University Press.

Larsen, C. (2002), 'Underdeklaration af personlig indkomst måt ved sammenligning af dansk skatte- og nationalregnskabsstatistik' (Unreported personal income estimated by examining discrepancies between Danish national accounts and tax statistics), mimeo, Institute of Economics, University of Copenhagen, Copenhagen.

Le Grand, J. (2003), *Motivation, Agency, and Public Policy. Of Knights & Knaves, Pawns and Queens*, Oxford: Oxford University Press.

Mackscheidt, K. (1984), 'Konsolidierung durch Erhöhung von Steuern und Abgaben?', In H.H. von Arnim and K. Littmann (eds), *Finanzpolitik im Umbruch: Zur Konsolidierung öffentlicher Haushalte*, Berlin: Duncker and Humblot, pp. 145–61.

Pedersen, S. (2003), *The Shadow Economy in Germany, Great Britain and Scandinavia: A Measurement Based on Questionnaire Surveys*, Copenhagen: Rockwool Foundation.

Pickhardt, M. and J. Sardà Pons (2006), 'Size and scope of the underground economy in Germany', *Applied Economics*, **38**, 1707–13.

Pittman, T.S. and J.F. Heller (1987), 'Social Motivation', *Annual Review of Psychology*, **38**, 461–89.

Pommerehne, W.W. and B.S. Frey (1992), 'The effects of tax administration on tax morale', unpublished manuscript, University of Zurich.

Pommerehne, W.W. and H. Weck-Hannemann (1996), 'Tax rates, tax administration and income tax evasion in Switzerland', *Public Choice*, **88**, 161–70.

Pommerehne, W.W., A. Hart and B.S. Frey (1994), 'Tax morale, tax evasion and the choice of policy instruments in different political systems', *Public Finance*, **49** (Supplement: *Public Finance and Irregular Activities*), 52–69.

Sandmo, A. (2006), 'The theory of tax evasion: a retrospective view', *National Tax Journal*, **58**, 643–63.

Schanz, G. von (1890), *Die Steuern der Schweiz in ihrer Entwicklung seit Beginn des 19. Jahrhunderts*, Vols I–V, Stuttgart.

Schneider, F. (2004), *Arbeit im Schatten: Wo Deutschlands Wirtschaft wirklich wächst*, Wiesbaden: Gabler.

Schneider, F. and D. Enste (2000), 'Shadow economies: size, causes, consequences', *Journal of Economic Literature*, **38**, 77–114.

Scholz, J.T. and M. Lubell (1998), 'Trust and taxpaying: testing the heuristic approach to collective action', *American Journal of Political Science*, **42**, 398–417.

Scholz, J.T. and N. Pinney (1995), 'Duty, fear, and tax compliance: the heuristic basis of citizenship behavior', *American Journal of Political Science*, **39**, 490–512.

Skinner, J.S. and J. Slemrod (1985), 'An economic perspective on tax evasion', *National Tax Journal*, **38**, 345–53.

Slemrod, J. (2007), 'Cheating ourselves: the economics of tax evasion', *Journal of Economic Perspectives*, **21** (1), 25–48.

Slemrod, J., J. Whiting and J. Shaw (2007), 'Tax implementation issues in the United Kingdom', paper prepared for 'Reforming the Tax System for the 21st Century: The Mirrlees Review', Institute for Fiscal Studies, London, www.ifs.org.uk/mirrleesreview/publications.php) (accessed 7 October 2007).

Smith, K.W. and L.J. Stalans (1991), 'Encouraging tax compliance with positive incentives: a conceptual framework and research directions', *Law and Policy*, **13**, 35–53.

The President's Advisory Panel on Federal Tax Reform (2005), *Simple, Fair and Pro-Growth: Proposals to Fix America's Tax System*, report to the President, Washington, DC, November.

Torgler, B. (2005), 'Tax morale and direct democracy', *European Journal of Political Economy*, **21**, 525–31.

Torgler, B. (2007), *Tax Compliance and Tax Morale: A Theoretical and Empirical Analysis*, Cheltenham, UK and Northampton, MA, USA: Edward Elgar.

Tyler, T.R. (1990), *Why People Obey the Law*, New Haven, CT: Yale University Press.

Yitzhaki, S. (1974), 'A note on income tax evasion: a theoretical analysis', *Journal of Public Economics*, **3**, 201–2.

15 The environment
Kim Mannemar Sønderskov

Introduction

Social capital helps solve collective action problems. In the presence of social capital, groups of actors are able to cooperate and provide collective goods not provided in other groups. That is the main message from the growing literature on social capital (Coleman, 1990: ch. 12; Putnam, 1993: ch. 6, 2000: ch. 16; Uslaner, 1999; Paldam and Svendsen, 2000; Ostrom and Ahn, 2003; Rothstein, 2005: ch. 1; Nannestad, this volume). Collective action problems arise in association with provision of non-excludable goods – that is, goods nobody can be excluded from enjoying (Musgrave, 1959). Every potential contributor to a non-excludable good thus faces the dilemma: should I contribute even though I can enjoy the good without doing so? Most of us face such dilemmas in many aspects of life: should I pay a higher price for fair trade products such as TransFair or Max Havelaar? Should I occasionally give up my right of way to help the traffic flow more smoothly? Should I vote? Sign petitions? Demonstrate? And so on. Collective action dilemmas crop up in many aspects of life and are relevant to all the social sciences. In political science, collective action dilemmas have been proclaimed *the* central issue (Ostrom, 1998). Given the expected beneficial effect of social capital on collective action problems, the popularity of the concept is not surprising.

There are also collective action dilemmas in relation to the natural environment. Pollution abatement and a sound environment are paradigm cases of a collective action dilemma and a non-excludable good, respectively (Weale, 1992: ch. 1). Which countries are to reduce CO_2 emissions, which corporations must comply with environmental regulations to avoid more rigorous regulation, which farmers should adopt environmental management practices, should I help bring down air pollution by riding my bike to work instead of using my car, should I donate money to an environmental organization, should I join one, should I pay a premium for environmentally friendly products or just try to avoid unfriendly ones? All these actions provide non-excludable goods that can be enjoyed by anyone, whether or not she too performed these actions. Collective action dilemmas like these abound in relation to the environment.

Surprisingly few scholars have explored this abundance to test whether social capital actually helps solve collective action problems. Similarly, an equally small number of students of the environment have investigated the environmental effects of social capital. Only a few studies have looked into the relationship between social capital and solutions to environmental problems. This chapter reviews the scanty literature available and argues that both the social capital literature and the environmental literature can benefit from further investigation of the relationship. With its numerous collective action dilemmas, the environment is an excellent testing ground for social capital hypotheses. Thus, the environment can broaden our understanding of if, how, why and when social capital affects cooperation. Likewise, the literature on environmental behavior (of actors) and environmental performance (of states) would benefit from the social capital concept. If social capital really does help solve collective action problems, it must affect environmental behavior and performance, and integrating social capital would improve our knowledge on these matters (cf. Rudd, 2000). Furthermore, it may help us in developing new solutions to environmental problems as well as specific policy recommendations.

However, as will be demonstrated in the review below, the existing environmental social capital literature is as yet too scattered to draw any conclusions. Therefore, in addition to the review, this chapter also proposes some guidelines for future analyses of the environmental effects of social capital. A general definition of social capital is suggested and scholars are urged to theorize more thoroughly on the relationship between social capital, collective action and the environment. The chapter is organized as follows: the next section provides a first review of the scanty literature on social capital and the environment. The third section proposes a framework for analysing environmental problems using the social capital toolbox and draws on the concepts of collective action and trust. The fourth section concludes.

Reviewing the environmental social capital literature

This section reviews 25 empirical studies that all investigate if social capital – variously defined – affects the natural environment. Only studies that specifically relate their analysis to social capital are included. This implies that studies that do not relate components of social capital – for example trust or associational activity – to social capital are excluded (for example, Binder and Neumayer, 2005). It is most probably not a complete review, but all studies known by the author are included. The literature on the relationship between social capital and the environment is quite heterogenous. To structure the review the literature is subdivided into four groups. The first two groups consist of studies where the actors are professionals – farmers, fishermen or corporations – who affect the environment through their professional behavior. This literature is further divided into studies dealing with professionals using a common resource without external interference, and studies dealing with professionals who participate in public, semi-public or non-governmental organization (NGO) sponsored environmental programs in relation to their profession. The third group of literature deals with citizens who affect the environment through their everyday actions. The last group consists of a single miscellaneous study that defies categorization.

Type 1: professionals' self-organized maintenance of common pool resources

Table 15.1 lists the studies that deal with self-organizing professionals and their usage of common pool resources (CPR). Elinor Ostrom's *Governing the Commons* (1990) is often used as the point of departure in studies on social capital, and usage and maintenance of such resources. A common pool resource is a good from which several actors can extract (a limited amount of) resources, for instance, an irrigation system, a forest or a fishery. Maintenance and usage of such resources often give rise to collective action dilemmas because it is impossible or very difficult to restrict access to them: they are almost non-excludable. Anyone can extract resources, whether she helps maintain the resource or not. Likewise, over-exploitation looms because no one controls the resource. Thus, there is imminent danger that the common resource will cease to exist because of insufficient maintenance and overexploitation. This was the disheartening prediction made by Garrett Hardin in his article, 'The tragedy of the commons' (1968).

Ostrom analyses the conditions required to avoid this tragedy. Under certain specific institutional arrangements, groups can use and maintain a common pool resource on their own – that is, without interference from external authorities. In addition, she points briefly to the beneficial effects of social capital (1990: 184). Ostrom's study suggests that only groups with high levels of social capital are able to cooperate and maintain a common pool resource on their own.

This idea has been taken up by several authors, who have investigated self-organized initiatives (see Table 15.1). Apparently, social capital – however defined – helps CPR users to overcome potential collective action problems on their own in a variety of different CPR situations. Thus, social capital helps protect the environment from degradation, thereby preserving natural habitats and biodiversity. The study by Rodríguez and Pascual (2004) confirms the beneficial effect of social capital on collective action dilemmas, but it also shows that social capital may affect the environment negatively. It describes how the presence of social capital, and especially associational activity, helps Peruvian farmers act collectively when clearing

Table 15.1 Literature on self-organizing professionals

Study	Definition of social capital	Indicator(s)	Units of analysis	Hypothesized effect(s)	Results
Adger (2003)*	'the norms and networks that enable people to act collectively'	Institutions; networks; trust	Communities	Management of protected marine areas; better coastal defense against flooding	+
Katz (2000)	Rules and norms	Social coherence	Farmers	Less deforestation	+
Ostrom (1990)	–	–	CPR users	Sustainable use of common pool resources	+
Pretty and Ward (2001)*	Trust, reciprocity, rules, norms, sanctions and networks	Existence of CPR user group	CPR users	Sustainable management of common pool resources	+
Rodriguez and Pascual (2004)	'a subset of social interaction processes which generates durable externalities'	Associational activity; kinship; leadership	Farmers	Scrubland clearance (negative environmental effect)	Assoc: +; Kinship: ÷ Leadership: ÷
Sekhar (2007)	'norms and social networks that facilitate cooperation'	Reciprocity; informal institutions; sanctions	Fishermen	Better fisheries management	+

Notes:

* Not all effects are based on self-organization; some are caused by participation in governmental or NGO sponsored programs.

+ Indicator(s) has/have the hypothesized effect.

÷ Indicator does not have the hypothesized effect.

scrubland for farming, thus securing their incomes. However, land clearance may have negative externalities in terms of soil erosion and loss of biodiversity, causing detriments to outside communities. Interestingly, the study includes the level of bonding social capital within the groups of farmers as an explanation of scrubland clearance (measured by the existence of within-group kinship). The effect of kinship is negligible and insignificant, which indicates that bonding social capital does not lead to higher levels of clearance. Apparently, the imposition of negative externalities on outside communities is not undertaken because of strong internal bonds and skepticism about outsiders. I return to the bonding social capital issue in the third section.

Taken together, this body of literature indicates that social capital can help groups overcome the potential collective action problem associated with self-organized usage of CPR. These studies find that social capital makes sustainable usage of these CPRs possible, in most cases benefiting the environment as well as outside communities. By helping to prevent overfishing, soil degradation, deforestation, and so on, social capital affects natural habitats, biodiversity and the environment in general (cf. Pretty and Smith, 2004). Without social capital, these resources might deteriorate or require state intervention to survive.

Type 2: professionals' participation in (semi-)public or NGO-based environmental programs

The second strand of literature (Table 15.2) examines the role of social capital in CPR situations where some public or outside interference is present. Mark Lubell shows how social capital increases American farmers' participation in joint watershed management programs, thus helping to reduce fertilizer and pesticide consumption (2004). Expectations about reciprocity coupled with trust in fellow farmers and in the regulatory agencies raise the expected benefits from participation, consequently increasing participation, Lubell argues and shows. Using Swedish data Lundqvist (2001) shows how the absence of trust and negative experiences with earlier cooperation led to non-participation in a program designed to reduce application of fertilizer. The consequence of non-participation is eutrophication of marine environments. Krishna and Uphoff (2002) find similar effects of social capital in India, where social capital increases the participation rate of communities in governmental and World Bank sponsored programs. Communities with higher levels of social capital – defined in terms of how likely they are to undertake collective action – plant more trees and build more fences to protect these trees, thus benefiting both the community itself and communities downstream. In the Philippines, Cramb (2005; 2006) shows how membership of landcare groups leads to less

Table 15.2 Literature on professionals' participation in (semi-)public or NGO sponsored environmental programs

Study	Definition of social capital	Indicator(s)	Units of analysis	Hypothesized effect(s)	Results
Cramb (2005; 2006)	'Relationships of trust, communication, and cooperation that facilitate collective action'	Membership of landcare group; participation in landcare schooling	Farmers	Better soil conservation	+
Enevoldsen (2005)	Trust, norms of reciprocity	Trust between actors	Corporations	Decreased CO_2 emissions	+
Krishna and Uphoff (2002)	'Cognitive and structural assets that create propensities and capabilities for mutually beneficial collective action'	Index (formal associations, voter turnout, newspaper); preferences for individual versus collective action	Villages	Maintenance of watersheds	Index: no effect Preferences: +
Lubell (2003)	–	Trust in other actors	Governmental officials; NGO officials	Higher perceived effectiveness of environmental programs	+
Lubell (2004)	'norm of reciprocity, trust, and networks of civic engagement'	Trust in regulatory agencies and other farmers; expectations about reciprocity	Farmers	Increased participation in and support for watershed management	Trust: varies; Expectations: +

Table 15.2 (continued)

Study	Definition of social capital	Indicator(s)	Units of analysis	Hypothesized effect(s)	Results
Lundqvist (2001)	–	Trust in other actors	Farmers	Participation in water pollution reduction	+
Raymond (2006)	Trust	Trust between actors	Landowners	Establishment of Habitat Conservation Plans	÷

Notes:
+   Indicator(s) has/have the hypothesized effect.
÷   Indicator does not have the hypothesized effect.

soil degradation through collective action. Conversely, Raymond (2006) describes one of the few clear non-findings in this review: social capital and trust do not increase participation in American habitat protection programs.

In his analysis of a completely different environmental problem, CO_2 emissions, Martin Enevoldsen (2005) shows that the density of social capital and trust within Dutch industrial sectors affects whether corporations cooperate and reduce CO_2 emissions voluntarily. Sectors with high levels of social capital are able to reduce CO_2 emission, thereby avoiding further governmental regulation. In sectors with less social capital, free riding prevails and the CO_2 reduction goals set by the government are not met.

Taken together, this group of literature shows that social capital – defined in various ways – can increase participation in public-private environmental programs even when participation is not mandatory. Hence, social capital apparently raises the environmental impact and the effectiveness of such programs.

Type 3: citizens' involvement in pro-environmental behavior and environmental activism

While the literature reviewed above examined professionals engaged in production with environmental effects, this third type of literature (Table 15.3) deals with ordinary citizens and their everyday environmental behavior. Two types of behavior are analysed within this literature: pro-environmental behavior and environmental activism.

Pro-environmental behavior is individual behavior intended to improve the environment (Kollmuss and Agyeman, 2002). Examples are beach cleaning, recycling, and environmental purchasing behavior like buying environmentally friendly products or avoidance of environmentally unfriendly ones. Although pro-environmental behavior has been studied extensively (for reviews see Bamberg and Moser, 2007; Kollmuss and Agyeman, 2002) and produces non-excludable goods, very few studies have included the concept of social capital.

Two studies investigated the establishment of self-organized solid waste collection in Bangladesh (Bhuiyan, 2004; Pargal et al., 2002). They both find that communities with higher levels of social capital are more successful. Likewise, Edwards and Onyx (2007) find that an Australian community rich on social capital is doing well in regard to sustainable community development. This result is however based on a single case study and therefore lacks comparative validation.

The studies above deal with the effect of social capital in smaller communities where almost everyone knows each other and pro-environmental

Table 15.3 *Literature on citizens' pro-environmental behavior and activism*

Study	Definition(s) of social capital	Indicator(s)	Units of analysis	Hypothesized effect(s)	Results
Bhuiyan (2004)	'trust, social networks, and civic engagement'	Trust in other actors; membership; community events	Citizens	Establishment of solid waste collection	+
Birner and Wittmer (2003)	Personal networks (Bourdieu)	Organizational networks to mobilize voters and activists; political contacts	Interest groups	Influence on environmental policy making	+
Edwards and Onyx (2007)	'norms and networks that facilitate collective action'	Index (community trust, networks and more)	Communities	Sustainable community development	+
Kurz et al. (2007)	Sense of community	Index (community trust, associational membership and more)	Citizens/ communities	Increased recycling	+
Lubell (2002)	Civic engagement	Associational membership; (generalized trust)*	Citizens	Environmental activism (petition signing, environmental group membership)	Assoc: + Trust: +, but insignificant
Pargal et al. (2002)	Various	Trust; norms of reciprocity; sharing	Communities	Establishment of solid waste collection	All positive but significance varies

Study	Definition	Indicator(s)	Unit	Dependent variable	Effect
Sønderskov (2008)	–	Generalized trust	Countries	Increased environmental group membership	+
Sønderskov (2007, 2008)	–	Generalized trust	Countries	Increased recycling; no effect on organic food consumption	Recycling: + / Organic: insignificant
Torgler and Garcia-Valiñas (2005)	Trust	Generalized trust; membership of environmental organization	Citizens	Increased willingness to pay taxes that improve the environment	Yes
Wakefield et al. (2006)	'networks, norms and trust that facilitate community coordination and cooperation'	Trust in government; civic responsibility; group membership; environmental group membership	Citizens	Increased pro-environmental behavior and activism	Varies between indicators and dependent variable

Notes:
+   Indicator(s) has the hypothesized effect.
*   Generalized trust is not part of the employed social capital definition.

behavior benefits a relatively small number of people. The following studies deal with pro-environmental behavior that affects the environment on a larger scale and involves numerous actors.

Torgler and Garcia-Valiñas (2005) find a positive effect of social capital on large-scale pro-environmental behavior. People with generalized trust and members of environmental organizations state that they are more willing to pay taxes to help avert environmental damage. Wakefield et al. (2006) find that civic-minded citizens more readily recycle, and people with strong links to their neighborhood are more likely to reject environmentally unfriendly products. Kurz et al. (2007) and Sønderskov (2007) find that citizens in communities and countries with high levels of social capital recycle more, and the former study supports this relationship at the individual level. The latter study by Sønderskov also investigates whether social capital affects organic food consumption, finding no effect of generalized trust. I will return to this study below because it illustrates how comparisons of social capital effects can increase our knowledge of social capital.

While pro-environmental behavior is intended to affect the environment directly, *environmental activism* is intended to affect the environment indirectly by modifying other people's behavior. Four studies have investigated the effects of social capital on activism. Together these studies show that social capital – variously defined – has positive effects on environmental group membership, donations to environmental groups, number of applications on environmental issues to authorities, industries and media, participation in public meetings and demonstrations, and signing petitions (Birner and Wittmer, 2003; Lubell, 2002; Sønderskov, 2008; Wakefield et al., 2006). It should be noted, however, that Wakefield et al. use environmental group membership as an indicator of social capital, while Lubell and Sønderskov use it as an indicator of activism.

The literature on pro-environmental behavior and activism shows that social capital – defined in a variety of ways – enhances collective action on a range of different environmental problems spanning from local problems to larger environmental issues involving numerous actors.

Type 4: miscellaneous literature

The last study reviewed here (Table 15.4) fits none of the categories used above because the argued link from social capital to the environment rests on multiple arguments. This study argues that all the beneficial effects identified in the literature above should be reflected in the aggregate environmental conditions of nations. If the positive effects of social capital described in the literature above are real, one would expect that nations with high levels of social capital have better overall environmental

Table 15.4   Mixed literature

Study	Definition(s) of social capital	Indicator(s)	Units of analysis	Hypothesized effect(s)	Results
Grafton and Knowles (2004)	Putnam*	Trust; norms; associational membership; democratic accountability; corruption	Countries	Better national environmental quality	Varies between indicators and dependent variable

Notes: Putnam*: 'the features of social organization . . . that facilitate coordination and cooperation for mutual benefit'.

conditions. The study only vaguely supports this hypothesis. It investigates the effects of several social capital indicators on several indicators of national environmental conditions and finds both negative and positive effects of social capital. Actually, most social capital indicators have both negative and positive effects, depending on the environmental indicator examined. Thus, no clear results emerge from this study, but it should be noted that the analysis rests on relatively few cases. Nevertheless, the mixed results are dismaying and discouraging. If social capital does not have a robust effect on national environmental performance, then one might ask if social capital substantially contributes to the solution of environmental problems specifically, and collective action problems generally. This study therefore indicates that we should proceed with caution before concluding that social capital helps improve the environment. In the concluding part of this section, I point to some other reasons why the results from literature as a whole should be approached with some caution.

Discussion: does social capital have an environmental pay-off?
Other than the last study and a few other results, most results reviewed point to a positive effect on the environment of social capital. Apparently, social capital does benefit the environment on a range of different environmental problems, from local commons problems to more extensive ones like green taxes and CO_2 emissions. However, the literature as a whole is still far too undeveloped to conclude much on the relationship. Two points are especially problematic, namely, the variety of definitions employed and the lack of theoretical explanations.

Looking at Tables 15.1–15.4, it is evident that a myriad of social capital definitions are employed in the studies reviewed here. Nearly every study provides a unique definition of social capital, ranging from all encompassing, functionalist definitions like 'Cognitive and structural assets that create propensities and capabilities for mutually beneficial collective action' (for example, Krishna and Uphoff, 2002), over broad Putnamian definitions like 'networks, norms and trust that facilitate community coordination and cooperation' (Wakefield et al., 2006), and even Bourdieuan definitions 'personal networks' (Birner and Wittmer, 2003), and to narrow definitions focusing on trust between the involved actors (for example, Lubell, 2004). This myriad of social capital definitions is not unique to the environmental literature (cf. Paldam, 2000; Sobel, 2002), but it undermines the empirical support for a general environmental effect of social capital. Several studies on other topics have questioned whether social capital is a one-dimensional concept, positing instead that social capital is multifaceted, and that it consists of distinct elements with discrete societal effects (Bjørnskov, 2006; Knack and Keefer, 1997). If the different elements have different effects, some of the results reported in the literature above may be sensitive to the definition employed; another definition might yield different results. This is actually illustrated in some of the environmental studies. A few of them include measures for more than one element of social capital and find that they affect the environment differently (for example, Grafton and Knowles, 2004; Pargal et al., 2002). Thus, even though the literature as a whole supports an environmental effect of social capital, the evidence rests on studies that define social capital in various ways that may or may not be related. This gives reason to question the empirical support for an environmental effect of social capital.

In addition, some of the studies employ very problematic definitions. Some use functionalist definitions like 'relationships of trust, communication, and cooperation that facilitate collective action' and then go on to investigate if social capital enhances cooperation. Not surprisingly, these hypotheses are confirmed. Some studies take this even further. They find that factors other than the ones included in their original definition of social capital affect cooperation and then conclude that social capital has to be redefined to fit the particular context (for example, Bhuiyan, 2004: ch. 9). If the concept of social capital is defined differently in each study to yield positive results, then its value becomes negligible. Again, functionalist definitions are not unique to the environmental literature (cf. Durlauf, 2002; Portes, 1998), but functionalist definitions are not suitable for hypothesis testing. If social capital is defined as enhancing cooperation, not much light is shed on if and why social capital helps solve problems of collective action, and if and why it brings about environmental improvements.

The other overarching problem with the literature is the lack of theoretical explanations. All studies argue that social capital affects the environment through an effect on collective action. However, in most studies, that is about all the explanation provided. Quite a few studies throw in a few references to Robert Putnam and then proceed quickly to the test (for example, Wakefield et al., 2006). However, it is very seldom clear exactly why a specific conception of social capital is related to the solution of collective action problems. Consequently, it is often unclear which mechanisms lead to collective action and environmental improvements. A few studies have done a bit more theoretical footwork, and I will return to their arguments below.

To sum up this review, my conclusion is that the overwhelmingly positive message of the environmental literature should be taken with a grain of salt. Although quite a few studies uncover beneficial effects of social capital upon the environment, more thorough analyses have to be conducted before drawing conclusions on these matters. The next section offers some guidelines on how this could be undertaken. However, the section also argues that this work might very well be worthwhile because of the excellent testing possibilities within the environmental field.

Suggestions for future analyses
Functionalist definitions of social capital should be avoided when testing hypotheses. That is the one inescapable outcome of this review. Functionalist definitions do not guarantee a thorough test of hypotheses. Moreover, when defining social capital as multifaceted – that is, as consisting of more than one element – it should be discussed how the different elements are related. Do they express the same phenomenon or does one of them cause the others? Such a discussion will make it easier to judge the validity of the arguments and findings if it turns out that one of the elements does not affect the dependent variable in the test.

If the literature is to really move forward, a common definition of social capital is essential. Of the definitions employed in the studies above, the one used by Mark Lubell, seems to have the greatest potential as a general definition in relation to the environment and collective action. In two of his studies, Lubell defines social capital as trust and argues that trust is the central aspect in relation to collective action. However, the object of trust changes from study to study. The object of trust varies according to the actors involved in the collective action problem under examination (Lubell, 2003, 2004). To sharpen this definition, social capital can be defined as the density of trust between the relevant actors (cf. Paldam and Svendsen, 2000). Relevant actors are those with the potential to help solve the environmental problem in question, and the density of trust refers to how much these relevant actors trust each other. Using this definition in an analysis of local common pool problems, social capital should be defined as the density of trust between the users of the common resource. In analyses of larger environmental problems like urban or regional air pollution, trust should be defined as the density of trust between the polluters. The set of relevant actors in some instances becomes so vast that the actors do not know each other, and hence, do not have information about the trustworthiness of the other actors. In such cases social capital could be defined as the density of generalized social trust – that is, trust in other people in general (cf. Uslaner, 2002). This generalized trust definition was actually used in some of the above mentioned studies that deal with very large sets of relevant actors (Sønderskov, 2007; 2008; Torgler and Garcia-Valiñas, 2005).

By defining social capital as the density of trust between the relevant actors, our definition becomes consistent across studies and disciplines, while being flexible enough to fit most contexts, from the small closely knit group of people with bonding social capital, to the very large heterogeneous group whose actors do not know one another.

This definition might seem trivial, but in a certain respect it differs from most definitions employed so far. Most scholars distinguish between bonding and bridging social capital (between in-group trust and out-group trust) and argue that they produce different outcomes (see, for example, the introduction to this volume). In relation to collective action, however, both types of social capital might help overcome collective action problems, and both types might thus help bring about environmental improvements. Hence, the perspective advocated by this definition is that the distinction is rarely relevant in relation to environmental collective action problems. It may, however, still be relevant in some cases, for instance when collective action is undertaken not only due to dense in-group trust, but also because of strong out-group skepticism. Such out-group skepticism has been dubbed 'excessive bonding social capital' (Introduction, this volume) or 'particularized trust' (Uslaner, 2002). Colletta and Cullen (2002) describe how the disastrous genocide in Rwanda was so effective not only because of within-group social capital in Hutu clans but also because of excessive hatred towards Tutsis. This implies that the type of collective action being analysed leads to negative consequences for outside communities. In the Peruvian case of scrubland clearance described by Rodríguez and Pascual (2004) the distinction might be relevant. In such cases the definition and the indicators will have to incorporate levels of excessive bonding social capital or particularized trust.

Having proposed a common definition of social capital, I now turn to the other concern raised in the review, namely, the lack of theoretical arguments characterizing most of the studies. Only a few of the studies contain theoretical arguments that go beyond stating that social capital helps solve collective action problems. The most thorough theoretical footwork is found in the works of Mark Lubell and Kim Sønderskov, respectively. Both authors draw on a rational choice framework and argue that trust reflects how individuals expect other members of the collective to act. Will they act in a trustworthy manner and contribute to common goods or will they free-ride? If an individual trusts the relevant others, she expects they will contribute, and vice versa. If she expects that other people will fulfill their obligation, the benefits from cooperation increase. Furthermore, by cooperating, future cooperation by other players is more likely, which raises future benefits. Hence, if people expect others to cooperate and they expect to play within this collective again, then cooperation is the rational choice. This implies that trusting people will more often engage in collective action.

Obviously, there are other theoretical explanations for a relationship between trust and cooperation than rational choice. However, only the rational choice explanation has been advocated extensively in relation to the environment. On a general level, some authors have argued that the effect of social capital on collective action is due to non-strategic behavior. Pedersen et al. (this volume) argue that people prefer to cooperate if they may reasonably expect others to do likewise, because cooperation feels good. Other authors refer to higher degrees of altruism or civic-mindedness among trusters, which would explain the effect of trust on cooperation (Letki, 2006; Torsvik, 2000); however, the altruistic/civic-mindedness explanation is dismissed empirically in Letki (2006) and Sønderskov (2007, cf. below). Thus, other perspectives than the rational choice explanation ought to be explored.

With a common definition of social capital and more comprehensive theoretical footwork, the best place to start would be to investigate which theoretical perspective is the most fruitful – and other empirical questions as well. Owing to the large number of collective action dilemmas, the environment provides excellent testing possibilities. One strategy would be to compare the effect of social capital on similar kinds of environmental problems. A previous study can illustrate this. Sønderskov (2007) compares the effect of generalized trust on recycling behavior and organic food consumption to investigate if generalized trust promotes pro-environmental behavior generally, or whether this only happens when a collective action dilemma is present. There is a collective action dilemma in relation to recycling because it solely produces non-excludable goods in terms of reduced resource consumption. On the other hand, the collective action dilemma is of a much smaller magnitude in regard to organic foods consumption, because is also produces benefits for the consumer herself in terms of better flavor, quality, and so on. As mentioned in the review above, the study finds that generalized trust increases recycling but not organic food consumption. Thus, social capital increases provision of non-excludable goods in collection action dilemmas, but not pro-environmental behavior or civic behavior generally.

Several other comparisons are possible. One could investigate if there are limits to the effect of social capital. Can the relevant group of actors grow so large that trust is no longer feasible? This could be examined by comparing the effect of social capital on citizens' actions in relation to large-scale problems (for example, CO_2 pollution) with their reaction to medium-scale problems (for example, urban air pollution) (see also Rydin and Pennington, 2000). It would also be interesting to see if the effect differs according to the type of aggregation technology required to supply a non-excludable good. For example, does the effect vary between a situation where all relevant actors have to contribute in order to supply the good (for example, preservation of interdependent species) compared with one where just one actor has to contribute (for example, the establishment of a natural park) (cf. Hirshleifer, 1983; Holzinger, 2001)? The environment contains numerous possibilities to investigate if, how, why and when social capital affects collective action and the environment. Once more solid knowledge has been accumulated we may be able to provide specific environmental policy recommendations.

Conclusions

This chapter has provided a first review of the literature on social capital and the environment. The sparse literature has found positive effects of social capital on a wide range of environmental problems. The effects range from solutions to small common problems – like sustainable usage of fisheries – to massive environmental problems like green taxes and CO_2 reductions. Thus, in the presence of social capital, professionals and citizens within small groups, communities and countries are better able to solve environmental problems and bring about environmental improvements. This effect was unanimously explained by the beneficial effect of social capital on solutions to collective action problems. However, the review also made it clear that the results are based on very different conceptions of social capital, which implies that the effect may not be a general social capital effect, but isolated effects of various unrelated elements. Hence, it is far from certain that social capital affects solutions to environmental problems, and it is therefore not certain either that social capital affects collective action problems generally.

To take the literature a step further, this chapter has proposed a common framework, where social capital is defined as the density of trust between the relevant actors. The term 'relevant actors' refers to the actors involved in a collective action dilemma. Furthermore, this chapter has suggested future research on the relationship between social capital and solutions to environmental problems. This research could broaden our understanding of whether, why, how and when social capital helps solve environmental problems. This knowledge could also be applied to other collective action problems.

References

Adger, W.N. (2003), 'Social capital, collective action, and adaptation to climate change', *Economic Geography*, **79** (4), 387–404.

Bamberg, S. and G. Moser (2007), 'Twenty years after Hines, Hungerford, and Tomera: a new meta-analysis of psycho-social determinants of pro-environmental behaviour', *Journal of Environmental Psychology*, **27** (1), 14–25.

Bhuiyan, S.H. (2004), *Benefits of Social Capital: Urban Solid Waste Management in Bangladesh*, Münster: LIT Verlag.

Binder, S. and E. Neumayer (2005), 'Environmental pressure group strength and air pollution: an empirical analysis', *Ecological Economics*, **55** (4), 527–38.

Birner, R. and H. Wittmer (2003), 'Using social capital to create political capital: how do local communities gain political influence? A theoretical approach and empirical evidence from Thailand', in N. Dolšak and E. Ostrom (eds), *The Commons in the New Millennium: Challenges and Adaptations*, Cambridge: MIT Press, pp. 291–334.

Bjørnskov, C. (2006), 'The multiple facets of social capital', *European Journal of Political Economy*, **22** (1), 22–40.

Coleman, J.S. (1990), *Foundations of Social Theory*, Cambridge, MA: Harvard University Press.

Colletta, N.J. and M.L. Cullen (2002), 'Social capital and social cohesion: case studies from Cambodia and Rwanda', in C. Grootaert and T. van Bastelaer (eds), *The Role of Social Capital in Development: An Empirical Assessment*, Cambridge: Cambridge University Press, pp. 279–309.

Cramb, R.A. (2005), 'Social capital and soil conservation: evidence from the Philippines', *The Australian Journal of Agricultural and Resource Economics*, **49** (2), 211–26.

Cramb, R.A. (2006), 'The role of social capital in the promotion of conservation farming: the case of "landcare" in the Southern Philippines', *Land Degradation & Development*, **17** (1), 23–30.

Durlauf, S.N. (2002), 'Bowling alone: a review essay', *Journal of Economic Behavior and Organization*, **47** (3), 259–73.

Edwards, M. and J. Onyx (2007), 'Social capital and sustainability in a community under threat', *Local Environment*, **12** (1), 17–30.

Enevoldsen, M. (2005), *The Theory of Environmental Agreements and Taxes*, Cheltenham, UK and Northampton, MA, USA: Edward Elgar.

Grafton, R.Q. and S. Knowles (2004), 'Social capital and national environmental performance: a cross-sectional analysis', *Journal of Environment & Development*, **13** (4), 336–70.

Hardin, G. (1968), 'The tragedy of the commons', *Science*, **162** (3859), 1243–8.

Hirshleifer, J. (1983), 'From weakest-link to best-shot: the voluntary provision of public goods', *Public Choice*, **41** (3), 371–86.

Holzinger, K. (2001), 'Aggregation technology of common goods and its strategic consequences: global warming, biodiversity, and siting conflicts', *European Journal of Political Research*, **40** (2), 117–38.

Katz, E.G. (2000), 'Social capital and natural capital: a comparative analysis of land tenure and natural resource management in Guatemala', *Land Economics*, **76** (1), 114–32.

Knack, S. and P. Keefer (1997), 'Does social capital have an economic payoff? A cross-country investigation', *Quarterly Journal of Economics*, **112** (4), 1251–88.

Kollmuss, A. and J. Agyeman (2002), 'Mind the gap: why do people act environmentally and what are the barriers to pro-environmental behavior?', *Environmental Education Research*, **8** (3), 239–60.

Krishna, A. and N. Uphoff (2002), 'Mapping and measuring social capital through assessment of collective action to conserve and develop watersheds in Rajasthan, India', in C. Grootaert and T. van Bastelaer (eds), *The Role of Social Capital in Development: An Empirical Assessment*, Cambridge: Cambridge University Press, pp. 85–124.

Kurz, T., M. Linden, and N. Sheehy (2007), 'Attitudinal and community influences on participation in new curbside recycling initiatives in Northern Ireland', *Environment and Behavior*, **39** (3), 367–91.

Letki, N. (2006), 'Investigating the roots of civic morality: trust, social capital, and institutional performance', *Political Behavior*, **28** (4), 305–25.

Lubell, M. (2002), 'Environmental activism as collective action', *Environment and Behavior*, **34** (4), 431–54.

Lubell, M. (2003), 'Collaborative institutions, belief-systems, and perceived policy effectiveness', *Political Research Quarterly*, **56** (3), 309–23.

Lubell, M. (2004), 'Collaborative watershed management: a view from the grassroots', *Policy Studies Journal*, **32** (3), 341–61.

Lundqvist, L.J. (2001), 'Games real farmers play: knowledge, memory and the fate of collective action to prevent eutrophication of water catchments', *Local Environment*, **6** (4), 407–19.

Musgrave, R.A. (1959), *The Theory of Public Finance: A Study in Public Economy*, New York: McGraw-Hill.

Ostrom, E. (1990), *Governing the Commons*, Cambridge: Cambridge University Press.

Ostrom, E. (1998), 'A behavioral approach to the rational choice theory of collective action: presidential address, American Political Science Association, 1997', *American Political Science Review*, **92** (1), 1–22.

Ostrom, E. and T.K. Ahn (2003), 'Introduction', in E. Ostrom and T.K. Ahn (eds), *Foundations of Social Capital*, Cheltenham, UK and Northampton, MA, USA: Edward Elgar, pp. xi–xxxix.

Paldam, M. (2000), 'Social capital: one or many? Definition and measurement', *Journal of Economic Surveys*, **14** (5), 629–53.

Paldam, M. and G.T. Svendsen (2000), 'An essay on social capital: looking for the fire behind the smoke', *European Journal of Political Economy*, **16** (2), 339–66.

Pargal, S., D.O. Gilligan and M. Huq (2002), 'Does social capital increase participation in voluntary solid waste management? Evidence from Dhaka, Bangladesh', in C. Grootaert and T. van Bastelaer (eds), *The Role of Social Capital in Development*, Cambridge: Cambridge University Press, pp. 188–209.

Portes, A. (1998), 'Social capital: its origins and applications in modern sociology', *Annual Review of Sociology*, **24** (1), 1–24.

Pretty, J. and D. Smith (2004), 'Social capital in biodiversity conservation and management', *Conservation Biology*, **18** (3), 631–38.

Pretty, J. and H. Ward (2001), 'Social capital and the environment', *World Development*, **29** (2), 209–27.

Putnam, R.D. (1993), *Making Democracy Work – Civic Traditions in Modern Italy*, Princeton, NJ: Princeton University Press.

Putnam, R.D. (2000), *Bowling Alone*, New York: Simon & Schuster.

Raymond, L. (2006), 'Cooperation without trust: overcoming collective action barriers to endangered species protection', *Policy Studies Journal*, **34** (1), 37–57.

Rodríguez, L.C. and U. Pascual (2004), 'Land clearance and social capital in mountain agro-ecosystems: the case of Opuntia scrubland in Ayacucho, Peru', *Ecological Economics*, 49 (2), 243–52.

Rothstein, B. (2005), *Social Traps and the Problem of Trust*, Cambridge: Cambridge University Press.

Rudd, M.A. (2000), 'Live long and prosper: collective action, social capital and social vision', *Ecological Economics*, **34** (1), 131–44.

Rydin, Y. and M. Pennington (2000), 'Public participation and local environmental planning: the collective action problem and the potential of social capital', *Local Environment*, **5** (2), 153–69.

Sekhar, N.U. (2007), 'Social capital and fisheries management: the case of Chilika lake in India', *Environmental Management*, **39** (4), 497–505.

Sobel, J. (2002), 'Can we trust social capital?', *Journal of Economic Literature*, **40** (1), 139–54.

Sønderskov, K.M. (2007), 'Different goods, different effects: exploring the roles of generalized trust in collective action', paper presented at Dansk Public Choice Workshop, Copenhagen, 30 January, www.akf.dk/dansk_public_choice/pdf/soenderskov.pdf, accessed 2 September 2007.

Sønderskov, K.M. (2008), 'Environmental group membership, collective action and generalised trust', *Environmental Politics*, **17** (1), 78–94.

Torgler, B. and M.A. Garcia-Valiñas (2005), 'The determinants of individuals' attitudes towards preventing environmental damage', FEEM working paper, no. 110.05, http://ssrn.com/abstract=822044, accessed 2 September 2007.

Torsvik, G. (2000), 'Social capital and economic development: a plea for the mechanisms', *Rationality and Society*, **12** (4), 451–76.

Uslaner, E.M. (1999), 'Democracy and social capital', in M. Warren (ed.), *Democracy and Trust*, Cambridge: Cambridge University Press, pp. 121–50.

Uslaner, E.M. (2002), *The Moral Foundations of Trust*, Cambridge: Cambridge University Press.

Wakefield, S.E.L., S.J. Elliott, J.D. Eyles and D.C. Cole (2006), 'Taking environmental action: the role of local composition, context, and collective', *Environmental Management*, **37** (1), 40–53.

Weale, A. (1992), *The New Politics of Pollution*, Manchester: Manchester University Press.

16 The labour market*
Fabio Sabatini

16.1 Introduction

The positive role of social capital in economic development is now commonly acknowledged in the scientific and political debate. However, both social capital and economic development must be looked on as multidimensional concepts: the definition of what type of social capital may provide a positive contribution to the wealth and progress of a society is still a subject of major contention.

One of the most popular definitions of social capital refers to the set of 'features of social life – networks, norms, and trust – that enable participants to act together more effectively to pursue shared objectives' (Putnam, 1995). Drawing on more than a decade of empirical investigations, the literature has classified the elements in the set into three main types of social capital: *bonding*, *bridging* and *linking*.

Bonding social capital relates to networks between homogeneous groups of people, quite close to outsiders, that constrain members into their boundaries. Bridging networks are shaped by weak ties connecting people belonging to different socio-economic backgrounds. Examples are culture and sports clubs. Linking social capital refers to vertical connections with people in power, whether they are in politically or financially influential positions. Examples are voluntary organizations and social services agencies. Bonding social capital is generally considered as a source of backwardness, while bridging and linking ties are supposed to foster the diffusion of information and trust, with beneficial effects for economic activity and well-being.

The economics literature on social capital generally focuses on the relationship between networks, trust and economic growth. It is true that growth, by increasing total wealth, also enhances its potential for improving well-being and solving other social problems. However, there are other facets of social capital and economic development that should be accounted for. As stated by the World Bank,

> History offers a number of examples where economic growth was not followed by similar progress in human development. Instead growth was achieved at the cost of greater inequity, higher unemployment, weakened democracy, loss of cultural identity, or overconsumption of resources needed by future generations

... To be sustainable, economic growth must be constantly nourished by the fruits of human development. (2000: 7–8)

Acknowledging the importance of human development as one of the main factors of growth's sustainability implies the need for the empirical research to carry out further investigations on its relationship with social capital.

A relevant aspect of growth that has never been accounted for within the social capital literature is 'labour precariousness'. It is our belief that precariousness plays a crucial role in determining social cohesion and the agents' well-being. Precarious workers are generally characterized by low employment conditions in terms of pay, employment security, sickness and parental benefits, balance between work and private life. They are usually provided with less work-related training and enjoy scarce prospects of building a career. The high exposure to the risks of job loss, wage variability and intermittent unemployment raises the uncertainty on future incomes, making difficult any form of long-term planning of life activities such as marriage and procreation.

Labour precariousness can thus be seen as a barrier to social integration that may destroy human and social capital: a high level of flexibility on employment hinders training and qualification and, at the same time, hampers the consolidation of social ties, both inside and outside the workplace. While stable and satisfactory work provides not only income, but also an identity and a 'sense of belonging', precariousness generates discouragement and distrust towards labour market institutions that, at the macro level, may result in a more distrustful society.

Another interesting figure in the economic literature is the surprising lack of empirical studies addressing the role of bonding social capital, which has led to an underestimation of the possibility for strong family ties to act as a positive asset for the agents' strategies of survival and for the economy as a whole.

The need emerges to focus the empirical research on different types of social ties, as well as on aspects of economic development that may tell something more about the 'quality' and the sustainability of growth.

This chapter aims to shed light on the causal linkages connecting the three types of social capital (bonding, bridging and linking) to human development and labour precariousness. The main question of the chapter is, what type of social capital is able to mitigate labour precariousness and to foster human development?

This issue has been addressed through a review of the literature and an empirical investigation on the Italian regions. Social capital's dimensions have been measured by synthetic indicators built by means of a multivariate analysis performed on a dataset including 43 variables. Causal relationships have been assessed through the use of structural equations models.

Our contribution to the literature is twofold. First, we provide an empirical analysis that simultaneously accounts for all three forms of social capital, thereby introducing the first rigorous assessment of the role of strong family ties and shedding light on the diverse effects exerted by each social capital's dimension. Second, we introduce the theme of labour precariousness in the debate on social capital and economic developemnt.

The chapter is organized in three sections: first, we provide some definitions. Section 16.3 carries out a review of the role of social networks in reducing unemployment and precariousness. Section 16.4 describes the methodology and results of the empirical analysis. We conclude the paper with a brief discussion of the main empirical findings.

16.2   Definitions

Everyday life experience suggests that social networks may play a double-sided role in economic development and well-being. On the one side, they are a fertile ground for nurturing trust and shared values, that reduce monitoring costs and facilitate transactions. Repeated interactions among group members foster the diffusion of information raising reputations' relevance. The higher opportunity cost of free-riding in Prisoners' Dilemma kind of situations makes the agents' behaviour more foreseeable causing an overall reduction of uncertainty. Therefore, an increase in trust-based relations may reduce the average cost of transactions, just as an increase in physical capital reduces the average cost of production. However, networks can work in the opposite direction as well: members of a group may use their ties as a means for the pursuit of narrow sectarian interests, and organizations may lobby against the interest of other groups. The distinction between bonding, bridging and linking social capital reflects the different roles that networks may play in shaping the economic development of a society.

The term 'bonding' holds a negative connotation and generally refers to small circles of homogeneous people that do not cooperate with others outside the boundaries of the group. The literature has often focused on the family as a potential form of bonding social capital. In his pioneering study, Banfield partly attributed the backwardness of Southern Italy to the inability of citizens 'to act together for their common good or, indeed, for any end transcending the immediate, material interest of the nuclear family' (1958: 10). According to the author, any family activity was oriented towards the protection and consolidation of the isolated family unit. 'Moral' activity (that is, any action informed by moral norms of trust and reciprocity) was seen as limited to family insiders, with outsiders only being significant as a potential resource to exploit for the family. Applying Banfield's claims to the purposes of this chapter, we can argue that the bonding social capital of the family may act as a tool for job search actions, thereby mitigating labour precariousness, and, at the macro level, as a factor hampering the economic performance and development.

Bridging social capital is given by horizontal ties shaping heterogeneous groups of people with different backgrounds. The term 'bridging' refers to the ability of such networks to create 'bridges' connecting sectors of society that, otherwise, would have never come into contact. The common claim is that bridging social capital has positive effects on the diffusion of information and trust, thus fostering transactions and economic growth.

The term 'linking social capital' describes ties connecting individuals, or the groups they belong to, to people or groups in position of political or financial power. For example, civil society organizations allow citizens to come into contact with the institutions to carry out advocacy activities through collective action. This kind of network is critical for leveraging resources, ideas and information beyond normal community linkages and, therefore, may play a significant role for social well-being. However, the role of organizations in development is widely debated in the literature. Economic studies suggest that much depends on the context where non-governmental organizations' (NGOs) activities take place. Knack and Keefer (1997) sustain that cooperation and solidarity connected with the presence of voluntary associations work better at the level of smaller communities. In the authors' words:

> If the economic goals of a group conflict with those of other groups or of unorganized interests, the overall effect of group memberships and activities on economic performance could be negative . . . Although the ability of groups to articulate their interests is likely to be an important restraint on government, it also provides groups a way to capture private benefits at the expense of society. (1997: 1271)

In other words, organizations can behave pro-socially as well as anti-socially, just like all the other forms of social capital. Regarding labour precariousness, the effect of the associational activity has not been the object of empirical investigations yet. These hypotheses on the divergent roles exerted by the three types of social capital on precariousness and development will be tested in Section 4 within the empirical investigation on the Italian regions.

According to the United Nations Development Programme (UNDP, 2007),

> Human development is about much more than the rise or fall of national incomes. It is about creating an environment in which people can develop their full potential and lead productive, creative lives in accord with their needs and interests . . . Development is thus about expanding the choices people have to lead lives that they value. And it is thus about much more than economic growth, which is only a means – if a very important one – of enlarging people's choices.

Human development is generally measured through the Human Development Index, that is computed as the average of three indexes representing life expectancy, education and per capita income. In this chapter, the Human Development Index has been adjusted in order to take into account Italy's high level of wealth.

As regards labour precariousness, in its 'Classification of Status in Employment', the International Labour Organization (ILO, 1993) defines 'precarious' workers as either: (a) workers whose contract of employment leads to the classification of the incumbent as belonging to the groups of 'casual workers'; (b) 'short-term workers' or 'seasonal workers'; or (c) workers whose contract of employment will allow the employing enterprise or person to terminate the contract at short notice and/or at will, the specific circumstances to be determined by national legislation and custom. The ILO defines 'casual' workers as having an explicit or implicit contract of employment which is not expected to continue for more than a short period.

16.3   The labour market

The social capital literature has shown that workers have better chances of finding employment when using networks (Granovetter, 1973, 1974; Fernandez et al., 2000; Munshi, 2003). In economic theory, Boorman (1975) was the first to provide a formal network model which described the information structure of finding a job. In Boorman's model, networks are endogenous: contacts are developed by individuals who maximize their probability of getting a new job in the event that they lose their present job. Another formal model has been developed by Calvó-Armengol and Jackson (2004), to prove that the employment likelihood increases with the extent of social contacts.

An interesting empirical study by Datcher (1983), focusing on the impact sorted by informal networks on the probability of quitting a job, finds that workers with contacts before being hired are less likely to quit their jobs. In other words, a higher extension of the worker's social networks implies a longer job duration. Within an empirical study on Mexican immigrant workers, Aguilera (2003) has proved that increases in human capital are associated with shorter job tenure, apparently in an effort to improve employment conditions, while the use of social capital is positively related with job tenure. In general, it appears that acquiring employment is a social process, and those using personal networks find longer-lasting jobs. A following study on Mexican immigrants by Amudeo-Dorantes and Mundra (2004) finds that social networks, particularly strong ties, contribute to the economic assimilation of immigrants by raising their hourly wages. However, networks do not enhance immigrants' employability. Instead, strong ties allow for a lower employment likelihood possibly through the shelter against temporary unemployment provided by close family members.

This quick glance at the literature suggests the possibility of social networks generating virtuous circles, going from reduction of precariousness and the improvement of workers' well-being, to the accumulation of new social capital in the form of trust and more stable social ties. What should be the object of further investigations is the effect of such social networks-induced job-matching processes on the overall efficiency of the labour market. For example, Bentolila et al. (2003) argue that in the presence of imperfect information on jobs and workers' characteristics, networks can induce a significant mismatch of talents. This result has been empirically confirmed by Ferrante and Sabatini (2007) in their analysis of the effects sorted by human and social capital on the occupational choices of Italian workers.

The crucial role of precariousness in the determination of well-being has been stressed also by the recent happiness literature. Drawing on data from the Longitudinal Surveys of Australian Youth, Dockery (2005) investigates factors that influence young Australians' self-reported levels of happiness during the school-to-work transition, focusing on the role of labour market experience. The author finds evidence of declining well-being with duration of unemployment and of the importance of job quality, rather than just having a job. Some notable studies provide evidence that unemployment significantly reduces happiness in Europe and the USA (Di Tella et al., 1997) in Britain (Clarck and Oswald, 1994), and in Britain and the USA (Blanchflower and Oswald, 2004). Gerlach and Gesine (1996) find similar results for Germany.

16.4 Empirical analysis
The aim of this section is to shed light on what type of social capital plays a role in reducing precariousness thus improving well-being, and to assess whether there is a relationship with human development. The analysis is based on a dataset collected by the author, including about 200 indicators representing the 'structural' dimensions of social capital and different

aspects of the quality of economic development. Principal component analyses have been performed on three subsets of variables, with the aim of building synthetic, latent, measures of strong family ties (that is, bonding social capital), weak informal ties among friends, neighbours and acquaintances (bridging social capital) and weak ties connecting members of voluntary organizations (linking social capital). Principal component analysis (PCA) explains the variance-covariance structure of a dataset through a few linear combinations of the original variables. Its general objectives are data reduction and interpretation.[1] Rough data on social capital are drawn by a set of multipurpose surveys carried out by the Italian National Bureau of Statistics (Istat) on a sample of 20 000 households between 1998 and 2002. Data are aggregated at the 'regional' level, that is, there are 20 analysis units corresponding to the Italian regions, traditionally characterized by a strong North-South polarization.

The variables adopted in the analysis are as follows:

- The bonding social capital shaped by strong ties connecting family members. This variable is measured by the first factor obtained from a PCA performed on a dataset of 25 indicators representing family size, the spatial proximity among family members, the frequency of encounters and the quality of relationships. Variables are described in Box 16.1.
- Bridging social capital, as measured by the first factor obtained from a PCA performed on a dataset of 12 variables representing people social engagement, or what can be referred to as the consumption of relational goods, like frequenting sports clubs, dining out with friends, and talking with neighbours. Variables are described in Box 16.2.
- The linking social capital shaped by weak formal ties connecting people from different socioeconomic backgrounds within the boundaries of voluntary organizations. This measure is given by the first factor resulting from a PCA performed on a set of six variables representing different dimensions of associational participation, described in detail in Box 16.3.
- The Human Development Index, as adjusted to take into account Italy's level of wealth, different from that of most developing countries. The index of life expectancy has been computed adopting 50 and 85 years respectively as minimum and target levels, the index summarizing literacy and schooling has been replaced by the rate of high school attendance, and the index of per capita income has been computed adopting higher living standards as minimum and target levels. Basic indicators are described in detail in Table 16.1.

● As pointed out in the introduction, we have extended the ILO's notion of labour precariousness to comprise people looking for a job, who suffer from the highest degree of uncertainty. Labour precariousness is thus measured by the ratio between the sum of three variables representing precariousness (workers with provisional contracts, freelancers and people looking for a job) and the regional labour force.

BOX 16.1 BASIC INDICATORS OF STRONG FAMILY TIES (BONDING SOCIAL CAPITAL)

People aged 14 and over who have given unpaid help to strangers for every 100 people in the same area.

People aged 14 and over particularly caring for relatives other than parents, children, grandparents and grandchildren, or counting on them in case of need, for every 100 people in the same area.

Couples with one child, for every 100 couples with children in the same area.

Couples with three children, for every 100 couples with children in the same area.

Couples with children, for every 100 families in the same area.

Couples without children, for every 100 families in the same area.

Families with 5 components and more for every 100 families in the same area.

Single families for every 100 families in the same area.

People aged 15 and over with children living 16 kilometres away or more (in Italy or abroad) for every 100 families with children in the same area.

People aged 15 and over with children living within 1 kilometre (cohabitants or not) for every 100 families with children in the same area.

People having their brothers and/or sisters living 16 kilometres away or more (in Italy or abroad) for every 100 people with brothers and/or sisters in the same area.

People having brothers and/or sisters living within 1 kilometre (cohabitants or not) for every 100 people with brothers and/or sisters in the same area.

People meeting their brothers and/or sisters every day for every 100 people with brothers and/or sisters in the same area.

People aged 6 and over meeting family members or other relatives every day for every 100 people in the same area.

People up to 69 having their mother living 16 kilometres away or more (in Italy or abroad) for every 100 people with a living mother in the same area.

People up to 69 having their mother living within 1 kilometre (cohabitant or not) for every 100 people with an alive mother in the same area.

People aged 6 and over never meeting their family members and other non-cohabitant relatives for every 100 people in the same area.

People aged 6 and over having neither a family nor other non-cohabitant relatives for every 100 people in the same area.

People up to 69 having their father living 16 kilometres away or more (in Italy or abroad) for every 100 people with a living father in the same area.

People up to 69 having their father living within 1 kilometre (cohabitant or not) for every 100 people with a living father in the same area.

People aged 14 and more declaring themselves satisfied with relationships with their relatives for every 100 people in the same area.

Families with at least 2 components used to having dinner with other relatives at least once a week for every 100 families in the same area.

People meeting their children every day for every 100 people with non-cohabitant children in the same area.

People meeting their mother every day for every 100 people with non-cohabitant mother in the same area.

People meeting their father every day for every 100 people with non-cohabitant father in the same area.

BOX 16.2   INDICATORS OF THE INFORMAL NETWORKS OF FRIENDS AND NEIGHBOURS (BRIDGING SOCIAL CAPITAL)

Non-profit sports clubs for every 10 000 people in the same area.

People aged 6 and over attending bars, pubs, and circles at least once a week for every 100 people in the same area.

People aged 6 and over eating out more than once a week for every 100 people in the same area.

People aged 6 and over meeting friends more than once a week for every 100 people in the same area.

People aged 14 and over attending pubs and bars to listen to music concerts for every 100 people in the same area.

People aged 14 and over attending social centres to listen to music concerts for every 100 people in the same area.

People aged 6 and over never attending bars, pubs and circles for every 100 people in the same area.

People aged 6 and over never eating out for every 100 people in the same area.

People aged 6 and over never talking with others for every 100 people in the same area.

People aged 6 and over never talking with neighbours for every 100 people in the same area.

People aged 6 and over talking with others once a week or more for every 100 people in the same area.

People aged 6 and over talking with neighbours once a week or more for every 100 people in the same area.

BOX 16.3   INDICATORS OF LINKING SOCIAL CAPITAL

People aged 14 and over who have helped strangers in the context of a voluntary organization's activity, for every 100 people in the same area.

People aged 6 and over who, when meeting friends, carry out voluntary activities for every 100 people meeting friends in the same area.

Voluntary organizations for every 10 000 people

People aged 14 and over who have joined meetings in cultural circles and similar ones at least once a year for every 100 people in the same area.

People aged 14 and over who have joined meetings in ecological associations and similar ones at least once a year for every 100 people in the same area.

People aged 14 and over who have given money to an association at least once a year for every 100 people in the same area.

Table 16.1   The adjusted index of human development

Label	Description
ISUA	Adjusted Human Development Index, computed as the arithmetic mean of LIFE, SCHOOL and INCOME
LIFE	Dimensional index of life expectancy. Minimum value = 50 years. Target value = 80 years
SCHOOL	Dimensional index of high school attendance, given by the percentage of people aged from 14 to 18 who are enrolled in high schools. Minimum value = 0. Target value = 100
INCOME	Dimensional index of per capita income. Minimum value = €5000. Target value = €40000. INCOME = [log (effective value) − log(5000)] / [log(40 000) − log(5000)]

The causal relationships connecting variables have been assessed through structural equations models, a technique that has grown up in psychometrics and proves to be particularly suitable for the investigation of multi-dimensional phenomena like social capital and economic development.[2] Hundreds of models – accounting for all the possible linkages connecting variables – have been tested.

In the model that best fits the observed data, labour precariousness is significantly mitigated by bonding social capital and, to a higher extent, by human development. The linking social capital of voluntary organizations exerts a positive effect as well, while weak bridging ties connecting friends and acquaintances do not seem to alleviate precariousness. This result partly contradicts Granovetter's (1973) claim on the strength of weak ties: in Italy's Southern regions, the action of supporting people in their job placement can be motivated just by the existence of strong ties or, in other words, by what Banfield (1958) referred to as 'amoral familism', that is, the imperative of protecting and consolidating the isolated family unit. Weak ties may function as a means of fostering the diffusion of information, but do not concretely help workers in their job search actions. On the other hand, the analysis does confirm the negative effect of bonding social capital on human development. This view of the family as an isolated moral community is indeed strongly representative of the social reality of Southern Italy, where most people do not act morally outside the family. However, what to an external observer may appear just as a perverse mechanism hampering labour market's efficiency and, in the long run, development processes as well, deserves a more in-depth reflection. The mutual assistance mechanisms developed within the family unit should be looked on also as a defence reaction against situations of underdevelopment and 'social poverty', where both the state's and market's institutions are weak.

Linking social capital proves to exert a positive effect both on human development and on reduction of precariousness. This sounds like a proof of Putnam's claims on the role of voluntary organizations, therefore contradicting part of the economics and political science literature in the field. In Italy, the density of voluntary organizations is in most cases connected with a deep tradition of civic involvement and social participation, and the development of civil society has been largely informed by ideological principles, not directly related to the pursuit of personal or sectarian advantages. On the contrary, bridging social capital negatively affects human development, just like strong family ties. The consumption of relational goods within sport or culture clubs, music bars or restaurants is not necessarily related to those cooperative norms and behaviours that can benefit economic performance.

The analysis in the chapter shows that higher levels of precariousness significantly reduce bridging social capital. The lack of professional stability causes frequent changes in people's relational sphere, thereby leading to a continuous process of breaking and rebuilding social ties. Arguably, workers may react to such a situation of uncertainty by taking refuge in their private sphere, at the expense of social participation. A refinement of the model with a slightly lower goodness of fit clearly states that precariousness also reduces social participation. Precarious workers are probably too deeply absorbed in their daily struggle for survival, and little time remains for pro-social activities and collective action. Once again, the renouncement of social participation may be looked on as a defensive choice. Finally, linking social capital proves to be positively and significantly affected by human development.

16.5   Concluding remarks

In the introduction we posed the question: what type of social capital is able to mitigate labour precariousness and to foster human development? The empirical analysis shows that only bonding social capital mitigates precariousness on the labour market, while the weak ties shaping voluntary organizations are the only type of social capital that nourish human development, thereby fostering sustainable growth.

The literature generally underestimates the positive role exerted on well-being by the mutual assistance and social protection mechanisms promoted by the family. Through their ability to mitigate precariousness, strong family ties may act as a means of defence against high levels of unemployment. In other words, bonding social capital can be seen not only as a cause of backwardness, but also as one of its possible consequences.

However, the main factor reducing precariousness is human development: higher levels of wealth and schooling inevitably lead to an improvement in workers' well-being. The widespread idea that social contacts function as a powerful job placement factor is only partly confirmed by data. In Italy, strong ties support the reduction of precariousness, while weak ties connecting friends and acquaintances seem to be quite harmful to such purposes. What certainly deserves further investigations is the effect of social networks-induced job-matching processes on the allocation of talents: significant mismatches of talent and excessive job markets' closure to outsiders may reduce the efficiency of the labour market, to the point of compensating the beneficial effects exerted on workers' well-being by the reduction of precariousness. Anyway, it is clear that neglecting the social embeddedness of actors seriously invalidates the explanatory power of any economic analysis of the labour market.

Voluntary organizations are the only type of networks shown to be able to nourish human development, thereby fostering sustainable economic growth. Bonding and bridging social capital, on the contrary, negatively affect human development. In Italy, the associational activity is strictly connected to sound ideological or religious motivations, and generally implies the sharing of moral norms of trust and reciprocity that can counteract the negative effects of the 'amoral familism', as well as the tendency of organizations to lobby for the narrow interests of their members. Finally, it is noteworthy that the relationship between linking social capital and human development proves to have a double direction. Arguably, not only social participation through civil society organizations fosters the institutional and the economic performance, as claimed by Putnam, but the reverse effect is true as well: higher levels of human development encourage people to devote time to community affairs through collective action.

Notes

*   I am deeply indebted to Elisabetta Basile and Claudio Cecchi for their suggestions and advice. Needless to say, all views and errors are attributable only to the author.
1.   Although p components are required to reproduce the total system variability, often much of this variability can be accounted for by a small number, k, of the principal components. If so, there is (almost) as much information in the k components as there is in the original p variables. The k principal components can then replace the initial p variables, and the original dataset, consisting of n measurements on p variables, is reduced to one consisting of n measurements on k principal components. For an overview on PCA see Lebart et al. (1984) and Johnson and Wichern (1992).
2.   For an overview on structural equations models see Bollen (1989).

References

Aguilera, Michael B. (2003), 'The impact of the worker: how social capital and human capital influence the job tenure of formerly undocumented Mexican immigrants', *Sociological Inquiry*, **73** (1), 52–83.

Amuedo-Dorantes, Catalina and Kusum Mundra (2007), 'Social networks and their impact on the earnings of Mexican immigrants', *Demography*, **44** (4), 849–63.

Banfield, E.C. (1958), *The Moral Basis of a Backward Society*, New York: Free Press.

Bentolila Samuel, Claudio Michelacci and Javier Suarez (2003), 'Social contacts and occupational Choice', CEPR discussion paper, no. 4308.

Blanchflower, D.G. and A. Oswald (2004), 'Well-being overtime in Britain and the USA', *Journal of Public Economics*, **88** (7–8), 1359–86.

Bollen, Kenneth (1989), *Structural Equations with Latent Variables, Wiley Series in Probability and Mathematical Statistics*, New York: Wiley.

Boorman, Scott A. (1975), 'A combinatorial optimization model for transmission of job information through contact networks', *Bell Journal of Economics*, **6**, 216–49.

Calvó-Armengol, Antoni and Matthew O. Jackson (2004), 'The effects of social networks on employment and inequality', *American Economic Review*, **94** (3), 426–54.

Clarck, Andrew E. and Andrew J. Oswald (1994), 'Unhappiness and unemployment', *The Economic Journal*, **104** (424), 648–59.

Datcher, Linda (1983), 'The impact of informal networks on quit behavior', *The Review of Economics and Statistics*, **65** (3), 491–5.

Di Tella, Rafael, Robert J. MacCulloch and Andrew J. Oswald (1997) 'Preferences over inflation and unemployment: evidence from surveys of happiness', *American Economic Review*, **91**, 335–41.

Dockery, Alfred M. (2005), 'The happiness of young Australians: empirical evidence on the role of labour market experience', *Economic Record*, **81** (255), 322–35.

Fernandez, Roberto M., Emilio J. Castilla and Paul Moore (2000), 'Social capital at work: networks and employment at a phone center', *American Journal of Sociology*, **105**, 1288–356.

Ferrante, Francesco and Fabio Sabatini (2007), 'Education, social capital and entrepreneurial selection in Italy', paper prepared for presentation at the 2006 International Comparative Analysis of Enterprise (micro) Data (CAED) Conference, Federal Reserve Bank of Chicago, Chicago, 18 and 19 September.

Gerlach, Knut and Stephan Gesine (1996), 'A paper on unhappiness and unemployment in Germany', *Economic Letters*, **52** (3), 325–30.

Granovetter, Mark S. (1973), 'The strength of weak ties', *American Journal of Sociology*, **78**, 1360–80.

Granovetter, Mark S. (1974), *Getting a Job: A Study of Contacts and Careers*, Cambridge, MA: Harvard University Press.

ILO (International Labour Organization) (1993), 'International classification of status in employment (ICSE-93)', available at: http://www.ilo.org/public/english/bureau/stat/class/icse.htm.

Johnson, Richard A. and Dean W. Wichern (1992), *Applied Multivariate Statistical Analysis*, New York: Prentice Hall.

Knack, Stephen and Philip Keefer (1997), 'Does social capital have an economic payoff? A cross country investigation', *Quarterly Journal of Economics*, **112** (4), 1251–88.

Lebart, Ludovic, Alain Morineau and Kenneth M. Warwick (1984), *Multivariate Descriptive Statistical Analysis. Correspondence Analysis and Related Techniques for Large Matrices*, New York: John Wiley & Sons.

Munshi, Kaivan (2003), 'Networks in the modern economy: Mexican migrants in the U.S. labor market', *The Quarterly Journal of Economics*, **118** (2) 549–99.

Putnam, Robert D. (1995), 'Bowling alone: America's declining social capital', *Journal of Democracy*, **6**, 65–78.

United Nations Development Programme (UNDP) (2007), 'The human development concept', http://hdr.undp.org/en/humandev/ (accessed 4 January 2008).

World Bank (2000), *Beyond Economic Growth. Meeting the Challenges of Global Development*, Washington, DC: World Bank.

PART VI

MIGRATION AND INTEGRATION

17 Locational choice, ethnicity and assimilation
Gil S. Epstein

17.1 Introduction

The locational choice of migrants has an important role in determining the assimilation process into the local population. The social capital of migrants is developed by the fiscal and ethnic surroundings in the host country. This is determined by their choice of location, the networks they join and the level of ethnicity they choose. In this chapter we consider the different ways migrants choose where they live and analyse its effect on the assimilation process. This assimilation affects their social capital and, in the long run, has an effect on different migrants and their families.

Migration decisions take into consideration the migrant's ability to adjust to a new environment: for example, finding jobs and accommodations and the ability to continue consuming ethnic goods which is a function of the level of the network externality in the destination (see, for example, Epstein, 2002; Bauer et al., 2007). A migrant might decide that others have been making decisions based on better information than he has. That is, the migrant may take the position that so many other people cannot be wrong. If the migrant behaves in this way and discounts his/her private information he/she may adopt a decision rule that gives rise to herd behavior. Herd behavior and network externalities may have opposite effects (see Epstein, 2002; Bauer et al., 2007). While herd behavior may attract migrants, the network externality does the opposite telling the migrants not to join a certain location.

As we show below one aspect of assimilation is the ability to learn the local language. Chiswick and Miller (2002) show that linguistic concentrations reduce an immigrant's own local language skills. Moreover, immigrants' earnings are lower the poorer their local language proficiency and the greater the linguistic concentration of their origin language in the area in which they live. Better jobs lower the returns of investing in the local language proficiency and, therefore, the incentive for these migrants to learn the local language is great.

This choice of location also affects the immigrants' consumption of ethnic goods, which distinguishes the migrants from the local population and affects their assimilation. We consider the relationship between the migrants' consumption of ethnic goods and the willingness of the local population to accept them into the economy. This willingness affects the productivity and wages of the migrants, and thus their employment. The question of assimilation and integration into the labor market of the host country has been analysed in the literature (see, for example, Bauer et al., 2000; Boeri et al., 2002; Venturini, 2004).

Various indicators are used to measure the degree to which migrants have assimilated. The most common measures are wages and earnings. Constant et al. (2006) present the *ethnosizer*, which measures the ethnic identity of a migrant rather than his ethnicity, using information such as language, culture, societal interaction, history of migration, and ethnic self-identification. Using the GSOEP (German Socio-Economic Panel) 2002 data, they show that ethnic identity persists, being stronger in specific groups such as females, Muslims and those that are older at the time of entry, while those with closer cultures, such as Catholics and other Christians, assimilate more easily. There is mixed evidence on the impact of migrants on local worker's majority wages and employment – it depends on whether they are substitutes or complements (Gang and Rivera-Batiz, 1994).

The locational choice of migrants has an important affect on the social capital formation of the migrants. The question is, are these networks that the migrants join *Bonding* or *Bridging* networks (Svendsen and Svendsen, 2004)? Joining a bonding network will decrease the assimilation process and joining a bridging network will increase assimilation and the social capital of the migrants. According to the study by Chiswick and Miller (2002) these networks seem to work as bonding networks. Thus, as described above, herd affects will enhance the bonding networks rather than being a bridging network. On the other hand, Bauer et al. (2005) look at the location choice of migrants and connect the location decision with their language proficiency. Their results suggest that Mexican migrants to the US with good English proficiency choose, on average, a location with a small enclave, whereas those with poor English proficiency choose a location with a large enclave. Thus those with high English proficiency will choose smaller networks and thus increase the bridging social capital networks.

Migrants have to choose their actual level of social traits given their network surroundings, which determine the social practices they wish to uphold. Changing a person's traits has a cost. The choice of social traits level by migrants is a way of joining a bonding versus a bridging social network. Those that choose higher levels of social traits are joining the bonding network while those that are choosing the lower levels are going towards the bridging networks. For example, going to church every Sunday, praying a few times a day, not working on the Sabbath, not eating specific type of foods or at certain places, wearing specific clothes, and so on all have opportunity costs. On the other hand, there are benefits from keeping their ideal social traits, and any deviation also has a cost.

The growth perspectives of European Union member countries are seen to be crucially related to the challenge of mobilizing people to work. One issue is that non-economic migrants have more difficulties in economic performance and labor market integration, and provide a larger potential burden to the social security systems than economic migrants. Recent work in Denmark and Germany (see Schultz-Nielsen and Constant, 2004; Tranaes and Zimmermann, 2004; Constant and Zimmermann, 2005; Constant et al., 2006) has provided new evidence, which indicates that an ever-rising share of immigrants is unavailable to the labor force. Instead, migrants arrive as refugees, asylum seekers or for family reunification purposes. Differences in labor market attachment might be due to differences in individual characteristics across ethnicities and within ethnicities, as we claim in this chapter.

In the second part of this chapter we set up a model where migrants have to choose their level of social traits and consumption of ethnic goods. Each migrant has his/her own ideal social traits and, given the average level in the network, choose their consumption level. As the consumption of ethnic goods increases, the migrants become more unlike the local population and are less assimilated. Less assimilation affects the reaction of the local population to the migrants and their willingness to accept them. This affects wages and unemployment of the migrants in their local network and determines whether they are in a bridging or bounding network.

The chapter is organized as follows. Section 17.2 describes the locational choice of the migrants considering both herd and network effects, in the determination of the migrants' choices. Section 17.3 considers the locational decisions and its effect on the consumption of ethnic goods by the immigrants which directly affects assimilation. We round off with Section 17.4 which defines the main conclusions of the chapter.

17.2 The choice of location

When a migrant makes his/her decision where to emigrate to he/she takes into consideration different aspects of the country he/she wishes to emigrate to. One of the aspects is help in adjusting to a new environment, such as finding jobs and accommodations, and the ability to continue consuming ethnic goods. This is called 'network externalities' in the literature. The ability to speak his/her language in a foreign country is in itself helpful. The network allows the immigrant to preserve his/her traditions and history in the new environment and to continue consuming ethnic goods. Network externalities are not always positive. Increasing the number of foreigners in the host country increases competition for jobs suitable for immigrants, thus decreasing the immigrants' wages. Moreover, as the number of immigrants increases, the local population may become xenophobic. The locational choice of migrants has an important affect on the social capital formation of the migrants and whether their have chosen to be in a bridging or bonding network.

If full information were available about local conditions, migrants would choose the location where there are net benefits from network externalities. If such full information is not available, a choice is made under conditions of uncertainty. If you have imperfect information, which decision rule should you adopt? In the face of uncertainty, a common decision rule is to randomize, but here you confront an indivisible location decision. You may not know all that much about life in a particular location. You observe, however, that other people who are like you have recently been favoring this location. You have a feeling that the location people have been choosing is not the best from among the available alternatives. You, however, decide to discount this feeling which is based on your private information, and proceed on the assumption that others have been making decisions based on better information than you have. That is, you may take the position that so many other people cannot be wrong. If you behave in this way and discount your private information or your feelings to follow the decisions of others, you are adopting a decision rule that gives rise to herd behavior.

In order for a population of immigrants to produce network externalities that will attract other migrants, the population of immigrants must be sufficiently large. In many situations it is not clear how this critical mass of people arrived at a certain location. Informational cascades – herd behavior – help us understand the creation of the critical mass which creates network externalities. In order to create a herd in a certain location, the number of immigrants required is relatively small. Thus herd behavior may be an explanation for the creation of a mass of immigrants which is sufficient to attract others and which enjoys the positive externalities of the network. Informational cascades also help us understand why we observe immigrants deciding to emigrate to destinations where the negative externalities are stronger than the positive externalities of the network. The reason for this phenomenon is that individuals are uncertain regarding the effect of the network externalities and decide to follow the flow of immigrants rather than the stock of immigrants. Finally, herd behavior enables us to understand how an individual makes a decision when there is more than one country that provides the immigrant with the same level of network externalities (see Epstein, 2002). The immigrants will decide to follow the herd rather than the network externalities of previous immigrants' destinations.

Based on data from the Mexican Migration Project, Bauer et al. (2007)

investigate the location decision of Mexican migrants in the US. They show that both network externalities and herd behavior have a significant effect on migrants' location decision. Herd effects have significant positive consequences on the location decision of a migrant while network externalities has an inverse U-shaped effect, namely, when the size of the network is large, but not too large, increasing the network will increase the benefits the migrant will obtain. However, if the network is too large, it will decrease the benefits the migrants obtain from the network. In other words 'too big' is not always better for the migrant.

Let us try to understand the network effect better. A small number of papers investigate the reason causing the determination of immigrant's location choice in the United States. A common result of these papers is the importance of ethnic concentration on the location decision of migrants. It has been shown[1] that immigrants tend to locate in cities with high concentrations of ethnically similar immigrants. The results indicate that income and human capital affect the extent of ethnic segregation in the neighborhood chosen by a household. However, the existing literature overlooks the effect of immigrants' language proficiency on the location decision. Another line of the migration literature analyses the effect of enclaves on immigrants' educational attainment, language proficiency and labor market outcomes. Numerous empirical studies, such as Gang and Zimmermann (2000), have shown that ethnic neighborhoods have detrimental effects on the educational attainment of migrants. Chiswick and Miller (1996) explore the relationship among family networks, language enclaves and English language acquisition by immigrants. Chiswick and Miller (2002), using 1990 US Census data on adult male immigrants from non-English speaking countries, show that linguistic concentrations (enclaves) reduce an immigrant's own English language skills. Moreover, immigrants' earnings are lower the poorer their English language proficiency and the greater the linguistic concentration of their origin language in the area in which they live. Better jobs lower the returns to investing in English language proficiency and, therefore, the incentive for these Spanish speakers to learn English.

On the other hand, Bauer et al. (2005) look at the location choice of migrants and connect the location decision with their language proficiency. Their results suggest that Mexican migrants to the US with good English proficiency choose, on average, a location with a small enclave, whereas those with poor English proficiency choose a location with a large enclave.

Putting all these results together, we are able to paint a broader picture: immigrants with good English proficiency will choose to migrate to locations with relatively low concentrations of immigrants of similar ethnicity and language. If the size of the enclave is small it enables immigrants to improve their English proficiency over time, which in turn affects their earnings and assimilation into the local population. On the other hand, immigrants with poor English proficiency will choose to migrate to locations with large networks of migrants of similar ethnicity and language. This, in turn, decreases their ability to increase their English proficiency, which negatively affects their earnings and assimilation into the local population. We may conclude that large enclaves are a potential source for a 'language trap'; they attract poor proficiency English speakers and sustain their poor abilities.

17.3   Location decisions and the consumption of ethnic goods

One of the objectives of the migrants is to continue consuming ethnic goods. The network enables him/her to do so. Each migrant has to choose his/her social trait level. This social trait can be seen as ethnic goods consumed by the individual. The payoff of a migrant is given by v which is a function of five components:

- the ideal level of the social traits, which this individual (family) believes they should be at;
- the actual level of the social traits the migrant decides to follow;[2]
- the average level of the traits under which the migrant congregation is currently at;
- the earning of the immigrant and
- the effort invested by the migrant at the workplace is given, otherwise those that are unemployed invest zero effort.

Below we explain how each of the different variables affects the payoff function of the migrant.

We assume that the migrants differ in only one dimension, and that is the ideal level of social traits they believe they should hold. It is assumed that migrants are distributed uniformly across different levels of the ideal social traits.

The payoff function of a migrant is a function of two components:

1.   the utility of practicing social traits at its given level;
2.   the cost of choosing such social trait levels.

Let us now consider each of the components in more detail:

1   Utility
The individual's utility decreases if the individual deviates from his/her ideal level of observation. This deviation can go both ways. Increasing the

actual level over the ideal or decreasing the level below the ideal, which will cause the utility to decrease. It is clear that the migrant would prefer to be at his/her ideal point, however this is not always possible. On the other hand, if the migrant chooses a trait level, which equals his/her ideal level, he/she will be at the maximum utility level. Namely, deviating from the ideal point decreases the utility. Thus, if we change the actual level and get closer to the ideal point then the decrease in the utility will be smaller and thus the utility increases. If we increase the actual level beyond (or decrease it below) the ideal point, then the utility will decrease as a result of such a deviation.

2   Cost

Let us consider the second part of the migrant's payoff, the cost of consumption of a given trait at level. It is assumed that the average trait level in the sociality of the migrants is at given level. It is also assumed that it is easiest for the migrant to 'consume' at the average level. However, if the migrant wants to deviate from this level, it will cost him/her, since it will be harder to practice his/her social traits when they differ from the average level. This puts the migrant in the environment where he/she lives, and should he/she wish to deviate from it, he/she must invest more effort – thus the further away he/she wishes to be from the average social trait levels in his society, the harder it will be for him/her. The bigger the change in the 'consumption' of ethnic goods, from the average level which the migrant decides on (either increasing or decreasing it), the higher the cost of adjustment. However, as earnings increase, the cost of deviating from the average level decreases since the wages substitute for the deviation from the average trait level. The migrant can use his/her earnings to buy such ethnic goods (like traveling to their home country frequently, buying specific types of food, and so on) simply by a substituting effect. A different way of looking at this is that, as earnings increase, the migrant cares less about the average level in his/her society. The earnings of a migrant will equal the wages in the case of the employed migrants, and will equal the social benefits of the unemployed. Namely, if we get closer to the given average level, the cost of changes will be smaller for the migrant. It is assumed that the number of migrants is large enough so that each one does not have market power in terms of affecting the average level. In other words, each migrant sees the average social trait level as given, thus when determining the optimal trait level, the migrant does not take into account the effect it may have on the average level of the social trait in his/her society. Moreover, if a migrant wants to decrease his/her level below the average it also has its costs, as the surroundings will not always accept his/her deviation from the average social trait (this can be via different means, such as affecting the children, not receiving the basic social traits the family wishes to obtain, and so on). As the earnings of the individual increase, the individual's cost of deviating from the average level of consumption of traits in the society decreases.

We have assumed symmetric payoff functions. Thus a deviation in each direction has the same consequence on the payoff function of the migrant. In other words, increasing the trait or decreasing the trait, by one unit over or below the ideal level, will have the same effect on the migrant's payoff function. In reality it may well be that the cost and utilities are not symmetric, namely, increasing the level of consumption of the ethnic goods decreases the utility by less than the change in the other direction. This, of course, will be a function of the migrants' preferences. If the migrants care about their special social traits, they may prefer to increase their actual traits above the ideal, rather than decrease them. Moreover, it is assumed that migrants who work have a disutility from the effort invested at the workplace.[3]

A migrant chooses the optimal level of consumption of ethnic goods – stoical traits that maximizes his/her payoff function. Thus:

- The actual level of consumption of ethnic goods (social traits level) of a migrant will increase as his/her ideal social traits increase.
- Migrants with high ideal levels will actually consume higher levels of these traits and those with low ideal levels will consumer lower levels.
- The actual level of ethnic good consumption (social trait level) of a migrant will increase as the average level of consumption of social traits in the society increases.
- If the average level of consumption of social traits level is higher, it is easier for the migrant to consume higher levels. However, there is also a cost when decreasing or increasing his/her own social traits as there will be pressures from the different migrants surrounding him/her.

As the earnings of a migrant increase, the consumption of ethnic goods – social traits – will increase (decrease) if the ideal level is greater (smaller) than the average level in the sociality. Namely, as income increases, migrants will choose an actual trait closer to their ideal point.

Thus there is a substitution between the consumption of social traits and other products. In lower income levels, the migrant can increase his payoff by consuming at a level closer to the average level in his society. Since the migrant obtains a benefit from consumption of social traits and ethnic goods, the migrant can increase his payoff by increasing his social traits and making it closer to his ideal. As income increases the cost of deviating from the average level in his congregation decreases and enables him to be closer to the ideal level.

If we now substitute the optimal level of consumption of ethnic goods, into the migrants' payoff function, we would obtain the migrants optimal payoff in equilibrium. As would be expected, the equilibrium optimal payoff of the migrant is positively related to his/her earnings, is negatively related to the effort invested at the workplace and the optimal payoff depends on the difference between the ideal level of social traits of the migrant and the average level in the society. As the difference between the two increases, the utility of the migrant will decrease, since the cost to the migrant of changing his/her consumption of ethnic goods increases. If the ideal level of a migrant equals the average level of consumption of ethnic traits in the sociality, namely, for the migrant, his/her ideal level will equal the average level in the society, and this utility will be at maximum.

Assume for now that all individuals employed have the same wages. Remember that an employed migrant may have an increase in income as a result of moving from unemployment to employment. However, he/she also encounters a decrease in utility as a result of efforts invested in the workplace.[4] An unemployed migrant obtains a given level of unemployment benefits and has zero investment in effort at the workplace.

Let us now consider the case where an immigrant has to choose whether to be employed or unemployed. The migrant will choose to be employed if his/her payoff from being employed is greater than his/her payoff from being unemployed.

If the social benefits, of the unemployed migrants, equal the wages earned by him/her, it is clear that the migrants will prefer to be unemployed. Therefore, *in order for the migrants to be willing to be employed the difference, between the social benefits of the unemployed and the wages of the employed, must be sufficiently large.*

A migrant determines his/her social traits also as a function of his/her employment status. Therefore part of the consumption of social traits is a direct function of the employment status of the migrant. From comparing the optimal payoff of a migrant in the two different situations, being employed or being unemployed, we can calculate the level of the ideal social traits which will make a migrant indifferent.

We obtain two different values of the ideal level that makes the migrant indifferent. Thus for a given wage, for levels of an ideal level, which are higher than the high critical level or lower than the low critical level, the individual will choose to be employed, otherwise the individual will choose to be unemployed.

Expected consumption of ethnic goods

Let us now consider the expected amount of consumption of ethnic goods by both the employed and unemployed migrants. Individuals who have a higher level of ideal social traits than the higher critical level or lower than the low critical level will be employed and will consume ethnic goods which are a function of the wage level. Those individuals, who have an ideal level between the two critical levels, will be unemployed and will consume ethnic goods which are a function of their social benefits. Since we assume that the ideal social trait levels are uniformly distributed we obtain that the average level in the society of migrants will equal the median level of the distribution. So we may conclude that the relationship between the ideal levels of the migrants, the average level in the society, and the employed and unemployed status of the migrants are as given such that those with high and low ideal levels will be employed and earning wages, and those with ideal levels between the two critical values will be unemployed and will receive social benefits. In other words those migrants that have a low ideal preference (and want to be part of the community[5]), will have a higher probability of being employed. At the same time, the migrants with very high preferences will choose to be employed to help obtain resources and be further away from the average level of observation, closer to their own ideal level. These migrants have a high cost with loss of benefits from not being at their ideal point. In other words, migrants, with high or low levels of ideal preferences, will choose to be employed rather than unemployed. The cost, of being close to their ideal point, is high and thus, if their earnings increase, they will be able to be closer to their ideal point. Those migrants, who are in the center, will choose to be unemployed.

Earning and the consumption of ethnic goods

Let us now consider changes in wages and unemployment benefits and their affect on the employed and unemployed migrants. Increasing the wages of the employed will, first, increase the number of employed. Those who were employed and continue to be employed will be even closer to their ideal level, and the others who were unemployed and become employed will allow themselves to consume levels closer to their ideal. On the other hand, an increase in the unemployment benefits will increase the number of unemployed. Those who were unemployed will have an actual trait closer to their ideal level. As a result of an increase in the employment benefits those, who became unemployed, will move away from their ideal level and closer to the average level in the congregation. Therefore,

> Increasing wages will increase the number of employed and will decrease the difference between the employee's actual trait level and their ideal. Increasing unemployment benefits will increase the number of unemployed. Those, who were unemployed, will consume ethnic goods closer to their ideal level and

those, who were employed and became unemployed, will move away from their ideal level.

Consider the case where wages are a function of the consumption of ethnic goods. Consider a firm that has two factors of production: local workers and migrants. For simplicity, we assume that there is only one group of migrants. We assume that migrants and the local population are not identical. As long as the migrants hold on to their ethnicity, the local population will not recognize them as full substitutes for the local population, and the local workers will not always be willing to cooperate entirely with them. For example, if a Moslem migrant prays five times a day, this may well disturb his interaction with the local workers and, as such, the local worker may not want to work enthusiastically with him. In other words, migrants, who hold on to their ethnicity, may see their productivity affected via their interaction with the local population.

The difference between the migrants' productivity level and that of the local worker is a function of the level of consumption of ethnic goods. As a result of the consumption of these goods the level of efficiency of the migrants decreases; as stated above this can be a result of different activities by the local population such as harassing the members of the migration group, not cooperating with them, discriminating against them, and so on (see Epstein and Gang, 2006). Such activities decrease the migrants' productivity and thus their efficiency.[6]

The difference between the productivity of the migrants and the local population and, as such, the difference in their wages is determined by the actions taken by the migrant and the general attitude of the population to them. The attitude to the migrants is reflected in the average level of consumption of ethnic goods which is a function of both the employed and unemployed migrants. The more ethnic goods the migrants consume, the more they distinguish themselves from the local population. This will decrease the willingness of the local population to work with them and will increase their 'harassment' activities.

Since wages are negatively related to the consumption of ethnic goods of the worker, the employed migrants will decrease their consumption of ethnic goods relative to the level consumed when the wages are independent of its consumption. As a result, the employed workers will decrease their consumption of ethnic goods and so their average level of consumption in the economy will decrease.

17.4 Concluding remarks
In this chapter we have considered the reasons for the location choice made by migrants and its effect on the ethnicity level of the migrants

and their assimilation. This definitely affects the social capital of the immigrants.

As we have seen, it is important for migrants to go where other migrants are resident. Migrants may follow the herd or go to large networks but, in each of the situations, migrants will want to continue to consume ethnic goods. Both herd and network externalities play an important role in the locational choice of the migrants. The locational choice of migrants has an important affect on the social capital formation of the migrants. It determines whether migrants are joining birding networks with assimilation or bonding networks without assimilation.

This choice has an important effect on the ability of the migrants to assimilate and on the social capital of the migrants. As we have seen, those who choose large networks have lower possibilities of learning the local language and so will not do as well economically as those immigrants that emigrated to countries/areas which consist of smaller networks. Moreover, we have considered the case of self-selection in determining the location choice of immigrants. The self-selection argument states that migrants with low proficiency in languages will choose larger networks. The trap, for those with low proficiency who go to large networks, is that the larger networks will limit their ability to learn the new language and decrease the ability of the migrants to assimilate.

The networks also have another effect. The networks enable the migrants to continue consuming their social traits and ethnic goods. We considered the relationship between the employment of migrants and the choice of social traits. Employment and social traits have an affect on social capital. We have shown that migrants who have a low ideal preference (and want to be part of the community), will have a higher probability of being employed. At the same time, migrants with very high preferences will choose to be employed in order that they can obtain resources which will allow them to be removed from the average level of observation and closer to their own ideal level. These migrants have a high cost and loss of benefit from not being at their ideal point. In other words, migrants, with high or low levels of ideal preferences, will choose to be employed rather than unemployed. The cost of being close to their ideal point is high and, thus, if their earnings increase, they will be nearer to achieving their goal. Those migrants that are at the center will choose to be unemployed. Moreover, increasing unemployment benefits will increase the number of unemployed and increase the consumption of ethnic goods.

To sum up, migrants emigrating to large networks will increase their probability of being unemployed, consuming high levels of ethnic goods and decreasing the probability of assimilation.

Notes

1. See for example Jaeger (2000), Chiswick et al. (1996) and Borjas (1998).
2. One could think of the actual level as the level of ethnic identity as measured by the *ethnosizer* index (see Constant et al., 2006).
3. There exists a disutility from working (Shapiro and Stiglitz, 1984; Epstein and Hillman, 2003).
4. See for example Shapiro and Stiglitz (1984) and Epstein and Hillman (2003).
5. If they did not want to be part of the community, they would not have encountered a cost of being far from the average level. Therefore it is assumed, that these individuals wish to be in the community and their ideal level is greater than zero. Moreover, they cannot get such ethnic goods elsewhere.
6. This is similar to the cooperation and harassment activities described in insider-outsider theory (Lindbeck and Snower, 1988).

References

Bauer, Thomas, Gil S. Epstein and Ira N. Gang (2005), 'Enclaves, language and the location choice of migrants', *Journal of Population Economics*, **18** (4), 649–62.
Bauer, Thomas, Gil S. Epstein and Ira N. Gang (2007), 'The influence of stocks and flows on migrants' location choices', *Research in Labor Economics*, **26**, 199–229.
Bauer, Thomas, Magnus Lofstrom and Klaus F. Zimmermann (2000), 'Immigration policy, assimilation of immigrants and natives' sentiments towards immigrants: evidence from 12 OECD countries', *Swedish Economic Policy Review*, **7**, 11–53.
Boeri, T., G. Hanson and B. McCormick (2002), *Immigration Policy and the Welfare System*, Oxford: Oxford University Press.
Borjas, G.J. (1998), 'To ghetto or not to ghetto: ethnicity and residential segregation', *Journal of Urban Economics*, **44**, 228–53.
Chiswick, B.R. and P.W. Miller (1996), 'Ethnic networks and language proficiency among immigrants', *Journal of Population Economics*, **9** (1), 19–35.
Chiswick, B.R. and P.W. Miller (2002), 'Do enclaves matter in immigrant adjustment?', IZA discussion paper, no. 449, IZA, Bonn.
Chiswick, B.R., Y.L. Lee and P.W. Miller (1996), 'Longitudinal analysis of immigrant occupational mobility: a test of the immigrant assimilation hypothesis', IZA discussion paper, no. 452, IZA, Bonn.
Constant, Amelie and Klaus F. Zimmermann (2005), 'Immigrant performance and selective immigration policy: a European perspective', IZA discussion paper, no. 1715, IZA, Bonn.
Constant, Amelie, Gataullina Liliya and Klaus F. Zimmermann (2006), 'Ethnosizing immigrants', IZA discussion paper, no. 2040, IZA, Bonn.
Epstein, Gil S. (2002), 'Informational cascades and decision to migrate', IZA working paper 445, IZA, Bonn.
Epstein, Gil S. and Ira N. Gang (2006), 'Ethnic networks and international trade', in Dennis Snower (ed.), *Labor Mobility and the World Economy*, Berlin and Heidelberg: Springer Verlag.
Epstein, Gil S. and A.L. Hillman (2003), 'Unemployed immigrants and voter sentiment in the welfare state', *Journal of Public Economics*, **87** (1), 1641–55.
Gang, Ira N. and Francisco Rivera-Batiz (1994), 'Labor market effects of immigration in the United States and Europe: substitution vs. complementarity', *Journal of Population Economics*, **7**, 157–75.
Gang Ira N. and K.F. Zimmermann (2000), 'Is child like parent? Educational attainment and ethnic origin', *Journal of Human Resources*, **35**, 550–69.
Jaeger, D.A. (2000), 'Local labor markets, admission categories, and immigrant location choice', http://dajaeg.people.wm.edu/research/ (accessed 22 May 2006).
Lindbeck, Assar and Dennis J. Snower (1988), 'Cooperation, harassment, and involuntary unemployment, an insider-outsider approach', *American Economic Review*, **78** (1), 167–88.
Schultz-Nielsen, M.L. and A. Constant (2004), 'Employment trends for immigrants and

natives', in T. Tranaes and K.F. Zimmermann (eds), *Migrants, Work, and the Welfare State*, Odense: University Press of Southern Denmark, pp. 119–46.

Shapiro, C. and J. Stiglitz (1984), 'Equilibrium unemployment as a worker discipline device', *American Economic Review*, **74**, 433–44.

Svendsen, G.L.H. and G.T. Svendsen (2004), *The Creation and Destruction of Social Capital: Entrepreneurship, Co-operative Movements and Institutions*, Cheltenham, UK and Northhampton, MA, USA: Edward Elgar.

Tranaes, T. and K.F. Zimmermann (2004), 'Migrants, work, and the welfare state: an introduction', in K.F. Zimmermann and T. Tranaes (eds), *Migrants, Work, and the Welfare State*, Odense: University Press of Southern Denmark, pp. 15–29.

Venturini, A. (2004), *Post-War Migration in Southern Europe. An Economic Approach*, Cambridge: Cambridge University Press.

18 Making integration work
Peter Nannestad

Introduction

Over the last 25 years most Western European welfare states have experienced a rather dramatic increase in number of immigrants, especially from
non-western, less developed countries.[1] Consequently, the question of how
to integrate[2] these immigrants into the economic, social and cultural fabric
of the receiving countries is now a highly prioritized political and societal
concern practically everywhere.

A survey of the outcomes of various integration policies designed and
implemented in Western European welfare states results in a rather dismal
picture. While different integration models and approaches are adhered to in
different countries, the outcomes generally tend to fall short of expectations.
The bare facts seem to be that labour market participation rates among non-
western immigrants tend to lag far behind those of natives, their unemployment rates tend to be markedly higher, and the wage gap between immigrants
and natives remains substantive even after many years of residence. As a
consequence, non-western immigrants tend to be strongly overrepresented
among welfare recipients. This is especially marked in universalistic welfare
states with generous benefit levels. Likewise, social integration appears fragile
at best, as witnessed by strong segregationist tendencies – not least in housing
and education – and the quite low rates of out-group marriages observed in
non-western immigrant groups in many Western European countries. As
far as can be judged from available data, crime rates in certain non-western
immigrant groups also tend to exceed those in the native population, indicating problems of anomia in these groups. Lately, terrorist attacks in some of
the immigrant-receiving Western European countries, court convictions of
would-be terrorists with immigrant backgrounds in others, as well as riots
in the suburbs of Paris in 2005 or in Danish towns in 2008, and the turmoil
and confrontations engendered by the Danish Muhammad cartoons in
2006, have contributed to highlighting the persistence, and possibly even
exacerbation, of integration problems related to the presence of non-western
immigrants in Western European welfare states.

Approaching an understanding of integration problems

If this account is approximately correct, the existing situation with respect
to integration of non-western immigrants into Western European welfare

states is obviously suboptimal. Society as a whole, as well as natives and immigrants as groups, would gain from better integration. Since everybody ultimately stands to gain, everybody should have an interest in making integration work (better) and in contributing towards that goal. So why is integration so evidently not forthcoming, and why has the road towards integration so far proved so twisted and bumpy? A steadily growing body of literature is devoted to this question. Roughly, the explanations suggested may be divided into three groups.

One group of integration studies considers discrimination based on racial, cultural and other forms of prejudice the main obstacle to integration. This literature dates back to (at least) the monumental *The Authoritarian Personality* by Adorno et al. (1950) and draws on important later contributions to the literature on prejudice, for instance that by Allport (1954). The focus is primarily on the prejudices found in the majority (the natives) and their negative impact on integration, while attitudes among minorities (immigrants) are normally accorded less attention. Negative attitudes towards immigrants among natives are conceived of as basically irrational; they are sought to be explained by socio-psychological factors, not by negative minority–majority encounters in the real world, conflicts of interest, competition in various arenas or other types of grievances. A special branch of this literature tends to emphasize the role of the media and populist politicians in instilling prejudices in the native population through various forms of manipulation and by their deliberately negative framing of immigration-related issues. From this perspective, explaining the persistence of a situation of suboptimal integration is quite simple: since individuals (natives) are basically irrational, so will be the outcome of the choices they make.

A second group of studies focuses on cultural-historical explanations and champions a strongly constructivist view of integration (problems). Among the most distinguished contributions to this literature are Anderson (1983) and Brubaker (1992). According to this school of thought, integration fails because the native population constructs their individual and collective histories and identities in ways that are more or less exclusionary towards outsiders, and because they cling to and defend these constructions even when the very fact of immigration makes such constructions increasingly obsolete and dysfunctional. According to Brubaker, differences between Germany and France with respect to national inclusion regimes are thus rooted in historically determined differences in how 'nationhood' is constructed in these two countries. What stands in the way of successful immigrant integration are hence mainly certain (culturally and historically based) constructions in the natives' minds rather than more mundane real-world factors that may affect either natives, immigrants or both. This is similar to the explanation of integration failure offered by the socio-psychological literature, except that the root cause of the malaise is seen as cultural, not socio-psychological. From this constructivist-school point of view, suboptimal outcomes may result because individuals are not necessarily free to make rational decisions.

The aim of the present discussion is to examine the obvious integration deficits in Western European countries from a perspective which draws on some concepts and simple analytical tools from political economy (Mueller, 1989). The main theoretical claim is that one root cause of integration failure is that integration entails a collective action dilemma or 'rationality trap', where acting in individually rational and optimal ways results in a collectively suboptimal outcome. In the following I first unfold this theoretical argument in more detail. I then consider to what extent this collective action problem can be solved through regulation (or coercion), selective incentives or social capital. Finally, using empirical data on labour market integration of immigrants in the 15 'old' European Union (EU) countries, I demonstrate that both selective incentives and social capital do contribute to the solution of the collective action problem of integrating immigrants into the labour market, but that the impact of selective incentives is stronger than the impact of social capital.

The collective action dilemma of integration[3]

Benefits and costs of integration
There can be little doubt that for natives and immigrants alike integration must be considered superior to what appears the only plausible alternative[4] – segregation. Ethical considerations and lofty principles of liberal justice aside, integration must seem superior to the natives from an economic as well as a social perspective. Economically, the weak integration of immigrants into the labour market in many Western European countries means that scarce resources are wasted, since immigrants are barred from contributing efficiently to economic production in society. In addition, it also means that non-western immigrants tend to become an economic burden on the rest of society, as they have to be supported through various kinds of income transfers.[5] Conversely, integration into the labour market would turn non-western immigrants from economic liabilities into economic assets for society at large. Socially, integration of immigrants most likely prevents or reduces social tensions along ethnic lines and ameliorates concomitant phenomena like crime, thus leading to more social tranquility and stability than a situation characterized by ethnic segregation. To the immigrants as a group the primary prospect of integration is to escape from a situation of long-lasting economic and social marginalization and

to gain a more secure foothold in society, making elevating their status from denizenship to citizenship easier to achieve. In sum, integration must be considered a societal *good*, not least when compared with ethnic segregation as the alternative.

If full integration is indeed a situation that would benefit natives and immigrants alike, then it might be tempting to expect all individuals to contribute voluntarily to bringing it about.[6] That, however, is obviously not what is happening in the real world today. But nor is it a theoretically valid conclusion. There are two reasons. First, while integration is a good, one must also consider the costs to the individual actors of bringing about and sustaining this good. Secondly, integration resembles a public good in at least one important respect. Together, these two properties give rise to the well-known collective action dilemma (Olson, 1965), or rationality trap.

The costs (or disutilities) associated with integration – for natives and immigrants alike – are mostly non-economic.[7] That makes them no less real, however. In the process, both groups face adaptation costs. Immigrants typically have to spend time and energy acquiring command of a new language. They also have to invest in building new social competencies, that is, the ability to navigate and interact within a system of social and cultural norms and values which in some respects may be very different from those into which they were socialized in their countries of origin, and in establishing new ties abroad.[8] They have to adapt to acting in a public space where values like the rule of law, freedom of expression, gender equality, personal autonomy and so on overrule whatever their own values might be, although they are normally allowed (within certain limits)[9] to lead their private lives according to their own values. Natives have to adapt to a situation of much greater cultural heterogeneity and its concomitant ambiguity and openness of modes of interaction. They have to live rather than merely profess tolerance. And they have to accept situations where they must compete on an increasingly equal footing with minorities for scarce goods like employment, housing and 'the collective goods of the state' (Wimmer, 1997: 32) – with the concomitant risk of ending up as losers.[10]

The collective action dilemma in integration
If a utility-maximizing individual feels that the costs of integration exceed the benefits, this individual cannot be expected to cooperate voluntarily in bringing it about. Even if benefits exceed costs, rational individuals would still face strong incentives to not cooperate in helping integration along. The reason is that integration, like internal security, shares at least one feature with a public good: it is non-excludable in consumption.[11] Non-excludability means that once the good (integration) is there, nobody

can be excluded from enjoying the benefits of it, whether or not they contributed to creating the good in the first place. Since benefits cannot be linked to participation in costs and endeavours, rational individuals have no incentive to share the costs of integration: 'free-riding' becomes the rational strategy for both natives and immigrants (unless prevented by, for instance, institutional arrangements). As a consequence, integration will not be achieved at all, or it will be achieved only to a suboptimal extent – which seems to be the current situation in Western European countries.

Thus, in order to make sense of integration problems, it would appear that one should not be oblivious to the possible role of the collective action dilemma, or rationality trap, related to integration, and the concomitant strategy of free-riding. On the one hand, integration is beneficial to all, and it is hence the rational collective strategy. On the other hand, when faced with the individual costs of integration, free-riding becomes the individually rational strategy. If unrestrained, rational individuals will pursue their individually rational (cost-avoiding) strategy at the expense of the rational collective goal – integration.[12] Thus, integration problems and failure will be the outcome of individually rational strategies of cost avoidance.

Solutions to collective action dilemmas
Collective action dilemmas – or rationality traps – abound in social and economic life. Small wonder, therefore, that ways to cope with this type of social dilemma have been extensively explored theoretically, empirically and experimentally, not least in the wake of Mancur Olson's seminal work *The Logic of Collective Action* (Olson, 1965). In the following, I discuss three solutions to the collective action dilemma of integration: regulation (coercion), selective incentives and social capital. The first two solutions are the solutions to collective action dilemmas already considered by Olson (1965: 45); the third solution, the one involving social capital, is an attempt to revitalize the idea – explicitly rejected by Olson – that in some circumstances collective action dilemmas can indeed be solved, or at least ameliorated, through voluntary interaction.[13]

Regulation
According to the standard welfare economics literature one solution to collective action dilemmas is regulation (Barr, 2004). This basically means coercion: individuals are coerced by the state or some other external power to contribute their share of the costs of bringing about certain public goods. This undoubtedly works fine in many areas. But when it comes to the collective action dilemma of integration, the possibilities of solving it through regulation are rather limited. The main reason is that in western liberal democracies of today individuals – natives and immigrants alike

– are protected against a wide range of state coercion measures by a set of human and civil rights embodied in national constitutions and international law.

Traditionally, integration-relevant state regulation has primarily been applied to political integration, that is, to the naturalization of immigrants. Naturalization is the policy area where states have the strongest capacity to regulate with respect to the inclusion or exclusion of immigrants. States have a very high level of discretion to decide if, and under what conditions, immigrants can obtain full citizenship. Naturalization is not a human right, no matter how long immigrants have lived in the host country or how deserving they may be from some point of view. There is not even a right to equal treatment with respect to naturalization.[14]

According to at least some theorists (and some politicians), restricting access to citizenship is a serious impediment to integration (Nuscheler, 1995: 213–16). This is correct in a formal sense: immigrant integration remains incomplete as long as the host country withholds full citizenship. On the other hand, granting citizenship to immigrants is no recipe or guarantee for integration. In the last resort the importance of a state's naturalization regime for immigrant integration is contingent upon how immigrants construct the relationship between integration and the acquisition of citizenship, and not upon how some theorists construct it.

In a survey of the five largest groups of non-western immigrants in Denmark conducted in 2004 (SoCap04), the respondents were asked if they considered certain advantages associated with acquiring Danish citizenship 'very important', 'less important', or 'unimportant'. Among the advantages presented was that having obtained Danish citizenship, 'one can feel accepted as a full member of Danish society'. The percentage distribution of the responses is given in Table 18.1.

Table 18.1 indicates that – at least in Denmark – state regulation of access to Danish citizenship is not a powerful inclusionary (or exclusionary) device. The immigrants themselves tend to consider more mundane aspects of citizenship than 'inclusion in the national community' important. This means that even though the state wields strong regulatory powers when it comes to the naturalization of immigrants, this regulatory power is not the most effective policy instrument in furthering integration.

In other areas of integration the regulatory capacities of the state are mainly negative. The state can, within certain limits, proscribe types of behaviour and activity deemed detrimental to integration. It can interdict discrimination in hiring, housing and so on, thus 'levelling the playing field' where immigrants and natives interact. It can likewise forbid overt expressions of racism in public, incitement to racial hatred or libelous accusations against members of certain groups in society. Most Western

Table 18.1   *Percentage distribution of immigrant respondents considering certain advantages of obtaining Danish citizenship 'very important', 'less important' or 'unimportant' (n in parentheses)*

Advantage	Very important	Less important	Unimportant
Right to a Danish passport, making it easier to travel	81.76 (1183)	11.06 (160)	7.19 (104)
Right to vote in Danish national elections	66.86 (912)	19.79 (270)	13.34 (182)
Protection against being deported	45.29 (610)	22.35 (301)	32.37 (436)
Access to jobs requiring Danish citizenship	44.70 (603)	25.87 (349)	29.43 (397)
One can feel accepted as a full member of Danish society	33.73 (476)	20.55 (290)	45.71 (645)

Source: Data from SoCap04.

European countries have implemented such regulations as part of their efforts to further integration.[15] But there are limits to what the state can do in these respects. Regulations against 'hate speech' or public defamation of individuals or groups have to be carefully balanced against, for instance, the right of free speech and freedom of information. Likewise the protection of freedom of religion has to be balanced against the right of freedom from religion. Affirmative action initiatives have to be balanced against individual rights to equal treatment and equality before the law, and so on.

A liberal democracy will not be able to solve the collective action problem of immigrant integration through regulation alone. If the natives do not want to live next door to immigrants, do not want to see their children going to school with immigrant children or do not want to work alongside immigrants in the workplace – or if immigrants harbour similar aversions against natives – , the liberal state cannot force either group to do what they do not wish to do without seriously infringing on personal liberties and rights. In the absence of willingness among natives as well as immigrants to bring about integration and to take the unavoidable costs upon themselves, preciously little seems attainable by state coercion.

Selective incentives
Apart from outright coercion by an external enforcer, conventional theory offers only one solution to the collective action dilemma: selective

incentives (Olson, 1965: 44). Selective incentives are benefits that accrue only to those who participate in the costs of bringing about the public good, but not to others. If powerful enough, these benefits can outweigh the costs of participating, and hence render cooperation rather than free-riding the individually rational strategy.

For non-western immigrants it would seem there is at least one selective incentive to take it upon themselves to cover some of the costs of integration, namely the costs related to acquiring new language skills and social competencies. The incentive is that language skills tend to rather dramatically increase an individual's chances of finding work. Mogensen and Matthiessen (2000: ch. 5) show that for non-western immigrants in Denmark the level of command of the Danish language is by far the most important predictor of employment status.[16]

Similarly, one could argue that employers may face selective incentives to participate in bringing about integration by giving jobs to immigrants. If an individual employer can increase production and profits by hiring immigrants, there is a selective incentive for him to do so (Faist, 2000: 77), and at the same time contribute to the (labour market) integration of these groups, which is a collective good both to employers as a group and to society as a whole.

The effectiveness of such selective incentives in inducing individual actors to participate in bringing about integration cannot be judged in isolation, however. In the end their effectiveness will depend on the total institutional setup facing the actors and the incentives created by it. In that respect there can be little doubt that the dual development of the emergence of welfare states on the one hand and, on the other, of a human rights regime that has considerably circumscribed the traditional power of national states to dispense with non-citizens at will and at the same time entitled non-citizens to certain welfare provisions by the host country, has weakened selective economic incentives for immigrants to take their part of the costs of integration upon themselves.

Depending on their institutional setup, welfare states may have yet other negative influences on the incentives to participate in bringing about integration among native Danes and immigrants alike. They are, however, less specific than those mentioned above. As has often been noted, especially universalistic welfare states seem prone to 'clientelizing' groups which in some respects are considered 'weak'. Immigrants constitute one such group (Preis, 1996; Kamali, 1997; Rath, 1999). Clientelization implies that immigrants meet an all-encompassing system which can be relied upon to take care of nearly everything for them. While the intentions behind that system are certainly benign, the result can easily be loss of initiative, incentives and capacities to do something about one's own situation, what Lindbeck

(1986: 77) has dubbed the 'acquired helplessness' syndrome in the Nordic welfare state context. Thus, tendencies towards clientelizing immigrants found in, especially, the Nordic welfare states can hardly be considered conducive to the integration process. Furthermore, since the universalistic welfare state has become established as the main social problem-solving device in these countries, employing professional problem-solvers to this end, the native population may increasingly come to regard various social problems as belonging in the realm of public policy and therefore the responsibility of 'experts'. This attitude cannot but weaken individual incentives among natives to participate in the integration of immigrants and to pay their share of the costs. Unfortunately, as with state regulation, 'experts' cannot by themselves bring about integration.

Social capital
In his seminal book *Making Democracy Work* Putnam (1993) used the concept of social capital, later defined as 'features of social life – networks, norms and trust – which facilitate cooperation and coordination for mutual benefit' (Putnam, 1997: 31), as his central explanation of differences between the economic, politico-administrative and social performance of Italian regions. Since then, a growing body of studies has confirmed that there is indeed a relationship between the level of social capital endowment, especially the level of generalized trust, in a country and a wide array of economic and social outcomes, from economic prosperity and growth to governability.

There are two standard micro-level answers to why and how social capital might be economically and/or politically beneficial. Both answers were discussed by Putnam (Putnam 1993: ch. 6).

The first standard answer builds on the concept of transaction costs. Social capital (networks and interpersonal trust) is said to be beneficial because it reduces the transaction costs individuals face in economic or political exchanges, thus generally facilitating such exchanges and enabling individuals to engage in types of transactions which could not take place in the absence of social capital due to the prohibitive costs of, for instance, contracting and monitoring.

The second standard answer builds on the concept of collective action dilemmas. Social capital, especially interpersonal trust, is claimed to be beneficial because it enables individuals (and/or groups) to overcome collective action problems, hence avoiding being locked into collectively suboptimal equilibria ('rationality traps'). This is the interesting mechanism in the present context.

The intuition behind the idea that social capital can help solve collective action dilemmas is simple. The reason why 'defection' (or non-cooperation) is the dominant strategy in a Prisoner's Dilemma game is that it ensures the best outcome for a player *regardless of the strategy chosen by the other*. In particular, it ensures against ending up as 'sucker' if the other player is not playing 'nice'. So 'defection' is the strategy of choice if one does not trust the other player to cooperate and does not want one's pay-off to be utterly dependent on his strategic choice. But to the extent that one does trust the other player not to exploit one's cooperation, 'defection' is no longer the optimal strategy. Alternatively, it could be argued that social capital can help solving collective action dilemmas because as social capital enters into a Prisoner's Dilemma game, the pay-off of a particular strategy changes. If the choice not to cooperate implies that others lose trust in me, the potential gains from not cooperating will now have to be balanced against this loss. If there is some value at all to being trusted by others, then at the very least, the gain from not cooperating will be less than in a situation where social capital is at stake too. So we have to consider – according to Nannestad (2004) – if social capital could indeed help solve the collective action dilemma of integration too, and if variations in the level of social capital endowment in Western European countries explain variations in the extent to which these countries have so far been able to solve the problem of integrating their immigrants.

Social capital and immigrant integration in Western European countries – some empirics
In the following, I operationalize social capital as *generalized trust*. Thus, as a proxy for a country's level of social capital endowment I use the percentage of respondents in a given country who in the World Value Survey (WVS) answered the question 'Generally speaking, do you believe that most people can be trusted or can't you be too careful in dealing with other people?' by indicating that generally speaking, most people can be trusted. The reason for choosing this proxy is that generalized trust supposedly plays an important role in helping to solve collective action problems.

The level of generalized trust varies widely across Western European countries, as shown in Figure 18.1. The mean over the 15 'old' EU countries is 37.7 percent with a standard deviation of 16.8. The minimum percentage of respondents expressing generalized trust is 12.3 in Portugal, in contrast to the maximum percentage of 66.3 percent in Sweden (closely followed by Denmark with 65.5 per cent). Is this variation in the level of generalized trust reflected in the variation across countries in the extent to which they are able to integrate their immigrants? If so, that would suggest that social capital can indeed help solve or ameliorate the collective action dilemma of immigrant integration.

To answer that question, I use labour market integration as a proxy

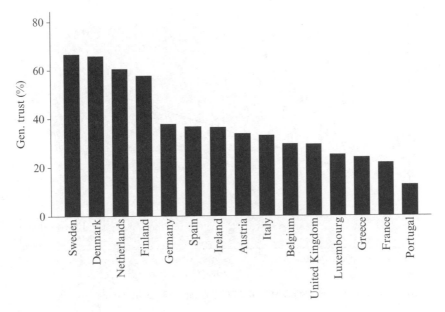

Source: WVS 1999–2000.

Figure 18.1   Levels of generalized trust in the 15 'old' EU countries

for immigrant integration as such. Obviously, doing so is not without problems. As exemplified by, especially, the United Kingdom, countries can be quite successful in integrating immigrants into the labour market, while in other respects segregation remains the dominant feature. On the other hand, while success in labour market integration does not necessarily guarantee success with respect to other types and areas of integration, it is difficult to imagine a situation where immigrants are well integrated in other areas, but are more or less excluded from the labour market. Thus, labour market integration can arguably be considered a necessary, but not sufficient condition for immigrant integration in other areas.

Immigrant labour market integration is operationalized as the immigrants' excess unemployment relative to that of natives.[17] In this way differences in national labour market conditions are controlled for. On average over the 15 'old' EU countries, the excess unemployment rate of immigrants is about 2, meaning that on average the unemployment rate of immigrants is twice that of natives, a ratio ranging from 1.4 in Ireland (best) to 2.88 in Sweden (worst).

Figure 18.2 shows the relationship between levels of generalized trust and the excess unemployment level of immigrants in the 15 'old' EU countries

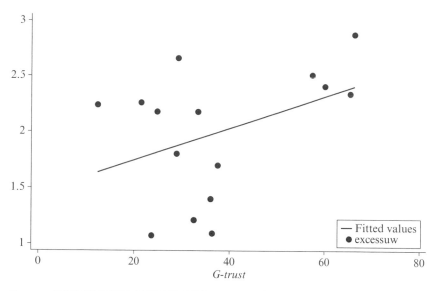

Source: WVS 1999–2000; SOPEMI (OECD, 2001) and own calculations.

*Figure 18.2   Relationship between generalized trust and the excess
unemployment of immigrants in the 15 'old' EU countries*

with a linear regression line added. Somewhat perplexingly, Figure 18.2
suggests a positive relationship between level of generalized trust and
excess unemployment of immigrants. This would indicate that social
capital in no way contributes to solving the collective action dilemma of
immigrant integration. On the contrary, the higher the level of generalized
trust, the higher the level of excess unemployment among immigrants!

However, the implicit model behind Figure 18.2 is most likely misspeci-
fied owing to omitted variables. An omitted-variable bias can seriously
distort estimations of the relationships between the variables included in
the model, even to the extent of changing their sign. Table 18.2 gives the
results of estimating a somewhat richer model in which welfare state type
and the educational composition of the stock of immigrants in a given
country are controlled for. Controlling for the type of welfare state (universalistic, corporatist, residual, cf. Esping-Andersen, 1990, with a special
category added: 'Southern European welfare state', cf. Jensen, 2005) basically amounts to controlling for the strength of the selective incentives for
immigrants related to labour market integration, as the strength of these
incentives varies across welfare state types. Thus, in the universalistic or
Nordic welfare state, benefit levels are generous and access to social benefits

Table 18.2   *Regression of excess unemployment of immigrants on level of generalized trust, welfare state type and percentage poorly educated immigrants in the 15 'old' EU countries (OLS; standard errors in parentheses)*

Variable	Coefficient (standard error)	Prob.
Generalized trust	−0.035 (0.015)	
Welfare state type (relative to universalistic)		
Corporatist	−1.484 (0.540)	0.023
Residual	−1.986 (0.608)	0.010
Southern European	−2.376 (0.569)	0.002
Pct. poorly educated	−0.001 (0.010)	0.922
Constant	4.478 (1.252)	0.004
R² (adj.)	0.679	
N	15	
Root MSE	0.330	

Source: WVS 1999–2000; SOPEMI (OECD, 2001); OECD migration database and own calculations.

does not in general depend on labour market participation and prior contributions. This means that in the universalistic welfare state immigrants, especially low-skilled, low-paid individuals, on the whole have weak economic incentives to enter the labour market. The corporatist or continental welfare states north of the Alps have quite generous benefit levels as well. In these welfare states, however, access to important types of benefits must be earned through prior labour market participation. Therefore, immigrants have stronger incentives to enter the labour market in continental welfare states (north of the Alps) than in universalistic welfare states. Incentives for entering the labour market are even stronger in the continental welfare states south of the Alps, since benefit levels are considerably lower than in the other two welfare state types. Finally, in the residual welfare state the state acts mainly as the 'insurer of last resort', covering only those unable to buy insurance in the market. Also this type of welfare state has low benefit levels, creating strong incentives for immigrants to enter the labour market. Controlling for the educational composition (percentage poorly educated) of a country's stock of immigrants would be necessary if the educational background of immigrants is related to how easily they are absorbed into national labour markets, which is most likely the case.

As shown in Table 18.2, the level of generalized trust now has a negative impact on excess unemployment among immigrants, indicating that higher levels of social capital are associated with lower levels of labour market exclusion of immigrants. This might be interpreted as indicating that social capital does indeed contribute to the solution of the collective action dilemma of (labour market) immigrant integration.[18] But it is equally obvious that welfare state type has an important impact on the extent of labour market integration. Here corporatist, residual and southern European welfare states tend to outperform universalistic welfare states (in that order). The educational composition of the stock of immigrants in the 15 'old' EU countries does not show any statistically or substantively significant impact on the excess unemployment among immigrants. This most likely reflects that the effect of the educational composition of immigrant stocks on excess unemployment is absorbed into that of welfare state type on the excess unemployment of immigrants, as the educational composition of the stock of immigrants is strongly correlated with welfare state type, residual welfare states having the lowest percentage of poorly educated immigrants and universalistic welfare states the highest.

What, then, is more important if we are to solve the collective action dilemma of (labour market) integration of immigrants – the level of social capital (generalized trust) in the receiving country or selective incentive structures (welfare state type)? The R^2 measure in Table 18.2 tells us that, taken together, selective incentives and social capital levels account for about 68 per cent of the variation in the excess unemployment level of immigrants across the 15 'old' EU countries. Decomposing the R^2 measure in Table 18.2 we find that even without paying attention to social capital levels we would still be able to account for 54 per cent of the variation in excess unemployment among immigrants. Social capital levels thus add 14 percentage points to the explanatory power of the model, or slightly more than one-fourth of the total R^2. This is not a negligible contribution, but it leaves little doubt that welfare state type (acting as proxy for the strength of selective incentives) has far stronger explanatory power than social capital when it comes to variation in the extent of (labour market) integration of immigrants across the 15 'old' EU countries.

Conclusion

Integration of non-western immigrants into Western European welfare states has been shown to entail a collective action dilemma, also known as a 'rationality trap': while integration is socially preferable to non-integration (segregation), adaptation costs make it the rational strategy for natives and immigrants alike not to cooperate in bringing about integration, resulting in a suboptimal outcome. This suboptimal outcome is evident in all immigrant-receiving Western European welfare states.

One classical solution to such collective action dilemmas, (state) regulation, is likely to be ineffective when it comes to integrating immigrants. The regulatory capacity of the liberal democratic state with respect to integration is constrained by human and civil rights embodied in national constitutions and international treaties. Selective incentives are more likely to be effective, but their effects are weakened by the institutions of the welfare state, depending, however, on welfare state type.

Recent research in the social sciences has focused on social capital as an alternative solution to collective action dilemmas. Macro-level data from the 15 'old' EU countries indicate that variation in the social capital endowment of these countries is indeed positively related to the extent to which their immigrants are integrated in the labour market. But this is only true when welfare state type is controlled for. If welfare state type can be interpreted as a proxy for the strength of selective incentives – such incentives being strongest in residual and weakest in universalistic welfare states – this finding indicates that when it comes to solving the collective action dilemma of immigrant integration in the labour market, social capital matters, but selective incentives decide.

Notes

1. In the following, the term 'immigrants' normally denotes non-western immigrants. No distinction will be made between immigrants and refugees.
2. The term 'integration' in the following denotes a process of mutual adaptation as well as its result. Thus, integration – in the sense of mutual adaptation – differs from assimilation, which is one-sided adaptation by immigrants to natives.
3. The following is heavily based on earlier work (Nannestad, 2004). However, on one important issue I have revised my point of view, see note 13.
4. It could be argued that assimilation would be an even better situation for the majority than integration, while for the minorities it would be inferior to integration. Since assimilation is not on the official agenda in Western European countries any more, it will not be considered an alternative option. *We Are All Multiculturalists Now* (Glazer, 1997).
5. Owing to the relatively modest size and the fragmentation of immigrant groups in many Western European countries, the possibilities of establishing alternative 'niche economies' (for immigrants by immigrants) are severely limited. This certainly holds true for Denmark, cf. Diken (1998).
6. This would also appear to be an implication of the prejudice-approach: integration would be forthcoming, were it not for the (irrational) forces of prejudice and xenophobia.
7. The Ministry of Economic Affairs in 1995 estimated the total economic costs of refugees and immigrants in Denmark to be about 12 billion DKK per year, net of taxes and so on (Ministry of Economic Affairs, 1997). However, a considerable part actually represents the costs of non-integration.

8.   Cf. Faist (2000: 127–8). See also Wadensjö and Orrje (2002).
9.   In some respects, these limits are actually rather wide. For instance some countries show considerable leniency – and administrative inventiveness – in their dealings with polygamous marriages in certain immigrant groups.
10. 'For blacks to gain may mean whites will lose' (Wellman, 1993: 56).
11. The other defining characteristic of a public good, jointness of supply, is of little importance in this context.
12. 'It is certain that a collective good will not be provided unless there is coercion or some outside inducements' (Olson, 1965: 44).
13. This represents a radical revision of my own views in Nannestad (2004), where I explicitly ruled out voluntary interactions as a possible way of solving the collective action dilemma of integration.
14. Cf. the privileged access of ethnic Germans ('Aussiedler') to German citizenship as compared to, for instance, Turks with long-time residence in Germany.
15. The effectiveness of regulations against discrimination is a different matter. There is little doubt that anti-discriminatory policies are more developed in Sweden than in Denmark. Nevertheless, there are no signs that integration problems are less severe in Sweden than in Denmark.
16. Strictly speaking, there may be a simultaneity bias here. Language skills increase the probability of being employed, but employment probably also leads to improved language skills. Therefore, not all of the strength in the empirical relationship between language skills and employment can be ascribed to the causal link from language skills to employment. There are nevertheless good reasons to believe that the interpretation offered by Mogensen and Matthiessen is correct and that (lack of) language skills has a relatively strong causal impact on employment among immigrants and refugees. These reasons have to do with three characteristics of the Danish economy. First, the biggest sector in the Danish economy is service. While some types of service jobs do not require much in terms of language skills, for instance cleaning, many others involve contact and interaction with consumers and clients, hence requiring both language and social skills. Second, most Danish firms are small, which means that the workforce comes to resemble a primary social group. Again, this characteristic puts a premium on social skills and command of the Danish language. Finally, ongoing changes in organizational structures in Danish firms – from steep hierarchical structures towards more flexible work organizations and flat structures of command – have further increased the importance of language skills and social competencies (cf. Rosholm et al., 2000).
17. Source SOPEMI (OECD, 2001, table 1.14), and own calculations.
18. There could be an endogeneity bias involved here if labour market integration of immigrants contributes to the level of generalized trust in society. This issue will not be pursued further in the present context, however.

References

Adorno, B., E. Frenkel-Brunswik, D.J. Levinson and R. N. Sanford (1950), *The Authoritarian Personality*, New York: Norton.
Allport, G.W. (1954), *The Nature of Prejudice*, Cambridge, MA: Perseus.
Anderson, B. (1983), *Imagined Communities*, London: Verso.
Barr, N. (2004), *The Economics of the Welfare State*, Oxford: Oxford University Press.
Brubaker, R. (1992), *Citizenship and Nationhood in France and Germany*, Cambridge, MA: Harvard University Press.
Diken, B. (1998), *Strangers, Ambivalence, and Social Theory*, Aldershot: Ashgate.
Esping-Andersen, G. (1990), *The Three Worlds of Welfare Capitalism*, Oxford: Polity Press.
Faist, T. (2000), *The Volume and Dynamics of International Migration and Transnational Social Spaces*, Oxford: Clarendon Press.
Glazer, N. (1997), *We Are All Multiculturalists Now*, repr. edn, Boston, MA: Harvard University Press.

Jensen, B. (2005), *Indvandringen til Europa* [Immigration to Europe], Copenhagen: Gyldendal.

Kamali, M. (1997), *Distorted Integration. Clientization of Immigrants in Sweden*, Uppsala: Multiethnic Papers.

Lindbeck, A. (1986), *Hur mycket politik tål ekonomin?* [How Much Politics Can the Economy Take?], Stockholm: Bonniers.

Ministry of Economic Affairs (1997), *Økonomisk oversigt december 1997* [Economic Survey], December, Copenhagen: Schultz.

Mogensen, G.V. and P.C. Matthiessen (2000), *Mislykket integration?* [Failed Integration?], Copenhagen: Spektrum.

Mueller, D.C. (1989), *Public Choice II*, Cambridge: Cambridge University Press.

Nannestad, P. (2004), 'A game real actors won't play? Integration of ethnic minorities in Denmark as a collective action dilemma', *International Migration Review*, **38** (1), 287–308.

Nuscheler, F. (1995), *Internationale Migration. Flucht und Asyl*, Opladen: Leske & Budrich.

Olson, M. (1965), *The Logic of Collective Action*, Cambridge, MA: Harvard University Press.

Organisation for Economic Co-operation and Development (OECD) (SOPEMI) (2001), *Trends in International Migration*, Paris: OECD.

Preis, A.-B. (1996), *Flygtninge, sandheden og andre gåder* [Refugees, the Truth, and Other Riddles], Copenhagen: Socialpædagogisk Bibliotek.

Putnam, R. (1993), *Making Democracy Work*, Princeton, NJ: Princeton University Press.

Putnam, R. (1997), 'Democracy in America at century's end', in A Hadenius (ed.), *Democracy's Victory and Crisis*, Cambridge: Cambridge University Press.

Rath, J. (1999), 'The Netherlands: a Dutch treat for anti-social families and immigrant ethnic minorities', in M. Cole and G. Dale (eds), *The European Union and Migrant Labour*, Oxford: Berg.

Rosholm, M., K. Scott and L. Husted (2000), '*The Times They Are A-Changin*', Working Paper 00-07, Centre for Labour Market and Social Research, Aarhus.

Wadensjö, E. and H. Orrje (2002), *Immigration and the Public Sector in Denmark*, Aarhus: Aarhus University Press.

Wellman, D.T. (1993), *Portraits of White Racism*, Cambridge: Cambridge University Press.

Wimmer, A. (1997), 'Explaining xenophobia and racism: a critical review of current research approaches', *Ethnic and Racial Studies*, **20** (1): 17–41.

PART VII

THE ECONOMY

19 Economic inequality[1]
Henrik Jordahl

19.1 Introduction

Inequality is a strong determinant of trust.[2] People in unequal societies trust each other to a much smaller extent than people do in more equal communities. Several economic and social mechanisms could explain this relationship. Political factors could also be important; political arguments and decisions are often influenced by notions of distributive justice. People's aversion to inequality has also been demonstrated in more systematic studies, for example by Fehr and Schmidt (1999).

The development of income inequality and trust in the US illustrates the negative relationship. Since about 1975 there has been a significant increase in income inequality (Piketty and Saez, 2003), and as observed by Putnam (2000) trust has declined during the same period. The coincidence of high trust and low income inequality in the Nordic countries provides an alternative illustration.

There are good reasons to care about this. A major economic advantage of trust is that transaction costs – especially costs of policing and enforcement – are reduced when buyers and sellers can seal an agreement with a handshake. Additional benefits enjoyed in trusting societies are demonstrated in other chapters in this volume.

This chapter's review of the literature on inequality and trust concentrates on economic inequality, which belongs to the category of inequality of outcome (or welfare) and excludes inequality of opportunity (which disregards inequalities that are due to differences in effort). In the empirical parts of the chapter the definition of inequality is even narrower. Probably since it is relatively simple to define and measure, annual income inequality has received most of the empirical attention. While the literature thus defined is quite small, it is also a growing literature with plenty of room for contributions in the future.

The weight of the evidence suggests that economic inequality reduces trust. Of the causal mechanisms proposed in the chapter, social ties appear to be more important than inference on social relationships, conflicts over resources or opportunity cost of time, but none of the mechanisms go hand in glove with all of the empirical findings.

The rest of the chapter proceeds as follows. Section 19.2 presents the four proposed links from inequality to trust in more detail. Section 19.3

discusses different measures of economic inequality. Sections 19.4–19.7 present the empirical findings under the headings 'Trust across countries', 'Individual trust across local communities', 'Causality issues' and 'Experimental evidence'. Some concluding remarks in Section 19.8 close the chapter.

19.2   The links from economic inequality to trust

Trust is fundamentally an actual or potential relation between two persons: one person (the truster) who trusts another person (the trustee) to cooperate rather than to cheat. Trust can be seen as continuous either by varying the value that the truster is willing to put at stake, or by varying the amount of resources that the truster is willing to invest to prevent the trustee from cheating.

The literature contains several suggestions of causal mechanisms through which economic inequality could influence trust. Some of the mechanisms are more precisely stated than others, but most, if not all, of them point to a negative influence. Most mechanisms belong to what Hardin (2006) calls the encapsulated interest conception of trust. Trust is seen as the expectation of cooperative behavior derived from the truster's knowledge of the incentive structure facing the trustee.[3] Even though the trustworthiness of a stranger will often be highly uncertain, it is likely that some information about his position in the income distribution is available, which together with the truster's own position can be used to infer how large a reasonable baseline level of trust might be.[4] This section presents the proposed mechanisms in four groups: social ties, inference on social relationships, conflicts over resources and opportunity cost of time.

First, social ties probably make people more willing to trust those who are similar to themselves, including in terms of income and wealth. The propensity to put more trust in someone who is closer socially has been suggested by Coleman (1990) and Fukuyama (1995). Hardin's (2006: 39) broad explanation is that familiarity normally is connected with social ties between the truster and the trustee. Social ties create incentives for trustworthiness and familiarity provides knowledge about this. If it is likely that two persons who belong to the same socio-economic group – and therefore have social ties to each other – will meet again, trust can be built on the expected value of forthcoming cooperative encounters. For similar reasons, much harm will be done to a person's reputation should he cheat someone to whom he is tied socially. In more unequal communities, enforcing sanctions and upholding social control may be more problematic.[5] Coffé and Geys (2006) argue that inequality makes individuals from different socio-economic groups less likely to have values and norms in common.

Second, inference on social relationships may matter to trust. Some people – for example, those who are influenced by Karl Marx – will see economic inequality as a signal of exploitation, that is, of untrustworthy behavior. Persons holding this belief will find it natural to reduce their trust in the face of rising inequality. By this logic, it should become particularly difficult to trust people at the top of the income distribution, but the trust reduction could also apply to people in general if income differences are thought to reveal that people seize every opportunity of exploiting others.

In a related argument Fischer and Torgler (2006) propose that envy and positional concerns have a negative effect on perceptions of others' fairness. People who feel disadvantaged by their relative income position may come to distrust the reference group of 'the Joneses' and extend this distrust to other people. This prediction puts additional focus on the relative income of the truster but downplays the position of the trustee.

Third, economic inequality creates conflicts over resources. According to this line of argument, inequality magnifies economic incentives for deceitful behavior directed against the rich, especially for poor people. If inequality makes people with fewer resources less trustworthy, it will make people with more resources less inclined to trust them. Note, however, that this explanation, based as it is on quite simplified incentive structures, implies that the poorest person is more willing to trust everybody else the more unequal is the distribution of income. If income differences are large, richer people have little to gain from cheating a poor person. The net effect of inequality is generally considered to reduce trust, but this is in the end an empirical matter.

In addition, there is a political dimension to conflicts over resources which could undermine trust. Income differences may give rise to a struggle over governmental resources, including over public goods and how they are financed (Boix and Posner, 1998; Coffé and Geys, 2006).[6] Rothstein and Uslaner (2005: 46) argue that people in unequal societies lack a sense of solidarity in the form of a 'shared fate'. Society is seen as a zero-sum game between conflicting groups and this is reflected in lower levels of trust.[7] Here inequality makes both the poor and the rich less willing to trust each other.

Fourth, the opportunity cost of time could provide a link from income inequality to trust. A change in income inequality will be accompanied by a change in the aggregate level of trust if each person's trust is sensitive to changes in his income (unless the individual effects even out). For someone who earns a lot of money, working and trusting is more attractive than spending time verifying that others are trustworthy.

Zak and Knack (2001) derive the proposition that an increase in wage inequality that keeps the mean wage constant will reduce trust. When their wages fall, people with low wages respond by reducing their trust in others.

A lower wage means that taking the time to ensure that others are trustworthy becomes more attractive than working and trusting. At the other end of the wage distribution, higher wages lead to more trust in others. The net wage effect follows from the supposition that a person is more sensitive to a wage change the lower his wages are.[8] It is worth noting that this mechanism will not show up as an effect of inequality in empirical studies where individual wages are controlled for.

19.3   Measures of economic inequality
Empirical studies of economic inequality typically focus on inequality of annual income. In the best of worlds this would not be so. Lifetime consumption is arguably more important than yearly earnings. Consumption is less variable than annual income since people tend to adjust their savings over the life cycle and save a relatively large fraction of temporary increases in their income. However, since data on lifetime income and consumption often fall short on quality and consistency, many studies use annual income despite its lesser relevance. Another shortcoming is that provision of public goods, which reduces consumption inequality, is normally omitted. To make inequality measures based on permanent income and lifetime consumption (including public goods) available would be a substantial contribution to a more encompassing literature than that reviewed in this chapter.

The Gini coefficient is by far the most popular measure of inequality. Almost all studies of inequality and trust use it exclusively. In cross-country studies, where availability, comparability and quality of data are often an issue, this exclusive use of the Gini is expected and acceptable. Studies within a given country are different in that they have better possibilities of working also with other measures of inequality. The choice of inequality measures should preferably be guided by the proposed social mechanisms in the hypotheses being tested. Table 19.1 briefly describes some measures of income inequality with focus on different parts of the income distribution.

Table 19.1 makes clear that there are different measures of income inequality and although the frequently used Gini coefficient incorporates inequality in the entire distribution of income, other measures may be more informative of why inequality matters for trust. The existence of a small group of people with very high incomes is very different from a situation with a wide gap between the poor and the middle class. Different measures of inequality will capture different mechanisms through which inequality may influence trust.

Although in theory a measure of inequality corresponds to a well-defined economic variable, the empirical studies are often characterized

Table 19.1   Measures of income inequality

Inequality measure	Description	Comment
Gini coefficient	The ratio of the mean absolute difference between all income pairs to twice the mean income. This gives a coefficient between zero and one	Captures inequality in the whole income distribution. Sensitive to differences about the middle (more precisely the mode) of the distribution
Percentile ratios	Ratios of incomes at different percentiles of the income distribution, e.g. income at the 50th percentile over income at the 10th percentile	Captures inequality in a certain part of the income distribution. Not sensitive to extreme values unless percentiles at the tails of the distribution are used
Top income shares	Share of income earned by the top x percent	Captures inequality in the form of concentration of income at the very top of the distribution
Standard deviation of logs	The standard deviation of the logarithm of income	Captures inequality in the whole income distribution. Sensitive to changes at the tails of the distribution

by less clarity. The cross-country studies of inequality and trust often use inequality measures from 'secondary' data sets – that assembled at the World Bank by Deininger and Squire (1996) has been particularly popular – without giving any information about the comparability of different observations. This practice neglects several of the problems that arise when using compilations of inequality data from a variety of sources. What is the reference unit: the household or the individual? Is it income or expenditure that is being measured? If it is income, is it gross or net of taxes? Atkinson and Brandolini (2001) discuss these and several related pitfalls in their excellent survey on the use of secondary data sets in studies of income inequality.

19.4   Trust across countries
There is by now a large number of cross-country studies that investigate the relationship between income inequality and trust. The four waves of the World Values Survey have made this line of research possible by providing a simple and internationally comparable measure of the average level of trust for a growing sample of countries. Virtually all of these studies use

the Gini coefficient as their inequality measure and the share of a country's population who say that most people can be trusted as their trust measure.[9]

Although cross-country studies are often considered problematic when it comes to causal inference, an attractive feature when studying trust is that there is a lot of variation between countries. In the latest, fourth, wave of the World Values Survey the share of trusting people ranges between 3 percent in Brazil and 67 percent in Denmark. Economic inequality varies almost as widely.

Income inequality and trust are strongly and robustly correlated in the cross-country studies – see, for example, Knack and Keefer (1997), Zak and Knack (2001), Berggren and Jordahl (2006), Leigh (2006a) and Bjørnskov (2007). Unlike the other studies, Leigh (2006a) includes observations of trust at the individual level (in 59 countries). Fischer and Torgler (2006), also with individual trust observations from 25 countries, show that trust is positively correlated with a person's relative income position. Since the estimated effect is larger for incomes below the reference point, inequality is expected to reduce trust in the aggregate. Figure 19.1 displays the negative relationship between income inequality, measured by the Gini coefficient, and the share of trusting people for 75 countries (the correlation coefficient equals −0.47).

Regardless of the strength of the correlation in Figure 19.1, cross-country studies are at best suggestive of a causal effect of inequality on trust. It is well known that cross-country studies are plagued by omitted variables, endogeneity, measurement error and influential outliers. One can hardly come to conclusions about individual behavior and attitudes by studying data at the country level. Conclusions about the mechanisms linking inequality to trust are even more distant.

19.5   Individual trust across local communities

The cross-country studies described in the previous section should be seen as a first tentative step towards establishing a causal effect of inequality on trust. Further investigations are needed to reach firmer conclusions. Combining individual-level survey data on trust with income inequality measures from local communities holds several advantages. Measures of income inequality are more readily comparable between geographical units within a country, although the variation in inequality may be smaller within than between countries. Another advantage is that individual determinants of trust (for example, education) can be held constant. Country-specific institutional determinants of trust are obviously held constant when a single country is studied.

Alesina and La Ferrara (2002) study individual level data from US

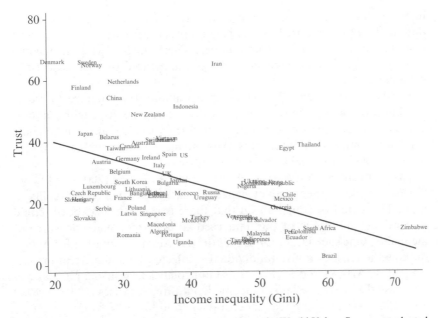

Notes: Trust is the most recent country average from the World Values Surveys conducted in 1997 and in 1999–2001, supplemented with a few observations from the Danish Social Capital Project (see Bjørnskov, 2007). Income inequality is the Gini coefficient from around 1995, from the UNU/WIDER World Income Inequality Database, Version 2.0b, May 2007. A line with fitted values from a univariate linear regression of trust on inequality is displayed in the figure. All Gini coefficients are calculated by WIDER and are based on sources with full coverage in terms of area, population and age, and with a quality rating no worse than 3. For most countries there are several observations to choose between. The primary preferences underlying the selection are as follows: household as the statistical unit, person as the unit of analysis and household per capita as the equivalence scale. The secondary preferences regard the income definition and rank disposable income before gross income, consumption, and expenditure (in descending order of preference). Most observations are from 1995; the Australian observation from 1989 is the largest deviation from this year. All else being equal, observations from the Deininger and Squire data set are chosen.

Figure 19.1   Income inequality and trust across countries

localities and find that trust is lower in metropolitan areas with an uneven distribution of income. However, the effect of racial heterogeneity is even stronger in their study and income inequality is no longer statistically significant when this variable is added to the empirical model. Their interpretation of the results is in line with the social ties mechanism. Trust is lower in heterogeneous communities since contacts between dissimilar people (arguably without social ties to each other) are more common. This is the case both for interracial contacts and for contacts between people in different income brackets. The alternative so-called 'local interaction' interpretation receives less support. This interpretation starts out from the findings that the poor are less trusting and that the fraction of poor people is higher in more unequal communities. Then, people living in unequal communities may trust less since they are influenced by their distrustful neighbors.

For Australia, Leigh (2006b) reports in a similar study that trust is lower in ethnically and especially in linguistically heterogeneous neighborhoods, but he finds no relation between economic inequality and trust. These results are obtained both for 'most Australians' (generalized trust) and for 'most people in my local area' (localized trust).

Taken together the studies by Alesina and La Ferrara (2002) and Leigh (2006b) provide rather weak evidence of a link from income inequality to trust. This could of course mean that there is no such link, but it could also reflect limitations of the data used to construct their measures of inequality. One such limitation is that the data do not contain information on how the trust of a given individual is affected by a change in income inequality. Alesina and La Ferrara's Gini coefficient is also a bit shaky in the sense that they use family income from three censuses (in 1970, 1980 and 1990) to generate annual data for the period 1974–94 by interpolation and extrapolation. This means that they measure income inequality with some error, which could lead to underestimation (attenuation bias) of its influence on trust. Given the strong relation between economic inequality and racial heterogeneity in the US it could also be problematic to distinguish the effects of those two variables empirically. Leigh uses data from one point in time (1997–98) so he does not have to do any interpolation or extrapolation, but the obvious drawback is that no changes in inequality and trust are observed. The neighborhood or suburb level could also be too small to capture all aspects of income inequality in the presence of residential segregation by income. Segregation could be an important mechanism through which inequality reduces trust.

The described data limitations are absent in a recent Swedish study by Gustavsson and Jordahl (2008) which combines individual-level panel data on trust with county level inequality measures computed from register based individual income data for a large representative sample. The results for the period 1994–98 show that income inequality is associated with lower trust – especially differences in the bottom half in the income distribution (measured by the 50/10 percentile ratio) seem to be important.[10] This suggests that measures of income inequality other than the Gini coefficient should be tested in other countries. The study also indicates that it is primarily inequality in disposable income rather than in pre-tax income that matters for trust. This means that consumption opportunities are more important than earnings capacity, and that redistribution of income could influence trust. Another result is that the proportion of people born in a foreign country is negatively associated with trust.

Given Sweden's low level of economic inequality, the study can arguably be seen as a tough test of the relationship between inequality and trust. On the other hand, Sweden's egalitarian political tradition may imply that trust is more sensitive to changes in income distribution than in other countries such as the US. In fact, the study demonstrates that a given increase in inequality brings about a stronger reduction in trust among people who would like to see a more even distribution of income. This is broadly in line with the mechanism based on inference on social relationships (since it is natural to prefer a more equal income distribution if inequalities are viewed with suspicion), with similarities to the argument and findings in Fischer and Torgler (2006). The mechanism based on the opportunity cost of time receives some support since individual income (which arguably reflects wages) is positively related to trust, but this mechanism cannot explain the negative relationship between inequality and trust that remains when individual income is controlled for.

Going beyond studies of trust, there is suggestive evidence in favor of the mechanism based on conflicts over resources to the extent that there is more crime in unequal societies (see, for example, Kelly, 2000). However, a problem with this interpretation is that the poor are generally less trusting than the rich. Unless this can be explained by deeper personal factors, it contradicts the mechanism based on conflicts over resources.

19.6 Causality issues

An important reason for the large interest in trust is that societies where people trust each other seem to work better in many dimensions. Given the large number of outcome variables that have been claimed to depend on trust, one has to wonder if any economic variable can be treated as exogenous.

When it comes to inequality, Alesina and La Ferrara (2002) mention that trusting communities may offer better opportunities for the poor. This could be the case if risk sharing and informal credit transactions are facilitated by trust. Leigh (2006b) mentions that less trusting people might move to more heterogeneous neighborhoods if they prefer to live there. There is also the possibility that trust influences inequality indirectly through an effect on economic growth.[11]

Some attempts have been made to identify the causal effect of inequality on trust by using instrumental variables. This section discusses what has been done in studies based on individual-level trust data. A valid instrument has to be both relevant (related to inequality on the basis of theoretical argument and by statistical correlation) and exogenous (not directly related to trust after controlling for the explanatory variables). In his cross-country study with individual-level trust data, Leigh (2006a) uses the ratio of the size of the cohort aged 40−59 to the population aged 15−69 as an instrument for the Gini coefficient. Since he includes individual age as a control variable, the most obvious objection to this instrument is neutralized. However, as in most cross-country studies, omitted variables are an issue. Especially worrying is the lack of income data at the individual level. Since the relevance of the instrument is established by the correlation of age and earnings, it cannot be exogenous − many studies report a positive correlation between individual income and trust.

Alesina and La Ferrara (2002) use the number of municipal and township governments in 1962, the percentage of revenues from intergovernmental transfers in 1962 and the share of the labor force in the manufacturing sector in 1990 as instruments for the Gini coefficient in 1970, 1980 and 1990. It should be safe to say that the exogeneity of these three instruments can be discussed. Leigh (2006b) uses the Gini coefficient and other variables at the regional level (about 460 000 people) as instruments for the Gini coefficient at the neighborhood level (about 20 000 people). This helps if locality choices are endogenous, but does not resolve other endogeneity problems.

Gustavsson and Jordahl (2008) use international demand for Swedish manufacturing goods as an instrument for the 50/10 percentile ratio of incomes. The idea is that international demand affects the income distribution differently across the counties depending on their industrial structure. International demand qualifies as an instrument as it is clearly exogenous and is not expected to have a direct effect on trust. The results from this exercise indicate that there is indeed an effect of income inequality on trust.

19.7   Experimental evidence

Several experimental economists have criticized the reliability of survey-based measures of trust, instead preferring to study 'trust games' in the field or in the laboratory (see, for example, Carpenter, 2000). Although experiments are often criticized for lacking external validity (inequality observed or induced in an experiment may not be relevant in real life situations), an important advantage is that they can be designed to discriminate between different explanations of a phenomenon. Of the four underlying mechanisms presented in this chapter, the one based on social ties have received most attention – and support – in the experimental studies.

The propensity to put more trust in someone who is closer socially is demonstrated in a seminal article of Glaeser et al. (2000), but see Anderson et al. (2006) for some dissent. Möbius and Szeidl (2007) report a strong and robust relationship between network flow measures of trust and trusting behavior in experiments. They explain trust as a function of 'social collateral' that can be used to enforce informal contracts in social networks. In a related study, Leider et al. (2007) show that favors granted to friends and strangers in a dictator game can be explained by enforced reciprocity (expecting repayment in the future) but not by signaling one's generosity or by preference-based generosity.

Although these studies indicate that social ties are relevant for the link from inequality to trust, they do not show how and to what extent income inequality affects the structure and density of social networks.

19.8 Concluding remarks

Economic inequality seems to be a strong determinant of trust. This relationship shows up consistently in different studies, although in a few of them it is not statistically significant. The detailed investigation of Gustavsson and Jordahl (2008), which addresses several empirical problems, confirms the negative association and indicates that income differences in the bottom half of the income distribution may have a particularly strong influence on trust.

Discriminating between the four proposed causal mechanisms is difficult, but social ties appear to receive the strongest support. Alesina and La Ferrara (2002) interpret their findings in line with this mechanism (dissimilarity reduces trust) and the experimental evidence is also affirmative. One can also mention a survey conducted by Johansson-Stenman (2006) which shows that the higher a person's income, the more he is willing to trust someone with high income relative to someone with low income. It is, however, less straightforward to explain Gustavsson and Jordahl's (2008) finding that inequalities in the bottom half of the income distribution are especially important.

The mechanism based on inference on social relationship also receives some support. It is consistent with the observation in Gustavsson and Jordahl (2008) that a given increase in inequality brings about a stronger reduction in trust among people who would like to see a more even distribution of income. The prediction that inequality reduces the trust of people all over the income distribution, and especially in rich trustees, has not been tested distinctly, but it is not inconsistent with the available evidence.

The mechanisms based on conflicts over resources and opportunity cost of time suggest the same influence of inequality at the aggregate level, but the underlying individual-level effects are diametrically opposed to each other. According to the mechanism based on the opportunity cost of time, inequality increases trust among people with high income and reduces trust among people at the bottom of the income distribution. The mechanism based on conflicts over resources predicts the exact opposite pattern. Since they have so little to lose, inequality is expected to increase the trust of people with low income.

At first glance, the fact that there is more crime in unequal societies makes the mechanism based on conflicts over resources attractive. But the observation that the poor are less trusting (Alesina and La Ferrara, 2002; Gustavsson and Jordahl, 2008) and appear to be more trusted (Johansson-Stenman, 2006: 17) contradicts this mechanism. The political formulation of this mechanism, stating that inequality makes both the rich and the poor less willing to trust the other group, is not at odds with the evidence. On the other hand, it has not been tested thoroughly.

The positive correlation between individual income and trust fits the opportunity cost of time mechanism, but this mechanism still fares worst in the sense that the estimated effect of income inequality on trust remains when individual income is held constant. This implies that there is much more to the connection between inequality and trust than what can be explained by differences in the opportunity cost of time.

Clear-cut tests of the four mechanisms would ideally be based on data with observations of various pairs of trusters and trustees, including the income of each one of them. Further studies – surveys and experiments – should focus on this kind of data and dig deeper into the four proposed mechanisms. Economic inequality seems to reduce trust and this probably relates to social ties, but much uncertainty remains about the underlying causal mechanisms.

Notes

1. I wish to thank Niclas Berggren, Andreas Bergh, Christian Bjørnskov, Justina Fischer and Daniel Waldenström for valuable comments and suggestions.
2. This chapter deals with trust and not with other conceptualizations and measures of social capital. Costa and Kahn (2003) and Coffé and Geys (2006) relate inequality to social capital in a broader sense. Alesina and La Ferrara (2000) relate inequality to participation in associational activities.
3. Yamagishi and Yamagishi (1994: 132) refer to this as 'assurance'. Other common conceptions of trust explain it as a moral commitment or as a disposition of character (Hardin, 2006: 25). A problem with these two conceptions is that it is not easily understood how economic inequality affects normative or psychological predispositions to trust and to be trustworthy. If such predispositions are genetic, they would probably not vary with the distribution of income. While it is also true that the rationalistic and instrumental conception of trust advocated by Hardin (2006) – and used by many economists – has been criticized for lack of relevance (Ostrom, 1998; Rothstein, 2005), its application in the area of economic inequality does not rule out different conceptual explanations of trust in other areas.
4. Berggren and Jordahl (2006) provide some discussion about how people extend (market-induced) trust in their trading partners to people in general.
5. The focus is here on reputation and informal sanctions. It is conceivable that formal sanctions in the form of legal punishment are easier to uphold in unequal societies where an upper-level citizen 'does not bear the sword for nothing'.

6. Both of these studies actually work with broader concepts of social capital rather than with trust, but the described explanation could be relevant for trust too.
7. Rothstein and Uslaner (2005) also stress inequality of opportunity in addition to income inequality. Compared with income, opportunities are harder to capture empirically. Therefore Rothstein and Uslaner do not investigate equality of opportunity as such, but focus on the universality of welfare state programs, arguing that discretionary − and sometimes arbitrary − decisions in selective welfare programs reduce trust.
8. A similar explanation could follow from Rothstein's (2005) claim that the possession of economic resources makes it easier to handle occasional acts of fraud and deceit. If poor people, through this mechanism, are more afraid to lose some of their wealth, the net effect of a mean preserving spread in wealth will be a reduction of trust.
9. In the latest, fourth version of the World Values Survey the question is 'Generally speaking, would you say that most people can be trusted or that you need to be very careful when dealing with people?' In the literature this is usually referred to as *generalized trust*, which is different from *particularized trust*. Unlike generalized trust, particularized trust entails trusting people that you have a personal experience with. Generalized trust is similar to *bridging* and particularized trust to *bonding* social capital (cf. Putnam, 2000: 22).
10. Quantitatively, the results in Gustavsson and Jordahl (2007) show that changes in the 50/10 percentile ratio can have a substantial impact on trust. Trust is predicted to decrease by 1.4 units on its 0−10 scale (the standard deviation of this trust measure is 2.2) if the 50/10 percentile ratio would increase from its mean of 1.82 to its maximum of 2.05 (in Stockholm).
11. For the link from trust to growth see Knack and Keefer (1997), Zak and Knack (2001) and Berggren et al. (2008). For the link from growth to inequality see Kuznets (1955) and Persson and Tabellini (1994).

References

Alesina, Alberto and Eliana La Ferrara (2000), 'Participation in heterogeneous communities', *Quarterly Journal of Economics*, **115** (3), 847−904.
Alesina, Alberto and Eliana La Ferrara (2002), 'Who trusts others?', *Journal of Public Economics*, **85** (2), 207–34.
Anderson, Lisa R., Jennifer M. Mellor and Jeffry Milyo (2006), 'Induced heterogeneity in trust experiments', *Experimental Economics*, **9** (3), 223−35.
Atkinson, Anthony B. and Andrea Brandolini (2001), 'Promise and pitfalls in the use of "secondary" data-sets: income inequality in OECD countries', *Journal of Economic Literature*, **39** (3), 771–99.
Berggren, Niclas and Henrik Jordahl (2006), 'Free to trust: economic freedom and social capital', *Kyklos*, **59** (2), 141–69.
Berggren, Niclas, Mikael Elinder and Henrik Jordahl (2008), 'Trust and growth: a shaky relationship', *Empirical Economics*, **35** (2), 251–74.
Bjørnskov, Christian (2007), 'Determinants of generalized trust: a cross-country comparison', *Public Choice*, **130** (1–2), 1–21.
Boix, Carles and Daniel N. Posner (1998), 'Social capital: explaining its origins and effects on government performance', *British Journal of Political Science*, **28** (4), 686–95.
Carpenter, Jeffrey P. (2000), 'Measuring social capital: adding field experimental methods to the analytical toolbox', in Jonathan Isham, Thomas Kelly and Sunder Ramaswamy (eds), *Social Capital and Economic Development*, Cheltenham, UK and Northampton, MA, USA: Edward Elgar, pp. 119–37.
Coffé, Hilde and Benny Geys (2006), 'Community heterogeneity: a burden for the creation of social capital?', *Social Science Quarterly*, **87** (5), 1053–72.
Coleman, James (1990), *Foundations of Social Theory*, Cambridge, MA: Harvard University Press.
Costa, Dora L. and Matthew E. Kahn (2003), 'Understanding the American decline in social capital, 1952−1998', *Kyklos*, **56** (1), 17−46.

Deininger, Klaus and Lyn Squire (1996), 'A new data set measuring income inequality', *World Bank Economic Review*, **10** (3), 565–91.

Fehr, Ernst and Klaus M. Schmidt (1999), 'A theory of fairness, competition and co-operation', *Quarterly Journal of Economics*, **114** (3), 817–68.

Fischer, Justina A.V. and Benno Torgler (2006), 'The effect of relative income position on social capital', *Economics Bulletin*, **26** (4), 1–20.

Fukuyama, Francis (1995), *Trust: The Social Virtues and the Creation of Prosperity*, New York: Free Press.

Glaeser, Edward L., David I. Laibson, Jose A. Scheinkman and Christine L. Soutter (2000), 'Measuring trust', *Quarterly Journal of Economics*, **115** (3), 811–46.

Gustavsson, Magnus and Henrik Jordahl (2008), 'Inequality and trust in Sweden: some inequalities are more harmful than others', *Journal of Public Economics*, **92** (1–2), 348–65.

Hardin, Russel (2006), *Trust*, Cambridge: Polity Press.

Johansson-Stenman, Olof (2006), 'Who are the trustworthy, we think?', working paper, no. 222, Department of Economics, Göteborg University.

Kelly, Morgan (2000), 'Inequality and crime', *Review of Economics and Statistics*, **82** (4), 530–39.

Knack, Stephen and Philip Keefer (1997), 'Does social capital have an economic pay-off? A cross-country investigation', *Quarterly Journal of Economics*, **112** (4), 1251–88.

Kuznets, Simon (1955), 'Economic growth and income inequality', *American Economic Review*, **45** (1), 1–28.

Leider, Stephen, Markus Möbius, Tanya Rosenblat and Quoc-Anh Do (2007), 'Directed altruism and enforced reciprocity in social networks: how much is a friend worth?', NBER Working Paper, no. 13135, National Bureau of Economic Research, Cambridge, MA.

Leigh, Andrew (2006a), 'Does equality lead to fraternity?', *Economics Letters*, **93** (1), 121–5.

Leigh, Andrew (2006b), 'Trust, inequality and ethnic heterogeneity', *Economic Record*, **82** (258), 268–80.

Möbius, Markus and Adam Szeidl (2007), 'Trust and social collateral', NBER Working Paper, no. 13126, National Bureau of Economic Research, Cambridge, MA.

Ostrom, Elinor (1998), 'A behavioral approach to the rational choice theory of collective action', *American Political Science Review*, **92** (1), 1–22.

Persson, Torsten and Guido Tabellini (1994), 'Is inequality harmful for growth?', *American Economic Review*, **84** (3), 600–621.

Piketty, Thomas and Emmanuel Saez (2003), 'Income inequality in the United States: 1913–1998', *Quarterly Journal of Economics*, **118** (1), 1–39.

Putnam, Robert D. (2000), *Bowling Alone: The Collapse and Revival of American Community*, New York: Simon & Schuster.

Rothstein, Bo (2005), *Social Traps and the Problem of Trust*, Cambridge: Cambridge University Press.

Rothstein, Bo and Eric M. Uslaner (2005), 'All for all: equality, corruption, and social trust', *World Politics*, **58** (1), 41–72.

Yamagishi, Toshio and Midori Yamagishi (1994), 'Trust and commitment in the United States and Japan', *Motivation and Emotion*, **18** (2), 129–66.

Zak, Paul J. and Stephen Knack (2001), 'Trust and growth', *Economic Journal*, **111** (470), 295–321.

20 Economic growth
*Christian Bjørnskov**

20.1 Introduction

In the early 1970s, the later Nobel laureate Kenneth Arrow (1972: 357) remarked that 'virtually every commercial transaction has within itself an element of trust' and went on to suggest that 'much of the economic backwardness in the world can be explained by the lack of mutual confidence'. Arrow had no way of knowing how right he may have been in his assessment as there were almost no data on trust in those days, and the few that were available were not to be used by economists for the next two decades.

That situation changed when the concept of 'social capital' burst onto the scene of the social sciences following Robert Putnam's (1993) book, *Making Democracy Work*. Putnam (1993: 167) defined social capital as 'features of social organization, such as trust, norms, and networks, that can improve the efficiency of society by facilitating coordinated actions' and argued that it was the key to understanding the vast and somewhat mysterious differences between Northern and Southern Italy in wealth and the quality of governance. The ensuing popular and academic attention gained by the book was more than substantial.

Since then, the concept of social capital has proven to be more than a mere fad even if Putnam's specific view of it as a unitary concept has been discredited (cf. Claibourn and Martin, 2000; Uslaner, 2002; Bjørnskov, 2006a). It has, for example, been demonstrated that features under the umbrella of social capital are associated with a number of beneficial outcomes such as educational volume, corruption, institutional quality and subjective well-being. Perhaps most importantly, one of these outcomes is the speed with which countries develop economically.

In this chapter, I provide a non-technical survey of this particular strand of the social capital literature. The remainder of the chapter is divided into three parts. Section 20.2 reviews the existing studies connecting social capital, and in particular social trust, with economic growth. The first half of Section 20.3 then surveys the association between social capital and a set of factors that are usually associated with growth, which may give some indication of the potential transmission channels connecting trust and growth. The final half of the section concludes and briefly discusses routes that would seem fruitful to take in future research.

20.2   Direct studies of social capital and economic growth

Even though the factors now placed under the umbrella of the social capital concept have been discussed in economics since Adam Smith (cf. Bruni and Sugden, 2000), it was to last until the booming interest in growth theory and growth empirics in particular in the early 1990s before such elements were included in empirical undertakings. As Putnam (1993) identified social capital as one of the main reasons for the affluence of Northern Italians compared with their Southern compatriots, it became a seemingly straightforward choice to also attempt to include it in more formal studies of economic growth.

20.2.1   Early studies

It was therefore only natural that the start of direct studies on the association between social capital and economic growth was heralded by Putnam himself in a joint paper with John Helliwell (Helliwell and Putnam, 1995). However, the paper employed three different proxies for social capital, none of which directly measures social trust: (1) civic community, capturing organizational density and voting; (2) institutional performance, capturing the quality and capacity of regional government, and (3) citizens' subjective satisfaction with regional governments, that is, a political confidence indicator. Again exploring the differences between Italian regions, the study showed that the social capital measures were significant long-term growth factors in most regressions. Helliwell and Putnam (1995) furthermore tentatively attributed part of the growth effect to the beneficial effects of social capital on regional governance, although stressing that this question needed more research.

Quickly, the topic entered the cross-country literature which had itself been exploding since Robert Barro's (1991) seminal work. An early related study was that of Gratano et al. (1996) who explored the growth effects of 'cultural values' of which social trust formed part of one of the two cultural components employed in the analysis. While their 'postmaterialism' factor proved not to be associated with growth in the 25-country sample employed in the paper, another factor which the authors termed 'Achievement Motivation' was. This factor, capturing the degree to which people place emphasis on thrift and determination as opposed to obedience and religion, to some extent measures the strength of economic norms and people's reliance on horizontal relations instead of hierarchical association, and as such can be said to be associated with both the second element of Putnam's social capital concept as well as with social trust.[1]

Jonathan Temple and Paul Johnson's (1998) paper also positioned itself broadly within the social capital literature. They employed a measure of 'social capability' developed in the early 1960s by Adelman and Morris

(1965) in order to test whether it is associated with economic growth. The measure, intended to embrace 'the attributes and qualities of people and organizations that influence the responses of people to economic opportunity, yet originate in social and political institutions' (Temple and Johnson, 1998: 966), turned out to be strongly and significantly associated with long-run growth rates. While Temple and Johnson stressed that their paper is not a direct test of any social capital variable, they devoted a section to discussing the relation between social capability and social capital, arguing that it may capture effects of both trust and associational activity. Yet, in the sample of 44 countries now available with data on both social trust and the Adelman-Morris index, there is no association between social trust and the index when controlling for gross domestic product (GDP) per capita in the 1960s. There is, however, a significant negative association between the index and associational activity and confidence in the parliament, respectively. Using the most recent data thus suggests that Temple and Johnson's results are unrelated to the literature on social trust even while the study clearly belongs within a broad discussion of social capital and thereby questions Putnam's original hypothesis that social capital in the form of associational activity drives economic growth.

In a much later contribution, Knack (2003) returned to directly exploring Putnam's hypothesis. In a sample of 38 countries, he found no support for Putnam's conjecture, noting that the beneficial 'Putnamesque' effects of social capital are probably outweighed by the negative effects of associations working as predatory special interests, as first stressed by Mancur Olson (1965) and later studied in a literature separate from the social capital studies. Splitting associational activity into activity in Olsonian organizations – professional associations, labour unions and political parties – and Putnamesque organizations – everything else from sports clubs to peace movements – replicates the finding. Knack nevertheless also used social trust as his alternative social capital indicator with findings discussed below. Coates and Heckelman (2003) further explore these factors, but split the sample in developed and developing countries. By doing so, they find evidence against Putnam but for Olson, as associational activity is *negatively* associated with investments in the Organisation for Economic Co-operation and Development (OECD) countries. Coates and Heckelman thus show that Putnam's positive view of networking effects is dominated by Olsonian 'institutional sclerosis' owing to organized special interests.

As the earlier studies summarized in Table 20.1 probably also failed to find evidence of Putnam's core hypothesis, the literature has in more recent years exclusively used the social trust component of social capital in growth regressions.

Table 20.1   Summarizing early studies

Study	Published in	Controls	Dependent
Helliwell and Putnam (1995)	*Eastern Economic Journal*	Initial GDP	Growth
Gratano et al. (1996)	*American Journal of Political Science*	Education, investment, initial GDP	Growth
Temple and Johnson (1998)	*Quarterly Journal of Economics*	Education, investment, initial GDP	Growth
Coates and Heckelman (2003)	*Public Choice*	Initial GDP	Investment
Knack (2003)	*Public Choice*	Education, property rights, inflation, initial GDP	Growth

20.2.2   More recent studies on specific trust effects

The paper by Stephen Knack and Philip Keefer (1997), which appeared in one of the absolute flagship journals of the social sciences – the *Quarterly Journal of Economics* – was the first to include separate measures of social capital in a standard empirical growth framework. Relying on the 29 country observations available at that time, it showed that social trust and a measure of 'civic norms' were positively associated with growth while Putnam's measure of associational density was not. As such, Knack and Keefer's paper was the first study to question Putnam's unitary view of social capital on a sound empirical basis, and thus to question Putnam's theoretical reliance on network effects. In other words, they split Putnam's network activity, social trust – defined as the confidence people have that strangers will behave according to shared honesty norms – and 'civic' or positive 'social' norms such as the (lack of) general acceptance of cheating on taxes, getting public benefits without being entitled to them and so on.

Knack and Keefer furthermore argued that part of this effect might come about due to their social capital measures, trust in particular, being associated with the level of human capital and the quality of governance (bureaucratic efficiency, legal quality), which the authors in a previous study had shown to be strong predictors of economic growth (Knack and Keefer, 1995); furthermore, they also discussed the potential influence of confidence in government, which they argued is associated with social trust. In a somewhat simpler research design, la Porta et al. (1997) also found some slightly weaker evidence for a growth effect of social trust as well as considerable effects on underlying factors of growth such as the quality of the legal system and average education. Both papers thus pointed to two potential transmission mechanisms for trust's effects on growth: education and institutional quality.[2]

A real worry at the time was that the trust results were fragile, proxying for other factors or simply spurious. British political scientist Paul Whiteley (2000) therefore replicated the basic findings of Knack and Keefer using a slightly larger sample (34 countries) and a broader trust measure, composed of trust in family, fellow national citizens, and people in general.[3] While he thus obtained qualitatively similar results to Knack and Keefer (1997), he also showed that once trust is included in the regression, the 'achievement motivation' factor of Gratano et al. (1996) turns out to be insignificant. In other words, the findings in the earlier study are most likely due to their specific cultural variable proxying for social trust. Finally, Whiteley also provided some simple robustness tests, showing that even though one might suspect that the effects of trust on growth might be due to the influence of single countries or groups of countries, this does not appear to be the case.[4]

At about the same time, Knack in a widely cited joint study with Paul Zak again replicated the main finding in Knack and Keefer (1997), this time in a sample of 41 countries (Zak and Knack, 2001). They first addressed the important question of causality: does social trust lead to growth or does growth lead to higher trust? Their results suggest that trust is *causally* associated with growth, and not just a consequence of economic development as was suggested in, for example, Jackman and Miller (1998).[5] Furthermore, they also provided the first formal attempt at modelling a theoretical mechanism connecting social trust with growth. In a simple economic growth model, they suggested that part of the effect comes about as investors have to either trust their investment brokers or bear monitoring costs. In a set of additional analyses, they provided evidence suggesting that social trust affects the investment rate in a way that supports this transmission mechanism.

As noted above, Knack (2003) in a subsequent study found no evidence for the effects of associational activity. However, his study did show an association between trust and growth very similar to that found in his joint work with Zak. Hence, even while social scientists supporting Putnam may surmise that trust simply proxies for the type of associational activity Putnam argued leads to growth, the 2003 study flatly rejected this option.

Two research teams, Beugelsdijk et al. (2004) and Berggren et al. (2008), have explored how robust the trust–growth association is, reaching slightly different results. Both papers employ extreme bounds analysis, which – put simply – tests to what extent an empirical result survives additional controls for potentially related effects. However, the two papers differ in important ways. First, Beugelsdijk et al. focus on growth over the period 1970–92, that is, their main focus is on long-run growth. Berggren et al., on the other hand, focus on growth in the periods 1970–90 and 1990–2000, that is, on growth in an intermediate time perspective. This might give rise to differences if social trust is a 'deep' determinant of growth. Second, Beugelsdijk et al. focus on the same 41-country sample as Zak and Knack (2001) while Berggren et al. employ both a 39-country sample and a 63-country sample for their later-period results, the latter encompassing more developing and postcommunist countries. Third, the latter also provides a somewhat more advanced test (called least trimmed squares) for the influence of small groups of country observations, that is, whether the overall findings survive the exclusion of country observations that might seem 'strange', instead of simply leaving out countries from the analyses.

The results of these robustness tests are nonetheless qualitatively similar. Beugelsdijk et al. note that the trust–growth association is very stable with respect to the inclusion of additional control variables and reasonably stable with respect to the inclusion of specific countries, and therefore judge social trust to be a better predictor of long-run growth than most other factors suggested in the growth literature. Berggren et al., on the other hand, find that social trust in their intermediate-run framework does not pass the standard robustness tests and is somewhat sensitive to the inclusion of certain countries. They nonetheless find reason to stress, as Beugelsdijk et al., that trust is a comparatively stronger growth factor than a number of other better known variables. Most notably, both studies find that social trust is a stronger direct predictor of growth than education even though a long tradition in economics treats this as a decisive factor in creating economic development.

Finally, only two studies so far try to estimate directly the influence of potential transmission channels, both of which are still unpublished but available as conference or working papers. Boulila et al. (2006) employ 35 country observations with full data coverage in the World Values Survey and perform a series of tests of the causality patterns between trust, potential transmission channels, and economic growth.[6] Their study comes to two conclusions. First, the estimates indicate that the main transmission channel of social capital works through trust leading to better quality of formal institutions, as also suggested by Porta et al. (1997) but contrary to the rather strong conclusion of Zak and Knack (2001) that formal institutions create trust. The second conclusion is that the analysis also leaves an unexplained part that could be attributed to a number of theoretical possibilities, for example those outlined in Whiteley (2000). As such, Boulila et al. (2006) find reason to stress the less tangible transmission channels such as the potential effects of social trust on overall transaction costs in the economy.

My own study on the topic, on the other hand, draws data from 64 countries in a set of similar tests (two-stage and three-stage regressions) to find evidence of two separate transmission channels that exhaust the full effects of social trust on growth (Bjørnskov, 2006b). The study first of all confirms the finding of Boulila et al. that social trust affects growth through its effects on institutional quality/governance, and thus again rejects the reverse causal direction implied by Zak and Knack (2001). However, I also find an indirect effect as trust is positively associated with educational attainment that in turn raises investment rates. In other words, I find concrete evidence of Coleman's (1988) original contribution that social capital is associated with educational attainment. This in turn causes higher investment rates, probably because the returns to investments increase with the tangible skills of the labour force.

While all these studies find that social trust increases economic growth, there are differences in the estimated size of this effect. In other words, while the studies all find that trust is positively associated with growth, they disagree as to how important it is. Table 20.2 lists the large-scale studies that have explored the effects of social trust/social capital on growth, including the four critical studies summarized in the next section. As can be seen in Table 20.2, virtually all cross-country studies focusing on the medium or long run find rather strong effects of social trust on the speed with which countries develop economically. The average effect in these studies implies that if social trust in a given country was increased by ten percentage points, the annual growth rate of GDP would increase by approximately half a percentage point. In other words, a ten-point trust difference between two otherwise average countries would in ten years grow to be a difference in average incomes of roughly US$300 per capita, as incomes in the country with average trust would increase by roughly US$900 while those in the higher-trust country would increase by roughly US$1200.

20.2.3 Questioning the findings

While the cross-country literature on medium to long-run growth surveyed in the above thus supports the notion that social trust is an important deep determinant of economic growth, five studies exist that question these effects. Four of those are on regional growth rates instead of national growth, which may be worth noting, while the last one consists of a recent small-sample panel data study.

The first critical paper dates back to 1996. In the paper, Helliwell (1996a)

Table 20.2   Growth effects of increasing social trust

Study	Published in	Controls	Growth effect
Helliwell (1996a)	NBER working paper	–	0%
Knack and Keefer (1997)	*Quarterly Journal of Economics*	Education, investment goods prices, initial GDP	56%
la Porta et al. (1997)	*American Economic Review*	Initial GDP	20%
Whiteley (2000)	*Political Studies*	Investment, education, initial GDP	40%
Schneider et al. (2000)	*European Journal of Urban and Regional Studies*	Investment, openness, initial GRP	Neg.
Zak and Knack (2001)	*Economic Journal*	Investment price, education, initial GDP	60%
Beugelsdijk et al. (2004)	*Oxford Economic Papers*	Robustness analysis	58%
Beugelsdijk and van Schaik (2005)	*European Journal of Political Economy*	Investment, schooling, agglomeration, initial GRP	0%
Berggren et al. (2008)	*Empirical Economics*	Robustness analysis	36%
Boulila et al. (2006)	Conference paper	–	16%
Bjørnskov (2006b)	Working paper	–	54%
Roth (2006)	Working paper	Education, investments, pop. growth, initial GDP	–

Note: The growth effects are calculated as the increase in the growth rate resulting from a one standard deviation shock to social trust, which in the largest sample available (in Bjørnskov, 2006b) is approximately an increase of 15 percentage points. Note that the effects of the robustness studies are averages, that GRP is gross regional product and that the Beugelsdijk and van Schaik study also controls for spatial spillovers.

strongly questions the effects of social trust across the nine US census regions and the Canadian provinces.[7] While he noted that the same exercise on Italian regions, which he had published the year before in collaboration with Robert Putnam, revealed significant growth effects of trust, the same effects could not be found in regional data from North America even though social trust differs markedly across states and provinces. Helliwell provides two potential reasons for the non-findings. First, since the 1950s in both countries income levels have converged at such a pace that it might make it impossible to discern any effects of social capital statistically. Secondly, Helliwell shows that social trust also has had migration effects in the US as states rich in trust also have had higher life quality. Consequently, people have tended to migrate to high-trust states with the effect that the trust differences across the states have not been stable while high-trust states still have had an inflow of productive workforce and thus a positive economic effect.

Schneider et al. (2000) subsequently performed a set of standard growth regressions using data from 58 European regions, as divided in accordance with the NUTS II categorization.[8] They found that while a variable measuring respondents' active interest in politics was positively associated with growth, social trust was *negatively* and significantly associated with regional growth rates in the period 1980-96. This puzzling result is hard to reconcile with the cross-country findings even if one asserts that social trust only affects national-level policies. It must, however, be stressed that Schneider et al. do not include data from the high-trust Nordic countries as Norway is not a member of the European Union (EU), Finland and Sweden became members too late to be included in these data, and regions in Denmark do not fit the NUTS II categorization. As such, the results may be biased downwards even though being thought-provoking.

Beugelsdijk and van Schaik (2005) provide a similar exercise with similar data from the European regions, including social trust and associational activity in standard regional growth regressions. However, they stress that no reliable data are available for gross regional product and therefore use regional average incomes *relative* to the national average income. Even while they fail to mention this point, they therefore analyse regional growth rates *relative* to national growth rates and not regional growth as such. Given the likely possibility that social trust mainly affects national-level policies, it may come as less of a surprise that they find no effects of trust. Beugelsdijk and van Schaik nonetheless find evidence supporting a positive influence of associational activity on regional relative growth. As such, even though the study does not note so, the results can be interpreted in two different ways: (1) as evidence confirming Putnam's hypothesis that associational activity has an economic value; or (2) evidence confirming an Olsonian hypothesis that regions rich in organizations get ahead of other regions in the country, thereby placing a negative effect on the rest of the country. The question therefore still remains whether associational activity has an economic value for a country as a whole. If not, Beugelsdijk and van Schaik actually show that organizationally dense regions exert a negative externality on the rest of the country in what can be termed a zero-sum economic game.

Casey (2004) instead explores the simple bivariate relations between economic performance across 11 British regions and three social capital indicators: (1) civic engagement; (2) overall associational activity including both civic and economic associations; and (3) social trust. While his study is not directly on economic growth, the persistence of the regional differences in the United Kingdom over several decades may make it reasonable to treat current economic performance as the *outcome* of past growth processes.[9] Given that this rather strong assumption can be accepted, the study confirms both strands of the social capital literature by finding positive correlations between economic performance and both trust and civic engagement, but also provides tentative support for the alternative Olson hypothesis, as economic engagement is negatively associated with performance. Casey thus provides what can be thought of as tentative evidence in favour of *all* hypotheses in the social capital literature: a positive effect of social trust and associational activity on long-run economic performance, but also a negative Olsonian effect of special interest groups on the economy.

Finally, Roth (2006) questions the entire literature – regional or national – by using a panel of 138 observations available from 1981 to 1999 from 43 countries. He thereby comes to focus on *changes* in social trust and their relation with changes in economic growth rates. As he organizes his data into five-year periods, he moreover focuses on the short run instead of the long run of most cross-sectional studies.

The interesting feature of Roth's paper is that he obtains two mutually conflicting results. When using total growth rates in the period 1990–2004, he finds a standard positive association between social trust and economic growth of the same size as most previous studies, and the same result applies when pooling growth in five-year intervals. When, on the other hand, he controls for time-invariant national features, Roth finds a significantly *negative* association between trust and growth. In other words, his findings suggest that in the short run, decreases in social trust are associated with increases in economic growth, which leads him to suggest 'that developed countries inherit too much trust' (Roth, 2006: 18). As such, Roth argues that citizens of rich countries may be *too* trusting, thereby making them particularly vulnerable to fraudulent behaviour, which can lead to deteriorating growth rates.

Whether his results using country fixed effects prove to be spurious are to be seen although they may seem puzzling given the evidence that social trust is indeed relatively invariant over time in most countries (cf. Bjørnskov, 2007). As such, for several reasons Roth's study raises more questions than it answers, not least because his country coverage is very narrow, which could bias his results in many ways. In addition, by focusing on *simultaneous* changes in growth and trust, he implicitly makes the assumption that trust immediately causes slower growth and that the changed levels afterwards have no growth effects over and above the short-run costs. Given the fairly strong cross-country evidence, it remains a possibility that increased trust slows down growth in the short run but leads to permanently higher growth after a transition period. Quite clearly, this remains an unsettled issue.

20.3   Social capital and growth – why, how much, and what now?

The academic interest in the concept of social capital has exploded since Robert Putnam's book on regional government in Italy appeared in 1993. Putnam conjectured that social capital – the mass of norms, trust and associational activity – was responsible for the historically higher growth rates in Northern Italy than in the comparatively poorer Southern parts, which gave rise to the present literature on the association between economic growth and social capital. The earliest literature, which Temple (2001) surveyed, provided what appeared to be tentative support for Putnam's notion.

As this chapter has shown, the large-scale cross-country studies exploring this association has established that countries' levels of social trust is indeed an important factor in explaining long-run growth patterns across the world. On the other hand, as in other empirical studies showing that Putnam's three social capital elements are actually separate social phenomena, it is telling that most growth studies tend not to support any effects of associational activity and only one study finds evidence of growth effects of positive social norms. These findings give rise to many directions for future research, because the social capital literature still leaves a number of questions unasked, some of them questions that we would not have asked before the empirical studies established the findings surveyed here: what are the transmission mechanisms connecting trust to growth, and how, if at all, can trust be created?

20.3.1   *Candidates for transmission mechanisms*

First, one must admit that even though we as a profession know – or at least strongly suspect – that social trust causes economic development, the question of exactly how this effect comes about is one that we are only beginning to explore. Two very recent studies attempt to estimate the transmission channels through which trust affects growth, suggesting that it mainly works through its influence on the quality of formal institutions such as the legal system and public bureaucracy, and through the general

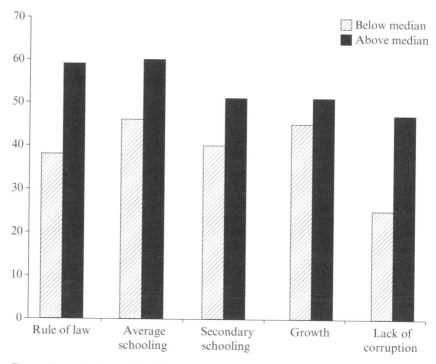

Figure 20.1   Trust-related differences

educational level of the population. More specifically, how these underlying effects come about is nevertheless still unknown, even though some studies have theorized on it.[10]

Yet, less tangible effects could also be responsible for part of the growth effects. Whiteley (2000: 448), for example, stresses that 'Trust promotes norms which abjure self-interest and reinforces the idea that individuals should act in the interests of the group in order to solve collective action problems', an idea often attributed to Alexis de Toqueville (2000) but already apparent with Adam Smith (1776). As such, Whiteley's main pick of a transmission mechanism is that social trust directly reduces transaction costs and principal–agent problems, and only indirectly affects growth by increasing investments in education and physical capital. A number of other studies have connected social trust to factors that one or more influential papers in the economic growth literature have argued are responsible for differences in national growth rates across the world. Figure 20.1, which plots the average growth rate along with average rule of law index, average schooling length, secondary schooling enrolment and the Transparency International lack of corruption index, provides a first glimpse of the broader set of possible transmission mechanisms.[11]

Another way to look at this question is to realize that economic growth can arise from two basic channels: factor accumulation, that is, increasing the inputs used in the production of goods – the labour force participation, usage of land and other resources and investments in real and human capital – or increases in *total factor productivity* (TFP), that is, increases in the efficiency with which resources are being used in production processes. Hence, even though some studies find social trust to be connected to factor accumulation – more education, higher investment rates – other studies find it to be associated with productivity. So far, only two studies have attempted to estimate the efficiency effects of social capital directly, and only in a very simple way. Helliwell (1996b) reports evidence that both trust and associational activity are negatively associated with how fast countries have been closing a gap in productivity with the US in the period 1962–89. He thus suggests that trust may *prevent* the adoption of modern production techniques. On the other hand, Knack and Keefer (1997) report evidence suggesting that trust is positively associated with the productivity of labour. Hence, the two studies point in completely different directions as one shows negative effects on efficiency growth while the other shows that workers in high-trust countries are more productive. The question as to whether social trust makes countries more efficient in particular remains open.

20.3.2   *Directions for future research*
Another related question is that of how social trust can be created, if at all. Indeed, possibly one of the most difficult questions in the research on the potential transmission channels connecting social trust and economic growth is that of causality. In particular, social scientists disagree which comes first: trust or institutional quality, and trust or education? Or do some different factors underlie the creation of trust? Figure 20.2 illustrates the causal relations found in Bjørnskov (2006b) in bold lines while also showing the potential opposite directions of the effects suggested in earlier work (dotted lines).

An influential strand of this literature represented by Rose-Ackerman (2001), Knack and Zak (2002) and Berggren and Jordahl (2006) argues that institutional quality creates trust by making life more predictable and safe. In an environment where you have confidence that the legal system will help you if someone violates your person or property, you are more likely to rationally trust other people. In other words, the Kierkegaardesque 'leap of faith' inherent in any act of trust becomes smaller when people are insured from the most severe consequences of having their trust betrayed.

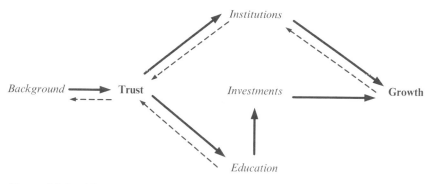

Figure 20.2   Transmission channels

However, the other strand of the literature argues for the reverse causal direction. The main argument is that if the economic transactions are protected by formal institutions such as the legal system, there is less need for interpersonal trust in such transactions. Hence, even if social trust may be important in the absence of formal institutions, increasing the quality of those institutions may not lead to more trust because it simultaneously undermines the necessity and returns to having trust (cf. Uslaner, 2002; Bjørnskov, 2007). The problem remains for this strand of the literature that if trust causes institutional quality and education, it may not be possible to create it through simple policy interventions, which obviously limits the readily applicable policy implications of the social capital literature.

As such, even if social trust is a deep determinant of economic growth, a number of questions remain open. Can social trust be consciously created? How does trust lead to economic growth? Are high-trust countries more efficient or do they simply use more inputs in their production? Are some conditions more enabling of the trust effects than others? And does the absence of results when using regional data suggest a real problem in the social capital literature or do they simply reflect that trust mainly affects factors operating at the analytical level of the nation state? The literature on social capital has come a long way since its inception, but profound insights are hopefully still lurking in the future.

Notes

*   I am grateful to the many people who commented on my work on the subject, in particular Niclas Berggren, Peter Nannestad, Martin Paldam, Fabio Sabatini and Gert T. Svendsen. Henrik Jordahl and Mogens Kamp Justesen, who helped complete the list of relevant papers and provided helpful comments on this chapter, deserve special mention. The usual disclaimer naturally applies.
1.   In the 25-country sample in Gratano et al. (1996), the correlation between both factors and the corresponding values of social trust is .43. Instead, using the factors scores

in Bjørnskov (2006a), the correlation between the achievement motivation factors in Gratano et al. and Bjørnskov's trust factor is .54 while the correlations between the other factors and the two factors in Gratano et al. are small. It may also be worth noting that the achievement motivation factor and the overall measure of associational density used in Knack (2003) are negatively related. As such, it must be emphasized that although the indicators used in the early studies make direct comparisons with the later literature difficult, the broad conclusions can be compared as long as the relations between the different measures are known.

2. To the non-technical reader, a transmission channel is the path through which an effect travels to reach its final destination. As an example, water contributes to plant growth through a transmission channel starting from the water being pumped into the plant by the roots – the first step of the channel – and ending by water reaching various parts of the plant where it performs its last job – the last step of the transmission channel.

3. The trust measure in Whiteley (2000) derives from a principal components analysis in which he forms a composite trust measure consisting of trust in family members, trust in fellow nationals and trust in people in general. As such, the results in Whiteley may not be perfectly comparable with the remaining literature.

4. One of the most frequently mentioned examples is that of Scandinavia where countries exhibit remarkably high levels of trust at the same time as the Nordic welfare state differs from other institutional designs. The possibility thus exists that the welfare state is responsible for high growth instead of the high levels of trust as what appears as effects of trust in the statistics could be driven by the welfare state. However, testing this properly reveals that it rather clearly is not the case.

5. It may be worth noting that in Bjørnskov (2007), I explore the alternative that growth causes trust by employing so-called instrumental variables estimates. The results reject this option, thus supporting Zak and Knack's conclusion that the relation is in one direction only, from trust to growth.

6. Specifically, Boulila et al. use instrumental variables and simultaneous equations regressions to control for reverse causality and to trace the influence of trust through a political-economic system.

7. One of the major problems with both Helliwell studies from 1996 (Helliwell, 1996a, 1996b) is that he writes about the results of estimating growth, but does not provide tables with the results. The reader therefore is not given the chance to assess the findings for himself.

8. NUTS II, the *Nomenclature des Unités Territoriales Statistiques II*, follows the regional divisions of federal states such as Germany and Italy and also divides other countries into similarly sized regions. Eurostat provides national accounting data for these regions.

9. Casey does not simply point to the stability of regional differences, but provides concrete evidence that while unemployment rates have converged since the 1970s, the differences between average incomes in British regions have remained remarkably stable. Whether the differences in social trust have been also been stable even though the average level has dropped remains an open question. All evidence in Casey (2004) must therefore be interpreted with considerable care.

10. Coleman (1988), in the first contribution of the 'modern' social capital literature, discusses how social capital can affect schooling outcomes. Knack (2002) provides some interesting thoughts on how social trust can affect political outcomes such as the long-run quality and capacity and effectiveness of public administration. However, in this context it may be worth mentioning that Beugelsdijk (2006) argues that social trust is so closely related to governance or well-functioning of institutions that the WVS trust indicator actually *measures* institutional quality.

11. Studies that find social trust to be negatively associated with corruption include Bjørnskov and Paldam (2004), Paldam and Svendsen (2002) and Uslaner (2002, 2004). As corruption problems are most often an indication of the failure of formal institutions, corruption to some extent belongs to a dimension of governance.

References

Adelman, Irma and Cynthia Taft Morris (1965), 'A factor analysis of the interrelationship between social and political variables and per capita gross national product', *Quarterly Journal of Economics*, **89**, 555–78.

Arrow, Kenneth (1972), 'Gifts and exchanges', *Philosophy and Public Affairs*, **1**, 343–67.

Barro, Robert (1991), 'Economic growth in a cross-section of countries', *Quarterly Journal of Economics*, **106**, 407–43.

Berggren, Niclas and Henrik Jordahl (2006), 'Free to trust: economic freedom and social capital', *Kyklos*, **59**, 141–69.

Berggren, Niclas, Mikael Elinder and Henrik Jordahl (2008), 'Trust and growth: a shaky relationship', *Empirical Economics*, **35**, 251–74.

Beugelsdijk, Sjoerd (2006), 'A note on the theory and measurement of trust in explaining differences in economic growth', *Cambridge Journal of Economics*, **30**, 371–87.

Beugelsdijk, Sjoerd and Anton B.T.M. van Schaik (2005), 'Social capital and growth in European regions: an empirical test', *European Journal of Political Economy*, **21**, 301–25.

Beugelsdijk, Sjoerd, Henry L.F. de Groot and Anton B.T.M. van Schaik (2004), 'Trust and economic growth: a robustness analysis', *Oxford Economic Papers*, **56**, 118–34.

Bjørnskov, Christian (2006a), 'The multiple facets of social capital', *European Journal of Political Economy*, **22**, 22–40.

Bjørnskov, Christian (2006b), 'How does social trust affect economic growth?', Aarhus School of Business, Department of Economics working paper 02-06.

Bjørnskov, Christian (2007), 'Determinant of generalized trust: a cross-country comparison', *Public Choice*, **130**, 1–21.

Bjørnskov, Christian and Martin Paldam (2004), 'Corruption trends', in Johann Graf Lambsdorff, Markus Taube and Mathias Schramm (eds), *The New Institutional Economics of Corruption*, London: Routledge, pp. 59–75.

Boulila, Ghazi, Lobna Bousrih and Mohamed Trabelsi (2006), 'Social capital and economic growth: empirical investigations on the transmission channels', paper presented at the fifth annual meeting of the European Economics and Finance Society, Crete, 18–21 May.

Bruni, Luigino and Robert Sugden (2000), 'Moral canals: trust and social capital in the work of Hume, Smith and Genovesi', *Economics and Philosophy*, **16**, 21–45.

Casey, Terrence (2004), 'Social capital and regional economies in Britain', *Political Studies*, **51**, 96–117.

Claibourn, Michele P. and Paul S. Martin (2000), 'Trusting and joining? An empirical test of the reciprocal nature of social capital', *Political Behavior*, **22**, 267–91.

Coates, Dennis and Jac C. Heckelman (2003), 'Interest groups and investment: a further test of the Olson hypothesis', *Public Choice*, **117**, 333–40.

Coleman, James S. (1988), 'Social capital in the creation of human capital', *American Journal of Sociology*, **94**, S95–S120.

Gratano, Jim, Ronald Inglehart and David Leblang (1996), 'The effect of cultural values on economic development: theory, hypotheses, and some empirical tests', *American Journal of Political Science*, **40** (3), 607–31.

Helliwell, John F. (1996a), 'Do borders matter for social capital? Economic growth and civic culture in U.S. states and Canadian provinces', NBER working paper, no. 5863.

Helliwell, John F. (1996b), 'Economic growth and social capital in Asia', NBER working paper, no. 5870.

Helliwell, John F. and Robert Putnam (1995), 'Economic growth and social capital in Italy', *Eastern Economic Journal*, **221**, 295–307.

Jackman, Robert W. and Ross A. Miller (1998), 'Social capital and politics', *Annual Review of Political Science*, **1**, 47–73.

Knack, Stephen (2002), 'Social capital and the quality of government: evidence from the U.S. states', *American Journal of Political Science*, **46** (4), 772–85.

Knack, Stephen (2003), 'Groups, growth and trust: cross-country evidence on the Olson and Putnam hypothesis', *Public Choice*, **117**, 341–55.

Knack, Stephen and Philip Keefer (1995), 'Institutions and economic performance: cross-country tests using alternative institutional measures', *Economics and Politics*, 7, 207–27.

Knack, Stephen and Philip Keefer (1997), 'Does social capital have an economic pay-off? A cross-country investigation', *Quarterly Journal of Economics*, 112, 1251–88.

Knack, Stephen and Paul J. Zak (2002), 'Building trust: public policy, interpersonal trust, and economic development', *Supreme Court Economic Review*, 10, 91–107.

la Porta, Rafael, Florencio Lobez-de-Silanes, Andrei Shleifer and Robert Vishny (1997), 'Trust in large organizations', *American Economic Review*, 87 (2), 333–8.

Olson, Mancur (1965), *The Logic of Collective Action: Public Goods and the Theory of Groups*, Cambridge, MA: Harvard University Press.

Paldam, Martin and Gert T. Svendsen (2002), 'Missing social capital and the transition in Eastern Europe', *Journal for Institutional Innovation, Development and Transition*, 5, 21–34.

Putnam, Robert (1993), *Making Democracy Work. Civic Traditions in Modern Italy*, Princeton, NJ: Princeton University Press.

Rose-Ackerman, Susan (2001), 'Trust and honesty in post-socialist societies', *Kyklos*, 54, 415–43.

Roth, Felix (2006), 'Trust and economic growth: conflicting results between cross-sectional and panel analysis', working paper, no. 102, the Ratio Institute.

Schneider, Gerald, Thomas Plümper and Steffen Baumann (2000), 'Bringing Putnam to the European regions: on the relevance of social capital for growth', *European Journal of Urban and Regional Studies*, 7, 307–17.

Smith, Adam (1776), *An Inquiry into the Nature and Causes of the Wealth of Nations*, Indianapolis: Liberty Fund.

Temple, Jonathan (2001), 'Growth effects of education and social capital in the OECD countries', *OECD Economic Studies*, 33, 57–101.

Temple, Jonathan and Paul A. Johnson (1998), 'Social capability and economic growth', *Quarterly Journal of Economics*, 113, 965–90.

Toqueville, Alexis de (2000), *Democracy in America*, Indianapolis: Hackett. First published in 1840.

Uslaner, Eric M. (2002), *The Moral Foundations of Trust*, Cambridge: Cambridge University Press.

Uslaner, Eric M. (2004), 'Trust and corruption', in Johann Graf Lambsdorff, Markus Taube and Mathias Schramm (eds), *The New Institutional Economics of Corruption*, London: Routledge, pp. 76–92.

Whiteley, Paul (2000), 'Economic growth and social capital', *Political Studies*, 48, 443–66.

Zak, Paul J. and Stephen Knack (2001), 'Trust and growth', *The Economic Journal*, 111, 295–321.

21 The macro perspective on generalized trust
Martin Paldam[1]

21.1 Introduction: the *G-trust* variable

One of the key variables in the social capital discussions is generalized trust.[2] To save words the average generalized trust for a country is termed *G-trust*. Table 21.1 gives the formulation and the aggregate of all answers in the World Value Surveys[3] that covers 188 pools in 83 countries during the last two decades of the twentieth century. Almost 30 per cent of the 255 399 answers say that 'most people can be trusted'. The individual country *G-trusts* are listed in the Appendix to this chapter.

Justified trust reduces transaction and monitoring costs. It saves time and trouble the higher it is in society. It is thus a factor of production – it will be demonstrated that it is not a powerful one.

Any country has a level of justifiable trust. If you have more trust than that, you are a 'sucker' that other people exploit. If you have less trust, you are a 'cynic', who creates costs and trouble for other people. Most prefer to deal with reasonable people, who are realistic by being close to the justifiable level. By the law of large numbers we get:

Thesis The *Rationality Theorem of Trust*: trust is rational for society at large.

We may measure it poorly and individuals deviate to both sides, but the *G-trust* is rational and an important characteristic of a society.

The *G-trusts* of the 188 polls are depicted on Figure 21.1, which shows that they have a strong correlation to *income*. The concept of income used is natural logarithm to *gdp*. Here gdp is GDP per capita – the distribution of that income is measured by another variable, Gini. The logarithm is used to make the income measure *relative*, so that an increase of 10 per cent appears equally big when it takes place at a low level or at a high level of income.

Figure 21.2 shows an almost equally strong correlation of *G-trust* and *LiSa*, high life satisfaction used in happiness research as a welfare measure (see Frey and Stutzer, 2002). The two – rather similar – figures allow us to make three observations about the *G-trust*:

Table 21.1   The G-trust *item in the World Value Surveys, 1980–2000*

Item A165: Generally speaking, would you say that most people can be trusted or that you need to be very careful in dealing with people?

Answer	Frequency	%
Most people can be trusted	75 466	29.55
Can't be too careful	179 933	70.45
Sum	255 399	100.00

Note: The WVS covers 188 polls covering 267 870 people in 83 countries in four waves. The *G-trust* item is included in all 188 polls done.

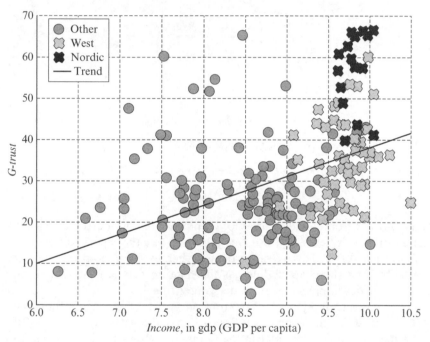

Figure 21.1   Scatter of the 188 G-trust *and* income

Obs 1:   It varies widely between countries, from close to 0 per cent to almost 70 per cent.

Obs 2:   It is related to other important matters in society as income and welfare.

Obs 3:   It contains a 'cultural' element so that some groups of similar countries cluster also as regards *G-trust*.

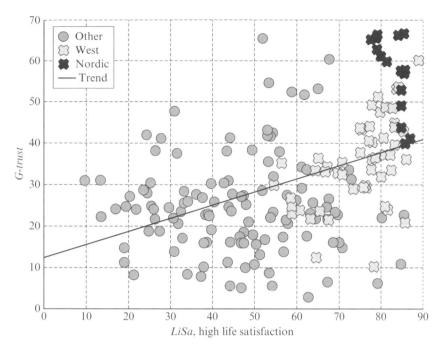

Note: Life satisfaction is missing in one of the 188 polls.

Figure 21.2   Scatter of the 187 G-trust and LiSa, high life satisfaction

As *G-trusts* from a wide variety of countries are considered, an organizing principle is necessary. For this purpose I use the theory of the *Grand Transition* (GT). This is the process, whereby poor countries become wealthy, and the chapter thus has the relation between the *G-trust* and economic development as the underlying theme.

The newest survey of the literature on growth and trust is Bjørnskov (Chapter 20 in this volume). It appears that the variables in Table 21.2 are the main ones that enter in the family of models tried, but a handful of other variables have been tried as well, though with less success, see, for example, Delhey and Newton (2005) and Bjørnskov (2006).

Section 21.2 offers a few notes on GT-theory. Figure 21.1 suggests that the Grand Transition is associated with a change from a *G-trust* of 10 per cent to about 40 per cent, that is, by 30 points. Section 21.3 discusses the time dimension: is trust a stable factor in the society? Section 21.4 looks at a set of the main variables – listed in Table 21.2 – which are related to the *G-trust* and discusses causality. Section 21.5 discussed the problematic

Table 21.2   The six variables considered in the paper

Variables	Definition	Source, see also netsources
G-trust	Generalized trust (see Table 21.1)	World Value Surveys
Income	Natural logarithm to gdp[1]	Maddison (2003)
LiSa	High life satisfaction	World Value Surveys
TI-hc	Honesty/corruption measure	Transparency International
Gini	Gini coefficient	World Development Indicators
Polity	Polity index for democracy/ dictatorship	Peace Research Institute, University of Maryland

Note: [1]gdp is GDP per capita. It is measured in PPP-prices.

relations between the *G-trust* and on one side development and on the other democracy. Section 21.6 contains concluding remarks.

21.2   A note on the Grand Transition and the GT-theory

The GT is the path of a country going from a low to high income, that is, from a poor less developed country (LDC) to a wealthy developed country (DC). The difference in gdp (in PPP prices) is about 40 times. Most socio-political and institutional variables also have large changes when countries go through the GT. Table 21.4 shows that this is indeed the case with the six variables we consider in the chapter.

For example, the *TI-hc* index (from Transparency International) for honesty–corruption has a range of 7.9, from about 1.8 in the most corrupt country to about 9.7 in the most honest. If we compare the *TI-hc* of the 10 per cent poorest to that of the 10 per cent richest countries, they differ by almost 7 points, so the GT is somehow associated with a transition of corruption of about 85 per cent of the observed range for the index, and the correlation between income and the *TI-hc* is 0.81 in the data sample of Table 21.5. Thus the two variables are strongly connected. Paldam (2002) argues that the main direction of causality is from the GT to corruption, and the arguments are supported by the causality analysis in Gundlach and Paldam (2007).[4]

The key idea of the GT-theory is that development is a path where the whole society changes in much the same way.[5] Thus the GT consists of a set of transitions in all proportions and institutions in society. The GT is not a unique path, but rather a zone around such a path. All countries deviate somewhat, but the GT does give a lot of convergence.[6] Thus, if we compare two countries that have both gone through the full transition, they are much more alike after the transition than they were before.

Poor countries have little physical and human capital, mortality is high, people live in the countryside, religiosity and corruption are high, and so on. Development changes all of that, and we speak of the urban transition, the demographic and the democratic transitions, the sectoral transition, the religious transition (or secularization), the transition of corruption, and so on. Here the GT-claim is that all these transitions are basically endogenous, but if one of them does not occur it turns into a development barrier.

Consequently, the GT is a highly simultaneous dynamic process, where everything depends upon everything else, resulting in much multicollinearity that makes it difficult to untangle causality as illustrated by a comparison of Figures 21.1 and 21.2.

GT-theory takes income/production as the most representative 'catch all' variable for the Grand Transition, and thus says that the key causal link expected is from the income level to the other variable. This is obviously a reduced form relation, as it covers the full web of simultaneity. All variables that are within the GT-complex can be used to explain each other – see, for example, Table 21.5. From nearly all sets of three variables from that table it is easy to present a model where any two of them explain the third in a seemingly convincing way.

Thus the key variable is income/production. We use the natural logarithm to gdp, which is the GDP (gross domestic product) per capita, as the best income variable.

Income is in gdp, where we use the gdp data, from Maddison (2001, 2003).

The concept of the Grand Transition thus implies that everything depends upon everything else. The big simultaneity has caused many researchers to look for a key: something that is *primary*, in the sense that it causes development, but is not caused by development. In order to work, such a key has to be reasonably stable and must differ substantially between countries.

21.3   The time dimension: are *G-trusts* stable?
The book that pushed the concept of social capital into its present status was Putnam (1993).[7] Two of its main ideas are:[8]

Claim 1   *Stability*: social capital stays stable for centuries. At present we take this claim to mean that the *G-trusts* are stable.

Claim 2   *Primacy*: social capital is primary to institutional and economic development.

Putnam's claim is that social capital is primary and hereby fills a crucial role. Claim 2 states that social capital is primary to institutions – or at least to the effectiveness of institutions.[9]

The same claim is also made – though in a different context – by Uslaner (2002) as regards *G-trust*. Uslaner takes *G-trust* back to the 'moral' foundation of society. It is thus something basic that even deserves to be primary.

To the extent that *G-trust* is a factor of production, the idea that *G-trust* changes slowly is a troubling idea, especially if it has to do with the moral foundation. Putnam's claim is that poor countries are deemed to remain poor for a long time to come, owing to something that was formed slowly centuries ago. Uslaner's idea leads to the conclusion that countries are – and maybe even deserve to be – richer *because* they have a sounder moral foundation.

Below we show that *G-trusts* do move more than enough to be endogenous, and that it is – at least in one important case – endogenous.[10]

21.3.1   The distribution of the changes 1: the numerical changes
Thus it is crucial if the *G-trust* is stable. The data contains 161 changes of the *G-trust* of a country, as seen in Table 21.3. The first three columns show average changes over five years, then the next two columns show average changes over ten years, and so on. The averages in row (A) are the absolute, while row (B) gives the average numerical changes. The last line in the table shows how many of the changes which exceeds 10 per cent – either upward or downward.

We first consider the numerical changes in row (B) of the table: two points are immediately obvious: (1) The five-year changes are rather large; (2) The changes are not much larger as the span increases to 10, 15 and 20 years.

This suggests that a good deal of the movements is due to measurement error, which includes short run reactions to 'random' events. Figure 21.3 gives an estimate of the order of magnitudes. The six dots are the unshaded averages from Table 21.3. If the average line is weighted with the number of observations it tilts marginally upward only. Thus Figure 21.3 suggests that the measurement error is of the order of magnitude of 5 percentage points:

Thesis 4   The *measurement error* in national polls of the *G-trust* is about 5 points.

Hence, the 'true' average movement in the *G-trust* is about 2 points over the 20 years or 0.1 points per year. This is rather modest – much as suggested by Thesis 2. But if the movement adds up over two centuries it does reach 20 points. Note also (from the last line of the table) that no less than 42 per cent of the 19 first differences that extends 20 years change more than 10 points, which is twice the likely measurement error. Consequently this measure of social capital is not stable.

Table 21.3   All changes ΔG that can be calculated from the 188 polls

About	5 years			10 years			15 years	20 years
Waves	W2–W3	W3–W4	All	W1–W2	W2–W4	All	W1–W3	W1–W4
App. years	1990–95	1995–2000	5 year	1982–90	1990–2000	10 year	1982–95	1982–2000
Number	31	41	72	20	39	59	11	19
(A) Average ΔG	−4.49	1.10	−1.31	3.08	−3.54	−1.30	−4.50	−0.57
(B) Average |ΔG|	5.76	6.73	6.91	5.44	7.25	7.39	5.68	8.74
Fraction of |ΔG| >10%	19.4%	14.6%	16.7%	10.0%	23.1%	18.6%	18.2%	42.1%

Note: The table covers all 161 pairs of *G-trusts* for the same country that can be calculated from the 188 polls.

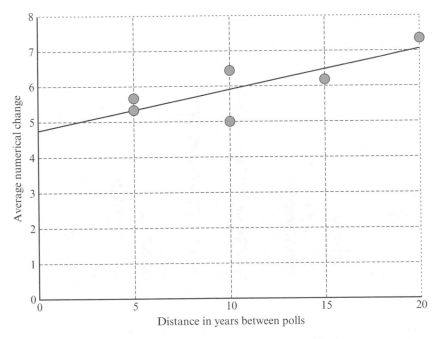

Figure 21.3   The average numerical G-trust *changes,* |ΔG|

If we take into account that the Grand Transition in most cases takes two to three centuries and that is associated with a change of about 20 points change in the *G-trust*, there is really nothing in these orders of magnitudes that prevents the full change in the *G-trust* shown on Figure 21.1 to be endogenous.

21.3.2   The distribution of the changes 2: the absolute changes
With such a large measurement uncertainty it is difficult to determine how much the results change. However, it may help to look at the absolute changes.

Figure 21.4 compares the distribution of the differences. It is obvious that they are almost as large over 20 years as over five years. Roughly half of the changes are above the measurement error. Hence, we know that these data show large, but not very *systematic* movement.

21.3.3   A large scale social experiment: the transition from socialism[11]
The period from 1982 to 2000 contains a large social experiment: The collapse of communism in East and Central Europe and the transition to a Western (capitalist/democratic) society. The collapse happened very

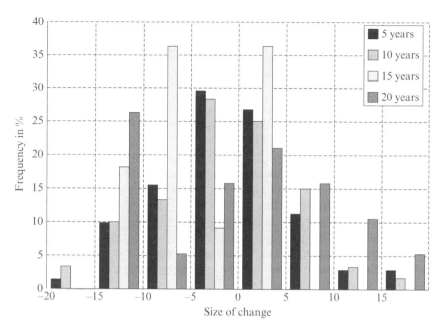

Figure 21.4   The distribution of all changes over 5, 10, 15 and 20 years

fast, during 1988–90. It came unpredicted, and it caused a large U-shaped economic crisis (Figure 21.5), where full recuperation has only taken place after 2000 in most of the countries, and it is not yet complete in some of the transition countries. It seems reasonable to treat the transition as a large, sudden, exogenous shock to the system. It is documented rather well in the World Value Survey (WVS) data, with two or three observations from 19 countries for waves two to four. However, there is only one observation from 1982, namely from Hungary, which was a unique communist country.[12]

The figure is calculated by taking the (one) change from 1982 to 1990 and adding the change from 1990 to 1995 (that is for 12 countries), and finally adding the change from 1995 to 2000 (for 19 countries). So it is all the available information, and the last two sections of the curve are reasonably well determined. From 1989 to 1991 was the time of the big political collapse and the starting year of the transition downswing, so it is unfortunate that the change out of the old system is only indicated by one observation.

It builds trust in the data that the path of the life satisfaction variable is similar to the one of the *G-trust*, although the *G-trust* moves a little less and turns a little slower. If we take these data to be representative, they show a large effect on the *G-trust* of the transition from communism. Also, we

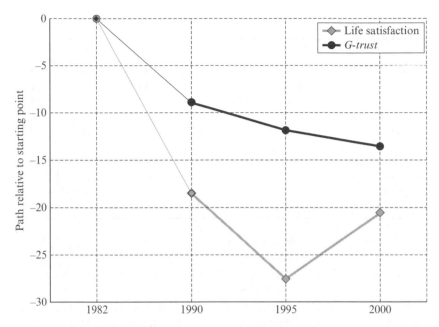

Figure 21.5   *The* G-trust *and life satisfaction during the transition from communism*

predict that (most of) the return to the previous levels of life satisfaction and trust will take place in the first decade of the twenty-first century.

We know only the level of *G-trust* in one old communist country and in two Asian communist countries. However, we also have three polls for the *G-trust* in Belarus, which is the ex-communist country that has changed least, so perhaps we can assess that the level in the old communist bloc in East and Central Europe was between 35 and 40. Thus the fall was about 30 per cent owing to transition that generated a fall of income that peaked at about 30 per cent in the average country. This suggests a strong endogenous reaction of *G-trust* to the economy.

The greatest 'social experiment' in our data consequently shows that the *G-trust* can have large endogenous movements. Thus we are not able to say that *G-trust* is fully primary – perhaps it is not primary at all.

21.4 The web of connections between the *G-trust* and other variables
The research on trust has found several variables that are related to the *G-trust*. The five main ones included are – as defined in Table 21.2:

Income, or production is (the natural) logarithm to gdp as explained. *LiSa*, high life satisfaction. *TI-hc*, Transparency International's honesty/

Table 21.4   Correlation matrix – pure cross-country

ti	G-trust	Income	LiSa	TI-hc	-Gini	Polity
G-trust	1	**0.38**	**0.45**	**0.49**	**0.52**	0.13
Income, Ln gdp	**0.38**	1	**0.73**	**0.81**	**0.33**	**0.71**
LiSa, High Life satisfaction	**0.45**	**0.73**	1	**0.71**	0.07	**0.46**
TI-hc, index for honesty/corruption	**0.49**	**0.81**	**0.71**	1	**0.29**	**0.57**
−1 x *Gini* coefficient	**0.52**	**0.33**	0.07	**0.29**	1	**0.25**
Polity index, last 10 years	0.13	**0.71**	**0.46**	**0.57**	**0.25**	1
Average correlation	0.39	0.59	0.48	0.57	0.29	0.42

Note: Variables in bold are significant at the 5% level.

corruption index. It is scaled from 10 for full honesty to 0 for full corruption. Here only data for the last period are available. *Gini*, the Gini coefficient. Here, the data has many gaps, and time series are not available. As it should be negatively correlated to the *G-trust*, the sign has been reversed, and we thus use – *Gini*. *Polity*, the Polity index of democracy/dictatorship, is scaled from 10 for a perfect democracy to −10 for a perfect dictatorship. An average for the last ten years is used.

The expected result from Grand Transition theory is that the variables contain much simultaneity, in the sense that all other variables contribute somewhat to explaining income, and the income contributes much to explaining all other variables. However, we hope to find that some variables are only indirectly related to income. That is, if *A*, *B* and *C* are used to explain income, then *C* is not needed, in the sense that *C* is insignificant, and contributes nothing to the R^2 when it is adjusted for degrees of freedom. In this case we say that *A* and *B* encompass *C*.

21.4.1   Correlations
Table 21.4 is a correlation matrix between these variables. Due to the scaling all coefficients of correlation in the table should be positive, as they actually are. Only two of the correlations are insignificant. The least significant is the one between the *Gini* and *LiSa*. This is puzzling, but not central to our story. It is much more important for that story that the correlation between the *G-trust* and the *Polity* index is insignificant.

Income is the variable that is most correlated to all the others, as it should be by the Grand Transition theory. The variable that has the least correlation to the others is the *Gini*. This is not unexpected given the quality of

Table 21.5   The links to income, *the central variable*

(1)	(2)	Corre-lation	Size in % of range	(1) → (2) Via growth	Comments to growth connection	(2) → (1) GT-pattern
G-trust	Income	0.38	50	Some	Social capital is a factor of production	Yes?
LiSa	Income	0.73	70	No?	Perhaps a link via productivity	Yes
TI-hc	Income	0.81	85	Weaker	Weak effect from TI → investment → growth	Yes
Gini	Income	0.33	50	Dubious	Much researched, but weak results	Yes
Polity	Income	0.71	60	Weak	Borderline significant	Yes

Note: Column (4) considers the difference between the value of the said index in the poorest 10 per cent and in the richest 10 per cent of the countries relative to the range observed for the index.

measurement for that variable, and the literature. The second least correlated coefficient is *G-trust*, which also has a large measurement problem.

As at most four observations are available, it is difficult to establish causality in most cases. However, many of the cells in the table have been the subject of a whole little literature, and some of this research has reached agreement.

21.4.2   The links to income via growth

By far the most researched connections are those to income via growth, dealt with in Table 21.5. The effects of hundreds of variables on the growth rate have been studied by a range of methods, and large-scale attempts have been made to determine which of these variables have a robust impact.[13] This literature shows that a few more than ten variables have a robust effect on growth, while another five to ten are borderline robust. None of our variables are among the robust ones, but two are in the borderline group. These results are helpful when it comes to untangling a pattern such as the one we consider.

Consider the observation that income and democracy have a correlation of no less than 0.71. The growth literature tells us that the many attempts to find an effect of democracy on growth have only led to a weak effect, see Doucouliagos and Ulubasoglu (forthcoming) for a new meta study

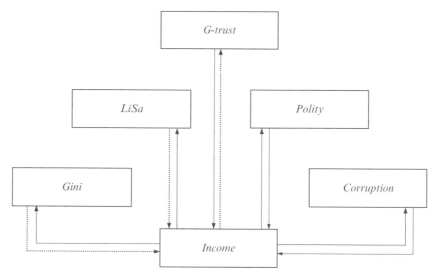

Note: See Figure 21.6b for some corrections, where arrows are dominated by the links which are not included.

Figure 21.6a   The causal links from/to income

covering the literature. At least ten other effects are stronger, and there is a considerable residual factor. So there is no way the causality from democracy to income can explain more than a small fraction of the correlation. Thus the large correlation has to be mainly a GT-effect, that is, a Grand Transition effect.

This is only a reduced form conclusion, for there are a number of possible channels whereby the Grand Transition may lead to democracy. One may be a pure demand effect saying that the income elasticity of people's demand for democracy is larger than 1. Another explanation goes via the vast expansion in education that is associated with the GT, and so on. However, our analysis contains no education variable. This allows us to start with the causal connections from/to income as drawn on Figure 21.6a. *Income* influences all the other variables, but they do in turn all influence *income* a little, as per the theory of the Grand Transition.

21.4.3   All links
The five links the other way have been investigated by a set of regression reported in Paldam (2008). This has given the pattern of causality shown in Figure 21.6b. There are still some uncertain links, which are indicated with a question mark and, of course, more variables may be included.

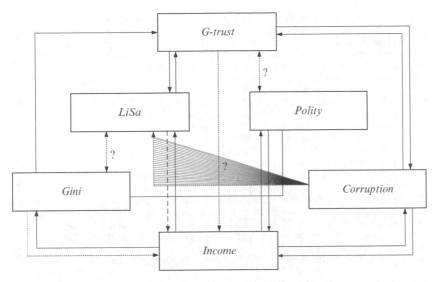

Figure 21.6b   All causal links between the six variables

Note that several of the links from Figure 21.6a are dominated by other stronger links.

How much can we trust the causal directions indicated? I am fairly confident that those on Figure 21.6a are trustworthy. Also the causal links from the *Gini*, *LiSa* and *TI-hc* to *G-trust* in Figure 21.6b seem reasonably well justified.[14]

21.4.4   *The links between the* G-trust *and* income

The correlation between *income* and *G-trust*, is 0.38 in Table 21.4 – also, the relation looks convincing in Figure 21.1. There is no doubt that the two variables are connected. However, the *income/G-trust*-relation is dominated by some of the other stronger relations. Thus we have to conclude that most of the connections are indirect and more of a general GT-nature than due to direct causality.[15]

The causality: *G-trust* ➤ *income*. A substantial literature from Putnam (1993), Dasgupta and Seargeldin (2000) and, in particular, Grootaert and Bastelaer (2002) argues that social capital plays a role in development. It is easy to argue that social capital is a factor of production. Social capital – certainly trust – makes transactions faster and cheaper, it reduces monitoring costs, and so on.

Thesis 2 and thesis 3 above claim that *G-trust* is *the* primary factor that explains development. This should give a clear causal link from the *G-trust*

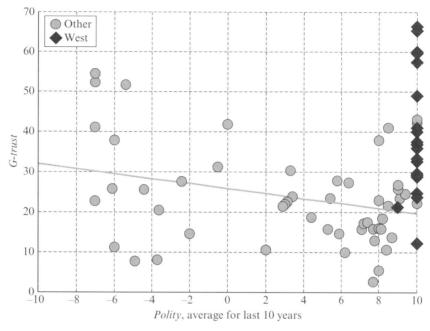

Figure 21.7   Scatter of the 80 G-trust *and the* Polity *index for the degree of democracy*

to income, but our finding is that the link is encompassed by other links. It must mean that the causal link operates through other variables. Thus it is difficult to argue that social capital is *the* primary factor for development we are all looking for. It rather appears as another endogenous factor in the complex causal net of the Grand Transition. This does not reject that it is an important variable to study.

The causality: *income → G-trust*. Here it appears that the link goes via other variables, and is a typical GT-effect. It is interesting that the link goes via two seemingly independent variables, the *Gini* and *LiSa*, so that *income → Gini → G-trust* and *income → LiSa → G-trust*. As the two intermediate variables are independent, we are dealing with a complex web where the influence of additional variables is likely to be involved.

21.4.5   The links between the G-trust *and* Polity, *the degree of democracy*
We then turn to the links between *G-trust* and *Polity*. Here the correlation is only 0.13 in Table 21.4, and Figure 21.7 shows a picture corresponding to Figures 21.1 and 21.2. It looks much less convincing. Also, it is strange that the line through *Other* countries has a negative slope, while the line

through all points (not included) has almost the same slope, but positive. Neither slope is significant. Also, the *Polity/G-trust* coefficients are weak in the statistical analysis.

The causality: *G-trust* ➤ *Polity*. A considerable literature discusses social capital as an important prerequisite for democracy, in particular see Deth et al. (2002). Also, many development aid agencies argue that it is important for development to build civic society and social capital. Thus we expect a positive link from *Polity* to *G-trust*. Our findings suggest that this link must be indirect and weak.

The causality: *Polity* ➤ *G-trust*. It is one of the cornerstones in the argument in Putnam (1993) that the difference in social capital in the north and south of Italy is due to the political history of the two parts of Italy in the previous 500 years, where especially the dictatorship in the Kingdom of the two Sicilies in the south prevented the development of social capital, while the north of Italy had a complex set of regimes that were often less oppressive, and hence permitted the building of social capital.

This idea has been developed in Paldam and Svendsen (2000, 2002) to explain the difference between West and East Europe, due to the democratic history of the West and the communist dictatorship in the East. This led to the dictatorship theory of social capital, which is that dictatorial regimes fear voluntary cooperation between their citizens and thus try to bring such cooperation under the control of the political system. Also, it is well known that many dictators use fear as a deliberate instrument.

Thus I expected to find a clear connection from *Polity* to *G-trust*. However, this did not work.[16] Part of the reason may be that the transition from communism in East and Central Europe was associated with a rather large depression, a chaotic period of rent grabbing, and a wave of high inflation that caused a large drop in life satisfaction. So perhaps a clearer connection may still appear over a longer perspective.

21.5   Conclusion: the trust transition
The chapter is a mixture of a survey and a basic exposition of the macro data on generalized trust, *G-trust*. It covers only one of the main series used to measure social capital. However, a great deal of data has been collected on this variable. The chapter has looked at the dynamics of the measured *G-trust*s, and at its relation to five other series.

The organizing framework is the theory/empirics of the Grand Transition, which sees the process of development as a broad transition of all socio-political and economic variables in society. All these transitions add up to the Grand Transition. It is not helpful to say that everything depends on everything else, so the literature on development has searched for *the* key to development: something that is primary to all other factors. Since Putnam (1993) it has been frequently claimed that social capital is that key.

It is clear from the results in the chapter that the data show a transition from low trust in poor societies to high trust in rich societies. Thus, there is a transition of trust. The chapter discusses how the transition of trust relates to development.

The chapter demonstrates that the measures of *G-trust* have a considerable element of measurement error, and though it normally changes slowly it does change enough so that it is perfectly possible that the trust transition is fully endogenous. Thus the Putnam claim that social capital is a deep constant in society and hence primary does not appear to hold as regards the *G-trusts*.

In the analysis of the relation between generalized trust and other variables a number of connections were found strongly significant: The main variables that appear to be causal to social capital is the *Gini* and *LiSa* (high life satisfaction), but also corruption matters. My interpretation of the literature (including my own research) is that these variables all have *income* as a key causal factor. Thus it is clear that the *G-trust* enters into the complex.

So whereas *G-trust* is an interesting variable that plays a role in the Grand Transition, it is hardly the key causal factor for the transition.

Notes

1. The chapter has been presented at the workshop and summer school on 'Social capital, corporate social responsibility and sustainable economic development'. I am grateful to the discussants, especially to Giacomo degli Antoni, Leonardo Becchetti and Felix Roth. I have also benefited from discussions with Gert Tinggaard Svendsen and Christian Bjørnskov. A longer version with the statistical analysis is published as Paldam (2008).
2. See Fukuyama (1995). The present chapter does not discuss the definitions of social capital; see Paldam (2000).
3. For easy replicability the World Values Survey data are used throughout this chapter. The data are documented in Inglehart et al. (1998, 2004). I use the full data set as available from www.worldvaluessurvey.org.
4. Some other authors claim that the reverse causality dominates, see, for example, Lambsdorff (2007). People who have worked with these things have not yet managed to agree on the causal structure explaining the strong correlation.
5. See Gundlach and Paldam (2007) for a discussion of GT-theory, and the relation between this theory and the main alternative, the Primacy of Institutions theory.
6. We do not observe convergence in cross country samples because countries are at very different stages in the GT.
7. Putnam's definition of social capital is network density, though he discusses its relation to trust. Thesis 3 is defended in Helliwell and Putnam (1995).
8. I should state that this is the standard interpretation of Putnam's book, and that it does not speak of *G-trust*, but of network density. Also, Putnam (2000) describes a large fall in social capital in the US over a couple of decades.
9. Consequently Putnam's claim encompasses the *primacy of institutions hypothesis* claim by Acemoglu et al. (see their 2005).

10. The argument contradicts the results cited in Bjørnskov (Chapter 20 in this volume) and Uslaner (2002) arguing the trust is primary.
11. This subsection uses the term *transition* for the transition from socialism.
12. Hungary was the communist country that was allowed the most market institutions and the most contacts with the West, also, it had a relatively easy transition to a market system.
13. See Doppelhofer et al. (2004) and Sturm and Haan (2005).
14. The significant coefficient to the Gini is common in this research; see, for example, Uslaner (2002) and Leigh (2006).
15. See also Berggren et al. (2007) for a study of the robustness of the relation.
16. An alternative way to study this connection is to analyse the relation between *G-trust* and economic freedom directly as done by Berggren and Jordahl (2006), who do find considerable correlation.

References

Acemoglu, D., S. Johnson and J. Robinson (2005), 'Institutions as the fundamental cause of long-run growth', in P. Aghion and S.N. Durlauf (eds), *Handbook of Economic Growth*, Amsterdam: North-Holland, pp. 385–472.
Berggren, N. and H. Jordahl (2006), 'Free to trust: economic freedom and social capital', *Kyklos*, **59**, 141–69.
Berggren, N., M. Elinder and H. Jordahl (2007), 'Trust and growth: a shaky relationship', IFN working paper, no. 705, Stockholm.
Bjørnskov, C. (2006), 'Determinants of generalized trust: a cross-country comparison', *Public Choice*, **130**, 1–21.
Dasgupta, P. and I. Serageldin (eds) (2000), *Social Capital: A Multifaceted Perspective*, Washington, DC: World Bank.
Delhey, J. and K. Newton (2005), 'Predicting cross-national levels of social trust: global pattern or Nordic exceptionalism?', *European Sociological Review*, **21**, 311–27.
Deth, J.W. van, K. Maraffi, K. Newton and P.F. Whiteley (eds) (2002), *Social Capital and European Democracy*, Abingdon: Routledge.
Doppelhofer, G., R.I. Miller and X. Sala-i-Martin (2004), 'Determinants of long-term growth: a Bayesian averaging of classical estimates (BACE) approach', *American Economic Review*, **94**, 813–35.
Doucouliagos, H. and M. Ulubasoglu (forthcoming), 'Democracy and economic growth: a meta-analysis', *American Journal of Political Science*.
Frey, B.S. and A. Stutzer (2002), *Happiness and Economics: How the Economy and Institutions Affect Human Well-being*, Princeton, NJ: Princeton University Press.
Fukuyama, F. (1995), *Trust*, New York: Simon & Schuster/Free Press.
Grootaert, C. and T. van Bastelaer (eds) (2002), *The Role of Social Capital in Development*, Cambridge: Cambridge University Press.
Gundlach, E. and M. Paldam (2007), 'Two views on institutions and development: the Grand Transition vs the Primacy of Institutions', working paper 2007-2, Department of Economics, Aarhus University; and working paper 1315, Institute for the World Economy, Kiel.
Helliwell, J.F. and R. Putnam (1995), 'Economic growth and social capital in Italy', *Eastern Economic Journal*, **21**, 295–307.
Inglehart, R., M. Basáñez and A. Moreno (eds) (1998), *Human Values and Beliefs. A Cross-Cultural Sourcebook*, Ann Arbor, MI: University of Michigan Press.
Inglehart, R., M. Basáñez, J. Díez-Medrano, L. Halman and R. Luijks (eds) (2004), *Human Beliefs and Values. A Cross-Cultural Sourcebook Based on the 1999–2002 Value Surveys*, México, DF: Siglo XXI Editiones.
Lambsdorff, J.G. (2007), *The Institutional Economics of Corruption and Reform*, Cambridge: Cambridge University Press.
Leigh, A. (2006), 'Does equality lead to fraternity?', *Economics Letters*, **93**, 121–5.

Maddison, A. (2001), *The World Economy: A Millennial Perspective*, Paris: OECD.

Maddison, A. (2003), *The World Economy: Historical Statistics*, Paris: OECD.

Paldam, M. (2000), 'Social capital: one or many?', *Journal of Economic Surveys*, **14**, 629–53.

Paldam, M. (2002), 'The big pattern of corruption. Economics, culture and the seesaw dynamics', *European Journal of Political Economy*, **18**, 215–40.

Paldam, M. (2008), 'Generalized trust. The macro perspective', forthcoming in volume from the conference 'Social Capital, Corporate Social Responsibility (CSR) and Sustainable Economic Development', organized by Lorenzo Sacconi, Giacomo Degli Antoni and Marco Faillo, Trento, July.

Paldam, M. and G.T. Svendsen (2000), 'An essay on social capital: looking for the fire behind the smoke', *European Journal of Political Economy*, **16**, 339–66.

Paldam, M. and G.T. Svendsen (2002), 'Missing social capital and the transition in Eastern Europe', *Journal for Institutional Innovation, Development and Transition (IB Review)*, **5**, 21–34.

Putnam, R.D. (1993), *Making Democracy Work: Civic Traditions in Modern Italy*, Princeton, NJ: Princeton University Press.

Putnam, R.D. (2000), *Bowling Alone. The Collapse and Revival of American Community*, New York: Simon & Schuster.

Sturm, J.-E. and J.D. Haan (2005), 'Determinants of long-term growth: new results applying robust estimation and extreme bounds analysis', *Empirical Economics*, **30**, 597–617.

Uslaner, E.M. (2002), *The Moral Foundation of Trust*, Cambridge and New York: Cambridge University Press.

Net links

Author's working papers are at www.martin.paldam.dk.

Maddison's data set is at www.ggdc.net/maddison/.

Polity is at www.cidcm.umd.edu/inscr/polity.

Transparency International is at www.transparency.org/.

World Development Indicators are at http://devdata.worldbank.org/dataonline/.

World Values Survey is available from www.worldvaluessurvey.org.

Appendix

Table 21A.1   All G-trusts *in the World Values Survey – first four waves*

	Country	1982	1990	1995	2000
1	Albania			27.0	24.4
2	Algeria				11.2
3	Argentina	26.1	23.3	17.6	15.9
4	Armenia			24.7	
5	Australia	48.2		40.1	
6	Austria		31.8		33.4
7	Azerbaijan			20.5	
8	Bangladesh			20.9	23.5
9	Belarus		25.5	24.1	41.9
10	Belgium	29.2	33.5		29.2
11	Bosnia			28.3	15.8
12	Brazil		6.5	2.8	
13	Bulgaria		30.4	28.6	26.8
14	Canada	48.5	53.1		37.0
15	Chile		22.7	21.4	23.0
16	China		60.3	52.3	54.5
17	Colombia			10.8	
18	Croatia			25.1	20.5
19	Czech Rep.		27.4	28.5	24.6
20	Denmark	52.7	57.7		66.5
21	Dominican Rep.			26.5	
22	Egypt				37.9
23	El Salvador			14.6	
24	Estonia		27.6	21.5	23.5
25	Finland		62.7	48.8	57.4
26	France	24.8	22.8		21.4
27	Georgia			18.7	
28	Germany	32.3	32.9	33.3	37.5
29	Greece				23.7
30	Hungary	33.6	24.6	22.7	22.4
31	Iceland	39.8	43.6		41.1
32	India		35.4	37.9	41.0
33	Indonesia				51.6
34	Iran				65.4
35	Iraq				47.6
36	Ireland	41.1	47.4		36.0
37	Israel				23.5
38	Italy	26.8	35.3		32.6
39	Japan	41.5	41.7	42.3	43.1

Table 21A.1   (continued)

	Country	1982	1990	1995	2000
40	Jordan				27.7
41	Korea S	38.0	34.2	30.3	27.3
42	Kyrgyzstan				16.7
43	Latvia		19.8	24.7	17.1
44	Lithuania		30.8	21.9	25.9
45	Luxembourg				24.8
46	Macedonia			8.2	13.7
47	Malta	10.1	23.8		20.8
48	Mexico		33.5	31.2	21.8
49	Moldova			22.2	14.6
50	Morocco				22.8
51	Netherlands	44.8	53.5		60.1
52	New Zealand			49.1	
53	Nigeria		23.2	17.3	25.6
54	Norway	60.9	65.1	65.3	
55	Pakistan			18.8	30.8
56	Peru			5.0	10.7
57	Philippines			5.5	8.6
58	Poland		31.8	17.9	18.4
59	Portugal		21.7		12.3
60	Puerto Rico			6.0	22.6
61	Romania		16.1	18.7	10.1
62	Russia		37.5	23.9	24.0
63	Saudi Arabia				53.0
64	Serbia			30.2	25.8
65	Singapore				14.7
66	Slovakia		22.0	27.0	15.9
67	Slovenia		17.4	15.5	21.7
68	South Africa		29.1	15.9	13.1
69	Spain	35.1	34.2	29.7	36.3
70	Sweden	56.7	66.1	59.7	66.3
71	Switzerland		42.6	37.0	
72	Taiwan			38.2	
73	Tanzania				8.1
74	Turkey		10.1	5.5	16.0
75	Uganda				7.8
76	UK	43.1	43.7	29.6	28.9
77	Ukraine			31.0	27.8
78	Ulster	44.0	43.6		39.5
79	Uruguay			21.6	

Table 21A.1 (continued)

	Country	1982	1990	1995	2000
80	USA	40.5	51.1	35.9	36.3
81	Venezuela			13.8	15.9
82	Vietnam				41.1
83	Zimbabwe				11.2
	Number	21	43	54	70
	Average	38.9	34.8	25.8	28.4
	Standard deviation	11.5	14.5	13.2	14.7

Note: Every poll in the WVS includes this item. The list thus also covers the 188 pools of the WVS data set.

PART VIII

MEASUREMENT

22 Mixed methods assessment[1]
Veronica Nyhan Jones and Michael Woolcock

Introduction

Social capital, in its best forms, contributes to economic, social and political development by enabling information-sharing, mitigating opportunistic behavior and facilitating collective decision-making (Woolcock and Narayan, 2000). Although theoretical and conceptual debates properly continue, and will be unlikely to ever reach a clean resolution (Szreter and Woolcock, 2004), these have occurred alongside efforts to enhance the quality and scale of empirical data available to assess the claims (and counterclaims) made regarding the efficacy of social capital, especially in the field of international development. The range of data sources now spans the full gamut of social science, from national household surveys, historical records and field experiments to case studies, key informant interviews and ethnographic investigations; all have been deployed in an effort to better understand the nature and extent of social relations in particular communities, its trajectories over time, and its consequences for human welfare.

Most research conducted on social capital in developing (and, for that matter, developed) countries, however, has been conducted using a single methodological instrument (for example, surveys or participant observation). With the notable exception of Anirudh Krishna (2002, 2007), researchers have worked predominantly with either quantitative or qualitative methods, a consequence being that opportunities for fruitful exchange between approaches have been lost. Moreover, the actual content of the tools used to collect data on social capital – as opposed to the final results obtained from them – have rarely been disclosed or made available to other researchers to draw upon. Seeking to correct this gap, this chapter provides a summary of two instruments (or 'toolkits'), one qualitative and the other quantitative, that have been field-tested by various groups of researchers inside and outside the World Bank.

Far from being the 'final word' on the subject of measurement, the approaches introduced here are more of a 'second word' – that is, an attempt to integrate and build upon select methods used by a 'first generation' of social capital researchers working on various issues in developing countries. The ultimate goal is to work iteratively towards approaches that are increasingly more refined, valid, reliable and useful. As with the conceptual debates discussed above, we have little expectation that a consensus set of 'gold standard' tools will ever emerge; rather, more modestly, our hope is that social capital researchers in diverse contexts will not have to start from scratch each time they begin their work, but will increasingly be able to access effective, field-tested tools and instruments. To this end, and because the salience and manifestations of social capital are so context dependent, researchers working with the materials outlined here are strongly advised to undertake the hard work of judiciously adapting the various component elements to suit the questions and situation at hand; as such, these tools are inherently and perpetually 'work in progress'.

In the sections that follow, we frame the measurement issues around six dimensions of social capital: (1) groups and networks; (2) trust and solidarity; (3) collective action and cooperation; (4) social cohesion and inclusion; (5) information and communication, and (6) empowerment and political action. We present first the qualitative approaches to assessing these six dimensions, and then the quantitative, though ideally both should be incorporated as necessary, whether sequentially or in parallel, given the type of research question being considered. In practice, however, the distinctive skill sets associated with each approach, plus limited time and resources, mean that only one approach tends to be adopted for a specific study. This practice is especially unfortunate in development studies, since the issues under investigation are typically very complex and rarely map neatly or obviously onto a single discipline or methodology. To make use of social capital research as part of efforts to improve people's lives, practitioners require a full understanding of how and why local social processes work the way they do.

In order to adequately understand development issues and establish a firm basis on which to draw project and policy recommendations, data that offers both context-specific 'depth' (usually obtained via qualitative methods) and generalizable 'breadth' (usually obtained via quantitative methods) is required (Bamberger, 2000; Rao and Woolcock, 2003). 'Social capital' is one such complex issue that benefits from the coherent integration of qualitative and quantitative approaches. Researchers in the field are thus encouraged to adopt the combination of qualitative and quantitative methods that best correspond to the specific nature of the issues under investigation. There are numerous ways to go about this; one example might be to conduct qualitative focus group discussions to feed into the design of a quantitative survey. Similarly, working with community groups later in the process to map local assets such as public meeting places may help to triangulate and interpret some survey findings. Ideally an iterative process including both qualitative and quantitative methods would be used, but when this is not feasible some infrequent, low-cost use of mixed methods can still add significant value. Given the context- and resource-specific nature of designing a mixed methods approach, it is difficult, and probably unrealistic, to prescribe such sequencing options in this chapter but other references exist to help in the design and implementation phases (for example, Tashakkori and Teddlie, 1998; Rao and Woolcock, 2003).

Assessing social capital across six dimensions

Given the diverse views in the literature about the key features (even the ontological status) of 'social capital', we are only too aware of the equally contentious views regarding whether and how social capital can be measured (and the additional concerns raised by having any such ventures endorsed by the World Bank; see Bebbington et al., 2004). Our view is that these differences are best resolved through practice rather than isolated or abstract theoretical debate, and through making increasingly more informed choices about which approaches to use in a given context on the basis of the best information and resources available. The overriding approach we have taken to organizing the vast empirical literature is to conceptualize social capital as a household or community-level (that is, 'micro') variable (as opposed to something that is a feature of, say, an entire nation) with six non-exclusive, overlapping dimensions. These dimensions were chosen inductively, largely for convenience and ease of exposition, though they are certainly consistent with the broader empirical literature. Importantly, they are also products of the valuable guidance we received from the two advisory groups[2] that reviewed the source documents from which this chapter is derived.

We provide here a brief summary of what each dimension covers, and then proceed to explore different approaches to assessing it, first qualitatively and then quantitatively. Schematically, the dimensions reflect the group membership characteristics and subjective perceptions of trust and norms that are most commonly associated with social capital (dimensions 1 and 2), the main ways in which social capital operates (dimensions 3 and 4), and the major areas of application or outcomes (dimensions 5 and 6).

Dimension 1: *groups and networks.* The questions here consider the nature and extent of a household member's participation in various types of social organizations, community activities and informal networks, and the range of contributions that one gives and receives from them. It also considers the diversity of a given group's membership, how its leadership is selected, and how one's involvement has changed over time.

Dimension 2: *trust and solidarity.* In addition to the canonical trust question asked in a remarkable number of cross-national surveys over many years, this category seeks to procure data on trust towards neighbors, key service providers and strangers, and how these perceptions have changed over time.

Dimension 3: *collective action and cooperation.* This category explores whether and how household members have worked with others in their community on joint projects and/or in response to a crisis. It also considers the consequences of violating community expectations regarding participation.

Dimension 4: *information and communication.* This category of questions explores the ways and means by which poor households receive information regarding market conditions and public services, and the extent of their access to communications infrastructure.

Dimension 5: *social cohesion and inclusion.* 'Communities' are not single entities, but rather are characterized by various forms of division and difference that can lead to conflict. Questions in this category seek to identify the nature and extent of these differences, the mechanisms by which they are managed, and which groups are excluded from key public services. Questions pertaining to everyday forms of social interaction are also considered.

Dimension 6: *empowerment and political action.* Individuals are 'empowered' to the extent they have a measure of control over institutions and processes directly affecting their well-being (World Bank, 2002). The questions in this section explore household members' sense of happiness, personal efficacy, and capacity to influence both local events and broader political outcomes.

Using qualitative methods to assess social capital in context
The case for qualitative research rests on the unique and important insights that it brings in its own right and, secondarily, on its capacity to address the weaknesses of quantitative approaches. Indeed, the respective strengths and weaknesses of qualitative and quantitative approaches are largely complementary – that is, the weaknesses of one approach can be compensated for by the strengths of the other. Qualitative tools can be used to explore issues of process and causality that cannot be inferred from quantitative data alone. Qualitative methods also allow unanticipated responses and issues to arise.

The tools summarized below are most closely associated with the qualitative tradition. While they can be used in their own right, ideally these tools should be part of a broader, integrated methodological strategy for researching social capital. The text that follows is not intended to provide 'how-to' guidance on the use of these tools. Rather, it seeks to give the reader a broad understanding of which qualitative tools are relevant to different aspects of social capital research. Additional resources are cited that offer detailed, practical instructions on how to apply these tools.

The first category of qualitative methods can be referred to as participatory approaches (Mikkelsen, 1995; Narayan, 1995; Robb, 2002). Introduced to scholars and practitioners largely through the work of Robert Chambers (see Chambers, 1997; Kumar and Chambers, 2002), participatory techniques – such as Rapid Rural Appraisal (RRA) and Participatory Poverty Assessments (PPA) – help development agencies learn about local poverty and project impacts in cost-effective ways.

The Rapid Rural Appraisal is especially useful with illiterate respondents (not all of whom are poor), allowing researchers to learn about their lives using simple techniques such as wealth rankings, oral histories, role-playing, games, small group discussions, transect walks (see the following section) and village map drawings. These techniques permit respondents who are not trained in quantitative reasoning, or who have little education, to provide meaningful graphic representations of their lives in a manner that gives outside researchers a quick snapshot of certain aspects of their living conditions.

The RRA can be said to involve *instrumental* participation through novel techniques that enable researchers to better understand their subjects. A related approach is to use *transformative* participation techniques, such as Participatory Rural Appraisal (PRA), the goal of which is to facilitate a dialogue (rather than extract information) that assists the poor and others to learn about themselves and thereby gain new insights that lead to social change ('empowerment').[3] In PRA exercises, a skilled facilitator helps communities generate tangible visual diagrams of the processes that lead to deprivation or illness, strategies that are used in times of crisis, and fluctuation of resource availability and prices across different seasons. Eliciting information in this format helps the poor to conceive of potentially more effective ways to respond to the economic, political, and social challenges in their lives in ways that are not obvious *ex ante*. The process and findings provide a potentially enduring foundation for community groups to discuss action and change beyond the scope of a specific research agenda.

Participatory methods are conducted in groups. It is essential, therefore, that participants include representatives from each of the major subgroups in a community. The idea is that if a group reaches consensus on a particular issue after some discussion, this consensus will then be representative of views in a given community, be it a village or slum neighborhood, because outlying views would have been set aside in the process of debate. For this technique to work, the discussion must be extremely well moderated. The moderator must be sufficiently dynamic while also deftly able to steer the discussion in a meaningful direction, to navigate his or her way around potential conflicts and, in the end, establish consensus. The moderator's role is thus key to ensuring that high-quality data is gathered from a group discussion – an inadequate or inexperienced moderator can affect the quality of the data in a manner that is much more acute than an equivalently inadequate interviewer working with a structured quantitative questionnaire. Even with a skilled facilitator, pre-existing relationships between local parties can either enable or undermine productive discussions.

Another important qualitative tool is the key-informant interview, that is, an interview with someone who is a formal or informal community leader or who has a particular perspective relevant to the study, such as women or members of an ethnic minority. Such interviews may be recorded using notes or a tape recorder. The researcher may find that it takes some time to establish rapport with the interviewee; some local greeting rituals may also need to be followed. Though some respondents may be intimated by recording technologies, some may find it cathartic to tell their story to someone from outside the community. Expectations and issues such as anonymity must be clearly addressed at the start. Life histories and open-ended personal interviews are additional tools that have long been used in qualitative research. Indeed, it can be illuminating to interview the same people over time, just as it is useful to repeat household surveys.

The qualitative investigator can also engage in varying degrees of 'participant observation' as an actual member (for example, a biography of growing up in a slum), a perceived actual member (for example, a spy or a police informant in a drug cartel), an invited long-term guest (for example, an anthropologist) or a more distant and detached short-term observer of a specific community. A final qualitative approach is textual analysis. Historians, archeologists, linguists and scholars in cultural studies use such techniques to analyse various forms of media, ranging from archived legal documents, newspapers, artifacts and government records to contemporary photographs, films, music, websites and television reports. This approach provides interesting insights into local culture and politics untainted by the presence of a researcher.

Applying qualitative tools to the six dimensions of social capital
Each of the qualitative tools described in the previous section can be used to research the effects of social capital in poor and non-poor communities alike. The subsections that follow provide analytical frameworks – that is, key questions for focus group discussions and interviews, as well as potentially useful group activities – for each of the six dimensions of social capital outlined in the introduction to this chapter. Because the six dimensions overlap in practice, some questions appear under more than one dimension. By the same token, an inquiry regarding one dimension may shed light on the other dimensions. Naturally, not all questions and issues included in the analytical frameworks that follow will be appropriate in every case. The entries below are therefore not intended as direct

questions to respondents, but to better focus the research team on relevant concerns. Effective (and ethical) data collection respects the valuable time of respondents, simplifies the analysis phase, and forces additional rigor on the conceptual design of research. It may also save money.

Dimension 1: groups and networks   Understanding the groups and networks that enable people to access resources and collaborate to achieve shared goals is an important part of the concept of social capital. Informal networks are manifested in spontaneous and unregulated exchanges of information and resources within communities, as well as efforts at cooperation, coordination and mutual assistance that help maximize the utilization of available resources. Informal networks can be connected through horizontal and vertical relationships and are shaped by a variety of environmental factors, including the market, kinship and friendship.

Another kind of network consists of associations, in which members are linked horizontally. Such networks often have clearly delineated structures, roles and rules that govern how group members cooperate to achieve common goals. These networks also have the potential to nurture self-help, mutual help, solidarity and cooperative efforts in a community. 'Linking' (vertical) social capital, on the other hand, includes relations and interactions between a community and its leaders and extends to wider relations between the village, the government, and the marketplace.

The questions listed below are intended to get at the nature and extent of peoples' participation in various types of social organizations and networks (formal and informal), and the range of transactions that take place within these networks. The questions also consider the diversity of a given group's membership and how its leadership is selected.

Focus on several formal and informal groups and summarize their explicit and implicit functions. How often are the groups activated? Are informal groups based on occasions (for example, weddings, births, or deaths)? What other triggers bring members of a group together?

What is exchanged (for example, goods, services, favors, information, goods, moral support, and so on) in community groups or networks?

What are the most important aims of the exchange (for example, to meet basic needs, increase income, meet basic social obligations, maintain or expand potentially useful relationships, or some combination thereof)?

What characteristics are most valued among network members (for example, trustworthiness, reciprocity, cooperation, honesty, community respect, and so on)?

Who are the most socially or economically isolated people in the community? How does this isolation correlate with the kind or extent of networks to which these people belong?

Who plays a leadership or mobilizing role in the groups or networks? How are they selected?

Dimension 2: trust and solidarity   This dimension of social capital refers to the extent to which people feel they can rely on relatives, neighbors, colleagues, acquaintances, key service providers and even strangers, either to assist them or (at least) do them no harm. Adequately defining 'trust' in a given social context is a prerequisite for understanding the complexities of human relationships. Sometimes trust is a choice; in other cases, it reflects a necessary dependency based on established contacts or familiar networks. Distinguishing between these two ends of the continuum is important for understanding the range of people's social relationships and the ability of these relationships to endure difficult or rapidly changing circumstances.

How would you define trust? What are some examples?

How long have people in a given neighborhood or community lived together? How well do they know one another?

Have new groups recently entered the community (for example, refugees or economic migrants)?

To what institutions (formal or informal) do people turn when they have individual or family problems?

On whom do people rely for different kinds of assistance (for example, goods, labor, cash, finding employment, entering university, and so on)?

How is trust distributed in the community (for example, primarily within extended families or clans or through specific networks and/or localities)?

Do patterns of mistrust and suspicion exist between households or among groups?

Dimension 3: collective action and cooperation   Collective action and cooperation are closely related to the dimension of trust and solidarity, however, the former dimension explores in greater depth whether and how people work with others in their community on joint projects and/or in response to a problem or crisis. It also considers the consequences of violating community expectations regarding participation norms. To understand this dimension, interviews with formal and informal community leaders or leaders of non-governmental organizations (NGO), associations, unions or other groups (key-respondent interviews) can prove very useful for triangulating data collected in focus group discussions.

Describe recent examples of collective action that have taken place in the
   community (or a segment of the community). What was the course and
   outcome of these activities?

Who initiated the activities? How were people mobilized?

Do social, cultural, or legal constraints limit the participation of specific
   groups (for example, women, young people, poor people, minorities,
   and so on)?

Are some groups, neighborhoods, and/or households more likely than
   others to work together, and if so, why?

Are some groups, neighborhoods, and/or households more likely to exclude
   themselves or be excluded from collective activity, and if so, why?

What kinds of constraints limit peoples' ability or willingness to work
   together (for example, lack of time, lack of trust or confidence in outcomes, suspicion toward the mobilizers, and so on)?

What are the social sanctions for violating expected norms of collective
   action in the community?

Dimension 4: information and communication   Increasing access to information is frequently recognized as a central mechanism for helping poor
communities strengthen their voice in matters that affect their well-being
(World Bank, 2002). The questions below are intended to explore the
ways and means by which households receive and share information
regarding such issues as the community at large, market conditions, and
public services, as well as the extent of their access to communications
infrastructure.

Inventory the existing communication sources, their actual and perceived
   reliability, veracity, availability and the extent to which these sources
   are used in practice.

What are the preferred local sources and channels of information?

What informal sources of information exist in the community? Which
   members of the community are included or excluded from such sources?

What information is available through different networks? To different
   households and/or groups (that is, is there differential distribution
   within the community)?

What information is not available to different households and/or groups
   (that is, what are the limits of differential distribution within the
   community)?

Dimension 5: social cohesion and inclusion   Social cohesion and inclusion are closely related to the previous four dimensions of social capital,
but focus more specifically on the tenacity of social bonds and their dual

potential to include or exclude members of community. Cohesion and inclusion can be demonstrated through community events, such as weddings and funerals, or through activities that increase solidarity, strengthen social cohesion, improve communication, provide learning for coordinated activities, promote civic-mindedness and altruistic behavior, and develop a sense of collective consciousness.

Are there recurring disagreements in networks and groups, or even demonstrated conflict?

What community patterns of differentiation and exclusion exist with respect to opportunities, markets, information and services?

What prevents public services and expenditures from reaching the poorest and most vulnerable groups? Are the reasons related to ethnicity, gender, a political agenda, or geographic isolation?

What are the patterns of inclusion and/or exclusion in political participation?

How often do people from different social groups intermarry?

What are the triggers for everyday conflict among members of a network and/or group (for example, resource competition, serious social cleavages, socio-economic inequities)?

What kinds of mediation have taken place to help the community resolve conflicts?

Have these worked? Why? For how long?

Dimension 6: empowerment and political action   Individuals are empowered to the extent that they have a measure of control over the institutions and processes that directly affect their well-being (World Bank, 2002). The social capital dimension of empowerment and political action explores the sense of satisfaction, personal efficacy and capacity of network and group members to influence both local events and broader political outcomes. Empowerment and political action can occur within a small neighborhood association or at broader local, regional or national levels. Each level has its own importance and should be considered separately, as well as in conjunction with the others. This dimension also considers social cleavages, whether related to gender, ethnicity, religion, regionalism or other factors. Key-informant interviews with political and labor leaders, together with representatives of the judicial system and media, are also important for exploring this dimension.

How do customary, informal laws constrain or facilitate the ability of citizens to exert influence over public institutions?

How do formal laws constrain or facilitate the ability of citizens to exert influence over public institutions?

To what extent can members of a community hold public institutions and officials accountable for their actions?

What kinds of formal and informal mechanisms are available to individuals and groups to demand accountability of local leaders and officials?

Which groups or segments of the community have the greatest influence over public institutions?

What is the source of influence of these groups (for example, group size, ability to mobilize members or expand member base, connections to power elite, economic importance)?

Which groups have the least influence over public institutions and why?

Applying quantitative tools to the six dimensions of social capital
These six dimensions can also be assessed quantitatively, using some form of household survey.[4] The value of quantitative data is that it can be readily aggregated, allowing for broad generalizations to be drawn over time and space about large numbers of people; as such, they are especially useful for determining the impact of projects and policies. In certain respects, survey data can also be seen as more 'objective', since the household survey format ensures that there is less scope for pressure from other community members to influence how questions are answered.

Examples of questions from each of the six dimensions are included below. Together, these questions constitute the 'core' list of 27 questions identified by the team members and advisory group for the quantitative component of the larger project. A full list of 95 questions is provided in the Social Capital Integrated Questionnaire (SC-IQ) (see Grootaert et al., 2004), but given that not all research teams will have the time, resources or inclination to ask this many questions, the 27 'core' questions represent our best collective effort to reduce the list, if required, to its most essential components.

Dimension 1: groups and networks
Social capital, in its best forms, helps the dissemination of information, reduces opportunistic behavior and facilitates collective decision-making. The effectiveness with which social capital, in the form of the associations and networks, fulfills this role depends on many aspects of these groups, reflecting their structure, their membership and the way they function. The SC-IQ makes it possible to describe organizations along three key dimensions, namely, the density of membership, the diversity of membership and network characteristics.

1. At the level of households, the *density of membership* is measured by the average number of memberships of each household in existing organizations (this can be normalized by household size). This basic

indicator can be cross-tabulated by location (region, province, urban/ rural) or socio-economic characteristics of the household (income group, age and gender of the head of household, religion, ethnic group) to capture the distribution of memberships. The indicator can also be broken down by type of organization. A functional classification focuses on the prime objective of the association (education, health, credit, and so on). Another useful classification refers to the scope of the group: whether groups operate only in the community, are affiliated with other groups (inside or outside the community) or are part of a federated structure. Groups with linkages often have better access to resources, especially from outside the community, such as from government or NGOs. Using information on memberships, organizations can also be classified as to whether they represent primarily bonding, bridging, or linking social capital (World Bank, 2000).

2. The SC-IQ data make it possible to assess the internal *diversity of membership* according to nine criteria: kinship, religion, gender, age, ethnicity/linguistic group, occupation, education, political affiliation and income level. Diversity information can be used separately or combined in an index. For example, a 'diversity score' can be calculated for each organization, ranging from 0 to 9. These scores can be averaged overall or weighted to emphasize the most important organizations to which households belong. It is not immediately obvious whether a high degree of internal diversity is a positive or negative factor from the point of view of social capital. One could argue, on the one hand, that an internally homogeneous association would make it easier for members to trust each other, to share information, and to reach decisions. On the other hand, these members may also have similar information so that less would be gained from exchanging information. Furthermore, the coexistence of a series of associations that are each internally homogeneous but along different criteria could render the decision-making process at the community level more difficult. Analysis in several countries has suggested that internally diverse associations yield higher levels of benefits than others, although homogeneous associations make it easier to bring about collective action (Grootaert, 1999, 2001).

3. Regarding *networks*, the SC-IQ provides items of information: the size of the network, its internal diversity and the extent to which it would provide assistance in case of need. Because 'network' is a difficult concept to define concretely in the context of a household survey, a pragmatic approach has been taken: a network is seen as a circle of 'close friends' – that is, people one feels at ease with, can talk to about

private matters, or call upon for help. The size of the network then is captured by the number of such close friends. The usefulness of the network is assessed by asking the respondents whether they could turn to the network in a series of hypothetical emergency situations. The answers to these questions can be aggregated to yield a 'mutual support score' for the network. Diversity is assessed in a simpler way than was the case for associations, by focusing only on whether the network consists of people with different economic status. This is a key feature to determine the network's ability to provide resources to the respondent in case of need, and thus the network's usefulness in the management of risk.

Sample survey questions

1. I would like to ask you about the groups or organizations, networks, and associations to which you (or any member of your household) belong. These could be formally organized groups or just groups of people who get together regularly to do an activity or talk about things. Of how many such groups are you or any one in your household a member?

2. Of all these groups to which you or members of your household belong, which one is the most important to your household?

3. Thinking about the members of this group, are most of them of the same . . .
   A. Religion
   B. Gender
   C. Ethnic or linguistic background/ race/caste/tribe

4. Do members mostly have the same . . .
   A. Occupation
   B. Educational background or level

5. How frequently does this group work with or interact with groups outside the village/neighborhood?
   Never   Rarely   Occasionally   Frequently

6. About how many close friends do you have these days? These are people you feel at ease with, can talk to about private matters, or call on for help.

7. If you suddenly needed to borrow a small amount of money [Rural: enough to pay for expenses for your household for one week; Urban: equal to about one week's wages], are there people beyond your immediate household and close relatives to whom you could turn and who would be willing and able to provide this money?
   Definitely   Probably   Unsure   Probably not   Definitely not

Dimension 2: trust and solidarity

Measurement of the more cognitive aspects of social capital in the SC-IQ is organized around the themes of trust and solidarity. Trust is an abstract concept that is difficult to measure in the context of a household question-naire, in part because it may mean different things to different people. The SC-IQ approach therefore focuses both on generalized trust (the extent to which one trusts people overall) and on the extent of trust in specific types of people. Trust is also viewed in the context of specific transactions, such as lending and borrowing. Because of the difficulties in measuring trust, the questions in this section have a degree of redundancy to them. In part, this serves the purpose of cross-validating the responses to different questions. It is possible to tabulate the answers to each trust question against the usual spatial or socio-economic characteristics, but because of the complexity of the concept of trust, it is recommended to use factor analysis or principal compo-nent analysis to identify any underlying common factors across the different questions. This approach has been successfully used in empirical work. For example, a study on trust in Uganda found that from a series of questions on trust, three factors emerged which identified three different dimensions of trust: trust in agencies, trust in members of one's immediate environment and trust in the business community (Narayan and Cassidy, 2001).

Sample survey questions

8. Generally speaking, would you say that most people can be trusted or that you can't be too careful in dealing with people?

    People can be trusted   You cannot be too careful

9. In general, do you agree or disagree with the following statements?

    A. Most people in this village/neighborhood are willing to help if you need it.

    B. In this village/neighborhood, one has to be alert or someone is likely to take advantage of you.

    Agree strongly   Agree somewhat   Neither agree nor disagree
    Disagree somewhat   Disagree strongly

10. How much do you trust . . .

    A. Local government officials?

    B. Central government officials?

    To a very great extent   To a great extent   Neither great nor small extent   To a small extent   To a very small extent

11. If a community project does not directly benefit you but has benefits for many others in the village/neighborhood, would you contribute time or money to the project?

    Will not contribute time   Will not contribute money
    Will contribute time   Will contribute money

Dimension 3: collective action and cooperation
Collective action is the third basic type of proxy indicator for measuring social capital. The usefulness of this indicator stems from the fact that in the vast majority of settings, collective action is possible only if a significant amount of social capital is available in the community. The major exception occurs in totalitarian societies where the government can force people to work together on infrastructure projects or other types of common activities. Thus, the validity of the collective action indicator as a measure of social capital needs to be evaluated against the political context of a society. The indicators of structural and cognitive social capital discussed previously can be helpful here. Collective action is an important aspect of community life in many countries, although the purposes of the action may differ widely. In some countries, collective action consists primarily of community-organized activities for building and maintaining infrastructure, and for providing related public services. In other countries, collective action is more politically oriented and used primarily to lobby elected officials to provide more services to the community.

The collective action section of the SC-IQ aims to collect: the extent of collective action, the type of the activities undertaken collectively, and an overall assessment of the extent of willingness to cooperate and participate in collective action. Each of these variables can be cross-tabulated against the usual set of spatial and socio-economic variables to obtain a pattern of the incidence of collective action. More interestingly perhaps is the cross-tabulation of collective action variables against the indicators of structural and cognitive social capital discussed previously. This would reveal whether communities with a high density of organizations and/ or high levels of trust also display higher levels of collective action. Any correlations revealed by such tabulations could usefully be the subject of further multivariate analysis.

Sample survey questions
12. In the past 12 months did you or any one in your household participate in any communal activities, in which people came together to do some work for the benefit of the community?
     Yes   No (skip to question 14)
13. How many times in the past 12 months?
14. If there was a water supply problem in this community, how likely is it that people will cooperate to try to solve the problem?
     Very likely   Somewhat likely   Neither likely or unlikely
     Somewhat unlikely   Very unlikely

Dimension 4: information and communication
Module 4 of the SC-IQ has a simple structure: it is a list of sources of information and means of communication. Analysis of this information is equally straightforward. Each item can be cross-tabulated separately against spatial and socio-economic variables to identify whether certain areas or groups have better or worse access to information and communication. The identified pattern can be compared against the pattern of structural and cognitive social capital established on the basis of the previous modules. If areas of low social capital are found to have poor access to information and communication, a further inquiry into possible causality might be warranted.

The information from module 4 can also be aggregated, either at the household level or at the community level, to obtain a single score for information and communication access. Factor analysis or principal component analysis are suitable techniques to that effect. Additional questions enable an assessment of the relative importance of groups and networks as sources for important information compared with 'impersonal' sources such as newspapers or television. Information on government activities and markets is directly relevant for the generation of income and/or for non-monetary aspects of well-being, and can therefore be included as an explanatory variable in multivariate analysis of household well-being.

Sample survey questions
15.   In the past month, how many times have you made or received a phone call?
16.   What are your three main sources of information about what the government is doing (such as agricultural extension, workfare, family planning, and so on)?

Relatives, friends and neighbors   Community bulletin board
Local market   Community or local newspaper   National newspaper   Radio   Television   Groups or associations   Business or work associates   Political associates   Community leader   An agent of the government   NGOs   Internet

Dimension 5: social cohesion and inclusion
Module 5 of the SC-IQ brings together three related topics: inclusion, sociability, and conflict and violence. The section on inclusion ranges from general perceptions of social unity and togetherness of the community to specific experiences with exclusion. The respondent is first asked whether there are any divisions in the community and, if so, what characteristics cause it. Questions on exclusion from services at the level of the community

are followed by more direct questions, such as whether the respondent has ever been the victim of exclusion. The most policy-relevant information will come from the detailed cross-tabulation of the presence of exclusion by type of service against the characteristics deemed to be the grounds for exclusion. This tabulation will reveal whether exclusion exists across the board, owing to characteristics such as gender or ethnicity, or if the reasons for exclusion vary by type of service or activity. Such information has a high diagnostic value in identifying sources of social stress in the community. To compare the incidence of exclusion across communities, an 'exclusion score' can be constructed by adding up the answers from several questions.

One of the positive manifestations of a high level of social capital in the community is the occurrence of frequent everyday social interactions. This 'sociability' can take the form of meetings with people in public places, visits to other people's homes or visits from others into one's own home and participation in community events such as sports or ceremonies. The section on sociability in module 5 covers each of these situations. In order to distinguish whether these daily social interactions are of the bonding or bridging variety, questions are asked whether the people with whom one meets are of the same or a different ethnic or linguistic group, economic status, social status or religious group. The diversity of social interactions can usefully be compared to the diversity of the membership of associations (covered in module 1). Put together, these two items of information on diversity give a good picture of the internal divisiveness or cohesiveness of a community and whether bonding or bridging social capital predominates.

The presence of conflict in a community or in a larger area is often an indicator of the lack of trust or the lack of appropriate structural social capital to resolve conflicts, or both. The SC-IQ brings together three important items of information on conflict and violence: the extent and trend of violence, the contribution made by internal divisiveness in the community and the feelings of insecurity stemming from fear of crime and violence. To match perceptions with fact, certain questions in this module ask about the household's recent experience of crime. It is useful to tabulate this information both at the household level and the community level. It is quite likely that perceptions of violence as well as experience of it differ between rich and poor households, old and young people, and so on. Likewise, different communities can have vastly different experiences with conflict and violence, even if they are geographically close. The comparison of communities will be made easier if the different questions on conflict and violence in module 5 are aggregated, either directly or by means of factor analysis.

Sample survey questions

17. There are often differences in characteristics between people living in the same village/neighborhood. For example, differences in wealth, income, social status, ethnic or linguistic background/race/caste/ tribe. There can also be differences in religious or political beliefs, or there can be differences due to age or sex. To what extent do any such differences characterize your village/neighborhood? Use a five-point scale where 1 means to a very great extent and 5 means to a very small extent.

18. Do any of these differences cause problems?
        Yes   No (go to question 21)

19. Which two differences most often cause problems?
        Differences: in education; in landholding; in wealth/material posses- sions; in social status; between men and women; between younger and older generations; between long-term and recent residents; in political party affiliations; in religious beliefs; in ethnic or linguistic background/race/caste/tribe? Other differences?

20. Have these problems ever led to violence?
        Yes   No

21. How many times in the past month have you got together with people to have food or drinks, either in their home or in a public place?

22. [If not zero] Were any of these people of different . . .
        Ethnic or linguistic background/race/caste/tribe?   Economic status? Social status?   Religious groups?

23. In general, how safe from crime and violence do you feel when you are alone at home?
        Very safe   Moderately safe   Neither safe nor unsafe
        Moderately unsafe   Very unsafe

Dimension 6: empowerment and political action

The final section of the SC-IQ takes a broad view that transcends social capital. Empowerment refers to the expansion of assets and capabili- ties of people to participate in, negotiate with, influence, control and hold accountable institutions that affect their lives (World Bank, 2002). Empowerment is brought about by a wide range of actions, such as making state institutions more responsive to poor people, removing social barri- ers and building social opportunity (World Bank, 2000). Empowerment is thus a broader concept than social capital, and political action is only one of many activities that can be undertaken to increase empowerment.

   In the context of the SC-IQ, empowerment is defined more narrowly as the ability to make decisions that affect everyday activities and may change the course of one's life. Respondents are asked to assess this ability directly.

As discussed above, political action is one venue to practice and possibly increase this ability. Module 6 considers a number of concrete political activities such as filing petitions, attending public meetings, interacting with politicians, participating in demonstrations and campaigns, and voting in elections. The analysis of this information can follow a pattern similar to that recommended for the previous module. The data can be aggregated both at the level of the household and the level of the community. Different households, depending upon their demographic, economic and social characteristics, will feel differently empowered and will participate in political action to differing degrees. It is useful to compare this pattern of empowerment with the patterns of access to information, fear of violence, sociability and other dimensions of social capital derived from other modules. By the same token, earlier analysis will already have provided a community score of social cohesiveness and inclusion, and this information can usefully be complemented with a community score of empowerment and political action.

Sample survey questions
24.   In general, how happy do you consider yourself to be?
        Very happy   Moderately happy   Neither happy nor unhappy
        Moderately unhappy   Very unhappy
25.   Do you feel that you have the power to make important decisions that change the course of your life? Rate yourself on a 1 to 5 scale, were 1 means being totally unable to change your life, and 5 means having full control over your life.
26.   In the past 12 months, how often have people in this village/neighborhood got together to jointly petition government officials or political leaders for something benefiting the community?
        Never   Once   A few times (<5)   Many times (>5)
27.   Lots of people find it difficult to get out and vote. Did you vote on the last state/national/ presidential election?
        Yes   No

Conclusion: integrating qualitative and quantitative approaches to assessing social capital
Increasing evidence shows that social cohesion is critical for societies to prosper economically and for development to be sustainable. Social capital is not just the sum of the institutions which underpin a society; it is the glue that holds them together. Social capital is multidimensional in nature. Given that it is most frequently defined in terms of groups, networks, norms of reciprocity, cooperation and trust, research on social capital must be able to capture this multidimensionality. In order to make use of social

capital findings to improve development processes and outcomes, it is also necessary to understand the dynamic nature of interpersonal and group relations in the context in which it is being studied. As such, social capital readily lends itself to a mixed-methods research approach. Employing both qualitative and quantitative methods allows researchers to uncover the links between different dimensions of social capital and poverty, as well as to construct a more comprehensive picture of the structures, perceptions and processes of social capital in a given locality.

Even if quantitative and qualitative approaches are construed as existing along a continuum (Bamberger, 2000), rather than being wholly distinctive, the fact remains that most individual researchers are trained in and hired to perform primarily only one approach. The organizational imperatives of large development agencies also tend to give higher priority to quantitative approaches, which provide the 'de-contextualized' (though putatively 'more objective') measures that enable such agencies to 'see' complex problems and diverse contexts in ways that comport with their particular capacity to respond to them (Scott, 1998). Using and/or integrating both methods requires a deliberate choice and sustained commitment on the part of a research team; informing and facilitating such choices is one of the primary goals of this chapter (and the broader project from which it draws).

Many researchers have stressed the limitations of different approaches and/or called for more methodological pluralism in development research. Indeed, starting with the work of Epstein (1962), many researchers have made important contributions to development research by working across methodological lines (Tashakkori and Teddlie, 1998; Bamberger, 2000; Gacitua-Mario and Wodon, 2001). Ideally, researchers should endeavor to understand the strengths and weaknesses of each approach and discern practical strategies for combining them on a more regular basis when assessing social capital (Kanbur, 2003; Rao, 2002).[5] It is important to note, however, that because qualitative research enables discussion on processes and, implicitly or explicitly, power relations, it carries the risk of aggravating local conflict. Well-intentioned researchers bear responsibility for that risk. In fact, both methodological approaches can unearth delicate relationship issues and raise local expectations; therefore careful planning, management and follow-through are essential to *do no harm*. At a minimum, researchers should plan to disseminate their findings to local stakeholders at various stages of the exploration and ideally would consider how local follow up can be integrated into ongoing government, civil, or private initiatives.

In summary, combining qualitative and quantitative approaches to the assessment of social capital offers practitioners several advantages. First, they gain a clearer, more nuanced understanding of the context of the communities and/or regions for which they design, monitor and evaluate development interventions. Second, the two methods in combination can provide baseline socio-economic information that can improve the design of both research tools (for example, a living standards survey or poverty assessment survey) and development projects. Third, quantitative and qualitative research methods together yield better impact and evaluation data, enabling teams to understand the full impact of projects on social capital (which can be positive, negative or both) and, conversely, whether areas with certain types and levels of social capital experience more successful project implementation than areas with other types and levels of social capital. Finally, when analysed and disseminated locally, integrated quantitative and qualitative findings can be sources of empowerment, enabling better understanding of the present and potentially new visions of the future. In this spirit, the present chapter will have served its purpose if it helps realize such goals; indeed, it is precisely through such pragmatic processes that the otherwise more abstract conceptual and methodological debates that continue to surround the idea of social capital should be (more than marginally) informed.

Notes

1. This chapter provides a brief overview of – while drawing extensively on and seeking to partially integrate – work originally presented in Grootaert et al. (2004), which developed a quantitative survey instrument of social capital, and Dudwick et al. (2006), which focused on qualitative tools for assessing social capital in context. Those interested in the details of these respective methodological approaches are advised to consult the original source documents. Our indebtedness to our respective colleagues on these projects is duly acknowledged. The views expressed in this chapter are those of the authors alone, and should not be attributed to the World Bank or the University of Manchester.
2. These advisory groups comprised members from both inside and outside the World Bank, and included leading scholars as well as development practitioners. The names of the group members are provided (and their valuable contributions duly acknowledged) in the original source documents (that is, in Grootaert et al., 2004 and Dudwick et al., 2006).
3. The Self-Employed Women's Association (SEWA) in India has used a related approach with great success, helping poor slum dwellers to compile basic data on themselves that they can then present to municipal governments for the purpose of obtaining resources to which they are legally entitled. Participatory approaches, however, have the potential for abuse – see Cooke and Kothari (2001) and Brock and McGee (2002).
4. Details on the methodological challenges of measuring social capital via a standard survey instrument are usefully outlined in Fafchamps (2006).
5. King et al. (1994) and Brady and Collier (2004) provide more academic treatments of the potential commonalities of quantitative and qualitative approaches.

References

Bamberger, Michael (2000), *Integrating Quantitative and Qualitative Research in Development Projects*, Washington, DC: World Bank.
Bebbington, Anthony, Scott Guggenheim, Elizabeth Olson and Michael Woolcock (2004),

'Exploring social capital debates at the World Bank', *Journal of Development Studies*, **40** (5), 33–64.

Brady, Henry and David Collier (eds) (2004), *Rethinking Social Inquiry: Diverse Tools, Shared Standards*, Lanham, MD: Rowman & Littlefield.

Brock, Karen and Rosemary McGee (2002), *Knowing Poverty: Critical Reflections on Participatory Research and Policy*, London: Earthscan Publications.

Chambers, Robert (1997), *Whose Reality Counts? Putting the First Last*, London: Intermediate Technology Publications.

Cooke, Bill and Uma Kothari (2001), *Participation: The New Tyranny?*, London: Zed Books.

Dudwick, Nora, Kathleen Kuehnast, Veronica Nyhan Jones and Michael Woolcock (2006), 'Analyzing social capital in context: a guide to using qualitative methods and data', World Bank Institute working paper, no. 37260, World Bank, Washington, DC.

Epstein, T. Scarlett (1962), *Economic Development and Social Change in South India*, Manchester: University of Manchester Press.

Fafchamps, Marcel (2006), 'Development and social capital', *Journal of Development Studies*, **42** (7), 1180–98.

Gacitua-Mario, Estanislao and Quinton Wodon (eds) (2001), 'Measurement and meaning: combining quantitative and qualitative methods for the analysis of poverty and social exclusion in Latin America', technical paper 518, Latin America and Caribbean Region, World Bank, Washington, DC.

Grootaert, Christiaan (1999), 'Social capital, household welfare, and poverty in Indonesia', Policy Research working paper 2148, World Bank, Washington, DC.

Grootaert, Christiaan (2001), 'Does social capital help the poor? A synthesis of findings from the local level institutions studies in Bolivia, Burkina Faso, and Indonesia', Local Level Institutions working paper 10, World Bank, Social Development Department, Washington, DC.

Grootaert, Christiaan, Deepa Narayan, Veronica Nyhan Jones and Michael Woolcock (2004), 'Measuring social capital: an integrated questionnaire', World Bank working paper, no. 18, World Bank, Washington, DC.

Kanbur, Ravi (2003), *Q Squared: Qualitative and Quantitative Methods of Poverty Appraisal*, New Delhi: Permanent Black.

King, Gary, Robert Keohane and Sidney Verba (1994), *Designing Social Inquiry: Scientific Inference in Qualitative Research*, Princeton, NJ: Princeton University Press.

Krishna, Anirudh (2002), *Active Social Capital: Tracing the Roots of Development and Democracy*, New York: Columbia University.

Krishna, Anirudh (2007), 'How does social capital grow? A seven-year study of villages in India', *Journal of Politics*, **69** (4), 941–56.

Kumar, Somesh and Robert Chambers (2002), *Methods for Community Participation*, London: Intermediate Technology Publications.

Mikkelsen, Britha (1995), *Methods for Development Work and Research: A Guide for Practitioners*, New Delhi: Sage Publications.

Narayan, Deepa (1995), *Toward Participatory Research*, Washington, DC: World Bank.

Narayan, Deepa and Michael Cassidy (2001), 'A dimensional approach to measuring social capital: development and validation of social capital inventory', *Current Sociology*, **49** (2), 49–93.

Rao, Vijayendra (2002), 'Experiments in "participatory econometrics": improving the connection between economic analysis and the real world', *Economic and Political Weekly*, 18 May, 1887–91.

Rao, Vijayendra and Michael Woolcock (2003), 'Integrating qualitative and quantitative approaches in program evaluation', in Francois J. Bourguignon and Luiz Pereira da Silva (eds), *The Impact of Economic Policies on Poverty and Income Distribution: Evaluation Techniques and Tools*, New York: Oxford University Press, pp. 165–90.

Robb, Carolyn (2002), *Can the Poor Influence Policy? Participatory Poverty Assessments in the Developing World*, revd edn, Washington, DC: International Monetary Fund.

Scott, James (1998), *Seeing Like a State: How Well-Intentioned Schemes to Improve the Human Condition Have Failed*, New Haven, CT: Yale University Press.

Szreter, Simon and Michael Woolcock (2004), 'Health by association? Social capital, social theory and the political economy of public health', *International Journal of Epidemiology*, **33** (4), 650–67.

Tashakkori, Abbas and Charles Teddlie (1998), *Mixed Methodology: Combining Qualitative and Quantitative Approaches*, Thousand Oaks, CA: Sage.

Woolcock, Michael and Deepa Narayan (2000), 'Social capital: implications for development theory, research, and policy', *World Bank Research Observer*, **15** (2), 225–50.

World Bank (2000), *World Development Report 2000/2001: Attacking Poverty*, New York: Oxford University Press.

World Bank (2002), *Empowerment and Poverty Reduction – A Sourcebook*, Washington, DC: World Bank

23 The sociability of nations: international comparisons in bonding, bridging and linking social capital
Roger Patulny

Introduction

It seems obvious to suggest that a sociable nation would be a good place to live. But how do we identify which nations are sociable and which are not? Anecdotal evidence is powerful but contradictory.

We might embrace the idea that the family and the local neighbourhood make up the backbone of a nation, and point to countries such as Italy and Spain as examples of sociable nations. We can picture rustic images of multiple generations of grandparents, parents and children playing and dining together in village squares, with open and obvious displays of mutual warmth and affection. This can be contrasted against visions of more restrained, isolated and atomized individuals populating the countries of central and northern Europe to complete a stereotype of socially 'warm' Mediterranean and 'cold' northern European countries.

However, if we take a broader picture of civil society as the key to a nation's sociability, the opposite picture emerges. The integrated and homogenous societies of northern Europe are archetypes of peaceful, safe and healthy societies, and offer stereotypes of people calmly riding bikes, obeying road rules and volunteering in broad-based civic associations that stretch beyond the boundaries of family and village. Contrast this against the chaos of traffic in Mediterranean Europe, the pattern of declining volunteering identified in the US (Putnam, 2000), and the destructive but family-based Mafia of Italy. The 'warm' south of Europe can seem anarchic and tribal, and the 'cold' north peaceful and prosperous.

Another possibility is to conceive of political involvement in democracy and the functioning of government as central to a nation's sociability. The much vaunted democratic institutions of the US create a stereotype of a healthy and robust democracy and an open, tolerant and diverse society, which can be contrasted against the poor democratic functioning and heightened corruption to be found in southern and ex-communist eastern European countries, and the sociability of countries seems to change once more.

Different anecdotes, world views and stereotypes will drive different pictures of the sociability of nations. The key question is whether there is some way to look beyond anecdotes, and measure the actual strength and sociability of nations? One concept for measuring a nation's sociability – which I define loosely as a nation's sense and breadth of social connection leading to social activity – is the multidisciplinary concept of *social capital*. This is a promising concept, but not without difficulty in theory and measurement.

Of the numerous definitions of social capital (see, for example, APC, 2003) nearly all conceive of an entity comprised of multiple components, the most important being social networks and norms of trust. A commonly quoted definition – that of the Organisation for Economic Co-operation and Development (OECD) – makes these explicit: 'Social Capital is networks together with shared norms, values and understandings that facilitate cooperation within or among groups' (Cote and Healy, 2001). Such a definition highlights the multiplicity; the fact that social capital is made up of many complex parts. Despite this, some analysts (Brehm and Rahn, 1997; Claibourn and Martin, 2000; Li et al., 2005) have reduced the measurement of social capital to the most simple and visible standalone indicator developed by Robert Putnam (2000): membership in civic associations. Others have combined volunteering with another popular measure, interpersonal trust (Paxton, 1999), and left it at that.

Is such empirical reduction valid? Social capital theory is contentious, and there are literatures just as willing to separate certain aspects of social capital – such as trust and volunteering (Uslaner, 2002) – as put them together (Paxton, 1999). However, with the odd exception (for example, Stone and Hughes, 2002), very few of the more advanced empirical attempts to measure social capital dwell on theoretical issues. This does poor justice to the voluminous amount of theoretical work that has gone into developing the definitions and subtleties of the concept over the past decade, most notably from Putnam (2000), but also from many others including Woolcock (1998), Paxton (1999), Narayan (1999), Burt (2000), Lin (Lin et al., 2001), Szreter (2002), Stone and Hughes (2002), Rothstein (2003), Svendsen and Svendsen (2004), Patulny (2004) and Patulny and Svendsen (2007), not to mention the earlier seminal work of Coleman (1990) and Bourdieu (1986).

I suggest that social capital analysis is rent by divisions peculiar to much social scientific theory and measurement, where theory and measurement are like stubborn parents. One should love them equally, but the jealous attention to detail each demands can overwhelm the harried researcher into privileging one above the other. We might perhaps have time to read, consider and critique the thousands of articles on the theory of social capital and related aspects of trust, government and civil society, and develop a full range of possible measures. Or we might have time to find and code enormous amounts of data spanning many years and national contexts, and learn the complex statistical techniques required to undertake panel and structural-pathway analysis of a few indicators of social capital. But we do not seem to have time for both.

Here, I want to defend theory. The various important theories of social capital cited above, when taken together, do not logically *prove* that social capital is exactly one thing or another, and should be measured accordingly. They do however provide weight to the idea that social capital is an entity comprised of a number of things that *could* quite easily belong together.

Given this likelihood, empirical attempts to measure social capital across nations have been poor and under-theorized. The most obvious omission is the failure to measure across nations key aspects of the three most important types of social capital networks. These three are known in the literature as *bonding*, *bridging* and *linking* (Woolcock, 1998; Putnam, 2000; Szreter, 2002), and are distinguished by bonding networks being based upon familiarity and intimate interaction in fairly closed circles; bridging networks upon more generalized and widespread social interactions with strangers in a civil society context; and linking networks upon perceptions and contacts formed between citizens, the government and the institutions of governance.

In addition to many dimensions, social capital has many parts. It is more than just *networks* of association. As I discuss more fully below, social capital networks are guided by *norms*, and are the site and guidelines for actions and *practices*. The measurement of a fully theorized version of social capital to capture the sociability of nations should try and account for all these things; multiple dimensions (bridging, bonding and linking) and multiple parts (networks, norms and practices).

The great difficulty in comparing nations is the lack of internationally comparable data to capture the many dimensions and parts of social capital. The advantage in comparing nations, however, is that data can be aggregated to the national level, and similar units of analysis can be compared across surveys. Sample sizes will be limited, which will preclude the undertaking of much complex statistical analysis. But a descriptive analysis is possible, and would form an important baseline step in 'eye-balling' the full range of social capital variables. This would begin to show both how they cohere and what they indicate concerning the sociability of different countries.

This chapter then examines international data from several international datasets, with the aim of producing a descriptive assessment of the social capital of nations. It will compare aggregated rates of different aspects and networks of social capital across countries using data from the World

Values Survey (WVS), the European Social Survey (ESS), OECD statistics, and various international Time Use Surveys (MTUS and HETUS). The aim is not to prove causal direction or even statistical association so much as to simply 'eyeball' the available data capturing the full range of theoretical concepts that comprise social capital. This will serve as a good base for later, more sophisticated research with potentially better data.

Aspects of social capital
Following on from the OECD definition above, the aspects of norms like trust, and networks such as voluntary associations seem appropriate aspects, and I would argue that time based activities are also important. Aspects such as socializing and volunteering time should also be examined as social capital measures, and I summarize the key elements of each below.

Norms
Norms are primary to any conception of social capital, and the most prominent social capital norm from the literature is trust. There are divergent views over the nature of trust, however. Political scientists (Fukuyama, 1995; Putnam, 2000) see trust as a culturally and historically derived artifact. Economists (Dasgupta, 1988; Gambetta, 1988) and certain sociologists (Coleman, 1990) see trust as a rational construct based on information concerning the trustworthiness of others. However, other sociologists such as Luhmann (1979) see it as a norm linked to a *lack* of information – by definition, we cannot know 'strangers', so trust is a necessary leap of faith that allows social interaction to occur in an information vacuum. This tension can be resolved, as I have previously suggested (Patulny, 2004) by recognizing the existence of two different types of trust, captured in Uslaner's distinction between particularized-rational and generalized-normative trust (Uslaner, 2002), the latter more moral, altruistic and oriented to what you should do in an altruistic sense (Mansbridge, 1999).

Networks
The different types of trust – along with any other potential norms that might accompany them – are best understood with relevance to different *networks*, and are likely divisible along the lines of the major social capital network types identified in the literature – bonding, bridging and linking (Woolcock, 1998; Putnam, 2000; Szreter, 2002) – which I examine in the next section.

Practices
This is a particularly important and often omitted aspect of social capital – *practices, or activities*. The emphasis on studying social practices can be

traced back to Bourdieu (1977), but Putnam (2000) makes the perhaps more relevant point that not all networks generate social and voluntary activity, as some voluntary members prefer to donate money rather than time, and it is thus important to measure activity as much as membership. Of the increasing number of time use researchers measuring social capital activity however (Robinson and Godbey, 1997; Putnam, 2000; Ruston, 2003) most fail to translate such activities as volunteering into bridging and informal care into bonding social capital, an easy theoretical match commonly overlooked. In addition, there are many activities relevant to linking – or political – social capital that are often left out of the analysis, such as engaging in political action, voting, and contacting politicians and officials. This will be discussed further in looking at linking capital in the next section.

The different social capital networks
The three types of social capital networks – bonding, bridging and linking – have been developed in great detail theoretically by the likes of Woolcock (1998), Putnam (2000), Szreter (2002) and Svendsen and Svendsen (2004), but little has been done to try and measure such networks empirically. Only Stone and Hughes's (2002) work to date tries to capture the different social capital network types in the one analysis, but they did not include practice and activity measures. Some might suggest that paying too much attention to such network distinctions denotes a misunderstanding that social capital is only a 'metaphor' for the advantage that flows from social strength (Wellman, 1988; Burt, 2000) or to cover up the neo-liberalization of social policy (Fine, 2001; Harriss, 2001), and was never intended to stand up to rigorous measurement and validity checks.

While not rejecting these views, I would point to the welter of academic and policy interest in strengthening American society in the wake of Putnam's *Bowling Alone* in 2000 as a strong indication of the value in measuring concepts such as social capital. Measurement allows us – however imperfectly – to move beyond anecdote, which (as demonstrated in the examples from the introduction to this chapter) can present completely conflicting pictures. Measurement should be cautious, but not rejected outright. Caution implies that we get the measure as theoretically correct as possible, which in this case means measuring all relevant network-types. I will describe each briefly in turn.

Bridging
Bridging networks are outward focused, inclusive and public-good oriented, and are best captured in Putnam's (2000) classical depiction of civic society, and in the example of northern European countries raised in the

introduction. Generalized trust is an appropriate norm for capturing the potentially fragile nature of relations between strangers, and questions asking directly about generalized trust in strangers seem appropriate as bridging norms. In addition, another norm that might potentially accompany trust as a measure of bridging social capital would be tolerance towards strangers. Tolerance has been included in a number of empirical studies of social capital (Onyx and Bullen, 1997; Putnam, 2000; Stone and Hughes, 2002), and is appropriate for bridging as it denotes a sense of generalised acceptance and inclusion.

Bonding

Bonding, as distinct from bridging, is inward rather than outward looking. It is focused upon experience, familiarity and private rewards, and is captured in the example of family-oriented Mediterranean nations raised in the introduction. Its theoretical essence, however, is captured in the phenomena of group closure examined by Bourdieu (1986) and Olson (1982), which sees rewards going to members though the exclusion of outsiders from access to the network resources. Bonding can thus capture many of the negative elements attributed to social capital by Portes (1998) whereby strong ties lead closed groups to operate in ways that work against the greater social good (that is, the Mafia). However, it is important to recognize that such negative actions are characteristic of an 'excessive' and 'parochial' kind of bonding only, and are intrinsic neither to bonding nor any other kind of social capital, as some critics might like to suggest.

I have previously proposed that bonding networks operate on the basis of particularized trust, while bridging networks operate on generalized trust (Patulny, 2004). However, questions about particularized trust cannot be asked directly of close family, friends and intimates, as responses will suffer a normative bias towards a favourable 'yes' answer. Other questions concerned with the degree of loyalty and intimacy people feel towards their close companions are likely better indicators, and these have not yet been widely examined in relation to social capital.

Linking

There is a possible third type of social capital – linking (Szreter, 2002; Woolcock and Narayan, 2000) – that is said to capture the ties between citizens and government, and was captured in the introduction with the example of the USA. This type of social capital is problematic, and may not even *be* a type of social capital, as it operates along unclear lines of trust and risks tautological overlap with concepts and measures of governance. However, it will do no harm here to operationalize linking in the same study as bridging and bonding, and leave it to the reader to decide on the appropriateness of including or excluding it. Linking norms would include confidence and trust in government, which Brehm and Rahn (1997) and Newton and Norris (2000) relate positively to both interpersonal trust and a desire to not 'cheat the system'. Certain authors (Knack and Keefer, 1997) see a propensity to 'cheat the system' as synonymous with generalized social attachment (bridging social capital), but I propose that it intrinsically captures perceptions of efficiency and corruption in the system of governance, and is thus a better measure of linking rather than bridging social capital. Linking activities would include such measures as engaging in political action, voting and contacting politicians and officials; measures which have not been examined in the context of linking social capital to date.

I do not insist that conceiving of social capital as a cross-tabulation of 'norms/networks/practices' with 'bonding/bridging/linking' is a perfect framework, or nullifies the many problems identified with the social capital concept. I discussed such problems in earlier work to which I refer the reader for more detail (Patulny, 2004), but note them briefly here: tautology, or the propensity to confuse social capital indicators with outcomes in measurement (Portes, 1998); ownership of social capital and whether it is the property of the collective (Putnam, 2000) or the well-placed individual (Bourdieu, 1986); different network types crowding each other out, and victim-blaming/negative social capital (Portes, 1998; Grieg et al., 2003).

However, many of these problems result from conflict between different network types – bonding and bridging in particular – and that measuring such networks here may shed some light on how these theories translate into practice with regards to whether different social capital networks support (cohere with) each other or conflict with each other.

Variables and data
Each of the dimensions of social capital can be operationalized using variables from a range of international datasets.[1] There are pros and cons with using this approach, but the overall result provides a useful, theoretically robust snapshot of social capital across many countries.[2] Variables used are detailed below.

Variables – bridging
Concerning variables for bridging social capital, the normative measures used were of generalized trust in most people and tolerance towards neighbours. Two trust questions were compared. The first was a binary question from the WVS asking: 'Generally speaking, would you say that most people can be trusted or that you can't be too careful in dealing

with people?' The second trust question was the 30-point 'Rosenberg' scale combining three questions about trust, care and helpfulness from the ESS, which is probably more methodologically rigorous (Zmerli and Newton, 2006), but available across fewer countries. The validity of the generalized trust question has been confirmed in correlations between trust levels across countries as measured by the WVS question and results from wallet-dropping experiments (Knack and Keefer, 1997). Tolerance is measured using WVS questions asking about whether one would prefer not to live next to stigmatized neighbours, in this case those of a different race and immigrants/foreign workers. I calculated the proportion of people in each country who did *not* perceive either of these groups to be unwelcome neighbours, and took such proportions as measures of the level of tolerance within each country.

Bridging networks have been measured by looking at the proportion of people who report being a member of at least one generalized, civic, 'Putnam' group, again comparing similar data from both the WVS and ESS. This follows on from work by van Schaik (2002) who attempts to separate organizations, dividing the voluntary groups from the WVS into 'Putnam' groups (religious, education/arts/culture and youth work) versus 'Bourdieu/Olson' groups (unions, political parties and professional groups), on the basis of the former being outward looking and collective, and the latter being inward looking and protective. Here, I code 'Putnam' groups to include: social welfare service for the elderly, education, arts, music or cultural activities, human rights, conservation, the environment, ecology, animal rights, youth work, sports or recreation, women's group, peace movement, organization concerned with health, and other groups.

Bridging practices have been measured by using the same 'Putnam' membership variables from the WVS and the ESS as for networks, but according to whether people have been active or done unpaid or voluntary work on behalf of those organizations. In addition, as a more direct measure of activity, time use estimates of the average number of minutes per day spent in volunteering have been calculated across available countries from MTUS and HETUS data.

Variables – bonding
As previously mentioned, bonding measures of 'trust in intimates' are likely to be confounded by a normative bias towards positive responses. Alternative questions about being loyal and close to people like or different from oneself are available in the ESS, and are also likely to have some positive bias, but not as much as a trust question. As the only question able to capture a propensity to bond with familiars available, I have chosen to make use of it.

Bonding networks have been measured in a similar vein to bridging networks above, but this time by coding according to membership of associations that can be described as 'Bourdieu' groups, which I code to include: labour unions, professional associations, consumer groups and religious organizations. In addition to these measures, there was an additional network measure available, which asked people 'whether they had someone they could discuss intimate matters with'.

As with bridging, bonding practices have been measured by using the same membership activity, unpaid or voluntary work variables from the WVS and the ESS, but this time with regards to 'Bourdieu' groups. Also, I estimate the average number of minutes per day spent in informal care of others across available countries from MTUS and HETUS data. I note that the category of 'informal care' is combined with other tasks under the heading of 'odd jobs' in the MTUS dataset, which means that the estimates of informal care derived from MTUS are likely greater than those from HETUS, and this should be taken into account in interpretation of the statistics. Finally, two other bonding practice variables were available from the ESS; how often people meet up with friends, neighbours and relatives, and how often people help other people informally (that is, help friends, family, or even strangers, but *not* as part of a formal voluntary organization; which suggests a more intimate, localized, bonding-oriented action). Each of these questions is graded on a seven-point scale, and means have been calculated for each country.

Variables – linking
For linking social capital, the most appropriate norms were confidence and trust in parliament – also termed 'institutional' trust – and being unwilling to 'cheat the system'. The question on confidence comes from the WVS, which I have converted into a binary form and calculated proportions answering that they have confidence in their parliament for each country. The question on trust is an 11-point question from the ESS, for which I have calculated mean scores for each country. Cheating, or an unwillingness to cheat on certain systemic features, is a more limited variable than the five item variable used by Knack and Keefer's (1997) from the WVS to denote 'civic cooperation'. It drops one of the items so as to maintain a focus on public services – and thus governance – and is comprised of four questions asking whether it is acceptable to claim government benefits to which you are not entitled, avoid fares, cheat on taxes and accept bribes. I have combined these questions into a 40-point scale where a higher score indicates greater disproval of cheating, and calculated mean scores for each country.

Linking networks have been measured in a similar vein to both bridging and bonding networks, but purely with reference only to membership in political parties, for both the WVS and the ESS.

Linking practices have likewise been measured by using the same membership activity, unpaid or voluntary work variables as for both bridging and bonding, though on this occasion with regards to political parties. In addition, there are three other measures of linking activities available. From the ESS, there are questions concerning whether people voted at the last national election, and whether people have contacted a politician or official in the last 12 months. I have calculated proportions of people who have answered yes for both these questions. And from both the WVS and the ESS, there are measures of political activity. I have restricted the measures provided to those incorporating only lawful political activity: signing a petition, joining in a boycott and attending a lawful demonstration, and calculated the proportion of people in each country who have admitted to doing at least one of these activities in the past 12 months.

Results

Bridging social capital
The data for all normative, network and practice-based measures of bridging social capital can be seen below in Table 23.1. To help interpretation, the top eight scores for each indicator have been shaded in a dark grey, and the next eight in a light grey, so that the general clustering of high scores in certain countries can be taken in at a glance.

In addition, it became necessary to sort the data in some way so as to generally concentrate the higher scores and shades across the variables at the top of the table. To this end, aggregated scores for all indicators from the WVS were subjected to principal components analysis to produce component scores for each country. Such scores are indicative of how well the various bridging scores for that country load against a single principal component dimension capturing aggregated bridging social capital. Only data items from the WVS were used, because the WVS covered every country except Israel, and thus a component and rank position could be produced for every country by restricting data to just this dataset. The component scores are listed below, and countries are sorted from highest to lowest according to such loadings.

It can be seen immediately that bridging social capital is more strongly concentrated within certain countries than others.[3] In keeping with findings from the literature connecting welfare and social capital (Rothstein, 2003; Patulny, 2005), it can be seen that the Nordic countries of Sweden, Denmark, Norway, Iceland and Finland, as well as the not dissimilar Netherlands, all demonstrate strong levels of bridging social capital, while

Table 23.1 Bridging

Country	WVS Prin comp	Norm			Network			Practice	
		Generalized Trust		Tolerance	Putnam member		Volunteer	Putnam Active	
		WVS	ESS	WVS	WVS	ESS	Time Use	WVS	ESS
		%	Mean (0–30)	%	%	%	mean min	%	%
Netherlands	1.9	61.2	17.4	93.8	87.8	70.3	11.5	46.1	46.0
United States	1.5	36.0		88.3	77.7		9.0	57.0	
Sweden	1.4	64.3	18.4	96.9	75.5	68.8	4.2	42.6	47.5
Australia	1.3	40.6		93.9	74.8		5.3	61.2	
Norway	1.2	66.3	19.5	88.7	71.4	66.0	2.0	46.4	46.5
Switzerland	1.1	38.4	17.6	88.4	69.3			53.1	
Denmark	0.8	65.9	20.1	88.6	63.8	68.4		34.2	45.5
Canada	0.8	39.0		95.3	62.8		8.9	43.3	
Iceland	0.7	40.2	19.4	95.8	60.1			28.9	
Belgium	0.6	30.6	14.7	78.9	59.0	55.5	4.7	33.3	49.3
Finland	0.4	55.9	18.9	82.4	54.6	42.3	5.0	32.8	35.9
Luxembourg	0.3	25.4	15.2	89.8	52.7	57.1		27.9	28.0
Austria	0.3	32.9	16.4	85.8	51.6	56.8	4.3	25.8	34.9
South Africa	0.2	11.2		60.0	50.8		4.4	36.8	
Czech Republic	0.2	23.8	13.5	76.4	49.5			28.5	

Greece	0.1	22.2	10.6	81.1	47.1	16.1		34.9	8.8
Ireland	0.0	36.0	18.2	84.2	46.3	51.1		26.1	33.0
Slovakia	0.0	15.3	12.1	70.2	46.1			38.6	
Germany	−0.2	32.6	15.4	89.1	41.8	53.9	7.8	17.4	41.6
Slovenia	−0.2	21.4	13.0	80.5	40.4	29.8	9.0	24.4	25.5
France	−0.4	21.6	14.6	85.3	35.5	42.9	1.0	24.5	41.0
United Kingdom	−0.6	34.5	16.3	81.4	32.1	49.8	3.0	28.1	47.0
Italy	−0.7	32.1	13.3	80.2	29.9	22.2	2.0	20.0	19.1
Estonia	−1.0	21.5	15.1	74.8	22.2		1.1	14.0	
Spain	−1.0	34.4	14.3	86.2	22.1	30.3	1.0	12.7	22.7
Portugal	−1.2	9.5	12.6	91.9	18.3	18.2		11.9	10.4
Latvia	−1.3	16.9		87.6	15.7		0.1	16.6	
Hungary	−1.4	22.2	12.6	69.2	13.3	15.1	0.2	10.7	16.1
Poland	−1.5	18.7	11.1	72.1	12.2	10.4	0.7	9.3	8.1
Ukraine	−1.5	26.1	12.9	80.4	12.0			6.5	
Lithuania	−1.6	23.8	12.9	72.1	8.8			7.4	
Israel	.	22.8	14.7		38.4				26.5

Note: All data is weighted and representative of national populations aged 20–74.

413

in keeping with findings about the effects of totalitarianism on eroding civic society, the ex-communist countries such as Hungary, Poland, Ukraine, and Lithuania all show lower levels of bridging social capital. Mediterranean countries such as Portugal, Italy, Greece, Spain and even France also show lower bridging social capital levels, though not as bad as the ex-communists. Non-European Anglo countries such as the USA, Canada and Australia show higher levels of bridging social capital, which provides an interesting contrast to Putnam's picture about declining social capital in the USA in that if it has gone down, it still remains quite high by international standards, at any rate. However, these higher ranks may be a consequence of the non-inclusion of these countries in the ESS.

In terms of the breakdown of scores between norms, networks and practices, it can be seen that there is a strong degree of coherence across these three components, with similar countries showing strong, medium and weak scores for each across. The possible exception to this coherence is the presence of strong bridging practices in several mainland European countries which otherwise lack strong normative or network bridging indicators. This can be seen in the higher rates of active membership and volunteering in countries like Germany, Slovenia, Slovakia and France, and also in the UK. This might be a feature of European Union (EU) directives specifying limits on working weeks and higher leisure time in those countries allowing for more social activity to take place. However, such a proposal is speculative and should be considered as an interesting point for future research.

Bonding social capital

The data for all normative, network and practice-based measures of bonding social capital can be seen below in Table 23.2. As with bridging, to help interpretation, the top eight scores for each indicator have been shaded in a dark grey, and the next eight in a light grey, so that the general clustering of high scores across countries can be seen. Principal components analysis was not possible for binding measures from the WVS, as there were only two bonding measures used from the WVS – membership and activity in voluntary associations. I thus added the proportions for each of these measures together so as to produce a rough ranking system. The component scores are listed in the table, and countries are sorted from highest to lowest according to such loadings.

It can be seen that, as with bridging social capital, higher bonding scores also tend to cluster among certain countries. However, it is interesting to note that higher bonding scores are much more widely dispersed across the full range of countries than are bridging scores.[4] So while the Nordic countries show levels of bonding as high as they do for bridging, countries such as Poland and Hungary also show high scores according to indicators such

Table 23.2 Bonding

Country	WVS mem	Norms Loyal similar people ESS %	Someone discuss intimacies ESS %	Network Bourdieu member WVS %	Bourdieu member ESS %	Caring Time Use mean min	Meet friends etc. ESS Mean (0–7)	Practice Bourdieu Active WVS %	Bourdieu Active ESS %	Help others ESS Mean (0–7)
Australia	136.0			69.1		33.0		44.2		
United States	134.7			70.3		39.3		43.3		
Netherlands	133.8	95.6	94.4	55.5	63.5	31.7	5.3	15.3	19.4	4.3
Switzerland	122.4	99.1	96.2	59.6			5.2	28.9		4.4
Sweden	118.1	92.7	93.0	89.3	80.8	8.2	5.2	32.7	18.3	3.9
Norway	117.7	89.5	97.0	68.8	70.2	8.0	5.8	26.6	20.4	3.6
Canada	106.2			48.7		28.1		25.1		
Denmark	97.9	97.8	93.3	62.8	84.8		5.2	9.3	23.1	3.9
Belgium	92.3	98.1	89.0	31.6	46.2	5.5	5.1	9.2	17.0	4.0
Iceland	89.0	98.3	95.2	86.4			5.5	9.2		
South Africa	87.6			61.6	68.9	21.1		42.6		
Finland	87.3	94.5	92.0	62.6		11.0	5.1	12.6	15.5	3.3
Slovakia	84.7	91.5	86.8	33.7			4.9	20.7		
Greece	82.1	96.5	92.4	24.3	12.1		3.8	14.0	5.7	3.2

415

Table 23.2 (continued)

Country	WVS mem	Norms		Network		Caring	Meet friends etc.	Practice		Help others
		Loyal similar people	Someone discuss intimacies	Bourdieu member		Time Use		Bourdieu Active		
		ESS	ESS	WVS	ESS		ESS	WVS	ESS	ESS
		%	%	%	%	mean min	Mean (0–7)	%	%	Mean (0–7)
Luxembourg	80.6	95.0	93.9	22.2	67.6		5.1	8.7	8.4	3.5
Czech Republic	78.1	89.3	83.3	21.5			4.2	7.3		3.0
Austria	77.4	95.8	92.0	41.8	61.1	29.9	5.0	9.9	17.3	4.5
Ireland	72.4	92.7	93.0	27.5	51.4		4.7	10.7	20.1	3.6
Slovenia	64.8	87.3	92.0	24.8	38.5	28.0	4.6	8.8	10.9	4.1
United Kingdom	60.2	93.6	92.8	21.3	54.9	9.0	5.0	11.9	21.7	3.7
France	60.1	91.1	88.9	10.1	20.2	9.0	5.1	5.3	12.7	
Germany	59.2	97.5	95.1	23.1	54.0	8.4	4.7	6.5	17.4	4.4
Italy	49.8		79.4	21.2	24.2	10.0	4.8	11.0	11.9	3.2
Estonia	36.2	93.9	34.7	14.0		13.7	4.3	4.4		
Spain	34.9	93.0	93.1	11.4	17.7	9.0	5.4	5.6	9.7	3.0
Latvia	32.3			16.6		11.3		6.1		
Portugal	30.2	86.1	90.8	8.0	14.5		5.9	3.4	9.5	3.4
Hungary	24.0	96.2	92.5	20.7	17.3	10.5	3.7	7.7	10.8	3.6

Poland	21.5	96.1	88.2		14.7	4.1	6.3	3.2
Ukraine	18.5	80.8	89.0	17.6		4.4	6.4	5.7
Lithuania	16.2			25.1	7.4	13.0	5.6
Israel		95.0	92.1		40.7	5.2	7.2	4.0

Note: All data is weighted and representative of national populations aged 20–74.

as 'caring time' and 'being loyal to people like oneself', and Mediterranean countries such as Spain and Greece also demonstrate better bonding than bridging capital. English-speaking countries such as the US and Australia also demonstrate better levels of bonding than bridging social capital, though again this may be a result of the limited use of WVS and not ESS data for both these countries.

The different distribution of bonding and bridging scores across countries is interesting in that it suggests that there is something in the theoretical separation between bonding and bridging. Countries which do not have high levels of bridging social capital, or else had such networks destroyed by the totalitarian influence of communism, may have developed or had to rely upon bonding social capital in compensation. It might also be the case that some countries have seen strong bonding networks 'crowd out' bridging ones, in that citizens of these countries privilege their familiar networks to such a degree that they discriminate and even fight against more public ones. However, these possibilities and the distinction between bridging and bonding should not be overplayed on the basis of this data. Ex-communist countries are still nearer the bottom of the distribution of bonding scores, and the same Nordic and English-speaking countries are at the top end and mainland and Mediterranean European countries in the middle. This means that bridging and bonding are more likely complementary than opposed as a general rule across countries.

In terms of the breakdown of scores between norms, networks and practices, it can be seen that there is still coherence across these three components, though it is not as strong as for bridging social capital. As with bridging, certain European countries such as Germany, Slovenia and the UK, as well as Austria and Ireland, show higher levels of bonding practices than these countries exhibit for any normative (Germany excepted) or network indicator. Again, this is an area for future research into the effects of EU work directives and free time to engage with.

Linking social capital
The data for all normative, network and practice-based measures of linking social capital can be seen below in Table 23.3. As with bridging and bonding, to help interpretation, the top eight scores for each indicator have been shaded in a dark grey, and the next eight in a light grey, so that the general clustering of high scores across countries can be seen. Again, as with bridging, principal component scores have also been calculated for each country using linking measures derived from the WVS.

It can be seen that the pattern of linking scores is very similar to that of bridging scores,[5] with Nordic countries showing as high levels of linking as they did bridging, ex-communist such as Latvia, Estonia and Lithuania in

Table 23.3 *Linking*

Country	WVS Princ comp	Norms			Networks				Practices			
		Conf Parl	Trust Parl	Cheat Unjust	Member Political Party		Active Political Party		Political Action		Vote	Contact Politic/Official
		WVS	ESS	WVS	WVS	ESS	WVS	ESS	WVS	ESS	ESS	ESS
	%	%	Mean (0–10)	Mean (0–40)	%	%	%	%	%	%	%	%
Iceland	2.40	71.3	5.9	31.6	19.2		3.5		59.7	63	92.9	33
United States	2.39	37		31.5	19.1		6.6		84.4			
Norway	1.68	69.6	5.4	32.5	15.4	8.7	3.2	3.9	69.8	51.2	75.9	24.5
Switzerland	1.30	40.4	5.5	31.3	13.4		5.4		69.4	51.4	70.6	16.4
South Africa	1.17	56.7		29.3	12.7		6.7		43			
Austria	0.96	39	4.7	31.7	11.6	12.1	3.4	6.4	61.9	38.1	72.4	21.8
Sweden	0.73	50.6	5.3	30.7	10.4	7.8	4.2	3.6	89.7	64.4	67.7	15.4
Australia	0.64	29.7		33	9.9		2.5		82.4			
Netherlands	0.41	54.7	4.6	31.2	8.7	4.9	2.8	2.4	68.6	29.7	83.3	14.3
Greece	0.30	23.9	4.6	27.5	8.1	4.3	5.3	2.1	67.6	10.1	77.8	15.2
Slovakia	0.11	39	3	27.3	7.1		5.3		65	32.4	71.1	7.6
Belgium	0.10	34.8	4.7	29.7	7.1	6.6	2.8	4.3	75.4	30.3	82.2	14.6
Finland	0.03	42	6	31.4	6.7	6.3	2.8	2.3	55	44.7	92.9	23.7
Canada	0.01	39.5		32.2	6.6		2.9		77.5			

Table 23.3 (continued)

Country	WVS Princ comp	Norms			Networks				Practices			
		Conf Parl	Trust Parl	Cheat Unjust	Member Political Party		Active Political Party		Political Action		Vote	Contact Politic/ Official
		WVS	ESS	WVS	WVS	ESS	WVS	ESS	WVS	ESS	ESS	ESS
		%	Mean (0–10)	Mean (0–40)	%	%	%	%	%	%	%	%
Denmark	−0.01	46.6	6.3	33.7	6.5	6.3	2.5	2.7	68.9	47.1	93.9	20.9
Luxembourg	−0.03	56.5	5.7	29.4	6.4	6.9	2.7	1.7	62.1	33.7	93.5	23.4
Italy	−0.45	32.9	4.8	32.1	4.2	3.1	2.3	2.3	65.6	24.5	83.5	13
Ireland	−0.49	30.6	4.7	31.7	4	3.8	1.8	2.1	64.9	28.2	81	24.2
Czech Republic	−0.60	11.8	3.1	30.8	3.4		2		66.2	19.6	83.3	18.4
Slovenia	−0.64	24.5	4.1	29.5	3.2	4.3	1.4	2.4	37.8	8.6	89.2	12.7
Germany	−0.68	34.8	4.2	31.8	3	3.4	0.9	3.9	59.1	46.9	78.7	12
United Kingdom	−0.79	35.5	4.2	31	2.4	2.1	1.2	1	73.9	44.5	84.6	16
Ukraine	−0.79	24.6	4.8	27.6	2.4		1.5		28	25.2	67.3	9.2
France	−0.85	38.5	4.3	28.8	2.1	2	0.8	2	74.9	48.8	63	16.9
Hungary	−0.91	33	3.6	27.2	1.8	1.7	1.2	1.8	17.1	10.9	82.9	10
Spain	−0.92	44.9	5.1	31.8	1.7	3.3	1.3	2.2	42.4	48.6	77.2	14.3
Latvia	−0.93	25.5		27.6	1.7		0.8		38.3			
Estonia	−0.98	25	4.1	30.2	1.4		1.1		29.9	9.9	56.8	10.4

Lithuania	−1.00	10.1		28.5	1.3		1.3		36.1	7.7		6.1
Portugal	−1.08	43.2	3.7	29.4	0.9	4.3	0.6	2.2	30		85.9	8
Poland	−1.10	30.2	2.3	31.9	0.8	1.9	0.6	1	27.6	13	83.2	
Israel		4.6		31.9		9.4		1.9	48.5	31.9	81.5	13.7

Note: All data is weighted and representative of national populations aged 20–74.

particular showing low levels of linking, and mainland and Mediterranean European countries showing middling levels of linking social capital. In contrast to bonding, the English-speaking countries tended to show slightly lower rather than higher levels of linking social capital, a testament perhaps to their natural liberal suspicion of big government. Their levels remain high in the overall ranking of countries, nonetheless.

In terms of the breakdown of scores between norms, networks and practices, as with bonding, there is coherence across these three components, though it is not as strong as for bridging social capital. As with both other types of social capital, European countries such as Germany, France, Slovenia, the UK and the Czech Republic show higher levels of linking practices than these countries exhibit for any normative or network indicator. Again, this is an area for future research into the effects of EU work directives and free time to engage with.

Conclusion

In seeking to examine the social capital – and thus the sociability – of nations, I have opted for a theoretically informed approach which operationalizes the many components of social capital. I have calculated aggregated country-level social capital indicators for normative, network and practice-based indicators of bonding, bridging and linking social capital. I have found a high degree of convergence between all such indicators across countries, and would conclude that descriptive evidence points to high levels of social capital of all types in Nordic and English-speaking countries whilst mainland and Mediterranean countries show middling levels, and ex-communist countries in Eastern Europe show the lowest levels; even of bonding social capital.

I reiterate that I have not proved a causal direction or even a statistical association between any of the social capital elements, and this was not the purpose of this chapter. More comprehensive data gathered within a single dataset is needed to engage in sophisticated statistical tests. What I have shown is that a descriptive presentation of social capital, derived from a theoretically robust set of indicators, shows an apparently strong sense of sociability in some nations and not others. This provides a useful theoretical base and an interesting empirical snapshot of social capital in Europe and other OECD countries that transcends anecdote. It will serve as a useful tool for students, policy-makers and those interested in advancing social capital research into the future.

Notes

1. Data came from three main survey datasets, the World Values Survey (WVS), the European Social Survey (ESS) and the Multinational Time Use Study (MTUS) combined

with the Harmonized European Time Use Study (HETUS). The WVS and ESS were both used to increase the scope of countries covered and the questions that could be asked, and to provide a validity check on similar questions used in both surveys for similar countries. MTUS and HETUS are two harmonized datasets agglomerated from similar national time-use surveys, but MTUS data is available at the unit record level, whilst HETUS has only aggregated tabulated records available. Where possible, I have used the tabulated HETUS data for each country, and calculated matching data using MTUS for countries not available in HETUS. I note that estimates for informal care in MTUS are likely to be higher than for HETUS (see the coding of bonding activities, below).

2. As a rule of thumb, I included all countries present in the most rigorous and consistent of the surveys, the ESS, and then any additional countries present in at least two of the other three datasets used. There was still substantial missing data, particularly across all four datasets, making complex multivariate analysis (that is, regression) difficult if not impossible.

3. Statistically, all country-level bridging indicators correlated well together. Indicators correlated with a Pearson's R ranging between 0.3 (for the ESS measure of 'trust' with 'time spent volunteering'), and 0.9 (for each of the WVS and ESS measures of 'membership' with 'activity' in Putnam associations). Most correlations were of the order of R of around 0.5 to 0.6, and Spearman's ranked order correlations produced even higher coefficients.

4. Most country-level bonding indicators correlated well together, though the coefficients were not as high as for bridging, and certain indicators were clearly of lesser relevance. The indictors for 'loyalty', 'meeting friends' and 'time spent in caring activity' showed poor correlations with each other and a number of other indictors, ranging from Pearson's R of −0.1 (for 'loyalty' with 'time spent in caring activity') and 0.5 (for 'time spent in caring activity' with both 'being active within a Bourdieu organization' and 'helping others'). Such poor correlations are likely driven by the limited response variation for the 'loyalty' and 'meeting friends' indictors. Other indicators showed better correlations, ranging from 0.1 (for 'being intimate' with 'time spent in caring activity') and 0.7 to 0.8 (for WVS and ESS membership and activity indictors with each other), and most being in the order of around 0.4 to 0.5. Spearman's ranked order correlations showed similar results.

5. All country-level linking indicators correlated quite well together, with the exception of 'voting'. Voting correlated negatively with the WVS and ESS measures of 'membership' or 'activity' in political parties, and also with the measure of 'taking political action', while its highest correlation was a Pearson's R of 0.3 with 'cheating'. The cheating indicator also showed no correlation with the WVS measure of 'activity' within political parties. The rest of the indictors correlated well, in a range between 0.2 (for 'confidence' with the ESS measure of 'activity' within political parties) and 0.8 (for the WVS with the ESS indictors for membership in political parties), and most being in the order of around 0.4 to 0.5. Spearman's ranked order correlations showed similar results.

References

Australian Productivity Commission (APC) (2003), *Social Capital: Reviewing the Concept and its Policy Implications*, Canberra: AusInfo, pp. 1–89.

Bourdieu, P. (1977), *Outline of a Theory of Practice*, Cambridge: University of Cambridge Press.

Bourdieu, P. (1986), 'The forms of capital', in J. Richardson (ed.), *Handbook of Theory and Research in the Sociology of Education*, New York: Greenwood Press, pp. 241–58.

Brehm, J. and W. Rahn (1997), 'Individual-level evidence for the causes and consequences of social capital', *American Journal of Political Science*, **41**, 999–1023.

Burt, R.S. (2000), 'The network structure of social capital', in B.M. Staw and R.I. Sutton (eds), *Research in Organizational Behavior*, **22**, 345–423.

Claibourn, Michele P. and Paul S. Martin (1990), *Foundations of Social Theory*, Cambridge, MA: Harvard University Press.

Claibourn, Michele P. and Paul S. Martin (2000), 'Trusting and joining? An empirical test of the reciprocal nature of social capital', *Political Behaviour*, **22**, 267–91.
Cote, S. and T. Healy (2001), *The Well-being of Nations: The Role of Human and Social Capital*, Paris: OECD.
Fine, Ben (2001), *Social Capital Versus Social Theory. Political Economy and Social Science at the Turn of the Millennium*, London: Routledge.
Fukuyama, F. (1995), *Trust: The Social Virtues and the Creation of Prosperity*, London: Penguin.
Gambetta, D. (1988), 'Mafia: the price of distrust', in D. Gambetta (ed.), *Trust: Making and Breaking Cooperative Relations*, London: Blackwell.
Grieg, A., F. Lewins and K. White (2003), *Inequality in Australia*, Cambridge: Cambridge University Press.
Harriss, John (2001), *Depoliticizing Development. The World Bank and Social Capital*, New Delhi: LeftWord.
Knack, S. and P. Keefer (1997), 'Does social capital have an economic payoff? A cross-country investigation', *Quarterly Journal of Economics*, **112**, 1251–88.
Li, Yaojun, A. Pickles and M. Savage (2005), 'Social capital and social trust in Britain', *European Sociological Review*, **21**,109–23.
Lin, N., K. Cook and R.S. Burt (2001), *Social Capital: Theory and Research*, New York: Aldine de Gruyter.
Luhmann, N. (1979), *Trust and Power*, Chichester: Wiley.
Mansbridge, J. (1999), 'Altruistic trust', in M.E. Warren (ed.), *Democracy and Trust*, Cambridge: Cambridge University Press, pp. 290–309.
Narayan, D. (1999), *Bonds and Bridges: Social Capital and Poverty*, Washington, DC: World Bank.
Newton, K. and P. Norris (2000), 'Confidence in public institutions: faith, culture, or perform-ance', in S.J. Pharr and R.D. Putnam (eds), *Disaffected Democracies: What's Troubling the Trilateral Countries?*, Princeton, NJ: Princeton University Press, pp. 52–73.
Olson, M. (1982), *The Rise and Decline of Nations: Economic Growth, Stagflation, and Social Rigidities*, New Haven, CT: Yale University Press.
Onyx, J. and P. Bullen (1997), *Measuring Social Capital in Five Communities in NSW: An Analysis*, Sydney: Centre for Australian Community Organisations and Management.
Patulny, R. (2004), 'Social capital norms, networks and practices – a critical evaluation', SPRC discussion paper, no. 134.
Patulny, R. (2005), 'Social capital and welfare: dependency or division? Examining bridging trends by welfare regime, 1981 to 2000', SPRC discussion paper, no. 138.
Patulny, R. and G. Svendsen (2007), 'The social capital grid: bonding, bridging, qualitative, quantitative', *International Journal of Sociology and Social Policy*, **27** (1/2), 32–51.
Paxton, P. (1999), 'Is social capital declining in the United States? A multiple indicator assess-ment', *American Journal of Sociology*, **105**, 88–127.
Portes, A. (1998), 'Social capital: its origins and applications in modern sociology', *Annual Review of Sociology*, **24**, 1–24.
Putnam, R.D. (2000), *Bowling Alone: The Collapse and Revival of American Community*, New York and London: Simon & Schuster.
Robinson, J.P. and G. Godbey (1997), *Time for Life: The Surprising Ways Americans Use Their Time*, University Park, PA: Pennsylvania State University.
Rothstein, B. (2003), 'Social capital in the social democratic state', in R. Putnam (ed.), *Democracies in Flux: The Evolution of Social Capital in Contemporary Society*, New York: Oxford University Press, pp. 289–333.
Ruston, D. (2003), *Volunteers, Helpers and Socialisers: Social Capital and Time Use*, London: Office of National Statistics.
Schaik, T. van (2002), 'Social capital in the European Values Study Surveys', OECD-ONS International Conference on Social Capital Measurement, London. 25–27 September.
Stone, W. and J. Hughes (2002), *Social Capital: Empirical Meaning and Measurement Validity*, Melbourne: Australian Institute of Family Studies.

Svendsen, G.T. and G.L.H. Svendsen (2004), *The Creation and Destruction of Social Capital: Entrepreneurship, Co-operative Movements, and Institutions*, Cheltenham UK and Northampton, MA, USA: Edward Elgar.

Szreter, S. (2002), 'The state of social capital: bringing back in power, politics and history', *Theory and Society*, **31** (5), 573–621.

Uslaner, E.M. (2002), *The Moral Foundations of Trust*, Cambridge: Cambridge University Press.

Wellman, B. (1988), 'Structural analysis: from method and metaphor to theory and substance', in B. Wellman and S.D. Berkowitz (eds), *Social Structures – A Network Approach*, Contemporary Studies in Sociology, vol. 15, Greenwich, CT: JAI Press, pp. 19–61.

Woolcock, M. (1998), 'Social capital and economic development: toward a theoretical synthesis and policy framework', *Theory and Society*, **27** (2), 151–208.

Woolcock, M. and D. Narayan (2000), 'Social capital: implications for development theory, research and policy', *The World Bank Research Observer*, **15** (2), 225–49.

Zmerli, S. and K. Newton (2006), 'Social trust and attitudes towards democracy: a close association after all?', conference paper for the Economic and Social Research Council (ESRC) Research Methods Festival, St Catherine's College, Oxford, UK, 17–20 July.

Appendix

Table 23A.1   Social capital variables, country data and years

Survey	Variables and abbreviations	Countries and years
WVS	*Bridging* – Trust others in general (*Norm*), Tolerance towards neighbours (*Norm*),[1] Member of a Putnam-organization (*Network*), Active in a Putnam-organization (*Practice*) *Bonding* – Member of a Bourdieu-organization (*Network*), Active in a Bourdieu-organization (*Practice*) *Linking* – Confidence in parliament (*Norm*), Cheating unjustifiable (*Norm*), Member of a political party (*Network*), Active in a political party (*Practice*), Undertaken a political action (*Practice*)	Australia (1995), Austria (2000), Belgium (2000), Canada (2000), Czech Republic (2000), Denmark (2000), Estonia (2000), Finland (2000), France (2000), Germany (2000), Greece (2000), Hungary (2000), Iceland (2000), Ireland (2000), Italy (2000), Latvia (2000), Lithuania (2000), Luxembourg (2000), Netherlands (2000), Norway (1995), Poland (2000), Portugal (2000), Slovakia (2000), Slovenia (2000), South Africa (2000), Spain (2000), Sweden (2000), Switzerland (1995), Ukraine (2000), United Kingdom (2000), United States (2000)
ESS	*Bridging* – Trust others in general (*Norm*), Member of a Putnam-organization (*Network*),[3] Active in a Putnam-organization (*Practice*),[3] *Bonding* – Loyal to friends like me (*Norm*), Have friends to discuss intimate matters (*Network*), Member of a Bourdieu-organization (*Network*), Meet friends (*Practice*), Help others (*Practice*), Active in a Bourdieu-organization (*Practice*)[3] *Linking* – Trust in Parliament (*Norm*), Member of a Political Party (*Network*),[3] Active in a Political Party (*Practice*),[3] Undertaken a Political Action (*Practice*), Voted in last election (*Practice*), Contacted Politician or Official (*Practice*)	Austria (2004), Belgium (2004), Czech Republic (2004), Denmark (2004), Estonia (2004), Finland (2004), France (2004), Germany (2004), Greece (2004), Hungary (2004), Iceland (2004), Ireland (2004), Israel (2002),[4] Italy (2002), Latvia (2004), Lithuania (2004), Luxembourg (2004), Netherlands (2004), Norway (2004), Poland (2004), Portugal (2004), Slovakia (2004), Slovenia (2004), Spain (2004), Sweden (2004), Switzerland (2004), Ukraine (2004), United Kingdom (2004)

HETUS *Bridging* – Volunteering (*Practice*)
        Bonding – Caring (*Practice*)

Belgium (1999), Estonia (1999), Finland (1999), France (1998), Germany (2001), Hungary (2000), Italy (2002), Latvia (2003), Lithuania (2003), Norway (2000), Poland (2003), Spain (2003), Sweden (2001), United Kingdom (2001)

MTUS *Bridging* – Volunteering (*Practice*)
        Bonding – Caring (*Practice*)

Australia (1997), Austria (1992), Canada (1998), Netherlands (2000), Slovenia (2000), South Africa (2000), United States (2003)

Notes:
1. WVS data on 'tolerance' from Hungary was unavailable in 2000, and is from 1995.
2. WVS data on 'cheating being justified' was unavailable for many countries in 2000. Data for this question is from 1995 for Estonia, Hungary, Latvia, Norway, Poland, Slovakia, Slovenia, Sweden, and Switzerland, and from 1990 for Iceland, Ireland and Portugal.
3. ESS data concerning membership and activity in voluntary associations was from 2002, and was not available for Czech Republic, Estonia, Iceland, Slovakia, Switzerland and the Ukraine.
4. While Israel is included in the latest WVS, most data is missing. Only data for Trust and Political Action questions is provided.

24 Building social capital
Robert Chase and Rikke Nørding Christensen

24.1 Introduction

The large amount of literature on social capital shows that, while the concept is multidimensional and its characteristics vary by context, social capital is a valuable development asset. Thus, many development activities seek to enhance it. This chapter presents evidence on how to build and enhance social capital by investigating whether and how certain World Bank operations enhance social capital.

Social capital is in broad terms defined by the World Bank as 'the norms and networks that enable collective action'. Social capital is a concept with broad intuitive and operational appeal. Social capital is a vital yet under-appreciated development asset, which refers to a class of assets that inhere in social relationships, such as social bonding and bridging, makes those with access to it more effective and can be enhanced for lasting effects. As a rubric encompassing many institutional characteristics important for development efforts success or failure, social capital represents an important asset for practitioners to understand and enhance. Further, evidence from many different contexts suggests communities and individuals, who are better endowed with social capital, enjoy better services, more effective governance and improved welfare.

Certain mechanisms in development operations seek to enhance and build social capital. The World Bank's growing portfolio of community-driven development (CDD) operations have been associated with building social capital. A recent World Bank study 'Thailand Social Capital Evaluation (2006)' finds that indicators of social capital differ significantly between villages that participated in CDD compared to villages that did not. For example, villages with more trust and stronger norms of collective action were more likely to participate, suggesting the CDD operation acts as a mechanism to select these characteristics. Furthermore, it also presented evidence that the CDD operation enhanced social capital characteristics, such as information sharing, leadership and empowerment. This chapter builds extensively on this evaluation and provides examples of how to build and enhance social capital in the Thailand context.

Social capital from the Thai perspective has by Thai scholars been realized as distinguishing characteristics of Thai rural villages and considered as positive social assets. The Thai 'community culture' school of thought, composed of prominent academics and non-governmental organization (NGO) activists, have produced significant research, articles, books, and other literary works since the early 1980s (for example, Apichart, 1983; Boonthien, 1984; Chatthip, 1984) which constitute a counter-narrative to the dominant modernization discourse. They argued that rural village communities had ideologies, worldviews, social relationship systems and values that differed from the capitalist culture. This perspective noted with alarm the decline of the culture-based rural economy resulting from commodification and differentiation.

Napaporn (2003) suggests that the strength of rural communities lies in their knowledge, social and spiritual capital. Social capital gained its strength from kinship ties and social networks within and across communities. In addition, Maniemai (2003) proposes that various mechanisms have maintained traditional networks within and across villages. Culturally, religious practices help maintain people's connection. Ceremonies, festivities and even life-course rituals rely on material and human resources from within and across villages. Economically, the exchange system – a form of survival strategy of rural people in the marginalized economy – maintains linkages among villages depending on who has or lacks resources. In times of crisis, such as droughts or floods, villages elevate the exchange to a moral principle that allows those in trouble to gain much more from the exchange than they give. In the past, migration for better lands enlarged people's connections; today migration for work expands their networks to urban areas. Anan (1998) suggested that social capital in Thai society was governed by the principles of reciprocity and communality. Labor exchange in farming as well as labor contribution in village public works are examples of reciprocity based on equality.

The chapter includes the following: Section 24.2 presents a World Bank operation: community-driven development. Section 24.3 presents the evaluation of the Thai social investment fund, which includes a short summary of the methodology, data and results. Section 24.4 gives the conclusions.

24.2   Introduction to World Bank operation: community-driven development

Community-driven development represents an approach the World Bank takes toward its operation. Many operations that adopt a CDD approach have the objective to build social capital. Further, CDD approaches explicitly work with existing community social capital. They generally involve competition among village groups that likely favors villages able to put together better proposals. Given this approach there are selection and impact effects. Through the *selection effect*, CDD approaches may act as mechanisms to identify and reward communities better endowed with social capital. Since CDD operations require collective action for program participation, communities with more social capital likely can participate in CDD operations more readily. Through the *impact effect*, participation in CDD procedures can directly enhance social capital, because they facilitate communities to identify and develop ways to collaborate more effectively. In general, CDD operations provide opportunities for communities to apply and compete for resources including a demand-driven process. Dimensions of social capital, such as willingness for self-sacrifice or links to formal local authorities, may increase the chance that a village will prepare a successful CDD financing proposal and thus become a participating or treatment village. Participating villages are involved in several activities designed to enhance social capital characteristics.

In response to the increasing prevalence of community-driven development projects, there has been increasing interest in evaluating their impact (see Mansuri and Rao, 2004). The World Bank's multi-country analysis of early generation social funds resulted in several studies that look at effectiveness of Social Investment Fund (SIF) projects in Honduras (Walker et al., 1999), Zambia (Chase and Sherburne-Benze, 2001), Bolivia (Newman et al., 2000) Armenia (Chase, 2002), Peru (Paxson and Shady, 2002), and Nicaragua (Pradhan and Rawlings, 2002).

The Thailand Social Capital Evaluation (2006) seeks to identify whether observed social capital differences between treatment and comparison villages result from *selection* effects, so that villages that participate in the CDD operation already had different social capital characteristics, or *impact* effects, wherein the activities of the CDD operation directly enhance social capital characteristics of participating villages. Hence, to identify a net gain from a project the study evaluates the differences in social capital between villages that participated in a World Bank project (SIF) and non-participating villages, and whether SIF participation impacted or built social capital characteristics. The empirical approach applies an innovative *ex-post* assessment of how the Thai Social Investment Fund worked with and changed village social capital, by breaking social capital such as social bonding and bridging into interrelated but distinct dimensions, and combining quantitative and qualitative measuring techniques. Using the most common case of inadequate social capital baseline information, it uses an innovative combination of quantitative and qualitative research methods to analyse the hypothesis that 'CDD builds social capital' and develop a more sophisticated understanding of the relationship between *selection*, *impact* effects, and different social capital dimensions in CDD.

24.3　Thailand social capital evaluation: Thai Social Investment Fund
Through understanding of social capital dimensions in context, development actors need to develop ways to support and enhance different social capital aspects. Based on experience, the World Bank's community-driven development operations seek to support local social capital. As an example of community driven development, the Thailand Social Investment Fund made strengthening village social capital one of its prime objectives.

The Thai government established the Social Investment Fund as a US$120 million component of a World Bank loan designed to provide relief from the Asian financial crisis. The SIF provided resources for local and community grassroots organizations to implement their development projects. The long-term objective of the Social Investment Fund was to enhance community-learning capacity for sustainable development through community empowerment. The purposes of the Social Investment Fund include the following:

Revive grassroots society through the use of decentralized procedures so that communities and localities can participate in development activities;

Enhance community organization and local administration capabilities in administration and management for long-term self-reliance;

Promote the emergence of self-sufficient economic systems and strong community economies; and

Stimulate widespread participatory social development by supporting the development of civic societies and good governance in the long run.

To achieve these objectives, the SIF built on available social capital to support highly desirable reforms towards decentralization, better governance, community empowerment and the forging of broad development partnerships involving civil society. To receive grants, communities followed sub-project procedures for proposals, management and monitoring. In addition to tangible assets that resulted from community development projects, the process of participating in the SIF was intended to help communities learn by doing, initiating a process to build institutional capacity and social capital that would strengthen the community in the long run.

As presented in Table 24.1, from September 1998 to August 2002, the SIF provided funding support in five categories in the amount of 4401 million baht to projects in 76 provinces. Identified through an outreach campaign, villages were given information about the SIF and the menu of options. With support and guidance from SIF staff, village organizations then prepared proposals for funding through one of these menus. The SIF central administration reviewed these proposals and decided which to

Table 24.1   Number of SIF projects and amount of SIF funding support by menu

Menu	Number of projects	Amount of funding support (million baht)
1. Community economy and community occupation	3184	778
2. Community welfare and safety	1207	354
3. Natural resource management and cultural preservation	790	194
4. Community capacity building and networking	2236	1060
5. Community welfare for the needy	457	2016
Total	7874	4402

fund. Villages then implemented the sub-projects themselves, with different types of support from the SIF.

24.3.1   Methodology and data

The methodology in the Thailand Social Capital Evaluation (2006) combines quantitative techniques to match treatment and comparison villages with qualitative field research to identify how and why villages that participated in the Thai SIF differed from others that did not participate. The evaluation presents a set of indicators for several dimensions of social capital that reflects the Thai context, disaggregating solidarity and social bonding and bridging into trust, groups and organizations, networks and linkages, cooperation and collective action, information sharing and communication, social cohesion and empowerment. Further, it uses an innovative and pragmatic mixed-methods evaluative approach to collect and analyse evidence about social capital characteristics in treatment villages that participated in the SIF and matched comparison villages that did not participate. From that evidence, it concludes that SIF acted both as a mechanism to select villages with pre-existing cooperative norms and as an effective instrument to enhance bonding and bridging such as networks, leadership, and villagers' capability to exercise voice to formal authorities.

The methodology used existing household survey data[1] to match each of 72 sample villages that participated in the SIF to six potential comparison villages within the same province.[2] Additional data helped to identify the most accurately matched comparison villages. The data used for this second stage matching included indicators on: urbanization, distance to nearest town, access to infrastructure, type of terrain, ethnicity, religion, longevity of settlement, population, out-migration level and land ownership structure. Using this field information, field researchers identified 72 comparison villages matched to the 72 treatment villages.[3]

24.3.2 Qualitative field data collection

Qualitative data is normally associated with case studies or rapid appraisals that involve small sample sizes. But in this evaluation the research faced a major challenge to develop a data collection methodology and analytical framework that would enable analysis of a large volume of qualitative data to produce credible and representative findings, without losing its richness, and contextual nature.

The field data team developed data collection instruments that captured the many social capital dimensions appropriate to Thailand.[4] The instrument included a semi-structured interview guide, which poses discussion questions organized according to the social capital dimensions described above, adapted to the Thai context, and inspired by the Integrated Questionnaire for the Measurement of Social Capital established by the World Bank. Interviewer's rating forms, scoring each village on a one to five scale on each social capital indicator was also collected.

Efforts to minimize errors that could enter due to researcher's subjective scoring were made by combining field researchers with differing perspectives, extensive piloting and training, anchoring vignettes[5] and asking villagers to validate social capital scores. Where there were differences the team would discuss and reach consensus on a rating. Analysis by Isham et al. (1995) suggests this is an effective way to reduce subjective errors. If necessary, additional interviews were conducted to verify results. These consolidated ratings forms were recorded on a consolidated ratings form, where field teams could record discrepancies and explain through illustrations the rationale for final consolidated rankings.

Using all these validation techniques, teams visited 144 sampled villages, spending on average three days in each village. They conducted interviews with key informants of village leaders and regular citizens. They interviewed three to five leaders per village including both formal and informal leaders,[6] and nine to twelve regular citizens, seeking to choose key informants representing major groups, including distribution by economic status, gender, age, socio-cultural group, housing location and beneficiary status with respect to development projects.

At the end of the analysis process the research team was brought together for a debriefing workshop to consider the quantitative analysis showing which variables differed between SIF and comparison villages.

They discussed which of these differences were likely due to characteristics that existed before the SIF started and which resulted from direct SIF impact. These qualitative study examples helped to attribute differences to selection or impact and gave a better sense for practical implications of SIF operations.

24.3.3   Ex-post quantitative analysis

The rankings scores themselves provide a detailed summary of social capital indicators for each village, which lend themselves to quantitative analysis to understand patterns in those indicators. Combining the SES household data with the social capital data, the study included extensive analysis of the links between socioeconomic characteristics, participation in the SIF and social capital variables.

There were three parts to quantitative analysis of this village level data. First, the team identified significant differences between treatment and comparison villages on each social capital variable. Second, it used regressions to find determinants of different social capital variables, using both SES variables from before the SIF started and participation in the SIF as potential explanations for social capital outcomes. Finally, it debriefed field teams to identify whether SIF selection or impact explains observed social capital differences.

24.3.4   Results

The main results from the evaluation showed that villages that participated in the SIF scored higher than matched comparison villages on several social capital dimensions (see Thailand Social Capital Evaluation, 2006: table 2). Especially solidarity and trust in treatment villages showed a greater sense of self-sacrifice for common benefits and trust among close neighbors. Their groups and organizations demonstrated greater diversity of leadership and were better able to learn and adapt to new opportunities. The largest distinction was in networks and linkages.

BOX 24.1   CHIENGWAE VILLAGE

Chiengwae village at Udornthani province is a good example of how SIF support, civic networks and multi-party forums have made people become more confident and able to act together to voice and solve their problems.

The village proposed a project to SIF with the aim to solve and prevent drug usage among village youths, and the project was approved. Under this project, village leaders collaborated with the village school in several activities, such as sports, drug education, rehabilitation, and occupational training. This project allowed the village to establish a 'civic network against narcotic drugs in Udornthani province', and was able to expand the network to other provinces.

This civic network later became involved in organizing civic forums to solve environmental problems arising from a large-scale irrigation project. The part of the project that affected the village was the construction of a feeder canal from Nong Harn lake to the sub-district land areas. The canal however obstructed the natural waterways and caused floods in both farms and settlement areas. The civic network therefore organized civic forums with several local organizations. Together they requested financial support from the Tambon Administration Organization (TAO), and were able to get a grant to solve the problem. They also mobilized people in the sub-district to contribute their labor to construct new feeder canals and drainage to change the waterways. This effort was successful, and the network expanded. Now, people can use the forum of this network to plan and discuss issues that arise.

Source: Thailand Social Capital Evaluation (2006).

Likewise, aggregate indicators of both social bonding and bridging were higher where there was a CDD operation. In addition, treatment villages also scored significantly higher on channels through which social capital was transmitted. Specifically, SIF villages showed a greater diversity of types of cooperation than comparison villages. In treatment villages, government officials were ranked as more accountable, responding to villagers' voices to a greater degree.

BOX 24.2   KOKGONG VILLAGE

Kokgong village in Udornthani province is a remote village. It would have been difficult for the village to achieve the development that has occurred without participating in the SIF program. The village is located in a new frontier, and is surrounded with sugar fields. Its inhabitants have a different ethnicity from the natives in the area. They are ethnic *Phu Tai*, who migrated from Sakonnakorn province. They were able to preserve much of their ethnic culture, including skills in silk and cotton weaving. An officer of the Tambon Administration Organization helped the villagers in drafting a project proposal to get funding support from SIF for a cloth weaving project. SIF gave not only financial, but also other technical support.

The products of the weaving group made possible by SIF's support won much recognition from local government agencies. Group leaders were invited to participate in several training sessions, such as those on group management (planning, accounting), production (dyeing, packaging), marketing, as well as on extended activities, such as how to start a savings group. Through their participation in these sessions, they came to know and got acquainted with other weaving and production groups as well as resource persons from GOs, NGOs and the private sector. These new contacts enabled them to have wider market channels. It is notable that such a small project offered a range of learning opportunities to both group leaders and members, resulting in more diversified capabilities.

Source: Thailand Social Capital Evaluation (2006).

Social Investment Fund treatment villages differed concerning social cohesion outcomes. Treatment villages were ranked significantly lower than matched comparison villages on tolerance for differences. Where the SIF had operated, village members showed less tolerance for community members different than the majority in the village. Finally, several empowerment indicators were stronger in SIF treatment villages. For example, SIF villages were judged better able to sustain development activities, demonstrating in the eyes of field research teams better capacity to make productive use of development opportunities outside of SIF funding.

The quantitative analysis on social bonding and bridging determinants were tested to measure how each of the social capital variables were dependent on the set of socio-economic variables, given that the community participated in the SIF. The results verified that SIF villages differed from matched comparison villages on several social capital indicators, also when controlling for these socio-economic characteristics. Nearly all the social capital variables, except one, tolerance of differences, were affected positively by participating in the SIF. Another finding was that villages where many people were tenant farmers tend to have higher social capital. In addition, higher consumption villages in the sample exhibited more trust of close neighbors and lower consumption villages were more able to cooperate.

However, more inequality was found in the village that was associated with higher social capital in many dimensions. When coupled with the agriculture findings this evidence suggests that social capital norms operate as a means of providing insurance, so that particularly in places with tenant farming and unequal consumption, cooperative norms were more prevalent. Finally, the evidence suggests that more education was associated with less social capital, so cooperative norms and networks were maintained and valued by the less well educated.

Among indicators that were not regarded as impacted by the SIF was trust among close neighbors, which is a longstanding characteristic of villages that takes a long time to develop. For example, there is a long and strong tradition of 'kum', or village solidarity, that researchers found in greater evidence in SIF villages, particularly in the Northeast of Thailand. While SIF villages generally exhibited higher trust than comparison villages, researchers attributed these differences to traits the SIF could not make an impact on in its short period of operation. The SIF selected villages where neighbors already trusted one another, which could allow those villages to put together stronger proposals.

Social Investment Fund treatment villages had greater diversity of leadership capability, which where attributed greatly to SIF impact. To prepare and implement a SIF sub-project, villages need effective leaders who can convince and inspire fellow community members. Moreover, these leaders must be informal or outside the formal administrative structure. The SIF supports the emergence of diversified leaders. While there were likely potential leaders in many villages, the SIF helps them emerge, encouraging them to explore channels outside of formal administrative procedures to get things done.

As a central operational tenet, the SIF sought to build information networks among villages and organizations. These observed differences were attributed to SIF impact, rather than to selection. The SIF encouraged learning connections between organizations and villages to understand what worked best. For example, the SIF organized and financed study tours among villages, so they could share approaches as to what worked and what did not. Further, when organizations identified, planned and implemented sub-projects, they gained opportunities to work with other similar organizations and to interact with village authorities.

Social Investment Fund villages showed more evidence of cooperating on a diverse set of activities than comparison villages. Field researchers attributed these differences to pre-existing village characteristics that enabled villages to be more successful in organizing SIF sub-project proposals. As further evidence of this selection effect, cooperative activities prevalent in SIF villages tended to be more traditional and culturally based, so that a pattern of village members working together on such activities likely existed before the SIF.

As additional verification that SIF selects villages with a proclivity for collective action, note significant differences between treatment and comparison villages concerning the prevalence of human-made irrigation systems and of pre-school nurseries. Organizing community members to maintain irrigation systems is a quintessential form of collective action that requires community capacity to work together over a long time horizon. The percentage of land under irrigation is a strong proxy for social capital. Likewise, if the community organized itself to provide pre-school nurseries, it suggests strong cooperation. Both qualitative and quantitative evidence suggests that SIF villages began with a greater capacity to cooperate to undertake joint activities.

Differences in sharing information and having more responsive government officials seemed to be attributed to SIF impact. Because implementing SIF sub-projects, organizations needed to share information and work together. Resulting partnerships improved communication with other communities and with local government officials. As Figure 24.1 illustrates, network support, which the SIF provided, had a significant impact on information sharing: when organizations compared notes on their operations, they learned from the examples of their peers. As noted, SIF treatment villages were less tolerant of differences than comparison villages.[7] This was attributed to SIF activities, because preparation and implementation of SIF sub-projects creates an atmosphere focused on achieving and adhering to project goals, which may exclude those of lower capabilities, whether those people be poorer or of a different language or ethnic group. These findings correspond to other research on community-driven development approaches in the region, for example research on the Kecamatan Development Project (KDP) in Indonesia, which investigated the effect of CDD operations on local-level conflict and found that CDD operations can be disruptive to make available extra resources through new channels. However, because that operation stressed clear and transparent operating procedures, it also provided a means to manage those conflicts without them becoming too heated. In support of the Indonesia CDD research, there is evidence of reduced social cohesion in Thai SIF villages as opposed to comparators. However, field researchers' explanation for the effects on cohesion in SIF treatment villages suggests a different source of potential tension, one that may operate through social exclusion.

Social Investment Fund villages appeared more empowered than comparison villages by showing greater ability to sustain development, and being more effective in voicing their problems to authorities. This was attributed largely to SIF impact, rather than to conditions that existed beforehand. Because the SIF promoted networks within and among villages and allowed villagers to articulate political voice, networks form to

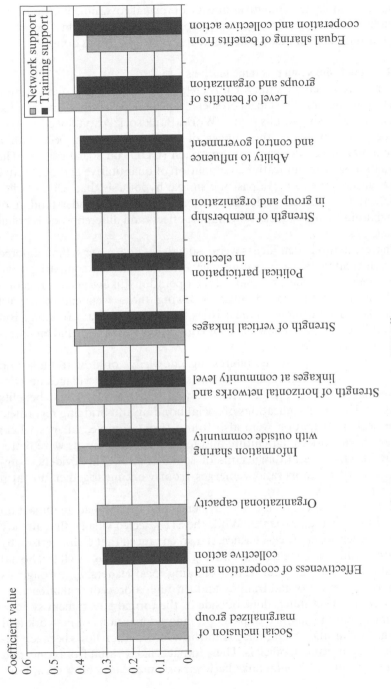

Coefficient value

- Network support
- Training support

Social inclusion of marginalized group

Effectiveness of cooperation and collective action

Organizational capacity

Information sharing with outside community

Strength of horizontal networks and linkages at community level

Strength of vertical linkages

Political participation in election

Strength of membership in group and organization

Ability to influence and control government

Level of benefits of groups and organization

Equal sharing of benefits from cooperation and collective action

Figure 24.1   Effects of training and network support in SIF villages

439

design and implement initiatives outside of formal government procedures. In addition, SIF operations generated opportunities for informal leaders to emerge and build confidence in their capacity to get things done.

24.4   Conclusions and recommendations

The main research question for this chapter is how to build social capital and how to measure the impact on social capital. This has been investigated by exclusively using results from a World Bank social capital study.

The study evaluates the impact of a World Bank project with a community-driven development approach (CDD) on social capital. The evaluation uses an innovative combination of quantitative and qualitative research methods to move past the simple hypothesis that 'CDD builds social capital' and help to develop a more sophisticated understanding of the relationship among selection, impact effects and different social capital dimensions.

The evaluation identified several social capital aspects that differed between treatment (participating villages) and matched comparison villages. The results showed that CDD operations likely act as selection mechanisms among communities, allowing those well endowed with particular social capital characteristics to receive program funding. But the results also showed how the CDD operation works with and enhances existing social capital.

The evaluation produced interesting knowledge on how to build and enhance village social capital. Social Investment Fund villages demonstrate that working together effectively attracts resources and benefits villagers. However, indications of social bonding and bridging regardless of project participation were also found. For example, villages where more people work in agriculture and fewer own their farms were better endowed with several dimensions of social capital. This evidence suggests a spirit of cooperation emerges from working together on farm necessities.

Finally, the evaluation provides evidence that the SIF had an impact on several social capital variables. While the SIF selected villages that already had a greater norm of self-sacrifice, it also enhanced that characteristic by demonstrating the benefits of sacrificing to improve village welfare. Social Investment Fund activities helped building local leadership, through its support for networks and training and through a procedure that encourages leaders to get things done outside of the formal government system. The intervention itself had impacts on many dimensions of network and linkages within and among villages and how information flows between villagers and government officials. These impacts likely result from concerted efforts to create horizontal links between organizations and vertical links

---

BOX 24.3   WHAT BUILT SOCIAL CAPITAL IN THAILAND?

Working together at village level
Supporting networks by:

- creating horizontal links between organizations
- enhancing vertical links to formal authorities

Training in leadership

Source: Thailand Social Capital Evaluation (2006).

---

to formal authorities. The main results of what worked in Thailand are summarized in Box 24.3.

However, the evaluation also found that SIF activities might have reduced social cohesion, particularly through its focus on reaching clear objectives, which seemed to exclude those viewed as least effective. In addition, SIF treatment villages seemed to be less tolerant of differences than comparison villages,[8] which might have been attributed to SIF activities that may exclude those of lower capabilities, whether those people be poorer or of a different language or ethnic group.

Hence, this illustrates the classic challenge of elite capture as the CDD operation is an approach that gives control of decisions and resources to community groups, which might not always include the poorest level in a society. This is an important result when replicating the approach in other countries. To reduce this outcome it is imperative to follow the operation procedure as carefully as possible and at the same time accommodate adjustment to the country context and development.

Community-driven development operations in other countries with different contexts and cultures can benefit from lessons learned when building and evaluating social capital. Box 24.4 describes some of the lessons learned on how CDD operation can build social capital and how the impact can be rigorously evaluated.

Using the Thailand Social Investment Fund as a case study, this chapter has highlighted the relationship between CDD and social bonding and bridging. Community-driven operations act as a development mechanism to select villages with strong social capital characteristics, and participating in a CDD operation had a direct impact on community social capital characteristics. The Thai CDD approach can usefully be adopted in other

---

BOX 24.4   LESSONS LEARNED REGARDING HOW TO BUILD AND EVALUATE SOCIAL CAPITAL IN A CDD SETTING

To build social capital:

- Analyse and define social capital in the country context
- Define objectives in the project that built social capital
- Analyse the selection and impact effect in regard to project/ program processes

To evaluate social capital:

- Develop an overall evaluation strategy
- Identify data
- Establish a control group
- What data exist already – baseline data
- What need to be collected – quantitative versus qualitative data
- Identify measurable indicators
- Analyse program/project process

---

countries seeking to build social capital as long as the project and the measurement techniques are carefully designed to the specific county context. Because CDD is a project approach, it is a guiding framework, with room for variation; social capital is in this regard a precondition for effective CDD. At the same time CDD can build and enhance social capital. Yet, CDD is not the only way of building social capital, but it is a promising approach under constant development. The next step may involve elements of how to insure that marginalized group will be targeted and included to benefit from their stock of social capital.

Notes

1.   Thailand socio-economic household survey (SES) from 1998 and 2000, that is, were used from before the CDD operation began. The SES includes indicators such as household income, change of assets, debts, consumption, education, occupation, expenditures and household characteristics in municipal and non-municipal areas. For the selected years these surveys sampled 2112 villages, of which 201 later participated in the SIF. The unit of analysis was villages and therefore this household level data was aggregated into village level data.

2. Using propensity function summarizes the relative importance of chosen indicators in determining whether or not a village participated in the SIF.
3. The field team sampled 72 treatment villages from the 201 identified because of budget and logistics constraints. Due to security concerns, they excluded villages in three Southern provinces affected by conflict.
4. These specific indicators fall into categories with more universal applicability: solidarity and trust, groups and organizations, networks and linkages, cooperation and collective action, information sharing and communication, social cohesion, and empowerment.
5. These short examples included in the semi-structured interviews would frame discussion, facilitating comparisons across villages and research teams.
6. In treatment villages this included people who had important roles in the SIF project.
7. The finding that treatment villages had lower social cohesion scores than treatment villages is statistically significant in the difference in means. However, it is not significant in the regression findings, suggesting that socio-economic characteristics explain part of this difference, rather than SIF participation.
8. The finding that non-treatment villages had lower social cohesion scores than treatment villages is statistically significant in the difference in means. However, it is not significant in the regression findings, suggesting that socio-economic characteristics explain part of this difference, rather than SIF participation.

References

Anan Ganjanapan (1998), *Karn radomthun puer sangkhom* [Capital Mobilization for Society], Bangkok: Local Development Institute.

Apichart Thongyou (1983), 'Tasana waduai wadanadharma chumchon [Perspectives on community culture]', *Sangkhom Patana*, **10**, 5–6.

Boonthien Thongprasan (1984), *Naewkid wadanadharma chumchon nai arn patina* [Community Culture Concept in Development], Bangkok: Catholic Council of Thailand for Development.

Chase, R. (2002), 'Supporting communities in Transition: the impact of the Armenia Social Investment Fund', World Bank Economic paper, World Bank, Washington, DC.

Chase, R. and L. Sherburne-Benz (2001), 'Impact evaluation of the Zambia Social Fund', Social Protection Department, World Bank, Washington, DC.

Chatthip Nartsupha (1984), *Thai Village Economy in the Past*, Bangkok: Sangsan Press.

Isham, Jonathan, Deepa Narayan and Lant Pritchett (1995), 'Does participation improve performance? Establishing causality with subjective data', *World Bank Economic Review*, **9** (2), May, 175–200.

Mansuri, G. and V. Rao (2004), 'Community-based and driven development: a critical review', *World Bank Research Observer*, **19** (1), 1–39.

Maniemai Thongyou (2003), *Thun chumchon, utasat krobkrua lae kongthun mooban* [Community Capital, Household Survival Strategies and Village Fund], Bangkok: Srinakharinvirot University.

Napaporn Havanon (2003), *Yanavidya mai nai karn sang kwamru puer kwam khemkhaen khong chumchon lae sangkhom* [New Epistemology for Community and Society Strengthening], Bangkok: Srinakharinvirot University.

Newman, John, Menno Pradhan, Laura B. Rawlings, Gert Ridder, Ramiro Coa and Jose Luis Evia (2002), 'An impact evaluation of education, health, and water supply investments by the Bolivian Social Investment Fund', *World Bank Economic Review*, **16** (2), August, 241–74.

Paxson, C. and N.R. Shady (2002), 'The allocation and impact of social funds: spending on school infrastructure in Peru', *World Bank Economic Review*, **16** (2), August, 297–319.

Pradhan, Menno and Laura B. Rawlings (2002), 'The impact and targeting of social infrastructure investments: lessons from the Nicaraguan Social Fund', *World Bank Economic Review*, **16** (2), August, 275–95.

Thailand Social Capital Evaluation (2006), *Thailand Social Capital Evaluation: A Mixed*

Methods Assessment of the Social Investment Fund's Impact on Village Social Capital, Washington, DC: World Bank.

Walker, Ian, Fidel Ordoñez Rafael del Cid and Florencia Rodriguez (1999), *Evaluación Ex-Post del Fondo Hondureño de Inversión Social* (FHIS 2), Tegucigalpa, Honduras: ESAConsultores.

Index